Gordon, Jason Thomas,
The singers talk : the
greatest singers of our time d
[2023]
33305256753108
ca   10/03/23

D0942045

THE SINGERS TALK

THE GREATEST SINGERS OF OUR TIME DISCUSS THE ONE THING THEY'RE NEVER ASKED ABOUT: THEIR VOICES

JASON THOMAS GORDON

PERMUTED
PRESS

A PERMUTED PRESS BOOK
ISBN: 978-1-63758-699-0
ISBN (eBook): 978-1-63758-700-3

The Singers Talk:
The Greatest Singers of Our Time Discuss The One Thing They're Never Asked About: Their Voices
© 2023 by Jason Thomas Gordon
All Rights Reserved

Please consult your doctor before taking any medications or remedies mentioned in this book.

This is a work of nonfiction. All people, locations, events, and situations described are transcribed from interviews between the author and artists and edited for clarity.

No part of this book may be reproduced, stored in a retrieval system, or transmitted by any means without the written permission of the author and publisher.

PERMUTED PRESS

Permuted Press, LLC
New York • Nashville
permutedpress.com

Published in the United States of America
1 2 3 4 5 6 7 8 9 10

For Papa. For the Dream.

CONTENTS

A NOTE FROM THE AUTHOR

Thank you so much.

Your purchase has helped save children's lives.

The royalties from this book will benefit St. Jude Children's Research Hospital through a campaign I started called Music Gives to St. Jude Kids.

My grandfather, Danny Thomas, founded St. Jude in Memphis, Tennessee, in 1962. As a fighter for human rights, he believed that no child should ever die because of cancer or any other life-threatening disease. His dream was to build a hospital where no family would ever be turned away because of their race, religion, or economic status.

I'm proud to say my grandfather's dream came true, and today, St. Jude leads the way the world understands, treats, and defeats childhood cancer. And at St. Jude, no family ever receives a bill for their treatment, travel, housing, or food.

To learn more about St. Jude and Music Gives,
please visit musicgives.org or follow us @musicgives

St. Jude was not involved in the creation of this book.
Please be advised that some interviews contain profanity and occasional
references to drug use that may be inappropriate for young readers.

INTRODUCTION

I'm talking to Eddie Vedder at a bar in Toronto. He's the lead singer of the legendary Pearl Jam and they are beloved the world over. I'm the singer and drummer of a rock band called Kingsize and it's safe to say by your reaction that Pearl Jam has the edge on us.

So here we are at the same party, having a beer, and Eddie is just as down-to-earth and cool as you'd hope he'd be. Our conversation spans various subjects, all centered around our love of music... "Yeah, Side B of *The Unforgettable Fire* is amazing!"

Then the evening ends, off he goes, and that's when it hits me: I've been a drummer almost my whole life and just recently started singing for my band. And I didn't ask Eddie Vedder—*of all people*—how he can scream his head off every night and still sound so incredible after all these years!

I'm an idiot.

Thousands of books have been written about every aspect of many musician's careers, plus millions of interviews, articles, and photographs, detailing their personal and professional lives. And, while there are some magazines like *Modern Drummer* or *Guitar World,* where you can learn about a certain player's technique, style, or gear... when it comes to singers—there's nothing!

As soon as I became the front man of my band, I discovered there was no resource to learn how a singer does their job night after night. No magazine or book reveals the physicality and danger involved in singing on a regular basis. There's nothing that tells the truth about how exhausting, frustrating, and fragile the human voice truly is.

For all their glory in the spotlight, there's one huge aspect of a singer's life that has been completely overlooked for years...

SINGING IS BRUTAL.

The Singers Talk is collection of in-depth conversations with some of the greatest singers of our time, discussing the one thing they never get asked about: their voices.

If you're a singer—trying to train your voice, protect your voice, help, heal, or even find your voice—you're in good hands here.

You'll learn how the best in their field keep their vocal cords in shape, how they protect themselves on the road, and countless other tricks, strategies, and philosophies that'll help you on your way.

But *The Singers Talk* isn't just a survival guide for singers.

This book will also give you a backstage look at how your favorite vocalists approach what they do onstage and in the studio. Packed with amazing stories you've never heard before, you'll also find sides of their personalities you didn't see coming.

I knew going into this that I'd hear things I wouldn't find anywhere else, but what I didn't see was just how spiritual some of these conversations would turn out to be. Some led to tears or unexpected revelations of self-doubt. Others were sermons, sacred, and holy. And some of them were just funny as shit!

My goals for the interview process were simple:

1. Ask every singer the same questions so we can hear the various ways each singer approaches the same subject.

2. Get specific with each artist about how they approach songs that give them trouble, and whether it be sickness or fatigue, what are the solutions to the hardest problems we face as singers on the road?

3. Be the fan you truly are. I'd be getting the chance to speak to some of my heroes, and I was not going to shy away.

I asked Stevie Nicks if she's ever fallen over while spinning around onstage; Mavis Staples about singing with Martin Luther King; Brian Johnson about replacing Bon Scott in AC/DC; Ann Wilson about singing "Stairway to Heaven" in front of Led Zeppelin; Michael McDonald about why he's everyone's favorite singer to impersonate. Anything I wanted to know, Chris Farley would be my guide!

Unfortunately, some of my favorite singers aren't with us anymore, but I still wanted to hear about their vocal approach, so I reached out to the people who were right beside them. You'll hear Steve Cropper remember Otis Redding, Nile Rodgers still bewildered by David Bowie, Clive Davis rhapsodize about Whitney Houston, and don't even ask me what Robby Krieger revealed about Jim Morrison!

This is not a technical book in any sense of the word, but by the time you finish, I know you'll find some new approach or helpful method that works for you. And like me, I think you'll feel less alone, and more freedom to fly. Because in the end, every singer within these pages knows what it takes to stand up to that mic by themselves, reach down into their guts, and give everything they've got for the sake of the song.

And what makes a great song work?

The soul the singer puts inside the vocal.

The Singers Talk is a celebration of that soul.

Jason Thomas Gordon
Los Angeles, Summer 2023

THE QUESTIONS

The singers in this book were asked most or all of these questions:

Who first exposed you to singing?

Were you emulating anyone when you started out?

How did you find your own voice?

Did you ever have any vocal training?

Are you nervous or confident before you perform?

Do you do vocal warm-ups before shows?

Do you have any rituals before you hit the stage?

Is there anything after the show that helps keep your voice in shape?

How do you take care of your voice on the road?

When you start getting sick, what do you do?

Are there songs where you wonder if your voice will be there that night?

Are there songs where you've had to adjust the key live?

What was your most embarrassing vocal mishap ever?

Do you remember a performance where you surprised yourself?

How are you with hearing your own voice?

Do you have a favorite vocal performance you're really proud of?

What's changed the most about your voice since you started?

If you could duet with one singer—living or dead—who would it be?

Who are your top five favorite singers of all time?

If you could ask any singer about their voice, who would it be and what would you ask?

BRYAN ADAMS

"LET'S MAKE IT... AAAAAAAAALLLLL FOR ONE, AND ONE FOR LOVE!" If you know that song, and you know that part, sung high above the stratosphere, well, then you know it's no joke. But to Bryan Adams, it's a good laugh because he nails it every time. But I don't. So, he's about to give me a vocal lesson.

Bryan Adams first entered our collective lives on MTV when it used to be "Music Television." I still remember being a kid and watching the video for "Cuts Like a Knife"—Bryan and his band playing in an empty swimming pool; a girl changing in a dressing room, about to dive in. It was pure rock 'n' roll with solid pop melodies. But what we didn't see coming was that iconic duet with Tina Turner, or for Bryan to wind up singing opera (and learning an important rule about pasta) with Pavarotti.

As a matter of fact, this Grammy Award–Winner has had so many hits and number one records that it would be impossible to recap right now, but how's this for a stat: he's sold over 100 million records.

And to think that all he wanted was a way to pay his rent.

Who first exposed you to singing?

Listening to records. I was quite taken with the sound of two people singing, so The Beatles, Simon & Garfunkel, Everly Brothers, those kinds of records really got me. And there was a defining moment where I remember being thoroughly blown away watching the *Joe Cocker: Mad Dogs & Englishmen* movie, thinking, *Wow, that's just the most incredible voice I've ever heard*. And Janis too! There used to be the Columbia Record Club where you'd get nine records for a dollar or something ridiculous. My father would allow me to have one or two records and one of them was Janis. I chose it because the most exotic thing I'd ever seen before that was a Flamenco dancer when I was in Spain with my dad.

Are you talking about the album cover of *Pearl*?

Yeah. You put that with the voice [*laughs*], it was the most incredible thing.

Were you emulating anyone when you started out?

I didn't really want to be a singer! I wanted to be the guitar player. I've been singing since I was fifteen because I couldn't find a singer for my band, so I stepped in on a temporary basis until we found somebody. But we never found anybody. I was really into hard rock, so I was into Deep Purple, Led Zeppelin, Bad Company, and The Who—Roger Daltrey's voice was seminal in my upbringing—and I wanted to be in one of those kinda bands. That's where my head was at. And then, later on, the Eagles and Jackson Browne. I would've loved to sing like any of the singers at the time, but I didn't know I had a voice.

How did you find your own voice?

I don't know that I ever did, it just came out. I used to go to auditions as a guitar player and it was always like, "Uhh, thanks very much, we'll give you a call." Then, I went to an audition and they said, "Can you sing?" It was like, "Yep... you know... sorta." I sang a song, and they went, "You got the job." So, I started playing with this club band, and I had to be escorted to the stage by a bouncer because I was fifteen. But after a while, I wasn't digging it. The guys were like thirty-five and they were all getting wasted and I just wasn't interested in that. Then, I met somebody who was doing studio work, and I said, "If you're looking for a singer, I'm a singer," and they gave me a shot. So, about once a month I would get a job, and that would be enough to pay my rent and keep me in hot food and shoes for another month.

What were you singing, like jingles?

I would sing anything. I would sing back-up for somebody, I would sing on jingles. It gave me studio work and experience. So, that really helped. I did that until I was probably seventeen.

Did you ever have any vocal training?

Not a lesson.

Do you feel nervous or confident before you perform?

You always get that butterfly feeling. Sometimes it's more for technical reasons 'cause you don't want to get up there and the microphone's not working. So, until you touch the mic and make sure it's on, I have this little daunting feeling.

Do you do vocal warm-ups before shows?

Not really. I think a lot of it comes from just working clubs. We did club shows where we did four sets a night so, there was no chance to warm-up. You warm-up, you're just basically giving away a whole set. Save it. Usually we do a sound check and that would work as vocal warm-up.

Is there anything after the show that helps keep your voice in shape?

Yeah, sleep. That's the key.

How do you take care of your voice on the road?

I try and get as much rest as possible. I don't drink, I don't smoke. I think alcohol is one of the worst things you can do for your voice. Truly. I think that's the killer right there.

So, when you start getting sick, what do you do?

If you're in a very humid, warm environment, and then it gets very cold, that's when I tend to have a little bit of trouble. This one gig I did in South Africa, my voice started sounding really good, and by the end of the song, it just disappeared. I walked over to my guitar player and said, "Keith, I can't talk. I can't sing." So, I sorta whispered into the mic [*laughs meekly*] "I gotta go have a cup of tea. I'll be back in five minutes." I went backstage, had a cup of tea, came back and finished the show.

Are there songs where you wonder if your voice will be there that night?

No.

Are there songs where you've had to adjust the key live?

I never really have much of a problem; touch wood. Hang on, let me find some wood. I don't sing songs that are out of my range, for starters. I can sing pretty high, but all my songs aren't like that. So, you pace things throughout the night.

What was your most embarrassing vocal mishap ever?

Oh, which one? [*Laughter*] The only thing really embarrassing for me is suddenly making up new words for songs onstage and everyone's looking around, like, *What*?

Do you remember a performance where you surprised yourself?

I've recorded demos and gone back to try and capture the moment of that demo and it was like, "Mmmm, you know what? There's no point in doing that again, that's great. Let's just record everything around the voice," and we would do that!

How are you with hearing your own voice?

I'm okay with it. I don't really analyze it that much, I kinda just do it.

Do you have a favorite vocal performance you're really proud of?

I'm pretty happy with a lot of them. For example, "Run to You" was a one take performance.

No way, that's a great take!

There are a lot of vocals that I recorded with "Mutt" Lange where he pushed me really hard to sing better and better. And he was always right. So, a lot of the things I did with "Mutt" I really like.

Yeah, "Mutt" Lange, he's a helluva producer, huh?

He got the best things out of me. Working with him was like going to the University of Rock because we learned so much.

What did you learn vocally from him?

That you can do better.

I'm so jealous of raspy voices and you have one of the greatest ones in rock. Is it just natural or is there a trick to pulling it off without blowing out your voice?

Thank you. I don't know. On my second album, I put a line in the credits that said, "Thank you, cords, for holding me up" because, back then, there were no monitors, and you'd have to open up for The Kinks with no sound and just have to belt it. Getting through it was kind of everything. I didn't have any more aspirations other than, *I just wanna get through and be able to pay my rent.*

But you must have cords of steel from those early club days.

From the time I turned thirty-eight, I decided I was gonna work ten days a month, like ten shows in a row. I would always keep my chops up that way. Sometimes it would be spread out over two weeks, but the most I ever did in a row was fourteen shows.

Fourteen shows in a row?! My God!

[*Laughs*] It didn't happen that often, trust me.

I'm curious about that high note on "All for Love," that note on the word "All." Is there a trick to nailing a note like that for you?

You're talking about the beginning of the chorus? [*Sings*] "ALLLLL!"

Yeah. Hitting that note and sustaining it, while staying in pitch? That's tough!

One thing about my voice: I don't sing.

What do you mean?

Note. Note. Note. Note. I scoop practically every note that I sing. I sing [*subtly ramps the note upwards*] "ALL FOR ONE" Every single note is a scoop.

But all the music stops and you have to hit that note.

It's not, [*sings, hitting the note dead-on*] "Let's make it ALL." It's [*runs his voice up to the note*] "AAALLL." So, you scoop up, that's how you do it. I'll do it slower for you. [*Starts small and eases his voice up into the note*] Everything I sing has a scoop to it. I don't sing any note straight on.

What's changed the most about your voice since you started?

Well, it's a journey. I recently re-recorded one of my first songs called "Hidin' from Love," and wow, my voice is so different now. I'm more comfortable. When I went into my first album, I didn't know what I was doing, so I was just winging it. Actually, I'm still winging it. [*Laughter*] I did this Bare Bones Tour, which was my acoustic tour, with my piano player, and I learned more in those years about my voice than I did in all the years of making rock 'n' roll tours because I could hear myself. What happens when things are really clear is you find a comfort zone for your voice. The more shows I did with my acoustic tour, the better singer I became.

If you could duet with any singer—living or dead—who would it be?

I really like Sam Smith's voice. We'd make a great duet. I think it'd be very beautiful. There's so many good singers out there. I got to sing with Paul Rodgers a couple years ago, who's one of my heroes as a vocalist, and could be the best rock singer ever. Really humble, sweet guy. It reaffirmed that I made the right choice when I follow some of these people. I sang with McCartney once. It was mind-blowing! I don't think I slept for two nights after that. It was the Prince's Trust and he appeared out of nowhere. We did "I Saw Her Standing There," and the mic was open, so I just went up and did a harmony.

Another major duet we gotta talk about: Pavarotti calls you up and asks you to do a duet with him on a live televised concert in Italy. There's a video of you guys singing "O Sole Mio" and it's a master class in cool under pressure. Man, you handle that moment like such a champ. You look totally loose, like you're about to burst into laughter, and the love between you as you're singing is so sweet. What was that experience like?

It was beautiful. I mean, it was farcical because it was broadcast live on Italian television and I'm singing in Napolitano. Okay? I don't speak Italian. So, during the recording of that, I just thought, *This is so outrageous, how did I get talked into this? I must be mad!*

How does Pavarotti call you up, first of all? I mean, that's huge!

I know! I don't know how he got my number! He called me up one day and I said, "Naw, who is this?" and he goes, [*mimics Pavarotti's deep, boisterous voice*] "I am Luciano." I said, "Who is this?" [*Explodes*] "I AM LUCIANO!" I said, "Okay!" But he was a big sweetheart and he just wanted his show to be fun and a success. Thanks for mentioning that. He's a beautiful, beautiful guy, and I miss him a lot.

It says so much about the instrument of your voice that he would seek you out. Did he tell you what it was about your voice that moved him so much?
No, he talked mostly about spaghetti.

Anything we need to know about spaghetti?
Yeah. And you heard this right from Luciano, okay? You *never wait* when people put pasta on the table. That whole thing about, "You have to wait until everyone gets served before you start." No. When your pasta comes to the table, you eat it then.

You sang with Tina Turner as well. What was that like?
When I was twenty-four, I was chasing Tina Turner to come and sing with me. I used to go and see her in clubs before she had her comeback—I just love her—and the day happened where she agreed to sing on ["It's Only Love"].

One of the top three greatest duets of all time. That's an actual fact.
[*Laughs*] I had never had any experience producing anybody before and we'd already done the track. All she had to do was come to the studio and sing my melody. But when she tried to sing it, it was too low for her. There was this awkward moment like, *Oh no, it's not gonna work*. And then, I thought, *Hang on, Tina, I'm coming out*. I went out into the studio with her and said, "Let's just sing the song, okay?" I started pushing the melody to a different area and it became more in her range, and we got it. One of those things where the chemistry had to happen in the room together.

That's so rad. Did you learn anything from singing with her?
She ended up inviting me to tour with her in Europe. We did twenty shows together and it changed everything for me. We suddenly had an audience and the record turned around. It was unbelievable. Every night, going up and singing with Tina Turner? Are you kidding? Oh man, every night was like someone dropped an atom bomb onstage. She was fantastic because she always *really* looked forward to the gig. If I learned anything, it was, you just need to go for it because with Tina you cannot hold back. She won't let ya hold back. If you don't go for it, she'll just blow you off the stage. I'm very grateful to her.

Who are your top five favorite singers of all time?
I'm gonna say Paul Rodgers, Freddie Mercury, Lennon/McCartney, Joe Cocker, John Fogerty, Janis, Crosby, Stills, Nash, & Young, Everly Brothers, let's put Jimi in there.

Okay, you're way past your top five!

Bob Dylan, Joni Mitchell, and don't forget Roger Daltrey! And new singers: I love Chris Martin and what's the singer from the Kings of Leon? [Caleb Followill] And I love Dave Grohl. "Monkey Wrench" is one of the silliest vocals ever where he just belts that high note the whole time! I remember walking up to him and saying, "Man, how did you do that?" Fuck. That is a seriously unbelievable vocal. James Hetfield is an amazing singer too. Ozzy is fantastic. I loved Ozzy when I was a kid. Oh, don't forget David Bowie. And excuse me, Mick Jagger as well.

This didn't work out as planned; that was your top twenty-five.

I could give you more, man! A lot more! You could put Bruce Springsteen in the top twenty-five easily too. There's a great singer. You should listen to the songs we did together live. There's a recording of us doing "Cuts Like a Knife" and "Badlands." Listen to it, man.

I'll check it out, for sure.

By the way, you could put Ray Charles in there because I love Ray Charles more than anything. And Sam Cooke, by the way, *and* Otis *and* Marvin. Put them all!

If you could ask any singer about their voice, who would it be, and what would you ask?

I would ask Marvin Gaye, "How long did it take to work out the arrangement for 'The Star-Spangled Banner?'" When he sang at the NBA game. Because I can't work out the timing, if it's being played to tape, or if there's musicians playing it. What if he fucked up on TV and went to a different part of the song? It's *flawless*.

It's such a trippy arrangement too. It's fluid.

It's the best version of the song. Ever.

I gotta go Whitney Houston on that one.

That is off the charts. But that's more traditional. That's just pure, extraordinary singing and deep church, you know? Hold it. Put her and Aretha Franklin in my list as well. [*Laughter*]

SETH AVETT

WANT TO SEE ONE OF THE BEST ROCK SHOWS OF YOUR LIFE? Check out the Avett Brothers sometime because they can do it with a banjo and a ballad.

Raised in Concord, North Carolina, Seth Avett and his older brother Scott did what I told my young nephews to do for years: form a band! Brothers in bands. Works every time.

But not since the Everly and Neville Brothers have two brother's voices played off one another so beautifully. Along with their melodic skill on most instruments, their honest to God songwriting, and their brilliant bass player, Bob Crawford, the Avetts have slowly built a career that has grown bigger with each new release.

That sense of family, community, and the life-or-death stakes of our everyday existence are ever-present inside of the vocal blend that Seth and Scott provide to each song. Over time, they've developed a trusted, creative relationship with producer Rick Rubin, and have received multiple Grammy nominations. But, more importantly, they've created a loyal and passionate fan base who come to see the brothers' band, as if it were a pilgrimage. And as you'll hear by Seth's choice of words, there is something sacred to all of this. If you're open and available.

So, "This might be a terrible idea, but..."

Who first exposed you to singing?

My dad, and church, for sure. Our grandpa was a Methodist minister—he died before I was born—but he and his wife raised three kids who all are the loudest voices in the sanctuary. Alice, who has since passed, my dad Jim, and Uncle Wally, all three of them are the loudest people in the congregation. [*JTG laughs*] My dad loves to sing harmony and it's funny when the person singing loudest in the church is singing a third or a fifth above everyone else. I learned a lot about harmonic structure because it was always around. He would sing harmony with whatever was on the radio. So, it's super easy for me to fall into that, singing a third or a fifth above that main line. It's very natural, completely because of Dad.

Were you emulating anyone when you started out?

In the earliest stages, it probably would have been Kenny Loggins, and Randy Travis, and Tom T. Hall. Then, as soon as I was aware of other forms of singing, certainly Robert Plant, and then Kurt Cobain. It's just a big playground, like, *Oh, this is how Harry Belafonte does it*! But when people are singing in their most honest voice, it's gonna be a brand-new treatment, with everything: phrasing, tone; there's always some new voice and the sky's the limit. That's what's so awesome about it.

How did you find your own voice?

It's been a long process. And you can hear this going back to the first Avett Brothers records; I had not found it yet. It's bizarre to me when someone's like seemingly fully formed. Like Billie Eilish: how can you be so formed so young?

Yeah, like Otis Redding.

Otis Redding. Or Sam Cooke, right out of the gate, sixteen years old, fully formed. That's one of those weird, Mozart, touched by God kind of things. But that has not been my path. My path has been much slower and it's taken thousands of performances. I don't feel like I really started understanding what my voice is capable of, or the best tone and texture for it, until I realized that it was not separate from the meaning of what I'm saying. I had it wrong, for myself, that the nuts and bolts of singing could be separate from subject matter. I found my voice through realizing whatever I'm singing, I need to be telling the truth as well as I understand it. That doesn't always have to be super literal, but I do have to be checked into it. Like a meditation. Enough not to focus on the aesthetic of my voice.

Did you ever have any vocal training?

I was in a chorus class in middle school, but, no, I'm a textbook example of on-the-job training. [*Laughter*]

Do you feel nervous or confident before you perform?

I feel pretty normal at this point. I don't know if "confident" would be the word, but it doesn't really occur to me to feel either. Scott and I have played thousands of shows, so it wouldn't really make sense to be nervous. But if I were to go onstage for a solo show, I would be nervous, for sure. Me and Jessica Lea Mayfield did a record of Elliott Smith covers a few years back, and we did a tour for that, and I was nervous. Especially the first few nights.

What is it about Elliott Smith's voice that compelled you to want to cover his stuff?

I really believe that what we respond to, as humans, is people being their sincere, genuine selves. There is an unspoken, inarticulable element that we are allergic to. If someone is not genuine in their singing—this might be too strong of a word—I think we feel repelled. Or repulsed. At least I am. It could be subconscious too, but if I feel I'm sensing that, I do not want to hear it. I do not want to hear when someone is not being themselves in their singing, which is why Elliott Smith sounds so good to me. In his case, vulnerability is a major element, and you're just getting a direct line to the sensitivity of the human soul.

Man, you couldn't have said it better.

Everybody has that. That's why that part of him speaks to them. It keeps you connected to your own sensitivity. That's what great singing does. Whatever element it draws on, whatever element it celebrates and amplifies, it is a mirror to that element inside yourself.

Do you do vocal warm-ups before shows?

I do, but I've only been doing that for a year or so. As I get older, I'm realizing the importance of it. I have a couple that Rachel from Lake Street Dive taught me, and a couple that my wife, who's an actress, taught me.

What's the routine?

I do the long "S" sound and then a low hum where I try to vibrate my vocal cords as much as possible with some super low notes. Then, an "M-U-M" sound, like [*hums low*] "MUM-MUM-MUM-MUM-MUM." And then, I do a scale with like a "GEH" sound. I try to do that ten or fifteen minutes before I go on. That seems to help.

Do you have any other rituals before you hit that stage?

Camaraderie is probably the most valuable component. The seven of us love each other and it's very familial, literally, and figuratively. There's so much love and appreciation, so it's less of a technical prep, but we all like to be together about twenty minutes beforehand just to laugh. We just get in the same room, and make fun of each other, and make stupid songs, and then we're in good shape to go out there, 'cause what we present musically is not especially rigid, professional, or studious. It's pretty loose and it's really more akin to a celebration of some sort, or a revival. So, checking into joy and camaraderie beforehand is more of a priority than practicing our instruments.

It's so true because your shows are like a tent show revival. People go bananas.

There is that element and that's what seems really special to me. Like, *it is available*, if you want to be in a celebratory atmosphere.

And pretty transformative too. I've been to shows of yours where you don't even realize it, and then you look down, and your feet are off the ground, and you're like, I'm hovering above the fucking floor.

Yeah, that's the thing! I feel like, as a species, we've become more and more wrapped up in overgeneralizing the doom, "Everything's going to hell," and all that. So, it seems more immediate and more important and more pertinent to have reliable events to connect.

Is there anything after the show that helps keep your voice in shape?

We used to drink alcohol a fair amount in the early days, but I have noticed that if I actively stay away from that, I have better longevity. So, I drink a lot of water, try to sleep a lot, and not overdo it.

When you start getting sick, what do you do?

I try to prioritize. Stop talking and save everything I can for the stage because then you're super aware that you only have a little bit in the tank. Every night, whether I'm sick or not, I have a little mug warmer that I plug in and I have a hot tea onstage with me. I do that in the studio as well. I like to have a mug warmer and a real ceramic mug with some good ginger turmeric tea with too much honey in it. I'll make sure that's flowing a lot if I have some throat health challenges. I'll have lozenges onstage too. And if I'm feeling like something's coming on with a cold, I'll warm-up a lot longer before a set.

Are there songs where you wonder if your voice will be there that night?

There sure are! "Ain't No Man" is a tough one. I sing harmony throughout and it's a pretty high harmony. The lead vocals are never an issue, it's the harmonies that are the most challenging. But that song, I take the third verse on my own, and it's just the drum kit and the vocal. I had this idea that it'd be the last song and I'll take that moment to do a big thank you and Scott will introduce the band. It's really fun, but that means "Ain't No Man" has to be last in the set, which generally is twenty-five to thirty songs, so it's always like, *God almighty*. When "Ain't No Man" is sixth or seventh, it's never an issue, but after two hours and fifteen minutes of full on singing non-stop, there's a couple things where it's like, *Well, that's not available, gonna do that an octave lower*.

Are there songs where you've had to adjust the key live?

Our first two or three records, we just tuned to the piano, and the piano was from like 1898 or something, but around 1900, I guess standard pitch changed. So, we recorded our first records like this, and it was a little lower. Then, to stick with that, we recorded *Emotionalism* a half step down. So, a lot of things from that era have been hyped up half a step just to make it more standard, and easier to remember, and easier to play. But I heard some song Smokey Robinson was singing recently, and I was like, *Man, he really brought that down a few keys, that's smart*. I can see that happening at some point. To me, all that stuff is super malleable. Any key can be changed at any time. We like the Dylan approach.

What was your most embarrassing vocal mishap ever?

Around 2003, I joined David Childers onstage at the Neighborhood Theatre in Charlotte to sing a song called "The Prettiest Thing." When it came time for my verse, I just choked, man. I loved the song so much, I got caught up in not wanting to let it down and forgot the lyrics. [*Laughter*] That'll happen. You can forget lyrics no matter how old you are, no matter how many times you've played the song.

Do you remember a performance where you surprised yourself?

The ending of "Bleeding White" was a big surprise. If you give that one a careful listen, there were some let-loose moments that were very exciting and a little surprising. And the same thing at the end of "Roses and Sacrifice," there's a big finale type outro. I'm a big, big fan of the let-loose-at-the-end-of-the-song moment. I love when a singer will just wail. And I have that extra gear, but for some reason, every time I go into that gear, I kind of forget that that's something I can do. I'm not Chris Cornell, but I can have moments where I can head into that fun, stratosphere range, and I love it.

How are you with hearing your own voice?

I'm okay with my voice. I don't really judge it as much as I used to. I can definitely get lost in judging if my pitch is on point enough to view something as a keeper, but I don't do that with a ton of emotion anymore, so that makes it a lot easier to review a vocal. It's hard for me to listen to some earlier stuff because of the pitch, but I think that as I mature and get older, I'll even be able to listen to that stuff with appreciation.

You and Scott have some of the best harmony vocals we've heard in years. I gotta understand what the key is to singing a great harmony. How do I maintain my own melody and not start singing in the other person's key?

[*Laughs*] That's just practice, practice, practice. I think it's important to see it as its own melody. If you listen to a master like David Rawlings, he's not just mirroring. It's not just an interval that goes everywhere the main line goes. If you took that lead vocal and some of the rigidity away and let it free flow a little more, you can get the best of both worlds where it is a backup vocal, but it's also adding more color and dimension and meaning to what the actual lyrics are.

Do you have to have guardrails up in your mind so that you don't veer into Scott?

No, we've just done it so much. That was built-in at a young age, again, just hearing my dad sing harmony all the time. And Scott did too, but he doesn't hear it like I do. To him, I think it's more of an abstract consideration. Because it's harder for him, a lot of times he will come up with a more interesting harmony line. Because I have an automatic leaning towards a certain type of harmony, I have to really let myself go emotionally, where I set myself free to land in a harmony line that's more interesting. Just like anything, once you learn to sing harmony, you can get into the curse of being formulaic. But if someone's trying to get better at singing harmony, I would say, sit down at the piano. It's all laid out in front of you. Play a C then play an E. Those two guys together. Then, you can pick out the melody, and then you can pick out the harmony. And you can hear it. You don't have to be trying to invent it all the time. It's the piano, man. The piano *is* the tool. A lot of times in the studio, it's like, "Why is this not working?" The only way to solve the mystery is to go sit down at the piano.

In the *May It Last* documentary, you mentioned that after seeing Doc Watson perform, you realized that power didn't have to come from playing loud but from character. Can you explain what you meant by character?

I feel like all great artists and performers have become great because they have character, because they are checked into who they are. It was very confusing for me as a twelve-year-old kid to look at Nirvana and understand that the power is coming from the character. It's not coming from the aesthetic and it's not coming from the volume. But since there is so much volume, and awesome, exciting aesthetic, and youth and energy, it's easy to get that confused. Kurt Cobain had a lot in his mind, he had a lot that he was considering and thinking about, and he was a very sensitive soul with quite a lot of grit to him. But he had a lot of character. And that's what makes Nirvana more of a lasting thing that we now understand it to be. Doc Watson, it's the same thing. And it's the same thing with Mos Def. You listen to any of his records and it's *full* of character. It's full of a guy checking into what he is, texturally, rhythmically, in his soul, in his understanding of the world around him. But that was a jarring reality for me and Doc gave it to me. He'll play you a song that puts you in the woods in the middle of the night by yourself, walking towards death, and man, it's all of the things. That's what great art does. You can present power, but you don't have to be presenting it at 125 db.

There's also a scene in the film where you're recording "No Hard Feelings" with Rick Rubin and you deliver this soul crushing performance. When it's over, you and Scott go outside and you're sort of struggling to come to terms with the beauty of the song versus the painful relationship that brought the song into existence. Scott's almost more emotionally distraught than you in that moment. Do you guys take on each other's joy or pain in a more significant way because you're singing about it together?

Yes, and that's generally more of an unspoken thing. That moment that was captured on film was a very difficult moment. And it's very uncomfortable for me, still, to view it because that song... it's really a once in a lifetime song. I feel like I got to be the little human channel for it. But it's been shown to me that it's a real important song for a lot of folks. And it's a special thing to be able to sing it and to connect with people. We finish the encore with it and it's extremely emotional. Last night, I gave my set list to the girl in the front row who was crying her eyes out. I don't know the specifics of what that song is bringing up for her, who she's lost, or who she's about to lose, it might be herself. But it definitely checks you into the temporary nature of this life and that's a weirdly beautiful and uncomfortable place to be sometimes. I wanted to see the song through, and stay the course to finish it, and be open to God to let me have it so that I could share with people that it's okay. Life is suffering, that's true, but it's a lot of other things too. We let go of things throughout and it's always a surprise. It's hard to get good at it, but in the end, you even let go of yourself. It's something we can't really understand but we are here together and we can try to understand together. We can try to come by compassion and forgiveness as much as we possibly can. But that moment in the film is evidence that it was an emotional thing to write the song, share it with Scott and Bob, and to commit it to tape. It's heavy.

Yeah. And Scott could've approached that song like, that's a sweet song my brother wrote, but it was almost like *you* needed to console *him*.

That's true. More often in a marriage or a significant other type of relationship, one person has to be the one that takes care of the other. And, a lot of times, you trade roles back. Scott takes care of me a lot and I take care of him as I can. So, it makes perfect sense that I would finish that song and be like, "Oh man, that was magic, that felt really good," and that he would be like, "*But what does it all mean?*" We certainly take turns with that. The moments that he's a little more tortured are generally not the same moments that I am, which is very convenient.

It's so interesting how you guys have to step into each other's mind frame in such a deep, powerful way to sing your brother's feelings. The empathy and transference that must go on is amazing.

It is amazing. And it's built-in, so it's easy to take it for granted sometimes, but it is a very special thing that we both got to get in this life.

Rick Rubin is one of the greatest producers of all time and you guys have done a bunch of records with him. How does he approach recording vocals?

The things I've learned from Rick can be applied to recording and life in general. He's really up for the experiment. He's really up for, "Well, let's just find out." He'll start a lot of statements with, "This might be a terrible idea, but..." For someone of such renown, it was really refreshing, especially early on, to see that he had that kind of humility in the work process. So, the thing that I've applied vocally is: just try the experiment. This isn't coming out tomorrow. You're just learning, you're just finding out. Is it great? Is it silly? Is it awesome? Is it powerful? Whatever, let's find out. The beautiful thing about Rick is that he's not Mr. Technical. He ain't gonna come in and say, "Oh, you should sing a third here." That's not his language. All of the conversation is about spirit. And that's helpful too, because you can have the greatest technical singing in the world, but if the spirit isn't there, it's not gonna invite your listener in. *Because you're not there*! For there to be a vocal that is connecting, you have to be connected to yourself in the first place, and the way I understand things, that means I need to be connecting to God. In whatever capacity that exists. That's a mysterious thing, but I believe it to be true.

Do you have a favorite vocal performance you're really proud of?

I'm generally partial to the newest thing, but I felt really good about "Fisher Road to Hollywood" for me and Scott both. And I have to say that I didn't get in the way of myself for "No Hard Feelings." I'm really glad about that.

Do you have a favorite vocal performance of Scott's?

I really love "Mama, I Don't Believe." I felt that was a great song and a great performance. And "When You Learn." When Scott is hitting that sensitivity, that really stands out for me, because, in my mind, he built his approach on his natural sort of abrasiveness at times, texturally. That really works for him too, but there's something really special to me when he goes into that very, *very* fragile place.

What's changed the most about your voice since you started?

I think it's gotten more nuanced and I've learned to explore more angles of it. To my mind, Mike Patton is possibly the greatest vocalist in the world and has been for probably thirty years. To me, he's the benchmark of what's possible as far as variety. I don't push it that far because he's superhuman to me, but I have been more open to like, when we're rocking, let's rock, let's scream. And when we're getting sweet, let's get really, really sweet. And when we get low, invite that Johnny Cash low in there. Don't be afraid to explore the textures on any given song. What. Serves. The Song? That's another big Rick thing, "What serves the song?" Whatever serves the song, that's what we're doing.

If you could duet with one singer—living or dead—who would it be?

Tom T. Hall.

Who are your top five favorite singers of all time?

Sam Cooke. Louis Armstrong. Shannon Hoon. Dolores O'Riordan. Chris Cornell.

If you could ask any singer about their voice, who would it be, and what would you ask?

Jeff Buckley. I would ask him, "What is the best path to the divine while singing?"

TONY BENNETT

ANTHONY DOMINICK BENEDETTO—IF YOU'RE ITALIAN, you probably know that name is short for Tony Bennett. A man who released his first single in 1951 and announced that he was slowing down in 2021. Now, I'm no math whiz, but I believe that's seventy years of recording music and touring the world. May everyone be so lucky to do what they love for that long. But Tony Bennett has always been a man in rarified air.

Following in the tradition of the great jazz vocalists and song stylists like Nat King Cole and Frank Sinatra, Tony has won nineteen Grammy Awards, two Emmy's, a lifetime achievement award, and is tied with Willie Nelson as the oldest living singer in this book. The man is ninety years old, proving what can be done if you have the talent, the will, and a little bit of luck.

I was lucky enough to briefly speak with him before he announced his retirement, having no idea that some of his advice would play such a crucial role in future interviews. Guys named Tony—they've always got a trick up their sleeve.

Who first exposed you to singing?

I was always singing from the minute I was born. My family was that way. My father was a wonderful singer in Italy. In all the different towns that he was in, they would listen to him and he had that reputation. And it was a big influence.

And your brother was a singer as well early on?

My brother was a wonderful singer as a young boy of nine or ten years old. My mom had him studying with an opera teacher, singing opera, and he was very successful, but he didn't like doing it. I couldn't believe it because we were a family that loved music. I said, "How can you not like it? It's the best thing in the world to entertain and make people feel good." So, I kept on. To this day, I love to entertain people.

Were you emulating anyone when you started out?

No.

How did you find your own voice?

I was taught by Mimi Spear at the American Theatre Wing on 52nd street, which was the great jazz street. She was a great teacher and she was a great jazz singer. She taught me to just be myself and don't imitate anybody else.

Do you feel nervous or confident before you perform?

Any performer who performs well is always nervous before they walk onstage. They hope everything goes good and that the audience is gonna like them. So, you never get over wondering if it's gonna be good every time you sing.

Do you do any vocal warm-ups before you go onstage?

No. I just sing.

How do you take care of your voice on the road?

You have to sleep well. If you have a good night's sleep, you're in top voice. You just don't want to let the public down. And I'm funny, I'm ninety years old, and I'm still singing in top voice.

Five years ago, at the London Palladium, you set down the microphone and sang "Fly Me to the Moon" with just a guitar, and your voice was reaching the very back of the theater, and I thought, *I don't know how he's doing this*!

I'm still doing that.

How are you exuding such power?

I just know how to sing. I love to sing. I love to make people feel good.

Have you ever had an embarrassing vocal mishap onstage?

No. [*Laughter*] It takes about seven years to learn how to sing right. That's what happened to me. It took me years to learn what to leave out, what to put in, so that the show is balanced, so you don't stay on too long, and that the public is satisfied.

What were you doing in the beginning that's different from how you are now?

Making an awful lot of mistakes!

Like what?

I can't remember. I made sure I forgot every one of them! [*Laughs*]

Aside from all the people you've sung duets with over the years, if you could do a duet with one singer—living or dead—who would that be?

Louis Armstrong. When he was alive, I always wanted to do an album with Louis Armstrong. He was the great jazz singer, you know, he was the best one.

Who are your top five favorite singers of all time?

Nat King Cole, Frank Sinatra, Ella Fitzgerald...that's about it.

If you could ask any singer about their voice, who would it be, and what would you ask?

Mimi Spear said, "Just be yourself. Never imitate another singer. Imitate musicians. Piano players, and trumpet players, and saxophone players...but don't imitate singers. Be yourself. The minute you're yourself, you're different than anyone else."

Nile Rodgers on
DAVID BOWIE

THERE PROBABLY ISN'T ANYONE mentioned in this book who has been more of an influence to singers everywhere. We all love David Bowie. Ziggy Stardust. Aladdin Sane. The Thin White Duke. He just kept on going, changing his style, his persona, his sound and vision. Always one step ahead, defining what we should dig next, delivering it to us in the shape of a hit or as a concept we would only fully grasp in retrospect.

He sold over 100 million records, was inducted into the Rock & Roll Hall of Fame, won multiple Grammy Awards, and is considered one of the greatest rock stars we've ever known. But for me, he was a perfect artist to the very end, and no one will ever come close.

In 2016, Bowie released his twenty-fifth and final studio album, *Blackstar*. Two days later, he was gone from cancer. His parting gift to us was his own eulogy, shrouded in bittersweet mystery, knowing full well this would be his last statement to the world.

Nile Rodgers, on the other hand, is a legend is his own right. Record producer, singer, songwriter, guitarist, co-founder of CHIC, the man is an absolute funk-filled force of nature. He's the winner of multiple Grammys and a Rock & Roll Hall of Fame inductee as well. You want to chart? You go to Nile. That's what Bowie did in 1982 when they recorded *Let's Dance*. It would be his bestselling album of all time and make Bowie a superstar in the process.

When was the first time you heard Bowie sing?

I was in a group called New York City and we were playing down in Miami Beach in the mid-'70s, and I met this woman, who was a photographer, at a Hawaiian restaurant. I don't know how she took a fancy to me or how we struck up a conversation, but somehow, she convinced me—with not too much arm twisting—to spend the night with her on a nude beach in Dania, Florida. She had a boom box and she played *Ziggy Stardust and the Spiders from Mars*, and it was amazing. The whole night was amazing!

And years later, you produce his bestselling album of all time. I heard you guys made *Let's Dance* in seventeen days, from recording to the mix.

Yes, absolutely. That's completely true.

That is something. Was he precious about his vocals or was he just goin' for it real quick?

It was very quick, but also really precious. Out of all the recordings I've done with David—and there were quite a few—because I did *Let's Dance*, "Dancing in the Streets," *Cool World*, and then, *Black Tie White Noise*. Out of all of those vocals, the only thing we ever had a slight disagreement over is when he sings, [*mimics Bowie singing "China Girl"*] "Tremble like a floooower," and his voice cracks.

What about it? I love that part!

He came back and said, "Let's punch in and fix that," I was like, "What? No way!" I convinced him to leave the cracking voice on because it sounded really emotional. As Luther Vandross would say, "When you make a mistake, make it loud and proud." I was going, "Dude, you made that loud and proud and I'm gonna make it even louder in the mix!" [*Laughter*]

What was his approach to recording vocals?

His demeanor was incredibly laid back because he was clear on what he wanted to do every time he worked with me. It may be a different experience with Tony Visconti [Bowie's longtime producer], but with me, he had a vocal concept, and he just looked to me for the musical concept and the content.

Was he punching in a lot or going for straight takes?

Surprisingly, there was a very small amount of punching in because he would have such a good idea of what he wanted to do. And, from living with him before we actually recorded *Let's Dance*, he would do a lot of homework. He would study and sing into his Walkman and he would have it all sort of mapped out. We never did a vocal that he had to come back and replace. We may have punched in a line or a note here and there, but not a lot.

Let's Dance kicks off with "Modern Love," where he speaks the intro, saying that he knows when to go out and when to stay in to "Get things done." It's such a random statement to open a record and I'm not sure how it connects to the rest of the song. Did you ever ask him what that line meant?

I didn't think about it at the time. It just sounded cool. Now that you say it, I realize it was very reflective of what we were doing. It actually made a lot of sense because it speaks to my concept of his preparedness. In that pre-production period, David really was out to do something. He really wanted to make a statement. He really did homework and breezed through everything. And it's interesting because we did it so well. He basically commissioned me to make a hit album. That was my directive right from the word go. He said, "Nile, I want you to do what you do best." I asked him what he thought I did best and he said, "You make hits." I said, "Oh. Okay!" [Laughs] David Bowie wants me to make hits after coming off Scary Monsters? Okay!

Did you ever see how he may have taken care of his voice?

No, we never discussed it. All I know is that whenever it was time for us to go, he was ready. When he says, "I know when to go out. I know when to stay in. Get things done." He always was ready to get things done. The most I ever saw him focus on vocals, to a degree that felt like he was really more meticulous, was on the Black Tie White Noise album because that was originally titled The Wedding Album. That was the music he played when he and Iman got married, so he toiled over that more than normal.

When you hear his voice now, what do you remember most?

The acting with his vocals. He could change his voice to play a scope of characters. For example, when we were doing "China Girl," he was being dramatic and sort of playful. That's what I notice a lot about him.

That track is so odd and so glorious at the same time.

Once I came up with that guitar part, I said, "Hey David, this seems to be a bit of an uncomfortable, racist riff. I don't even know why you guys are even calling the song 'China Girl.'" Because he had written that with Iggy Pop, and I don't think that when he wrote that song he was sober. I knew that he now was sober, so I didn't want to query him too deeply. But I came up with my own interpretation. I believe they were talking about speed balling because in the world of druggie's, "China White" was slang for heroin, and "Girl" was slang for cocaine. But I never wanted to ask him.

There've been a lot of interviews with him talking about that time in his life where he was using a lot and a lot of the terrifying imagery that was surrounding him and that's definitely in the song.

Right, so you gotta understand my discomfort because I was not sober at the time. I was using quite a bit and he had the Serenity Prayer tattooed on his leg.

He had the Serenity Prayer tattooed on his leg?

In Japanese, by the way. I asked him, "Yo, what does that ink mean?" And he told me that it's a kanji of the Serenity Prayer. And I don't think he lied to me. The only time I ever questioned whether David was pulling my leg was when he had written the framework of "Let's Dance," and told me he thought it was a hit. To me, it sounded like a folk song that would be a B-Side. I called his office and a bunch of his friends and said, "Is David saying this to me, thinking that I'm some kind of sycophant and I'm just gonna agree with everything he says?" They all said, "No, he's not like that. If he said he thinks it's a hit, he really thinks it's a hit." I said, "Oh my God. Now I gotta turn this song into a hit." [*Laughter*] So I re-wrote the arrangement right there in my bedroom at his chalet in Switzerland.

There's a great video where you show how that song transformed. You play what he played you and then you play how you changed it.

There's a recording which shows it perfectly. I told him, "Sing exactly what you sang when you were playing the folk thing over this new arrangement and see how you feel." You hear him singing and he's gently dancing around, but by the time we get to the end of it, he's formulated what he's gonna do and it sounds just like "Let's Dance." The phrasing is right, the vibe is right, he's completely convinced and fallen into the groove, and says to the whole band, "Okay, okay, got it." But he was talking to me. *Okay, Nile, I got it. It's a funk song*.

Do you have a favorite track where his vocals absolutely floor you?

I'm a huge fan of his vocal characterizations all throughout the *Ziggy Stardust* album, but I really love "Suffragette City." [*Sings*] "Awww Wham Bam, thank you, Ma'am," and all that. He's a great storyteller. I think when you have confidence in the story, you also have a certain confidence in your delivery of that story. And because he's such a terrific storyteller, it gave him ease of mind with what he wanted to say and how he wanted to deliver it. No one sounds like Bowie. That's what's terrific about him is that he really has a unique, individual sound.

Yeah. He was the best, man...what a loss.

I know. He was really amazing.

BEN BRIDWELL

IF YOU HAVEN'T HEARD Band of Horses, I strongly suggest throwing this book across the room and running for the nearest record store, because this is music you purchase.

Ben Bridwell's voice is a thing of beauty. He may not always think so, but he's wrong.

I first heard Ben's glorious vocal tone when the band's first single hit the radio. The song was called "The Funeral," and I still remember driving along, straining to sing along to that incredible, high, melodic melody. It was one of those pathetic moments where you realize your limitations as a singer.

After seeing Band of Horses live, and hearing the albums that followed, I'm in for life with these guys. Once you see it for yourself, you'll be stoked he's out there as well, makin' sure the pizza tastes right after the show.

Who first exposed you to singing?

I was lucky to grow up in a household with a lot of music around. I grew up with MTV, so I'd always envision myself as the dude in the video. I remember, even as a seven-year-old, being like, *Man, this is my story*.

How'd you make it a reality?

I was working at this café in Seattle and was a bit jaded by the way the kitchen staff was treated at times, and I was like, *I'm just gonna save every bit of money, every tip I get, and I'll show these motherfuckers one day*.

I know you started a record label from there, played a bit of drums, and then started singing. What drove you to make singing your focus?

By the time I got around to singing, it was the most foreign thing in the world. I knew I could hum a bar, but I never considered it something that would be a viable solution to my life. In some ways, I do think a lot of Band of Horses story comes out of me not wanting to flip eggs anymore. I could be stuck in a damn café for the rest of my life or I can try to do something different and make the type of music I'd want to listen to.

Were you emulating anyone when you started out?

Oh, I'm sure. That stems mostly from growing up listening to Neil Young. I remember the "A-ha" moment, driving back from a Rolling Stones concert with my parents in Clemson, South Carolina to Irma, where we lived. It was late at night and my dad had the new Neil Young tape, which was *Harvest Moon*. I remember being like, *I get this guy's voice*. There's so much emotion and so much story underneath the story because of the way that it's told.

Yeah, he's one of those guys who's purely himself when he's singing. It's not perfect, it's not supposed to be, and if it were, it wouldn't work.

Yes, exactly. *It is the point*.

He's one of the guys that gave me courage too.

He's under-recognized for his contributions to so many of us. You can seek some courage in someone that's seemingly so fragile a voice, but it's a show of strength.

One million percent. So how did you find your own voice?

As I'm going in to start my own project, I went to Guitar Center and got this little stomp box unit, like vocal processor thing. I was also listening to Built to Spill and Flaming Lips, and other bands where the singer has that higher range thing. I'm like, *I'll just make enough smoke and mirrors on this bitch and no one will know that I can't sing* or no one will know that my words suck or that I'm a hack. It's total imposter syndrome. The first shows that we did, the voice as another instrument was definitely the way of the game 'cause I didn't believe in myself as a songwriter, a singer, or a lyricist.

Did you ever have any vocal training?
Never.

Do you feel nervous or confident before you perform?
I'm rarely fired up and confident that we got this shit in the bag. I would honestly question my dedication if I felt that it wasn't a dangerous situation out there.

What do you do to calm yourself?
I'll have a cocktail. I'll be really quiet, think a lot. Probably think too much, get kind of freaked out. Sometimes the excitement does overrule the nervous energy, but most of the time there is a bit of a silent desperation going on.

What freaks you out the most?
The between song area is one of the scariest things in life for me, waiting for people to clap, and having to be the emcee. That part is daunting at best. I'm usually trying to get it on as soon as possible so we can kill dead time.

Do you do vocal warm-ups before shows?
Never once. Never have.

How do you take care of your voice on the road?
I don't. I talk shit all night long. I play damn corn hole after the shows and stay up 'til damn five in the morning.

Whaaat?
There's only been a couple times we've had to cancel due to my voice failing me, and usually that was due to like a sinus infection, and just being overworked. But it's been very rare in our almost fifteen years. I did recently quit smoking cigarettes, which is gonna be a big help, I hope.

Do you have any rituals before you hit the stage?
I've done every set list for this band so, that's something I take seriously. It might be like a tick I have, but I'll spend a lot of time making sure that the set list is different from other ones if we're playing the same town. I'll look up the set list from last time we played there and make sure it all works well. With all the weird guitar changes that we have, it's like this weird algorithm that has to get figured out every day.

Anything else?
If I can, I'll sleep for like forty-five minutes or an hour, getting ready for war, 'cause once I wake up it's kind of game time.

Is there anything after the show that helps keep your voice in shape?

No, it's always been counter-intuitive. We'll just get out some sporting game if we can. If there's some area that we can hang out at, we have these chairs that we keep. Even when we first get there, I'll set up the camp, and we hang out, listen to music, and party. It's not very civilized.

Are there songs where you wonder if your voice will be there that night?

I have that over-arching terror kinda built into all of them. For some reason, I chose to sing in this register and now I'm stuck with it. [*Laughter*] But I wanna do a great job for these people that spend their hard-earned money to be there. Our two biggest songs being "The Funeral," which is in a high reg, and then, "No One's Gonna Love You," I do have to get them right or the pizza won't taste right after the show.

Do you ever adjust the key live?

Sometimes. We've had to do that when you have to sing in the morning for promo stuff. You have to be there at like 7:00 and play the single. Well, it's the single because you sang it in this damn register, you dumb ass! It's a double-edged sword.

[*Laughs*] So then you take it down?

At times. We've all found that if we go down a step or step and a half, it just makes for like an awesome, more interesting take on the song anyways. But it's such a novelty to us because we don't ever do it. Shit, if we're allowed to be around for another damn decade or two, we may have to consider it.

On *Acoustic at the Ryman*, you sing "Wicked Gil" in a much lower register than you do on *Everything All the Time*, and it's really beautiful.

Oh, yeah! That's good looking out. I wrote it just like *that*. I mean, that was my intention always. With the full band, electric, sometimes it's really kind of dense. I've always had this torch I've carried for the original, and the Ryman offered an opportunity for a new twist on an old favorite. Or an old twist on a new one.

I also love what you did with "No One's Gonna Love You" on the *Stockholm Version*. That song was already so incredible on *Cease to Begin*, and then you release this single like eight years later and it's even better. The vocal take is really naked and raw. What made you decide to re-record it like that?

I was contacted by my manager about this fella who had died from an act of terrorism in Sweden. He leaves his wife and two babies in the wake of this tragic murder and the widow was wondering if I'd be willing to come and sing "No One's Gonna Love You." Actually, she asked me if I'd do "The Funeral," dog, and I was really like...freaked. I'm just a fragile person when it comes to that kind of stuff, especially when kids are involved. Like, I cannot trust myself that I can even carry out this duty, much less the irony of singing "The Funeral" at a funeral. Well, I gathered enough courage to say, "Okay, I'll come out there, but let's do this song instead." Luckily, these brilliant local musician dudes made this arrangement for me and said they'll play it with me. Since I had the night off before the funeral, I said, "Let's record it and maybe we can raise some funds for anything his wife needs."

Man, that's beautiful.
Yeah, Chris Bevington. It was really tough, man, I barely made it through. We did Nick Cave's "Into My Arms" and our song.

Band of Horses released a single of "Into My Arms." What is it about Nick Cave's voice that you love so much?
I have friends that love Nick Cave and the Bad Seeds and The Birthday Party, but it never really got to me. I mean, there's songs that I liked, but I never really *got it*, until I got it. Much like that night driving with my parents and Neil finally got to me. It kind of hits you like, *Duh! Why didn't this break through earlier?*

Things find you at the right time though, don't they?
Yes, exactly. I'm a firm believer in that. There's always something waiting for you. So, the Bad Seeds came to me at the right moment. Seeing them perform onstage also, seeing their whole *sermon.*

Yeah, that's the perfect word for it.
Just the command of the audience. It's just so inspiring, man. It's like this motherfucker will command the entire room and maybe some of the space outside of it.

And with a voice that isn't what people think of as technically proficient, yet it's incredible and carries with it the weight of the world in the most beautiful way.
The Silver Jews have a great line in a song that I always keep under my cap. It's "All my favorite singers couldn't sing." And that's kinda it too. We don't like the classically beautiful sounding things. We want the twisted and fractured beautiful.

You have so much balls right now even speaking like this. Your voice is so fucking great! It's crazy how good your voice is. You can't sink down to our level. [*Laughs*]
Damn, dog. No, man. I don't know...that's really kind of you, that's really kind.

What was your most embarrassing vocal mishap ever?
Oh God. It's a ghost that lives with me. We were in Sydney, Australia on the big promo tour for *Why Are You OK*, and we were playing the Sydney Opera House. We do this big, drive time radio show in Melbourne, and I remember the voice was not doing well. Then, we had to take a plane to Sydney and that didn't go well because we started partying a little bit. We were doing so much damn press and so much damn performing all the time, partying too late,

staying up too late, and I was smoking like a damn freak. It was maybe five songs in and my voice won't get sound. It just went to nothing. Even my middle range was starting to go out. Then, I had nothing at all, but tears pouring down my eyes. This was great drama. This was better than any Shakespeare community theatre. This was real life and death on the stage. For the first time in my life, my voice just won't work. And it's this huge stage and huge exposure and huge wave that we're riding.

What'd you do?

Our buddies from the opening band came and played a couple songs with us to help out, but it was just a disaster.

Do you remember a performance where you surprised yourself?

I just can't think of any time I've been impressed with myself ever. I over-prepare everything. Before I even share anything with the other band members, or ever go to our studio, I've got my shit kind of sorted.

Are you the kind of singer who hates their own voice?

Very much. Yeah, I'm definitely one of those guys, but I've learned to live with it because I also want to do better at my job. But I can say whole heartedly that I don't like the way it sounds.

That's so crazy! Do you have a favorite vocal performance you're really proud of?

I'm kind of proud of all of them. The fact that they happened at all always seems so unlikely. I'm sure there are some where I'm like, *Damn, good job*, but I don't think of it like that.

I'm a huge fan of the way you approach your vocals in the studio because it seems like you always find different ways to keep it fresh. You have what I would consider to be the classic "Ben Bridwell sound," which would be something like what you'd hear on "Wicked Gil." That's just you double tracking in your higher register, right?

Yeah, a lot of the times it is a good double vocal.

But then sometimes you'll layer your vocals in really unique ways. I'm thinkin' of songs like "Laredo" or "Infinite Arms" where it sounds like you're double tracking yourself high, but then you're doing one in your normal head voice, I think.

I got four of myself.

What are you doing, two high and low?

I can't remember exactly how many I was doing, but that *Infinite Arms* album is rife with Benji vocals everywhere. There's ones where I understood what an octave was now, *We gotta put it down! Dumb ass thinks he sounds good*. I was so over-focused on that at times, I started to overcook things with too much layering and stacking of vocals. Just because anyone can, doesn't mean they should.

Well, one of the things I dig about you is that you're always finding new ways to experiment with your voice. You're not just leaving it in one place.

Shit. I hope. God, you know more about my voice than I do. [*Laughter*] I appreciate that.

Let's talk about your appreciation for the lost art of background vocals. Songs like "Dilly" or "Shut-in Tourist" have some really creative melodies goin' on.

I love backing vocals. I honestly don't think about them enough. I'll hear a song that's got good "Doo-Wops" on it, or "Sha-na-na-na's" or something, and I'm like, *Damn! That sounds bad ass! Don't forget, man, that shit is fun!*

What's changed the most about your voice since you started?

I've noticed I can get a good falsetto. I'm not afraid to sing soft now and retain pitch. I'm trying to be better at nuancing and working with the mic that's in front of me because they do sound different and your energy sounds different on it.

Explain that.

You might think that your extra energy is going to be the thing that injects the song with its life, but, in reality, you might just be sounding a little too aggressive. It's trying to find ever wider boundaries of dynamic. I find by doing that, I'm able to sing really personal on the mic. And not being afraid of the microphone and being able to still get my character without fucking up the whole vibe of what the song needs. And trying to be *anonymous* in the song at times, trying to be anonymous as a voice, like not trying to put my inflection in there. Maybe I'm understanding more about what my role can be. I feel a lot better about it than when I started, that's for sure.

If you could duet with one singer—living or dead—who would it be?

Oh shit. Otis Redding. My God, that's a terrifying question. But he's the greatest singer in my opinion, living or dead. It would just be the greatest honor.

Who are your top five favorite singers of all time?

Well, Otis goes first. Neil Young would have to go second, I guess. Dang, dude, this is gonna bother me all night. You must've seen people lose their minds on this.

Yeah, it's great.

You're a sadist! Okay, this is not the be-all, end-all of what my list is: Leonard Cohen, number three. Number four. *Oh my God*. It hurts every time. I'll go for Stephen Malkmus from Pavement. He informed my ass more than even I know. For real. He was a huge influence for me growing up, and still.

Alright, you got one more.

Hell, I'll go with something contemporary. I'll go with damn Kendrick Lamar right now.

If you could ask any singer about their voice, who would it be, and what would you ask?

Oh, my goodness. Man, you really pull the tough stuff at the end, don't you? I'd ask Neil Young, "When you write the song and you're playing the guitar or the piano, or whatever it is, are you saving something for when you got the song figured out? Or are you immediately singing full bore, even while you're writing the song, through all the tedious moments that it takes to write a song? Are you using the voice that you know you're going to use later or saving it so you can focus more on the details?"

That's interesting. My problem is I'll hold back, and then when we get full band, I'll realize, *I wrote it out of my range!*

Ohhh. But I bet you still find a way, don't you?

You gotta find a way, right?

Exactly! [*Laughs*] Absolutely.

Andy Wallace on
JEFF BUCKLEY

DAVID BOWIE ONCE SAID that if he could only have one record on a desert island, it would be Jeff Buckley's *Grace*. It was the only official record Buckley would release in his young career before drowning in the Mississippi River in 1997.

When *Grace* was released in 1994, Bob Dylan called him "One of the greatest songwriters of the decade." Robert Plant and Jimmy Page, both heroes to Jeff, sang his praises at every turn. His voice to them was "Mind-altering," and "Scary." Bono, PJ Harvey, Thom Yorke, and Chris Cornell have all said the same in their own ways. Many demos and live recordings have been released since his death, but that debut album will always be the crowning achievement of a once in a lifetime artist.

Andy Wallace was right there beside him. As a Grammy Award–Winning producer, mixer, and engineer, Wallace has worked on many of your favorite albums and is credited on records with over 120 million sales. But it was on *Grace* that Andy used all his skills behind the board to share an artistic vision and create a timeless classic. It was a true honor to speak with one of the kindest guys in the business about this incredible moment in both of their lives.

When was the first time that you heard Jeff sing?

When he signed to Columbia, they were looking at possible producers, so I met with [A&R executive] Steve Berkowitz and Jeff. Jeff and I really hit it off nicely. Shortly after that, I went down to see him do his solo act with just an electric guitar and a small amp in a little club, and I was blown away. I heard that he was an exceptional artist from Steve, but I was completely amazed, not only by his incredible voice and his command of the songs he was doing, and his original approach—because he did a lot of interesting covers of songs—but he was very entertaining. He had a good sense of humor and a real off the cuff style of talking to people.

Yeah, it's interesting when you listen to those live recordings. His songs were so deep and intense. Then, between songs, he's a total goofball, and doing impressions and weird voices.

That's right. He'd be doing some goofy take on Led Zeppelin or just talking to someone in the audience, but always with a humorous thing. Then he'd start blending in some musical stuff with his talking and it would gradually morph into the intro of "Hallelujah" or something. He'd go off on that, transitioning the audience from laughing and giggling to having their jaws drop while they got sucked into the whole vibe of his performance on these heavier songs. He really was amazing. I said, "Wow. This is a good move."

Had you ever heard anything like him before?

Not like Jeff. Jeff didn't particularly like to hear this, but his voice was reminiscent of his father, Tim Buckley. I don't know his catalog backwards and forwards, but I certainly was aware of his albums. But Jeff was unique.

He could sing so low as if he were talking just to you, and then a second later, push his voice to these incredible heights. From there, he could twist it and control it in ways that just don't seem possible. Especially for some white kid that didn't grow up in India or the Middle East singing that way.

That's right. And he didn't wanna be perceived as a white kid singing the blues.

I don't even think of the blues when I hear Jeff. He's got his own world going.

The song that really centered around was "Forget Her," which was not only intended to be on *Grace*, but a lot of the people at the label were really pulling for that to be the lead single. I think he got self-conscious about that. There were other issues too, and I can't verify this, but my impression was that it was about a relationship and he still had a friendship with the person and felt self-conscious about the negative attitude in the lyric. I was really disappointed that it was off the album. I was very glad to see when they did the *Legacy Edition*, that it was the first song on the second disc. At least it got a chance to be heard.

When he was recording demos for the second album, I read that someone from the label heard "Everybody Here Wants You" and immediately started pushing for it to be the lead single and Jeff got pretty emotional. Almost like it was so commercial that it disturbed him, 'cause he didn't want to be pigeon-holed by the obvious thing. Maybe "Forget Her" had that same kinda vibe around it. It's such a great song, but if it were on _Grace_, it may have been too poppy or too commercial for the record. The fear may have been that it would overshadow the other stuff he felt was more important.

Possibly. The structure of it isn't as intriguing as the song "Grace," which I think is an absolute brilliant song. _That's the one_. When I first saw him at Sin-é and he sang "Grace," I looked at his manager and said, "Where did that song come from?" He said, "That's one of Jeff's originals." I said, "Hooooly cow."

The magnitude of Jeff's talent is a given here, but one of the major reasons that _Grace_ is such a masterpiece is because you knew exactly how to capture him on tape. When it came to recording his voice, what was that process like?

Jeff did most of the work as far as the voice is concerned. He's just a killer singer and we didn't have problems getting good takes. He would often want to do more takes than I felt were necessary. The main thing was to get the vibe right, which is what you have to do producing anyway, and that was one of the things Jeff really wanted as well. He wanted to get out of the city because he had become the darling of the East Village scene and everybody wanted a piece of Jeff. Bearsville was a residential studio out in the woods, up in Woodstock. It was fairly remote, which was good.

How did you get the vibe right to record the vocals?

After dinner, we'd go back out into the studio and we'd round up whoever was around, whether it was staff members or a friend who was up visiting for a day, and there was generally wine involved. [_Laughs_] I told him, "We're not making a record here. We're just making a recording of your performance, so go out and do your solo thing just the way you would. Don't stop and start a song over. Treat it as if you were at Sin-é doing a show." We had an audience in the control room, but within view, so he wasn't all alone out there, and it was nice. It created a relaxed environment. He would go out and basically entertain as he was doing in the club. A couple of things came out of that, "Hallelujah" being one of them. "Corpus Christi" might have come outta that. So, that was a nice thing and kind of bridged that gap.

"Hallelujah" has gotten so much attention, but "Lilac Wine" and "Corpus Christi Carol" are just as intimate and vulnerable. Were you doing anything else to pull that out of him?

A lot of it had to do with not getting in the way too much. I'm pretty sure that I encouraged him to work up close to the mic with a pop screen in front of it, just to get a very intimate up-close sound. The U 47 is a nice warm sounding mic so, that's why I chose it. I generated a little reverb back to him so he wouldn't be hearing himself super dry right in your face.

That's a smart move.
Yeah, but not too much. I don't like to swamp it in reverb. Some of the songs, obviously, like "Corpus Christi" for instance, have a little more reverb than some of the other ones, but that was a mixing decision.

Was he pretty confident about his vocal abilities or was he insecure about that?
He was pretty confident about it. And not to get to hung up on this "Forget Her" thing, but he had the basic track for the music recorded before he had written the vocals. He came in one time and said, "I wrote some vocals," and I said, "Great, let's do a reference vocal track so I can hear it and you can live with it." He basically sang what's on the record. Even though, in his mind, he was recording a reference vocal, he went for it. He didn't just do it lackluster so we could hear the melody. He wasn't inclined to do things halfway like that. He was truly a performer. Even goofing around in the studio about something, it always felt like a performance.

Are there any standout moments for you when you listen back?
His performance on "Corpus Christi Carol" always kind of gives me a little shiver. And the note he holds at the end of "Hallelujah." I honestly don't know how he held the note that long.

There're things he does toward the end of "Grace" where he's already as high as he can be, and then he kicks into another gear and goes even higher, while remaining fully in pitch. The control and mastery he had over his voice is just insane.
Yeah, I know exactly what you're talking about, particularly on "Grace" where he just goes [*mimics Jeff, taking the scream even higher*]. You're like, holy mackerel! [*Laughter*] And with such enthusiasm and commitment. You mentioned pitch too. I can guarantee I did absolutely no pitch correction on any of his vocals anywhere. And I'm pretty sensitive to pitch, I really am. It's one of the areas that gets under my skin.

I'm gonna ask you a hypothetical, just as a producer: you hear a performance and you have to choose between the one that's perfect pitch or the one that's a little off-pitch but has the "Thing" to it. Which do you go for?
It depends on how out of pitch it is, but I would rather have some exciting moment that makes the hair stand up on the back of my neck, as opposed to something that is absolutely pitch perfect but not as exciting. You have to know the singer's ability. Is it that they're just always gonna be a bit pitchy? I might ask someone to do it again, but not even call their attention to the pitchiness because I don't want to make them start thinking about pitch. That should be something that your instrument just goes to. And I'm not a big fan of punching in because I'd rather have somebody sing another performance, unless I feel that it's gonna wear them out.

Do you know if he was nervous or confident before he went onstage?

He was not a person that was particularly nervous. When he made the transition to playing live with the band, in big rooms instead of coffee houses, I do know he was concerned about how to make that transition properly. Part of him just wanted to rock out. He really wanted to be a metal band. But he knew that was not the thing to do so, *How calm do we have it? How wild do we get?* This type of thing.

Do you know if he did vocal warm-ups before shows? Or even in the studio?

In the studio, I believe he did. It's hard to believe he wouldn't. But maybe I'm wrong.

Did he come off as the kind of guy that was protective of his voice?

Nothing that he expressed. He tended to live kind of recklessly. Unfortunately, it may have led to his demise. Going in the river fully clothed. Not a good plan. I remember when I first heard about it, it was just like, *What? It can't be.* I had my plane reservation to go down in a week, and I was just...*I can't believe it.* Anyway, I never got the vibe that he was outwardly expressing a great deal of concern about, "I can't do this" or "I gotta do this with my voice." If he did, it wasn't any big, long regime of [*mimics a singer running scales*].

What is it about Jeff's voice that made him so special to you?

Oh boy, I guess they're obvious things, but his commitment to the lyric, and expression verbally, was as good as anybody I've ever worked with. So sincere in his expression, and intense. The other thing is just his beautiful voice. His ability to sing like an angel as people have described it, and yet, at the same time, he could scream, like at the end of "Grace." But he certainly had this incredibly clear voice. Those are the aspects that stand out for me.

When you hear his voice now, what do you remember most?

It varies a lot. I just remember sharing a sense of humor with him. He had a good sense of humor and I do too, and we laughed a lot. One of the songs on *My Sweetheart, The Drunk*, "Morning Theft" has a line "I miss my beautiful friend." Whenever I hear that I get all choked up. I get choked up now just thinking about it because I really do miss my beautiful friend.

BELINDA CARLISLE

THERE IS A FIRST TIME FOR EVERYTHING, and in 1978, The Go-Go's were it. Before these five feisty females were inducted into the Rock & Roll Hall of Fame, they were a part of the LA punk rock scene, doing things no other band made up of women had ever done before. Yeah, there were revolutionary girl groups, soul outfits, and rock bands, but the Go-Go's were the only ones writing all their own material and playing all their own instruments at this level.

"Can you hear them? They talk about us." Buddy, did they ever?

When the Go-Go's released their debut album in 1981, you had no other choice. They immediately became a pop culture phenomenon, owning the airwaves, MTV, and the thrift store fashion sense of young girls everywhere. And that gorgeous creature behind the microphone, leading the charge, was Belinda Carlisle.

Her vocals took inspiration from the California sound and playful energy the Beach Boys had defined. But Belinda wouldn't stop there. In the decades that followed, she'd continue to rock out with her band, but would also chart another vocal path on her own, going deep inside herself, battling her personal demons, and finding a completely different voice that embraced other forms of language and new ways of communicating from the heart.

Still doing exactly what she wants on her own terms, you can take the girl out of punk, but you can't take the punk out of the girl.

Who first exposed you to singing?

My mom had a beautiful voice and she used to always sing to me. That's some of my earliest memories, was being in my crib, and my mom would sing some of the hits of the times, like in the late '50s, early '60s. After that, television was of a certain genre and I was exposed to Judy Garland and Della Resse and Ethel Merman. I've always been attracted to the female voice from a very young age.

Were you emulating anyone when you started out?

I was trying to sound like Julie Andrews. [*Laughs*] I remember when Mary Poppins came out, singing "Spoon Full of Sugar" in an English accent at like age nine.

How did you find your own voice?

When the Go-Go's started, we were literally sitting on a curb at a party and picking which instrument we were gonna play. I had never sung before, but I always fancied myself a singer—I didn't know if I could sing or not—but I thought, *Sure, I'll sing*! [Guitarist] Charlotte Caffey used to say in the beginning days, "Wow, the way you pronounce your S's and that natural vibrato kind of sounds like Bryan Ferry." I was a huge Roxy Music fan and I loved Bryan Ferry, so, of course, that was a compliment. But then I heard a recording of our third show at Rock Corporation in the valley, and I was horrified because I sounded awful, and I knew I had a lot of work to do.

What was the work you had to do?

You learn technique and how to breathe. I had a naturally unique voice—I can carry a tune—but I had to work on technique. With experience, you know your strengths and weaknesses. A strong point of mine has always been knowing my capabilities as a singer, what I should and should not do. But that just comes with time. I had to work a long, long time, *and really hard*, to get to a point where I sounded at least listenable.

Did you have any vocal training?

I couldn't afford vocal lessons, but my manager paid for my lessons. I think I went through all the vocal teachers in LA at that time. [*Laughter*] I still take vocal lessons by Zoom. A really important thing for me was to learn about breath, control, and how to use the voice so you don't lose it. Singing was always a work in progress, learning as I went along.

Are you nervous or confident before you perform?

I never went onstage without a few drinks, but then, when I got sober, I was like, *Oh God, it's gonna be impossible to ever sing onstage again*. What I found is that it's so much easier!

What's the main difference, other than being sober?

When you're singing, at the risk of sounding really pretentious, you can tap into something that's greater than yourself, and you can just fly. It's the most amazing feeling to sing when that happens. Now, I can kind of click into that. I never used to be able to do that. Singing, for me, is almost like channeling. It's almost like an energy exchange with the audience. It's an amazing thing to have, an amazing thing to feel. *I love, love, love* singing. When it's great, it's great, and when it's terrible, it's really bad. [*Laughter*] But most of the time, it's a great time.

Do you do vocal warm-ups before you perform?

Now I do. I have like a library of vocal lessons. I'll do a warm-up before sound check. Then, before the show, I'll do vocal warm-ups in my dressing room, which usually has at least one or two humidifiers going.

How long are you warming-up?

Ten or fifteen minutes. That's all I need. You can do scales, transitioning from your chest to the head voice. There's an area between the chest and head that's like a danger zone, so opening that up. And trills, which are really good. Some of these are guttural sounds that you can make and do scales with.

Do you have any rituals before you go onstage?

I take an Aleve, which is an anti-inflammatory. It was a really good tip that a vocal doctor told me because it kind of shrinks your vocal cords a bit, any sort of inflammation you might have. I drink lots of Throat Coat, which is a tea that has licorice. And the humidifier thing I'm a real stickler for. That's really important to keep the room moist. I travel with two humidifiers. And no air conditioning. I make sure the air conditioning system is off in my room.

Is there anything after the show that helps keep your voice in shape?

I don't talk and I go straight back to my hotel. Absolutely no fun. I used to be able to do everything, but now my voice is pretty fragile. I can only sing two shows in a row and I have to be really, really careful with it. I just know my limits. Sometimes I do scales after a show, but not religiously.

How do you take care of your voice on the road?

Try to keep the talking and socializing to a bare minimum. I don't go out to dinners. I don't really do much except stay in my room and get in bed and make sure my humidifiers are filled up. I think the humidifiers are the most important thing actually. It's like a jungle in my room, hot and humid. [*Laughs*] There's a lot of pressure on the singer because if the voice goes, everything else goes too. And I don't like to fly on the day of a show because that's a lot of dry air.

When you start getting sick, what do you do?

I panic. [*Laughter*] There's nothing else to do. I'll get Silver Collodial, take throat spray. I try not to think about it, but sometimes it's really, really difficult to sing through a cold. Sometimes you have to take Prednisone, a steroid, which I do not wanna do, but sometimes you just have to do it. If it gets really bad, that will usually save me.

Do you have songs where you wonder if your voice will be there that night?

That doesn't happen too often, thank God. Some of the songs that you might've been able to sing as a twenty-year-old you can take down half a key or a key. I've done that on some of the songs that could possibly get me into trouble. With vocal lessons, you learn how to handle those high notes, so I'm usually okay. And if there is a song you might have a problem with, you can change the melody on it, and it kind of keeps it interesting for the audience and makes it easier for you.

What was your most embarrassing vocal mishap ever?

God! It happened at a corporate gig a couple years ago. It was outside, in Bali, which is really humid. I was totally fine, talking to some friends who were smoking cigarettes. I hate cigarette smoke, and hate cigarettes, especially being a singer. It's really difficult to be around. But I thought, *Oh, it's fine, it's humid out, and humidity is good for the voice.* So, I got onstage and started singing, and my voice completely went. I had never had anything like that happen to me before.

How did you get through that situation?

I just cut some songs. There's nothing you can really do about it. If it hits you and you start freaking out, that just makes it worse and closes it up more. You just try to not hit the high notes, try to talk through it, but it's awful. [*Laughs*] I'm embarrassed again.

Do you remember a performance where you surprised yourself?

I had a French album called *Voila*. Being able to sing a whole set in French and doing a good job with it, *that* was probably one of the high points of my career.

I was gonna tell you that "Avec Le Temps" is probably my favorite vocal performance of yours. Your voice is incredible on that track.

[*Laughs*] It's one of my favorite French songs ever. You don't even need to know what it means, you know it's a really sad song. You can hear it in the melody. Of all the songs on that album, that was probably my favorite song to sing.

You also sing in Gurmukhi on *Wilder Shores*. *Wilder Shores* and *Voila* are miles apart tonally, but they both show a totally different side of your voice than that little punk in the Go-Go's. These records show how expansive it really is and how truly gorgeous it is. Do you feel like you found an entirely new voice by singing in a different language?

Yes, I did. The French album, especially. I lived in France for twenty-five years, so I always felt like a bit of a chanteuse, like play acting almost, playing the part. It was super fun. *Wilder*

Shores gets into a whole other thing, which is kirtan and devotional music. I've been chanting for over twenty years, and I know the power of chanting. A lot of great kirtan and devotional singers have what's called naad in the voice, which is almost like a transference of energy. It's a real thing in Indian devotional music. When I think of Maria Callas, the naad in her voice is what people respond to. When I hear Maria Callas sing, it does something on a very primitive kind of level to me. That's what all the great kirtan singers have. So, it's being able to access my naad. It sounds like a ridiculous thing, but with mantra music, that's what you want to do. So, that was a whole other way of singing and that was a really interesting process because I wrote a lot of the melodies on those Gurmukhi chants, which are taken from Kundalini yoga, and are meant to be very powerful when you chant them or listen to them. I wanted to develop the naad in my voice to be able to change atmospheres or change feelings when people listen to it. The good Kundalini singers are able to do that—change things. Energy, I guess. Internal and external energy.

Do you have a favorite vocal performance you're really proud of?
I think "Avec Le Temps" is my favorite vocal performance.

We both have the same one!
That album is really dear to me because it really kept me sober in my early days. But it was also the first time in my life that I was able to experiment with the arrangements and with my voice. I think out of all the albums I've done in my career, that's probably my favorite for that reason. It was the first time I was able to work and sing from my heart.

How are you with hearing your own voice?
You know something, it's really hard to listen to a lot of stuff that would be considered classic, like *Beauty and the Beat*. I can't listen to my voice on that album. Now I can because I appreciate the album as a piece of work, but I could not listen to my voice for years and years and years, no.

How come?
I never really thought about singing. I kind of took it for granted. I'd go onstage, I'd drink and smoke and do whatever, and never really took care of it. After I got sober, my voice actually sounded like it had some depth and character. It's only within the past fifteen years or so that I've actually appreciated my voice and am proud of my voice. I know it's not the best voice, but it's unique and I like that. I think that's one of the secrets of the longevity that I've been blessed with, is that *it is* unique. You know when one of my songs comes on the radio. That's one of the secrets too, being able to sing such amazing songs. My catalog, I'm forever grateful for it. It took me a long time to be able to listen to it and say I like my voice.

You released your first solo record, *Belinda*, in 1986, and correct me if I'm wrong, but it sounds like your vocals were even stronger than they were in the Go-Go's. Even your vibrato feels more pronounced. Did something change for you around that time in regard to how you wanted to use your voice?

The nature of the music was a bit different. The Go-Go's is a specific kind of style. It's not a lot of theatrics. It's very kind of punk, straight forward, not a lot of vibrato. And this is not taking anything away from what I've done with the Go-Go's, because that's like my favorite thing to do, but my solo career did allow me more freedom as far as being able to sing differently. I think I probably found my style on my third album, *Runaway Horses*, where I kind of clicked into what my voice was all about.

I was eight years old when the first Go-Go's album came out. [*Belinda laughs*] But my sister is four years older than me and she was a Go-Go's *FANATIC*: posters all over the room, your albums blaring. That's how I grew up. But I was all into AC/DC and Def Leppard, so for me it was like girl's music, because you're a kid and you're an idiot. It wasn't until I got older that I realized how important the Go-Go's were as this band of women, writing and playing all their own stuff. I'm curious how that affected you as a vocalist. Did you approach that microphone like you had something to prove?

No, never. We were loving what we were doing. We weren't trying to prove anything. We did not think it terms of gender. We wanted to be a good band. After we disbanded in the nineties, we felt a bit slighted because the Go-Go's were kind of written off, and nobody understood where we came from, how we happened until the documentary, and I think it woke a lot of people up.

To what in particular?

They didn't know we were self-taught, that we put ourselves together, that we came from the punk scene. But we knew what we did, we knew what we achieved, and we were really proud, whether we got recognized for the achievements or not, but that was my favorite part of the documentary, being able to show people where we came from. People were like, "Oh my God, I had no idea!" It's not like *American Idol* or *The Voice* or one of those shows. We came from the garage. We came from the street.

That's right. And loaded with awesome songs! Like I said, you just don't know any better when you're that young, but when you're older, hopefully you're just like, a great song's a great song. And the songs are great!

Yeah, they are. I never appreciated that either. I never, ever, really thought about us in that way. Seeing that documentary, it was like, *Oh my God. That first album is incredible*. Sorry for tooting my own horn, but I didn't really appreciate the overall—well, the songs, the package, the sound, how important it was. But it *is* considered an important album, and an influential album, and now I can see that.

You're also overlooked for how great the backing vocals are. You guys were so young and performing these beautifully crafted background parts. What was the inspiration for that?

We grew up with the Beach Boys. Charlotte and I are native Californians. [Guitarist] Jane Wiedlin moved to California when she was very young, so I'm sure she would say she was very influenced by the "California sound." When I was a child and summertime came around, I would put on 93KHJ, lay down next to the speaker, and just sing from eight in the morning until six at night. Just sing, sing, sing. The music that was on the radio at that time was so great and the Beach Boys were the biggest part of my DNA.

And Brian Wilson sang background vocals on one of your albums! How did that come about and what was that like?

He used to come to Go-Go's shows in the early days and I worked with him through the years and sang backgrounds on a couple of his albums. I had a song named "California" on *A Woman and a Man*, and I just asked. It was probably the most amazing studio experience in my life. He comes in and goes, "I worked out all the parts." He had this cassette player and he would play the track and sing the parts over the track. It sounded like, "Oh my God, this is horrible. What are we gonna do? What are we gonna say?" The producer said, "Just let him go in and do his thing and then we'll deal with it." So, he was in the vocal booth doing all these parts, and when they were put together, it was like a symphony. It was so emotional, I felt like I was seeing Mozart work. It was the most incredible, emotional experience, watching a genius at work like that, and someone who means so much to me in so many ways. After he did his thing, and it sounded incredible, it was like, "Okay, let's just take the rest of the day off." It was emotionally exhausting. I can't really put it into words, but it was an unforgettable experience. It was amazing.

That's so cool. Do you have a favorite Go-Go's background vocal track?

The song that comes to mind is "Here You Are," a song off *God Bless the Go-Go's*. The background vocals are really beautiful.

What's the key to great backgrounds?

We used to have this thing when we recorded where somebody would be in the booth doing their vocals and somebody in the control booth would say, "You've been accused of barbershoppery!" You can over-do background vocals too. Don't make it a barbershop quartet cause that can sound really dorky. It's finding the balance. But I love BVs. That's always been one of my strong points, actually, is coming up with background vocals.

What's changed the most about your voice since you started?

I think it's a better voice. Your voice changes as you get older anyway, but it's deeper and richer. It's more confident too. I have more confidence. I never really had the confidence about singing until probably the last twenty years or so.

If you could duet with one singer—living or dead—who would it be?

Oh my God, Barry Gibb! There's a quality in the voice that does something to me. It's like, with some people, Go-Go's music transcends being music and becomes moments, or a memory, or something more than music, and Barry Gibb's voice just really affects me, and transcends just being that voice or music. It means so much more that it's hard to put into words. Plus, I met him a couple times, and he's so nice. He's probably my favorite songwriter.

Who are your top five favorite singers of all time?

Okaaay. Maria Callas, Barry Gibb, Chrissie Hynde, Dinah Washington, and oh-oh-oh-oh-oh, I know, there's somebody else. Neil Finn, I would say!

Neil Finn's so amazing! Stoked you brought him up. So, if you could ask any singer about their voice, who would it be and what would you ask?

I would ask Chrissie Hynde about her phrasing because I always thought her phrasing was really unusual. When I heard the Pretenders first album, it was different from anything I'd heard. How does she come up with her phrasing?

It's awesome 'cause sometimes she'll be singing a melody, and then, all of a sudden, she'll like speed it up and then slow it back down again.

Yeah! She's an incredible singer, and I've always been curious about that. And David Bowie. His voice too. One of the best voices ever. I don't know what I would ask him.

NEKO CASE

NEKO CASE PERFECTLY DESCRIBED how a lot of us feel as vocalists when she said, "It's not that I feel I'm good at it so much as, when you start singing, it's like you turn on a light, and that light keeps you safe." Whether it's with her solo material, a side project, or playing with The New Pornographers, Neko's voice keeps you safe. Her warm, lyrical tone stretches from country to indie rock to folk and pop, but there's something else that's not as easy to describe. It has a mysterious, compelling magic, rooted in the dust of the earth. If you've followed her career, you know exactly what I mean, and you're well aware of how respected and beloved she is by critics and fans alike.

But, if you've yet to hear her voice and haven't had the chance to fall deeply under her spell, I say you crank up "Hold On, Hold On" from her 2008 release *Fox Confessor Brings the Flood* and see what I'm on about. You'll be on about it too!

Who first exposed you to singing?

My parents and grandparents were avid music listeners, so it was just always there. It was like a constant soundtrack. I don't remember discovering it, but I remember appreciating it.

Who made you feel that you could do this?

Me. [*Laughter*] It wasn't like, I think I'm good at this so I need to do this. It was more like I just had such a desire I couldn't turn it off. It was more desire than ability.

Were you emulating anybody when you started out?

I wasn't.

How did you find your own voice?

I just kept making records. My first solo record was more of a country record and I think I overdid it. I'm singing at full volume and it sounds a little hokey to me. I sound really afraid. I didn't know what my own voice was yet, but I owned it.

Did you ever have any vocal training?

I went for a vocal lesson once when I was nineteen and I hated it. It didn't feel like singing, it felt like calisthenics. I'm glad I didn't do that because it molds people in a certain direction sometimes. It's good for some people, I just don't think I'm one of those people.

Are you nervous or confident before you perform?

I usually feel *pretty good*. Not that I feel like I'm good at singing so much as when you start singing, it's like you turn on a light, and that light keeps you safe. It's like, I have to keep doing this part, I don't have a choice. You're on an exercise bike that generates electricity. If you stop, *it stops*, and then everyone's in trouble. *Okay, I'll keep doing this, and everything will be okay.*

Do you do vocal warm-ups before shows?

I usually treat sound check as vocal warm-up. We start with songs that are in a lower register and easier to sing and then build up. But, I'm just now thinking about doing vocal warm-ups, which is sad because people should do them. It *is* good for your voice, it's good for your throat, and it's good for you physically. It's stretching. And stretching is so important for you if you want to have good form because singing is so physical.

How do you take care of your voice on the road?

I get as much sleep as possible. I don't drink or smoke, I don't eat sugar, and I try to eat healthy. And I exercise because the lungs are a part of your voice and you gotta keep the lungs healthy.

Is there anything after the show that helps keep your voice in shape?
One thing that's kind of a bummer is I used to sell my own merch and get to talk to people after the show because it's nice to talk to fans and hear about what they're doing. But because it's such a loud atmosphere, I would be speaking in a higher voice to have these conversations with so many people. I had to quit doing that because I would get really hoarse. I was really sad because it wasn't that I didn't want to talk to them or that I was too busy for them. You can't overuse your voice because it will actually stop working at a certain point.

Are there songs where you wonder if your voice will be there that night?
In "Hell-On" there's some screaming that is in a certain key and I gotta hold that note for really long. It's something that you do in your throat, which is dangerous already. It's not your head voice and it's not your stomach voice, it's in your throat, so it's like the most vulnerable part of your singing voice.

And how do you not blow it out?
I do most of it from my stomach and I just try to do all the other things: sleeping, etcetera. There are days where it sounds different, but I've always—knock on wood—hit it thus far.

What was your most embarrassing vocal mishap ever?
I don't think there's *one moment*. I've made sooo many mistakes and had so many moments like that, but I've noticed that if you make a mistake and have fun with it, the audience really loves it. If you can just embrace it or acknowledge it, I think that makes the audience feel really invested, and they like to break the tension by laughing.

Do you remember a performance where you surprised yourself?
I get the most joy making up harmonies. I try to do the weirder ones and that's when the surprise and the joy comes in.

Your harmonizing is so beautiful. I'm thinking of songs like the live version of "Hex" on *The Tigers Have Spoken*. Is there a trick to singing harmony with someone so flawless like that?
Get really good harmony singers to sing with you. Kelly Hogan and Carolyn Mark are singing on that. That's kinda their thing. They love to harmonize. Some people are really good at it. I'm not, in a way. Because my voice is so nasal, I have a hard time blending. Sometimes it works.

I always start veering into the other person's harmony.
Oh, it's so bad!

How do you stay on your own note?
Practice, practice, practice. It's taken me a really, really, really long time. I didn't know what harmony singing was 'til I was about twenty-six. I thought unison singing was harmony sing-

ing. Carolyn Mark and [New Pornographers singer] Carl Newman kind of taught me what harmony singing is. Oh my God, they were Canadian and patient with me. [*Laughter*]

How are you with hearing your own voice?

There are times when I hate it, but mostly I find that, after a while, I can't hear it anymore because your ears can become fatigued to a certain sound. Like when you hear the same thing over and over again, you can't hear its nuances after a while. You just don't have the perspective, even if you wanted it, so it's just about balance. *I can't hear this anymore. It's time to leave off for the day or work on something else.*

Do you have a favorite vocal performance you're really proud of?

One of the funnest I ever did—and it's not like my greatest performance, it just means a lot—is Edith Frost and Kelly Hogan and myself all sang back-up on a Mekons record *Journey to the End of the Night*. Whenever I hear that I just feel so, so good. It was such a fun time. I'm such a huge Mekons fan, on a personal and musical level. It was so wonderful.

That's awesome. "Bought and Sold" drives me crazy 'cause when I hear it, I feel as though I can sing along with you. But the second I open my mouth, I immediately become aware of my limitations as a singer. You just make it seem so effortless. Does that happen to you with certain people?

I always write songs that are too hard for me to sing. So, I have to learn them and get good at them. I expand my range that way. But then you think, *Am I always singing up here? Should I move around?* One thing I really miss in the world, and it's rare, is ladies with low voices. That might be my favorite sound: women who can sing in lower registers. I always want to cultivate more of that, but I can only go so low.

How do you suggest singing outside of your register? Is there a way to build that muscle?

By warming-up and practicing. I don't know if I can get any lower or higher than my range is now. I think I've really pushed it.

What's changed the most about your voice since you started?

I realized I don't have vibrato. It used to make me really sad because a lot of my favorite singers do. I think the change has just been accepting it.

Vibrato is such a mysterious thing.

It is. There's like a relaxation you have to use to make vibrato. I don't know if your throat has to be a certain shape, it would be interesting to find out, but I've gotten into trying to keep a clear, solid note without vibrato because, since I'm subconsciously trying to have vibrato, it turns more into a goat sound. Like *mahhhh*. I don't want that to happen. I would rather have it be clear and long.

Alright, tell me about a positive change!

I have a lot more stamina than I did. I keep the muscles in good shape. There's always the period of having to sharpen them before I go on tour. If you're chopping wood every day, you're great at chopping wood. But if you stop, and then a month later you come back to chop wood, your muscle memory, and your natural muscular ability has decreased so, you gotta work back up to it. Bodies are frustrating. You have to prime them before they want to do what you want. It's hard because you can hear what it is you want, but you have to work toward it, where we like things to be immediate.

If you could duet with one singer—living or dead—who would it be?

Probably Nick Lowe. But he and I are so different, I don't know that it would work. He just always makes me swoon. Everybody always talks about Frank Sinatra's timing and cadence, but I think Nick Lowe is actually slipperier. He's actually got him beat.

Who are your top five favorite singers of all time?

It's not an answerable question, but here's a few: Catherine Ringer, The Women of Trio Bulgarka, Dexter Romweber, Herb Reed, Bessie Griffin.

If you could ask any singer about their voice, who would it be and what would you ask?

Maybe I'll get to ask this someday, but Catherine Ringer of Les Rita Mitsouko, who are French, has an incredible range and can sing really high, but she can also sing really low. She can also do vibrato that actually imitates a Leslie speaker getting slower and faster on one of her recordings, and it always just makes me—"Oh my God, you're the greatest!" That's on a song about one of my other favorite singers called Umm Kulthum, an Egyptian singer who's a national treasure in Egypt.

So, your question for Catherine would be?

How do you keep the lows so velvety?

NICK CAVE

ASILY ONE OF MY FAVORITE SINGERS of all time, Nick Cave brings something to his vocals so deeply human and profoundly primal that it can move you to tears or scare you to death. His poetic baritone is at its best when he seems to be reaching out for salvation while embracing the chaos of this broken world.

If you've never seen Nick Cave and the Bad Seeds live, it's something that has to be done. It's a baptism, an exorcism, a hypnotism, where EVERYTHING is left on the stage, and you will leave a different person than when you arrived.

A singer, songwriter, composer, author, screenwriter, and whatever else he damn well pleases, Nick Cave has the one thing that all of us need to succeed as artists: his own voice.

And no matter how many awards he's been given or how loyal and rabid his fan base, he's still in the fight, struggling, searching, and yearning for that place just out of reach, that place where the soul of a vocal truly lives.

Who first exposed you to singing?

I was in a school band and I was the singer because no one wanted to be the singer. I was a little more of an extrovert than some of the other people around and I was part of their group. Even though it was generally understood that I had major issues as a singer, I would say. [*Laughs*]

"It was generally understood?"

Amongst the other people in the band, right? I was the least musical one. This is a bunch of fifteen-year-old kids. They were learning real instruments—guitars, drums, bass—and I wasn't innately musical. The singer, to them, was seen as the very bottom of the musical ladder because I didn't actually play anything. I remember the bass player saying to me, "Well, you're the least musical one," and weirdly enough, that stuck with me into my—now I'm sixty. That kind of remark still rattles around in my head.

But you wanted to be the singer and were drawn to music?

Well, I loved rock 'n' roll music and I loved certain singers hugely, but it wasn't what I wanted to be, for sure. I wanted to be a painter and that's what I was pursuing at school and really interested in. But my heroes were Elvis Presley and Johnny Cash. As a young man in the country town that I grew up in, in Australia, the *Johnny Cash Show* had a huge impact on me as a child. And, strangely enough, the actual voice that I have is in that basic ballpark of those kind of singers that sing effectively at a particular volume.

I can see how Johnny Cash would've been a great touchstone for you.

Johnny Cash is not a rock 'n' roll singer by any means. He sits within a particular range and a particular volume and a particular pressure on his voice where he sounds really amazing. But he's not a screamer or a rock 'n' roll singer. Anyway, he influenced me very strongly.

Were you trying to sing like him when you started out?

No, I was just trying to [*chuckles*] *sing*. It was enough just to get through the song, let alone try and sound like somebody else.

How did you find your own voice?

All through The Birthday Party, I'd been a screamer, and everything was extremely agitated and aggressive. The Alex Harvey Band had *a huge, huuuge impact on me*, and he's a classic rock 'n' roll singer who pushes his voice into that register. But he was an extremely expressive singer and that really inspired me, that kind of high drama of his vocal style. I screamed everything basically. And my voice actually isn't built for that.

What was it built for?

It wasn't until the third Bad Seeds album, *Kicking Against the Pricks*, that I realized my voice wasn't the voice that I thought it was supposed to be. It was a cover versions album where

I was covering people like Johnny Cash and some of the crooners I realized that if I sang softly, I actually had a rather rich, liquid, melancholy kind of voice that was quite pleasing. I was never a good pure rock 'n' roll singer and that really was life changing for me. It really changed the direction of the music I started to make.

Almost like your voice began to tell you who you really are?

I remember Shane MacGowan from The Pogues saying to me very early on, "You're a fucking crooner!" I'm like, "*I'm not a fucking crooner!*" [*Laughs*] and taking it as kind of an insult because I wanted to be the kind of singer that was confrontational and aggressive and violent. He said that as a compliment, but I didn't want to be someone who sat on a stool crooning. I wanted to be screaming in people's faces and kicking their teeth in. But he was quite right. I am a crooner.

Isn't it wild that, years later, you guys did that *What a Wonderful World* EP where you're crooning together?

[*Cracks up*] Yeah, trying our best!

Did you ever have any vocal training?

No. I should've, but I didn't. [*Chuckles*]

Are you nervous or confident before you perform?

I don't ever remember being nervous onstage. But, to this day, I remain full of anxiety and dread *before* I go on. I'm nervous now because I've got a bunch of festivals coming up and I'm thinking, *Can I do this?* and *Can I do that?* And *Is this gonna work in a festival way?* The songs we're gonna play will be quite challenging for a festival audience and that makes me full of dread for these festivals. Very, very nervous. But I have to say, as soon as I walk onstage, anything like nerves disappears immediately and I feel like I'm just stepping into a place where I belong. I really feel more and more that I belong in front of an audience singing.

For some people it's home. That's just the way it is.

Yeah. It's home.

Do you do any vocal warm-ups before your shows?

I started doing vocal warm-ups around the Push the Sky Away Tour and the positive effect they had on my voice was immeasurable. I'd never done anything like that up until that record. To walk onto a stage with a voice that was ready to sing rather than kind of sucking it up in the first two songs has changed things hugely. My singing has improved on the last couple records because of that.

What's your vocal routine?

A thing called the *10 Minute Vocal Warm-up* that I get off the internet. It's just this schoolgirl doing her vocal warm-ups and I just follow what she does. They're really good, they really work. You know, you don't want to think of your singers doing vocal warm-ups before they walk onstage, in a way. [*Laughter*] But, actually, I pretty much have to do them now. I'd feel greatly challenged if I didn't because of the huge difference it's made for me.

How do you take care of your voice on the road?

My basic routine is that I turn up as close to going on as possible. I do this ten-minute warm-up thing and then walk straight onto stage. I don't hang out before I go on. I hang out afterwards with everybody. But no one even sees me before I go on. My band'll turn up an hour or so before and they sit around and do whatever, but I don't talk to anyone before I go onstage. *Anyone*. I don't group hug or say the Serenity Prayer or any of that sort of behavior either.

Is it like a silence for you, is that part of your ritual?

Yeah. It's completely silent. And it's completely silent as I go to the stage, it's completely silent as I wait to go onstage, and there's something I find meditative about that. Sort of a beginning of a process of freeing myself from my...How'd you say, my?

Self-consciousness, maybe?

Self-consciousness and anxiety. So, I walk onstage in a calm state. But I'm not calm about performing, I have to say. I'm absolutely frightened of it—this is before I go onstage—full of dread, very neurotic about it. I don't like people to say certain things before I go on like, "Break a leg," or something like that. I have a whole group of things that really put me off. I find it a really delicate time, that five minutes before I go on. It can be quite profound actually.

Are there songs where you wonder if your voice will be there that night?

My biggest impediment onstage is that I am extremely physical, so there are breathing issues. When I start running out of breath, my voice dips and the tuning goes, and it gets a heavy, lugubrious tone, which I really don't like. I find that quite unpleasant. That has to do with running out of breath. But the physical performance is hugely important to me and I don't know how else to perform. The physicality of my performance is almost a nervous tick in the sense that I just keep moving and everything seems to be alright. But it's a bit of a trade-off.

I went through the same thing. Being a drummer, you're moving all of your limbs, going crazy, and then, I got up in front of the mic and I'm trying to move as if I'm a drummer still. Not air drumming, but my body has that drummer's rhythm. And I was noticing, *God, if I rock out and then try and hit some note that's a bit out of my range, I'm screwed*. I couldn't breathe.

It's like talking to someone when you're running. It's not ideal. If you look at someone like Iggy Pop, he moves a lot onstage, but when he sings, he's still. He kind of comes up to the mic, stops, and sings, *and then* does his bit of dancing. This is a really good way to go about things, but I don't do that. I'm moving all the time, and singing at the same time, which I'd eventually like to work out a bit better. [*Chuckles*] The other problem, of course, is I do very quiet songs at the piano up against very loud, physical tracks. So, I can sit down at the piano really exhausted from doing some eight minute piece of extreme physical movement.

"Stagger Lee" to "Push the Sky Away."
Yeah, exactly! And I have huge pitching problems because of that. But I have the most generous and forgiving audience on earth. They accept that. In America, they're less accepting of bad technique. In Europe and Australia, you can get away with like charm, right? You can be a bit pitchy and all the rest of it as long as there's a certain amount of charm. In America, I always noticed they would pick you up for being out of tune and these sorts of things. [*Laughs*] The critics have a higher level of technical standard in America.

I remember watching a documentary, and, at one point, you're reading a review of your show and the critic says something unflattering about your voice, and you're visibly pissed. I've been on the receiving end of that myself, and it sucks, but I have a theory, not that this pertains to me, but I do believe that all the greatest lyricists have unconventional, misunderstood voices: Bob Dylan, Van Morrison, Leonard Cohen, Tom Waits, Neil Young, Shane MacGowan, and you. Lyrically, that's a Mount Rushmore.
Well, I'm now taking myself out of this equation so I can speak freely about these people, but you've just basically gone through my list of favorite singers. I don't know how they see their own voices, but I always feel under par as a singer. I always have. If I'm sitting around with a bunch of good musicians, I always feel like I don't really belong in that club. I feel like I belong in another club. My club is a club that is to do with writers, not musicians. But there is something about tuning being slightly off that can be extremely moving in a way, do you know what I mean?

Yeah. That's the other half of my theory. I feel like if your voice is effortless and you can do all these gymnastics and stay in perfect pitch, it may sound amazing, but there is a different type of soul that gets lost. Like you don't have to try as hard. And there's something about having to dig deeper with your voice, *because you don't have this natural, crazy voice*, that gives the songs a closer connection to the soul in a way. Take your song "Love Letter." Any pop artist could take that song, thump it out with slick production, and twist it into some radio friendly single. But you would never, *for one second*, actually believe that the singer you're listening to sat down and wrote that love letter. Only a certain type of voice can do that and that's where the soul inside a vocal really lives. For me.
Okay, well, I'm enjoying this interview very much. [*Laughs*] I like that theory. I think it's that idea of *reaching* for something. And I have to reach a long way to get where I want to be with things. There's a sense of yearning and longing and *need* in that reach that certain other singers who are just already there don't have. And I say this with a lot of respect for all singers,

but there are certain singers where there isn't a lot going on because there isn't that sense of reaching.

In 1996, you recorded this incredible lecture for the BBC called *The Flesh Made Word*, and in it you speak of how, at the age of thirteen, your father began to usher you into his study, lock the door, and read aloud from authors like Shakespeare, Nabokov, and Dostoevsky, waving his arms about. Then he would point at you and say, "This, my boy, is literature." You go on to say, "I would watch my father lose himself in the outpourings of his own creative energy, and although he would've laughed at this notion, what my father was finding in his beloved literature was God. Literature elevated him, tore him from normality and lifted him out of the mediocre, and brought him closer to the divine essence of things." When I hear you sing, I feel like I'm listening to a man desperately trying to grab hold of "*The divine essence of things*."
Well, that is the reach, right?

It sums up what it feels like to be a singer, doesn't it?
I would say, yes. It's becoming more and more that way for me. Earlier Nick Cave stuff was much more straight narrative, much more storytelling, much more didactic, and the way I presented it was like, "Here it comes. Look out." There was no attempt to involve. It was something I kind of unleashed upon the audience and the audience took from it what they would. That's changed hugely as I've grown older. Especially in the last couple of years, there feels to be much more of a communal nature about the way that I sing.

Can you explain what's happening for you?
I feel it's to do with what you're talking about, that that reach is going into the audience and swinging back around into something that is much more to do with community as such. It's also something to do with the fracturing of the imagery, which requires the audience's imaginative involvement in the whole thing. That is becoming very powerful to me as a spiritual person. It feels that it's the same for the audience as well.

Your shows have become much more spiritual in a way.
I do believe in the idea that we are connected by our suffering and that we have an enormous capacity to rise out of that, that we are built for transcendence, and we all have that opportunity. I think that these concerts can be like that for everybody. I think that a rock show, in general, is a great place to find that. Not always, obviously, but often, it is a place where we reach beyond ourselves. I've been lifted and my life has been changed on a spiritual level and on a transcendent level by watching other people. Some of the most profound moments in my life have been watching someone perform onstage.

Can you recall any of those moments?
A Nina Simone show that I saw where I walked out of the concert a different person, for sure. And seeing The Saints performance when I was a young guy, trying to work out what I was

wanting to do, just standing there and watching *everything* changing in front of my eyes. I could feel myself changing on all sorts of levels. The rock concert can really be a place where that happens beyond a lot of these kind of temples of worship where this stuff is supposed to be happening. That's a hugely sweeping statement, I understand that, and I have had transformative experiences within churches and so forth as well, but the communal aspect of a rock concert is extraordinary.

I don't think there's any difference when it's done right.
It's an absolute disgrace to go to a concert and see people up there just going through the numbers. They had the opportunity to do something in a way that can be hugely generous and hugely giving, and sometimes you go to a gig and you can just see this opportunity is being squandered in some kind of way, and I find that pretty difficult to watch sometimes.

Do you remember a performance where you surprised yourself?
I'm working towards it. There are still things that I have a lot to learn about as a singer, I really feel that. It feels quite exciting to make new records because I feel like I'm finding out stuff, especially over the last few records in regards to vocals.

Like what?
How they're recorded, what I can sing, and what I can't sing. What is effective for me to sing, and what isn't effective for me to sing. What's happening lyrically. Things in regard to spontaneity, first takes, improvisation. A lot of that has been working very closely with [bandmate] Warren Ellis. He's a great believer in first takes. When you do three takes of something, I can guarantee, even though it may not be as good, Warren will go for the first take because he believes there's some sort of intrinsic sense of adventure and honesty within the first take, that kind of lovely not quite knowing what you're doing. So, he's inspired me on a more general level, in the way that I sing, by the way he goes about making music.

How are you with hearing your own voice?
I have a nice voice to listen to if I sing in a particular way and don't push too hard.

What was your most embarrassing vocal mishap ever?
My entire career is an embarrassing vocal mishap. [*Laughter*]

Are there songs where you've had to adjust the key live?
That's been done occasionally. Not that they're too high, it's that they're too low. I might've sung something like "Do You Love Me?" in a low whisper. That song is always a struggle to do live because it feels like a loud song, but actually the vocal is kind of down there. It's quite difficult to get anything going behind that range. It sounds great on the record because it's almost whispered. There's things like that where we sometimes change the key.

Do you have a favorite vocal performance you're really proud of?

No, not really. I don't make a habit of sitting around listening to my own music. I never, never do that. But that's not to say that I'm not proud of it. I just have a hyper-critical mind of what I do. I'm always trying to get to this place, which I am yet to get to, and this is a huuuge asset. I don't think there's a song I can listen to and think, *Oh fuck, I wish I hadn't of written that line*, or *If I hadn't of used that word*, or *Why didn't someone edit this song?* There's something that I generally have an issue with. Pretty much everything.

Why do you feel that's a "huge asset?"

That's the sort of motivating engine to keep doing records and to *care*. The motivating engine *to care* for what you're doing. Despite what anyone might think about what I do, I *care*. I can sit here and say that. Huuuge amounts of effort go into what I do and huge amounts of time go into songwriting. That idea of complacency and kind of squandered opportunities that I sometimes see around me, I find very difficult to cope with. I have friends that are way more talented than I am, way greater lyric writers, and better singers, that just didn't have that thing of being able to pursue their ideas in a kind of ordered way. It really kills me to see these *incredible* opportunities just go to waste with people.

That's a theme in my life with people around me too. But it fits into the overarching theme of the next question because I love the evolution "Jubilee Street" has made from the studio to the stage. On the record, you guys loosen the reins a bit by the end, but it's still pretty restrained. But the live version has become this animal that's completely explosive by the end, especially when you're screaming, "*I'm transforming, I'm vibrating, look at me now*!" [*Nick laughs*] I mean, it's everything you pray for as a vocalist, as a songwriter, and as a performer, all wrapped up in this one ecstatic release. The question is: *how fucking great does that feel to play?*

Yeah, it's really good. You know yourself when you look at your set list, there's songs that are like, "Okay, I got to do this song," and it's something of a trial to get through. And there's other songs that don't require anything but for you to just lose yourself in the song. That's pretty much like that. It has its momentum and it just builds and builds. It's always a huge relief to see that song come along in the set list. [*Chuckles*]

It was interesting to originally hear "Shoot Me Down" on *B-Sides and Rarities* and be like, "How did this song get ignored?" It's such a great vocal performance. I love that tune! But, recently, you put the song on *Lovely Creatures* [*The Best of Nick Cave & The Bad Seeds*], and I was psyched to see you finally give it the respect it deserves. I always wondered why that song didn't make *Nocturama* and I'm curious what made you pick it up again and go, "I was wrong about that one."

Yeah, you sometimes are, and it was a good song, right? *Nocturama* was an odd record because there was a bunch of songs that we didn't put on that we should've and songs that we shouldn't have put on that we did. Unfortunately, we didn't make the right decisions. There was a lack of nerve. It's got that long "Babe, I'm On Fire" and stuff, and it would've been a better record if it didn't have that and had "Shoot Me Down" and some of those songs. Really, you can lose confidence in something very quickly. Part of going into the studio and being a singer and a band leader, it's bluff. It's going in there and pretending you have every-thing in hand. You don't go in there saying, "Look. I've got nothing and I don't know what the fuck I'm doing." You have to rally the troops. [*Laughs*] But sometimes it's a very precar-ious thing when you make a record. The more nervous I feel and the more precarious the nature leading up to the recording, you can feel that you're moving into something that has the capacity to be really special. Because now you're moving into areas that you don't quite understand.

So being a bit scared or uncertain should be a part of it?

If you're feeling comfortable going in to make a record, I would be pretty worried. Chances are, all you're doing is repeating what you did last time. It's that kind of complacency around songwriting and making records and repeating yourself with tried and tested formulas that's generally the death of a band.

Your abandon and lack of self-consciousness in that area has always been really inspiring to me. Even on the first Grinderman album you're buzzing like a bee on "Honey Bee (Let's Fly To Mars)," and you're doing that with 1,000 percent commit-ment. There's a giant fucking bee on that mic, you know?

[*Laughs*] My finest hour. Well, thank you. Thank you.

In 1998, you wrote another lecture called *The Secret Life of the Love Song* that should be required listening for every singer. It's the most beautiful, bloody, truthful, and terrifying meditation on music I've ever heard. And your delivery, that ominous bass in your voice, just makes it all the more brutal. Where does that come from when you're recording these lectures? Is it your father in the library, waving his arms about, and you've partially taken on that persona? Or does it come from somewhere else?

I don't know about that. I do know that when I discovered what I liked about my voice, I was able to sing soft and have the mic up really, really loud so it was ultra-sensitive. It was picking up every little breath and all of that sorta stuff. There was a tone that existed in there that had a certain sort of gravitas to it and I really liked that. There were rich, dark tones in there that I didn't realize I had. A kind of certain...mournful...demoralized...[*Laughter*]

Oh man, it's something. [*Nick continues to chuckle*] It's a warning though.

Yeah, but I love those lovely high voices like Neil Young and Alex Chilton. I love that fragile-ness of where they are up there. They're very, very sad voices in a completely different way. There's a lightness of touch about the way they sing that's immediate in the tone of their voices that I find extraordinary.

You love your Memphis boys.

Indeed. Alex Chilton's another one who crashes around with his vocals, unbelievably so. Sometimes you're literally hanging on by your fingernails when you're listening to one of his vocals. It's terrifying, but incredibly beautiful.

What's changed the most about your voice since you started?

It's definitely stronger. There's more control than there used to be, in the sense that it doesn't actually make things more exciting when you just scream your head off. A certain amount of control can just have a lot more impact. I used to think the more abandoned I was vocally, and in every way, the better the song was. I'm not so sure that was true. But that's not to say that I don't really love The Birthday Party. It was incredibly wigged out stuff, that singing, but I'm very proud of that.

I love The Boys Next Door! What's going on? You're just gonna leave them out of the equation every time?

Yes. [*Laughter*]

If you could duet with one singer—living or dead—who would it be?

Elvis. No, I'd just look terrible. I take that back. I wouldn't want to duet with Elvis. I don't know, I'll have a think, and send you the answer. *

Alright. Who are your top five favorite singers of all time?

This is a ridiculous question, just letting you know up front.

I know.

Okay, I'll give it a go. In no particular order, I would say, Elvis, John Lee Hooker, Nina Simone, Bob Dylan. Oh, shit, I have to put...well...*oh God*...I'm leaving out so many people, it's ridiculous. How many is that, four? Look, I'm gonna throw Van Morrison in as well. They would change again if you asked me in ten minutes time, but Elvis would always be in there. Elvis is my man.

If you could ask any singer about their voice, who would it be and what would you ask?

A conversation with Bob Dylan about constantly changing the way he sings, I think more than any other singer I've ever encountered, is a really interesting conversation. The perverse nature of his singing, that sometimes he's the most beautiful singer on earth, and other times he's like the worst singer on earth? He's such a wonderful singer, but also an incredibly perplexing vocalist. But he's someone that's constantly played around with his instrument and has been brave enough to take it to places that are different and sometimes terrifying. But always beautiful too.

This was Nick's email answer:

Dear Jason,

I had to think about this question. There are many singers I would have loved to sing with just so I could be in the same room as them—Elvis, Nina Simone, Frank Sinatra, etc., but really my voice would be little more than a nuisance—but maybe I could have sung a duet with Karen Dalton. That may have sounded nice—her hard tops with my low tones. Who knows?

—Nick

Jody Stephens on
ALEX CHILTON & BIG STAR

NOT MANY PEOPLE have a number one single in the charts when they're sixteen years old. But Alex Chilton did just that when he sang "The Letter" with his first band, The Box Tops, in 1967. By 1971, Chilton had joined Big Star in his hometown of Memphis. The group was comprised of singer/guitarist, Chris Bell, bassist/singer, Andy Hummel, and drummer/singer, Jody Stephens.

The vocal blend in Big Star, combined with the melodic structure of their sound, is some of the most beautiful, exciting, and heartbreaking music you will ever hear. The Beatles had it. The Byrds had it. King's X comes to mind as well. But man, there is something about this group that just aches a little bit more. And while their records eluded the commercial success they clearly deserved, their music inspired everyone from the Replacements to R.E.M. and paved the way for the alternative and indie rock movements of the '80s and '90s.

Sadly, Chris Bell died in a car accident at the age of twenty-seven, after recording *I Am the Cosmos*, a brilliant solo album. Andy Hummel and Alex Chilton passed away in 2010, long after the band had broken up. And although there have been various reunions and incarnations of the group throughout the years, the one constant has been Jody Stephens, a true southern gentleman. When Jody isn't busy singing and writing with his new band, Those Pretty Wrongs, he helps run Ardent Studios, the legendary home for all of Big Star's recordings, among many others!

Always cool, calm, and humble to the bone, Jody Stephens is here. For you.

When was the first time you heard Alex sing?
Probably The Box Tops' "The Letter."

And then, he's suddenly joining your band a few years later.
Chris was primarily the mover, and possibly Andy, in getting Alex to join the band. I thought it'd be cool. I had a lot of respect for Alex and The Box Tops. It's interesting, he'd had some success, but I didn't even consider his voice and how it would fit in with Big Star. But then, we'd get together, and he had this different kind of voice.

When you say, "Different kind of voice," what do you mean?
From what I've read [producer] Dan Penn coached a lot of the way he was singing The Box Tops material. And that was great! It obviously worked incredibly well for The Box Tops, but then he comes to Big Star, and I think a few windows opened up to Alex whenever he sang. It was more about channeling whatever emotion he was feeling rather than trying to channel somebody else's direction of what his voice might be. I think that's probably the difference. What he brought to Big Star was his own voice.

How did Alex approach vocals in the studio? The sense I get is that he could be really meticulous about some tracks, and then not care at all about others, but sort of in the best way possible. Is that accurate?
I just see Alex stepping up to the mic with this confidence and delivering the performance. You always knew he was gonna nail the notes and I don't know that it ever required too many takes. I think he just knew when to quit. He just knew when, *That's it. I got what I wanted to relate.*

So he didn't obsess about his vocal parts really?
I think he certainly cared, but he didn't need to obsess.

That's interesting 'cause the band had so much complexity to the vocals *and* the background vocals. They're really well thought out and so deep and layered.

Alex and Andy both contributed a lot, but that was Chris and his guidance there. He was sort of the producer for *#1 Record* with John Fry, certainly with the sonics and the way the parts fit into the mix. We got to *Radio City* and it wasn't a practical thought to have a lot of lush background vocals because after Chris left, we were a three piece, and only two of us sang.

Chris Bell's vocal contributions were so honest, almost haunting on the songs he sang. Even on his solo album, there's so much going on inside there, ya know?

Oh yeah, even more so on his solo album.

Heartbreaking.

Indeed. *Man*. Some of that stuff, he digs deep, in this gut-wrenching voice that just—I don't know that anybody's ever sung devastation the way he did.

What a great way to put it. You sang some great Big Star songs as well!

Yeah. I enjoyed it. "Way Out West" was a great song and certainly one I could deliver. It's not a big range or anything. It was the character that the song needs and I was perfectly comfortable doing that because I was being myself.

"For You" is really beautiful too.

Oh thanks. Andy gave me the guitar and Alex taught me some chords and I wrote "For You" around the chords he taught me. [*Laughs*] That was fun. I enjoy singing. I do a lot more of it now with Those Pretty Wrongs because I sing lead on all the songs and it's just a good time. It took me a minute to adjust from sitting behind the security of a drum kit to stepping out in front of the stage. But, once you get over that, the connection with the audience is pretty cool. It's closer, so communication is easier.

Do you remember anything about the recording of "Morpha Too"? That's one of my favorite Big Star songs. It's 1:28 minutes long, packed with melody, beautiful vocal harmonies, an out-of-tune piano, and it's perfect.

It is perfect. I think Alex just went over and probably sat down at the piano, sang it, and that was it. From what I remember, that was one of those later night recordings.

Did he do vocal warm-ups before going onstage?

I never saw Alex do warm-ups, which kind of blew my mind! I was singing "Way Out West" or "For You" or something, and Alex said, "You know, just think about the note before you hit it. Just picture yourself hitting that note." That's probably the best vocal advice I ever got. I consider myself vocally challenged. I do warm-ups, big time. It helps tremendously in the studio and live. Makes a huge difference.

Isn't it wild how we beat the shit out of our drums without a care in the world, and then you step up to sing and, all of a sudden, this other instrument you play is like this dainty, fragile, thing?

Yes! That's weird! It is. And it kind of blew my mind because I always thought, *Wow, lead singers, what a piece of cake. They don't have anything to lug around. They just show up and deliver.* I discovered otherwise.

It's much more difficult than playing drums.

Well, I'm not gonna be able to have forty years of singing the way I've had with playing drums. But I would think, if I did it with any regularity, I'd get more comfortable with it, and maybe more relaxed with how protective I am of it.

Was Alex nervous or confident before shows?

He taught me a lot with this. He would finish the song and then possibly say, "Thank you," turn around, walk back to his amp, grab his cigarette pack, and take a cigarette out—just very casually, not with any hurry in mind—light it, take a few puffs, then kind of saunter back up to the mic and say a few words to the audience, and sing the song. He was nothing but confident and comfortable.

When you hear his voice now, what do you remember most?

Ardent had a little record label. It's inactive at the moment, but we get demos, and this one person sent in a demo, just a voice and a guitar, and I'm thinking, *There's not a lot of connection there.* They would say, "Yeah, but when you hear it with production, it'll work, it'll be that much nicer." Then, I happened to hear some of Alex's demos for the *Third* album, and it all came back to me that Alex's voice and a guitar were all a song ever needed. You didn't need anything else there. That's really what I remember about Alex's voice...and still hear.

What about Chris?

Chris was the same way. Chris could sit down with an acoustic guitar and there was a complete emotional deliverance there. You didn't need anything else.

CHUCK D

WHEN HE WAS A LITTLE BOY, Carlton Douglas Ridenhour wanted to become a sportscaster. Thank God he became Chuck D instead.

His prophetic, revolutionary voice would go on to change the face of hip-hop—and the world—for good. Along with hype man Flavor Flav, Chuck created Public Enemy, where they immediately began to "Fight the Power," bringing social and political consciousness to the forefront of music in a way that hadn't happened since Marvin Gaye asked, "What's Going On?" Using the strength and command of his voice to irritate and educate, Chuck has rightfully earned himself a place in the Rock & Roll Hall of Fame and a Grammy Award for Lifetime Achievement.

With his band, solo, or collaborating with other artists, Chuck's unique delivery always makes you stand at attention. Prophets of Rage, his side band with the members of Rage Against the Machine and B-Real from Cypress Hill is another prime example of what Chuck has to offer. He may be filling your head with knowledge, but he's making you bang that head like mad! So welcome to the Terrordome. And thanks for havin' us, Chuck...

Who first exposed you to singing?

I grew up in a household with music. I'm born in 1960, so you're talkin' 'bout the convergence of radio and television. Your grandfather's show [*Make Room for Daddy*] was a mainstay as far as the television was concerned. And the voices that came through the records, whether it was Ella Fitzgerald or Ray Charles, were always ringin' loud in my house.

What made you go, "I wanna use my voice in the world?"

First thing I wanted to do with my voice was become a play-by-play sports announcer in the '70s. That use and command of my voice happened to be at the right place, right time, right phase, where rapping really started to develop as an art form. Rap pretty much carried the same rhythms as my influences of the sports world like Marv Albert. So I developed my style of rapping by being able to put two and two together and create a vocal style that was reminiscent of sports casting and Black radio DJs.

Were you emulating anyone when you started out?

Marv Albert, Gary Byrd, the well-known DJ, and the beginning rappers—people like Melle Mel, DJ Hollywood, Eddie Cheeba. Those guys set a nice little template for me to follow.

How did you find your own voice?

I found my own voice as a DJ myself. I kind of knew who was doin' what and what somebody wasn't doin'. James Brown was definitely helpful in that because James Brown was a combination of singing, rap, and everything in between.

Did you ever have any vocal training?

I had vocal projection because my mother had the wherewithal to start the Roosevelt Community Theatre. Being in the theater and speaking your parts, you learn how to project. Also, if you're in the park, actually sportscasting, you're projecting quite automatically, lettin' it be heard, lettin' it be known. With singing, you hit notes. With rapping, you hit rhythms and tones. Your tones are your notes and your rhythms are your flow. A lot of times your tones and your flow are accompanied by synapses that pop off when you say certain things that seem like they fit. Like, there's some science behind Dr. Suess's *The Cat in the Hat* that we still can't explain. How it works on kids. [*Laughs*] "I took a cat in a hat and I beat him with a bat." Why does that happen to make you bop along with it? It has somethin' to do with your receptors. That's why rhyming is rhyming. We didn't invent rhyming. Grandmaster Caz said, "It didn't invent anything, but it reinvented everything."

Do you feel nervous or confident before you perform?

If I would be nervous, it would just be about knowin' my part. I don't have the greatest memory. I'm still not good to this day after 5,000 performances. That's repairable with repetition, but I get stuck in a box sometimes, knowing that I gotta spend twice as long to get it as somebody else. I have a photographic memory when it comes down to places, art, matter of fact,

I got total recall, but vocally, I don't. It's always been difficult, but if I had to paint a picture of somethin' I saw four weeks ago, I could paint it perfectly. I could name all the things in the place. It must be a glitch I just haven't got over. Maybe I need to work on it.

Do you do any vocal warm-ups before shows?
LL Cool J and Ice Cube call me "Mr. Iron lung." Very few times did the voice ever shut down. But I'm not doin' anything to warm it up, no.

Do you have any rituals before you hit the stage?
B-Real, my Prophets of Rage/Cypress Hill brother, started gettin' me into a ritual of drinkin' hot tea before we start. That's been helpful. Big props to B-Real, my brother.

Is there anything after the show that helps keep your voice in shape?
I'm drinkin' my fluids. I like to STFU, ya know? [*Laughs*] I like to be quiet, not say shit.

How do you take care of your voice on the road?
I don't do a lot of talkin'. I don't smoke, I don't drink, so maybe that's been helpful. And then, I was blessed from my father to have a very, very, very strong voice. He had to be the strongest voice that I ever heard. No question.

He had more bass than you?
WHAT? [*Laughter*] I'm not half the man my father was, trust me. My father would yell across the town at me or my brothers and you could not come home and say, "No," when he said, "Didn't you hear me call you?" *Everybody heard!* My father was a U.S. Marine, and sure enough, when he yelled, it was heard. Amazing.

Are there songs where you wonder if your voice will be there that night?
We have a motto, "You have to do the songs or the songs will end up doing you." The types of records that I've written and performed you have to be in shape to do. Your cardio has to be seriously on point. So there's no excuses, no chillin' out on the stage. These are very beat-oriented, powerful songs that you gotta be ready for. You gotta know when to move and when not to move.

Let's get into that.
Sometimes, if you're caught movin' the wrong way and do a fast verse, you gotta find air somewhere. Because everything is output, your input has to be perfectly timed to the point that you're not wasting your movement, you're not wasting anything. You gotta find the air to continue to kick out.

Right, even if it's finding a breath between a syllable.

Yeah, you gotta learn how to cycle air. Like you're doing a vocal, but you're really breathing as you're vocaling out. MC Hammer was great at it—another underrated guy who they never talk about. He would dance, do all kinds of incredible things, but he's still rapping, and he's moving. You have to make all three work. It requires everything just to keep your tone, and your breath, and your performance. Bottom line: people gotta like the performance. It's not whether they like the song. Your job is to perform to make them dig the song.

Plus you're not singing a melody that you can switch up if you run out of breath. You're inside of this rapid-fire momentum where there really isn't much time.

Yep. And you have to keep your tones 'cause there's some words that are stronger than others. You have to emphasize. Since you're not hitting notes as much as words, your emphasis on hitting a word has to be heavy, and you have to be on that one. This is like rugby; you know what I'm sayin'?

Are you doing any physical workouts to keep your stamina going?

I don't do hard physical work outs, but I've taken Pilates for the past five years and that's helped my core. Everything's about diaphragm and core at that speed.

Are there songs where you've had to adjust the key live?

Part of my challenge is to take on something that's very difficult to do at a difficult speed. I don't wanna adjust the song. I gotta adjust myself and step it up or leave it alone.

What was your most embarrassing vocal mishap ever?

I got cocky. Public Enemy was playing a town in California and I was showing off my chops. We did a three and a half-hour performance and, the next day, I hosted a gigantic, all-day event for eight hours and did the close out performance. That night, we had a gig in San Diego. By the time I got onstage, I had pushed it to the point where nothing came out. Voice was gone. And I paid the price because the audience was *packed*. Having no voice and looking at a packed audience is probably the worst thing that can happen, man.

What did you do?

Other people had to pick up the slack and do some of the other songs that they're featured on. The only thing I could do was hug babies, sign chests, and shit like that. [*Laughter*] Sign everybody's autograph in the place 'cause they sure 'nuff wasn't gettin' no voice outta me.

How are you with hearing your own voice?

I'm alright listening to my own tracks, but I've burned myself out once the song is released. I don't wanna hear it no more. I hear it so many times before I release it, and then, when it's released, I'm like, alright, now everybody else is talkin' about it; I'm done with it.

Do you have a favorite vocal performance you're really proud of?

"I Shall Not Be Moved," "Welcome to the Terrordome," and "Bring the Noise."

One of my favorite things you do is you'll ramp your vocal up into the line. In a song like "You're Gonna Get Yours," you'll go, "*Iiiiiiiiiin* this corner with the '98." First album, first track, first line, and you're already doing what would become a signature of your style. How did that move come about?

Mimicking somebody else that was mimicking Schoolly D. Schoolly tells me he got his influence off of Melle Mel. And Ice Cube tells me he got his offa me. [*Laughter*] Right there you got four emcees who all bit off of each other to develop their own style.

We should mention your partner in crime. Tell me about Flavor Flav's vocal style and the importance of having a hype man in Public Enemy?

You can't un-hear him. He fills the air spaces and has the most irritating, grating voice in the world. He's perfect for hip-hop and rap music and he's irreplaceable. Often imitated, never ever duplicated.

Do you have a favorite vocal performance of his?

"911 Is a Joke." I gave him the job to write the song, to come back to me a year later with a completed song. Came back to me a year later with that gem. I'm most proud of him over that fact. I thought it was an unbelievable job by Flavor.

Let's talk Prophets of Rage. You and B-Real join forces with the guys from Rage Against the Machine to form this supergroup and part of the job is stepping into Zack de la Rocha's shoes on the Rage songs. Not only is Zack one of the greatest rock voices ever, but tonally, his voice is so connected to that sound. I honestly didn't feel it could work with anyone else, especially someone like Chuck D with all that bass in your voice. But then, I went and saw you guys live, and I left drenched in sweat, from head to toe. One of the greatest concerts I've ever seen. Saying that it works is an understatement. What was that experience like for you, taking on Zack's role?

Not only were you takin' on Zack's role, you're takin' on Zack's role at twenty-one or whatever. When [guitarist] Tom Morello first approached me with that idea, I was like, hell no! But then, he said, "Would you be open to B-Real?" and that's when it clicked. I would be shadowin' B-Real and that's how we could go about putting a different power and speed to the vocals that Zack had already made. If you don't do it right, you're catchin' the L. But Tom Morello is not gonna accept anything less than us rehearsing it a million times 'til we get it right. So I got my blessings from Zack. And now, with the reformation of Rage Against the Machine, Zack has to go face his twenty-five-year-old self at fifty! So good luck with that one, Zack! [*JTG laughs*] It took two of us to manhandle those songs. But I got Public Enemy songs where the sixty-year-old Chuck has gotta take on the twenty-eight-year-old Chuck.

What's changed the most about your voice since you started?
It's definitely deeper. There's certain recordings where we would shave bass and I would speed it up in the mastering so it made it a little lighter and quicker. You have to take into consideration that a lot of times, if you have too much bass in your voice, you'll drag the track. You don't wanna drag the track.

If you could duet with one singer—living or dead—who would it be?
Bobby "Blue" Bland, one of the most proficient R&B/Blues singers of the past. But a high note of mine is, I done a song with Mavis Staples called "Give We the Pride." I love that song. That combination. That's utopia for me. Me and Miss Mavis.

I spoke with Mavis about her involvement with the Civil Rights Movement, singing for Dr. King, and really using her voice for change. If you can speak truth to power, unite people, educate them in a way that doesn't feel like a lecture, and still have a kick ass chorus you can rock out to, I don't have to tell you that there's an art to riding that line. And from the second you dropped *Yo! Bum Rush the Show*, that's all you've been doing.
Thank you. I appreciate it, man.

Who are your top five favorite singers of all time?
Oh shit! Levi Stubbs, Mavis Staples, Walter Williams of the O Jay's, Melle Mel, and I would say Marvin Junior of The Dells.

If you could ask any singer about their voice, who would it be, and what would you ask?
I did. I asked Miss Mavis about her voice and she said people thought she was like thirty-five years old, and she was fourteen. [*Laughter*]

Butch Vig on
KURT COBAIN

IN 1991, HAIR METAL RULED THE AIRWAVES with its pouty lips, puffy shirts, skin tight leather, and guitar god shredders, until a raggedy ass trio from Seattle released their second album called *Nevermind*. Their name was Nirvana.

An entire genre of music got swept away in one extraordinary, apocalyptic explosion. Everything shifted to a new sound a lot of people called "grunge." But here's what it really was: great fuckin' rock songs filled with pain, soul, and self-doubt.

And that voice giving you everything he had was Kurt Cobain. In four short years, Kurt would be gone. But what he left behind is an enduring legacy that goes well beyond any Grammy they ever won or their induction into the Rock & Roll Hall of Fame. Nirvana would become one of the greatest selling bands of all time as well as a cultural phenomenon who continue to influence the musical landscape today.

Producer Butch Vig was the man they chose to capture the sound of *Nevermind*. His work with the Smashing Pumpkins, Sonic Youth, and his own group, Garbage, would define the sound of the '90s. Being a drummer himself must have helped. Because he came in at just the right time and helped change the world as we know it.

When was the first time you heard Kurt sing?

In Madison, Wisconsin. I was in a band called Spooner. We were sort of a New Wave Pop band and our guitarist ran a record store and was a member of the Sub Pop Singles Club. It was a split single with Mudhoney, I think.

How did you start working together?

I was running Smart Studio and I got a call from Jonathan Poneman from Sub Pop. He said, "I think you should work with Nirvana." A couple days later, their first record, *Bleach*, showed up and I was kind of unimpressed because I thought it was one dimensional, except for the song "About A Girl." I heard that and a lightbulb went off. I thought, *This is like a Lennon/McCartney arrangement* with the melody and the way Kurt was singing. I love good hooks and great melodies, so that's what attracted me to them. I was lucky enough when Nirvana showed up that Kurt had written a whole bunch of new songs and they were all miles above where he was on *Bleach*. The chords were more interesting, the melodies were gorgeous, and I found his singing way more expressive. He had really grown as a writer and as a singer.

What do you think changed in him? If you listen to *Bleach* and *Nevermind* back-to-back, it's a major evolution.

He had a love for pop music. But, for him, authenticity meant punk rock in the attitude and the lifestyle that brings. I think he sometimes had to disguise his love for melodicism because it wasn't really thought of as being punk rock if you're singing something that's pretty.

So he kept the music raw, but embraced the pop sensibility within his vocal.

Yeah. And as we worked on the songs, he just set the bar much higher in terms of what he could do dynamically. So what you hear in his voice are these incredible, quiet, fragile, vulnerable moments and then, this incredible pain and frustration and anger in the same song. He used that dynamic in the tone of his voice from section to section and it really made the songs incredibly powerful. Later, he made fun of the quiet-loud-quiet arrangements, but we weren't the only band and producer doing that. A lot of people used that and still do.

Right, but you guys brought that style into the mainstream.

We kind of put that on steroids.

There's that *Classic Albums* documentary about *Nevermind* where you're at the board explaining how you tracked the chorus vocals for "In Bloom" and you mention that Kurt hated double tracking his vocals. What do you think that was about?

He thought it was fake. He wanted to record every song live and I wanted to spend a bit of time going back and doubling some things or re-recording things if I thought they could sound better. I told him, "The live experience is unique because you're in a room and you're performing and it's of the moment and it's done. But we're in the studio. You're making something completely different. People are gonna listen to it over and over again. When you're recording something, it's an artistic statement too, it's not just a performance statement." Once I got his head around that, he became open to it.

I'm realizing that more and more. Like when was the last time I saw the Beatles live?

Kurt was a huge Beatles fan and I actually used that sometimes to get my way in the studio. I'd reference McCartney or Lennon in terms of something in an arrangement or if I wanted to double a vocal. He didn't want to double "In Bloom," and I said, "Well, that's what John Lennon did." He'd pause and go, "Okay, Butch, let's do it," and he was great at it! [*Laughter*] I just wanted the choruses to have this incredible power and to sound larger than life. When you double his voice and double the guitars, it just makes everything bigger. It's still a really simple recording. We did the record in sixteen days.

In that documentary, you also show how great Dave Grohl was as a singer, doing the high harmonies against Kurt.

Dave's voice was very sympathetic with Kurt's. They both had a very similar timbre in that range. Listening back, I can't even remember who sang what, but Dave did sing a lot of the high harmonies on the record.

Was there any inkling, like, *This guy could go off and make his own album singing*?

No, I had no idea. I don't think he wanted to put that in anybody's face. He was the drummer, that's what he was there to do. I didn't know it 'til after Kurt passed away and he told me he was working on a solo record. I was like, "Huh?!" Lo and behold, he knows what he's doing! [*Laughter*]

In the third verse of "Smells Like Teen Spirit," Kurt sings, "*And I forget just why I taste*," and his voice breaks a little on the word "taste." At that time, the radio was chock full of bands trying to be perfect in every way. Were things like his voice cracking ever discussed within the band or the label or was everyone on the same page as far as what you were goin' for?

They were all really happy with the choices that we made in the production. If anything, I was looking for those moments where his voice *would* break and crack and when he would shred a little bit, like at the very end of "Teen Spirit" when he holds that note out, "A denial." It's like his voice just loses it. That happened many times where he would do two or three takes and would sing so hard he would blow his voice out. He wouldn't even be able to talk. I had to know when I could get a vocal out of him, depending on how his voice was holding up.

He really gave everything he had on those recordings.

The human voice, it's the most fragile and expressive instrument there is. It's way more expressive than a saxophone, or a piano, or a guitar, or a cello, because it's the combination of using words with melody and how they push or pull back on their delivery that gives the word so much character. Kurt had immense character. He was not a perfect singer by any means. If you listen to "Smells Like Teen Spirit," there's moments in the verses where he's sharp or flat, but I didn't care about that, and the band didn't either. He sounds really human. And there's something about his voice that really resonated with people when that record came out because in the same song you would hear this vulnerability and this fear and this rage and anger, all at the same time. Few artists were on the radio like that back in 1991.

I don't know if any were.
It was like, "What is this? We've never heard someone sing like this." It's impossible to imagine someone else singing with Nirvana. It wouldn't be the same. I've heard people sing to karaoke tracks and it's not the same. [*Laughs*] Kurt had this incredibly unique, powerful voice, and it was just loaded with character.

At the end of "Territorial Pissings," he's doing some amazing screams that crack all over the place too. That thing is a monster to sing. How would Kurt approach something where he's just shredding his voice? You're saying he would just blow it out completely?
Yeah, I only got a couple takes on that. I did what I call a "Warm-up take," but I would always record it because I didn't know how long his voice would hold out. Then I did two more takes. And rather than ask him to double, at points, I just turned on two of the tracks, side by side, and it was close enough for a double because he would sing so consistent. That's all performance. He didn't hold back when he sang, so it's not perfect, but there's real, raw emotion.

Did he blow his voice out a lot?
A lot. There's maybe one or two songs where I got him to do four vocal takes. For the most part, there was only two or three on every song we recorded and I had to make a vocal comp out of those. I would go through and pick the best lines from each verse and chorus and put those together for a master take.

He could also be just as powerful with the softer, more vulnerable side of his voice. Songs like "Something in the Way" are so haunting because of how he could draw you in. Can you talk about how you guys recorded that?
That was the most difficult to record. We attempted to record it live in the main room at Sound City. Kurt had his guitar dialed down, Krist [Novoselic] played bass, and Dave was trying to play drums really quietly, but that room is loud no matter what you do. They tried it several times, but it did not sound very good. Out of frustration, Kurt threw his guitar down and laid on the couch in the control room. He was playing his guitar on his back, singing the song in barely a whisper. I was like, "Stop everything, let's record right now." I unplugged the phone, shut the door, told Dave and Krist to stay out of the studio, and just set up a couple mics and recorded him. I did two or three takes of him just lying on his back, and it was powerful. He sang that so quiet that it's incredibly intense.

It says a lot about you as a producer that you could see that as the solution.
It's doing the opposite. Everyone else thinks that in order to convey intensity you have to scream or really push your voice. But sometimes using understatement, or pulling back, takes it to an even higher level of intensity. When you hear "Something in The Way," I can see this guy living under a bridge. It's so understated, but it sounds so real, like you've never heard someone so vulnerable when they sing. It's my favorite song on *Nevermind*.

Do you know if he did any vocal warm-ups before going onstage?
[*Laughs*] He didn't do any vocal warm-ups.

Yeah, that's a hard one to picture.
He never had any proper training. That's why I think he would blow his voice out so quickly.

Do you know if he took care of his voice on the road?
He used to drink tea a lot and I know that can help some singers.

I wonder how he survived on the road, singing his ass off the way he did every night.
I thought he did this as a joke, but he would sing like an octave lower. He'd sing "Teen Spirit" down an octave and sort of talk-sing it. Maybe part of that was because he couldn't get the high notes from night to night, but there's no way to know that. It didn't matter because I think the flaws in his singing is one of the things that drew people to the music.

Do you know if he was nervous or confident before shows?
He would get a little nervous like anybody, but he wasn't one of these people that's pacing around. Some people have to have their own space, they have certain rituals they go though, and some people get sick before they go onstage—they throw up or have a nerve attack and then they're fine—but he seemed to take it in stride. Being a punk band, it is what it is, and having that attitude takes the pressure off of thinking you have to be perfect every single night.

When you hear his voice now, what do you remember most?
We had so much fun. The sessions were fun. The band, despite all his demons, were in a really good place. Kurt would have these intense mood swings where he would be really focused and funny and just into it, and then, a light switch would go off, and he would withdraw into himself. Sometimes, he'd just go sit in a corner for a couple hours and nobody could say anything. He just didn't respond to things. Then, all of a sudden, he'd pick up a guitar and go, "Let's go," and he wanted to record. I had to be ready to go when I knew his green light was on. I never put on records that I have produced at home, I just don't listen to them like that, but I hear them. They're out in the world, on the radio, in clubs and car stereos. To me, *Nevermind* still sounds as powerful as it did when we recorded it and I think that's a testament to great songs and great performances.

CITIZEN COPE

THE DEBUT ALBUM BY CITIZEN COPE arrived on my doorstep a couple weeks after I did something sorta nuts. The year was 2002 and I had recently met a legendary music business executive. Feeling frustrated, I wrote him a seven-page, Jerry Maguire-type letter expressing my feelings about the state of the music business and how record companies were falling short. Rock 'n' roll felt like a thing of the past and the new music being released seemed formulaic, "Wallpaper for shopping malls." This icon needed to remember the days when that wasn't the case, the days when "Music came home with a broken bottle in its hand," whatever that flourish meant. The point was, we don't need any more over-produced, "Perfect" voices. We still wanted real voices with something to say!

I had totally forgotten I had sent the letter—until the executive wrote me a kind and thoughtful response, followed by a box of CDs, "From my library to yours." It was also a subtle message: "You're not 100 percent accurate, pal. There's still some great new music out there." Inside that box was the self-titled debut by Clarence Greenwood, aka Citizen Cope.

It's been over twenty years since that day and I've been a fan of this guy ever since. His music is as soulful, funky, and profound as the man himself. So, if you're up for meeting a challenge, really taking a look at who you are, then this cat may be your man. Citizen Cope has the ability to blend R&B, folk, rock, blues, and hip-hop into one sound and create something that feels completely original.

He just speaks to you. And sometimes that's all you need.

Who first exposed you to singing?

I was just listening to what was in the car that my parents were playing or people around me. My sister liked music. She would buy 45s, so I guess the genesis of it was as a listener.

What made you want to sing?

It sounds a little strange, but when I would see a school play or kids singing during recital. In Junior High School in Washington DC, they had a gospel choir that sang a song called "Thank You Lord," and that was pretty powerful. So I was exposed to some cool things and I would just kind of sing around a little bit and discovered I had a voice.

Were you emulating anyone when you started out?

I don't think so.

Where were you coming from with it?

It was more of a calming, meditative thing than kind of a "Wow" factor because I have a limited range. But the voice is really about a connection and the phenomenon that is created because of that is really a mystery. It's probably connected to a high level of consciousness. It just feels good to get to a note. It's just the purest thing. There's so many different levels to emotion and singing that contribute to something that touches somebody. I think it has a lot to do with being on that higher vibration.

How did you find your own voice?

I think you have to find a meaning behind it and what it represents. I'm sure there's people that said, "I wanna sound just like Otis Redding," and listened to a bunch of Otis Redding and had the capacity to sing like him, right? I was always interested in the emotion that somebody brought. Yeah, they could have a great voice, but what they were saying, and how they were saying it, and the whole universe of what I was hearing wasn't just put into the voice. There's all these other elements that add to what somebody ends up listening to. I know my voice touches people because it probably emanates some kind of energy that people recognize. So I think that a voice is just something that is able to have a conversation with the listener.

That makes sense because your voice is so conversational. When I put you on, it's like, I'm gonna hang with this guy for a minute. You seek out different voices for different emotions and Citizen Cope is like, I need to cool out and sing this refrain 'cause it makes me feel good. You bring that to the party.

That's the beauty of music. When the artist connects with his soul, that's what people want to hear. There's people that can hit Pavarotti's notes, but are they connecting to their soul like

Pavarotti is connecting to his? [*Laughs*] I don't say Pavarotti just to use a name of a singer. I think he emits what I'm talking about. It's more than just a technical instrument, it's a vessel to the soul. We have a hard enough time connecting to our own souls on this planet. Music is showing us where we should be, not just the person doing it, but the person hearing it, and that's connecting to our true being.

Are you nervous or confident before you perform?
There's a level of intimidation, stage fright, and camera shyness, but I'm really challenging that and looking at where the fear comes from. It's a good adrenaline to have, but I can feel a lot more comfortable onstage and allow myself to give a lot more in that sense.

Where do you think fear like that comes from?
I guess, in its most basic form, insecurity. Artists have insecurities. There's a reason why they were attracted to being an artist in the first place. It was probably because they thought differently than their peers or their parents or they just had a different outlook on life. A lot of times that look isn't celebrated. Many times, it's viewed as *odd* or *awkward*, and sometimes there's an isolation in actually becoming an artist that you need to endure.

People never really talk about how much alone time it takes to be an artist.
There's a woodshedding kind of thing where you spend a lot of time alone. Then, you're out there onstage [*cracks up*] in front of all these people. I think it comes back to the human need of what you do being valuable, and, most likely, artists grew up not feeling valuable. In the best cases they did, but, unfortunately, in many cases, there were things culturally, personally, racially, or intellectually that made them feel alienated from the mainstream culture.

And then, you put yourself up there to be judged. It's a wild thing to be that vulnerable.
You get up there and your core existence, not just your talent, is being judged on a listen. But I probably, subconsciously, put myself in that position. I looked at myself one time in the mirror and said, "Why the hell are you doing this to yourself?" I was serious. I was like, "Why did you put yourself in *this*." [*Laughs*] I was mad at myself. "*Why did you do that?*" But, ideally, you go to things in life that challenge you because the challenge is what you grow from. I've had challenges that I haven't met in the best frame of mind. As you get older, you hopefully realize that your relationship to the challenge is what's important, not the challenge itself. I don't want to be motivated by fear, that's not my intention, but we're meant not to be comfortable. This is like the hardest thing in the world for somebody like me.

I'm finding that out, man. It's true.
Being anxious about performing, or being on television, or having a taped interview, or something where your mind is psyching yourself out in that situation is taking you away from the source, which is the music. It's not anything but the unconscious mind operating on a lower

frequency, worrying about what other people are thinking about. So trying to have a more conscious approach of your performance is important, however you get to that.

Did you ever have any vocal training?

I didn't start any vocal training until 2006. I started using a teacher who just recently passed away who was really amazing and who taught understanding of the breath and the instrument. She was a genius. She would be on the phone and know that I wasn't standing up straight. She would know if you were sitting down or if your jaw wasn't in the right place.

What's one of her lessons that you hold dear?

How to streamline your breath up to the note. It comes from your bottom and it goes up to the roof of your mouth, the top of your head. You're essentially trying to push the air up there without the throat being involved. How you breathe and what kind of breath you put into that note is important. If you don't hit a note sometimes it's because you didn't breathe enough.

Do you do vocal warm-ups before shows?

I do like fifteen to twenty minutes of scales just to get my voice going.

Do you have any rituals before you hit the stage?

I'll do a little meditation or prayer, so that's helped.

Is there an intention behind the prayer or is it just like a surrender?

It's just a gratitude prayer. I'm grateful for the people that come to the show, the people on the stage, grateful for their safety because there's all these components you don't think about. You drove overnight in a bus, somebody was in a truck and got there safely, put all the stuff on the stage safely, people who drove to the venue got there safely. Just on a complete gratitude level, sometimes it's good to acknowledge all the things that could've gone wrong during that day that didn't. Sometimes, I'll pray to make sure that I have a good show, and sometimes I just say, "Thank you for love and life."

Is there anything after the show that helps keep your voice in shape?

No. I know Matisyahu used to always warm-up after his set. He'd go before *and* after, I think. It depends on how you use your instrument. I know people that don't even warm-up that really fucking sing! But I think, intuitively, they know how to sing. [*Laughs*]

When you start getting sick, what do you do?

Just take the natural shit to fend it off. I had a couple shows I had to cancel because my voice shut down. That's why I started doing the vocal stuff in the first place.

Are there songs where you wonder if your voice will be there that night?

I don't necessarily think about that. But you know when you didn't get it. [*Laughter*] And you know when you got it.

Are there songs where you've had to adjust the key live?

When I do "Brother Lee" acoustic, I do it in a lower register just because I think it feels cooler there.

Do you remember a performance where you surprised yourself?

Yeah, when I sang the "Ooo-Ooo's" on "Back Together," it's kind of beyond my range, but I did a falsetto for that. But mostly, just connecting to a song, and being like, *Oh, yeah, I did that.* It's taken a long time for me to be comfortable with my recorded voice.

Do you have a favorite vocal performance you're really proud of?

I don't consider myself a vocalist. I think I'm a purveyor of an energy. The voice in there is just what it is. I can go back and listen to "Sideways" and go, "I don't like the way I sang that," but it connects. [*Laughs*] I'm not trying to downplay what my voice does at all. See, it's not just the notes, it's the energy that's tied to the notes. I'm very proud of the energy that I've put out in my music.

What's changed the most about your voice since you started?

Early on, I started to do this to write songs and produce. I didn't think I was gonna be the singer. It was just the progression of finding who I was as an artist and my point of view, and now it's about accepting this calling from a higher frequency, where this phenomenon lives, and feeling what you're singing from your heart. It's a universe that keeps on growing. Some people go, "How can you sing the same song every night?" It's not the same song every night, you know? You're in a different place, under a different moon, under a different star, inside a different venue, in a different year. All these things are different about your circumstances. So there's completely new energy in that song. That's where you have to get.

If you could duet with one singer—living or dead—who would it be?

Probably Sade.

Oh, that's perfect! What is it about Sade's voice for you?

She's just able to tap into some kind of eternal grace and truth with her voice.

She sure is. Who are your top five favorite singers of all time?

That's really hard, man. Otis Redding. John Lennon. Probably Sade. Stevie Wonder. You should time everyone on this one, see who's fastest and longest. Alright, I'll give it to Shelby Lynne. Or Aretha. Alice Smith too. But I also wanted James Brown in there! Wait, did I put Marvin in? That's a cruel question you're asking, bro! [*Laughter*]

If you could ask any singer about their voice, who would it be, and what would you ask?

Bob Marley. I would ask him about singing live or in the studio and if there was a difference. Just his technique for projecting.

Why is that specific for him?

I think Bob had an understanding of where the voice should sit in that paradigm. It would be interesting to pick his brain about how much he's projecting when he's projecting. For Marley to have sounded like he sounded on those live records is amazing because he's not really projecting that much and that band is crankin'. He's not in a range where it's like Robert Plant. Led Zeppelin are so loud, right? And Robert Plant is already singing in a higher register so it's automatically gonna be pushing. You're gonna be able to hear it.

Plant's pushing to get over and Marley was mixed in with the band somehow.

Right, and he's not up there in a falsetto where that frequency's gonna cut easily. He wasn't a baritone. Bob was probably a tenor, but that was one aspect of Marley's voice to me that was a bit underrated. He was able to take that voice and sit it within that vibe.

Yeah, now that you're saying it, that makes total sense.

Marley had a real ability to use that microphone. All the greats did: Sinatra and Nat King Cole. If you ever listen to Aretha's old records, her voice was so powerful that a microphone couldn't handle the way they were recording in those days, so they recorded her voice distorted a lot. It's just a philosophy on how we sing, I guess. Ideally, what a singer is trying to say is like…

"How do I get louder than my band?"

You know what I'm sayin'? So, you end up pushing! I'm listening to my live tapes like, *Goddamn, I'm pushing my voice*! I guess that goes back to being a pro, but I think Marley was a real master at it. You know who was great at using the microphone was Al Green. He was a genius at that shit. His vocal on "Simply Beautiful," Al was barely singing, but it's not like he's whisperin'! [*Laughs*]

Tom Morello on
CHRIS CORNELL

IF YOU LOVE ROCK 'N' ROLL with all your heart, Chris Cornell's touched it, he's made it beat faster, and he's torn it apart. That's just the way it's going to be every time you hear his voice. He and Soundgarden redefined the boundaries of rock. These four genius musicians from Seattle inspired Nirvana, Pearl Jam, Alice in Chains, and so many others to create a new musical movement.

With his wild hair and sparkling eyes, Cornell was as handsome as they come, but it was his voice, *that voice*, that made us believers. In his time, he won three Grammy Awards: two with Soundgarden and one as a solo artist. And while his solo career was just as exciting and prolific, he also formed Temple of the Dog and became the singer for this other band: you may know them as Audioslave.

Audioslave rose from the ashes of Rage Against the Machine. One of the most influential bands ever, RATM fashioned a whole new style of hard rock themselves. When they (indefinitely) lost their singer, Zack de la Rocha, and were looking to start something new, guitarist Tom Morello and his bandmates found exactly what they wanted in Chris Cornell. And commercially, it took them all to new heights.

Tom also has his own solo career, podcasts and radio shows, has toured as part of Springsteen's E Street Band, and founded Prophets of Rage with Chuck D and B-Real. But most importantly, not since Angus Young has one man written more classic rock riffs to melt your face! Simply put, he's the Chris Cornell of guitarists.

When was the first time you heard Chris sing?

I was on tour with my pre-Rage Against the Machine band, Lock Up, and the club that we played had a big bedsheet video screen where they played videos. It was like a live Soundgarden thing from the EP era. First of all, it was crazy because until bands like Soundgarden and Jane's Addiction, when people played riff rock that was loud and heavy, it was normally about the devil and groupies. This was not. Whatever this song was, it was what we would later associate with grunge. I had never heard grinding—riff rock music with a guy singing in a kind of Robert Plant voice—but like a punk rock version of that. He clearly had *ideas and stuff!* [*JTG laughs*] It was a bustling atmosphere in the club, but I was riveted to the screen. I was like, I don't even know what's going on here, man, but it's kind of kickin' my ass and on a different wavelength than any other music ever. So I bought the cassette. The rule in the van is whoever's driving gets to pick the music, so I would play that, driving everybody crazy.

Rage comes out a couple years later and these are now two of the greatest bands of all time. Then, somehow you all find yourselves taking breaks from the bands that made you famous and you come together. Explain to me how you go, "Well, we don't have a singer. Let's just form a new band and have Chris Cornell sing."

[*Laughs*] Sure. Not a bad choice. The *Badmotorfinger* cassette was hugely influential on the first Rage Against the Machine record. It was *Badmotorfinger* and the first Cypress Hill record that we were all listening to and you can really hear that in that music, from the drop D tuning to the big riff stuff. When Rage broke up, Tim [Commerford] and Brad [Wilk] and I knew we still wanted to play together and we were spending a lot of time over at Rick Rubin's house just listening to records and watching videos. The one we kept coming back to was "Slaves and Bulldozers." Chris's voice on that is so baritone menacing at the beginning and then grows into this elemental howl that just tears the speakers apart. I'm not sure today even what that song's about, but I know that I believe every word of it. [*Laughter*]

It's so true. I feel that way about Rage too. Sometimes I'm singing along to you guys and I have no idea what's going on, but somebody was wronged, AND I. AM ON. THE SIDE. OF RIGHT! [*More laughter*]

"*And I'm on the sides of those guys!*" *Yeah*. We would listen to that song again and again and his voice was sometimes both beautiful and he could also turn a switch and make it absolutely terrifying. TERRIFYING. In that song, you felt it. I was never scared by Robert Plant; he's great, he's phenomenal. I was never scared by Ronnie James Dio, but there was something elemental in Chris's voice that was very unnerving. I think it was a big part of his power. While he did wrestle with demons his entire adult and teenage life, he channeled those demons into really, really great art through the funnel of his unbelievably gifted voice.

m sorry, man.

o a radio show on SiriusXM and I play his various bands and solo work all the time. When
putting those shows together, a little smile comes to my face. Whenever the terrifying
t of "Slaves and Bulldozers" comes on, a little smile's on my face. But, honestly, it's a little
cult to listen to. If I'm out somewhere and it comes on, or if it's on the radio and I'm in the
vith my kids, or when I'm on tour after gigs, I'll find some little metal bar and DJ and I'll
the stuff then. When I'm able to enjoy it in front of the company of others, it feels like
bration and that I'm okay to do. I will tell you this though, some of my favorite, most
g Chris Cornell vocals were not sung by Chris Cornell. It was after Chris passed, on tour
rophets of Rage and my own solo shows, we would do an instrumental version of "Like
" with the lights on the empty microphone and the crowd would sing the whole song.
beautiful.

is. I've been there singing along.
such a testament to him that that gorgeous melody is in everybody's mind forever.
re in the world. [*Sings "Like a Stone"*] "In your house." When that chorus comes in, it
eal spiritual celebration, and a memorial every night in a way that felt really good
at.

When you guys joined up to see if Audioslave would work, what did you play to see if there was any chemistry?

We just started trying to write songs. I had a big backlog of riffs and ideas and everyone was just pitching in ideas right and left. Chris, who had been a principal songwriter in Soundgarden, explicitly wanted to concentrate on singing and writing lyrics in Audioslave. He was like, "You guys be the music writers." Later, Rick Rubin pointed out just how extraordinary it was, like, "You don't know how lucky you guys are. I work with hundreds of singers and for someone to be so effortless in their ability to conjure compelling melodies out of the ether is very, very unusual." Chris is uniquely gifted in that regard.

His melodies are so great.

We took it for granted, whether it was throwing him a simple chord progression like "I Am the Highway" or "Like a Stone," or a more complicated, heavy riff like "Light My Way" or "Bring 'Em Back Alive." We would jam through the song a couple times and he would sort of hum a melody into the mic as we were recording stuff. He'd sing a wordless version of that melody, and we'd go, "Okay, great. That one sounds good, let's work on the next one," not realizing the magic that was unfolding before us. But it propelled us and challenged us because in order to get the most out of Chris's voice, we had to push ourselves in sort of different chordal structures. It was less linear with regards to rhythm and riffs and maybe a broader palette of sonic colors that allowed him to shine. In a way, he brought stuff out of us that was really special.

People know you as one of the greatest guitarists ever, but you're a singer as well. Did you learn anything that you were able to apply to your own voice by working with Chris?

The first thing I learned was: don't ever try to sing like Chris Cornell. [*Laughter*] Only he can do that. Stay in your lane, that's what I learned. Singing earnest folk songs in my rich, milk chocolate baritone is my lane. I feel *very comfortable* in that lane. That's how I'm going to be able to be authentic, and, to the best of my abilities, be compelling as a vocalist and be who I am. The one thing about Chris is that he never sang loud. When you hear those blood curdling howls, it's really soft in the room.

Explain that to me because you can't get more glorious than the scream he does in the breakdown section of "Cochise."

Yeah, it's glorious, but he's not blowing his head off.

What's he doing?!

I don't know! I would watch him in rehearsal and, of course, I asked him that question. He could rehearse those songs thirty times in a row and it wasn't like it was some intense vocal strain. First of all, he was blessed with some sort of otherworldly vocal cord abilities, but then, the way he harnessed his ability to sing in a range from nuanced beauty to full throttle shrieking power, it never was out of control. It was soft in the room. You can watch it on video and stuff, the veins are not popping on his forehead.

He's been doing that his entire career and it sounds like he's tearing his throat apart. Now I can do that scream, but we've got two takes.
Yeah, you can do it once. And then you have to cancel the tour. [*Laughter*]

When you guys would perform, was he nervous or confident before going onstage?
Chris was always very confident in his ability. He knew that he had a presence that was compelling and that he could sing like nobody else. You can't take those points off the board, so, I wouldn't say nervousness, no, I don't remember that at all. We came from two very well-established bands, and then, we're entering a world of "Who knows what anybody's gonna make of this?" But my theory, which I imparted at the time, was the Between the Monitors Theory. If you rehearse, know how to play your songs, and you're confident in your ability and your bandmates abilities between the monitors, then you're untouchable. We can take that setup anywhere. You can put it in a stadium, you can put it in a basement. As long as you can look each other in the eye and know that "I'm gonna hold down my end and I know you're gonna hold down your end."

That's so true.
The first time we ever performed was outside the Ed Sullivan Theatre on *Letterman*, on top of that awning.

I remember, it was almost like a rooftop performance.
Which was a bizarre first show. None of us had ever played a show like that. And here we are, a brand new band, playing all brand new songs for the first time in history in front of an audience. But we reminded ourselves beforehand, as long as we're straight between the monitors, it doesn't matter. You can put us anywhere. And it worked out. We were also very well-rehearsed. We take the crap seriously. [*Laughs*] We knew what we were doing and it was a mission. We knew that we had history, but we wanted this to be Audioslave and to stand on its own two feet. We wanted to establish that band as a thing on its own. And that first record was huge. It was something that we had never really had to that extent: those kind of big crossover radio songs.

Did Chris do vocal warm-ups before going onstage?
Yeah, he did some, but a lot of it was really ingrained, inherent, natural ability. He was not one of those guys that was doing "Ma-Pa-Ma-Pa-Ma-Pa" like fifty times before. Sometimes there'd be tea and honey, but it was a minimal amount of preparation for him to be able to sing like that. Here's the thing about Chris: he loved playing a long set. The longer, the better, like, let's give the people their money's worth.

That's awesome. How was he warming-up? Was it the same every nigh
Yeah, there would always be an acoustic guitar around, and it might just be
some songs, but there were no vocal gymnastics. I remember we were reh
to Ronnie James Dio—the tallest singer and the shortest singer rehearsing
other—and I got to sit in on a conversation between Chris and Ronnie in t
were talking about warming-up and they had very similar points of vi
was even more militant. [*Laughs*] Ronnie said, "If you gotta warm-u
singer." [*Laughs harder*] That's what he said! If you're warming-up, tha
is the way he looked at it. We were all just laughing, like, "You don't w
who else never warms-up? A fella by the name of Bruce Springstee

I know, I interviewed him, and knew he was gonna be super
He doesn't warm-up and *he* sings loud! He blows his head off!
loud, power, children's playground, screaming and yelling. And

Yeah, he's a monster. So, how did Chris take care of his
That was one thing we did notice. There were times whe
and it impacted his voice. There was a certain barometer
and his voice, that you could hear sometimes in the vo
a warrior with regards to his voice and there was no b
song's got too much screaming in it, let's take it off the
someone who could sing like that would've coddled th
didn't need to.

Did you ever have to adjust the keys live?
No, never.

Do you have a favorite vocal performance
I wrote the chord progression to "Like a Stone
*This is not a song that Soundgarden would play
would play. This is almost like the folk world th*
it into the room, but Chris didn't bat an ey
one that's on the record. It really gave u
to always maintain his unique vocal pe
around it.

When you hear his voice now, wh
It's honestly a little hard to listen to
but his death really haunts me in a
I'm still in it.

ROGER DALTREY

"*YEEEAAAHHH!*"

He'll probably kill me for leading off with that, but it is one of the most iconic, blood-curdling screams in rock 'n' roll history: Roger Daltrey of The Who, letting you know what it's all about as he enters "Won't Get Fooled Again."

But don't let the scream fool you. He's so much more as a vocalist on every level. As the singer of one of the most influential bands of the 20th century, Roger has sold more than 100 million records worldwide, was inducted into the Rock & Roll Hall of Fame, and along with his mates in The Who, helped redefine what a concert experience should be—raw, energetic emotion, visceral power, chaotic, shambolic excitement.

"Gimme a bum note and a bead of sweat." Get ready for Roger's philosophy on singing rock, a genre he helped create, and one he continues to revolutionize every time he steps foot onstage. As wild as ever, I find him compelling, hilarious, and still fully engaged in the art of being one of the greatest singers ever.

Man, do I love this guy?

"*YEEEAAAHHH!*"

Who first exposed you to singing?

My Uncle Len, my mother's youngest brother, used to play me records by people like Hank Williams. I used to *love* that music. From there, I heard people like Little Richard, Jerry Lee, and Elvis, of course.

And you sang in the church choir as well, right?

When I was seven years old. I had a very similar upbringing of the Black community that came from the gospel field, except I was singing High Church of England songs. [*Laughs*] But equally, we had to sing in tune, in pitch, in harmony, and *loud*. I've always had a loud voice. Then, along came a Scottish guy from Glasgow called Lonnie Donegan who was singing all kinds of Lead Belly songs and chain gang songs from America, the kind of music we used to call Skiffle, very simple, blues-based music. But the way Lonnie did it turned my head into thinking I could really do this! [*Laughs*]

What was he doing that inspired that thought?

This guy throws his head back and howls, he just sings from his guts. Everyone else is putting on a show, putting on a front, but this guy's singing came from somewhere *really* deep, and it just grabbed me by the ears. That's all I ever thought about then was becoming a great singer and carrying that ethos through. I sing like my life depends on it. I found that so many other singers didn't used to do that. They were great singers, don't get me wrong, but it was show time. I've always tried to sing like I'm singing for my life. Lonnie's like that.

Were you emulating anyone when you started out?

I was copying Lonnie! [*Laughter*] You go through those teenage years and anyone who has a hit record, you emulate them. I learned harmonies like the Everly's with my work mates and I could do a bloody good Roy Orbison. That's where we learned our chops because we used to play in the bars and people wanted to hear whatever was in the Hit Parade. The Hit Parade in those days was *incredibly* diverse, traditional jazz through to Johnny Cash, Del Shannon. It just went on and on and on, they were all so different.

How did you find your own voice?

My voice was easy. That really came out of [guitarist] Pete Townshend's writing. I suddenly *really* had to get to grips with living what I was singing. There was a period when my head met my heart and my heart took over. But the head kind of knew what it was up to rather than struggling in the dark. Townshend's writing was so different from anything else that was out there. It was something kind of left field. And it's some of the best lines rock singers would ever be presented with.

What did that do to your voice?

I had to think about it like, *I've gotta make this live. Otherwise, it's gonna fall on deaf ears.* It just came naturally, I suppose. Then, you've gotta present it to the public, and I never actually put on an act, I just do what I feel like doing at the time. In between the words, I just leap about. I'm not a great dancer, I'll never out dance Mick Jagger. He's the best front man in the business. You can't have another Mick Jagger, so I just have to be *me*.

Did you ever have any vocal training?

Nooooo. God forbid. That'd knock the balls off you! [*Howls laughing*] Then you end up with the antithesis of what rock should be. Obviously, you need to be able to pitch a song and you need to be in tune, but I've got a distinct dislike of the trained voice. Although I do admire the breathing, I dislike the sound of it. That's why I don't think there will ever be a Who musical because I don't think a trained singer could sing Townshend songs eight shows a week and make it sound good. You have to sing it a different way and that's not where Townshend music comes from.

Where does it come from?

It comes from the guts. You can't do that eight times a week.

Are you nervous or confident before you perform?

I was always confident. Once I open my mouth to start singing, I'm in another world.

Tell me about that world.

I'm much better now. I used to see the audience as an enemy. [*Cracks up*] It's kind of the nature of Who music. We always used to feel we had to drive our music through the audience to touch them because they were all so stoned and wacked out. We thought, *We gotta get this lot up*, [*laughter*] because in the late-'60s, early-'70s period, we would be playing things like *Who's Next*, and all that, and the fucking audience would be sitting down cross-legged on the floor! You'd go, "Well, fuck you lot! This ain't what this is about!" [*Laughs*] The only way to do that was to make them your enemy and say, "Right, you wanna fight? We'll give you a fight!"

But that's changed for you over the years?

I've suddenly realized that these are all my friends and I've become very, very fond of them. What I have learned, and it took me a long time to learn it, is that you can do 10,000 perfect shows with perfect pitch and get all the words right and everything's fantastic, the sound is perfect, but the one show the fans will remember was the one you screwed up. *Screw up so they'll remember you!* [*Laughter*]

Do you do vocal warm-ups before shows?

Noooo! I can't be bothered. I did for a while. I had a pre-cancerous condition on my vocal cords that I didn't realize was there until I did my first solo tour and things got really tough. Singing was becoming hard and I just happened to get recommended to see a voice doctor who looked at it and said, "Whoops! You got a problem."

What was it?

There were these great big white patches all over my vocal cords and they looked terrible. I was very worried. I thought, *Well, this might be the end of my career.* But it wasn't. A guy called Steven Zeitels did the surgery. There aren't many world-class singers who haven't been in Steven's hands, and I recommend that anyone who gets a vocal problem, if they can, get to see Steven, who runs the Voice Institute in Boston. He is fantastic. I did warm-ups during that period because we were doing a three-hour show, often six shows a week, which is an incredible high work rate.

Man, that's taking your life in your hands!

Especially for singers! Singing is the hardest job in the band, whatever anybody will ever tell you. I mean, guitarists, we shit 'em. [*Cracks up*] It's tough, man. It is really tough.

I thought the drummer had the hardest job in the band, but with singing there's a hundred psychological things going through your head whereas with drums, I'm just in it.

There's a different kind of power than just drumming or guitaring. And we don't have the luxury of changing the strings like the guitarist either.

Do you have any rituals before you hit the stage?

Yeah, you kind of build yourself a rock star these days. It's not quite as easy as it used to be! I just take the piss out of it all now. It's half an hour of getting dressed and mucking about. The main thing is to have a laugh. You gotta have a laugh. At our age, the journey we've been through, you just gotta laugh at it. It's amazing we've survived it all. The worst problem I had in my whole career was the fact that I didn't realize I was going deaf. *And I wonder why?* [*Laughs*]

Yeah, exactly!

We were called the loudest band in the bloody world at the time and I used to be in front of that lot every night. When your hearing goes, you over-sing which is basically what gave me the voice problem in the first place.

So, you have this surgery. What do you change to protect your voice?

I changed the whole monitor system from the old-fashioned, up-front sound—everything at high volume—brought the volume of the band down and did it all through the PA. And I found something interesting: don't play loud, just play well. You can play better when you're quieter. Everyone's much tighter. You can certainly sing better when you can hear yourself. I probably went the first fifteen years of our career and only heard myself *clearly* maybe one in ten gigs. Bloody hard work, I tell you.

How do you take care of your voice on the road?

I eat well, I keep fit. You gotta keep your lungs up. And sing properly. Sing with your real voice, don't try and put on a voice. All the people who try and put on a voice are now suffering. I won't mention any names, but you can hear them. You can tell that their voice isn't their natural voice and they try to squeeze it into a certain sound. Eventually, it gets them.

When you start getting sick, what do you do?

I've learned not to soldier on. If you get signs of a cold coming on or you get a cold, cancel the show. You're only gonna go backwards. Once you go backwards, you go back a long time with voices. A voice is incredibly fragile. I used to soldier on and we'd end up canceling more shows than if I'd just canceled the one or two and moved them until later in the tour.

It must be hard to cancel a show at your level.

I used to beat myself up terrible onstage sometimes, just desperately trying to get some kind of noise out, just because the crowd had turned up and they were expecting a show. I won't do that anymore. It's a horrible feeling for a singer to have to do it, but what can you do? We're not robots.

Are there songs where you wonder if your voice will be there that night?

I don't worry about it. I always go for it, even if I don't think I'll hit it. I'm quite well known for that phrase, "Gimme a bum note and a bead of sweat." That's what rock is. I'd rather have that than someone going through the fucking motions.

Are there songs where you've had to adjust the key live?

I've adjusted some keys onstage—very, very few—because I'm seventy-six years old. But "Baba O' Riley" and "Love, Reign O'er Me," they're in the same keys as ever. The highest note in "Love, Reign O'er Me" is a high B. [*Laughs*]

What was your most embarrassing vocal mishap ever?

I was playing with a friend's band at a charity show in LA and we were doing a version of "Born to Run." We did the intro, and when it came time for the vocal, I was just—*Oh Fuck*—a complete and utter blank. I mean, not even a clue! [*Laughter*]

Do you remember a performance where you surprised yourself?

Nothing surprises me, really. It's always trying to get the best out of the narrative of the story. So, rather than it just being a collection of words, the words are moods for touching people. And the emotion of the words, it's all connected. It can't be just words for word's sake.

How are you with hearing your own voice?

I don't actually like listening to myself, but I know when I've got it right. I know when I'm good.

Do you have a favorite vocal performance you're really proud of?

No. [*Laughs*] Everything I do, that's it. If you want it better, go get someone else to sing it! That's as good as I can do.

I wanna give your first solo album some love because it's such a great record, but you're also singing a bit differently than you were with The Who at the time.

That was all very, very deliberate because I did that when we were having a year off. Pete was writing *Quadrophenia* and singers can't have a year off.

"It's a Hard Life" and "Giving It All Away" are two of my favorite vocal performances of yours. I just really love the way you sing on that record.

"Giving It All Away" is an extraordinary song when we play it live. When I do it live with my own band, you can always hear a pin drop. There's something about the way that song starts, the chord changes, and the simplicity of it, that puts shivers up your back. "Paid all my dues, I picked up my shoes, got up and walked away." You can just feel the audience go [*makes a breathless sound*]. It's really weird. And it's palpable onstage. You can feel it.

Let's go back to 1965 for a second. The Who put out their first couple singles and then you release "My Generation," and you're stuttering the lyrics. This has to be the ball-siest choice you could make at that time because no one really knew you yet. How did that come about and did you have any reservations that it wouldn't work?

No, I knew it would work. There was something about the aggression of what [drummer] Keith Moon brought to the piece that amplifies the power of the whole thing. It was on the one beat, which was what was so different about Who music. It was rock, not rock 'n' roll.

You've said recording the *Tommy* album really changed you as a singer. How so?

Prior to *Tommy*, Pete was writing some very strange singles. We did "I'm a Boy, Pictures of Lily," and that's when I had trouble finding the voice for his songs. But *Tommy* wasn't particularly the album that did it for me, it was the stage performance that really developed me as a singer. I had to become Tommy. I had to become *the* character. If I hadn't become what I became at the time, which was a Rock God with all the fringes and shit, I don't know whether Tommy would've had the power that it achieves. Again, it's about touching people and making them feel.

Since Pete writes the majority of the songs, does he demo them up with his own vocals and then you take it from there and make it your own? What's that part of the process like?

He does a rough vocal and then I put my own vocals on and move notes about and look for the expression of it. I only take his top line as a rough guide to the melody.

A few years ago, I read an interview where the journalist was impressed by the fact that you could still hit the high note in "Won't Get Fooled Again," and you said, "All that bloody singing and all everyone remembers is a scream." Does that scream haunt you?

It's starting to. I'm getting to the age where it's my least favorite song to sing. I love it when we do it acoustic because it's more of a blues song for me. The way it was done on *Who's Next* is great, but it's too rigid for my taste. I much prefer to bend it around and play with it. And the scream is part of the original format so, yes, it drives me nuts.

It *is* one of the most iconic screams in rock history. Did you do it a few times to get it just right or did you just hit it that once?

I can't remember, probably a couple times. I think it's double tracked. I'm not sure.

Where do you place that scream when you do it? From your throat or your head?

I just scream. It's from my guts.

Another thing that follows you around is the legendary pandemonium that you guys brought to your live performances. You think of The Who and it's Keith and all his chaos, you guys trashing your instruments, and Pete doing windmills. No one ever approached music with as much abandon as you guys did. But the thing that always felt the *most* dangerous to me was you swinging that microphone around by its chord and catching it. Every time I see you do that, I'm fucking terrified for you and everyone around you. Has it ever gone wrong? Did it ever swing back and crack you in the face?

It's hit me in a lot of other parts that are quite more painful. [*Laughter*] I've never hit anyone in the band onstage, ever. I'm very aware of where it is, even when it's traveling at high speed, which is probably a couple hundred miles an hour when it's really spinning.

What's changed the most about your voice since you started?

It's just grown up. It's mature now. It's got a lot more life and a lot more living.

If you could duet with one singer—living or dead—who would it be?

Nooo, I don't like duets! [*Laughter*] So, there you go, that's easy. No one!

Who are your top five favorite singers of all time?

If I had to choose any, I'd have to say Lonnie Donegan would be my inspiration that gave me the impetus to go, "Yeah, I can do that." Elvis, because he was the coolest dude ever and he had something in his voice that was a quality to gain. Johnny Cash, Jerry Lee, Little Richard, but all for different reasons. They all had something in their voices. I hope I have something of what they all had in mine.

If you could ask any singer about their voice, who would it be, and what would you ask?

I can't name anyone in particular, but some of the singers that always use an electronic effect on their voice that gives it a particular sound.

Like Auto-Tune?

Auto-Tune. Oh, God, I can't stand that! Yeah. "Why the fuck do you do that?"

BRITT DANIEL

THE BEATLES, THE STONES, LED ZEPPELIN, FLEETWOOD MAC. Some bands are household names, while others most definitely should be, yet somehow remain one of the best kept secrets in music: Spoon is that band for a lot of us.

Those who know, know. And those who don't, should.

Led by the visionary voice of Britt Daniel, Spoon has built a steady career off their inspired songwriting, artistic integrity, and critical acclaim. From their 1994 debut EP to their latest album, few artists have a catalog this consistent. And few have a voice this confident and cool. Just listen to "The Way We Get By," "New York Kiss," or "Can I Sit Next to You," and you'll get the picture. Even his side project, Divine Fits, is one of the raddest records out.

So, I was thrilled to get into it with Britt and talk about Afrin, whiskey, and milk, his vocal approach, and why I think he and Phil Lynott are two of the best phrasers in rock 'n' roll history.

Who first exposed you to singing?

My dad played guitar and would sing a few songs like "(Ghost) Riders in the Sky" to me before I went to bed. He wrote a song called "Britt Lost His Coat," so that was maybe the first. Then, when I got into third grade, there was a choir in school, so that was where I really started singing. I just always liked it.

When did it become serious for you?

Some friends were getting together to play instruments and they said, "Why don't you come over and sing?" They thought I'd be up for it.

Were you emulating anyone when you started out?

I don't know if I was emulating anyone. I was just trying to sound good. I was really into Robert Smith right then, but I didn't sing like Robert Smith.

That was my first guy too. How did you find your own voice?

I've always gravitated to people that showed some humanity and personality in their vocals. I love Joe Strummer and the dude can't traditionally sing, but there's nothing like that vocal. He's just pure soul. When I heard Jonathon Richman for the first time, you could feel his personality in his vocal, which was not too different from how he spoke, and that really appealed to me—somebody who had their own personality just from how they sang the lines.

Did you ever have any vocal training?

No, other than being in choir as a little kid. I loved being in choir. I stuck with it through middle school. I think something about that did give me a sense of when to breathe and what that timbre was like, just being cognizant, so it became natural to do it without thinking about it.

Are you nervous or confident before you perform?

I get nervous before shows, but I'm never thinking, *Is my voice gonna go out?* Unless I'm sick. I'm pretty lucky with my voice. It's pretty dependable and I've never had to do much for it.

Do you do vocal warm-ups before shows?

I've never been one of those warm-up guys. I wonder if John Lennon or Marvin Gaye did vocal exercises. I kind of doubt they did. I bet they just went out there. Iggy Pop, he went out there. The only time I've done that is if I'm sick and my voice feels like it's a little out. Then, if I just belt through some songs, maybe three or four times, ones that are like real shouters, then my voice gets a little better.

You just shout through it backstage?

We played on TV a few years ago and I had a cold. There was so much mucus back there that my voice wasn't performing. I couldn't hit the notes that I normally could. I couldn't do a falsetto. There's a song called "The Beast and Dragon, Adored" that we've got that's a shouter.

At some point, I figured out that if I sing that backstage three or four times before I go on, it kind of clears everything out, and then I can sing normal again.

That's interesting.
I think it depends on what kind of sick you are. If you get laryngitis, that's not gonna help things. But if you just have a cold, for me that's what works.

Do you have any rituals before you go onstage?
Tequila rituals.

How many shots?
A couple.

Is there anything after the show that helps keep your voice in shape?
One thing I've noticed when we're starting a tour is if I haven't sung for a while, after the first show, I can be a little hoarse. But after that, it's kind of warmed-up. I don't understand why that is.

How do you take care of your voice on the road?
My overall health can be affected by staying up all night and drinking, but there's nothing I've specifically considered for my vocal. I don't know if that's good or bad for your book!

***You're ruining this book, bro!* So, what do you do when you start getting sick?**
I've done the thing where you gargle whiskey or tequila or something. If you're sick, that probably helps a little bit. Sip it or gargle it.

You gargle whiskey? I've never heard this.
I think the alcohol going back there is sort of clearing things out. The problem that's making you not be able to sing in a lot of these situations is there's phlegm back there in your throat and it's preventing your voice box from being able to do what it normally does. If you clear that out, you're a little bit back to normal. Have you ever heard that Paul McCartney said that he would drink milk before he did a vocal, which is what you're supposed to *not* do?[1]

Yeah, that seems like the worst idea!
Sometimes, if I'm stuffy, I'll do Afrin [Nasal Spray] 'cause that'll make you have less of that nasal sound if you clear out your sinuses.

Afrin and whiskey's gonna be the new thing on the streets.
[*Laughs*] Afrin, whiskey, and milk.

---

[1]	Note: Paul McCartney has been both vegetarian and/or vegan since the '70s, but did claim at one point that milk was his favorite drink.

Are there songs where you wonder if your voice will be there that night?

Not really. There are things I can't sing, but I figure that out ahead of time.

Are there songs where you've had to adjust the key live?

Yes. "Beast and Dragon" is one of 'em. I think it's in C on the record and we always play it in B. There may be two or three songs where we play it down a half or a whole step. That's something I do quite a bit when I'm writing a song. I'll try it out in different keys to see where it feels best.

Dude, we've released one full-length album and four EPs and just finished writing our second album. And it's *the first time* where I've actually gone, "Can we work out the keys beforehand?" I never knew that's what you should do 'til now. It took me this long!

So much of the personality you're gonna convey is dependent on the key. Sometimes you're gonna be singing at the top of your range, which is great if you're doing "Modern Love" by David Bowie. It's right at the top and you want that kind of energy, right? Then, sometimes you want it to be [*lowers his register*] way down. That's gonna affect how the song is performed and the impression of the emotion.

What was your most embarrassing vocal mishap ever?

There was a time when Feist and I were supposed to sing together. We talked about doing "You Really Got a Hold On Me" by The Beatles and I went down to her soundcheck. I had learned the Beatles version and she had learned the Smokey Robinson version. They were different keys and I couldn't pull it off. I just lost my way. I was all set with The Beatles version. [*Laughs*] We were singing a two part harmony and I kind of figured out what my voice could do and I just felt lost. I said, "I can't do it. I *wanna* do it, but I can't do it."

Do you remember a performance where you surprised yourself?

If I've sung for four or five hours, my voice starts to get buttery and malleable. It feels like it can do anything and then things happen that I wasn't quite expecting. The vocal gets a little torn up and more soulful. "Out Go the Lights" was a song where I remember I was singing it all day and when I got to the end of the day I could finally do these things I couldn't do before.

How are you with hearing your own voice?

Usually, I like it. I've kind of figured that out because I have a somewhat nasally voice. I don't usually wanna hit a microphone straight on. I wanna sing just a little off-axis. Something about that's a little less mid-rangey and I've got plenty of mid-range already.

So, where do you angle your mouth when you're off the mic?

I'm angling it a little to the side. Maybe the same height as the microphone, but off to the left a bit. Every vocalist is different, every voice is different, so everybody's gonna have a different trick. But, for me, it seems to be a little cooler, slightly more sultry, if I sing off-axis.

Do you have a favorite vocal performance you're really proud of?

I remember liking "Lines in the Suit" a lot when I did that one. It's a two-part harmony and right around then I was getting into that sort of throaty, sultry vocal that I definitely hadn't done on the first couple albums. But you hear it on "Believing Is Art" and "Lines in the Suit."

Right, because on *Telephono* and a lot of your earlier stuff, you were a bit punkier with vocals. But on *Girls Can Tell*, another side of you begins to take over. Did you make a conscious change around that time, like, "I don't wanna scream all this stuff forever. I better knock it off and find a different approach?"

Yeah, I think I just got a little tired of that approach. I wanted to try different things and *Girls Can Tell* was way more soulful than the records that came before it. It was much more about oldies radio, and Motown, and Elvis Costello, and the Supremes. Those were the big touch points for that record, so it was just bound to happen that the vocal would change a little bit.

I honestly think you may be the greatest vocal phraser in rock 'n' roll history. [*Britt laughs*] No one strings words together as rhythmically as you and it's all done with this really effortless swagger. A perfect example would be the final line of "Anything You Want" where you go, "Since you were nineteen, and still in school, waiting on a light on the corner by Sound Exchange." It's so rhythmically perfect!

That song had been sung at a certain speed and had a certain rhythm to it. But something about changing the rhythm and making it go really fast and packing all these details into this one line at the very end I knew would make you take notice. You're talking generally about a relationship, and then, right at the end of the song, there's this sort of zoom-in to this particular time, this particular place, where she was standing at a light on the corner by Sound Exchange, and it just felt right to me, like, this is gonna make time stop for a second. After that record came out, I remember a lot of people saying that vocal sounded like Thin Lizzy.

I can't believe you just said that because, to be fair, you really are tied with Phil Lynott for best phraser! We actually have a song on our new album that feels a bit Thin Lizzy. That kind of phrasing. And one of my best friends heard the demo and went, "Dude, that kinda sounds like Spoon!" [*Laughter*]

Oh, that's funny. I'd never had a Thin Lizzy record and I checked it out and I saw what people were talkin' about, but I don't know where it came from.

Something else I really dig about your vocals is that you have all these subtle affectations, like the way you'll hit your Ds with such specificity. You'll hear it on songs like "Don't Let It Get You Down" where you're like [*mimics Britt*] "DOUUN' let it get you DOUWN." [*Britt laughs*] You'll hit those Ds stylistically.

I hadn't thought about that, but yeah, it's cool. All of that stuff makes a difference. I don't know if I can define why, but sometimes singing a word very succinctly like "Down," and then sometimes it's gotta be, "*DOUWN.*" Who knows why? Sometimes it makes sense to do it one way and sometimes it makes sense the other. It's all a matter of taste and it all kind of paints a picture.

It's like what you were saying earlier about Joe Strummer. The way he's delivering the vocal *is* what's great about it. It's not about the technical proficiency, it's more like him howling in "London Calling," you know what I mean?
Yeah, I remember thinking about the Ramones a lot and John Fogerty does it too, but they say these words with this sort of style. One Creedence line where he goes, "Thought I HOID a rumblin.'" You know it's, "Thought I *HEARD* a rumblin'," but he wants to say, "Thought I *HOID* a rumblin.'" Why? I don't know, but it's fuckin' awesome. It adds something to the performance. It's just giving you these little bonus points.

There's a moment I love on the *Transference* album during "Trouble Comes Running." Right after the break, out of nowhere, you shout, "Well done!" and then start singing the verse. [*Britt laughs*] Was that intentional or were you really saying that to someone?
That was recorded at a rehearsal. I brought in my 4-track to record whatever we were doing and that was the first time we'd gone over that song. The guys hit on something that I really loved, so I said, "Well done." We could've taken it out, but I thought, *That feels good*.

What's changed the most about your voice since you started?
Knowing when it's the right time to scream. That first album, as you mentioned, had a lot of screaming, and some of it I like, some of it I don't care for as much. I was finding my way, writing songs for these tiny clubs, and I wanted to play loud, fast songs. I don't know, maybe you can tell me. Do you think it's changed?

I've noticed there's more creative care given to the vocal. Like most bands, when you're starting out, you're just trying to get the songs that you jam on tape. As you progress, you go, "What are the textures, the production, the engineering?" Now every song is treated as its own universe and you produce and engineer the vocal for *that song*, and the next one might have something totally different.
Right, right.

But when "Hot Thoughts" came out, it sounded like you were having fun! It was like you were freer than you had ever been. I had never heard you shout, "*Woo!*"
Yeah, that was a good "Woo." We played "Hot Thoughts" on *Ellen*, and she came to the rehearsal where we played the song two or three times. I was not doing the "Woo." It was something that I'd kind of forgotten about, and she came up and said, "You know, it sounds great, but I'm really missing that "Woo" you were doing." I was like, "You're right!" From then on, I started doing the "Woo." I want to put a little bit of fun into the performance if it's appropriate for the song. I like to feel that kind of presence from a singer.

If you could duet with one singer—living or dead—who would it be?

I'll go with Prince just because I wanna hang out with Prince.

What is it about Prince's voice that you love?

He's just going for it. He's playing a role in just about every song. It's almost like he's acting. He's taking on the character of the person and conveying that with his voice and he's very funny. Humor was big to him and you can really sense that in his inflection in those songs. You know, [*mimics Prince's performance of "The Ballad of Dorothy Parker"*] "Let me get a fruit cocktail." He's talking about being in a restaurant at the end of the night, he's low energy, and just wants a fruit cocktail [*laughs*], and then she responds in this way that's sorta sassy, "Sounds like a real man to me." All that is conveyed in a matter of, what, four seconds, these two parts that he's playing? Beautiful.

Who are your top five favorite singers of all time?

Dylan 1966. You know, talkin' like "Desolation Row," that era. Joe Strummer. Let's say Chan Marshall. Marvin Gaye. Q-Tip. And we haven't even mentioned Bon Scott yet!

If you could ask any singer about their voice, who would it be, and what would you ask?

I'd ask Stevie Wonder which vocal he is proudest of.

JOE ELLIOTT

WHEN I WAS EIGHT YEARS OLD, I had a crush on my camp counsellor. She had gorgeous, sparkling eyes, a beautiful, bohemian energy, an amazing smile, and wild, dirty blonde hair. But she was older. Much, much older. So this shit hurt. And no one on earth could possibly understand the magnitude of the pain I was feeling. No one but Joe Elliott.

Def Leppard had just released their second album and the song "Bringin' On the Heartbreak" was Joe letting me know I wasn't alone. In my opinion, it remains the greatest power ballad ever and the greatest promise of things to come. And it wouldn't be long before these lads from Sheffield, England conquered the world, from the radio to the video to the stereo to the stadium. They have been inducted into the Rock & Roll Hall of Fame and have sold over 100 million records, making them one of the bestselling artists of all time.

With his melodic ear, incredible range, and the unique ability to still kick ass at his age, Joe Elliott knows exactly what he's talkin' about. The question is: "Armageddon it?"

Who first exposed you to singing?

The Beatles, probably about four years old. I was told by relatives over the years when things like "Love Me Do" and "She Loves You" would come over the radio, I would walk to the radio and just gravitate to where the sound was coming from. I used to stand on this little stool, play a plastic Paul McCartney guitar, and sing along with these songs. Obviously, I was just magnetized by this as a child.

When did you know this is what you were gonna do?

I never once said to my parents, "I want to sing for a living." It never occurred to me that people like us could do something like that. But I had a musical upbringing. My mom taught herself to play guitar, then she taught me to play guitar. Then you start realizing you can write your own songs and I wrote my first one at the age of eight. I thought I had all the tools to be a singer until I started singing and realized I didn't. [*Laughter*] I'm a singer by trade, but I would've played tambourine or flute just to get into a band because I was so into music.

Were you emulating anyone when you started out?

I was just trying to find a voice when I first joined Def Leppard, which is the first band I ever sang with. Certain singers, you hear 'em, you go, my God, they're a big fan of such and such a person. I didn't have anybody in mind cause I liked everything, whether it be Kate Bush or Lemmy. As Miles Davis once said, "There's only two types of music: good and bad." I liked what I liked. Pop, rock, country, new wave, it didn't matter. All I did was try to sing melodies I thought were appropriate over the tracks that the guys were writing. In many respects, I was fortunate that I didn't sound like anybody else because it gave me my own identity eventually.

How did you find your own voice?

I'm still looking to be quite honest.

Did you ever have any vocal training?

Yes, but not until way into my career. It wasn't to learn to sing, it was to learn to not lose my voice, which is a totally different thing. The coach I used was a guy called Roger Love based out of Los Angeles. He said, "Look, I'm not gonna try to change your technique or introduce a vibrato you don't have or want. I'm just gonna give you exercises to stop you losing your voice."

Were you losing your voice a lot?

The reason I started losing my voice is because nobody in our old management knew anything about singing, and, in fairness, *neither did I*. I just thought you blindly went onstage and everything would be fine. Then, all of a sudden, you lose your voice like I did once in 1983 where we had to cancel like ten shows. One doctor said I'd never sing again and another one said, "Course you will, you just have to shut up for ten days." Then it came back.

Were you just doing too many nights back-to-back?
We'd just gone from forty-five minutes to an hour and a half, literally overnight, six shows a week. It was too much for an untrained voice. I was working off instinct, being totally fine up until that moment, but schedules are what started to rip me to shreds. There isn't enough recovery time in the twenty-two hours that you've got between your last word of one night and your first word of the next.

I feel like a lot of singers are afraid of coming off like prima donnas, so they try to trudge through when they really shouldn't.
It takes a tantrum or two from the lead singer of any band to lock the door with all the rest of the band and management in the room and go, "Listen, ASSHOLES, I can't sing three in a row anymore. It's not gonna be done. I just won't turn up." We realized it was better for all of us because everybody sings backing vocals in Def Leppard and they suffer too. So, the more days off we have, the better we perform. I said, "We can still play a finite amount of shows, we just have to do it over a couple years more. We don't have to do 5,000 shows over 5,000 days. We can do them over 20,000 days." It gives a longevity to the band. There's a logic.

You're right that communication is key as well.
With the greatest of respect, it wouldn't be a problem for Leonard Cohen or Lou Reed. Things that they've never done: cancel a concert because they've lost their voice. But for somebody like me or Bryan Adams or Robert Plant, anybody where there's a bit of histrionics going off, where you're trapped by your youth, you know, things that you thought were a great idea at twenty-one, but you didn't realize you'd still be doing at thirty-one, forty-one, fifty-one, and then *sixty*-one, they become issues.

Yeah, you don't think about longevity when you're writing those parts.
In my line of work, the only vocalists I'm aware of that remotely sound like they always did are Steven Tyler and Sammy Hagar. Bruce Dickinson as well. I've kind of got back there, but I lost it for a while because I got sick. And when you get ill in the middle of a tour, there is *nothing* you can do about it. You just have to suck it up and don't read the reviews. It's a horrible place to be.

How do you survive those moments with any sort of peace?
You have to have really thick skin because people like us have only got this inch long piece of steel to hide behind called a mic stand. *We can't hide! We're out front and center!* So, if you aren't on your game, everybody knows about it, and there's *nothing worse* than hearing, "I'm really sorry, everybody, but I've got a cold." [*Laughs*] I mean, get the point across somehow but don't do the "Woe is me, gimme some sympathy here." That's worse than just being rubbish.

So, the vocal training did the trick for you?

I got pneumonia twice in an eighteen-month period and it just destroyed my voice. I had to build it back from scratch. I spent eighteen months working with Roger and he not just physically built my voice back, but built the confidence back that I could do this, because there were times where I thought I'd never do it again.

What was that rebuilding process like?

Just the fact that he would say to me over a three-month period, "You've gained a semi-tone back comfortably," and then six weeks later go, "Now you're a tone higher than when we started." It's like, *That's a big deal.* All of a sudden it just kind of fell into place. And then I had middle that I never had in my life! They say you can't teach an old dog new tricks. Bullshit! Yeah, you can, if the dog's willing to learn. Most singers deteriorate from their late-twenties downwards and I was determined to not be one of them. So, you're never too old.

So, now you do vocal warm-ups before shows?

Every day. Every single show. We all do. We put on the Mp3 that Roger Love gave to us, in the dressing room, and whoever wants to join in does. If we're onstage at 9:30, we'll start warming-up as soon as the opening act goes on. And while we're doing that, we're kind of just ambling around the dressing room. I don't sit there in a chair, staring at the player like I'm in a lesson. You're just opening drawers and closing drawers, and washing your hair, and drying your hair, going, [*sings*] "Da-da-da-da-da-da-da." And then ten to fifteen minutes before you go on, you make a bit more of an effort to concentrate. I might put a recording of the opening song on and sing along with it in the showers. If it's, *Yeah, that sounds like me*, then you know everything's gonna be fine. If it *doesn't sound great*, you do some more exercises in that register which'll maybe open your throat up a little bit.

Do you have any other rituals before you hit the stage?

I'll have a shot of whiskey sometimes, me and Vivian [Campbell]. Just a tiny drop in a Dixie cup. I mean, it could be water for the amount that's in it. It's just a ritual. Irish whiskey, *boom*, and off we go. We might pace up and down a tiny bit while the intro tape's playin'. Me and Phil [Collen] share a tent, and Rick [Savage] and Vivian share a tent, and Rick [Allen] is already up on his kit, behind the curtain. Me and Phil are mostly just checking ourselves in the mirror to make sure we've not got cabbage in our teeth. [*Laughter*]

Are you nervous or confident before you perform?

You stand somebody in front of no people to take a field goal, or do it front of 100,000 people, there's a difference in how you approach that ball. It's the same difference with singing. Nerves become a big part of how you perform. It comes and goes. We can do these tours where we sell out night after night in arenas, and then, we'll take four years off to make a record. After four years of not singing live, you're back onstage like you're ten or twelve years old again, like, "Oh my God!" because it's been so long since you did it. [*Laughs*] You're nervous before you go on, but once you get onstage, after the first two or three minutes, it all settles down, and you go, *Oh I remember this*. It's like ridin' a bike.

Is there anything after the show that helps keep your voice in shape?
Yeah, just be quiet. We have a quick knacker about how the gig went, but we don't scream and shout about it. We just go, "That was pretty good," or "We need to change the order of these songs around," at the volume that I'm talking to you at now. For the last two decades, we've finished the set with "Photograph" and "Rock of Ages," not the easiest two songs to sing. The last thing I need is to keep going after that. You just learn to say as little as you can. And then, when you've got guests, you talk as need be. But if I have a day off tomorrow, I can talk a lot more than if I have a gig tomorrow.

How else do you take care of your voice on the road?
Thank God for Netflix and stuff like that because on days off, I don't go out looking for night-clubs. I don't stay up 'til six in the morning, ordering champagne and having to shout because you've got [*mimics thumping nightclub music*] going off in the background. We travel over-night, so we wake up in the next town, which is always better than traveling on show day, and you put on a movie. What's the last thing you wanna do when a movie's on? *Talk*. Other than that, I notoriously take a DVD of the gig and watch it back to find fault with what we've done so we can correct it tomorrow and to see how I sounded.

It's so funny because most people think a singer's life is what they're selling in the music video and so much of the job is the exact opposite.
I think singers at best are neurotic, and, at worst, probably as manic depressive as comedians. The singer's union is a limited membership that doesn't really deem explanation to any other form of musician because they just go, "Ahhh, shut up your moanin'." You can play smokin' hot solos on a guitar with the flu. *You can't sing with it*. Why don't you go sandpaper your finger ends, then play me that smokin' hot solo. Then we can talk.

And then you have to willfully make these choices that go completely against your nature as a front man because you wanna celebrate after a show!
There are times where I've overdone it on a night where we've had such a great gig that I've drunk too many whiskeys, stayed up too late, and sat with other people's smoke. You got to bed at 4 a.m., you've woke up the next morning going, *What the fuck did I just do?* And you sing like a bird the next gig. Then, there's other nights where you're like a nun. You finish your last word, you go to bed, you don't speak, you drink tea, you suck lozenges, there's nothing wrong. You get onstage the next day and you can't fucking hit a note to save your life. Like you say, it's a thankless task! There's no rhyme or reason why these things happen to singers, they just do. But you adapt to your environment. And my environment is to not do damage to my voice. The best way to do that is to be solitary. It's not like I'm lonely—I still see people—we just talk less. We nod!

When you start getting sick, what do you do?

I was doing what all neurotic people do in them situations, eating lozenges twenty-four hours a day. They don't do nothing, I know that. It's a psychological plea for help. For a start, it's the wrong hole. You got two holes down your throat. You breathe through one, you swallow down the other. And it's the one that you breathe down that needs the help.

So, what helps you in those moments?

Steam helps a lot. If you can get under a towel of a steaming bowl of menthol in boiling water, that can help a bit, but it's putting a Band-Aid on a massive open wound. So, you just drink lots of hot liquids and you warm-up all day. I get in a steaming hot shower and put my tape on and I'll see how I sound, knowing full well I'm going to have to do it again at 2, and then I'm gonna have to do it again at 4, and then again after soundcheck just to get through the gig. Sometimes, by the time I sing the first song, I've technically been singing for five or six hours, just doing warm-ups. It's either that or be really, really bad onstage. You know, I *just* about get through these gigs by doing this. I take a lot more supplements these days as well to be on the safe side. You don't just pop Vitamin C in the morning anymore, you pop every vitamin there is. They don't make me feel any better, but I haven't been sick since. Touch wood.

Are there songs where you wonder if your voice will be there that night?

Yeah, of course! Because a lot of our stuff is so bloody high. Then, there's the ones that you have to really sing. "Love Bites" is a singer song, whereas "Photograph" and "Rock of Ages" are kinda screamers where you can get away with a bit of rasp. But if you sound too much like Bonnie Tyler on "Love Bites," it's detrimental, so you have to be really careful. A lot of these are fingers crossed and hope for the best. I find if you put the effort in, it's like God watches over you and goes, "Okay, you've worked really hard today, so I'm gonna give you a bit of a voice." If I just got out of bed, smoked a cigarette, walked onstage, and expected to sound like Paul Rodgers, that's just ridiculous. To be in the same league as half of these great singers that I grew up listening to, I have to work ten times as hard as them. And I have no problem with that. If I wanna play in the big boy's playground, I gotta wear big boy pants.

Are there songs where you've had to adjust the key live?

In fairness, we have for thirty years to save all of us a lot of grief. We tune down a semi-tone and we did it guilt-free once we learned Hendrix and Thin Lizzy did it. Phil Lynott and Jimi Hendrix don't really sing in high registers and *they* were tuning down a semi-tone. Lots of artists tune down a semi-tone. I know some bands who tune down an entire key. That would be too low for us. E and D would be like, *ugggh*, too much. But a semi-tone, it just helps on everybody's voice. Over a period of 150 gigs, it saves you canceling ten or twelve, probably, and that's a big deal. And it gives you a bit more edge as well, when it's down a semi-tone. You get a bit more power in the bottom end, so everybody benefits. It's not a noticeable difference.

There's a weird stigma around it for some people.

I was talking to Mike Garson, David Bowie's keyboard player for decades, and sometimes he'd drop the key of "Life on Mars?" a fifth from the original because it just suited his voice at that time. David Bowie sang "Life on Mars?" when he was twenty-three, twenty-two, even? To expect him to still be able to hit those notes after fifty songs a day at the age of forty-five, fifty years old? You're dreamin'!

What was your most embarrassing vocal mishap ever?

We were on tour promoting the *Sparkle Lounge* album and doing this song called "Bad Actress," which has got this stop section in it, which is very similar to a Creedence song called "Travelin' Band" that we used to perform twenty-five years before. When it came to the stop section, I inadvertently sang "747 comin' out of the sky," and the rest of the band just plowed through, lookin' at each other like, *What the hell did he just do?* And then, halfway through, I'm like, *What did I just do?* Your brain goes into rewind and you got to try and pick up. Most people can't start on line two. Just coming blind to line two or three is an *insanely* difficult thing to do. You need to know line one 'cause it cues you up to line two. Somehow, I managed to do it and we carried on. Nonetheless, three days later, I did it again!

[*Laughs*] *Nooo*. Now it's a thing!

I just went in the dressing room afterwards going, "Guys, I don't know where that came from!" Most of the time it's stupid things like you sing the sign that somebody's holding up in front of you. You'll be halfway through some really important song and you sing, "Gimme a backstage pass, please," or "I love you, Joe," because you're reading it. This is one of the reasons I tend to sing verses with my eyes shut. [*Cracks up*] I'm okay once we get to the choruses, but it's the verses; especially if it's a new song and it's not in your DNA and you're having to use every bit of your brain to remember how the lyrics go. The last thing you wanna do is start reading a sign.

Do you remember a performance where you surprised yourself?

Not particularly. I've been singing in studios for forty odd years. I've had every experience you can possibly have from, "Wow, that was easy. I thought that was going to be really hard and I'm done in an hour," to, "Why am I still singing this song after three weeks?" I've been through every emotion you can have and it's all down to your mood, the key of the song, and your relationship with the song. I've spent weeks where I've tried to nail down a song on say, "Hysteria," and then I go in and nail "Animal" in a day.

How are you with hearing your own voice?

I'm not really keen on it. I don't mind so much these days because this new found tone that I have in my voice. It's like it's genuinely me. There's some performances where people are like, "I love your voice on that song," and I'm goin', "Really? 'Kay." [*Laughs*] "I don't." Certain things resonate with people more than they resonate with their creator. This is an art issue throughout history. People probably went up to Leonardo Da Vinci and went, "That painting!" and he went, "Oh, God, don't talk to me about that painting." It becomes the most famous painting in the world and he would've gone, "Well, not in my eyes." I've read so many interviews with bands who've made albums that are considered this genius record and they've gone, "We've made better records that just didn't resonate with the general public." It's the same with vocal performances.

Do you have a favorite vocal performance you're really proud of?

"Love Bites" and "Animal" off *Hysteria*. I'm pretty proud of them. On the last album, there's a song called "Man Enough." It's like, this is the new Leppard, like when Queen stopped being the old Queen and started doing things like "Another One Bites the Dust" or "Radio Ga Ga." There's another song called "Invincible" that I'm immensely proud of because I was able to use my singing chops, which I've always had. Those are the songs that resonate with me now because they're who I am now, not who I used to be, and I have to forever try and pretend to be that guy. I'm actually a pop singer dressed up as a rock singer. I sing pop much better than I sing rock. It's just a fact. Took me decades to actually admit or figure it out, but it's true. I sing pop music, which is why I think we were able to cross over, because when I sang songs that became pop hits like "Photograph," "Love and Hate Collide," or "Animal," I could actually do it.

You're one of the great scream-singers. "No No No" off *High 'n' Dry* is a great example. How were you not blowing out your voice on those early tracks?

Funnily enough, I don't remember too much about the individual performances on that record, except for say "Bringin' on the Heartbreak." That was the one song that [producer] "Mutt" Lange figured, if we were gonna get a chance at something on the radio, that was the song. He really pushed me to the limits on that song to the point where I actually stormed out of the studio halfway through, going, "I can't fucking do this! What you are trying to get out of me, I don't have it in my locker!"

What was he trying to get out of you?

A performance better than I thought I was capable of delivering. I remember I went next door where Whitesnake were recording. David Coverdale was singing a vocal and he did it in one take. That just about killed me off. I went into this rant, and he got the brandy out, and he's trying to calm me down, and put a bit of the wise old head on the young shoulders vibe, and I just got blind drunk on Coverdale's fucking brandy. [*Laughs*]

So, how did you nail the song?

I slept it off, came back in the next day, and went, "Okay, let's do this. What is it that you want me to do?" "Mutt" was probably right, I just doubted my own abilities, so I just bit my lip every time he said, "Not quite right, keep going, keep going." Eventually, when we got there, even the band were going, "Fucking hell! Is that really you?" That's when I was like, "Okay, I get it now." I didn't realize what I was gonna go through when I worked with "Mutt." So, when we came into *Pyromania*, I already knew he was gonna keep pushing me further and further to be better than I was on *High 'n' Dry*. Then, when it came to *Hysteria*, to be better than I was on *Pyromania*. I'm fine with that because he's making me a better singer than I probably would be under my own steam. But when I think back to "No No No," other than "Me and My Wine," it was the last vocal I did because we knew that I'd be toast after that one. They'd spent a lot of time getting the drums and bass and guitars right, and then, not quite as much time as we'd liked on the vocals. But we got the important stuff down. Things like "Lady Strange" were just blasted through in a couple hours.

I love the scream you do at the end of "Lady Strange" and the way it tails off.
That was me just doing my little Robert Plant impersonation. "Let it Go" was a big learning curve because it starts off almost whispering, then it goes into the high, screamy stuff. Every type of singing in a four-minute song, and it's the opening track. And then, the rest of the record was mostly full on. *Hit and Run* was just full on all the way through.

There's that breakdown section where you sing, "No, you ain't got no respect, and you hit me when I'm down," and then you kinda whisper something into the mic a couple times. Are you saying, "Bastard?"
I do, indeed. It was one of them things where "Mutt" was going, "Just go on, I dare you. Whisper the word 'Bastard'" "Okay, fine, I will." [*Laughter*]

Who yells "One-two-three!" to kick the band back in?
It was Rick coming through the cymbal mic probably.

Speaking of great count-ins to a song, there's nothing better than "*Gunter-Glieben-Glauten-Globen.*" What's the story behind that?
It was "Mutt." When we wrote "Rock of Ages," we were trying to come up with a song that was a cross between "I Love Rock 'n' Roll" by Joan Jett and a couple other tunes that were based on dropping the guitars out and singing over the drums. It was very glam rock. When you've got a song like that but you haven't got any lyrics for it, there's no cue for the guitarist to come in, so "Mutt" would count it out and instead of saying, "one-two-three-four," he'd come up with all these mad phrases. "Gunter-Glieben-Glauten-Globen" became one of them. It just became the cabin fever in-joke. We'd been in the studio for God knows how long, and by the time we got to mixing these songs, somebody said we should stick it on the intro of the song, and we did! It doesn't mean anything, it's total gibberish, just "Mutt" goofing about.

You were just teenagers when you released your first album and the background vocals were already such a big part of your sound. That was a pretty mature move

for the type of music you were playing. It's not like everybody was doing that. What inspired you guys to go, "We're gonna be a background vocal band?"

The background vocal thing was inspired by me and Sav. We wanted the band to reflect the melodic stuff that we loved like T. Rex, Queen, Sweet, any of the bands that had been in the British charts with harmony vocals. It got better when Phil joined the band. And it was totally understood and taken on board when "Mutt" started producing us.

Do you have a favorite Def Leppard background vocal track?

"Armageddon It" is hard to beat when I hear the guys singing that a cappella at soundcheck. If I'm not singing, I might go out and watch them perform it. I understand why people think we use tapes. We get accused of using background tapes all the time, but we've never done it in our lives. I turn around to our sound guy and go, "Jesus. You can totally see why people think we're faking it!" Most people don't sing very well. You see guys singing background vocals and they always move away from the mic halfway through the last word. That's when you can tell they don't really wanna sing. Our guys stay on mic 'til the last syllable of the last word is out. That's the difference.

What's changed the most about your voice since you started?

My ability to not lose my voice. I've just become a better singer. The recent DVD that we released, *London to Vegas*, has got the two and a half hours of us live in Vegas, doing the residency, and the entire performance of *Hysteria* from the O2 in London. There isn't one fix. Every single note outta my mouth is real. I didn't drop in or cheat on any of the songs. That is something I'm extremely proud of. There's thousands of great records out there that apparently aren't even really live, but I've never cheated. If you listen to our live album, *Mirror Ball* from 2009, it's a decent vocal performance, but the performances of me nine years older are twice as good. That is something I'm extremely proud of because, *by nature*, most singers get worse as they get older. Very few maintain or improve. I definitely improve, for whatever that's worth. I definitely improve.

If you could duet with one singer—living or dead—who would it be?

I would say Bowie.

Who are your top five favorite singers of all time?

Bowie, Bolan, Ian Hunter, Gary Holton from a band called Heavy Metal Kids, and Paul Rodgers.

If you could ask any singer about their voice, who would it be, and what would you ask?

I've probably already had these discussions with Lou Gramm, Bryan Adams, and a couple other people who've worked with "Mutt" Lange... "*How was he with you?*" [*Laughter*]

PERRY FARRELL

PERRY FARRELL CAME TO US as the singer of Jane's Addiction, fully formed, and unlike anything we'd ever known. Easily one of the most influential bands of the early '90s, selling millions of records, Jane's Addiction not only helped define the sound of the Los Angeles underground, but created a new type of rock 'n' roll that defied labels.

When he and the band weren't working, Perry released a string of solo records and side projects, always shape shifting into his latest artistic endeavor. And just like a shape shifter, the man himself is not easy to describe. In fact, I've been sitting here the past ten minutes, trying to find the words to do just that. And for the life of me, I can't.

How would you describe lightning? Or meeting an alien?

So, I asked three trusted friends to give me one word each to describe Perry Farrell. These were the responses: "Iconoclast," "Cosmic," and "Bohemiomythccentrifugalforce." That last one is obviously gibberish, one of my buddies messing around, except that she's dead on. You can't define or describe the awesome and artistic power of Perry Farrell in a few words.

So, I won't.

"HERE WE GOOOOOOO!"

Who first exposed you to singing?
My big brother and big sister. They were a good ten and twelve years older than me, so I was this kind of accident that happened almost towards the middle of my mother's life. But it worked out really great for me because I was introduced to The Beatles, and The Stones, James Brown, Sly & The Family Stone, Jimi Hendrix, and all these great groups my brother and sister were listening to. We lived in New York back in the early '6os. My brother is a rock 'n' roller and ended up singing in this group called the Left Bank. And he danced on this TV show, *Hullabaloo*, which was like *American Bandstand*. And my sister was into funk and soul, so I got this really wide array of music that we played. They were really into dancing and singing and I would entertain *them* when they would have their make-out parties.

How were you entertaining them?
I would be able to go if I tended bar and did the Monkey for them, and the Frug, and the Jerk, and the Hully Gully, all these dances. And I'd have to sing for them, so that's when I started actually entertaining people. Then, on the weekends, we would sit on the front porch and play 45s. Kids in the neighborhood would come over and we'd all be singing the Young Rascals "Good Lovin', Gimme that good, good lovin'." *That song* used to set my house crazy. I can still remember all of us running around when that song went off and the dogs would be barkin' at the top of their lungs and we would all scream, "Good Lovin!" We'd be so into it.

Were you emulating anyone when you started out?
No.

How did you find your own voice? It's so distinctive.
Oh, thank you. I really didn't have any designs to be a musician. I was just a runaway kid who came to California on a Greyhound. I spent seven years in the restaurant services industry as a busboy and a waiter. [*Laughs*] But it was the early '8os and punk rock had opened a window for people to come in who were creative souls that were maybe disenfranchised. It wasn't like the best-looking guy or the jock that wanted to be a musician, it was usually a kid that was a deeper thinker or an oddball, cut somewhat strange lookin'. With punk rock, it was cool to be strange.

How did singing become a profession for you?
Check this out: I was a liquor delivery guy and I would drop off bottles of booze to nightclubs and liquor stores. One place was a nightclub in Newport Beach, and they were having these modeling shows, and I was just waiting for the lady to sign off on my delivery, and I was gonna leave. The lady says, "Hey, do you model?" I lie to her and go, "Yeah, I'm a model. I can sing and dance and do impersonations too." She said, "Okay, come back and I've got a gig for you."

What'd you end up doing?

I started to do her show, which was really just walking on the runway. I would come out like Frank Sinatra, Bowie, Jagger. I would dress up like them and do a couple numbers. Afterwards, the girls would be lining up to talk to you. So, then I thought, *You know what, Perry? I think you should go for music because this is where the oddball can thrive. The reaction I'm getting is pretty cool; I'm gonna go in this direction.* You can be a strange personality, the stranger almost the better, and my life always seemed to light up when I was performing. It was so much fun living the life first, and then writing about the life, and then singing about the life. Those were the foundations of my success.

Did you ever have any vocal training?

There was a woman in the back of Music Connection that said she taught Exene from X to sing. Now, I'm sure she gave her lessons, but she didn't teach Exene how to sing because Exene sings really strange and definitely not opera. I probably took two or three lessons from her and what she taught me was the voice begins in the diaphragm and that's what I retained.

Is that something you've found useful?

What I've discovered about my body and my voice is that my highest notes are always generated from the lowest parts of my tummy. There's almost no air coming out. I have my vocal cords closed and tight. You know how bagpipes work? You gotta get the air in, and then, he slowly presses on that bag, and he's manipulating his fingers with holes that are letting it out, right? So, we don't have holes, we're fretless basically. As a vocalist, you're working on feel, and you need to get a certain amount of air. But if you take too much air, you won't be able to control it as it comes out. So sometimes, to get those high notes, I take in very little air because I don't intend on a lot of air escaping. *Now* I have such a control on it that what I want to accomplish is from a standpoint of expression. Every song is a different expression and you're expressing your feelings telling that story. If your story is a sad story or a tender story about love, you don't want to be screaming. You have to use your voice to express a tender sound, a tender feeling to tell a tender story. Now I feel like I can take any song and make it a really good song. I don't just walk in and walk out; I take my time. I work on the vocals alone for probably three days. I consider the harmonies of it, the interpretation, the delivery. Was every word delivered the way I intend to tell the story? Does it sound like I'm a phony? Could I do better? Could I give more emotion to it? All those things add up to whether your song is great or a throwaway.

Can you give me an example of great diaphragm vocalists?

I enjoy singers that belted it like Frank Sinatra, Jim Morrison. I like the sound of a man singing like a man, crooning. David Bowie even had a beautiful crooning voice. He had a great vibrato, like Anthony Newley who he learned from. [*Mimics Bowie*] *"Heeeeyyyy."* He's pulling from his diaphragm, but he's understanding and controlling the sound that's coming out of the diaphragm with his voice box. I guess it's his larynx going up and down that creates a wavering vibrato.

What sound were you going after?

I decided I wanted to be my own character and I wanted to sing high-impact rock. I wanted to sing high notes and I looked at the people I wanted to get high notes from: David Bowie, Robert Plant, The Who. These guys had these super high, soaring voices. Another trick that I use for my voice to get super high notes is, you notice that I move a lot onstage? That movement causes me to be just enough out of breath that I have to catch my breath. I catch that breath and I use that breath to create soaring notes. [*Sings*] *Aaaaaaaaaaahhh!*

Are you nervous or confident before you perform?

There's no doubt that I'm gonna go out there and sound good. You just give me some material and I'll put it in my heart, and I'll put it out to you, and it'll be fine. It's gonna be nice. I could sing a cappella and it will be beautiful. That's half of it. The other half is technique. You can start out with heart and soul, and if you don't have much of it, that's what it's gonna sound like. [*Laughs*] But if you have a lot of it, you can go a long way. Bob Dylan, Lou Reed, you know?

Are you doing vocal warm-ups before shows?

If you look at yourself as a dancer for just a moment, you would never go out and just start dancing. You're gonna be called upon to do some pretty great tricks and impress people. Now if you're a singer, it's the same thing. You wouldn't just go out there and try to hit high notes because you need to stretch out your vocal cords.

What's your routine?

I'm probably blowing this for vocal coaches that charge a lot of money, but this is what I do, and you can do the same thing. After that, it's just practice, practice, practice. But you will start to hear, and start to feel, as a singer should feel when they're singing. To start out with, do you remember *Sesame Street?* Kermit the Frog? [*Mimics Kermit*] "And he talked like this. Kermit talked like this. Do that for a second. Act like you're Kermit the Frog and talk. "Mmmm, hello, hello, how are youuu? I'm fine today." Try that for a second. See if you can do it.

[*Sings like Kermit*] "Someday you'll find it..."

That's it. That's it, you got it! That is your warm-up. What you're doing there is you are stretching your vocal cords, getting them ready. That's all you need to do.

Are you telling me you sing like Kermit the Frog as your warm-up?

Yep. I do that in the morning. I just start going [*hums like Kermit*] "Mmmmm-mm-mm-mm-mmmm." That's easy to do. Start out by humming like Kermit, then you start singing. Honestly, that Kermit the Frog positioning in your throat is how opera singers condition. They go [*hits an operatic note that sounds exactly like Kermit*] "Fiiii-gaaaa-roooooo! Fiiiii-gaaaaa-roooo!"

Holy shit, you're right! [*Cracks up*] That's insane!
Isn't that crazy?

How long do you do that for?
If you know you're gonna be doing an hour and a half show, you wanna start doing that two hours before the show. You can stop and rest. [*Kermit*] "Mmmmmmm. Heeeeyyyy." [*Operatically*] "Ahhhh-eeeeee-yaaaaaaa." I don't wanna sound like an opera singer, but it's the best way to stretch your voice out. When you first start to do it, if you're tight, and you can't do it, then you shouldn't be singing. So, it's almost like your watermark as well. If you're having a hard time doing it, you're not ready yet to sing. Only when your voice is ready to *talk like Kermit the Frog*, then it's almost like an indication that your voice is stretched enough.

How do you take care of your voice on the road?
You have to warm your voice up, do your show, and then warm your voice down. That's the other part of it. You have to be very dedicated. I've been performing over thirty years so, now I know that this is like being a professional athlete. It's even better because those guys all retire by the time they're like thirty-five, and I'm pushing sixty. I'm going into the best years of my life as a musician. I've learned so much and now I know how to maintain it. So, you need to have rest. Limit your talking because talking is a stress too. I love to keep my throat warm. That's why I always wear scarves. Then, you do the things like the teas. I like to have some booze with my tea, and there's nothing wrong with that, you know, you have a couple of drinks so it loosens everything up before I go out there. I'll have a Throat Coat tea with vodka and that feels nice.

So, what's your warm-down after the show look like?
Get in the shower. You don't have to sing real hard now because your voice has got adrenaline still. If you don't warm-down, you'll end up waking up really sore and stiff. You'll find that when you warm-down, it's kinda like you put the blood back into your throat real carefully. You don't have to go [*aggressive*] "Ahhhhh!" Just go [*hums, super mellow*] "Aaa-buu-daa-baa-duum," you know, "Mmm-mmm-mmm—Iii-yiii-ya-ya-ya-yiiii—Mmm-eeee-yeah-eeee-yeah-eeee-yeah." Wanna hear a funny thing? When I know that I'm ready, I do this thing, I just go, "Myyy-eee-yiiii. Myyy-eee-yiiii." It's a little falsetto. If I can do that, then I know that I'm gonna sound great onstage. If I can't do that, and go [*strained, gruff*] "Mmeeeggghh," I know that I gotta warm-up more.

Do you have any other rituals before you hit the stage?
I like to do sit-ups sometimes, definitely stretching the body too. And I love getting dressed around the dancers. That gets me kinda hot, you know what I mean? We're all getting dressed together backstage. All them girls are sexy and the guys are gettin' sexed up too.

I heard you have a little backstage jam as well.

We have a backstage jam room where we'll sing at least three songs, maybe five. But you don't wanna sing too many. I usually invite between twenty to thirty people at the most so it becomes this cool little party before you go on. By the time you go out there, there's no fear at all. There's no stage fright. You've already been performing for people, you're looking good, you're all dressed and made up and warmed-up, and it kinda gets you in the right mood to go out there.

Are there songs where you wonder if your voice will be there that night?

Yeah, for sure. The hardest one is "Jane Says," the first note. [*Chuckles*] And it's my last song. What I do is, I put it last so that I get my voice warmed-up, warmed-up, warmed-up, and the only way to make sure that note comes out right is you can't hesitate. You have to just put it out. Sometimes what you *can do* is put a little lead sound out [*sings, ramping up*] "Jaaaaaane Saaaaays." You know, kinda flow into it like that. It's called a glissando.

What was your most embarrassing vocal mishap ever?

Well, that happens all the time. [*Laughter*] Occasionally, there'll be a song or two where I can't even pick up the note. I'll just have this horrible feeling that I'm not even in key. I'm looking at them, and they're looking at me, and they know that I'm in Hell. [*More laughter*] I swear, I do it all the time. It'll only be like one song or so, but you can count on one song where I'm just thinking to myself, *I can't make out where to sing, I just can't do it.*

What do you do when that happens?

I get really embarrassed and I think to myself, *This is the worst feeling in the world*, to know that I suck right now, and I can't climb out of this. I have to wait for the song to end. [*Laughter*] I'll know that some people in the crowd picked up on it too because their applause won't be as great as the other songs. It's like a questionable crowd being like, "Huuuuuh?" [*Laughs*]

Do you remember a performance where you surprised yourself?

On the song "Three Days," the ending is all ad-libbed. I really had to give it the old, *We're heading out of town on the highway*. The emotion has to be just like that. You're finally free. *We're leavin' this dirty old town and we're hittin' the road!* It's just like that. It's just pure [*shouts*] *Woooo-hoooo!* I just let it rip because you can't write that kind of stuff out. That worked out really well.

Do you have a favorite vocal performance you're really proud of?

Well, I love that performance. That has to be one of the great performances by Jane's Addiction because that was all done in one take, and everybody just thought, *Don't touch it. Don't mess with it.*

How are you with hearing your own voice?

I love working on vocals and coming up with some song where you go, "God, I'm really proud of that." You have to work very hard on it. My method of working on songs is, I work on the vocals at my home. I have an engineer and they will come, let's say, 1:00, and they might not leave until 10 at night. So, we have a chance to listen to it, add, try harmonies, attach a second voice.

You have this "Perry sound" that's totally yours, with all these different voices mixed in. Do you triple track, double track, what's goin' on there?

I'll use so many voices, man. I double track the lead, but then from there I start thinking about what beautiful harmonies can happen. Even background vocals that are not harmonies. I love singing, so I wanna lay out a beautiful song that other people will love to sing. I really consider that. I put my time, efforts, and my life into how to tell that story, becoming the great storyteller. And how do you tell that story? You use your voice. You can become quiet. You can use mystery and create tension.

You're also the king of entering a song. I've studied this at length and could make a great case for this in court if I had to. No one kicks off a song better than you. The opening riff is always punctuated by a long moan, a scream, or an announcement that sorta says, "I'm here! The singer's coming in!" [*Perry laughs*] The first song on your first album is "Trip Away." You give this slight moan, and then you howl like a banshee, and it continues throughout your whole career. "Stop!" and "True Nature" both have these amazing "Here we gos!" Is that something you're consciously aware of?

Well, I do realize that the first five to ten seconds will make a person either not want to hear a song, or... you know what I mean? So, I make sure that people lock into the song.

What I love is that even if it's the first line of the song, you'll somehow manage to make the line itself part of your entrance, like "Mountain Song." The music stops, there's a breath, and then it's [*sings*] "Coming down the mountaaaain!"

Right.

"Ain't No Right" has, "I am skin and bones!"

[*Laughs*] Right.

My favorite one is "End to the Lies" because the first line of the song is, "You sit around there, tellin' stories," and you kick it off by just leaning into that "You" as hard as you possibly can. You're like [*sings*] "YOOOOUUU sit around there..."

[*Laughs harder*] Yeah, yeah. That first line, man. Everybody sings that first line. You might not know the first verse, but you definitely know the first line. You gotta make it count.

What's changed the most about your voice since you started?

I feel like I can be more gentle. And I can choose more gentle material and not be worried, like it needs to be harder, it needs to be stronger, it needs to have more impact. Maybe it's out of boredom, but I've really tried to discover or understand the other sides of my voice.

There's definitely a warmth on *The Great Escape Artist* that feels new to me, like you've found this lower register that you've begun to experiment with harmonically.

Yeah. Yeah.

If you could duet with one singer—living or dead—who would it be?

Etty Farrell. We've been working on our voices together for what, twelve years? We have a new project with Tony Visconti producing it and Etty's singing duets with me. That's honestly who I want to sing with now. Her voice as a woman suits my voice as a man. And I look forward to singing duets and romantic things—as well as powerful—but with a partner so, she's the one I chose as my partner. You'll be so impressed.

Who are your top five favorite singers of all time?

Iggy Pop, Lou Reed, Robert Plant, David Bowie, and John Lennon.

If you could ask any singer about their voice, who would it be and what would you ask?

I would probably ask David Bowie a question about his voice because I heard that he had studied, and was very fond of, this singer from the '60s by the name of Anthony Newley. These guys were crooners, but they were British crooners. Now that I've spent so many years as a singer, I've really come to appreciate the crooners of yesterday. You know, we had Old Blue Eyes, Frank Sinatra! Bing Crosby was before him. And these guys that sang in this manner, I just have a great deal of respect for. I mean, Tony Bennett. How amazing is he?

PATTY GRIFFIN

IF ANYONE CAN BRING TEARS TO YOUR EYES with just the sound of their voice, it's Patty Griffin. With some of the purest singing ever heard, she's won a Grammy for Best Folk Album and another for Best Traditional Gospel, but she can also rock your face off! Yet it's always Patty's depth and undeniable soul that keep you wanting more no matter what genre she tackles next.

Mavis Staples, Emmylou Harris, Robert Plant, and Neil Young are just a few of the iconic singers who love singing with Patty and many of the greats have covered her songs. The Chicks even won a Grammy for their version of "Top of the World," one of the songs that brought me to tears the first time I heard Patty sing it. Just try and deny its emotional power. Driving down a lonely highway, late at night, surrounded by stars, the expanding universe, and your aching regret, with that voice of the ages, telling you something so deeply personal and hauntingly melodic...*Waterworks*!

And then there's Patty's death-defying strength. But we'll get into that...

Who first exposed you to singing?

Like your family, I grew up surrounded by singers. It was just the old school way of learning to sing. It was just in the house. But the first thing that made me *fall in love* with singing was hearing my mother's voice. My mother sang constantly, so her voice was really strong, professionally great, and with beautiful tones. Still one of my favorite tones. She came from a family where everyone could sing, but it was those times where most people didn't think of that as something you would do for a living. Everybody just sang really well and that was that. [*Laughs*] You just kind of did it at church and sang around the house.

Were you emulating your mom, or anyone else, when you started out?

I wasn't consciously doing that. I was just trying to launch different things in myself off of hearing different singers. It was hard to hear Paul McCartney sing certain things when I was a little kid and not want to get some of that tone inside of me. I'm also not a very big person and I don't come from genetically strong, loud people. [*Laughs*] Everybody in my family's very soft spoken. So, I focused on volume through different singers, starting with Aretha Franklin and Linda Ronstadt—big belters—and tried to do that.

How did you find your own voice?

It took me a really, really long time. But I remember a certain moment in my very late-twenties that what was coming through my body was the essence of me. I was very conscious of that. It's sort of like an artist learning to oil paint. There's something to studying realism for a long time and building those wings until your technique is really solid. And then it kind of takes off on its own. I think part of that is life experience and just learning how to be in the world, who you are in the world. For me, it took a little time to get to that personally, but when that started to emerge in my life, my voice followed along.

Did you ever have any vocal training?

I took some coaching early in my twenties and I learned a couple of tricks about warming-up, but I didn't want to spend too much time with it because it was a little restrictive and there were rules involved. But it did save me from getting into the wear and tear that other singers suffer from. Doing the kind of work that I do, the night after night of singing with the band through God knows what sound system, it's pretty hard on the voice. I think mine survived and went a long way because of that training. Probably a little farther. There's a lot of athleticism.

It's interesting how many singers compare what they do to being athletes.

I think singers and drummers are really similar because they are the athletes of the band. [*Laughs*] The guitar players can go off and smoke and drink after the show until all hours and manage the show the next day. But if the singer and drummer do that, it's not gonna go very well.

I've obviously made poor life choices. Are you nervous or confident before you perform?

When you're really young, you think, *Oh, wow, if I get to do this all the time, I could be this happy all the time!* But once you get out there and you're doing it all the time, the pressures are different, and you have to bring it in a certain way every night at a certain level, and then, come in at a higher level, and a higher level, and a higher level. You never really get that exact kind of feeling of the first days of getting to do that—just dressing up, dancing around, and singing songs for the love of the music and not caring whether you're doing it very well or not. Just getting to do it is the whole point.

All these years later, do you still have fun when you bring it out there?

I do have fun. It's a different way of having fun.

Well, you had some vocal problems for a second there, right?

I actually had the experience of losing my voice. A few years back, I got breast cancer and had a surgery that removed a large portion of muscle I built up over the years that I used to sing. It was followed by some treatments that atrophied a lot of that area, so the breathing and air control was not what I had known. Then, there was the fatigue that took the muscle away, and then, there were the drugs that changed the way I could sing for a while.

How did you find your way back?

I had to start singing from scratch, getting my voice into certain parts of my body that I was used to having it in. Like, *How do I get any sound out at all?* But I still had to do shows so it was a pretty humbling experience. One of the things that changed for me was that I had to learn to interact with the audience in a much warmer way to get through the night. [*Laughs*] Now I'm having more fun onstage. My voice may not have the same level of athleticism I used to have access to, and I'm older, so I don't know if that will ever come back. But it's still there and my voice can still tell a story. It still has presence and it can reach people. When I don't get to do it, I get very antsy, so I'm gonna keep at it with what I've got.

What you've got is still incredibly enviable, so I should hope so! [*Patty laughs*] Do you do vocal warm-ups before you go on?

I do now. I'm dependent on them. They've helped me put everything back into the right place. There's a great App that I use called *Warm Me Up!* It's really well put together. I use it every day.

What's your routine like before you go onstage?

Probably about a half hour of warming-up with exercises. Then I do a little guitar and repetition of something. You're not trying to bring in the performance, you're just kind of going through something with a little bit of challenge.

Do you have any other rituals before you perform?

There's a silly thing that we started doing. I think it's because the guitar player that I work with has some professional dance background and some of it is in Flamenco. We started doing pseudo-flamenco countdowns of how many shows we have on this tour. We made ourselves do *PEP-PEP-PEP-PEP-PEP* with our heels in rapid fire. By the last night, we had one *STOMP*. That's our dumb, little ritual, but it's really fun and it gets your heart up, actually!

Is there anything after the show that helps keep your voice in shape?

I don't drink alcohol. [*Laughs*] That helps a lot. I know people who eat after the show and that's a terrible idea. If you wanna ruin your tour, eat food before you go to bed after you've sung, because it goes back up on you in the night and fries your throat. You don't want it "repeating on you," as somebody's mother once said to me. [*Laughter*] Sometimes you're starving after a show, and you have to eat something, but you have to be really careful. [*Laughs*] It's boring being a singer, isn't it?

***For real.* Any other ways you take care of your voice on the road?**

The main thing I try to do is get some sleep. It's hard because I love staying up and having fun, but I try to make myself go and be quiet because I'm not on the road to socialize every night. I'm on the road for the people who bought the tickets to the shows. Is any other singer you've talked to as boring as me? Am I like the most boring singer?

No! That's why I wanted to write this book! It's a hard job.

It's really amazing how you're in this tiny tribe that way. It's fun to talk to singers. It's very mysterious to me. And it's lonely. The lonely part is probably wearying for everybody, but I think you also have some perks that come with the job that other people don't.

You're talking about Groupies?

Groupies?!

I'm kidding! [*Laughter*]

I do know people where that is one of their perks! But you do have that direct interaction with the audience that the other people with you don't get to have. So, you're getting something from that that's unique

When you start getting sick, what do you do?

Do you want my full list of pharmaceuticals? [*Laughs*]

If you wanna give it to me!

I go to a pretty serious nutritionist and every day I take stuff for my immune system. After I went through the cancer, your immune system's so spent that it doesn't have any time to fight off a cold, so I had a cold for a year. It was pretty hard on the voice and trying to sing with that was just a nightmare. So, post-cancer, I do acupuncture for my voice. I also take these little brown seeds, put them in water, and they explode and look like somebody took a poop in your teacup, but it makes your voice work when it's locked up from being sick.

I haven't tried them yet, but I heard it's called Boat Sterculia Seed [Pang Da Hai].[2]
Everybody's different, but singers who are doing this professionally might have to work on their immune system a little bit better and I recommend a nutritionist. Especially one who has a knowledge of supplements because I haven't been sick for—knock wood—three, four years. That's pretty good. And I've been on the road.

Are there songs where you wonder if your voice will be there that night?
Yeah, there's certain things that I wish I hadn't written the way I have. [*Laughter*] It's like, *Why did you have to sing so loud all the time? Loud and high! What was your problem?*

Any songs where you've had to adjust the key live?
Over the years, yeah. As you get older, it's probably natural to not want to sing loud as much because you just don't *need* to. I used to have to do an angry yell in a lot of my songs and a grasping kind of, "*Why?*" As you age, what you want to express is not quite like that, or for me it's not. Not that I don't have a passion, and a need to understand things, and a quest to do that with my work, but I feel a certain softness coming into my voice and coming into my being. It is a little different, what I'm writing now. It's probably based on my physical limitations, but it's also how they're interacting with each other. What I need to express, and what I've learned from that, has changed how I want to use my voice.

I was gonna plead with you to make an all-out rock 'n' roll record. [*Patty laughs*] Songs like "Flaming Red" and "Silver Bell" are two of my favorites of yours!
Oh, wow! Lately, I've been listening to rock bands and I haven't for a while. So, I'm still interested.

You're such a badass on those songs. I'd love to hear more of that side of your voice.
Oh, thank you. I do love singing rock 'n' roll, but that's not really that hard on your voice. The hard stuff are those ballads where I'm trying to make this little, tiny speaker sound loud and big. *With sustain*. I have a small vocal cord. That's the stuff I no longer have any desire to write. [*Laughs*]

What was your most embarrassing vocal mishap ever?
It's kind of painful in a sad way, but I'll tell you. After I had all the cancer treatment, I took a gig with a friend of mine who had a Sirius radio show. I went out, got up onstage, and tried to make a sound on *live* radio, and...nothing. I hadn't realized it, but I had completely lost my

---

2   A Chinese herb.

voice. I was like, *Oh. I probably should've checked this out*. [*Cracks up*] That was kind of humbling. I just sat back down. "Oh well. I'm really, really sorry." The dumb, early days of singing, when I was in my cover band, I had a really sore throat, and I went out and got a milkshake and did a show. That's a really quick way to completely lose your voice if anybody's wondering. [*Laughter*]

Do you remember a performance where you surprised yourself?
The first record I did [*Living with Ghosts*] had a song called "Every Little Bit." The ending just showed up when I sang it in the studio. It's really high. I think my first year of touring I could still do it. [*Laughs*] It's physically incredibly challenging to pull off and play that guitar part at the same time. When I recorded it, I was riding my bike to work every day, or walking six miles a day, so I was, thoracically in pretty great shape.

That must have helped as well.
In the privacy of my own home, every now and then, I'll try to sing that part. But onstage, I never dare to go there anymore. It's too much. Too scary.

How are you with hearing your own voice?
It really depends on the day. But I've always admired saxophones for voices. People who have a lot of girth in their voice. I'm less of an admirer of a flute or a violin kind of voice and I think I have a flute. Or a violin occasionally. Or a cello. But not a saxophone. My favorite voices are definitely saxophones. I've been a cello trying to play a saxophone part at times, but I'm not really built like one.

You are not a flute. By any stretch.
[*Laughs*] Maybe a string instrument then, but something on the more mellow side.

Who has the saxophone tone you're looking for?
Mavis Staples is a baritone saxophone and it's so beautiful to me. It's so sexy and warm. Stevie Wonder has a saxophone. I do have an understanding of the qualities of my voice and what the pros of it are, but if I'd gotten my choice, I would've chosen the saxophone. [*Laughs*]

Do you have a favorite vocal performance you're really proud of?
I am kind of surprised about a performance I did on this record called *Downtown Church*, which is all gospel music. I did a song with Mavis Staples for a benefit project and this Christian label in Nashville offered me a gospel record. I wanted to try it because I felt like some of the language of God, especially in this country, is so controversial and divided. It's sort of taken on this tone of self-righteousness and not healthy and loving. I wanted to take some of that back for myself. But one of the deals for this record was they made all the artists record a real, live hymn.

What hymn did you choose?

My producer pushed me towards "All Creatures of Our God and King," which is taken from a St. Francis of Assisi text. It gets a pass from me because I think St. Francis was alright. But as a person who grew up Catholic, I had a real problem with the patriarchal language of a hymn. So, right down to the wire, I was trying to change the lyrics. [*Laughs*] He finally said, "You can't change this. St. Francis wrote this. Just do it, you're a singer." There was a moment in the studio where the lightbulb went on as I was singing, about what was in the writer's heart when they were writing it, and I connected to it. It was somebody else's song and somebody else's moment that they were capturing with the text, and I got it. I'm usually singing my own songs, so to connect with somebody else's song that way was something I can't forget. And when I listen to it, I can hear that. I can hear that moment. Hopefully other people can too.

Songs like "Top of the World" or "Dear Old Friend" can bring you to tears if you're listening to 'em at the right time. I know this from experience, by the way. Have you ever made yourself cry singing one of your own songs?

I have, yeah. Different things get me in different ways at times. [*Laughs*] I don't know why that is. That's pretty mysterious stuff. There's no conscious choice on that, you know, you couldn't try to make that happen.

What's changed the most about your voice since you started?

It's getting deeper. I would've preferred for it to start deeper. I wanted a deeper voice; I didn't wanna be a soprano. [*Laughs*] I wanted to be an alto. I loved the way that sounded. But what's amazing to me about it is that it's never done. It's ongoing. As you age, as you bring in more life through your body and gravity is happening, you're never done cookin'. I don't know one singer who hasn't told me about a million transitions that they've had to make, and find new voices, and cultivate new voices.

It's incredible, huh? An instrument that changes sonically with time.

I personally know singers that have spent time woodshedding new voices as they went along in their career. I certainly have. I'm surprised that I'm nearly sixty and I'm still learning; I'm still working on the parts and tunin' 'em up. If I'd known it was this much work this late, I probably never would've done it. [*Laughter*]

If you could duet with one singer—living or dead—who would it be?

I got to sing with one of my heroes already, Mavis Staples, so that was like a CHECK. And it would be cool to sing with someone like Leonard Cohen, wouldn't it? To try to find your voice around that kind of gravel. I love his backup singers. I love how he used that contrast all the way through and it would be cool to be one of them. [*Laughs*] Or just be one voice with his.

It'd be amazing. Emmylou Harris has sung harmony on a bunch of your songs over the years. Tell me about singing with Emmylou.

It's wild! Emmylou has boundless creativity with harmony singing. There's a reason why she's done it so much. She really knows how to fold herself in and wind herself around just about anything. She really has a set way of doing it. She'll sing a line, it sounds great, and she'll say, "Go back and let me do that again." She'll do it five more times and then she'll say, "And then I could try this," and, "I think I wanna try that on it." It's a little flavor, a little move that she hears. The idea is to just make that tension a little stronger. It's all about creating a tension. I learned that from her, and Gillian Welch, and Dave Rawlings, from sitting with them while they were working, how harmony singing is about tension. It's about a relationship, [*cracks up*] which is about tension!

Speaking of relationships, I have to ask you about your working relationship with [Patty's ex] Robert Plant. You guys have sung on each other's records and your voices always work so well together. What's it like singing with him?

It's a blast. He's got an interesting voice. He's not a saxophone. He's definitely a violin and it's loud! It's also fun because he's one of the most dynamic performers out there, still. He's pretty courageous in the way he approaches working onstage. He's not afraid. I learned a lot about having fun onstage.

Who are your top five favorite singers of all time?

Oh wow. Aretha Franklin, for sure. Definitely my mother. Gladys Knight is definitely in there. Mavis Staples. And I love Peter Gabriel's voice. He emotionally moves me, beyond, every time. He never disappoints me. [*Laughs*]

I'm so glad you brought him up because he's such an underrated singer and to hear that he's in your top five is so great. What is it about Peter Gabriel's voice?

He's very driven in this emotional way and he's very pure about it. For a man in our time, especially a white man, that's really rare. He's just been courageous to me, emotionally. His vulnerability's right there in the voice.

You're so right. It's that vulnerability, isn't it? "Come Talk to Me." He isn't afraid to say, to beg, "*Please, come talk to me.*" and have that aching in his voice.

Yeah, yeah. He's pretty special.

If you could ask any singer about their voice, who would it be, and what would you ask?

Sinéad O'Conner. I've never met her, but I'd love to talk to her about singing one day. I would love to know where she learned to sing because I'm half Irish, so that voice is from this world I understand a little bit. I'd love to know her background. I'm thrilled that people were smart enough to record it and make a lot of it, because I don't know, in the times we're in right now, how many people would get to hear a voice like that? That's a crazy, beautiful, unique voice. She's singing from this very mysterious, mystical place, and it's not always pretty, but it's beautiful. It's always beautiful.

SAMMY HAGAR

THERE ARE A COUPLE OF PEOPLE IN MY LIFE who led to you holding this book in your hand. Sammy Hagar is one of 'em. Sam came along at just the right moment in my youth, having set aside his solo career to join Van Halen. The band's iconic singer, David Lee Roth, was no longer in the group and had left some larger-than-life shoes to fill.

But when Sammy sang with the guys, that was all it took. Van Halen had the first number one album of their career. I met Sam soon after that and the next few years changed my life. He was a big part of it and I'll always be grateful that he didn't ruin it for me. I'm still a fan!

Starting off as the lead singer of the rock band Montrose, Sammy found even more success as a solo artist, was inducted into the Rock & Roll Hall of Fame for his work with Van Halen, and would later form projects like Chickenfoot and The Circle. But no matter who he's performing with, Sammy Hagar is one of the greatest rock 'n' roll singers ever. So, let's line up some-a-Sammy's Beach Bar Rum and get into it. But whatever you do: no shellfish!

Who first exposed you to singing?

Elvis Presley. I loved Elvis Presley. I'm tellin ya. I had a paper route and I went and bought "A Big Hunk o' Love / Hard Headed Woman." I bought the fuckin' single without havin' a record player.

[*Laughs*] Who made you feel you could do this?

I had a strange thing about lyrics. When I was a teenager, we'd have the radio on, and I knew the lyrics to every friggin' song. I don't care if I only heard it once or twice. All my buddies, and girlfriends, they used to say, "Man, how do you know that?" I'd say, "I don't know!" I just dug singin' along to the radio. So, they'd play this game where they'd turn the radio off and say, "Okay, what about 'The Lion Sleeps Tonight?' Sing that!" I'd go, [*sings the melody*], and they'd go, "Oh fuck!" Then it was like "Let's try and stump Sammy" basically, and they couldn't stump me. I knew all the lyrics.

When did you think this could be a career?

My older buddy, he got a guitar and an amp and asked me to sing. So, him and I would duet early Beatles songs and Beach Boys songs and stuff that was popular on the radio back then. And I just became a singer. It was totally organic. I just did it and kept doin' it. And the second I made a livin' at it, you know, a hundred bucks a week or whatever, I said, "That's it, I ain't doin' nothin' else ever again."

Were you emulating anyone when you started out?

At first it was Elvis. I did that "Uh-huh-uh-hu-uh" kind of silly shit. Then, when I was about fifteen, The Stones came to the Swing Auditorium in San Bernadino where I lived. I went and said, "Oh man, I'm gonna be like Mick now." My goal as a singer was to be like Mick and Keith. Or later on, Jimmy Page and Robert Plant, or Jeff Beck and Rod Stewart combined. I looked at the lead guitar and the singer and I said, "I'm gonna be both those guys." That was the attitude I took. And I'll tell ya somebody that I never talk about: Gary Brooker from Procol Harum. He's the guy that gave me my supersonic range. If you listen to "A Salty Dog" and some of those songs, he started off singin' low, and then he'd always go up higher, like "Whiter Shade of Pale." [*Sings*] "And so it waaaaas..." I'm goin', *Wow! How can he get up there and hit them big notes?* He loosened me up.

I totally hear that in you! So, how did you find your own voice?

I don't know how long it took me to sing like myself. That's why it took me awhile to write my first song, "Bad Motor Scooter." For me to able to sing my own song, it was wicked, man. I had a hard time with it because I didn't like hearin' myself. I would sing more like a Black guy. I would put a bluesy, R&B kind of twist on my voice.

What got you more into singing like yourself?

Rod Stewart was the first guy that got me interested in saying, *Man, how the fuck did he develop that style? Listen to him. You know that's him*. That got in my head a little bit. Rod has got the most unique friggin' voice on the planet. I still don't understand how he sings like that. And he doesn't sing loud; he's not a screamer. When I've heard him sing live, he kind of whispers, and it's a raspy old whisper, very cool. Paul Rogers too. Those two were the guys that I said, "Man, listen to these guys." It enlightened me to try and sing like them and it felt more comfortable than when I was tryin' to sing like Mick Jagger. It was just a learning process. I'm still puttin' on a little bit when I sing.

In what way?

The epitome of singin' with your own voice is a guy like James Taylor. His voice is so beautiful and pure. [*Casually sings "Fire and Rain"*] "Just yesterday mornin'..." He's just singin' and I think that's so special. I don't know if I'm quite in that place, but I'm gettin' real, real close. I made big headway in Chickenfoot. Van Halen, a little bit, but Chickenfoot, I made a giant step because I really became myself more than ever in that band.

Well, I would say that "Eagles Fly" is probably your "Fire and Rain." [*Sings mellow*] "Sunday morning, 9 a.m." You know, *that's you*.

You're right. That came right from my soul. That's a clean note. I hit that motherfucker clean. I'm not sure I can hit it that clean now. When I hear that performance, I'm still shocked. That last note at the end. I hit that thing for maybe twenty years. I was always able to sing in a higher register than I was born to sing in and it's bitin' me in the ass now! [*Laughter*] It's kind of where my sound comes from. But I don't go for that note every night, let me tell ya. [*More laughter*]

Do you find that you write outside of your range?

In Montrose, when I would write a song by myself, I was conscientious of the register, like "Make It Last" or "Bad Motor Scooter." But then, when Ronnie would write a riff like "Space Station #5" [*sings the guitar riff*], and I'd just sing to it, I didn't care what key it was in. I would naturally jump right up into that range and that's what [producer] Ted Templeman wanted in Van Halen because my voice could cut above those big guitars and big drums into that little screech range. That's a lot easier for a producer to get the band soundin' big and fat. That's why AC/DC's guys always sang in that register. It's the only way you're gonna get heard. You have to scream to get through. It was how I developed my style.

I think you're one of the most underrated screamers in rock 'n' roll. You're the white James Brown, man. [*Sammy laughs*] 'Cause you can sing/scream, you know? That's an art form.

Yeah, it's true. I gotta say, the classic one, the epitome of it is "Dreams" in Van Halen.

Let's take a trip back to 1987. I'm fourteen years old, been playing drums for about two years. Alex Van Halen is my drumming hero and you had just replaced David Lee Roth in Van Halen. The combination of all that really hit me at just the right time and pretty much cemented the fact that I wanted to be in a band for the rest of my life. As fate would have it, one of my best friends ends up moving down the street from Alex in this gated community. [*Sammy starts laughing*] And because I was such a spazz and would always hang around his house, I guess he felt bad enough for me that he started giving me tickets to shows. The next thing you know we're basically inseparable for a decade. I'm going to your rehearsals and driving to the shows with Alex and Eddie in the limo. It was kinda like that movie *Almost Famous*. I'm just this wide-eyed fan who's suddenly hanging out with one of the biggest bands on earth. And you really put up with me, man. [*Sammy laughs*] You really did.

That's a miracle what happened to you, you realize that? You could tell that story to about five million Van Halen fans around the world and they'd be followin' you around, wantin' to hear more, "What were they *really* like?" Alex Van Halen is a great fuckin' guy to do that for somebody. I love Alex. [*Pauses*] I love Eddie too.[3]

I love 'em too. With all my heart. They changed my life. You all did. But seeing you live so many times and being in rehearsals with you, something I noticed you're a master of is finding an alternate melody to sing when you're not hitting those high notes. Certain nights on "Dreams" or "When It's Love," if it was just too high, you would switch the melody, but the audience is still hearing it high somehow. You're really good at that.

Wow. That's interesting because I know I'm pretty good at it, but you nailed it. I think people are singin' it in their head, almost like they're hearin' the same note. That's a very good observation because when you're on tour you cannot hit every note, every scat, everything. I skim around that pretty good without givin' up the integrity of the song, that's for sure.

Another fascinating thing to observe was how you could run all over the stage, rock out, and still sing on key. That's so hard to do. How do you pull that off?

I think I have really good pitch naturally. It's not hard for me to sing on key, honestly. Some guys, it's a struggle. They don't know where the key is. Well, I do. So, I can sing on key if all I need is enough breath to do it. And from all the runnin' around I did, I was always in great shape. I've been a runner and an athlete my whole life. I don't go to the gym and workout, but I'm a walker, I'm a hiker, I do push-ups and sits-ups every frickin' day to keep my stomach and back in shape so that I can hit the notes and have the strength to sing. That's the key: havin' the wind to sing on key. It's the wind.

---

3 Sadly, Eddie Van Halen passed away on Oct. 6, 2020, after this interview took place.

Are you nervous or confident before you perform?

I'm totally nervous all the time. All I care about is being able to sing. I just don't wanna get out there and blow my voice out. Anything that happens to you physically fucks with your voice. Your strength is in your back and your stomach. If you have a hurt back, you cannot sing without fuckin' dyin'. It gets so hard to push them notes out at the end of a show. I'm still really an insecure performer because I painted myself into the corner of being the Red Rocker: high energy, come out, give it up, jump around, scream your ass off. I can't do it any other way. Sometimes to the point where I don't want to do shows.

I think the perception is that singers can just go out there and do it, no problem.

Man, there's times where I'm goin', *I don't think I'm ready to do a tour. I'm not in shape to go out and do forty shows*. It's a trip. A lot of it's in your head. I'm goin' through a process right now of gettin' my voice in shape for a tour I have in a month. I'm already working on it because to get out and sing for a couple of hours, in the range I sing in, when I haven't really been singin' hard...I can't even come near doing it for more than fifteen or twenty minutes without blowin' my voice out. It takes weeks. I can hit all these high notes real clean and clear for about fifteen minutes. And then, *nope, nope*, and it goes *lower and lower*, and pretty soon I can't even hit my mid-range without crackin' and soundin' like shit. Like I said, it makes me not wanna tour sometimes because I want people to walk away from my shows sayin', "That's the best he's ever been," or "That's the best show I've ever seen in my life." If I'm a little overweight, I haven't been workin' out enough, or been gettin' lazy and haven't been singin' enough, I can't give it that.

Plus those songs and those notes, at your age...things change.

Before for my seventieth birthday, I went and did twenty-two shows in a month to see if I could do it and it was really hard. There were nights where I was like, *I don't know if I'm gonna be able to sing standards*. I ain't out there collectin' a paycheck, I'll tell ya that. I really care. I always wanted to be rich and famous. I wanted it so bad you could see it in my early performances that I was willing to die onstage, but once that came tenfold, I ain't out there collectin' a paycheck, man. I'm out there wantin' to blow people's minds and make 'em happy and give them more than their money's worth. That's what I try to do every night and I put pressure on myself. I'm gonna make you so fuckin' happy and have so much fun; half the show I want you to have been laughin', but I take it very seriously.

Did you ever have any vocal training?

Oh, hell no. I tried in my twenties; I tried before Montrose; I tried during Montrose; I tried after Montrose. The last time I tried was ten years ago or somethin'. What happens is they try to retrain you. I can't sing the way they try to get me to sing. I don't sound like myself anymore. Steve Perry sings proper. He only hits vowels and that's why he's a great singer because he sings in a trained manner. Whether he was trained or not, I don't know. But I know he sings, A-E-I-O-U, and so does Barbra Streisand and so does Celine Dion and so did Whitney Houston.

What's A-E-I-O-U mean?

People that can sing those high melodic notes and hold 'em...you have to hold the vowel. You can't sing "Love," and go [*harshly sings the V in love, sounding awful*]. You can't put a V in there. You go [*sings, holding out the O but as a U sound, sounding great*] "Luuuuuuuuuuuu...." I know all that now through experience onstage. I think all of us who have been singin' long enough learned that A-E-I-O-U are easier to hit and hold. You turn a word into one of those vowels and you can hold it better at the end.

That makes perfect sense! You know, before those Van Halen shows, I always hung out with the rest of the band, but I never saw you. Were you doing vocal warm-ups?

Oh, yeah. Starting a little bit lower, I'll do my vowels. [*Sings some scales in his lower register, using A-E-I-O-U*] And then I'll start going up [*singing vowels in his higher register*]. Then, I'll start doin' my new trick, which is: [*sings the vowels even higher, using the combination of his head voice and a mid-range falsetto*] and see if I can do it without a glitch. When I can do that, I'm sayin', "I'm ready." I don't over warm-up because if I'm gonna have to sing two hours after warmin'-up for an hour, that's a three-hour show! I don't think I can do a three hour show anymore.

How do you take care of your voice on the road?

The number one thing I've learned: I cannot eat shellfish. [*JTG bursts out laughing*] And I don't care if I've got a night off, twenty-four hours later I'm still goin' [*clears his throat*]. I can eat a couple oysters. I can eat one piece of shrimp, but if I have like scallops, clams, Lobster Bisque and then a fuckin' lobster or a big pile of shrimp...

I would expect this answer outta Jimmy Buffett. What's happening here?

I found it out in St. Louis, one of my biggest cities. I used to always do two nights. When you sell out the first night, the promoter used to give us this big feast backstage: lobster, shrimp, clams, oysters, this giant ice tray full of every kind of shellfish on the planet, champagne. So, after the first show, I would eat that. The next night, I couldn't sing. I always thought it was because I wanted it so bad in St. Louis, 'cause they loved me so much, I wanted to give them the best show ever. I used to think, *Man, I overdid it again*. Probably three years in a row I did that. Then I meet Robert Downey Jr. one time in London after a Van Halen show. I'm sittin' there, eatin' shrimp, and he goes, "Man, what're you doin'? You can't eat shellfish. Before we do voiceovers for movies, it's in a contract in Hollywood: no shellfish, no red wine." I said, "You gotta be kiddin' me?" And he was 100 percent right. I thought back to St. Louis and went, BING! There you go. If you eat it, you're fucked a few hours later *and the next night*. Red wine too. The tannins: coffee, citrus, lemon.

But you always hear singers say how they put lemon and honey in their tea.

I've seen so many singers go around with their lemon and honey in their tea and I'm goin', "Man, don't drink that lemon!" You'll get that acid comin' up in your throat and will not be able to sing for shit.

Do you have any rituals before you hit the stage?

My band always says the same prayer every night. It's thanking God for your blessings, for the love and the light, and for allowing the love and the light to pass through us and to touch all those we come into contact with. "We wanna thank God for this wonderful opportunity to bring love and joy to all these people here tonight and for the ability to do a perfect job." And then we say, "I am the resurrection and the life" three times. If I ever forget to do that, I'm standin' there in the middle of the show goin', *No wonder this shit's fucked up. We forgot the prayer.* It has become a real ritual. I do it when I'm by myself and I'm gonna jump out and jam with someone else. I do it with my wife or my friend or whoever's standin' there next to me. [*Laughs*] I say, "Hey, you got a minute?"

That's really beautiful, man.

We "circle up." Our tour manager comes in and says, "Okay, five minutes, let's circle up." We circle up, do the prayer, go out, and hit it. I believe in prayer. It's like affirmation. It is so important to acknowledge the lifeforce you have. You're just like a tree. Same as everything on this planet. Everyone says God is the whole universe and all that, well, you are part of it. More people acknowledging the same thing brings that power together. I believe in it; it's totally real. I'm not a religious guy; I don't go to church, but my goal would be to give people hope so that they don't give up, so that they don't commit suicide, so that they don't do bad things and kill someone else. If you have hope that everything's gonna be okay, even if it never quite materializes, you're a better person. You're more giving, you're more ready, you're open, you go around sayin', "Maybe this is my chance to do something great and to be somebody and to help this person." Hope is a beautiful thing and I don't know why, but I do write about it. It's not intentional at all, it just comes to me all the time. Eddie would bring me the music and I'd start thinkin' of lyrics and they'd usually come out: "Dreams," "When It's Love," "Right Now," "Love Walks In."

Hey, since we're on the subject. "Love Walks In." There's that part where you sing, "Simply pulls the string?" What string are we pulling here? [*Sammy laughs*] What're you talking about? I've never understood that line. What is the string?

That's just a metaphor. That song was written about Ruth Montgomery and her book *Aliens Among Us*. She was an automatic writer. She claimed she wrote that book without even knowing it. She just started writing and all that information came in through her. "Pull the string," was just kind of one of those things. "Hey, can you pull any strings?" "Hey man, the guy can pull strings, he can get you in." You know what I mean? [*Almost to himself*] "Pull the strings..." *What the fuck does it mean?* [*Laughter*] It means I'm gonna get in! [*More laughter*]

Is there anything after the show that helps keep your voice in shape?

We were doin' a couple shows with Jon Bon Jovi and he had a vocal coach on tour with him. This coach would fuck with Jon's muscles with acupressure around his neck, in the back of his head and shoulders and chest and stomach and do all kinds of weird shit. One day I wasn't doin' so good and I said, "Hey Jon, let me talk to your guy." He said, "Sure, man." So he puts on a pair of rubber gloves, sticks his finger down my throat, and massages the side of my tonsils with his finger. I'm gaggin' like a motherfucker, 'bout to throw up. Then, he did some acupressure stuff around my throat and head and face, and man, I went out there and sang like a bird. So, I said, "What other tips does he give you, Jon?" He said, "I warm-down. Everybody warms-up. He taught me how to warm-down." I go, "What do you mean?" He goes, "I get in the shower and steam, I grab a towel, hold my tongue, pull it out, and go [*runs the scales with his tongue between his fingers*]. Do the vowels and warm-down, don't try to get up high, just warm-down for about ten minutes. I seldom do it, but every now and then, after a show, I'll feel like, man, I really pushed myself tonight, and I'll do it. I gotta say, I believe in it. A runner, after you run ten miles, what do you do? You stretch. You stretch before, you stretch afterwards too.

Are there songs where you wonder if your voice will be there that night?

Well, the bridge on "Poundcake." [*Cracks up*] "Right Now." Those two songs. Yeah, man, and if I do "Eagles Fly," that big note at the end.

What's the highest note you've ever sung in a song?

Well, it's gotta be "Dreams." [*Sings*] "We'll get higher and *HIGHER*, who knows what we'll find..." That's gotta be it.

Is there a trick to hitting those high notes when you know it's approaching and you're like, *Here it comes*.

The last thing I wanna say is, "Here it comes." I wanna forget about it and just do it. That's when I hit it. Every time I try to prep for it, you've already fucked yourself out of it. [*Laughter*] I'll just skirt around it. I'll scream it.

Scream it how?

Like "Right Now," the way we do it with The Circle, there's a big, "*Right NOOOOOOOW*," at the end [*mimics cymbals ringing out, the band holding out the chords*]. And it's a big note, right up there with the "Eagles Fly" kind of note. If I feel like I can't hit it properly, I'll scream it, I'll just go, "Right NOW!" So, it's the same effect.

So, stopping more abruptly instead of sustaining it.

The most important thing is hit the frickin' note. That's my newest enlightenment about singin'. Hit the note any way you can. If you gotta go into a falsetto, fine. Just hit the fuckin' note. [*Laughs*]

What was your most embarrassing vocal mishap ever?

Ohhh man, there's been so many, are you kiddin' me? The Monsters of Rock Tour, Van Halen, I fell down in the first song of the opening show and I busted my tailbone. I ruptured it and it was bad. I'd wake up in the mornin' and couldn't stand; I couldn't get up; I couldn't sit down on a toilet. I was spendin' the night in the hospital after shows and they're shootin' me up with steroids right into my tailbone area, which is dangerous as fuck. Then I got a sinus and ear infection from flyin' back and forth to my doctors in LA and I sang like shit every single night. I cried a couple times after a show, I felt so horrible. I never sang good the whole tour until the very last show. I finally sang "Eagles Fly" and hit the note.

That sounds miserable.

The worst was Texxas Jam. Walked out in front of 80,000 people in Dallas and couldn't sing. First song I knew it was over. Halfway through the show I apologized and said, "We will come back and do a free show."

I vividly remember that.

That's right and we did eventually. It was the right thing and I'm proud we did it. I'll betcha the fans were happy and proud of us. I didn't know what else to do. You bein' a singer, now you know there's nothin' worse than walkin' out there, "Hey man, I'm a fuckin' rockstar! We're the biggest band in the world, but guess what? I can't sing." And you can't sit there and tell 'em all night. Pretty soon they'll start throwin' shit at you. I won't do that again. If I can't sing, I'm not gonna go sing.

How are you with hearing your own voice?

I dig it now. I like the rasp in it. I like my honesty. I think the reason I couldn't stand my voice when I was first startin' was because I wasn't singin' like myself. I'm goin', "Who the fuck is that guy?" [*Laughs*] I couldn't relate to it. I was singin' in a fake voice and it made me cringe. I'd be like, "Oh, God, turn it down. Don't play that for nobody." I'd have to go outta the room. I'd tell Ted Templeman—first Montrose record—"Don't you think it's too loud?" I'm still that way with my headphones in the studio. I bury my voice when I'm singin'. But now I like my voice because it's me and I like myself. It's not an ego trip. It's not narcissistic. It's just that I do like myself. And I like the way my voice sounds when I hear myself sing back.

Do you have a favorite vocal performance you're really proud of?

A ton of 'em, man. Damn near any performance I've ever done I'm proud of because I wouldn't have let it out if I wasn't. But I think "Dreams" is the biggest accomplishment as a singer because I never sang in that range before, and when I did it, I went, "Wow. How did I do that? I hope I can do it again." And I did it again and again and again. "Don't Tell Me (What Love Can Do)" from Van Halen, of course "Eagles Fly," one of the great performances. There's a song on Chickenfoot's first record called "Learning to Fall." *That* is a great vocal performance. Chickenfoot's got a lot of great vocal complexity. That's when I discovered myself, I'm tellin' ya.

In what way?

Almost every vocal on that record was taken at the same time the band got the take. I sang every take. If we sang the same song for three days tryin' to get a take, I sang it every fuckin' time. And my voice was in the best shape of my life. I'm so confident in my vocals on that record. Bryan Adams did all the photos for that record for charity. We paid him $25,000 and he had this charity he would donate to and he's a really great photographer. So, he was in there with me when I was singing the real take for "Runnin' Out."

Bryan Adams was in the actual vocal booth while you were singing?

He's there with no headphones and *I had* headphones where the music was cranked. All he could hear was my voice, screamin'. And he's in there shootin', and I'd look at him every now and then and he was lovin' the fuck out of it because I was singin' so good and he knew it, him being a singer. Man, when I came outta that room, he was goin', "That was so awesome. I can't believe I fucking sat in there and listened to you sing like that just a cappella. It was the coolest thing ever." It was really special for me to have the confidence. That's how confident I was with my voice during that Chickenfoot record. I just sang every day so much, my voice was killin'. I had chops, I had range, I had tone. *And to be able to sing in front of Bryan Adams like that?* If I wasn't in shape, I would've been too insecure and kicked him outta there! [*Laughs*] Very proud of that record vocally.

I'm gonna exclude any Van Halen stuff here because it was such a big part of my childhood. So, aside from that, I think that "Peephole" may be my favorite vocal performance of yours. It's just a fucking monster.

Wow, I forgot about that. You're killin' me. That song makes me cry. I can't even sing that song, that song makes me so angry. That's a true story. I was on an airplane, goin' through a newspaper and read that. [*Shares a horrific story of child abuse, which I won't include due to its graphic nature. Fortunately, the child escaped*] I wept like a baby every time I thought about it. And when I sang it, I was so angry that, yeah, that vocal performance could be my greatest vocal performance ever. I could never sing that song again. I've never sang it live and I would never sing it live. It's too much for me. I'm way too soft hearted. That's the most angry performance you'll ever hear from Sammy Hagar, that's for sure. By maybe anyone. Johnny Rotten ain't got shit on that one. [*Laughter*] They weren't that angry, let me tell ya. I'm glad you brought that up. That's an important song.

Alright, let me give you one of my favorite Van Halen songs, which is "The Seventh Seal." There's something so awesome about your phrasing, the way you go, "Don't let me drown, drown, drown, drown in mother earth's soooooouuuuul... *YET!*" The spacing between "soul" and "yet" is so good. [*Sammy laughs*] "*YET!*" The punctuation of it after holding it out so long is just brilliant.

Well, you're bringin' up the good ones. I love the phrasing in that. It's like a drum part. [*Laughs*] That shit is deep and works and has a statement and, rhythmically, is badass. I remember [producer] Bruce Fairbairn really gettin' excited about my singin' on that song.

What's changed the most about your voice since you started?

Confidence, less pretention, and less seriousness; in the sense of not tryin' so hard. I used to over-sing, in Van Halen, especially when I listen back now. I should've shut up and let Eddie take that guitar solo and not made up any whoops and hollers and wooos and that shit. I've eliminated a lot of the trying to be the "Star of the show." You know, you listen to the song goin', "I gotta stand out, man, I gotta be in there every second!" I'm not like that. That's what's changed the most: my attitude. I'm not trying too hard anymore. I just wanna sing the song, sing the lyrics, get the point across. And I like singin' in a lower register now, not because I can't sing the high stuff. I like the way my voice sounds. It's seasoned now. I have more soul when I sing low. When I used to sing low, I had to fake it.

Can you give me an example?

"Finish What Ya Started" is a classic example. I was tryin' to sound like Billy Gibbons. [*Mimics Gibbons*] "If you wanna see other guys..." I was usin' a fake voice. Now I just sing it the way Sammy would sing it. I think that's the main difference. If you hear my new record, *Space Between* with The Circle, and listen to Chickenfoot, I ain't fakin', I'm singin'.

If you could duet with one singer—living or dead—who would it be?

Fuckin' Elvis, man. Shit. [*Laughter*]

Who are your top five favorite singers of all time?

Woooo! Gary Brooker, Paul Rogers. I gotta say Stevie Wonder. Maybe Janis Joplin. Damn. I'm gonna call you about twenty more times in the next month and say, "No! No! I wanna switch out so and so for so and so!" I forgot about James Brown. Come on, yes, him too!

If you could ask any singer about their voice, who would it be, and what would you ask?

Somebody like Bryan Adams. I think Bryan Adams is one of the great singers in rock 'n' roll. His voice sounds so raspy, but yet he sings high notes, he sings on pitch, he holds notes and all that. I need to pick his brain a little bit about how he gets that consistent sound in his voice. He sings dead fucking on key, he's got a range to die for, he's convincing, and he holds the notes, man, pure. And the idea is to hit the note. I don't care if it sounds Joe Cocker. Some of my favorite singers are like that. The most important thing is to hit the fuckin' note, not what it sounds like. That's personality. Otis Redding, Wilson Pickett, James Brown, they hit the fuckin' note, man. And I don't care how fucked up it was, sounded like blood was comin' outta their throat, they hit the note.

EMMYLOU HARRIS

"AND TO THOSE UNSUNG, WE LIFT OUR GLASS. May their songs become the traveling kind."

I'll drink to that. And I'm sure all my other brothers and sisters, singin' their hearts out, feel the same. "The Traveling Kind" was a duet Emmylou sung with Rodney Crowell and is about the path that a lot of us have chosen as musicians. The song was one of 47 Grammy nominations Emmylou has received in her fabled career. She's won 14, including a Lifetime Achievement Award and a membership into the Country Music Hall of Fame.

One of the great solo artists and duet singers of our time, Emmylou was also part of a supergroup called Trio made up of herself, Dolly Parton, and Linda Ronstadt.

Brown hair, white hair, don't care. Emmylou has always been a striking beauty inside and out, a fact that became even more resoundingly clear after coincidentally seeing her live in concert the night before the interview you're about to read took place.

As always, Emmylou makes you wanna lift that glass, then take your own leap of faith.

Who first exposed you to singing?

I was in Kindergarten and I was asked to sing a song someone had written. We had graduations at five and six years old, and I was the farewell. But I wasn't really conscious of my voice or being a singer or anything like that. It was something that just kind of fell to me. All of a sudden, I was dubbed as being musical. But I never really focused on my voice until the folk revival when I was in high school in the '60s and wanted to become Joan Baez. [*Laughter*] That's what started me on where I ended up today.

Were you emulating anyone when you started out? Were you emulating Joan?

Oh yeah. And then there was Judy Collins and Buffy Sainte-Marie and on and on. There were a lot of wonderful female folk singers, but it was a sidebar. I wanted to be an actress and knew all the songs to *Camelot* and *West Side Story*, where the woman took the lead. But I never got the chance to be in a musical.

How did you find your own voice?

I really feel like I found my own voice when I started working with Gram [Parsons].

What did you learn from that experience?

Singing country music, you're just focusing on the story, not your voice or how many notes you can sing, or showing off. It's just about telling a story and really singing harmony. Singing with Gram, it might seem like it's a secondary position, but I was really singing second lead, but following his lead. Somehow, that just focuses you on singing the lyrics to that melody and accompanying someone else. So, you're not thinking about yourself, really; you're giving yourself over to the song and the story.

Did you ever have any vocal training?

[*Laughs*] I've never had any vocal training. Over the years, I've had to go to vocal coaches just to keep the muscle because the vocal cords are a muscle. Like any athlete, you have to do stretches. There was someone that Linda Ronstadt turned me on to in Los Angeles. Then, later on, Buddy Miller hooked me up with a gal, and I would record the exercises on my phone. It's like running; you just stretch.

So, you're doing vocal warm-ups before shows?

Always. Just these recordings I've made with the vocal coach. And they're really awful sounding things. You wanna closet yourself away.

[*Cracks up*] I know, I know.

Just odd sounds that make your vocal cords move in a certain way. I will say though, when I was on the road with Linda, she would do vocal exercises and they were beautiful. Everything that came out of her mouth was beautiful. [*Laughter*]

Do you have any other rituals before you go onstage?

I always try to do a Nettie pot just to clear out any gunge, while I'm washing my hair or something like that. And I write my set out. I like to change up the sets or put in a song that we haven't done in a while, just to keep yourself focused so you don't get into a thing where it's a routine. You wanna be fresh and excited about what you're gonna sing.

Are you nervous or confident before you perform?

I guess I'm confident. I think it's more about talking between songs [*chuckles*] because sometimes I go off, and I know that everything I'm saying is just completely going over the head of the audience and it makes no sense, but I can't seem to shut up! [*JTG laughs*] But I've found over the years, audiences are very forgiving. I mean, last night, as you saw, I had to start a song over. I can't believe I started repeating the second verse. But I want the song to have its best performance, and that means getting the words right.

And the audience loves that.

I think they do because that's part of it. You're human up there, and I like to think I'm amongst friends, so to speak.

Is there anything after the show that helps keep your voice in shape?

I find that eating after a show is not good, and that's when you wanna eat! But having acid reflux is a real enemy to the voice. I try to be careful, but sometimes I *fail*. My boys really like to eat, and when that food arrives on the bus, it's a hard thing to resist. But I'm pretty tired, so I try to get as much sleep as possible.

How do you take care of your voice on the road?

I'm not real precious about it. I know that you shouldn't talk that much. I really am a sound-check fiend. I love doing it. Sometimes the sound will change anyway when the audience comes in, but making yourself familiar with the stage, getting a sense of how everybody sounds. And this may sound silly, but if I'm on tour, I'll have several outfits, so I'll think, *What am I gonna feel good wearing tonight on this stage*. And we should probably talk about the ear monitors....

Let's do it! I saw you messin' with 'em at your show last night.

I usually use just one ear, but last night at soundcheck, I felt more comfortable having both of them in. I hadn't done that in a long time, but I'm glad I did because I could really hear my voice clearly. The monitors are so important. You need a comfortable space, sonically, to get the balance of the guitar with the voice and the band. For the first twenty years that I performed with a band, I just used wedges. There were some times I did get nodes and lost my voice just by going out and singing every night over the top of the band. But when I did *Wrecking Ball* [1995] and actually had to take it on the road, Daniel Lanois, who produced the record, put the band together. Even though it was a smaller band, it was very loud, so I realized I was gonna have to go to using in-ears. I think that's what saved my voice. Twenty years later, I'm still able to perform onstage because I don't have to sing as loud, and I can hear my voice intimately.

It was interesting when you took the monitors out of your ears to do "Calling My Children Home" a cappella with the band.
That's a very different thing because you're singing around one microphone. We carry an omnipresent microphone because we usually do one of two a cappella songs every show. It's a change for the audience, visually. But also, to hear a song without any instruments after you've got the whole band playing is very interesting and emotional for the audience.

When you start getting sick, what do you do?
There've been times when I've had to go get a shot of steroids and get a dose pack if I'm in the middle of a tour. You don't want to do that very often because steroids aren't good for you. But there are times where you just need that little bit of help. There's only been a few times when I've had to cancel because I literally couldn't croak out a note. If you have a really bad cold, there are times where you can still get those notes, but there are times when the vocal cords fail you, and you've got something going on where you just can't—oh, it's just awful when that happens. You feel so vulnerable. But let's face it, that's who we are. I know people who say, "Well, you shouldn't judge yourself," or, "You shouldn't think of yourself only by your work," but with a singer, that's who you are. At least that's the way it is for me. Obviously, there's other parts to my life, but that's how I see myself, so I'm just gonna be doing it until they bring the hook out.

[*Laughs*] You mentioned that you had nodes and lost your voice. How did you get your voice back after that?
I had a wonderful doctor when I was in LA, and he discovered them. They were very minor, but he said, "I want you on vocal rest for a month." That took care of it!

Are there songs where you wonder if your voice will be there that night?
Fortunately, I have enough material. [*Laughs*] If I'm really worried about it, I'll work on songs before the show. I like to have a guitar in the room with me to kind of see where my voice is at. This would be more on the ballads, but I have enough songs where I can insert something where my voice is in a better place for that particular song. It usually doesn't impact the show.

Are there songs where you've had to adjust the key live?
A song has to shimmer with your voice and that really depends on the key. I've had to change some of my keys, but I don't worry about that because it's still about the song and it's still about the story. But this is one example I've always found rather fascinating: when we went in to record *Wrecking Ball*, I really wanted to do "Sweet Old World" by Lucinda Williams. I

See, that's my thing! Is there a trick to blocking out the other person's harmony so it doesn't throw you off? I always start veering the car into the other lane.

I don't know what the secret is. You're following the lead, and the melody is the main thing, right? So, you're looking for another melody that compliments it. In a duet especially, you're creating a third voice that's not there, that's hopefully gonna add some emotional impact to the song. I suppose it's like a painter choosing a color that makes the whole picture shimmer. I'm not sure if I'm answering the question.

Yeah, you are spiritually, for sure. But you've sung with so many of the greats over the years. From Dolly, Linda, and Patty to Willie Nelson, Roy Orbison, Neil Young, Mavis Staples, John Prine, the list goes on. All those singers are so different, and everybody has their own style, but then, you come in and sing with them, and it's so locked in and so perfect.

Over many takes! [*Laughter*] But a duet for me is like a second lead. It's kind of an over-used analogy, but the whole thing of Fred Astaire with Ginger Rogers. You're having to dance backwards *and* in heels, but you're in sync. It is a dance. Now, it is different when it's three parts. You're having to fit in more. I'm not gonna name the singer, but I came to sing on this artist's record and we had wonderful, long sessions, and I just loved singing with this person who I had never sung with before. They loved it, and I was really pleased with it. Then I heard the record, and I went, *Wait a minute, it's lost something*. I found out later that after they heard my harmony, they went in and replaced their lead. To anybody else's ear, maybe it sounded fine, but for me, it was not the same. It was once removed.

We briefly spoke about him earlier, but out of all these singers, you and Gram Parsons will be forever linked through those early days of singing together. Can you talk to me about singing with him and how important his voice was to the history of music?

[*Sighs hard*] Oh boy. He was a bit ahead of his time. He never liked to call it country rock, but he might as well give up on that because it's become country rock. He had a beautiful voice. I came into it completely not understanding country music. I just thought it was a good gig and jumped in. There's things on that first record that I don't really like what I did, but I quickly learned.

About what?

First of all, I fell in love with country music and singing those duets with him, serving the song, and serving what Gram was singing. It really helped me find my voice because I don't have what you would call a pure country voice—either a pure mountain voice like Dolly, or an original country voice like Tanya Tucker or Tammy [Wynette] or Kitty Wells, those extraordinary, authentic voices. Mine was always more of a folk voice. I don't know who came up with this quote, but it's "Style is a product of your limitations." [*JTG laughs*] Otherwise, we would all sound the same. Everything would be Muzak. What's wonderful about disparate voices singing together is that you create that third voice.

Yeah, there is a third voice. I never really thought about it like that.

I love to hear different people singing together. Obviously, you have the sibling voices: the Louvin Brothers, just magnificent, bone-chilling harmonies. Then, you have the beautiful sounds of the Everly Brothers. The McGarrigles. Unbelievable. Their voices have that sister blend, but they are different, and boy, you want to talk about some harmonies? I had to learn some serious harmonies from Kate and Anna when I worked with them, things I would never, ever come up with. It's not like anything else on the planet. When we wrote "All I Left Behind," they came up with this thing in the middle, this humming that was basically the lead instrument for the solo. This was not like a third part on a bluegrass song. This was some serious intervals, and I do have trouble sometimes with intervals, especially on minor chords. You have to have serious discipline. Kate had to teach me my part, and I had to put it on a cassette recorder and just sing it over and over again. Now, it is so imprinted on my brain. [*Laughs*] It might be the last thing I hear when I leave this world.

That's interesting because it's not like you're just glorious right outta the gate. Even *you* have to sit there and learn your part over and over.

Well, I'm saying, that's rare. Most of the time, I just open my mouth and whatever comes out. [*Laughter*] But I am not this savant you're kind of making me out to be. [*Laughs*]

If you could duet with any singer—living or dead—who would it be?

Leonard Cohen. He really influenced my sensibilities early on in those folk days when I was gobbling up everything, listening to everything. Bob Dylan and Leonard Cohen, lyrically, set the bar for me. There's so many but that's the first thing that pops into my mind. And I will say there's an artist and a record that I think is right up there with my top ten records of all time. Jennifer Warnes did an album of Leonard Cohen songs called *Famous Blue Raincoat*. If you wanna go to a special place, [*chuckles*] you need to drop the needle on that record and listen to it all the way through.

Okay! I wanna go back to something you said. If you have more of a folk voice, and Dolly was more of a mountain voice, what type of voice was Linda Ronstadt?

She's just one of the greatest singers of our generation. I've never heard anybody who sounds like her. She could sing anything. There are certainly singers who have her range. she has an extraordinary range. But there is just a heart-stopping beauty in the sound of her voice that's just there, and I really can't categorize her in any way.

What's changed the most about your voice since you started?

It's gotten lower, a little rougher, a little grainier. But that hasn't stopped me. If I want to sing a song, I'm gonna sing it. And even though the age makes it a little worn around the edges, it has more emotional impact because it's not as pretty.

Who are your top five favorite singers of all time?

That's really difficult, but I'll unquestioningly say there's a fella named John Starling who was the lead singer in a bluegrass group called The Seldom Scene. He sang for the love of it and was so into the zone. He passed away a couple years ago, but every time I hear him, and he comes up on my little shuffle, I'm still so moved by the sound of his voice. And the two big influences that affected me as to why I became a singer were Joan Baez and Gram Parsons.

You've got three right there. Do you have two more you can throw down?

Oh, did you ask me for five? [*Groans*] Oh, this is tough! There's so many singers that I love. It's a brutal question; I'm not gonna answer it.

[*Cracks up*] Alright. If you could ask any singer about their voice, who would it be and what would you ask?

You know, that question has never crossed my mind.

That's cause you've sung with all these people, and you sing like Emmylou Harris!

Well, I've been thinking lately, maybe I should seek out a vocal coach as I get older. [*Laughs*]

DAVEY HAVOK

HOW MANY VOCALISTS have so many different styles that they have to be in at least four bands just to cover them? Off the top of my head, I can name only one...

Davey Havok appeared on the scene in 1991, singing for the punk band AFI. Since then, AFI have continued to evolve, stretching their sound to anthemic gothic rock and atmospheric melancholy. But no matter what you wanna call it, Davey Havok is not only one of the best front men in music today, but he can wail into the stratosphere and scream/sing with such an impeccable sense of melody that you instantly become insanely jealous.

And it doesn't stop there. He's got a synthpop band called Blaqk Audio, a hardcore band called XTRMST, and Dreamcar, a new wave supergroup with the guys from No Doubt—all different styles, all different sounds, and all very different ways of approaching the vocal to a song. At times, we may disagree on what sounds better, but I know two things for sure:

Dude can sing for real. And I'm still insanely jealous.

Who first exposed you to singing?

I have vivid memories of my grandfather carrying me around as a toddler, singing old war-time standards to me. I remember a song called "Oh Mister Moon" that he would sing, and I would sing it back to him. He was the first to really imbue me with that very innocent love of singing. From there, I just continued to sing as a child and would play my mother's records and bounce on the bed. She had the *Rocky Horror Picture Show* soundtrack on vinyl, which I was fascinated with, which you can really see. [*Laughter*] Then, when I was five years old, I asked for an AC/DC record for my birthday. That was the first rock record I ever owned. But as I came into a better understanding of music, and deeper involvement in music, and deeper love of the culture surrounding music, and becoming parts of different musical communities, there were so many singers who influenced me. MTV had a huge impact on me when I was young. Everyone from Madonna and Annie Lennox to David Byrne and Tears for Fears, Devo, Duran Duran, Culture Club, and a lot of the British Invasion that was happening at the time really hit me hard. And then, I found Siouxsie and Robert Smith. I could go on and on.

Who really made you feel that you could do this?

I never had much trepidation with my ability or desire to sing publicly, so I suppose pointing back to my grandfather instilling a lack of shame and singing being something so natural and so much a part of my life. I remember going to family reunions as a little boy, and they would hand me a wooden spoon and pay me a quarter to sing the songs that my grandfather taught me. I've been professional since I was five. [*Laughter*] Now, I certainly wasn't brought up by show people; however, I definitely became show people! [*Laughs*]

Were you emulating anyone when you started out?

I was fifteen years old when we started AFI. It was the first band that I was in and still am to this day. Being unable to play our instruments, we were working from a place of direct inspiration. We were trying to emulate the ethos, the sound, DIY ethic and path of many bands that we saw in a lot of the early DC and LA hardcore that showed us, *Look, you don't have to be able to play. It doesn't matter.* Just do something, say something, and be something. We took a lot of inspiration from Teen Idols, 7 Seconds, Black Flag, Minor Threat, Germs, and a lot of that early '80s hardcore, long after those communities had changed and moved on, because there was a lot that inspired us that didn't seem tangible when we were also listening to The Cure, Skinny Puppy, Ministry, and Pet Shop Boys. None of that made any sense to us. [*Cracks up*] *No idea* how one could possibly do that! But as far as vocal influence, one of my sentiments as a teenager was that if I came back from a show and my voice wasn't thrashed, I didn't do a good job. [*Laughs*]

Well, that was definitely part of that scene, right?

Yeah, that visceral energy and extreme presentation. I would come to high school the next day, my voice would be shot, and I couldn't sing in choir. And the teacher would tell me, "You're blowing it, stop doing that." I'd be like "You can't tell meeee. This *shows* I'm doin' it right." He was right. What I didn't know then was there's absolutely a way to be able to healthfully sing *and* convey the emotion that you want to convey while not hurting your voice. It's just a matter of knowing how to do that. In fact, I later found out that it allows you to emote *more* and express yourself *more* when you have better vocal technique.

Did you have any vocal training?

I would sing in choirs and musical theater when I was young, and there was plenty involved in that. Then, early in AFI, I would have different vocal coaches in Berkeley. Unfortunately, it never truly connected with me in the way it needs to. There has to be a language that connects to allow you to understand the physical mechanism needed to sing properly, which, especially for me, having come from a place where damage was positive, it is counter to sing properly. I eventually hurt myself badly after years and years of singing, even though I had training.

How'd you hurt yourself?

AFI had just released what is to date our most commercially successful record [*Sing the Sorrow*], our sixth record. Ten years into being a band, I damaged my voice so badly at the end of that tour, I had to cancel ten days, which were all in a row. I had to go to the hospital and get surgery with the first show I had ever canceled.

You had to get surgery on your vocal cords?

Yeah, I had it twice. The first time was in 2003. That was harrowing because the thought of not being able to sing anymore is terrifying. After that surgery, I ran into the Wolf Child [Ian Astbury] at Swingers in the midst of this fear and he was like [*in British accent*], "Davey Havok, how are you? It's great to see you." I'm like, "Ian, I'm freaking out. I don't know what I'm gonna do, man. I have nodes." He just casually looks at me and goes, "Oh, we all get them. David Bowie had them." [*Laughter*] As you know, which your book points to, it's such an interesting insular community with singers that there is a connection that we know how fragile our voices are. We know how difficult it is to maintain vocal health on the road, or in the studio, night after night, while traveling and being sick. Guitarists can change their strings, drummers can change their heads, and DJs can do whatever they want. [*Laughs*] But if anything goes slightly wrong with us, we cannot perform to the best of our ability, and we can't give the audience what they deserve.

Yep. So, wait, you said you had another surgery after that as well?

A couple years later, while recording the follow up to that AFI record, I found out I needed to have surgery again. The Cure had offered us the *Curiosity* tour, and we had to turn it down because I had to go and get surgery.

Ohhh! Fucking heartbreaking, man!

Yeah, it's fucked up, right? [*Laughs*]

But how did you know you needed surgery, number one?

I would damage my voice on tour consistently. Traditionally, in the mid-'90s, we would be on tour, and the day off would heal it. By 2003, the day off wouldn't heal it. Then, it would be two days off, and it *still* wouldn't fully heal. And my ability was lessening onstage. There was a rasp, my range wasn't there, and I could hear a strange, inaudible buzz in my speaking voice that was never there before. No one else could hear it. Then, I remember feeling my first pang of pain in my vocal cords. It was like a swell of pain in my voice, which was already shot, and when that hit, I knew. I remember saying to [drummer] Adam Carson, "Something's really wrong. I'm in trouble."

And then, surgery number two, is it the same thing? Nodes?

Mine was a cyst both times, which acts very much like a node. The cyst was a result of the same poor singing technique that causes nodes. I'm sure you probably know him well, Dr. Sugerman.

That's my man!

Of course it is. Joe took great care of me on both occasions, and the surgeries went perfectly. But then, it was a matter of relearning. I went to many different vocal coaches that weren't working for me. Then, Joe recommended this wonderful woman in Santa Monica, Carol Tingle, who has helped me profoundly. I continue to go to her. She was able to teach me in a way that connected with me.

I wanna get into that. But are you nervous or confident before you perform?

Oh, totally confident because part of where we were coming from, and this sounds trite, but we just didn't fit anywhere. We were punks, so we didn't care what people thought. If people disliked us that meant that we were doing something right. To be honest, I still feel that way. [*Laughs*] If you look at the majority of people, I have so little in common with most everyone in the world, and I feel so strongly about many aspects of life and behaviors, and I have very defined beliefs that I'm passionate about that are unshared by the majority of people on this planet. I generally feel that if a lot of people don't like it, then it's probably saying something positive. [*Laughs*] But being that I grew as a vocalist and there were more vocal *demands* that I was imparting on myself, there was more to aspire to. And so, when there were notes to miss, if I'd miss them, it was less fulfilling.

Right. You're suddenly not so punk anymore.

But as far as having the courage to sing in front of people and the drive to sing in front of people, unapologetically, that was part of me my whole life. From a very young age, I decided to commit myself to being in a band with the intention of self-expression, and being part of a community, and making music that I loved, and looking for fulfillment in that regard rather than in a commercial way, which a lot of people do seek. It was also a conscious decision to eschew any normalcy or any standard way of life. I never thought I would have a home, or be able to enjoy constant relationships, or necessarily feed myself regularly. But it was okay because I was choosing to do what I love and that was singing. I don't get stage fright *unless* there's some sort of external circumstance that imparts that on me. If Morrissey's there or Robert is there, an artist or a singer that I respect and who inspires me, that I don't already feel comfortable with, I get a little nervous. [*Laughs*]

Do you do any vocal warm-ups before shows?
Every day. I warm-up before I'm going to sing, always.

What's the routine?
I have different exercises recorded from Carol Tingle. If I'm performing live, I will do my vocal warm-ups about forty-five minutes before set time. My warm-up's about forty minutes, but it's not full on singing. It begins with verbals or horsie-lips, then singing falsetto. There's a lot of breathing, staccato sounds. It focuses on placement. Ideally, I like to be warmed-up and go onstage about fifteen minutes after. Right before I walk onstage, if someone's around me, you'll probably hear me singing Erasure or The Smiths. Those are generally in my repertoire right before I walk on.

How do you take care of your voice on the road?
Being diligent with my warm-ups and getting as much sleep as possible. I found that to be the most beneficial thing, which is the most difficult to do on tour. That is the catch-22. But I've never done drugs of any sort, including alcohol or nicotine, so that certainly helps with vocal health. I'm also vegan.

No dairy to worry about.
Dairy will cause phlegm, which will get on your vocal cords whether you're highly lactose intolerant or as lactose intolerant as all humans are, so issues of acid reflux are less. In general, I try not to eat deep fried foods or greasy foods. I try to eat very healthfully, so that falls in line with vocal health as well. I can't go out because the worst thing for my voice is speaking over loud music. In fact, last night I went out. I was speaking over loud music and now my voice is fatigued.

Do you have any rituals before you hit the stage?
I get dressed, I stretch, because I'm physically active onstage, get my monitors taped on, and that's it. Hydration is also very, very important. I'm constantly drinking as much water as possible, which really helps with vocal health and with health in general. I've found other than hydrating and sleep that most of the "Cure Alls" that people suggest that you ingest have no effect on the vocal cords, which makes sense because, with the exception of phlegm coming down on your vocal cords from your sinuses, your vocal cords aren't in your digestive tract. They're in your bronchial tract. If you're eating something, it shouldn't go anywhere near your vocal cords when you swallow. It just goes down your esophagus.

Is there anything after the show that helps keep your voice in shape?

I'll do warm-downs and I'll steam. I'll steam before the show, and I'll steam after the show. I just have a personal inhaler. There's all sorts of different kinds. You can get them at any drug store. One of my tour managers from Dreamcar got me this really fancy one that looked like...what's Dennis Hopper's name from Blue Velvet?

Frank.

Frank! It looks like the inhaler that Frank has.

Oh, so it's like a mask you put on and breathe through?

Well the one that I frequently use is just a little personal steamer. It's got a little face mask on it, and you just pour some eucalyptus oil and water in it, then you lean over it and breathe for ten minutes. It's a diffuser that acts like an ionizer.

So, you'll do that before the gig and after?

Yeah. I know, it's such a pain in the ass! [*Laughs*]

Are you doing warm-down exercises as well or just the steam?

Warm-down as well.

And what does that look like?

I'll just do some scales with the verbal up and down a few times. And then, my brother works for Headspace, which is a meditation app. It teaches mindful meditation on a secular level, and he recommended that I do it because I'm generally an emotional disaster. I found that the language used by the teacher I listen to every day was very similar to that of my vocal coach in her teachings and in the warm-ups and breathing I do. And *that* further helped me understand how to make that mind/body connection. As you probably know, being mindful of your breath and *relaxing* to distill it down to something more basic is really what you need to not hurt yourself onstage.

Are there songs where you wonder if your voice will be there that night?

There are moments in songs that are more difficult, and I don't like screaming, so...[*JTG chuckles*] I don't like to scream. I haven't liked screaming for most of my adult life, not simply because it damages me, but because I really don't have any interest in screaming.

Hold on... you don't like screaming?

I don't like it at all.

But, isn't that... *ARE YOU KIDDING?* [*Davey bursts into laughter*] *WHAT ARE YOU TALKING ABOUT?* You have some of the best screams in rock history!

Oh, that's nice. Yeah, I don't enjoy doing it.

Then, why are you writing it?

I'm not. With the exception of XTRMST where I felt it appropriate for the content of the record, which was entirely screaming. But I don't write screams. *Well*, there's quiet moments of it you'll hear after 2006, but they're accents.

Regardless, you play old songs where you have to scream. How do you do that live? Or are you now remaining silent for those parts?

Oh, I do it. Again, that's about placement. The more relaxed you are in that scream, the more effortless it is, the bigger and crazier it sounds. If you're clenching and restricting and banging your vocal cords together, it sounds screechy and bad like you're damaging it. So, when it sounds like [*roars like an audience cheering*] that means you're doing it right. But when it sounds like [*roars but tightens his throat*] you're not gonna be able to talk tomorrow. [*Laughs*]

My favorite vocal track of yours is "Affliction" because it combines everything I love about what you do into one song just perfectly.

That's the exact example of me doing it wrong! So, what you said is correct. When you hear that and you're like, *He's gotta be hurting himself*, I was. I was singing that poorly. It's funny because, a few years ago, I was learning something off of *Decemberunderground*, and "Affliction" came on, and I hate to say it, but I was so embarrassed of the vocal on it!

Well, you're wrong!

To compare, the delivery of the scream in "Death of Seasons" is good, and the delivery of the screams on the entire XTRMST record is good and sounds bigger. I could hear on "Affliction" that I was doing it wrong. I remember [producer] Jerry Finn trying to get the right take out of me, and I was just an emotional mess. I couldn't sing. [*Laughs*] The more he was like, "This doesn't sound right," the less I could do it. That's how you get that really damaging sound because I was really damaging myself.

There are moments on "Kill Caustic" or "Endlessly, She Said," that have to be some of the most melodic screams on record. And that's really tough to make a blood curdling scream melodic. Most singers would end up in the hospital for even trying some of the stuff you do, and you toss it off repeatedly like it's not a big deal. How do you scream properly without tearing your vocal cords apart?

It's a very specific technique that involves filling your ribcage and making sure you have enough breath before you engage in the scream. Your soft palette is raised, and your throat is relaxed, and it's the same placement as falsetto. The black metal singers are the best at it because they can go from the [*growls, revving into a scream*] and you hear them just traveling that path, controlling from their diaphragm, just relaxing that soft palette, and going up and down, up and down. It's a similar placement.

That's why I keep mentioning the melodic nature of your scream.

Thank you. I think you would find that the best singers are the best screamers. Not to say that I'm the best singer or the best screamer, certainly, but I assure you, Axl Rose could really scream, and I assure you Karl from Earth Crisis, and Johnny Pettibone [Himsa] can sing. It's all the same mechanism. If you choose to scream, it's the same as choosing to sing. The true screamers, if they're candid enough, will admit that it's a very specific technique and they're very relaxed, and it's much like singing in your head voice.

XTRMST has to be the most hardcore thing you've ever done. This is after two surgeries, and it's really different from the kind of screaming that's going on in AFI. So, you're using that exact same approach for XTRMST?

Yeah. I was able to deliver those vocals with ease, which was even shocking for me because, at that point, I'd become better trained in singing. I had a better understanding of what it is I should and shouldn't do physically when I was screaming, and that came out very naturally.

But it sounds like, *This guy really doesn't care about his voice at all. He's willing to die on the mic*. And you're saying it's really focused, and not hurting you at all?

[*Laughs*] Yeah, right, right, right. Most of those vocals were between one and three takes. I was doing that with really good technique.

I assume that being in Dreamcar must be a welcome break from all that.

The Dreamcar record was a delight and exhibits my finest singing ability. Every song that we wrote, those guys would sit down, and I'd sing the melody, and then they'd change the key three times to see where my voice was strongest.

Man, I'm so late to the party on that one, but I've made it a rule now with Kingsize. I'm so sick of writing melodies I can't hit.

[*Laughs*] I empathize with that. That was the majority of songs that I've written in my life too. Then, the band goes, "Oh, we'll just do it in the studio," and I was like, "What about live?" "Don't worry about it." Two surgeries later. [*Laughs*]

What was your most embarrassing vocal mishap ever?

It was the AFI headline tour on *The Blood* record. I got sick, and my voice was so bad that, for the first time in the history of me performing, did I say something to the crowd about me being sick. It was so egregious that I apologized, "I'm really, really sorry. I'm so, so sick. It's just not working. Please, help me if you can." It was in Dallas, Texas, and they were so wonderful. If I hadn't said something, I don't think I would've been able to continue, and they were really supportive.

Do you remember a performance where you surprised yourself?

I can't say that there is because when we record, it's always so clear what I'm going to do. I don't really freestyle at that point. I know what I'm trying to achieve.

How are you with hearing your own voice?

I don't mind listening to my vocals. It just takes so long for us to write and record that by the time the record comes out, I've heard the songs so many times. I hear how the final version sounds, and that's it, especially being that we tour so much, and that we're playing all these songs live. Many of the songs are such a part of my life that I rarely go back to listen. But not because I don't like the sound of my voice. Unless there's poor performances.

Do you have a favorite vocal performance you're really proud of?

"The Assailant" on the Dreamcar record. I think it really showcases my true voice and a lot of the emotion coming through in the delivery in a very, very pure way.

It feels like Dreamcar allows you to have this real clean, new wave sound. Then, with Blaqk Audio, you get to explore your lower register and get real goth with it.

Yes.

I'll bet there's a lot of singers who feel they're a prisoner of the genre they've had success in. But you've found a way to keep expressing yourself and exploring your voice through all these other outlets. Was that a conscious choice for you?

Absolutely. I wouldn't be in other groups if those groups were going to mirror what I do in AFI, which is my longstanding group. So, the whole reason for doing Blaqk Audio, Dreamcar, or XTRMST, was a desire to do something that was vocally different for me.

What's changed the most about your voice since you started?

My technique and my range. As I learned to sing with more technical consciousness, and my ability to understand how the voice works, and the mechanism in the body, and being able to connect the intention and the execution, I've been able to sing better. Louder. And my range has increased, my stamina has increased, and I really have my vocal coach to thank for that.

If you could duet with one singer—living or dead—who would it be?

Just one? It's hard. You wanna pick living because that makes it more tangible, but then you're leaving out Freddie [Mercury] and Ian [Curtis]. But then, my mind also goes to Sia. [*Laughs*] It also goes to Nick Cave, which would be really interesting. Nick sang with Kylie [Minogue]. I'd love to sing with Kylie. *Oh God*, then there's *Madonna* and *Elizabeth Fraser, and, oh my God,* you know who I'm gonna say?

Of course, I do! But is there a way to explain why we love The Cure and Robert Smith's voice so much?

It's so pure. His purity comes through in his delivery. His words, and the passion, and the true love for what he does, and the true intention of what he creates, and the honesty of what he creates, comes through in his voice. And his ability to change musically within the context of a singular record, and over the years, create many different vocal stylings from "One Hundred Years" to the post punk of "10:15" to "Hot Hot Hot!!!" It's unreal. They're all genuine. None of that is forced. You can tell that he never does anything other than for the sake of expression and the desire to *do* it and to *be* it. It is who he is, and it's evident in what he creates. And that man sings for three hours a night! Which is insane! It's so high. [*Laughs*] He sings so high for three hours a night.

Who are your top five favorite singers of all time?

David Bowie, Robert Smith, Peter Murphy, Morrissey. *Oh, God*...I'm leaving out so many people...Ian Astbury.

If you could ask any singer about their voice, who would it be, and what would you ask?

I'd ask David Bowie, "If you're really not using it anymore, may I borrow it?"

Eddie Kramer on
JIMI
HENDRIX

Let's talk about arguably the greatest, most influential guitar player ever... and not get into his guitar playing at all.

Jimi Hendrix had a voice too. And although he may not have thought so, it was damn near perfect—the perfect voice for his own trip. The effortless creativity, originality, and passion that emanated from Jimi Hendrix was so unreal, it was as if he came down from another planet, then returned home, leaving the rest of us to figure out what just happened. Luckily, Eddie Kramer was there to capture it.

A multiple Grammy Award–Winning producer and engineer who has worked alongside everyone from Led Zeppelin to KISS, Eddie's long-lasting relationship with Hendrix is the one closest to his heart. He was behind the board for Jimi's first album, and has remained there to this day, making sure each posthumous release sounds just the way it should.

When was the first time you heard Jimi sing?

Jimi was discovered in New York at the Cafe Wha? by Chas Chandler. I hadn't started working with him as of yet, but after he did the first single, "Hey Joe," everybody knew about him in England, particularly us young engineers. I was basically an assistant engineer at Olympic Studios at that point in '66. It was a brand new studio, and I was the young kid on the block, doing experimental stuff with a lot of fellow jazz musicians. One day, I got a call from the studio manager and she said, [*mimics British accent*] "Hey Eddie, there's this American chap here, and he's got big hair, and you do all that weird shit anyway, so why don't you record him?" That's how I got the gig.

What was your initial impression of him?

Jimi was a revelation because no one had ever heard or seen anything like him. It was a very interesting first meeting because he was extremely shy and was pretty much huddled up in the corner waiting for us to get set up. But once we started getting sounds, he was totally into it and loved what I was doing. It was a camaraderie. We had a sort of meeting of the minds where I could get him sounds that he was thinking about, and that started the bond of engineer/client thing.

What was he like when it came to recording his vocals?

[*Chuckles*] Being extremely shy, he didn't want anybody to see him sing, so I constructed a three-sided screen facing away from the control room, dimmed all the lights, and inside this little booth that I made for him—headphones, microphone, music stand, very small lamps. Yeah, it was pretty much an uninterrupted quiet time. But generally speaking, it'd be Chas, myself, and Jimi, and nobody else. They all went to the pub while he was doing vocals. When we started to record his voice, it was amazing to hear how he could phrase because he wasn't a great "singer." He was a great song stylist and a great interpreter of his own material, *and others'*. But he thought he had the worst voice in the world. He hated the sound, so it was this constant reassuring Jimi that, "Man, that was cool! That sounded great!" We loved his *style*. It was the *style*, the *phrasing*.

He had this unassuming, laid-back delivery that really pulled you in.

Oh yeah, that unassuming, laid-back, casual phrasing was part of the beauty of what people were attracted to. When you met him or saw him play, he exuded this sexy, cool, casual thing, but with a lot of fun. One of the things that comes to mind is how much fun we had in the studio. I have outtakes of him *cracking up*.

Jimi also wins for the coolest laugh on record. I mean, who laughs cooler than him?

You're absolutely right! He had a cool laugh. It was relaxed, and it was kind of inviting. It was *share the joke with me*.

Was Jimi trying to get his takes in one or were there a lot of punch-ins going on?

He was pretty good. In some cases, he would do multiple takes, but not that many. I can't remember doing more than three or four takes on a vocal at the most.

A lot of praise has to go your way for how you were able to place his vocals so perfectly in the mix. With so much chaos going on throughout the songs, he really feels right there with you, like a friend singing you his thoughts. What was the key to placing his vocals just right?

Well, that's very nice of you to say, but I think credit must go to the time period when I started mixing. The vocal was so critical and where you place it. Jimi always wanted his vocal further back in the track. He would fight us on that. [*Mimics Jimi*] "Ohh man, my voice!" "Shhhh, Jimi, it's cool, your voice is great, man." Finally, he got used to it. I think we came up with the idea of trying to place him within the track so it's not too far forward, but enough that you can really understand what he's saying. As a great songwriter, it was really important to hear what he was singing about.

During the breakdown of "If 6 Was 9," is he chewing gum? That's gotta be the first gum-chew on record.

I don't know, but, oh yeah, Jimi chewed gum *all* the time. Big time. In between stuff you can hear the smacks. It's great.

Was Jimi nervous before shows?

I'm sure he was. But as soon as he strapped on a guitar and plugged in, it was all over. The main thing for Jimi was, "Can I hear my voice in the monitors?" That's what drove him mad. In those days, the PA systems weren't that great. Then, towards late '68-'69, he found this guy, Abe Jacobs, who was his front of house guy, and it really helped to get his vocal through because that was the main thing for him.

Did he do vocal warm-ups before recording or before going onstage?

I don't think *anybody* did vocal warm-ups. Nobody *knew* about that. I don't think that started until the mid-'70s-early-'80s.

Do you know if he worried about taking care of his voice on the road?

Noooo. He smoked, he drank a bit, like any other artist in the time. They pushed themselves. But I think it was fortunate because I don't think he had to scream. He was cool with his vocals. It wasn't as if he was pushing himself all the time. In the live shows, you can hear he's pushing it a bit, but not in the studio. He had good control.

When you hear his voice now, what do you remember most?

Gentleness. And the fact that he could take a song like "Little Wing," which to me is one of my favorites, and transport it to someplace else. I was always a big fan. I loved his voice. We'd do a take, and then we'd stop, and he'd poke his head around the side of the booth, look up and say, "How was that, man? How was that?" "That was cool, Jimi, that was great!" "Alright. I'll do another one." [*Laughter*]

Clive Davis on
WHITNEY HOUSTON

IF I WERE TO LIST every chart-topping success and record-breaking achievement from the woman often regarded as The Voice, we would never get to this interview. But you should look it up sometime and contemplate the magnitude of her talent because it is truly staggering. Or you could just listen to her sing. To say that Whitney Houston was a cultural icon doesn't even come close to the impact she had and the incredible legacy she left behind.

She has sold over 200 million records, won eight Grammy Awards, sixteen Billboard Music Awards, twenty-two American Music Awards, and was inducted into the Rock & Roll Hall of Fame. She's one of the bestselling artists of all time and is accurately considered one of the greatest singers ever.

Clive Davis is one of the great titans of the music industry. He has been the president of Columbia Records, founder of Arista and J Records, and CCO of Sony Music Entertainment. Often referred to as The Man with the Golden Ears, Clive was also inducted into the Rock & Roll Hall of Fame as a non-performer. Helping to guide the careers of too many to name, Clive has signed some of your favorite artists: Janis Joplin, Bruce Springsteen, Santana, Chicago, Billy Joel, Barry Manilow, Aerosmith, Pink Floyd... and Whitney Houston.

Tell me about the first time you heard Whitney sing?

I heard Whitney at a club called Sweetwater in New York. She was doing two songs in her mother's [Cissy Houston] act. She was nineteen. And I think this really sums up the essence of what a great singer is: the two songs that she chose as part of her step out were "Home" from *The Wiz* and "The Greatest Love of All." Now she didn't know this, but "The Greatest Love of All" was a song that I had commissioned for a movie soundtrack that was based on the life of Muhammad Ali, *The Greatest*. I had recorded that eight years earlier with George Benson and it went Top Ten R&B.

That's wild.

What knocked me out, apart from the stunning beauty of Whitney, was here she was finding meaning in both songs that the composers didn't even know were there when they wrote it. It was not only the technical ability of a powerful, natural, far-ranging voice, but it was the natural genius gift for finding meaning in the lyrics and bringing them to a new plateau.

You knew right away?

Whitney and I hit it off right from the beginning. There was other label interest, but for the one and only time in my life, in view of the competition, my parent company approved a [contract clause] saying that we're signing because of me, and that if I ever left the company, she could leave with me, because I would never otherwise do it. With that clause and with the connection, and the choice of material, and what she did with that material, I signed Whitney.

To that point, had there ever been a voice that affected you in that way?

No. I'm not taking it away from Aretha, the Queen of Soul, or Dionne Warwick for that matter. Both are all-time, peerless, unique, individualistic, wonderful singers. But I didn't discover Dionne and I didn't discover Aretha from scratch. I believed in them, and I did something equally satisfying, which was saying, I don't care that they're both approaching or over forty, they should be heard *forever*. I signed Aretha and Whitney and Dionne to make sure that their careers continued into their forties, fifties, sixties. But hearing what Whitney was capable of doing was the most impressive discovery, vocally, ever.

So, you sign this voice from Heaven. Are you in the studio during recording?

No. I never went into the studio with my artists.

Oh, really?

Never. I would find the material, I would speak to them individually before they went into the studio, and then I would critique it afterwards. There were two or three times with Aretha where I said, "Aretha, this could be a single and therefore we gotta be a little..." Because she was a natural genius in her own right, and Aretha would come to the studio so well-rehearsed in her head, never would do more than two or three takes of any song. But where we felt close to a hit single, which is all so valuable, if she strayed too far from the melody on the final hook, even Aretha, would go in the studio to make sure she nailed the chorus of a potential hit.

Do you know how Whitney approached recording her vocals?

I knew when I found "I Wanna Dance with Somebody," it would not be an Olivia Newton-John song as the demo was. Whitney would bring heat to it, sexuality to it, and she did. She knew instinctively, it's not that "I wanna dance with somebody," as compared to the demo; she brought out, *I wanna go to bed with somebody*. I remember after she had done *The Bodyguard*, *Waiting to Exhale*, and *The Preacher's Wife*, there was like an eight-year period where she was not in the studio. And we came to the *My Love Is Your Love* album. Obviously, the knives were out: *Could she repeat? Could she continue to sell tens of millions of records?* She came to my bungalow at the Beverly Hills Hotel. I remember playing for her the demo of "It's Not Right but It's Okay," and she said, "Let's play it again." I'll never forget, by the third time I had played it, she had every word. She, in her nightgown and bathrobe, started dancing through the bungalow with me following her, and already was bringing to the vocal such instantaneous, spectacular feeling, emotion, reading, interpretation. She was amazing in her gift.

Interpretation is a great way to put it because there are so many ways things can wind up.

Take a song like "I Will Always Love You." The version that Dolly Parton wrote was the arrangement that [producer] David Foster and Whitney worked with for *The Bodyguard* movie. But when you see the version of "I Will Always Love You" that she performed in South Africa in honor of Nelson Mandela before 100,000 people, you see her in a turban, amazing beauty, with that pregnant pause, with her interpretation of that lyric, knowing when to come in, knowing when to go to the climactic chorus, letting the words sink into the audience, you know that she was incomparable in her ability to bring home the song in a way that the composer did not even know was there when she wrote it.

Yeah, that performance is incredible. You know, I think the toughest thing for a singer would be "The Star Spangled Banner." It's like that song was written to see what kind of singer you truly are. And to go out there at the Super Bowl, millions of people watching around the world, I can't even imagine the guts it must take. One slip and you're toast. Have you ever seen anything like that performance in '91?

No. Nor do I think there ever has been. That probably is the quintessential definition of a song who everybody in the world who sings has tried or done. Whitney's version is, without question, the greatest performance of "The Star Spangled Banner" ever.

And she seemed so loose and casual. She's in a track suit like she was just hanging out at the Super Bowl and someone dared her to sing, and she was like, "Sure, I'll give it a go." Then, she goes out there, just smiling, no nervous energy at all, and delivers this powerhouse performance.

She did just that, no question.

Is there one performance for you that sums up who she was as a vocalist?

Well, it's like saying, "Which of your kids do you…"

I know, it's tough.

Every time she performed was special. I don't know if you saw my documentary [*The Soundtrack of Our Lives*] on Netflix, but when I was leaving Arista, she thought we would not be working together. Two or three years later, when we were reunited, the Princess Grace Foundation was honoring me on a national television show. She sang two songs to me, directly and personally. One was "I Believe in You and Me," and the other was "I Will Always Love You." Those performances were so personal between the two of us, and her ability to reignite those classics with personal meaning between the two of us will always stir me and affect me in a unique way.

BRITTANY HOWARD

I'LL JUST GET THIS OUT OF THE WAY RIGHT NOW: I'm all in on Brittany Howard. She and her band, Alabama Shakes, released their debut album in 2012, and with the first note from her lips, it was clear that something powerful, soulful, and exciting had returned to music. Their live show was even better. But when they released their second record, *Sound & Color,* just three years later, it was an artistic leap forward in a way that only people like Stevie Wonder, David Bowie, and Prince have pulled off.

Brittany has gone on to win multiple Grammy Awards, not just with Alabama Shakes, but with her debut solo album, *Jaime,* which hadn't been recorded when this interview took place. But rest assured, that record is another artistic triumph as well.

What can I tell you? We are witnessing greatness. And right now, she's all yours.

Who first exposed you to singing?

Me and my cousin used to sing when we were little kids. We were pretty young, maybe seven, so we would just come up with songs. At the time, TLC was huge. We'd sing the whole record, *CrazySexyCool*. We didn't know what the words meant, [*laughs*] but we sang it.

So, who made you feel you could do this?

Nobody. For a long time nobody knew I was singing. But I had a lot of different styles of singing because I liked all different types of music. I was being informed by punk music at one moment, and then at another time, prog rock, and then at another time, '60s doo-wop. I had so many different voices.

What prog rock were you into?

Yes, and King Crimson, things like that. Even my mother didn't know I could sing until I was probably sixteen years old. She didn't know what I'd been up to. It was just a matter of, I'm writing songs, I need to sing the songs. It wasn't like I thought I was particularly talented or anything like that. I was playing guitar. That was the thing that made me write my own songs, picking up a guitar and teaching myself how to play it.

Were you emulating anyone when you started out?

I sang to whatever music I was making. If I'm making punk music, I'm singing like the Ramones. Or trying to. But I never could. So, of course, I am doing it in my own way, but in my head, I'm saying, *This is a punk song, and this is what punk singers sound like*. Then, when I got into more prog rock, I liked thinking of layering harmonies. *Okay, everything has to have harmonies because that's the cool thing to do. It's gotta be complex and it's gotta be different*. I would look at the genre and I would try to emulate it. But, no matter what, it still sounded like me trying to emulate it.

How did you find your own voice?

My voice became more comfortable to me when I started playing with the band. It took years to find someone to show up every Tuesday and Thursday. It's hard getting people to dedicate. It was with this group of guys, Alabama Shakes, just writing songs, and not having a PA system. I'd be singing as loud as I could. Somewhere in between, I just found that comfortable range. *Okay, this is my range where I can sing really loud, and it feels good and is comfortable*.

Did you ever have any vocal training?

I never had any training. I tried once, but it just didn't stick. It wasn't very interesting, and I couldn't see immediately that it was helping because I was so young. I didn't think about the future. I just sang along to things and taught myself how to make the pitch solid. The voice is an instrument like anything else. You can practice it, of course. But I've had some emergencies where I would go in and they would give me like an elixir and then we'd do some warm-ups together so I could go onstage.

What was that about?

At the time, nobody had really heard of us. It was like rumblings of this group, and we were gonna perform at CMJ Music Festival in New York City. It was our first time in New York City, and it was this really big deal for the band, and here I am, I don't have a voice. It was bad. We had to go to Celine Dion's vocal coach. We go to his house, and he had me gargle carrot syrup, salt, warm water, and baking soda silently for two minutes, which is harder than it sounds. Two entire minutes of your life, gargling. It cleanses your vocal cords, and you're able to warm your voice back up. Then, we ran out of that place, and I just basically ran right onstage. We did the show, and everything sounded fine. It was a hit.

The last time I saw you perform was at the Greek Theatre in LA, and the word on the street was that you weren't feeling that great vocally before you went on. But I'm not exaggerating when I say that show was the greatest, most soulful vocal performance I've ever seen live in my life.

Oh, wow, thank you.

Really. And I've seen you guys live so many times, but I felt like even the band was playing more dynamically, and you were really pushing through something. When things are tough, do you find yourself stepping up like that and transforming?

Absolutely. One thing I love about being in this group, whenever things are hard, we always push back, never crack under pressure at all.

Are you nervous or confident before you perform?

I remember doing talent shows, and I was nervous. But I was also definitely focused on making it go off, like, this has got to be good because I don't want to embarrass myself. One thing I always tell myself is you have all the time in the world, and you don't have to rush. I don't get nervous anymore. I'm not really a public speaker. Some singers are really good at that, at communicating and being eloquent when speaking to the crowd. I don't feel comfortable in that role. Some nights are better than others; it depends on the crowd. Everyone's staring at me, and I don't know what to say. But if people are more interactive then it's easy because I'm talkin' to somebody.

I'm curious how you're able to give so much of yourself night after night and still do it again the next day, 'cause I don't feel you hold back.

Well, after a show, a lot of people go get drinks, or explore the town, or see another band, and I usually can't do that because I have to sleep. You have to get enough sleep. In my opinion, that is the most important thing as a singer. That's the only way your body heals whatever damage you're doing to your vocal cords. If I don't sleep, I'm not gonna be able to do my job the next day, and that's what we're out there for.

Do you do vocal warm-ups before your shows?

Our backing singers taught me lots about warming-up and the difference you feel. And you do notice a difference. We do some breathing exercises for your diaphragm, holding air and breathing air out. We'll do background exercises and then we'll just do some scales and that's usually it because you don't want to warm-up too much. You gotta warm-up just enough. I think the most important thing for me is doing the diaphragm exercises because of the way I sing.

What does the diaphragm exercise look like?

You're just breathing in air for a certain amount of time, and then breathing it out for a certain amount of time.

You breathe in for how long and breathe out for how long?

You start off short and then you go longer each time. So, you find your hard notes, whatever note that is, you'll wanna practice holding that note out as long as you can.

So, you're basically breathing in, picking your note, and then holding it out?

Exactly. And you can do scales that way. Holding out those notes and just getting your body prepared to sing.

How else do you take care of your voice on the road?

I don't drink, don't have coffee before a show, try not to dry your throat out. If you're having an especially difficult day, don't talk too much, which is the worst for me. I hate going on vocal rest. It's so lonely, not being able to talk. And people always think there's something wrong with me. It's like, "No, no, I'm on vocal rest. I love to talk!"

Do you have any rituals before you hit the stage?

Well, there's nine of us in the [touring] band, and the only ritual we have is we fist bump everybody in the group and any crew members we see. It's just a sign of like, let's do this. Solidarity. "I see you, we got this." And, usually, we just try to make each other laugh. It doesn't always work, but it's good to be jolly when you go out there.

Is there anything after the show that helps keep your voice in shape?

Just a real low hum to vibrate those vocal cords and whatever is building up on them. I'm not sure what it does, it's just something I do. Nobody taught me that. It's just nice. It probably has meditative properties too. You know, you go onstage and you have this huge leap in endorphins and dopamine, and your brain's going through so many things, and then after a show it's just a huge drop off. So, maybe it's good to take a second, be alone, and kind of focus on one thing, and bring yourself back down.

Are there songs where you wonder if your voice will be there that night?

It's really a night-to-night basis. If my voice is healthy and it's the beginning of a tour, I can sing everything with no problem. But after you've been singing for a solid week, your voice starts to get tired. It's gonna happen to everybody. I sing very loudly, and I sing from my diaphragm, so if I can't hear myself onstage, I start pushing from the back of my throat. I start trying to hear myself sing, and that's where you can damage your vocal cords.

So, what do you do when you feel your voice getting ragged?

On those occasions, we try to protect my voice and cut songs that are loud, or any song where I'm basically yelling for the entire song. "Heartbreaker" is one of those songs where if it's not there, I don't even want to attempt it because there's parts of the song where I have to hit these notes, and it'll do damage. So, it's like, *Whoop, don't do that*!

What's your most embarrassing vocal mishap ever?

Going for a note where everybody's like, "Oh, here it comes," and then it's just like, [*makes a hollow sound*] and you're like, *Awww!* But that's not all the show's about; that's the cool thing about seeing bands live. Whenever I see a band live and they're perfect, I find it kind of boring. I like to see how people react when something's going wrong. To me, that's what live is. It's a risk you take every night. You try to do it great to the best of your ability, and when I do make a mistake, I definitely don't beat myself up over it. It happens.

Are there songs where you've had to adjust the key live?

The only time that we changed the key was when we had to slow down the tape because of the overall feel of the song, like on "Dunes." That song be in E flat whereas when we play it live, it's in standard [E]. On the recorded version, it was just too fast. We finished the entire song, and it was time to sing on it. I was like, "I can't reach that. It doesn't feel right." We slowed it down, and that changed the tuning.

Do you remember a performance where you surprised yourself?

Oh, that happens all the time. Especially like in "Gemini," which is my favorite song to play live because I don't know what's going to happen. At the end there's always an improvised solo, and some nights I sound like Prince and those are my favorite nights. You know, like you take a solo, and it's really good, but it was an accident, but it was awesome? That's what I'm going for.

How are you with hearing your own voice?

I just don't want to put anything out that I don't respect so, that's pretty much where it stands. There's no pitch correction, I don't subscribe to Auto-Tune, anything like that. Strictly, just do it again. If you can't do it today, do it tomorrow, but you gotta do it. Anything that's left the studio and has been brought to you, I approve of.

What's changed the most about your voice from when you started?

When I was younger, it was higher and squeakier. Now that I'm older, it's like a fine wine. It's settled. I just know more about myself in general because I'm older and take it places where it's comfortable. Before, it was always searching, searching, searching, and now I know my voice can do this. I'm more comfortable with it.

If you could duet with any singer—living or dead—who would it be?

Probably David Bowie. I think I got *Hunky Dory* before I got *Ziggy Stardust*, and just being like, *This music is crazy*, and the songs; what he's singing about is crazy, and everything's like no genre. Or rather, ALL genres! I've always loved music like that, that wasn't like, *I'm a rock band*. You could be everything. Those are always my favorite artists, that do their own thing. I always wanted to sing with him. I mean, I've been singing with him since I found out about him, but...[*Laughs*]

Who are your top five favorite singers of all time?

Oh man, that's changing all the time because I'm always finding out about new singers. Recently, I found out about Betty Carter who's a jazz singer. She has the most beautiful voice that reminds me of a French horn. It's bold, it's not too bright, it's a little sad. And, of course, Nina Simone. Love her voice because it's so full of character. And Prince. Let's talk about those high notes he can hit, right? That falsetto of his—so controlled. And Curtis Mayfield. I always thought he had a really cool voice. I know I'm forgetting...Oh, there's this band now, they're called Chicano Batman. I love his voice. Bardo Martinez has the most unusual voice I've ever heard. You gotta check them out. It's really different. And Gil Scott-Heron. I like his voice for his speaking voice, mainly.

He's got like a molasses voice.

Yeah. And, of course, Freddie Mercury. If I had to name two records that taught me how to sing, it would be *By the Way* by the Red Hot Chili Peppers and *A Night at the Opera* by Queen. When I was around fourteen, I would play those songs over and over again. I really do think this is how I learned to sing. I would make my voice stay in pitch. First, I would do Freddie's harmony, and then I would do Roger Taylor's harmony, and then, I would do whoever else's harmony. Just going over and over, learning about harmonies that way. And because John Frusciante had such a big role in *By the Way*, I learned a lot about harmonies from that too— how to keep that note straight.

You know what harmony absolutely floors me, and I had to listen to like 70 million times? [*Sings the melody from "Sound & Color"*] "It must be I'm fallin' awake..."

Oh yeah, that one! [*Laughs*]

Something about the way you do that throws my heart across the room.
Those harmonies aren't perfect harmonies either. That was the whole fun experiment on "Sound & Color." One of them is never a third or a fifth, or what have you. It's always dissonant, and that's what makes it sound so creepy. It's lovely and creepy.

If you could ask any singer about their voice, who would it be, and what would you ask?
It was hard when you asked me my top five singers because I'm literally thinking of more right now. You know who Louis Prima is? My God. You actually gotta put him down as one of my top five because I love his personality inside his voice.

I remember when I met you for the first time, and I had to know about your laugh on "Gimme All Your Love." That laugh is so amazing to me. So, that was my big question to you: how did that laugh happen?
What'd I tell you?

You said that you laughed at something you did, right?
Yeah, I was doing this run in the song, and it failed. I just started laughing at myself, and we kept it in. I literally just wasn't singing well. [*Laughs*]

That's another one where you rewind it a million times and you just go, "Whoooo!" It's just so amazing, and the way it's mixed in with all the reverb and the echo. So, what's that moment for you with a singer where it's like, "How'd you do that?"
I'd like to know more about James Brown's squeal. Because he can hit those freely, at will. If I'm gonna squeal, I gotta be slightly raspy. Maybe his voice is already raspy, and he can hit those at any moment. He can just call on them and they're always there. I think that's really cool. I'm pretty sure if I did get a chance to ask how he did it, he'd probably just say, "I just do it." I don't think there'd be an answer. But I've always wondered about those.

CHRISSIE HYNDE

CHRISSIE HYNDE DOES NOT SUFFER FOOLS. So, now we're in a pickle. 'Cause this fool's a fool for Chrissie Hynde.

When I was growing up in the early '80s, you couldn't turn the radio dial or watch MTV without the Pretenders giving it to ya day and night. Led by the no bullshit, street swagger of Chrissie's voice, the band took their message of love all the way from Akron, Ohio, to the Rock & Roll Hall of Fame. A place they deserve to be, because very few out there are as truly rock 'n' roll as Chrissie Hynde.

Packed with melody, confidence, and personality, Chrissie's voice tells the story of what it takes to build a steady and solid career. But it's hard for some people to fully appreciate how influential or consequential they are to the history of music. Whether she's unaware, unimpressed, nonchalant, or humble, I can't be sure Chrissie cares either way. But her beautiful voice, unique phrasing, and punk rock attitude means so much to so many of us. So, it was truly an honor to speak with the great Pretender.

Who first exposed you to singing?

I listened to the radio. I wanted to be a singer since I was four years old. I think a lot of people who know their calling, you just know it all your life. I was always like that with singing. But I was too shy to play with the guys in the classroom, you know, the art room, so I just had to make up my own little songs. I didn't like to do it in front of anyone for a long time. I never really thought I'd get in a band, but then I kinda snuck in there during the punk thing. By then, I was playing guitar.

Were you emulating anyone when you started out?

I don't know that I've ever tried to be like anyone else. I don't even wanna be like myself!

[*Laughs*] How did you find your own voice?

I'm a rock singer, so I don't think you have to think about that too much. Rock 'n' roll isn't really as much a technical skill as just a personality. Iggy Pop was a huge influence, and he showed me that you could have this kind of unattractive, midwestern voice. He had one, so I thought, *Oh, I guess it's cool then*.

Did you ever have any vocal training?

The one place you cannot learn rock 'n' roll is in school. So, vocal training, that's good if you're gonna get into a West End musical, or go on Broadway, but it's not for me. I'm very much self-taught—not because I'm proud of it—I'm just a shitty student. I just have to do my thing. I wasn't even sure if I could sing, but then when everyone else would go out to work, I'd go into a closet and try to sing some R&B songs, just to see if I could. I loved Hendrix, James Brown, Dionne Warwick, The Beatles. That's how you learn to sing. You just listen to them.

Are you nervous or confident before you perform?

I used to feel very nervous. *Very, very nervous.* And I *hated* it. But after a few hundred gigs, you start to get used to it.

Do you do any vocal warm-ups before shows?

No, I think that's all psychological. An opera singer may have to do some calisthenics or scales, but my voice, if I haven't sung for two years and I step in front of a mic, it's exactly as it always is. I think training in my field can probably castrate the voice a little bit, but I don't know. I can only speak for myself.

Is there anything after the show that helps keep your voice in shape?

The only thing I've ever done that I think benefited my voice was quit smoking. That destroys your voice eventually. I always used to get bronchitis because I smoked, so every year, I'd have a bout of that. Maybe my voice wasn't very good, I don't know. But I got away with it. I didn't even quit smoking 'til I was in my sixties.

Oh my God. Wow. So, how do you take care of your voice on the road?

There's a couple of things actually. Air conditioning, especially in the states, really fucks your voice up. So, if you're in a hotel room in a hot climate, you probably should get a humidifier to put some moisture in the air just because the temperature dries your throat out. That's important.

When you start getting sick, what do you do?

If you lose your voice, game over, there's nothing you can do. The whole thing comes down. Anyone who's a lead singer lives in fear of that happening. Until about seven years ago, I'd only canceled about five shows in my life, and they were almost life and death kind of things. On our last tour, I had about five days where I had some sort of flu, and a fever, and had to get doctors in. We would soundcheck, and I had no voice, and we'd have to call it off. That really upset me because the whole crew's there, they're all set up, people are in the place, and it's horrible.

Are there songs where you wonder if your voice will be there that night?

Not really. I'm a rock singer. You just have to get out there and do it. The other thing that's helped is the in-ear monitors. They're really good if you're in a rock band. Rock bands like to play loud, and certainly use shouting, and that's not good. So, I use in-ear monitors just to make everything quiet. Anytime I've ever done a show where we have normal monitors, like on television, I'll have them turned off altogether and just use the house. I just don't like hearing my voice. I like to have it real quiet. Really quiet. Everyone I've ever worked with says I have the quietest mix of anyone they've worked with. I suppose I sing quite conversationally. I sing loud at times if I need to, but the in-ear monitors saved me from shouting. That isn't a nice sound anyway.

Are there songs where you've had to adjust the key live?

If I sing in a very low key for the record, to give it a bit more power, you might want to put the key up. There might be two in the repertoire where we've changed the key.

What was your most embarrassing vocal mishap ever?

I have had one. But I wouldn't say because I don't like to talk about things that embarrass me. I've done a few recordings I think are awful and I'm kind of ashamed. But what can you do? It's out there now, and I don't want to bring attention to them.

[*Laughs*] Okay. Do you remember a performance where you surprised yourself?

I'm always surprised that I can even do it because there's only one lead singer there, and I think, *Fuck, it's me!* [*Laughter*] That's kind of surprising, especially when I look around me. I have some really great guitar players, and I work with really good people.

How are you with hearing your own voice?

I can listen to my singing voice, but I can't listen to my speaking voice. I never watch anything I'm in, which is kind of a drag, because there's a lot of things I've been in that I want to watch, but I can't watch them cause I'm in them. No documentaries, nothing. I don't read any press, reviews, interviews, and I never have. I've never gone on social media. I'll post a blog every once in a while, if my office reminds me, but I would be self-conscious, and I don't want to be self-conscious. I don't wanna get depressed. I try to avoid all that. I'm not comfortable in the limelight unless I'm actually onstage with the band.

Do you have a favorite vocal performance you're really proud of?

I don't think I'm proud of any of it. Like I said, I just got away with it! [*Laughter*]

"The Phone Call" will never cease to amaze me. The song kicks off with that opening riff, and any other vocalist would probably have gone straight into some "Let's party" rock melody, but you completely subvert what's expected, and come up with this awesome, layered, multi-voiced, spoken word deal. I still can't even comprehend how you got there. What inspired that approach?

I'm untrained, that's why. Jimi Hendrix had a very conversational manner, and that's who I grew up with. He was like a number one.

You also have this beautiful vibrato that appears in songs like "When I Change My Life" and "Criminal." Is that something that you can just turn off and on at will?

I don't really know how that works. It's not done on purpose; I'm just trying to get through the song. I'm not trying to affect it. I don't know, even talking about it is creepin' me out a little bit. [*Laughs*] Because I just do my thing. There's no tricks or smoke and mirrors. I just hope for the best.

It's fascinating to me because you're saying you just hope for the best yet there are things you do with your vibrato where I'm like, *Man, that sounds like Aaron Neville*! But, so far, anytime I ask singers about their vibrato, nobody knows how they're doing it!

I'm not saying I'm one of them, but there are certain people who just have a voice when they're born. Elvis Presley. There was a voice. Tom Jones. There's a voice. Very few people in the world have it. Jim Morrison. John Lennon. Paul McCartney. James Brown. Amy Winehouse, what a great voice she had. She had her own thing. Their voices are distinctive. That's what's good about a voice; when you know who it is, and I don't think you can learn that.

Earlier, you were saying that you're just a rock singer, and I want to acknowledge the solo album you made with the Valve Bone Woe Ensemble because you're singing these gorgeous jazz melodies and stretching your voice in ways we've never heard from you before, and it turns out, you're also this really incredible jazz singer.

Well, I listened to jazz when I was a kid too. The reasons I wanted to do those songs is because they're melodic, and I like melody. The only thing that I've never got to do is opera, which I regret, because I do love opera. I'd love to be able to use the top end of my voice and falsetto, but it's just not in my wheelhouse because I'm in a rock band. I would've loved to have done that. For the pleasure of singing, that would be *fuckin' great*.

What do you feel has changed the most about your voice since you started?
I don't know.

Yeah, I don't either. [*Laughter*] I don't know if your voice *has* changed. I mean, it seems like it's just better.
I really appreciate you being so complimentary. We're just working on a new album. We've done all the backing tracks, and I sang along to guide the band through it. I listened back to them and I thought, *I don't need to replace any of the vocals*. They're just all the live vocals. I just sang all the songs in one take, over the phone. The technology has improved. I mean, you can record anything on them now, so it doesn't take much.

That must make you feel good.
Yeah, it's a relief. I don't have to go in and fuck around with it. But then, other times, you'll go in and try to do something and—it depends who you're working with too—you'll do like ten different takes, and they comp it and all that, and that's not always the most satisfying way. I'd much rather do it in one take.

If you could duet with one singer—living or dead—who would it be?
I don't know, there's a lot of singers that I like. I've guested on a lot of albums. I sang with Michael Hutchence. Mick Ronson. That was great that I got to sing on his last record. It's amazing that I've been able to be on so many people's records. It's fun!

You also did a duet with Frank Sinatra on "Luck Be a Lady" for his *Duet* recordings. Tell me about that experience.
Well, he wasn't there. And I didn't really research the song, so I had to jump an octave. I don't know what key I sing in best. I never found that out either.

The thing that I find so wild about you doing a duet with Sinatra is he's considered one of the greatest phrasers of all time. But you're vocal phrasing is every bit as iconic to so many of us. It's just so cool. But that's not something you're even paying attention to, is it?
I'm not paying attention. I guess it's natural. I mean, how much can you pay attention to that? You're not writing it out in a chart, you know; it's not like reading music.

I know, it's just a personality thing, but that's what makes you one of the greatest in my opinion. Could you name your top five favorite singers of all time?

There's so many singers, I couldn't even start. I love rock 'n' roll. I love bands. Hearing all those bands on the radio when I was a kid, that's what informed my whole destiny. And, to all those singers, I'm eternally grateful. God, we could talk about it for hours and hours, but it would be impossible to narrow down. There's hundreds. Literally. I'd be calling you back every ten minutes, going, "Oh, and what about?"

If you could ask any singer about their voice, who would it be, and what would you ask?

I wouldn't. It's like asking someone their medical condition. It's personal.

Well, obviously, I would!

Well, that's why you're in a rock band. You do your thing, I do mine. [*Laughter*]

JIM JAMES

A S THE SINGER OF THE CRITICALLY-ACCLAMED Americana, psychedelic, experimental, rock 'n' roll... Man, I hate labeling music! Some artists just have their own thing goin' on!

Jim James is the singer of My Morning Jacket, and whether he's playing with the band or solo, it's always a journey worth taking. He's one of those vocalists who thrives best outside of what's expected, constantly searching and evolving. But there's something else that's become even more intriguing over time: the spirituality he brings to every performance, whether he's singing softly or rocking out. That spirituality extends to his vocal approach as well, where the "Good Jim" lives. Some singers have voices that sound as though they're praying out loud, or striving to reach another realm beyond the one we experience here on earth. Listening to Jim sing, you get that feeling. Interviewing him, you understand why.

Who exposed you to singing?

Kermit the Frog. I'll just never forget bein' a kid and seein' Kermit the Frog sing and thinking, *What is that? What is that feelin'?* Jim Henson and that whole scene at *The Muppets*, they were masters at letting kids know that they knew that kids aren't idiots. [*Laughs*] They spoke to children in this very real way. There was this real, deep kind of sadness or depth to those songs like "It's Not Easy Being Green," or "Rainbow Connection." You're a little kid, and you see this cute frog singing these songs that are hitting you in this crazy way when all the other bullshit for kids is usually so trite. I just remember that feeling, so I'd have to say Kermit.

Were you emulating anyone when you started out?

Oh my God, yes, tons of people. I didn't have any older siblings, and my parents weren't really into music, so I was just observing what was popular on TV or whatever. And I just feel so fortunate that the whole grunge thing hit and formed my teenage years. Some of those bands did such a great job of turning us on to older bands and people like Neil Young. I'll never forget reading about Chris Cornell saying the way he got his voice so high was through years of screaming. [*Laughs*] I kind of took that advice and screamed a lot in the early bands. I really loved Nirvana. And I always loved Shannon Hoon from Blind Melon. I feel like he's one of the most underrated singers in the history of music. His voice is like sword of light, a light beam. I thought of him a lot when I was singing, really tried to stretch my voice as far as it could go. Sometimes it worked and sometimes it didn't. But it felt like I was doing somethin' because of what Chris Cornell had said, that when you're reaching for that note, a lot of times you don't hit it, but you're expanding your voice every time.

So, how did you find your own voice?

In my first band, our guitar player's brother was the singer for a while, and he had a really great smokey, kind of husky, Chris Robinson voice. But he was like five years older than us and wanted to do different things, so we still had the band but nobody to sing. So, I started trying to sing, but I was really self-conscious and hated my voice. Then one day, somebody accidentally left the reverb turned up on the amp I was singin' through, and it was like a revelation. When I heard my voice hit that reverb, it was insane. It was like, this is what I'm supposed to do. It turned me into a superhero or something. I just found it.

It's true. You have this atmospheric, reverby vocal sound that's almost like you're singing from a shower in outer space.

Totally. And over the years I've played with that. Sometimes I've ditched it, and sometimes I've liked other things, but, as a very insecure teenager, the reverb was my vehicle to say, *You're now okay. You don't have to judge yourself.* It was almost like putting on a cape; I could now become Superman. Reverb took away my fear.

Are you nervous or confident before you perform?

Only recently have I gotten over feeling like I have to hide. Just in the last two or three years, I've learned that it's okay to be myself, and that I am what I am, warts and all.

Did you ever have any vocal training?

About ten years ago, we were on tour, and I was about to lose my voice, so we went to this famous vocal coach to the stars here in LA named Roger Love. We saw him for an hour, and he saved the tour. He gave us this vocal warm-up that I still do before every show. It's just an mp3 that you sing along with for ten minutes. I think there's value in learning techniques, but I never had any training.

What's your warm-up routine like?

Runnin' scales and stuff. One of the things is trying to sing cartoonishly deep and as weird as you can. Like Roger was saying, try to pretend like you're Yogi Bear while you're singin' these things. I do that before every performance.

Perry Farrell told me he sings like Kermit the Frog before he goes onstage.

That's funny. Perry Farrell was another one in my formative years that really inspired me too. What an amazing voice he has. People like him were *really* tryin' to throw their voice way out there. Like Roy Orbison or Aretha Franklin. That was so inspiring to me. It was almost like an athletic feat when Perry Farrell or Shannon Hoon would hit those crazy notes, and you're just like, *Geeez*. But I also love a great Lou Reed or Bob Dylan vocal where most of the time they're pretty laid back.

Do you have any other rituals before you hit the stage?

I don't really subscribe to any religion or anything, but I pray to the spirits of the place we're playing, and I pray to some of my loved ones that are like my counsel that passed away. I kind of pray with them. Whether it's My Morning Jacket or whoever I'm playin' with, we'll get together and do a little huddle and just kinda give each other good energy before we go out there. I usually get down on my knees and just try to feel the energy of wherever we are and give thanks and also recognize the helplessness of the situation in my gig.

In what way?

So many times, it's not in your control. I try to realize that *before* I walk onstage and be grateful for it. You can do all the preparing you want, have everything set up exactly like you want, and have a terrible show, just for whatever reason, beyond your control. I try to recognize that. And also, just being grateful for your health, because if you get sick, you're fucked, show's over. That's the shitty thing about bein' a singer. You feel like you're carrying this whole organization on your back—this whole show, this whole team, and all these people. If you get sick, it all goes down. That's probably the scariest part.

When you start getting sick, what do you do?

Man, it sucks. I try to stay pretty healthy, eat pretty healthy. But just like any other time when you're gettin' sick, you start slammin' the Airborne and all the wellness tonics you can think of. Sometimes it works and sometimes it doesn't. I was talkin' to some natural doctor and they were like, "You have to remember that all that honey and lemon and stuff is going down your esophagus. It's not going past your vocal cords, so all that stuff isn't helping you at all, especially the honey. It's just tons of empty calories and sugar you're pumping into your body." He was like, "Just drink as much water as you can."

Is there anything after the show that helps keep your voice in shape?

I went and sang with Brandi Carlile a while ago. She had a vocal coach, and they did warm-downs after the show that I was really fascinated by. I need to investigate that more. But there's been so much build-up to the show, and doin' the warm-up before the show makes sense, but then after the show, you usually have people waiting that you wanna hang out with. Or you're exhausted and you just wanna go to bed and get out of the club. You've been in the club all day, so you really don't have the patience to sit back there and do another fifteen minute warm-down. [*Laughs*] I don't know, maybe one day I'll be changing my tune, but I was really impressed with Brandi. It's working for her, obviously.

How do you take care of your voice on the road?

You try to respect it. Even if we partied, I'd make sure that I partied when we had a day off the next day. I don't ever drink onstage, and I've never been a smoker, so I feel like a lot of that stuff's helped me. I have gotten sick several times and had to cancel shows and cancel tours, so I really just try to respect it.

Are there songs where you wonder if your voice will be there that night?

Oh totally. Especially when we're doin' a song where I have to hit a high note, or there's some crescendo or part that's a little difficult. It's so nerve-wracking. In a lot of our songs, I'll try to go for these notes, but sometimes you don't get there. [*Laughter*]

Yep. And you hope that adrenaline pushes you over?

I'm always giving 110 percent when I'm out there, but within that, there's *gonna* be some mistakes. There's *gonna* be notes I don't hit, there's *gonna* be chords I miss. That's the truth of every live thing. But the audience is along for the ride too. It's so visceral that I think everybody is accepting and giving and taking of each glory and each failure. But when the microscope's on and you're doin' TV or some highly scrutinized performance, you're just like, *Oh fuck, man*. The pressure's tremendous.

Are there songs where you've had to adjust the key live?

Oh my God, yeah! We're actually workin' on a new Jacket record, and I don't quite understand, but a lot of the songs will come to me in a key, out of the universe or wherever, and I grab a guitar, and kind of figure out what it is in the real world, and then, I'll do a voice demo of it, and send it to the guys. We'll go to the studio, and when we're tryin' to play it for real, I'm like, *Fuck, man, this is way too high!* I can't even remotely try to hit these notes unless I'm in falsetto. But we've recorded tons of songs where I've pitched them down like eight whole steps until I finally found the place that felt good.

What was your most embarrassing vocal mishap ever?

[*Laughs*] I'm sure there've been times on TV where I've had a crack or somethin' and you're like, *Awww!* and you just have to live with it. Of course, I'll get bummed about it, but when I look back, it's like, I've never for a second claimed to be a good singer. [*Laughter*] Tryin'. Tryin' my best, you know? That's why so many people love Kurt Cobain or Lou Reed who are like, we're just tryin' our best. Nobody's comin' out here sayin', [*affects a pompous voice*] "I'm gonna blow your mind." It's like [*in his normal voice*], "We're gonna try and do this." That's as far as it goes. "I've got the passion for it. I've got this song I wanna share with you. I'm not the greatest singer in the world. Okay, here we go."

Do you remember a performance where you surprised yourself?

Oh yeah, there's so many times. That's half the fun of playing or recording is when you have those moments where's it's just like, *Holy shit, this thing just came outta me that I don't even know where it comes from.* Like everything that's ever come outta me, I don't fully understand where it comes from. Or why there's this thing that goes, okay, now at this part go, "*RAAAAA!*" Or now try to hit some high note, or some really long scream or whatever.

How are you with hearing your own voice?

I've gotten used to it. But I almost have to think about myself outside of myself. I used to feel self-conscious about it, but in the past couple years, I've had this new part of myself come out that's almost like my caretaker. It's like the Good Jim comes and gives me a hug and says, "Hey man, don't be so hard on yourself, you're tryin' your best. You gotta take care of yourself." So, I try to think in that regard. I try to be kind to myself. Of course, I'm still hard on myself.

Do you have a favorite vocal performance you're really proud of?

Nah! I feel like I'm always tryin' to do different things. There's quieter things I'm proud of, there's louder things I'm proud of. I try to be proud of everything when I do it. One thing that I was blessed with is the ability to move on. It's like I'm so obsessed with what I'm working on, or what I'm performing in that moment, for that period of time, and then once it's done, I'm gone. It's almost like it doesn't exist anymore because there's this other thing now I need to work on. Lots of times, by the time we have go play it live, I'm like, *What are these songs? What are the words? What are the chords?* I have to totally relearn them because I'm usually working on one or two other records. That's the crazy thing about timing and the music industry. I write an album about falling in love, then I have to sing it while I'm breaking up. Or vice versa!

I really dig hearing laughter in songs for some reason, and I think that's you laughing at the beginning of "Smokin' from Shootin'," is that you?

God, I don't even remember, honestly. I haven't listened to that recording since we did it.

There you go. Just proved your own point. You really walk the walk. [*Laughter*]

It's fucked up because one of the things we love to do is three or four nights where we don't repeat a single song. It's really fun for us, and the fans too, because you know each night, you're gonna get a completely different show. So, we'll make set lists, and I'll be scratchin' my head, bein' like, *Fuck, how do I play song X? Or how do I play song Y?* Then, I'll usually check the last live version I can find. *Okay, how were we doin' it two years ago?* instead of, *How were we doin' it twenty years ago?* A completely different person made that record in a lot of ways.

Yeah, your approach to singing or playing something evolves with you in real time.

I try to explain that to people when I talk about how difficult touring can be. I'm now a forty-one-year-old person, trying to sing the songs that a twenty-year-old version of me wrote. I still like the songs, but a lot of nights you're like, *Shit, man, I don't know if I feel like feelin' the sadness of this twenty-year-old me right now.*

What do you do for yourself in those moments?

You have to find it in there somewhere to go for that wail, or go for that scream, and connect with that part of you that you may not want to connect with again. It's like, *Man, that was a tough time*, but you try to roll with it because I still love the music, and I'm still proud of the music. You have to revisit all these past versions of yourself, which sometimes is really fun and sometimes is just really, really difficult.

I feel like around the *Z* album you became much looser, allowing yourself to have more fun with your vocals. You're screaming and yowling and really going for it. Did something happen mentally that freed you up? I'm thinking of things like the end of "Wordless Chorus."

Yeah, man. I just started dancing more and trying to take things less seriously. While we were makin' *Z*, our buddies were DJing, and we would go dance a lot, which is somethin' I really like to do. When you're out on the dance floor, you're feelin' that euphoria of somebody sing-ing. You're hearin' "Rock Steady" and Aretha Franklin just fuckin' crushing it, and you're like, *Whoa, this is possible?* As a younger person, most of my music was about dealing with being alive in the world because it hurt so much. It was this exploration of pain, and how do we deal with this pain, and how do we deal with this sadness, but then you start getting into Stevie Wonder or Curtis Mayfield or Prince, and you're just like, *Holy shit.* There's this other way to deal with being alive and it's called dancing. It's called having fun. But it's not trite. Within that, there's also room for melancholy, and there's room for that darkness. But you're out on the dance floor workin' it out instead of sitting with your guitar and crying in your bedroom. That's such a cool feeling.

As a solo artist, you made an album of George Harrison covers [*Tribute to*]. I was wondering what it is about his voice that resonates so strongly for you?

I feel like George and Alice Coltrane are some of our best spiritual leaders that show you that music can be used for a higher purpose. You know, music is God, and God is love, and love is expressed through music. It's all part of the same thing. I always loved how George used his phenomenal fame and power to be this spiritual vehicle for love, for acceptance and peace and equality. I love how much he showed the world what his beliefs were, but he never seemed judgmental, and always seemed so open. His energy's just unbelievable. His recordings stand the test of time, and they always will. You just hear that deep spirit in his voice.

I feel like "A New Life" is you writing and singing your own George Harrison song.

Oh yeah, there's definitely parts of that spirit in a lot of the things that I do.

What's changed the most about your voice since you started?

I feel like it's gotten deeper. But I've deliberately changed my voice a lot over the years because sometimes I'll find a new way of singing that I like at the time. That's the beautiful thing about music, it's so formless. It's really one of the most magical things about life other than love itself, this thing called music, and how it cannot be defined. It can only be captured in snapshots. You can have a snapshot of a song as a folk song, and then another snapshot of the song as a fuckin' blistering rock 'n' roll song, or you can make it funky. You can literally do anything with any song. There's so many avenues; there's no need to try to hold onto something because it's always changing.

If you could duet with one singer—living or dead—who would it be?

Nina Simone. She's just what I was talkin' about—the depth of her voice and her spirit. She could take any song and completely reimagine it into her own universe. If she were still alive and I had a chance to duet with her, I would shit my pants with fear. I'd be quaking in my boots.

Just from how she might behave in the studio!

Well, yeah, that too. But just because of how much I love her voice. Her voice is a temple.

Who are your top five favorite singers of all time?

I'd say Dylan, Aretha, and Nina, and Bob Marley, and Curtis Mayfield.

God bless you. No one's said Curtis Mayfield yet, and I'm shocked.

Yeah, Curtis was such a spiritual force. I feel like he's part of the George Harrison, Alice Coltrane, John Coltrane core of spirituality. Curtis was always preaching love, always preaching acceptance, always preaching tolerance. And just the sound of his fuckin' voice, man. Changed the way I did everything. It's like, *Oh my God! I didn't even realize falsetto existed.* I'd heard it before, but once you hear him do it—*Fuck, this is the source of all life.* You can hear it in his voice. Think about Nat King Cole. Talk about this phenomenal, effortless expression. They build towers with every fucking note without lifting a finger.

Oh, man. Well said. So, if you could ask any singer about their voice, who would it be and what would you ask?

I feel like most people would probably agree that Dylan has the most mysterious voice of all. His voice has changed so much over the years. A lot of people say every voice is an act. Not an act in like a fake way, but it's part of his character, part of his persona. For years now, he's had kind of the gruff, grumbly, touring voice where you're like, "What song is he singin'? Oh shit, it's 'Tangled Up in Blue.'" But a couple years ago, I saw him do some old Sinatra standards live, and it was fucking crazy watching him go from singing his own songs [*imitates Dylan*] "Grrraaa-rrraaa-rrraaa," and then sing these Sinatra songs. It was like he turned into Édith Piaf or somethin'. His voice was huge and smooth and incredible.

You sang with him once too, right? What was that like?

We went on tour with him, and I got to sing with him a couple times. Just being that close to him onstage and trying to feel his energy. It's like the look in his eyes, he's somewhere else. In a good way. He's like off on some other planet.

So, what would your question to Bob Dylan be?

I wanna know what planet he's visiting! [*Laughter*] *Where is he getting this shit?* His genius is just so profound, you're constantly trying to figure it out. He's definitely the most controversial singer of all time, definitely the most influential, definitely one of the greatest, just in terms of talent. Most people joke about his voice, but his voice is so versatile and so powerful.

JOAN JETT

"GIRLS DON'T PLAY ROCK 'N' ROLL."

Those were the words from Joan Jett's first guitar teacher. No one knows his name, but they do know Joan's. And her philosophy is simple: "Tell me I can't do something, and you'll make sure I'm gonna be doing it." Thank God she did, because it led to one of the greatest revolutionary acts in music history when she co-founded the all-female rock band, The Runaways, in 1976.

Their debut single "Cherry Bomb" blew the doors wide open, and it wouldn't be long before Joan was kickin' ass as a solo artist. Backed by the Blackhearts, Joan Jett was soon pumping out of every radio in America, singin', "I love rock 'n' roll!" It took her all the way up the charts to #1 where she stayed for seven straight weeks.

And she's still here, singing with the same rebellious spirit that took her off the streets and landed her in the Rock & Roll Hall of Fame. She has weathered every storm the "business" or the changing times have thrown her way and has influenced everyone from the Germs to Miley Cyrus. She's also got too many stories you can't believe: the rejection and sexism; Mike Tyson and Cal Ripken; and hit after hit after hit.

It's amazing what staying true to your own voice can do.

Who first exposed you to singing?

I don't know that I was exposed in any sort of formal way. I don't even remember my parents singing around the house. They played a lot of Frank Sinatra and Johnny Mathis, that ilk of music, and I'd probably sing along. But I guess junior high would be the place I was first exposed to singing, in chorus class.

What made you want to sing?

I saw *Cabaret* when I was twelve or thirteen and was in love with Liza Minnelli. She knocked me out. That movie has it all. It's visually exciting and pushes the envelope, especially for a kid. So, I wanted to be onstage first, like Broadway. That was fleeting. Then I wanted to be an actor and did high school drama class, some chorus classes. But then, all of a sudden, it switched to guitar.

What made you switch?

I heard [Free's] "All Right Now." I still can hear the guitar. On the back end of that riff, it would bend a little bit out of tune. I don't know if it was the timing because I was just hitting puberty, but you could feel it not just hit your ears but hit your groin. I'm like, *I just have to do that. I have to make these sounds*. I was also influenced by British glitter music, which a lot of American kids never heard. "Bang A Gong" by T. Rex was a another big one.

Were you emulating anyone when you started out?

I think I learned to scream from Marc Bolan, those little "*Ow!*" screams.

I never put those together until now! You actually *do* have a Marc Bolan scream.

When I moved to California from Maryland, I was maybe fourteen, and I found this club I had been reading about in *Circus Magazine*: Rodney Bingenheimer's English Disco. They played all the British glitter songs: Sweet, T. Rex, Suzi Quatro. I was influenced by all of it.

How did you find your own voice?

It just came out. If I thought something should be sung harder, I sang harder. And if it was a softer song, I'd back down. I could sing in a variety of ways. When I sang show tunes in school, I had plenty of vibrato and that whole deal. So, technically, I'm able to sing properly, but once I went to playing rock 'n' roll, all the technical perfection stuff went out the window. What I do doesn't really call for technical perfection, though it definitely helps if you breathe right, and I do that—breathing from your diaphragm, really getting a full breath.

Did you ever have any formal training?

In school they taught us a scales, warming-up, those sorts of things. But I did *The Rocky Horror Picture Show* on Broadway for about eight months in 2000, and those people really helped me. Broadway is serious, serious, serious! All these arts are more difficult than people would think, but Broadway's really a kick-ass thing. I picked things up from them that I'd never really learned.

Like what?

Like opening your mouth to hit the high notes. People don't think about that, but it really works. You gotta open your mouth—wide! I also learned some exercises to relax your mouth. If you have to smile a lot in pictures and your mouth gets tired, just do [*does a lip trill*] and get your face all relaxed. One I use a lot onstage is making the sound of a squeaky door.

A squeaky door?

Say I'm onstage and I'm singin' really hard—I'm not singing *wrong*, I'm just singing *hard*—and my voice is gettin' scratchy. I need a second, but I don't have a second. So in between the verse and the chorus, I'll make the sound of a squeaky door, which is like stretching your vocal cords. Same thing you do when you're stretching your hamstrings. You'd go like [*makes the "Eeee" sound of a squeaky door*].

So, you'll go off the mic and squeal like that?

Yeah, I'll turn toward the drummer and look down, but I'm sure people on the side of the stage still see me. [*Laughs*] I look like I'm makin' an O-face with my tongue out. Not the greatest look, but these are the things you have to do—*and they work!* I don't care if it looks stupid.

You mentioned breathing before. Can you explain what you're doing?

Breathing in deep! It's tough, especially for women because they're trained that their bodies need to have a flat stomach. "Oh my God, I can't breathe into my diaphragm cause it makes my belly big!" For real. To really get a full breath, that belly has to come out, like you just had a huge meal or something. It's only there for a second, but people have trouble with it.

Especially in tight leather pants.

[*Laughs*] Well, no leather for me anymore.

Oh, that's right, you're vegan, yeah?

Yeah, as close as I can get.

Are you nervous or confident before you perform?

I've always been kind of a nervous person in a way, and I'm shy, so I was petrified when I started. I've always felt better in a group. I didn't feel good being singled out or being the focus; it just was hard for me. I'm more of a team player. I guess that's why I play rhythm guitar. I like to be part of the unit. I remember being in the studio for the first time and I had to sing in the dark with the lights out so nobody could see me in the control room. I just felt better.

Is it still that way for you?

Eventually, I got over that. I'm not petrified. I get amped up. It's almost anxious, almost nervous, but not quite. It's more like excited to get out there, trying to keep that energy channeled and not going in a scary direction, not thinking too much. Just trying to keep the energy contained because it's easy to lose your train of thought and start thinking about something weird or stressful at home, and then you've lost your focus.

Do you do vocal warm-ups before your shows?

I do some scales, I do some "shooos" and "sheeeees." I "swoooop," especially if you're in a bathroom, it sounds good. I do a [*sings loud and stretches the sound up*]. I do a "swoooo" as high as I can go, and a "sweeeee" as high as I can go. And keep trying to see how high I can go before I get a bit of a break. Then I can tell how strong or easy my voice is gonna be that night and if I have to really loosen up. Then I always do a bit of the squeaky door thing and sing the first line of "Bad Reputation" over and over just to make sure my voice is coming out strong.

Are you doin' "Bad Reputation" at full force?

Oh yeah, full force. Loud. [*Sings*] "I don't give a damn! I don't give a damn!" Full volume. And I'm talkin' about within a minute of goin' onstage.

Do you have any other rituals before you hit the stage?

A nice one we got into was having dinner with the band. I'm in a separate dressing room, so it'd be very easy to go to the stage like that. But I don't like that. I wanna feel like the unit, so, after I get dressed, I go over and hang out with the band until it's time to go onstage. We go on as a unit so we're immersed in each other. We're friends, we all like each other, we usually talk about baseball because we're in the summer and watching games and paying attention to the scores. Sometimes I have it on my phone on the stage so I can check the score. [*Laughter*]

Is there anything after the show that helps keep your voice in shape?

Just try not to talk too much.

How do you take care of your voice on the road?

I try to have humidifiers in all the rooms, at all times, to keep the air as moist as possible. I take very hot showers in general, and I'll stand there and breathe the steam for a while.

When you start getting sick, what do you do?

I don't really get sick that much, so if I do it's usually something like losing your voice completely from too much traveling and working at strange hours. You can lose your voice every once in a while, and I have over the years, here and there. So, if I *have* to do a show, they have little Pregnazon steroid packs you can take that bring down the swelling of the vocal cords. You can pretty much go from not being able to talk to being able to sing really well. But it's not somethin' you wanna do a lot. And I don't know if that's really "taking care." To really take care of your voice, you just have to not use it and get some rest. If you had time to chill, I'd definitely recommend that over steroids.

Are there songs where you wonder if your voice will be there that night?

Not really. I'm just aware that they're high or whatever the issue is. [*Laughs*] So, that's where all these things can help each other, the breathing with the high notes and opening your mouth. It's very helpful when you can execute all that correctly. It gives you more range, for sure. And if I can't hit a note, I have alternative notes I can go to, or change the melody and stuff.

Are there songs where you've had to adjust the key live?

Oh yeah, I've made the key lower. And also you work with different tunings.

What was your most embarrassing vocal mishap ever?

I don't even know what that would be. Can you give me an example?

I've heard all sorts. Sam Moore told me that he went for a high note onstage and farted.

[*Laughs*] But, if he farted, did the audience hear it?

I don't think so.

So, why did he tell everybody?

No, he told me!

Yeah, but you're gonna tell everybody! [*Laughter*] There've been times that I've forgotten words onstage. I remember I forgot some, like a couple nights in row, but a different song each night. And then, the night before the next show, I said, "Well, I'll know we're really screwed when I forget 'I Love Rock 'N Roll.'" What do you think I did that night? [*Sings the verse melody and jumbles the words*] I had to go, "Stop, stop, stop. We're gonna do that again." Just admit your fuck up and start again. Audiences like that. They like being inside that stuff. "Don't give me perfection. Let us see the little things that go wrong." It makes them feel like, "Hey, you guys are just like us."

Do you remember a performance where you surprised yourself?

If you're listening, Kenny, do you have any comments? Sometimes he remembers things better than I do.

Joan's manager and songwriting partner, Kenny Laguna, a legend who's been with Joan since her early days as a solo artist, gets on the phone.

KENNY: We could only afford one hour in the studio, and we wanted to demo what turned out to be the *I Love Rock 'N' Roll* album. She went into an iso-booth with her guitar and played "Crimson and Clover" and sang it, and that's the record. For someone to do that in 1981 was very unusual.

JOAN: I didn't realize it was that unusual until afterwards 'cause of everybody's reaction.

JTG: Hold on, so "Crimson and Clover" is a live take of you and your guitar?

KENNY: Yes, that's exactly what she sang. There's nothing punched in. She was very inspired, and felt it in her core, and it was a top five record. I'll remember that the whole rest of my life.

JOAN: And you know what one I'm impressed with? Loooong ago, when I used to drink, I was doing a vocal on a cover of a Who song called "Call Me Lightening," and I was so drunk. I couldn't stand up. That's why I don't drink anymore. So, I laid on the floor, on my back, with the mic in my hand, and just sang the lead vocal in a falsetto voice where I was able to hit all the notes. I thought it came out great.

How are you with hearing your own voice?

That's a really hard thing, to listen to your voice in the studio, soloed. You do a vocal and they listen back to it with no music, no nothin', just your voice, and it's bare and doesn't have any effects on it. It's a horrible feeling, even if you're on key and you sing it okay. I don't know, I think because it's just meant to be a part and not the whole thing. I really feel the part-ness of it. I can listen to it if it's mixed in the record. If it comes on the radio or somethin', I crank it up and roll down the windows because that's what you dreamed of. Being in a band and havin' a hit record and it comes on the radio? Why not enjoy it? You have so few things to enjoy these days, so I'm gonna enjoy the accomplishments that were so difficult to achieve. Nobody would sign us. They rejected all our hits. And then to form a band, make a record company, and actually do it?

It's so crazy that you had all those hit songs and no one would sign you?

We sent demos to twenty-three labels, all the majors and minors. They heard "I Love Rock 'N Roll," "Crimson and Clover," "Do You Wanna Touch Me," "Bad Reputation," and a song called "You Don't Own Me."

"You Don't Own Me," that's a great vocal too!

Thank you. Four of those became big hits! One was a number one! All these letters were sent back saying, "We're not really into this kinda artist right now," just a bunch of "Nos." So, when you get turned down like that and left for dead because they thought we were not capable, we did our own label, got it out, and had *more than one hit*. Big hits! Hits that they said they didn't hear. We have the letters to prove it.

And it's all because, at that time, men didn't think women could rock.

Rock implies sexuality. If women are playing rock 'n' roll, they're owning the sex act, and that makes a lot of men very uncomfortable. It's not even something they're aware of, but people are uncomfortable with girls talkin' about sex. But they're gonna do it and talk about it. Whether you're aware of it or not, it's happening. And why should girls have to shut up?

It's still part of their life experience, and it's important for your mental development, and your sense of self. It can be very empowering, or it can screw ya up. I think it's something that's more important than people realize: for girls to have channels to get things out in a healthy way.

Do you have a favorite vocal performance you're really proud of?
There's a lot of them that I'm pleased with, so I don't really have a favorite. I could pick a hard song like "Fetish," which is just straight up rock 'n' roll, or a soft song like "Little Liar," which is a ballad. The voices are completely different, but they're both me.

I'm fascinated by people who can get up at a sporting event and sing the national anthem. It's certainly not a move that most rockers have the guts to do, but you've done it a few times. What's that experience like for you?
That's really scary. That's not like singing rock 'n' roll onstage. It's really different. But I'm a big Orioles fan, like I mentioned earlier. My dad took me when I was eleven, and my first game was a no-hitter by Jim Palmer against the Oakland A's and Catfish Hunter. If you're into baseball, that is about the highest you can go. After we had hits, I think we sent them records and posters and stuff. And it turns out, a rookie that year was a big fan: Cal Ripken. So, they invited me down and asked if I wanted to sing the anthem. Even though I was petrified, it was such an honor to be asked, and such a weird thing to be asked, that I kinda had to do it. [*Laughter*]

KENNY: Hold on, I have to jump in here. [Publicist] Howard Bloom worked it out that if we went to see a ball game we could go into the locker room. So, we go downstairs, and there was only one guy left. It was Jim Palmer.

JOAN: And that's the guy I'd seen pitch a no-hitter!

KENNY: He was such a nice guy. He didn't know Joan from a hole in the wall, but was willing to take a picture with her. Well, within a couple of months, Joan had the biggest record in the world with "I Love Rock 'N Roll," and we played the Sportatorium, which was a big venue in Miami. Jim Palmer comes with his two teenage daughters and is beaming. "Man, I'm so glad I did that favor for Joan because now I'm a big shot to my daughters!" [*Laughter*] And that happened to be the start of the streak.

JOAN: Cal Ripken played for like fourteen years without missing a game, which only Lou Gehrig had done.

KENNY: Cal wanted Joan to sing the anthem when he tied the record. Joan had done it a couple of times, and she hates it because if they lose the game, she feels she's a jinx. She said, "No way am I ever doin' the anthem again." But Cal and his wife started bustin' Joan, and she finally gave in and was part of that incredible group. We were in a room where the President [Clinton] and the Vice President [Gore] were together in public for like the first time in a hundred years. There was Willie Mays, Joe Dimaggio, Frank Robinson. Everybody gave Cal a present, and she sang, and afterward, presented him a gold record.

JOAN: It was storybook, absolutely storybook.

KENNY: Joan has a connection to sports that's unbelievable. She was Mike Tyson's wake up call all during his career. The first time she didn't wake him up, he got knocked out by Buster Douglas.

JTG: When you say "Mike Tyson's wake up call" tell me what that means?

JOAN: Literally his wake up call. On a regular phone. This is pre-cellphone.

KENNY: So, sometimes Joan would have to wake up at some ridiculous hour because he was in Japan or wherever around the world. Then, I would place the call, and...

JOAN: "Time to wake up and kick ass!" [*Laughter*]

JTG: You would say, "Time to wake up and kick ass" to Mike Tyson every morning?

KENNY: From the sixth fight until the fight before Buster Douglas.

JOAN: Right up until Don King started workin' with him and they shut all his old friends out.

Joan, what's changed the most about your voice since you started?
I suppose the tenor of it. It's gotten thicker, fatter, deeper, and I've learned to sing properly, which helps me execute. It's like putting it in an oak barrel, rolling it around for forty years, and aging the vocal cords just right. But sometimes I'm surprised at how deep my speaking voice is. It's kinda weird.

You have a great tone to your speaking voice. You could do voiceovers.
Thank you. Yeah, I'd like to do that sometime.

If you could duet with one singer—living or dead—who would it be?
The first thing that popped into my head is doin' some kinda strange duet with Keith Richards. I think that would be fun.

That'd be great! Keith has one of the most underrated voices to me. I wanted to interview him for this 'cause I love it so much.
And what, he won't talk to you?

"I'm a guitar player."
Well, so am I, Keith! [*Laughter*] I think his voice has gotten better over the years. For his voice, he's learned to sing as well. It's a better timbre. You learn what you can do and what you can't.

I suppose that's another thing as you get older, you know your limitations, and then, you know where you can push yourself. But knowing yourself is part of it.

You and Paul Westerberg wrote and recorded the song "Backlash" together, and I know you cover "Androgynous" a bunch on tour. Paul's one of the singers who really gave me the confidence to do this when I started out. Can you tell me what it's like to work with him and what you dig about his voice?
He's got one of those great rock 'n' roll voices that's not trying to achieve perfection. That's what bothers me about today's records. Everybody fixes every little mistake. I like the mistake, or the little parts that might not be right on. I think his songwriting, his sense of melody, are all really special and different, but it's the fact that he's *not* a perfect singer. To me, that's perfection, when you have some of that humanity in there.

Who are your top five favorite singers of all time?
Oh God. Well, let's say Bowie... ohhh man... Okay, Daniel Higgs from Lungfish. Great underrated band. *Rainbows from Atoms* and *Talking Songs for Walking*. Debbie Harry. She's a good one. And The Stones are like my favorite, so Jagger. But it's favorite for a moment, you know what I mean? This isn't favorite forever.

Of course not!
I'm gonna say Liza Minnelli for the fifth voice.

If you could ask any singer about their voice, who would it be, and what would you ask?
I'd be too scared to go up to someone. Like I said, I'm shy! I'd stand against the wall, that's more my speed, you know? But I really worship Liza. I'd like to talk to her about the kind of stamina it takes to sing the way she does. She has to use her body, she's gotta breathe correctly and all that stuff. When she had to sing those *Cabaret* songs, what was that like? I'd probably ask her about making *Cabaret* because that movie really set me off on a path to want to be in show business.

BRIAN JOHNSON

IT SEEMS LIKE BRIAN JOHNSON AND AC/DC have been in my life since I was born. But doing this interview left me dead to rights! Brian's storytelling, humility, and sense of humor, combined with the melodic lyricism of his British accent, had me smiling so wide and laughing so hard that my face hurt when we finally finished talking.

Brian's iconic voice burst onto the world stage after AC/DC's original singer, Bon Scott, passed away in 1980. Bon was a rock 'n' roll legend, and Brian stepping into his shoes could have easily meant the end. Of Brian. And AC/DC.

How can you replace someone so beloved? There's really only three things you can do: honor the past, hire Brian Johnson, then hang on tight.

AC/DC's first record with Brian was *Back in Black*, the second highest-selling record of all time. *The what*? The second highest. Of all time. They've sold over 200 million records, have been inducted into the Rock & Roll Hall of Fame, and Brian Johnson, with his trademark newsboy cap upon his head, is one of the main reasons why.

And to me that makes good, good sense...

Who first exposed you to singing?

Well, it's kind of a strange thing. I was born in a mining village in the northeast of England called Dunston. We didn't have a record player. There was a radio, but there were no pop songs on at the time. It was pretty bleak. But I was in the Sea Scouts and every year they had a thing called The Gang Show where all the scouts from the area got together and put on this show, and I ended up signin' a lot of the lead songs. Then, the local Catholic Choir asked me if I wanted to sing in the choir, and you got paid two schillings and sixpence. I went, "Wow!" After three weeks, I became head choir boy, got a gold thing 'round me neck, and I *got four schillings* for mass on Sunday. *This was big time*. I hope you realize I'd broken into the big time at fourteen years of age. It was fuckin' wonderful.

So, the church led the singer of AC/DC to this?

What happened was, one afternoon on a Saturday, the TV came on, and this beautifully plummy BBC voice said [*mimics a regal British accent*], "And now for something quite different. We have a young man from America, and his name is Little Richard singing 'Tutti Frutti.'" Suddenly, it cut to this dapper fella with the fuckin' hair back, standin' in front of this piano and he went "A-wop-bop-a-loo-lop-a-lop-bom-bom. Tutti frutti!" My jaw dropped. I'd never heard *anything* like it in me life. And that was me gone.

That must have been such an incredible thing to see firsthand.

I didn't have a record. I was *never* gonna hear this thing again. But a couple of days later, I was walking back from school, and I heard it coming out of this house. I ran round and banged on the door. This woman said, "What do you want?" I said, "That record. C-c-c-could you put it on again, please?" She said, "Go to the window." She opened the window and played it again. Then she came out on the front step and did the hand jive. She taught me how to do that. That was it. That song changed everything for me.

Well, I love that you said that because as much as I love The Beatles, people usually tell that story and it's The Beatles or Elvis, and Little Richard is the guy that always gets overlooked. *He's the king of rock 'n' roll!*

Ab-so-lute-ly. And I never got it out of me.

Were you emulating anyone when you started out?

I just wanted to sing like him. And God love us, *I could!* I was fifteen, The Stones, The Beatles, they weren't big yet, but the buzz was starting to happen, and *everybody* was starting bands. There was only one problem: I didn't have any money. There were four kids in our family. Me dad wasn't exactly what you would call a top earner, and the wages there were pretty piss poor. I remember going with me dad to Miller's Music Store in Newcastle and buying a 10-watt Selma amplifier and a microphone. It came to twenty-three pounds and six schillings, and I had to pay it back. *With pride*. [*Laughs*] I'll never forget, we basically rehearsed early Stones and Chuck Berry songs, and my voice was high. I was goin' [*sings "Walkin' the*

Dog" by Rufus Thomas] "Baby's back, dressed in black!" I was just up there. I couldn't help it! And I sang with me eyes tight shut, just in case I was rotten, because I'd never sung with guitars and all that before. I suddenly thought, *Oh, this is fuckin' cool*. I enjoyed it.

How did you find your own voice?

It just came out. I thought I had a high voice until [producer] "Mutt" Lange gotta hold of me for *Back in Black*. He said to me "Eh, you know, Brian, I think we can go a little higher." I was goin', "Are you fuckin' kiddin'?" He went, "No." And it was there, I couldn't believe it. Of course, when I first heard Robert Plant doin' his stuff, I'm goin', *Look at that*. He gave a polished feel to that high end voice, that beautiful sustained strength. When you think about it, a lot of people sing from the stomach. I never did. That's why there's always a pained look when I'm really reachin', 'cause I'm singin' through the neck. That's what I sing through.

That's what's so crazy to me. The work horse nature of your voice is just so impressive. The durability it must have to crank out all those ball busting rockers night after night. You're all sandpaper and sawdust, man. How the hell do you do it?

It *does hurt*. It was getting to a point where the sets and the gigs were getting longer until I said, "Listen, this is fuckin' daft." I've never lost me voice. *I never. Ever. Lost me voice*. If I did, I sang through it.

I'm starting to think that maybe singers who came up in bars have a strength to that muscle in a way that others don't.

Before I joined AC/DC, I was in Geordie. We played all the clubs and pubs, and you had to sing a variety of songs. You had to entertain the workin' man, so you had to do Bob Seger, and Zeppelin, Free, Joe Cocker, and you had to do it good. We used to play about five, six nights a week, and it never bothered me. But once I got into the high end, doin' AC/DC stuff, you got a lot more responsibility. This is a big band that people don't expect second best. So, I'm pleased you're doin' this for singers, and the voices, because a guitarist can get up there and play through the flu. They break a string, or the drummer breaks a skin, they're replaced instantly. A singer, that's all you've got. There's nothin' to replace if you're fucked.

What you've accomplished as a singer is astounding. AC/DC was about to make their seventh album before you joined the band. *Their seventh album!* That's a lot.

[*Laughs*] I know.

And for fans who were already locked in and in love, that's such a hard thing to penetrate. Especially because Bon Scott is one of the greatest singers in rock 'n' roll history, and then he tragically passes away. I read an interview with Angus Young where he said that Bon saw you live with Geordie and really dug your voice, so they called you in for an audition. Within months, you're off recording *Back in Black*. Then the album comes out, and you literally pull off the impossible: you're embraced. By

the whole world. *Back in Black* goes on to become the second highest selling record *OF ALL TIME!*
[*Cracks up*] Who woulda thunk?

But that does not happen without the one thing that will be scrutinized above everything else when the record comes out—*your voice*.
Well, thank you so much, Jason, that's very nice of ya, but I never think about it like that. Bon *had* mentioned my name. Geordie were playin' a gig in Torquay, and the band that were on before us was Bon's band. It was a freezing cold night. I remember it like it was yesterday. Bon didn't look anything like Bon did now; he was playing flute and singing. [*JTG laughs*] He had a little beard and all that—it was a bit of a hippie band—and then, I started singin'. And I had this *severe pain* at my side, and I went down.

What do you mean?
It was an appendicitis type thing. I was goin' "Whuughghh" on the stage, but I kept on singin'. [*Laughs*] I think that impressed him. I was in fuckin' agony, but I just kept on goin'. [Rhythm guitarist] Malcolm Young told me Bon said, "I gotta tell ya, this guy, what an act!" [*Laughter*] He thought I was doin' a James Brown. [*Exhaustedly*] "I can't go on, man. I can't go on." I was just young and full of spunk and vinegar. I was unbeatable. Nothin' could knock us down. But it was so wonderful that he remembered me. It was a lovely, lovely way to get the gig.

So, Malcolm remembered what Bon had said and gave you a ring?
The telephone rang and this woman said [*in a German accent*], "You are Brian Johnson? You must come to London to audition for ziz band." I went, "Well, who are they?" She went, "Ziz, I cannot tell you." [*Laughs*] As always, AC/DC, just *surrounded* in mystery. I said, "Well, I'm not drivin' down to London to jam with some band. I don't even know who they are." She said, "No, *you must come!*" It's about a five-hour drive from Newcastle, so I drove down to Vanilla studios and had a game of pool with the crew. Somebody came out and said, "Has anybody seen that Geordie boy called Brian?" I went, "Oh, that's me," and he said, "The fuck you doin' playin' pool? The boys are up here waitin' for ya!"

You were playing pool instead of jamming with AC/DC? [*Laughter*]
I went upstairs and there they were. Malcolm came up, shook me hand and said, "Here's a bottle of Newcastle." I said, "I could fuckin' murder this. Thanks, mate." The lot was goin', "What do you wanna do?" I thought to meself, *If I do one of their songs, I'm already stuck behind the 8-ball.* So, I said, "Do you know 'Nutbush City Limits,' Tina Turner, in the key of A?" They started playin' and I went, "That's the fucker!" [*Sings*] "Church house, jailhouse!"

Man, they must have been so stoked.
You could see that somethin' had hit somebody between the eyes somewhere. Then they said, "Can you do any of our songs?" I said, "'Whole Lotta Rosie?' I do that with me little

band." That was basically it. I got a call from Malcolm and he said, "Would you like to make an album? We're goin' to the Bahamas next week." I said, "Where the fuck is that?" That's how dumb I was! I went out there and met with "Mutt" Lange and they said, "Can you write lyrics?" I said, "Well, I'll give it a shot." Literally. That was it. The rest is history.

Did you feel the weight of Bon's spirit upon you as you recorded the vocals?
Yes. Absolutely. At the very beginning. Then, absolutely not, because of the work rate. We were only there six weeks and we had to get it done. It was just every day, "Have you got the lyrics ready for this?" Like at the start of "Rock 'N' Roll Ain't Noise Pollution," "Mutt" just went, "Brian, could you just say something over [*hums the opening guitar riff*]. And I kid you not, I had a cigarette in me hand, which you can hear, and I just walked up to the mic and said [*quotes his opening vocal vamp that ends with*] "'cause rock 'n' roll ain't no riddle, man. To me it makes good, good sense." "Mutt" went, "Yeah, I suppose that'll do." [*Cackles*] So, needs as needs must, and we needed to do that right then, right there. That shit just came right out. And I'm pleased to this day that it does make good, good sense. Still.

Not a bad first run, my friend.
Yeah, the only trouble is, after thirty years, you still have to sing the same fuckin' songs! [*Laughter*] The funny thing is, I can still do it, and it just makes us so happy. The thing that got me at the end was me ears. I just couldn't hear anymore, and that was a dreadful thing. But it's one of the hazards of the job. I'm seventy-two now, and I just wanna finish the way I started, up onstage.

Did you ever have any vocal training?
Of course not. We once had this nasty manager who said, [*pompously*] "Right, we should spread our wings on this, Brian. I'm gonna send you to a vocal coach." I went, "What for?" He said, "Well, I think we should change the style of some of the singing. We should change the clothes too." I said, "What do you mean, change our clothes? We wear fuckin' t-shirts and jeans, that's it." And he said, "We'll see about that."

Did you go?
I'll go anywhere. So, I went along to this woman, God bless her cotton socks, who had a list of clients you wouldn't believe. But most of them were musical stars from the theater. She said, [*in a posh accent*] "Right, Brian, I want you to get ahold of the end your tongue and pull it out, and [*speaks in gibberish as if holding his tongue*] I said, "Not in this fuckin' lifetime." [*Laughter*] She said, "It opens up your stomach to your..." I said, "But I sing outta me neck." [*Whispers mischievously*] "Keep the fee, and don't tell anybody I didn't stay. Come on, can I take you for dinner?" She went, "Oh. Absolutely!" She was a lovely lass, but I think a lot of that is beyond someone like me. I can't think and sing. It's a spontaneous thing. And it toughens your voice up, it does. It's like Roger [Daltrey]. He's up there all the time, just givin' it whatever he can, and he's *still* fuckin' great.

Yeah, the only thing I can think is that from all your early years singing Bob Seger and Tina Turner, it trains your throat in a way. Like how a percussionist's hands are calloused. It does that in your throat; it forms it like a rock.

It does, and it's a great apprenticeship to play all these songs. "Just take those old records off the shelf." And, of course, Zeppelin. We even did a Satchmo [Louis Armstrong] song. And it taught you, so when you come to do your own, you would *know* how to end a line. You would just *know* what sounded good before the chorus came in.

Are you nervous or confident before you perform?

I think anxious is the word. *I gotta remember the fuckin' words*, which is an awful thing when you're learnin' a shitload of songs all in one shot. When I first went out with AC/DC, the very first gig was terrifying. It was a month before *Back in Black* was released, and we were playin' one of those new Euro halls in Belgium. I was pacin' in the back, tryin' to remember allllll these songs, and I came out, and there were all these signs: RIP BON ~ GOOD LUCK, BRIAN. I went, "Oh, look at this." [*JTG laughs*] The band started, and we did "Shot Down in Flames," and then we did "Bad Boy Boogie," and to this day, I don't know which lyrics I sang to which song. I mean it. I was so fuckin' shell shocked when I walked out. But the great thing about AC/DC for me was that I didn't have to be the front man—which I never fuckin' liked anyway. [Lead guitarist] Angus [Young] was the iconic figure out front. I would sing me bit, turn round, and walk back to Mal and it had this great symmetric thing about, like all the boys at the back. Nobody wanted to be in the limelight. Angus was just off. Seriously, he's just off, he's taken. Taken by the Angus devil. [*Laughter*]

Do you still get nervous before you perform?

I never get nervous, but I'm twitchy 'cause in the back of your mind, you're only as good as your last gig. You do one rotten gig where you're out of tune and people who've watched you for twenty-five years will go, "Oh, I saw him last year, he was crap. I'm not comin' back." And you're goin', "Hang on a minute, lads. It was a bad night." The worst thing is now people are recording shows from their iPhones. I think they should be banned. Some of these female entertainers spend eight, nine million on a beautiful show, a set full of surprises and dancers and different effects, and then some fucker films it all so people know what's gonna happen next. It's just not fair. They're cheatin' the public. And the music sounds *awful* on those things. *It's a fucking phone.* But unfortunately, these guys are just givin' the game away, spoilin' it for the people. A lot of singers now, you can hear them sayin', "Put your phone down. Please, join in with me here."

It is wild when you see people watching this incredible technicolor show through this tiny, little screen, and you're like, *What are you doing?*

It's daft. It's like people smokin' three packs of cigarettes a day. *They have to have their phone.*

When are you gonna watch it? You're not gonna watch it again.

They send it out, [*in a moronic voice*] "This was me last night." It's all about the fucking ego and what a great dude they are.

Alright, enough of them. Do you do vocal warm-ups before your shows?

No. I walk into the nearest toilet or shower and just go, [*screeches at the top of his lungs, raising the volume of his voice*] "Eeeeeeeeeee-YOU!" I'm ready!

That's it?

That's it.

One time?

That's it.

Oh my God. Do you have any rituals before you hit the stage?

I walk back and forward singing the lyric to the first song 'cause it's usually one off the new album, and I don't wanna be seen lookin' at the cheat screen. It has to be full on, confident, loud, proud, BANG! I just go back and forward, back and forward, and recite these words again and again, and then I feel good.

Are you just reciting or are you singing it full on?

I'm singing it. Just to meself. Then, I'll stop and chuck some water down us 'cause I know I'm gonna be sweatin'. You just dehydrate so badly on that stage. I take a bottle of electrolytes on with me. Sometimes you can touch my skin and it stays white. We *always* need oxygen when we come off. Angus is just a bundle of rags when he comes off. Literally. He has to have oxygen for at least four or five minutes because right to the end he's chuckin' himself around like a fuckin' maniac. None of us are gettin' any younger, ya know? But that's the great thing about this band: nobody can tell. We just keep on doin' daft shit. [*Laughter*]

Is there anything after the show that helps keep your voice in shape?

I go straight for a glass of wine!

How do you take care of your voice on the road?

When we have a day off, I just stay in me room and don't talk. That's literally all you can do. Just self-imposed silence. Keep quiet and drink lots of water, big bottles of water. I just pound 'em, pound 'em, pound 'em. Get room service. It can be kinda lonely on a long tour, but everybody's got their own way of gettin' through it.

When you start getting sick, what do you do?

You get a doctor in! A lot of guys carry these pills with 'em, like a steroid pill, which I don't believe in. It's the "Get Out Clause" if the throat's completely fucked up. But you're only good for two or three hours. It's like Cortisone for a football player to get 'em through the game. You're doin' irreparable damage 'cause you can't feel anything.

Are there songs where you hope your voice will be there that night?
There are songs that are tougher. "Back in Black" is a very difficult song to sing, mainly because of the breathing. "Shoot to Thrill" is another one. If you try singin' that and catchin' your breath at the same time, it becomes a bit of an art. Especially when you finish, you go, "Yes! I've done it thirty-five years ago, and I've just done it exactly the same." [*Laughter*]

Are there songs where you've had to adjust the key live?
Yeah, I think we started that on the Black Ice Tour. We took it down just a smidgen, but it was a smidgen enough to make everybody happy, 'cause it weren't just me, even the backing vocals on some of them *Back in Black* songs, or "For Those About To Rock," [*sings the high backing vocal*] "We salute you!" So, just to make it comfortable. And of course, we're playin' a lot longer than we used to. In the early days, it was like an hour and ten minutes. Now it's like two and half. *Paul McCartney does fuckin' three!*

Well, the more hits you have, the harder it becomes!
[*Laughs*] I know! "*We can't leave that out!*"

What was your most embarrassing vocal mishap ever?
We had a big wreckin' ball onstage, and I used to climb up on it and sing "Ballbreaker." They'd send me up there on this thing, and they'd swing it. It was fuckin' scary up there, I'm tellin' ya. I could only hang on with one hand 'cause I had the mic in me right hand. So, they sent me up and to start it swingin' they gave a little jut, and I grabbed the rope with both hands, and dropped the fuckin' mic. [*JTG cracks up*] It was like forty feet below, and I'm looking down at the guy that's doin' the swingin', goin', "I'VE DROPPED THE FUCKIN' MIC!" He just waved back at me. Of course, the band have got their heads down, goin' [*hums the guitar riff*]. And as I'm gettin' angrier, the ball started to spin. I'm goin', "SOMEBODY GET ME DOWN!!!" I think it was Mal looked up, "What's wrong with him?" Nobody could figure it out. I pointed and said, "Look!" and there was me mic. I thought, *Are they gonna let us down?* NO. Somebody tried to get the mic and throw it up to me! I went, "That's not gonna..." By the time we got down, the song was nearly finished. [*Laughter*]

Do you remember a performance where you surprised yourself?
That's a tough one because there's so many memories. You just go in and try the best you can, and you get surprised afterwards when you hear it and you go, "Oh wow, that's not fuckin' bad. I got a hold of that one."

How are you with hearing your own voice?
I'm fine with it. But you very rarely hear an AC/DC song in my house, mainly because people think you're a fuckin' creep if ya do.

Do you have a favorite vocal performance you're really proud of?

It's not somethin' I would like to talk about. I would just be embarrassed.

Well, do you have a favorite vocal performance of Bon's that you really love?

Yeah, I think "Ride On." It just sums it all up. [*Sings*] "I'm gonna ride on, ride on." It's just beautiful. He was a poet, Bon, he really was. He's one of me favorite rock 'n' roll singers and he just came up with some amazing stuff. Amazing lyric, cheeky but fun, to the point, naughty, sexy, dirty, bad lad, dangerous—all those good things.

One of my favorite vocals of yours is "Safe in New York City." There's a sneakiness about some of the melodies you do to switch up the chorus. It's really intricate, almost invisible, but it does so much energetically to keep the song moving. That tune ran the risk of being monotone and one-note, but you're doin' these really cool inflection points.

[*Sings*] "I feel safe in New York City." That was good. I remember we felt a lot for that as we were doin' it. When I sing in the studio, I don't sing with the headphones on and a big mic hanging down with a fishnet on it. I stand behind the board with the producer and the engineer. I have an old SM54 in me hand and no headphones, just the music there—obviously not too loud, that would be bad—but you can *just about* hear my voice through the microphone.

What's that do for you?

What you get from me is basic raw power because that makes me want to perform. If I can't perform, I can't sing the song how it should be sung. If you see the lads just tappin' their feet, you go, "Yeah." I jump around, I knock shit over. It's terrible, I get carried away, but to me, it's just bein' part of the band, bein' part of the process, instead of bein' in a studio with a box around us. That's my way I like to do it, and it's worked quite well, so I'm pleased with it.

The intro of "Thunderstruck" was instantly iconic the second it came out. [*Sings the background vocal part*] "Ahh-ahh-ah-ah-ah-aa-aa-aa—Thunder!" Can you walk me through how you guys recorded the vocals for that?

We knew it had to be a team effort, so we all went in. [Bassist] Cliff Williams was one of the main contributors. Him and Malcolm were the main ones. They double tracked their voices. It had to be punchy, and it had to be real sinister. That all just came together perfectly, all the way up to [*sings the first line*] "I was caught in the middle of a railroad track." The syncopation was just brilliant. And then, Angus put on that unbelievable guitar. I remember as soon as I heard it, goin', "Fuuuuuck. Everybody's gonna wanna learn to play that." The boys have this thing with riffs. They really do just come up with the most wonderful things. Kind of a lost art now, isn't it?

There's no better riffs in rock than AC/DC.

It's just a joy for a singer to walk into that. It really is still one of me favorite tracks. What I love about AC/DC is the "Yob Vocals," which was named by "Mutt" 'cause he said the backing vocals in AC/DC are nothing more than a bunch of yobs in the corner goin' [*mimics thuggish, gang backing vocals*] "YAAAAAA!" It worked.

What's changed the most about your voice since you started?

I think it got bluesier. I think it got feel. It got more experienced, more educated, and warmer *I'd like to think*. And I've learned to enjoy it more. When I first started, it just seemed so important. It had to be just perfect and right. Now, you don't worry. You know what's gonna come out, and it's cool. You can mess with songs. With "Back in Black," I can actually bend the notes in there now and again, just makin' 'em a bit more floaty. I like doin' that. Rather than painting by numbers, I can go in and make the song me own. That's what every singer wants to do, make it their own. Even if there's better singers than them, they'll never sing it like that.

If you could duet with one singer—living or dead—who would it be?

McCartney. Or Roy Orbison! Or Paul Rodgers! Joe Cocker! Bob Seger, I never sung with him. I'd love to do it. I mean, fuckin' hell, I'd love to do it with Satchmo!

Brian, you gotta pick one.

One? [*Sighs hard*] I'd have to say McCartney because Roy Orbison's too fuckin' high. He'd make us look stupid.

Who are your top five favorite singers of all time?

Robert Plant. Paul Rodgers. Elvis. Little Richard. Roy Orbison.

If you could ask any singer about their voice, who would it be, and what would you ask?

Satchmo. I would talk to him because Satchmo always said he didn't have a voice. He called himself a "Non-singer," which fascinated me because I think he's fucking brilliant. That's why he never got the words right. He'd just scat, [*does an incredible, spot-on, imitation of Louis Armstrong scatting*] "Boo-boo-daa-daa-boo-boo-vaaa-vaaa-boo-boo-zzzeee." He was just fantastic. When I first heard that song ["A Kiss to Build a Dream On"] it was [*sings a straight-laced rendition of the verse*]. It was shite. HE got a hold of it, and it was, "Bom! Bom!" [*Mimics Armstrong*] "Give me a kiss to build a dream on, and my imagination." And then, when he rocked, he rocked the fuckin' joint. I'm just fascinated how anybody could call that a non-singing voice, 'cause singing is how you express yourself from the heart, from the soul, from your very being. He was creatin' his own style. I wouldn't know what to ask Satchmo, really, because he probably wouldn't know the answer. He would probably just look at you and go, "Man, I don't fuckin' know."

That's probably what you're thinkin' about me!

It's a toughie talkin' about your own voice, 'cause, to me, I'm just another guy doin' a gig and havin' enormous fun doin' it. There's ups and there's downs. But, thank you, Jason, for puttin' up with me blather.

NORAH JONES

I F YOU HAVEN'T TRULY FOLLOWED Norah Jones' career, then you've been had. I know, she was everywhere when her debut album came out. No matter where you were, no matter who you are, we all heard *Come Away with Me*. You couldn't escape it. And sometimes that can seal the deal on how we view an artist.

The album sold over 27 million copies, won five Grammy Awards including Album of the Year, Record of the Year, and Best New Artist. And she was only twenty-two years old. I think I crashed my Camaro at twenty-two. So, who's the real winner?

But if *Come Away with Me* is how you think of Norah Jones, then come away with me and go deeper. This is a catalog, baby!

With her alluring tone and inspired skill, Norah can glide through any genre— jazz, country, blues, folk, and pop—and make it all sound cohesive. But what's most impressive is her down to earth approach to her instrument. She knows she's at her best when she can just "Sing the Story." Whether she's doing it with Dolly Parton, Ray Charles, Willie Nelson, or by herself, Norah is truly touched by something else.

I guess it doesn't hurt to be the stepfather of Jesus.

Who first exposed you to singing?

All music was pretty much through my mom. She used to send cassettes of us talking to her sister who lived overseas at the time. This was early '80s, so it was easier than phone calls, funner than a letter, and it was how they would communicate. So, there's a tape of me singing along to Pavarotti somewhere aged two or three, and I'm pretty sure it was "O Holy Night."

Of course you were already singing Pavarotti that young!

I was in a children's choir at age three or four. I grew up in Grapevine, Texas, and we went to this Methodist Church that had this amazing choir director. I remember taking it very seriously, listening very hard to her, and enunciating because she told us to "*E-nun-ci-ate*." To the point where all the other kids were looking at me like, *What is your problem?* I'm like, "What? I'm just doing what she said." [*Laughter*] But I got the solo at age four because I was really doin' it good! Then I had another solo at age five or six in the church program, which was like a musical. The choir performed "Our God is an Awesome God," and the teenage girl got a solo, and then, I got a solo doin' something else. It was like I always got the solos, so I just felt good singing.

Were you trying to sound like anyone when you started out?

Mimicking is something that was fun for me, and growing up, that was how I learned to sing; singing along with Aretha Franklin and trying to mimic Sarah Vaughan, who had an incredibly unique way of singing. So, I have my Sarah Vaughan impression, my Billie Holiday phase, my Aretha...attempts. [*Laughter*] I've gone through many phases of mimicking.

So, how did you find your own voice?

When I was in high school, I was still into jazz and mimicking all these other singers. But I am so clearly not gonna sound like any of them in real life. I had this great Etta James album where she did the songs of Billie Holiday, but sounding like Etta James. I have this recording of me doing "I'll be Seeing You," but ripping off the exact Etta James version of the old Billie Holiday version. It's like a real game of telephone. If you listen to them back-to-back, I'm imitating it exactly, but I still don't sound like Etta James! I sound like me! At a certain point, I feel like no matter how much you're trying to mimic, your own voice starts comin' out and there's very little you can do to stop that.

Did you ever have any other vocal training besides the choir?

No, but I was in choirs from then on. I even auditioned for the part of Mary in the church play. She had a really beautiful solo. I got cast as Joseph! [*Laughter*] *And I was sooo pissed*. I was like a foot shorter than the girl cast as Mary. But it was my first time using a microphone. The microphone had been hung from the ceiling of the gymnasium just to pick up the sound from the stage. I have a video of me doing my song as Joseph. The entire video, my neck is craned up, and I'm trying to make myself taller, just staring at the microphone the whole time and trying to sing into it. A very tiny, frail, little Joseph. Father of Jesus. Or do they call him the stepfather of Jesus?

That's a good question!

[*Cracks up*] He *is* a stepdad!

If you don't write a song called "Joseph was a Stepdad," I'm gonna be pretty upset.
"Joseph was a Stepdad," that would be great! [*Laughs*]

Like Springsteen, [*earnestly sings*] "Joseph was a stepdad."
[*Joins in, mimicking Bruce*] "Joseph was a stepdad."

So, you had a pretty confident upbringing when it came to your voice.
Yeah. Middle school choir is where I had all these hardcore teacher ladies who were really into warming-up and that kinda stuff, so I definitely don't feel like I was untaught. I had been taking piano lessons though, so I knew a lot about music theory already.

Are you nervous or confident before you perform?
If I'm doing a song I don't know that well, I'm nervous. But usually I'm not, no.

Do you do vocal warm-ups before shows?
Yeah, and I have for about ten years. Because your voice is a muscle, right?

That's what they're telling me.
[*Laughs*] So, when you're young, it's sort of fluid and supple and forgiving. But I found in my late-twenties that I actually had more control over it when I warmed-up.

What do your warm-ups look like?
It's the simplest thing. I just do [*sings scales*] "Du-du-du-du-du-du-du" up and down. I start as low as I can, I go as high as I can. And then I go back, all the way down.

You do this right before you go on?
I started doing it before soundcheck because at soundcheck, you don't want to blow it out and hurt yourself. I don't usually do it again. If I do it once a day, I'm good, as long as it's not too early in the morning.

Is there anything after the show that helps keep your voice in shape?
I've heard that you're supposed to warm-down, but I've actually never done it. I always forget. I guess it's like stretching after you run or something. Is that what it is?

I've never done a warm-down in my life, but I've had a bunch of people say that they recommend it. So, now I'm like, *Okay, do I do this?* And then, I hear Norah Jones doesn't do it, and then I have to question that. But you obviously have to do what works for you.
You do have to do what works for you.

It does seem to make sense though. I'll probably give it a go after the next show.

You also have to remember that age really does affect your voice, just like it affects your whole body, all your muscles. It's so much harder as you get older, but also better. I like the way my voice is with age. I always wanted to be old so I could get that old lady voice.

There is something beautiful about an aged, experienced, and weathered voice.

Some of my favorite Joni Mitchell records are from the '90s when her voice was like a completely different person. She went from having that high sort of soprano, to this low, like smokey—she's a lifelong smoker, so maybe that contributed to it. I remember smoking in my twenties and thinking, *Maybe I'll scratch my voice up a little, rough it up*. Then, this singer friend said, "You know, when you're smoking, it's like if you were a guitar player and you're just dragging your guitar behind you on the ground. That's what smoking is like for a singer." I was like, Oh my God! Talk about shaming me! I quit right after that.

How do you take care of your voice on the road?

I can't go to bars and talk loud. That's the main killer. Don't blab your head off to somebody at a bar. Just sit and listen! [*Cracks up*]

Are there songs where you wonder if your voice will be there that night?

Yeah, there are. I've always been this sort of quiet, hushed singer, but I've definitely stretched out more and written some new songs that have parts that are kind of intense. Sometimes I go for it, and sometimes I do the interpretive dance version where it's not quite the same note as on the record. [*Laughs*] I sing the note lower. But I'm also not the kind of singer that strains a lot. I'm not like an acrobat out there.

Are there songs where you've had to adjust the key live?

Yes, but more the opposite: higher. Sometimes the husky sort of thing is awesome when I'm recording, but it's a little harder to pull off live, so I've pitched up a couple times. There's maybe one song from my first record that I put down a half step. But it's less that I can't hit it and more that you don't want it to come off strained.

What was your most embarrassing vocal mishap ever?

Dolly Parton invited me to sing with her on the Country Music Awards, and it was like a dream come true. I had done a song of hers on a tribute record, and she loved my version so much she flew me down. We had dinner, we rehearsed, and she offered me her tour bus to get ready with her. I mean, her hair lady did my hair. It was like the funnest. And she's the coolest, right?

She's amazing!

So, we're doing the song, and she does her verse and then I come to my verse, and I'm singing and just hit a turkey! I'm just like, *What the hell?* [*Laughter*] It's not a hard song, it's not like a high note I can't hit, it's literally just a melody note in the song, and I don't know what happened. Just like "Eeee-awww!" So, that was funny, but what're you gonna do?

I love "Creepin' In" off your *Feels Like Home* record with you and Dolly singing together. You got that great Dolly laugh at the end of the track as well. What was she laughing at?

I feel like she laughs a lot! I don't think it was a joke or anything. But she came in, and most people pre-record stuff, but I was like, "No, we gotta do this live with Dolly! Let's do it right!" I'm not gonna bring Dolly in here and then my band won't actually get to play with her.

You're amazing. That's such a cool thing to do.

Well, it's kind of normal, but it's not anymore, right? She was just a delight. We did one or two takes, and it was super thrilling. The tempo went up a lot because everybody was so excited.

I think harmony vocals are a real art form, and you're so natural at it. What's the key to doing a great harmony vocal?

Ohhh, now you're talking my language. I have to fight not putting harmonies on everything possible. I think if I hadn't have become successful, I would be a harmony singer for whoever wants it. [*Laughs*] In fact, I'll still do it.

But is there a key to doing a harmony just right? My natural, untrained instinct is to veer off into the other person's melody. So, you gotta really stand guard.

I think if it's too perfect, it's too perfect, actually. I mean, you have to be in tune enough, right? That's a given. Sometimes if you move exactly with the melody, like all the same turns, a third up or a fourth up, it's too angular sounding, and you have to kind of be fluid. Aretha Franklin's records had some of the most amazing harmony singing. And Dolly's one of the best. You ever look at those old videos of her and Emmylou [Harris] and Linda Ronstadt?

Yeah. And I recently heard a tune where Neil Young sings with them too!

Oh yeah, he's also a great harmony singer. So is Willie Nelson. I remember the first time I sang with Willie. I was opening for him in San Francisco before my first album came out. They asked if I wanted to sit in with him and I said, "Yeah, but I don't understand how this works. Am I not gonna meet him before I go onstage? What the hell?" [*Laughs nervously*] That's so weird, right? Same thing happened to me with Bob Dylan.

That's really wild.

But Willie is such an easy, giving musician. He sang his line, then looked at me and kind of nodded, and I knew exactly where I was supposed to sing. When it came time to do the part together, I wasn't sure whether to take the melody or harmony 'cause we hadn't talked about it, but Willie will do whatever you're not doing. So, as soon as I started with the melody, and I was gettin' ready to jump to the harmony, he started with the harmony. Then, I jumped to the harmony, and he jumped back down to the melody. He's always listening and knows exactly where there's space and takes that.

So, your approach to harmonies is that they shouldn't be too perfect, and what else?
You really just wanna get out of your head, forget all the warm-ups, forget all the training, and be in the moment. You just wanna tell the person the story. You wanna sing the story. But you don't wanna think about singing too much. *You don't wanna be thinking about singing at all*. You just wanna be delivering the story. That can be said about all music and all instruments, but for singing, especially, because people relate to the human voice in ways that they don't relate to piano or saxophone or drums. It's so primitive, and it just goes straight to your heart. *If it does!* [*Laughter*]

Do you remember a performance where you surprised yourself?
On my first record we did this cover of a JD Loudermilk song that I had learned from Nina Simone called "Turn Me On." Our version was not like Nina Simone's. I just loved the song, and she's someone who I've loved for so long. But there's this part in the end where I'm like, [*sings a beautiful run on the word "you"*] in a soul singer way that I am usually not able to do at all, but it was an accident! I have a lot of limitations with my voice. I can't roll like those runs Stevie Wonder does. In gospel and Indian music, they do it a lot. I didn't really do *that*, but there's a little thing I do that I've never been able to do again. [*Laughter*] But I'm glad we got it on tape!

How are you with hearing your own voice?
I'm okay listening to it if it's right. I hate it if it's wrong. If I'm not capturing what I wanna convey, I'm not into it. I HATE my speaking voice. Like whenever you're listening to a recording and you catch a bit of the beginning or the end, like, [*speaks cartoonishly high*] "Oh, that was a great take!" It's like, "Oh my God, shut up."

Do you have a favorite vocal performance you're really proud of?
Nothing's coming to mind. But the natural thing is always better. The overthought take is not ever good. Like "Don't Know Why," which was my hit on the first record.

Never heard it.
[*Laughs*] That was the first take we recorded in a demo session before I got a record deal. When I got the record deal, we remade the album, but the song didn't have the magic, so we ended up using the demo, and that became the first single. It was like "The hit." It just had a natural quality about it, and that's the important thing for me. That take conveyed the story, and in the end, that's the most important thing.

That's why I love your voice so much on "Tryin' to Keep It Together," because it sounds like you're really trying to keep it together.
Ohhh! Thanks! I was! [*Laughs*]

It's so haunting and lonely, almost like we're hearing your inner thoughts.

Yeah, I was having a little bit of a hot mess moment.

If you could duet with one singer—living or dead—who would it be?

Johnny Cash. There's something so special about a baritone. It's rare. Also, he just seemed like such a special human. I loved his music so much, and it was so conducive to harmonies. But he was such a storyteller and had a beautiful voice. I don't think I've ever sang with someone who has a deep baritone since choir.

He's also the one person you haven't sung with.

Yeah, I've gotten to duet with a lot of my favorites. Ray Charles, Willie, Dolly...

...Mavis, Tony Bennett. I mean, the heaviest hitters of all time.

Oh my God. Mavis makes me wanna cry just thinkin' about her. She's so incredible. The Staples Singers, I mean, the harmonies on those albums. But it doesn't sound like a rehearsed choir. It sounds like they're just tellin' you the story, and that's the key with any singing.

Who are your top five favorite singers of all time?

No, you can't do that. I could do twenty. I'm not gonna do top five, then leave out one of my favorites! It's just too hard!

If you could ask any singer about their voice, who would it be, and what would you ask?

I wouldn't. I just wanna hang out and sing a song. I don't have any questions about singing.

Okay, you're talking to a guy that's writing a book, asking everybody!

I think it's cool that you're writing a book on it! I'm just saying, I don't have any questions! [*Laughter*]

So, you might ask somebody to just sing with you, is what I'm hearing?

Or sing *for* me, *my God*. The best thing about singing with Ray Charles is I got to stand three feet away and listen to Ray Charles sing. I got to be there while he was singing in a tiny room. *And I got to sing with him*, of course, but just hearing that voice that I've heard my whole life, coming from this person who is right there was incredible.

Well, it says a lot about your voice that all the greats have wanted to sing with you.

It's been the most surprising thing about my career, getting to sing with all these different people. It's been my honor. Young people too. Tank from Tank and the Bangas. I did some stuff with Rodrigo Amarante who I *love* singing with. He's Brazilian, he's amazing. Yeah, it's so fun. So fun.

Peter Albin on
JANIS JOPLIN

CEASELESSLY BULLIED BY HER CLASSMATES IN SCHOOL, misunderstood by her parents, and disgusted by the racism in her hometown of Port Arthur, Texas, it wasn't until Janis Joplin opened her mouth to sing that there was suddenly a place for her that made sense.

Finding herself inside the psychedelic, kaleidoscopic, and electrifying Haight-Ashbury music scene of San Francisco, Janis would soon meet Peter Albin, one of the most underrated bass players of the '60s and a founding member of Big Brother and the Holding Company. From there, Janis and Peter would meet the world.

With a voice unlike any other, Janis packed all her loneliness, pain, insecurity, and passion into every syllable she sang, becoming one of the most iconic, exciting, and charismatic singers of all time. Janis and Peter would make two official records together, including *Cheap Thrills*, their second album that shot directly to number one for eight consecutive weeks. It has been included in the National Recording Registry by the Library of Congress, and, along with her solo album, earned Janis a place in the Rock & Roll Hall of Fame, the Grammy Hall of Fame, and a Lifetime Achievement Award from the Recording Academy.

Janis' life was tragically cut short in her late twenties. But the power of her voice will live forever, reminding all of us that we are loved and not alone.

When was the first time you heard Janis sing?

It must have been in '63 or '64 because she was out here in the folk music days. I was doing a sort of bluegrass, old-timey duo with my brother called The Liberty Hill Aristocrats. The first time I saw Janis was at the studio called KPFA for a show called *The Midnight Special*. It was like a circle of chairs around a huge hanging microphone, and each person or group had a chance to sing a song. Janis was sitting right beside me with her guitar. My brother and I did some old-timey country song and then, I looked over at this gal who looked a little disheveled and off the street. She opened up her mouth and started singing, and it was in-fucking-cred-ible! She was really loud and really good. She sounded like a Bessie Smith, blues type singer with a little bit of country in there.

When did you realize she should sing for Big Brother and the Holding Company?

That happened in early '66. Big Brother was kind of a jam band, and we started looking for a female vocalist. All these other groups like The Great Society and Jefferson Airplane had these great female vocalists. *Why can't we have one?* We started auditioning, and Chet Helms [promoter and counterculture figure deemed "The Father of the Summer of Love"] said, "Do you know Janis Joplin?" I said, "Yeah, I know her from some time ago." He said, "Well, she's back in Texas, but if I work it right, maybe I can get her back out here." She had left on not great terms. Her friends in the early '60s knew she was going in the wrong direction, taking drugs and drinking a lot.

That's right, they got together and basically helped her get back home to sober up.

She was caught stealing wine out of a store, so her friends gave her a one-way ticket back to Port Arthur. "Clean yourself up. Get straight." I even have a copy of her mug shot. But Chet called her, and she liked the fact that there was a band that might want her to sing.

When she arrived back in San Francisco, what was her audition like?

We were pretty loud. *But she's loud! She didn't need a microphone!* At the first rehearsal, we didn't even say, "We'll call you," we said, "Well. Our next gig is Saturday." It was obvious she fit in really well, and very quickly, we started rehearing songs that she knew and brought into our repertoire. And her style started to change. She was into a folk-blues kind of voice when she started singing with us, but she realized that she had to put out more from her diaphragm and sing even louder. So, she really started being a rock 'n' roll blues singer. We were practicing in this old converted firehouse, and we get a knock on the door, and there's two cops standing outside who said, "We've gotten some calls about a woman screaming at this location, and we want to see if there's any problems?" "Oh, no. That's just Janis Joplin singing." [*Laughter*]

How did she approach recording her vocals in the studio? Was she going for whole takes, or was she really meticulous and punching in a lot?

She went for whole takes, and she usually got it around the second or third take. She was a lot more professional than we were.

The "Ball and Chain" performance on *Cheap Thrills*. I'm just gonna step back and you feel free to say what you want.

We were at a club called The Both /And to see Big Mama Thornton, and she sang "Ball and Chain." We went backstage after her first set and asked her, "We'd like to do this song, and maybe we'll change it a little bit here and there, but it's a terrific song. Can you write down the lyrics for us?" She kinda looked at us funny, but she wrote down the lyrics, then handed it to us and said, "Okay, here it is. 'Ball and Chain.' Now don't fuck it up!"

Well, she sure didn't. That vocal performance is easily one of the greatest ever. I love how wrecked her voice gets by the end, but she keeps pushing through and just pulls her guts out and hands 'em to you. That reserve she could find was unbelievable.

Every once in a while she would go back to some reserved space and bring out some line and it was like, *Wow!* And sometimes her voice would crack.

Giving that much to each show, how did she not blow her voice out singing that way?

Sometimes *it would* be a problem. I think she would try to medicate by drinking hard liquor. But that didn't work! [*Chuckles*]

Did she ever do vocal warm-ups before going onstage?

At one point, she went to Judy Davis, a vocal coach famous for doing some work with Barbra Streisand. She said, "You keep singing the way you're singing, your voice will be gone in a couple of months." She was given some warm-up stuff, and maybe she did them by herself, but I don't remember her doing warm-ups at shows. I think after a while she just said, "Screw it. I'm gonna sing the way I sing."

Was Janis nervous or confident before shows?

I don't think she was too nervous. She knew that she was a good singer. *But* she was always asking for reassurance. "Was I good tonight? Did I sound okay? Did I screw this thing up? I don't know."

The *Little Girl Blue* documentary really breaks your heart, just to see how vicious and cruel people can be toward someone who doesn't fit into their idea of beauty, or their flaccid perception of who a person should be. That scene where she goes back to her high school reunion, to this place where she was tormented only a few years earlier. It says so much about her spirit, the way she tried to fight those demons away through singing, and ultimately lost the battle, but won the war. If she could have only known how many people she empowered with her voice.

Yeah, going back to that reunion was like "I'm gonna show you guys," and it didn't turn out that way. It was just the opposite, really, and she was kind of defeated.

It was almost like she was still a freak to them, and even though she was famous, they were never gonna understand her.

Yeah, it's tragic.

But it was amazing how she could channel all that experience through her voice. I don't know that I've ever heard somebody sing more vulnerable. I mean, pleading with men to come back and exposing herself the way she did. In a normal soul song, it might just be a passionate, melodic vocal. But with Janis, it was like, she really means this. It was real. She's really begging right now.

[*Chuckles*] The song is "Women Is Losers." That is definitely a Janis song.

Do you have a favorite vocal performance of hers?

I don't really have any favorite ones, but I do like "Bye, Bye Baby." I like the way she sang that.

When you hear her voice now, what do you remember most?

The pain. I feel like she put herself in some of these painful situations, believing in something that wasn't gonna happen. And those situations are reflected in her voice and in some songs. But other songs she could do in her sleep! [*Laughs*] We were all living together in this big old vacation house, close to the State Park in Marin County. It was made with paper thin walls, hardly any insolation. It was a cold place. We had the fire going most times. I had a child that was just born in May, and this was June. [Guitarist] James Gurley had a child who was about six months old. We're talking about infants who needed their sleep. My wife and I are upstairs, and someone turned on the record player and was playing a Joan Baez record. I could hear "Silver Dagger" or one of those songs, and I thought, *Shit. I have to get up, go downstairs, shut the fucking record player off, and tell these people to be quiet*. So, I go down the stairs and here's Janis with the guitar, singing that song. It wasn't the record player. It sounded just like Joan Baez. But our band will have to take credit for getting her into a rock 'n' roll situation where she really had to sing differently and had to develop her own thing.

SIMON LE BON

I F YOU WERE ALIVE WHEN MTV ARRIVED, chances are this is how you met Simon Le Bon from Duran Duran: racing through the jungles of Sri Lanka in pursuit of a wild and elusive tropical woman with face paint while his bandmates scoured the island searching for him. Or maybe he was singing from the bow of a yacht in Antigua, intercut with various women having fun at the group's expense, toying with them. But what these bastards were really doing was toying with us! Because anybody watching the videos for "Hungry Like the Wolf" or "Rio" at that moment in time all thought the same thing: Duran Duran have the greatest job on earth.

I was a kid at the time, and this was one of the most outrageous things my young eyes had ever seen. The colors, locations, and exotic personalities were as vibrant and enticing as the synthesizers, throbbing bass lines, funky drums, and catchy hooks the band were laying down. And what an adventure it's been.

Simon Le Bon and his Grammy Award–Winning mates have now been inducted into the Rock & Roll Hall of Fame and have sold over 100 million records, making them one of the bestselling bands ever. And Simon's about to give you a master class on everything from voice problems and trade secrets to whole body operations, wasting energy, knowing it's Christmas, and having a view to a kill—onstage and off.

Who first exposed you to singing?

My mom. My earliest childhood memory is lying in a little cot with cream plastic sides. She used to put me down to sleep with a radio on. Back then it was called the Light Service, which is now BBC Radio 3, which was mainly classical music. I remember hearing the music and having an idea in my head of where it was going to go. Then, at four or five years old, I started doing singing competitions and singing in the school choir, but it was my mom who really encouraged me and made me feel that I could do it to begin with. She was a singer herself, but kind of gave it all up to have babies.

Were you emulating anyone when you started out?

Just me singing. That's all it was, definitely.

How did you find your own voice?

It wasn't really the voice, it was the music that I was singing that led me. I just served the music. In a funny way, that's one of the things that remains the same. I believe that what we have to do is serve the song.

Did you ever have any vocal training?

I did have a singing teacher, but she was also my piano teacher, and piano lessons for me were *torture*, absolute torture. I literally had my knuckles rapped with a ruler at times. Then, probably about age nine, a friend from school suggested I join the church choir. So, I joined, and things started happening differently. I had a fantastic choir master. His name is Michael Turvey, member of the British Empire. He's an amazing man. BBC made a documentary about Duran Duran about four years ago, and there's a bit where I go back to my church and we listen to the record that I made *in the church*.

That's right! So, are you nervous or confident before you perform?

Well, I have a mantra and it goes like this: "It's not fear, it's adrenaline. It's just your mind and your body preparing you to do something extraordinary. *And you will* do something extraordinary." If I ever get the butterflies and all that stuff, that always makes it okay and changes the way you feel about being nervous, which is all you can hope for. I heard that from an actor being interviewed on the radio and I decided to make it my own. It might've been John Gielgud. He had a lot of great sayings like that.

Do you do any vocal warm-ups before your shows?

I had an episode in 2011 where we'd been on a very, very intense promotion schedule. We had a press day in Cannes, and then around midnight, we went to the casino to do a performance for Bono's charity. We were doing "All You Need Is Now," and there's a bit where I go, [*scats the lyrics and melody, landing upon the "Whoa-oh!"*]. I reached out for that note and something went *BLINK*, and I thought, *What the?*

I don't like the BLINK. What was it?

It was weird because generally I've got a three-octave range. But I could only get up to A. I was four notes short of my high end. And a lot of our stuff is in the high end. I couldn't work out why I could only get up to a certain note. We managed to kind of busk it to the end, but the next day I woke up, and it was the same problem. We went back to London immediately, and I went to see a voice specialist called John Reuben. Fantastic Otolaryngologist. He got his little camera out and he said, "You've had a bleed on your vocal folds." I had a hemorrhage, and that's why the whole thing shut down. Part of my rehab was going to Ruth Epstein who's a voice pathologist. Magnificent lady, she is, absolutely *wonderful*. She gave me a warm-up file where she does the exercises, and I just sing along with it. It only takes twelve minutes, but at the end of it, I'm ready for anything.

What are the exercises?

You start off with relaxation exercises. You hang your head onto your chest, and you very gently sway it from side to side like you're watching a ball roll across your lap. Then you do your shoulders. You lift your shoulders up and then you relax them. Then you look at the ceiling, but you relax your jaw. And there's funny things that you say like, "Ice, Ice, Ice, Ice, Ice." [*Chuckles*] Whenever I do that part, I can always hear the rest of the band going, "Baby, baby." I usually do it in the corridor, or the toilet, or in the corner of the dressing room. And then, you start making noises like [*does some lip trills, moving up and down the scales*]. And [*makes a "bra" sound, but rolls his tongue along with it*]. And then, you work on your larynx and your pharynx with sort of yawning type things but making sound at the same time. Kind of [*long yawning sigh*] type stuff. It sounds silly, but it really, really works. We do tongue exercises as well.

What's the tongue exercise?

You'll stick your tongue as far out of your mouth as you possibly can, and you'll feel underneath your jaw, that part of it lifts. You're stretching it out as though you're trying to reach somebody across the room with it, or even just down your chin like a member of KISS. [*JTG laughs*] But really push it out there. It does feel a little uncomfortable, but most stretches do. Do that ten times. The other one is humming. You put your tongue at the top of your teeth, and [*sustains a long hum using N*] so you can feel the buzz on your lips, and "Nnnnnnnn-ya! Nnnnnn-ya!" [*Does a few more in short bursts that almost sound like a hyena laughing while doing the scales*] At the end, you finish off with like a siren with your mouth closed, your pharynx engaged, your larynx dropped, and you can feel it in your head. I think it's really saved my voice and really helped me.

Is there anything after the show that helps keep your voice in shape?

It becomes a TVR. Total Vocal Rest. I completely take a rest and won't talk to anybody.

How do you take care of your voice on the road?

Not taking drugs, not smoking, trying to drink moderately. We all know alcohol *dries you out* like a motherfucker. I drink lots of water, warm drinks. I like ginger tea. But I went a bit crazy with ginger in the early-2000s. I used to make fresh ginger tea, and it used to get stronger and stronger. By the end of that tour, *nobody* else could palate my tea because it was so strong. But I'm going, "It's a natural anti-inflammatory!" Six months after that tour, we got some cats, and my nose was running, my eyes were itchy. I went to this clinic in Surrey where they tested me for all kinds of things, and do you know what I'm most allergic to? *Ginger*. I'd overexposed myself to such a degree that I gave myself a great big sensitivity to it.

Have you replaced it with something?

Just warm drinks. No sugar. People talk about honey and lemon, but the lemon and honey thing doesn't work for me. The honey is counterproductive. People say, "Oh, it cuts through the mucus." What a load of rubbish. "Cuts through the mucus?" Since when did drinking something into your tummy get rid of the mucus that's in your breathing tubes?

So, when you start getting sick, what do you do?

Mucinex. It's amazing stuff. You know how it works, don't you? Guaifenesin. Guaifenesin works on the vagus nerve, which is a big nerve right down from your tummy up to your head, and it makes all of your mucus secretions much more fluid. So, easy to clear. Much less likely to get stuck halfway down your throat. I do also take Sudafed, but you gotta be careful with it because if you take too much of it, it's bad for your heart.

Are there songs where you wonder if your voice will be there that night?

Absolutely. Notoriously, the bit at the end of "A View to a Kill," which was made very obvious when we did Live Aid in 1985 [when Simon's voice cracked]. And then, the high notes at the end of "Ordinary World." [*Sings the high melody at the end of the song*] "Every wooooorld is my wooooorld! *Any woooooooorld!*" The third phrase, that's the difficult one.

Okay, so, you're onstage singing "Ordinary World," and that part is coming. What do you do to get yourself relaxed for it?

I stand up straight. I pull my chin in. A lot of times, if you get nervous or if you're pushing, you tend to stick your chin out. Say you get a cardboard tube from a piece of kitchen roll. If you hold the bottom of it with one hand and the top of it with the other, and you slide one hand in the opposite direction to the other, what happens to that tube? It flattens. That's what your larynx and your throat is like. If you stick your chin out, you flatten and squeeze that tube. You want it to be as open as possible. This is all my personal theory about the physicality of singing.

Well, give it to me because that was a great example!

To really start with, it's a whole body operation. You have to have a good base to start with so get your legs strong. It's no good having weak knees or wobbly legs. You've gotta be able to stand up straight and support this frame which expands. You have your ribcage which expands, and your diaphragm which goes down, but you want to maintain rigidity without tension. It's quite difficult. Everything has to be made as wide as possible.

So, having a strong posture, which not a lot of people talk about.
I always put my shoulders back, my chest out, my chin back, so I've got that straight tube and allow the resonance. The chest is a great resonator. I think my chest is a really big resonator. Different singers are different physically. I've got a small head and a big chest.

And how do you see the chest playing a role in the power of your voice?
It's the provider of the power. It's the engine room, really. The diaphragm and the lungs expand, you take in air, and then you slowly, in a relaxed manner, squeeze it out. That's your bellows. It's like the bagpipes. But it's also a resonator. You know what bagpipes sound like when the bag gets floppy? They go [*makes a pathetic, whimpering sound*]. It's this whole idea of maintaining space. Rigidity without tension, which allows things to really resonate and vibrate. I feel it in my chest when I'm onstage. I feel it in my head. I feel it in the back of my ears. I can feel my whole body resonating. Not so much my legs. This is the kind of shit you learn about when you have really bad vocal problems, by the way. I wouldn't know any of this stuff had I not lost my voice in 2011. And I did have times in the '90s where we canceled a few shows because of my voice.

What was that problem?
It could've been the same thing. I went into this hoarse mode and couldn't sing notes. I think it was partly a very, very punishing schedule. We did two weeks of rehearsals at Barker Hangar in California, and it was *hot*. It was really, really hot, and our rehearsals used to go on for about eight hours, and we didn't have days off. Two days later, we played our first show, and I felt that I'd started the tour with my voice already deteriorating. It didn't go immediately, it just went slowly, slowly, slowly. By the time it went, we were onstage in the Netherlands, started the song, I opened my mouth, and nothing came out. I managed to say, "This is really not fair on anybody in here. It's definitely not fair on you guys, and it ain't fair on me. I can't carry on. I can't sing anymore." I walked offstage, the band played some songs instrumentally, and then, shit hit the fan. It took over two months for me to get my voice back.

Are there songs where you've had to adjust the key live?
There might be.

[*JTG cracks up*] Are you being coy all of a sudden?
Yeah, I am. [*Laughter*] So, "Wild Boys," we recorded in the key of E. We now perform it in the key of D because that's got some proper high notes in it. And it's a *very* demanding song energy-wise. I really appreciate the dropping of that one tone.

You might've said it, but what was your most embarrassing vocal mishap ever?

I've had more embarrassing mishaps than that. My pants split, and then I got one of the roadies to staple them together. And then all the staples opened and dug into my leg.

Oh shit!

But vocally, the Live Aid one is still a horror. I still have nightmares about it. There's not many people who can top that one, believe me.

What was your feeling when you got offstage? Was the whole show null and void?

No, because we did some other good stuff. In fact, the rest of that song was good. Again, it was all down to over-rehearsal. But now I've got a couple of little principles that we tend to adhere to, and that's we *don't do* a rehearsal the day before our first show.

Do you remember a performance where you surprised yourself?

Yeah! Lots, actually. I mean, hitting certain notes that I never thought I'd be able to hit. Those notes at the end of "Ordinary World," they've got a quality to them that is—it's up there. It has a slightly kind of Robert Plant feel to it for me. But I'm sure there's lots of Robert Plant fans out there who'd go, "DON'T BE SO RIDICULOUS, SIMON!" But I'm a huge fan of his singing style. He's absolutely amazing.

Are you doing that note in falsetto, or are you straight on?

It's kind of halfway between falsetto and full voice. It's got a bit of rasp to it. When Robert Plant does it, he has even more rasp to it, and that's what makes it sound so amazing when he sings those high notes. I'm sixty-two years old now, and I've made sure I've kept my top end going. I've kept it really good.

How do you keep your top end?

You know how I said singing is a whole body operation? That's how you keep it going. You keep all of your body fit. You keep the frame fit, you keep the bellows fit, you keep the whole body strong. Those are the things that make it work. If you can maintain strength in those areas, you can keep your voice as long as that strength stays up. It's the *relaxed* feeling; the *not* pushing that I love.

How are you with hearing your own voice?

I don't dislike my own voice, but I don't like watching myself and I don't like listening to myself because it's not natural. It doesn't help. It just makes me feel self-conscious. And I'd rather not. I'd rather be inside the singer, singing out, communicating something than standing outside of the singer, trying to watch myself and see myself as other people see me.

That makes sense. But do you have a favorite vocal performance of yours?

There's a track on *Astronaut* called "The Point of No Return," and it's a double track vocal, but you can hardly tell. It's all done by me, not by machine. Nile Rodgers is the producer of that song, and he just did the most amazing job of getting that performance out of me.

What did he do?

He just helped lock it in. He helped by saying, "No, that's not the right one…no, that's not the right one…" We were singing a line at a time. Sometimes we would sing *a word* at a time. I know people who've created entire records like that. Bryan Adams used to be a neighbor of mine, and he said "Mutt" Lange likes to make his comp one word at a time. When I heard that I was like, "You're crazy! You lose the natural flow of a great take!" We're a little more loose about it, but sometimes, *sometimes*, you find a syllable from one take matches a syllable from another take, and you get a better performance sticking those two together. I'm giving away terrible trade secrets now. I really shouldn't be

But this is all part of what singers go through. Everyone has their thing. Some of the most successful pop singers of our time refused to be interviewed for this book because they're singing to tracks live and they're embarrassed about it. I talked to Michael McDonald, and he spoke about using Auto-Tune when he wants. There's tons of people who do all sorts of stuff, so to act like it doesn't happen, it's like, it's part of a choice people can make or not.

So, with Auto-Tune, I'm loathe to use it because I think it would be very easy for me to use it as a crutch, and for my actual singing skill to deteriorate because of it. However, *there are those times* when you sing something and you just know you're never gonna sing that line like that again. And there's one almighty bum note in the middle of it. But *the way* you sang it is great. It just needs to go up a quarter of a tone to hit the note right. Performance has to be king. But I do think we have to maintain the skill, the singer's skill. We have to practice and sing *a lot*. I sing every day, even if it's just sitting down with a guitar and playing a tune over and over again, you know, something the grandchildren like.

I wanna ask you about a tune that should've been a massive hit. "Danceophobia" off *Paper Gods*. [*Sings the chorus*] "I know what it is comin' over ya! You don't dance. Danceophobia!"

Ohhhhh! Riiight! Absolutely, absolutely! Haaa-haaa!

That track is so damn irresistible. You put that thing on, and you can't be mad, you can't be sad, it's just such a jam! Do you remember anything about recording those vocals?

I just wanted it to be really, really rhythmic. A song called "Danceophobia" has got to be rhythmic and really dancey. It's one of my favorites, it really is.

I don't know who decides what your singles are, but if it's you guys, you fucked up. And if it's the record company, they fucked up.
Let's blame the record company.

Well, I don't feel like you guys have given it enough love.
Yeah. I agree with you actually. I'm so grateful to you for turning people onto it.

What made you think of having Lindsay Lohan for the spoken word section?
We did *Regis and Kelly*, and Lindsay was getting her make-up done. I walked past and I just sorta did a double take and went, "Oh, hello!" And she goes, "Stop!" I go, "What?" And she said, "Last week I had my birthday party, and I dressed up as you from the '80s." And we kind of bonded over mutual admiration, which is always a great thing to base a relationship on, [*laughter*] and we stayed friends, actually. So, this came up, and somebody said, "Who should we get for this record?" I said, "What do you reckon about Lindsay?" And it was kind of when she was a really bad girl and had all the negative publicity, and everybody said, "Absolutely!" And we got it. She was amazing.

What's changed the most about your voice since you started?
I've got more relaxed, I've got stronger. I used to waste a lot of energy.

Tell me about "wasting the energy" as a singer.
Trying to put on too much of a physical performance. Trying to dance and sing at the same time when I'm not even a good dancer, to put it mildly. Trying to "Wow" the crowd with energy rather than singing the song properly. People come for the songs. The songs are the most powerful things. There's a little mantra that we all have before we go onstage: "Let the songs do the work." We wrote those songs. We know they're great songs. All we have to do is serve the songs. We don't have to do a "Performance." We just need to serve the songs, and everything else falls into place. Any of those songs—"Ordinary World," "Save a Prayer," stuff off the new album—when that gets performed right, and the whole band is locked into each other and the music, *that* is what makes a great concert.

Amen. So, if you could duet with any singer—living or dead—who would it be?
Oh, wow. Well, you know, I did duet with Pavarotti. It was an amazing experience. It was really amazing because my mom was in the crowd, and she was sitting directly behind Princess Diana. My mom used to sit there with her chin up, a big smile, showing her teeth with her eyes wide open. The message is, "Eyes and teeth, Simon. Eyes and teeth." [*JTG cracks up*] I kept looking at her, and I think Diana thought I was looking at her and got a bit bashful about it. After the concert, when I was talking to Diana, I said, "You do know my mom was sitting directly behind you, don't you?" [*Laughter*] I think she thought, *What's he looking at me like that for*? I like duets. Èdith Piaf would be an interesting one. But what about Patsy Cline? Do you think I'd sound good with Patsy Cline?

I love that answer. That would be the most fascinating duet to hear.

Yeah, because we're so different. But I think we could really mesh. I love the way she sings. I would also have to say Patti Smith. I'd love to do something with Patti Smith.

Speaking of duets, let me take you back to 1984. Bob Geldof puts together a project called Band Aid to send relief to the victims of the Ethiopian famine, and you're among some of the biggest artists of the day who got together and recorded the song "Do They Know It's Christmas?" That song was everywhere when it came out. It was such a smash. And you, Sting, Bono, George Michael, Boy George, and Paul Young all take turns singing on that first verse. Did you all get to pick your lines? How did that work?

No, not really. I was one of the first people who said yes to doing it, and I actually rehearsed the entire first verse *and* the second verse. I wasn't quite sure how much of the song I was gonna get. Nobody knew how many people were going to be there. And you got in there and think, "Oh, I've got that line, I've got that line...*what are these guys gonna do?*" And then, [producer] Trevor Horn goes to the others, "Right, you're doing this line. You're doing that line." I'm thinking, *There's other people doing my lines!* [JTG laughs] And then, you suddenly think, *Don't be stupid, of course it was gonna be like this. Who're you tryin' to kid, thinkin' that you were gonna get a whole verse?* No, but it's one of the greatest Christmas songs. I have to say, I think Bob thoroughly deserves his knighthood for it.

Who are your top five favorite singers of all time?

[*Gasps*] Favorite singers? Okay, I've got a very special one to start with. He's also one of my top five guitarists, and that is John Lee Hooker. Then, Robert Plant. Mick Jagger. Patti Smith. One more...Stevie Wonder.

If you could ask any singer about their voice, who would it be, and what would you ask?

I think I'd ask Robert about his high notes, and if they're a strain, or if he's found a way of really relaxing and doing that high stuff, because it's quite relevant to me. Actually, if you look at him, if you look at the way his body seems when he hits those high notes, his upper body becomes quite upright, and just like I've been saying, his chin comes back, and he pulls the microphone into his body. He doesn't stick his chin out.

Are you paying attention to the posture of a singer when you're watching them? Do you study that stuff?

Yes, absolutely. Mainly because I might learn something useful!

GEDDY LEE

HAVE YOU EVER HAD BLOOD STREAMING DOWN YOUR FACE as you sing your ass off, while playing bass at the same time? I'll let Geddy Lee tell you that story...

What I can tell you is that when I was growing up, any self-respecting radio station was playing "Tom Sawyer" at least ten times an hour. With a voice so impressively high it could possibly shatter glass, Geddy Lee ruled the school. On top of that, this Rock & Roll Hall of Famer is widely considered to be one of the greatest bass players of all time. But he didn't stop there.

Geddy kept exploring other sides to his voice, taking his instrument as seriously as he does his bass, his band rehearsals, and those germs just waiting to attack us! That's why he's also considered one of the greatest rock voices of all time.

Yet somehow as kids, there was always a dividing line. You were either fully obsessed with Rush, knowing every single vocal lick and drum fill by heart, or you were outside the gates, wondering why their fans were so insane. I was outside the gates. I dug "the hits" like everyone else, but it wasn't until much later that their music got me. Like all the best music does—when you're ready.

So, to all my jealous friends who've been so smugly inside the gates for years, here's me with Geddy Lee. Just kickin' it. A couple of bros hangin' out. You guys should really meet sometime. He's a great guy.

Who first exposed you to singing?

I was in the school choir when I was quite young. Unsurprisingly, I had sort of a soprano voice. I wasn't a regular, but I was a supplemental player. If somebody got sick, then I would sing, and I always enjoyed it. Then, when I started playing music with other kids in my neighborhood, it always seemed to default to me to do the singing because nobody wanted to do the job. Like many people who become major league catchers or hockey goalies, it's usually, "You be the goalie!" For me it was like, "You be the bass player. Oh! You sing too!"

Were you emulating anybody when you started out?

Any singer that I thought was good influenced me. If I go right back, my first favorite bands were like The Beach Boys, which were highly vocal. And as they got more adventurous in their music, I stuck around. But I also used to work in my mother's variety store, and we always had the radio on, which was mostly R&B and Motown—'course some great singers there—Aretha Franklin, Diana Ross and Smokey Robinson. Although there's nothing in my singing that emulates any Motown singer [*laughs*] because of the nature of the music that I've grown up playing. But I *was* paying attention to those singers when I was a kid.

How did you find your own voice?

My own voice developed as a tool needed in the context of the kind of music I was doing. I was drawn to singers like Steve Marriott in Humble Pie, and of course, Robert Plant, and the high energy, high octane, multi-range singers of the mid-'60s-early '70s. Because the kind of music Rush was playing in our formative years was very much heavy rock, my voice adapted to what was necessary. It needed to cut through this kind of dense, loud music, and that's sort of how my style began.

Did you ever have any vocal training?

Just some lessons at school, but I never had any proper vocal training, no.

Do you feel nervous or confident before you perform?

Obviously, the first few shows there's opening night jitters, but once you get past the first song, those go away pretty quickly. I've always felt pretty comfortable onstage, pretty at home onstage. Every once in a while, you'll be doing a show that you either have a lot of friends at, or you feel is special in one way or another, and you might tighten up a bit. That's how nerves present themselves to you. It's usually by tightening up your body and tightening up your hands, but it seems to affect players more than singers, I think.

Do you do any vocal warm-ups before shows?

Yeah, I warm-up for about twenty minutes before a show. I sit in a dressing room and do scales, and after that I sing different songs from our repertoire. I start in a lower range, and I slowly increase the range a bit. I try to not over-warm-up because I find I hit the stage in a better voice, but run the risk of running out of gas after the three hour mark. Because we *did* a very long show, I had to pace myself. Otherwise, I could run out of voice by the end. Especially as I get older.

And you guys increased your set as each record came out. Other bands would cut songs to make way for the new stuff, but you guys wouldn't really cut anything, you would just keep adding to the set.

It was normal for us to play three hours on the last few tours we did. We did have a twenty-minute intermission, which was a huge, huge help. Also, the fact that we have so many instrumental songs. I would always build those in to give my voice some rest.

How would you take care of your voice on the road?

I had a voice doctor that would recommend certain things to me, like diet was really important. Certain foods create mucus, like spicy food, acidic food, white wine, too much citrus. And mucus, as a singer, is something that's your enemy. I would avoid those foods. So, I would be on a very strict diet from a month before a tour started, right through 'til the tour was over.

And what about when the tour is in full swing?

I tried not to speak on days off. I stopped doing back-to-back shows because the next day my voice was pretty ratty. So unless it couldn't be avoided, I always took a day off in between each show. When I was younger, I used to get out and see the town and do all kinds of stuff. But in the last few tours we did, I would just stay indoors mostly, on my own, so that I could avoid talking on my day off and just let my voice rest. Usually, I would get together with [guitarist] Alex Lifeson or one of the guys for dinner, and of course, I would do a little talking and have some red wine. But, for the most part, my days off were pretty fucking boring.

When you would start getting sick, what would you do?

Freak out! [*Laughter*] Because for the last twenty years, I've increasingly become a germaphobe from being a singer. I have quite a few friends who play baseball, and a lot of them are pitchers, and they're equally as paranoid about their pitching arms as I am with my voice. So, I always wear a scarf, I avoid extreme swings in temperature, I *never go near* a freezing cold, air-conditioned room. I make sure that my room fan is set so that it doesn't get too cold, or that wind isn't blowing on my face, crazy shit like that.

I know, it sounds nuts, but it's true.

It's weird being a singer because your instrument is so affected by environment, whatever stress you're going through, and all those things come to play in your voice. That's what made me a germaphobe, really. Fear of getting a cold and not being able to do the gig. That's why I stopped shaking people's hands.

Well, how does that work in meet and greets?

I really try to avoid it. But sometimes you can't. And then I wash my hands like three times after every meet and greet. I use antiseptic gel and shit like that. I've been doing book signings for this book I just released [*Geddy Lee's Big Beautiful Book of Bass*] and I don't shake hands. I'll fist bump, but that's it. That's a hangover from those days, even though I'm not singing. I'm still afraid of getting sick. Because I've sung with colds and it's a fucking nightmare. I've done shows where I'm losing my voice halfway through, and they keep either burying your voice in the mix, or somehow trying to add more echo to it. [*Laughs*]

Would you rather trudge through with the cold than cancel the show?

I try not to cancel a show if I can help it because it's so much effort for people to come and get tickets and for us to get there. But I've sung through some horrible circumstances. One time I had a terrible ear infection, and I was supposed to get on a plane and fly to Montreal. The air pressure from the plane would've been excruciating, so I had to go to see my throat doctor, and he basically had to puncture my ear drum in order for me to get on the plane and do the show *that night! Which I did do*. Even though my ears were bleeding through the whole show.

What?

The procedure itself was one of the most painful things I've ever experienced in my life! When he did it, I just screamed from the actual pain. And then when I walked out of the doctor's office, there was a kid sitting in the waiting room, and I felt so bad for him [*laughter*] 'cause he must've heard this blood curdling scream, and thought, *Oh my God, I have to go in there next?* I have a lot of stories like that. Or going on with a nosebleed and you can't stop the nosebleed and have to keep doing the show.

So, you just have blood streaming down your face while you're playing?

Yeah. I'm prone to nosebleeds. I remember a show where I had a nosebleed in the middle of the set. It's really gross, but you have to swallow the blood as you're playing. Then, in between songs, you're trying to stop the bleeding and you're spitting out blood. That just continued through the whole night.

Geddy wins, y'all. That's a new one. Do you have any rituals before you perform?

The backstage thing is, we do a twenty-minute soundcheck every day, which is like a mini warm-up as well. I don't sing full out in soundcheck just as I don't sing full out in rehearsals. I try to break my voice in. Then, it's chill time. We have dinner at like five, do a meet and greet, and then after the meet and greet, it's vocal warm-up. At the same time, I'm warming-up my fingers, I'm warming-up my voice, and then pretty much go straight on.

Is there anything after the show that helps keep your voice in shape?

I drink a beer almost immediately. [*Laughter*] A cold beer after the show is about the best drink you're gonna have all day.

Are there songs where you wonder if your voice will be there that night?

Yeah, most of 'em. Especially "2112." That's the only song, as I got older, that we actually changed the key down a step because it's a very difficult song to sing. It's really on the edge for me, so I always have to pace that song at the right part of the set.

Alright, let's get to it. Is there a man on earth who can sing higher than you?

I always thought Jon Anderson had a wider range than me. And he was blessed with such a mellow tone. You know, my voice can sound quite harsh when I'm pushing up to the upper ranges, and his voice always sounds so pure and beautiful. But it's hard making your living up in the stratosphere.

There's a sonic shift in your voice from the *Fly by Night* album in '75 to *2112* which only came out a year later. What happened during that time for you vocally?

The early tours, I was screaming a lot, and I tried to learn to sing more after *2112*. I started becoming more aware of what key I was in. We wrote songs without any consideration for the key when we were young. We didn't know the rules to songwriting and modulations and all that. So, we just wrote what we thought was cool, and then I would do the vocals, and regardless of what key we happened to be in, I would just have to make it work. That kept going right up until we did the *Hemispheres* album.

What changed on *Hemispheres*?

That was the breaking point because we pretty much wrote and recorded that whole album in the studio. And then, I went in to do the vocals, and realized this key is impossibly high for me. I had to duke it out for two weeks until I hit all those notes, so I swore I would never put myself through that again. That's when we started taking more consideration to what key we were writing in and how my voice sounds in different keys. Ever since then, that's been a rudiment of my songwriting, to take that into consideration. But it's amazing, for years we didn't consider it at all. And, ironically, my sort of recognizable vocal style came from that inexperience. So, now when I sing in a lower voice, the producer's always saying, "Why don't you sing it up? Go an octave up." [*Laughter*] They all want me to sing like that screaming Mimi when I was younger. I'm like, "Dude, I'm tryin' to develop here."

I feel like you have another major shift in your vocal tone around *Grace Under Pressure* in '84, and it carries on through the rest of your career. I really love it. Even songs like "Still" off your solo album, there's a warmth to your voice that just feels so full and round.

Oh, why thank you. I really worked hard at being a better singer as I progressed. One of the main reasons I changed producers after *Grace Under Pressure* was I felt I wasn't getting enough direction as a singer. I wasn't working with people who had worked with great singers and could recognize things I was doing wrong and could be improved. That's why I wanted to work with Rupert Hine so badly because he is a great producer of singers, has a great sense of melody, and a great ear for trying to sing effortlessly. So, we did two albums with Rupert, and it was a really incredible learning experience for me. It started changing the way I approach vocals.

What was the new approach?

I was doing a lot of recording on my own at home. I was learning how to use my voice by experimenting with keys and layers of harmony, harmonizing with myself. And there's a whole bunch of records around that period of vocal harmonies, which is me singing with me! That taught me so much about how to structure a vocal part and how to create a melody. And it really tuned my ear, and helped me become a better singer by working on my own, and having the flexibility of a digital system in my home that I could spend hours experimenting with.

Do you remember a performance where you surprised yourself?

It's hard to pick one of those moments out. But almost all the vocals for *Clockwork Angels* I wrote at home, likewise, a good portion of the vocals from *Snakes & Arrows*. When I started working with [producer] Nick Raskulinecz, I was layering a high part and a low part. And very often he would say, "You don't really need that low part. Let's pull the low part and use the high part." So, what I considered to be a harmony, he considered to be the lead. And that's why you see—as of *Snakes & Arrows*—my voice creeping into the higher ranges again. Because he had that ear for the old Geddy Lee style, and I had felt that I had progressed as a vocalist. And that was surprising, to pull out some of the backing vocals and see how that high vocal line stood out. Yet, I wasn't screaming. It was more melodious. That was sort of the end result of a huge evolutionary protocol.

What was your most embarrassing vocal mishap ever?

The most embarrassing moment was in Leeds in the '80s. We started the song "Closer to the Heart," and I completely forgot the lyrics. I just stood there with nothing coming out of my voice, looking at the audience as *they* were singing the song and trying to help me remember.

How are you with hearing your own voice?

I don't enjoy it, but I'm used to it. I started to learn a lot of the ins and outs about my voice by working alone. And I always like to have a producer. I think a producer is invaluable in remaining the objective ear in the room because you hear yourself so many times in a row and can't possibly be objective anymore. But, still, it's a great way to get to know your strengths and weaknesses, by working on your own, and pushing yourself in the privacy of your own studio if you're lucky enough to be able to do that.

Do you have a favorite vocal performance you're really proud of?

There's a few songs on the last couple records I'm really proud of. "Headlong Flight." The fact I was able to do those live successfully surprised me every night. [*Laughs*] It's a tough song to sing, and it's one of my favorite songs that were ever written so, I'm pretty proud of that vocal performance.

People always talk about how high you can sing, or how insane your bass playing is, but there's another area I don't think you get enough credit for: you're probably the greatest multi-tasker in rock 'n' roll history. [*Geddy bursts into laughter*] You're juggling so much at once! First off, memorizing all the lyrics that [drummer] Neil Peart has written, and let's be honest, some may as well be a chapter from a Russian novel.

Yeah, there's a lot. It was a busy life being a third of Rush, that's for sure.

So, you gotta memorize the words, sing your balls off—in your case, almost literally—and then, play these incredibly intricate bass lines with all these complex rhythms and time signatures. How are you capable of doing all that at once? I'd love to break it all down. We can start with the lyrics. Was Neil just giving you sheets full of stuff, and then you were writing to that?

Yeah, Alex and I would get together and start jamming, and Neil would send us songs in various forms of completion, like *first drafts*. So, I'll have four or five songs in front of me. Some of the lyrics will speak to me as a singer, and some won't. So, I gravitate to the lyrics that move me, and we work with those. Neil was so great at collaborating because he is not possessive about, "You have to use all this stuff." He's not like that, there's no ego there. So, if I say to him, "This verse is great, but the other parts of the song don't work as well rhythmically. Can you rewrite the song so that it has the cadence of this verse?" He'll go, "Sure, no problem," and it'll go back to him, and we'll work back and forth. Other times, he'll write something that just flows, and I don't wanna touch a note, and I'll make sure that I can make the vocal and the music serve that lyric without interfering. So, it's all down to the quality of the idea. As it should be.

But he was never singing the vocal melodies to you?

No, no, he never had vocal melodies in mind. As he writes a song, he has a kind of melody in his head, but Neil can't carry a tune. [*Laughter*] He writes his own melody, and his own rhythm to it, but sometimes it doesn't jive with the way that I hear it, and he had great respect for that. As a writing partner, he was really pretty much ideal.[4]

How do you make all those the lyrics stick? Do you have a photographic memory?

What happens next is, I write the bass part that suits the song the best, sing the vocal melody—of course, that's done separately—and then I have to figure out how the fuck I'm going to do it live. [*Laughter*] And that involves rehearsal, rehearsal, rehearsal.

Alright, let's whittle it down some more.

So, I would just learn my bass parts until I could play them in my sleep. When I'm at the point where I don't have to watch my hands to play the bass part, *then* I'd start introducing the vocal parts, and rehearse them until I could do it. The three of us are rehearsal freaks, so we would

---

4   Rush retired from touring in 2015, about two years before this interview took place, and Neil Peart passed away in 2020.

each rehearse at least two weeks *on our own* before any tour. Then, we would rehearse as a band for two or three weeks without production. And then, we would rehearse another two weeks with production. Oftentimes, you're rehearsing for a full two months before you're playing one note in front of human beings. That's how you get good at something. [*Laughs*]

All those moving parts at once. It just seems insane that you can pull it off so well.
There's a lot of shit goin' on! Oh dude, I would love to be on a tour with a band where I'm just playin' bass, are you kiddin' me? That would be like vacation. [*Laughter*] There's moments, of course, where what you're singing *rhythmically* just cannot be in the same space as what you're playing as a bass player. So, you keep the essence of the bass part, but maybe not exactly what was recorded. You just play with the vocal or the bass a slight bit until you feel it's right.

I see. But you still got all those words to contend with! [*Laughs*]
The last few tours, I've actually used a teleprompter onstage in case my memory fails me. And that helps the whole tour because we have screens all over the stage, and there's a lot of vocal cues that cue prop changes. It benefits everyone, including lighting guys and prop guys, and especially the singers, to be able to see where you are in the song.

I wanna talk about your final Rush concert in 2015 because you guys closed with "Working Man" off your first album. How hard was it to sing that song, knowing that this would be the last show for the band you started as kids?
I would say the last part of that song was tough to sing. Even though we kept saying, "Okay, this is the last show," part of me didn't really wanna believe it. I think I got through that night by saying, *Naw, we'll do it again*. You know, *We'll take a break, and then, we'll talk and we'll see*. I was kidding myself to a certain degree. But part of me also did accept the moment. It was harder for me to say goodnight to the audience that night than actually do any singing. The singing, you just slip into professional mode and do your job. But when it came to talk to the crowd after, especially after Neil came out from behind his drums and gave us all a hug. He never did that before, and he swore he wouldn't do it that night. So, when he came out, I kind of knew that this was probably it for him. That was a tough, emotional moment. The crowd felt that too.

What's changed the most about your voice since you started?
Man, so much. So much learning. When I was a kid, I didn't know what the fuck I was doing. I didn't really know how to use my voice; I just pushed it in the direction that the song required. Now I feel like I have respect for the role of the singer as someone that needs to express the lyric with authenticity. I think that makes the difference between a song that endures and one that doesn't. When you hear a song, and that singer feels like he or she means it, *that's* the mark of a great vocal performance. That's something I don't think I realized as a kid. Of all the technical things I've learned along the way, the essential truth is one about authenticity.

If you could duet with one singer—living or dead—who would it be?

Oh God. I don't know why she'd ever wanna do it, but Billie Holiday would be a thrill.

Who are your top five favorite singers of all time?

Well, Jon Anderson, Robert Plant, Björk, Roger Hodgson from Supertramp—fantastic vocalist, I mean, really beautiful voice—and Billie Holiday of course.

If you could ask any singer about their voice, who would it be and what would you ask?

It wouldn't matter what singer I admired I was talking to. I would just ask them how much of their singing is what they were born with, and how much of it was actually schooling. There are some singers, great singers like Paul Rogers, who's another singer I have tremendous respect for, that has so much soul in his voice. Does it come right out of your voice naturally? Or did you have to educate yourself and teach yourself how to make that sound real?

Well, I asked you a similar question early on, and it just came outta you. This wasn't something you were trained in.

Yeah, I suspect that every singer will probably have the same answer, "That's how I was born." But you have to learn some of the rules along the way, and that helps you express yourself in a better way. I've worked as a producer on a couple of different projects through my last forty years, and the thing I always try to tell the singer is, "Let's find the key that works best for you first, and let's find the cadence of the lyric that allows you to express your voice in the most open way." Those are two very important things.

Steven Van Zandt on
LITTLE RICHARD

"WOMP-BOM-A-LOO-MOP-ALOP-BOM-BOM!"
In 1955, that wasn't just some fun gibberish to sing. It was a battle cry! The song was "Tutti Frutti," the singer was Little Richard, and none of us would ever be the same.

Richard Penniman's passionate voice, ecclesiastic piano playing, and dynamic showmanship broke the color line, integrating blacks and whites in a way no one had before. And Lord, did it sound great! From Elvis to The Beatles to Prince, Little Richard's influence on popular music can be felt across the very foundation of rock 'n' roll. That's why they called him The Architect, The Originator, and The Innovator. And that's why he was among the first group of inductees into the Rock & Roll Hall of Fame.

"Good Golly Miss Molly," "Long Tall Sally," "The Girl Can't Help It," "Rip It Up," sorry, Elvis. Those are just a few of the reasons Little Richard has got to be The King. He had a voice jam packed with the glory of the gospel, the pain of the blues, and the sweet release of sexual ecstasy, all rolled into one of the greatest performers you'd ever see.

And if he were here, he'd tell you the same thing himself.

So, how does "Little Steven" Van Zandt fit into all this? Best known as the guitarist of Bruce Springsteen's legendary E Street Band. Or as Silvio on the Sopranos. Or Lilyhammer. Or as the lead singer of Little Steven and the Disciples of Soul. A Rock & Roll Hall of Fame inductee, songwriter, producer, activist, host of Little Steven's Underground Garage, and one of our finest living musicologists. He was also friends with Little Richard, so I felt he may have some insight on the man. Or just be a ton of fun to talk to. Turns out it was both.

When was the first time you heard Little Richard sing?
Oh, I know! *The Girl Can't Help It*, the movie. He sang the title track and performed in it.

What was your impression of him?
The pioneers, at that age, you're kind of conscious as to their contribution, but I didn't really understand it 'til later. I was responding to the artists that I loved, which were the '60s artists, and they were telling us about the '50s artists, and how the pioneers were very important to their artistic growth.

You mean, like The Beatles covering their songs?
Yeah, that was the only reason we heard about these guys 'cause they were mostly gone by the time I got to be a teenager. They really kind of disappeared at once. Chuck Berry was in jail, Bo Diddley became a sheriff in Texas, Little Richard retired because of Sputnik—he thought that was a sign from God—Elvis went in the army, Buddy Holly and Ritchie Valens got killed in a plane crash, Eddie Cochran got killed in a car crash—Gene Vincent was in the same car and almost died—Jerry Lee Lewis married his thirteen-year-old cousin...

So, by the end of the '50s, all the pioneers were pretty much over.
They were curiosities at that point. If the '60s hadn't come along, those '50s pioneers would've been considered novelty acts, temporary teenage distractions. There was no connection to a bigger art form until the '60s guys came along and literally created the art form, and then, of course, credited *them* with being the roots of that art form. So, all of a sudden, they went from being novelty acts to being *extremely* important elements, and the naissance of the renaissance.

And where does Little Richard fit in during all this?
He is, in fact, the *embodiment* of rock 'n' roll. Chuck Berry I consider to be the most important of all the early pioneers, and Elvis Presley obviously popularized the genre.

Well, Elvis gets credited with being the king, but in my opinion, Little Richard is the king of rock 'n' roll. Where do you fall on this?

The king for me is always gonna be Chuck Berry because he was the storyteller. He brought the story, and he also brought the guitar. Between his lyrics and guitar playing, you have to credit Chuck Berry with the more significant elements of what became rock 'n' roll. But Richard embodied the actual spirits of rock 'n' roll in the sense of, he opened his mouth and out came liberation, okay? He was the most uninhibited. He *was* rock 'n' roll. And he embodied rock 'n' roll more than any other performer.

Explain what the embodiment of rock 'n' roll is to you.

Everything about him defined the genre. His androgynous sexuality, the whole uninhibited way he expressed himself was bigger than just his talent. It was a philosophical statement saying, "This art form not only tolerates your reinvention as a person, it actually demands it." You're able to be whoever you want to be. That's what Little Richard communicated, that kind of freedom and liberation, so, yeah, you certainly can call him the king of rock 'n' roll, I wouldn't argue with you. I mean, he was certainly the originator, but we must give some credit to Llyod Price who gets no respect at all and never gets mentioned. If Llyod Price hadn't gone in the army, there wouldn't have been any Little Richard.

I don't know much about Llyod Price.

Little Richard was basically signed to follow in Llyod Price's footsteps. So, we must mention Llyod who was arguably the first rock 'n' roller. And Fats Domino. People argue about what the first rock 'n' roll record was. You could make an argument that "Lawdy Miss Clawdy," 1952, was in many ways the first rock 'n' roll record because the other ones that are usually sighted like "Rocket 88" the year before, were still very blues oriented or boogie woogie. But "Lawdy Miss Clawdy" had that different rhythm that became the standard rock 'n' roll rhythm.

But if we're talkin' about the voice: Little Richard. Greatest rock 'n' roll singer of all time. True or false?

Yeah, I'll tell you why I would say yes. If you go back to his gospel records, you can certainly hear it. But I had the remarkable good fortune to hear the greatest Little Richard performance ever. And it was at a soundcheck. I was touring with The Dovells at the time and doing The Oldies Circuit, as it was called in 1973. Part of that circuit was doing those Richard Nader Extravaganza shows, which came about because the British Invasion put all their heroes out of work. You know, unintended consequence. They were put out to pasture in their prime, late thirties-early forties, completely cut off from the industry for the rest of their lives. If you had two hits on the charts when The Beatles came, you played those two hits for the rest of your life.

It's so crazy how all those amazing artists basically got cut off overnight.

It was a shame 'cause that first generation was the *only* one that really had that happen. Every other generation after that the audience grew *with* them. Who were the biggest artists in the '6os? The Beatles and Stones. Who are the biggest artists right now? The Beatles and Stones. And that's fifty years later.

That's so wild.
The first generation got screwed, they really did. For some reason.

So, now you're doing this gig with The Dovells.
We get to Madison Square Garden, my first time playing Madison Square Garden, and Little Richard was headlining. He had as much time as he wanted for the soundcheck. There's nobody there, a few people in the audience hanging around, and he just went through this incredible repertoire of things. He did blues, country songs, gospel, he did a Rolling Stones song, he just was singing like I'd never heard him sing.

Where is he in his career at this point?
At the height of his jive performance thing. He'd sing a little bit, and then he'd take his shirt off and stand on the piano and wave it around, *really* just fucking around. You never would've seen what he could do vocally at that stage of the game. I just happened to catch him in a good mood, and he did an hour of the most incredible singing I have heard in my life. I wish everybody could have heard him sing. I just happened to catch that and turns out: *Yes. He is the greatest singer of all time probably.* [*JTG laughs*] But you wouldn't necessarily know it. You'd have to go back and listen to the gospel records. And, of course, he's got the great style. All his hits are in that one style which is fantastic and really unequalled in terms of excitement.

It's just incredible how he sounds like he's singing through a distorted amp, but it's his vocal cords! You listen to something like "True Fine Mama," and it's just unreal and so pure.
Yeah, he just had it. He just had that gift. And we're lucky, through circumstance, that he ended up in the business, 'cause their first session wasn't going well. I don't know what they were trying to do with him, make him into a crooner or something. They went to lunch in this bar, and there's a piano onstage, and Richard jumped on the stage and started singing all these crazy, obscene songs, and they said, "This is what we have to do." Then, they brought in a woman to clean up the lyrics. "Long Tall Sally," and all of them, they changed the words around. But if he hadn't jumped up on that stage and just gone crazy for a minute, just to relieve the tension, who knows what would have happened?

It's important to note that Little Richard is basically your namesake as well. He was one of the guys who inspired you not just to be known as Steven Van Zandt or Miami Steve with the E Street Band, you're also known as Little Steven.
That's right. He was an inspiration for my name, and he was also the preacher at my wedding. Did you know that?

Yes! Usually for this section of the book, I have a band member, an engineer, or a producer of an artist who's no longer with us, talking about how they did their thing. But this is a unique situation because you weren't really any of those things to Little Richard. But you were his friend and one of our greatest living historians. So, what I'm hoping is that you may be able to shed some light on his process; like do you know how he went about recording his vocals in the studio? Was he a perfectionist, or did he just hit it and quit it?

I loved workin' with those '50s and '60s guys and worked with as many as I could. The Drifters and Coasters, Ronnie Spector, and, of course, the great Darlene Love who is the female version of Richard in terms of the greatest female singer in history. And why I loved working with those pioneers is, in those days you really had to be talented. Okay? You had to have real talent. [*Laughter*] They were not overdubbing; they were not fixing things. They sang things live. And they had to be exactly right every time. That required a different level of talent, it just did. And a different level of concentration. It was all done that way. There was no exceptions to the rule, and he was just naturally fantastic.

Do you know if he was nervous or confident before he would perform?

He always had that little bit of nervousness. Always.

There's like an undercurrent of jitter in him at all times, it felt like.

Yeah, I think so. He just had a lot of energy, and a lot of adrenaline pumping all the time. He was a little nervous before our wedding because it was the first one he ever did. We were like, "Let's take it easy on the religious stuff, we're not very religious, so let's take it easy on that," and he's like, "Yeah, yeah, yeah." And then, we got in there and he starts screaming about Jesus immediately. [*Laughter*] "Jesus has blessed this marriage!"

Are you guys still together?

Oh yeah!

Well, maybe he has, baby! [More laughter]

He's onto something, yeah!

Did he sing at your wedding too?

No. He left right after the ceremony. Percy Sledge sang "When a Man Loves a Woman" when we walked down the aisle. And then we had the band from the Godfather movie. Little Milton was playin'. The Chambers Brothers were hangin' around.

What a wedding you had, man.

Yeah, it was crazy, it was crazy.

I don't think any singers back then did this, but do you know if he did any vocal warm-ups before going onstage?

Nooo. No, no, no way. There was no such thing. It was all very casual, very natural.

Do you have a favorite Little Richard track?

"Long Tall Sally." After all these years, I still come back to that one. The way he moves the melody very adroitly. There's a lot of subtleties going on in that vocal, there's a lot of nuance, and you kind of take it for granted because he's Little Richard [*laughs*], but there's a lot going on actually.

"I Don't Know What You've Got, But It's Got Me" is one of my favorite vocals of his. It's so fascinating because if you really pay attention, it sounds like it's a love song between two men. I'm not sure if this is the first openly gay song or not, but his best friend comes to his job and confronts Little Richard about cheating on him. Who did that in '65? That's bold.

I think they were still hoping that people weren't paying attention. You couldn't really be that up front about it back then. They changed all of those songs. They were *all* gay songs, all of them.

Is "Jailhouse Rock" the first gay rock 'n' roll song?

[*Laughs*] Naw, naw. I mean, it was...it was...

"Number 47 said to Number 3, 'You're the cutest jailbird I ever did see.'" You know the rest. Pretty revolutionary if it was.

Yeah, but they were joking. [Songwriters] Leiber and Stoller had a very good sense of humor. Jerry Leiber was a comedian really, so no, I think it was makin' light of the fact that there were no women in jail, so they had to pretend. [*Reconsiders, laughing*] You know, you could make an argument for it, but I don't think so.

Well, since this is a celebration of singers, I have to mention how much soul *you* have whenever you step up to that mic, not only within the context of the E Street Band, but in your solo career as well. All anyone has to do is listen to you sing "Inside of Me."

Well, thank you. It was the era I grew up in. Most of my stuff is directed toward the soul music side of things. You're hearing my version of David Ruffin and Levi Stubbs and Sam Cooke. You can't ever get there, but they were so inspiring in those days. Smokey Robinson, Marvin Gaye, Otis Redding, Wilson Pickett. You're just trying to capture that emotion they communicated to you. It just becomes a part of you, and then you hope to communicate that same thing through your own songs. That's what it's all about.

When you hear Little Richard's voice now, what do you remember most?

For me, he embodies the pure liberation of our art form, which is unlike any other art form in terms of personal expression. It's really the most personal and the most emotional of all the art forms. His entire lifestyle, and persona, and flamboyant character, was also liberating for people, to look at him and think, I can be whoever I can imagine, and that's what comes across when I think of Richard. He opens his mouth and out comes liberation. Doesn't matter what the lyrics are, just singing syllables. [*Sings the intro to "Tutti Frutti" and laughs*] It doesn't matter. He's such an amazing communicator, it comes across, no matter what he's saying. He transcends lyrics. That's how strong a singer he is.

JOHN LYDON

IMAGINE BEING IN A BAND that releases one record, changes the world, then breaks up!

If you're John Lydon [aka Johnny Rotten] you don't have to imagine it. When *Never Mind the Bullocks, Here's the Sex Pistols* lashed out onto the streets in 1977, this guy became public enemy #1 overnight. Not since Elvis shook his hips on Ed Sullivan had anyone caused such a riot. The Sex Pistols were officially taking the punk rock label into the mainstream and leaving hordes of terrified masses clutching their pearls.

A year later, it was all over, but John was just beginning.

With his exuberant irritation still intact, John quickly formed a more experimental band called Public Image Ltd, revealing an entirely new approach to his voice, and changing our perceptions of what music could be. Again. His days with the Pistols may have earned him a place in the Rock & Roll Hall of Fame, but he told them off instead. With his iconic legacy as the outspoken king of the punks, I'd be lying if I said I wasn't slightly nervous going into this one.

You just never know what will set him off, but interviews usually do. So, it was a beautiful start when he got on the phone, knowing that the royalties from this book would benefit St. Jude, and wickedly announced, "If you got the cause, I got the claws!" After bursting into laughter, what transpired was a fun and revelatory conversation. I love John Lydon interviews, but this was something new, because I was genuinely surprised by so many things—his vulnerability, his honesty, and how he r-r-r-ripped off Speedy Gonzalez!

Who first exposed you to singing?

The Sex Pistols. Never really thought about it up until the point of being asked to join, and purely because of the way I was dressed, I suppose. That's as good a reason as any because if you're dressed like an individual, you're certainly gonna sing like one! [*Laughter*] I perfected the art of non-singing and just really being as off as I could so that I would never, ever, be accepted. That was an uphill climb from there on in.

Were you emulating anyone when you started out?

I suppose the Hunchback King [Richard III], the Shakespearean character, Olivier. Yeah, much more over the top, amateur dramatics gone insane kind of thing. It was the character I was looking for rather than the voice at first. That seemed to bode me well for a couple of sessions. Then, when I actually heard myself on monitors for the first time, I was horrified.

That's right, I heard that you kicked over a monitor.

It was such a shock. Such a, "Oh, what a nightmare I am. How did they ever put up with me?"

So, the first time you really heard yourself was live?

Yeah, onstage, supporting a band called Eddie and the Hot Rods. What a lethal moment to find out. [*Laughter*] We had a little speaker thing in rehearsals, but you really couldn't hear it. Once [guitarist] Steve Jones started up, that was it. If I was trying to pitch to anything, it would be his guitar, and he was in the process of learning too, but I found that *really, really* freeing. I started out with the concept that there's no such thing as a bad note. It's all just thrilling sounds, and if I could *just* get myself in there with what I had to say in my writing, then I was off. And, indeed, I was—off to the races!

How did you find your own voice?

Through the written words, really. Through what I was writing. I thought, *Well, God, I'm writing these words not to sing like some doo-wop artist, because I really mean it.* Loud and proud Londoner. Yak on! [*Laughs*]

Did you ever have any vocal training?

About six months in [former manager] Malcolm McLaren suggested I go to a singing instructor, and she was soooo upper class! Music Hall was her thing and showtunes, and there's no way I can do that. I'm a full belter, right? Put as much energy from your lungs into every single word and expression that the song was crying out for, not [*mimics someone fancifully doing scales*] "Do-Re-Me-Fa-So-La-Ti-*Ha-Ha*" No. Sorry. Didn't work. You don't wanna sound like everybody else. The end.

Are you nervous or confident before you perform?

OH GOD, the nervous end of it. To this day, I've still got that before I go on. Just dying inside, shaking like a leaf. It's a personal execution, really. [*Laughter*] You're puttin' your head in the chopping block, and you're demanding to be judged, and you're just hoping you get off lightly, your honor. [*More laughter*]

Do you do any vocal warm-ups before shows?

No, I usually sit in dead quiet. I don't like a lot of people around me either. I don't like confusing conversations because I'm trying to focus on what it is I'm about to do. I don't wanna discuss the price of bread or "Have you seen the headlines lately?" That's not going to work with me. Small talk really is fuckin' annoying. I suppose that's where you get the impression that I'm difficult to work with because I can't have a small talk conversation even at the best of times!

Do you have any rituals before you hit the stage?

As I said, the silence. And the fear. And trying to confront it and come to grips with it. It's an absolute nightmare though, to think that I could let people down. I can't have that. There's many a time before going on that I've thought about running away. It gets that frightening to you. *It may be false demons you're conjuring here inside myself,* I'm thinking, but they're my demons and I have to come to grips with them. But onstage, a totally different thing happens. A light goes on and then, I'm well and truly into it. I like being onstage, I just can't come to grips with the agony of beforehand. If anything, it's more intense now than it ever was.

Do you feel like you have to be a certain person or you're gonna let people down?

We have a catalog of about two hundred songs! It just adds to the stress! [*Laughter*] Trying to remember the lyrics in your head before you go on. *Oh my God, I hope I get that right!* I developed the idea of bringing a songbook on and having the songs written out. But I can't write them out like that. I have to underline them for emphasis, where the ups and downs are, so it really looks like a child's coloring book at the end of the day. That's kind of helpful except that my eyesight's going, so I'm really just looking at a blur. It's kind of a safety blanket.

Would you never do the teleprompter?

Ohhh, I can't read that! I'm half blind, aren't I? I tried that once. Somebody suggested it on a TV show, and I hated it. I'm sorry, my focus is going into people's faces, not words on a clear piece of Perspex in bright green, glaring at me. Monitors are what's really important for me onstage.

Massively important. What's your relationship to your monitors?

We work with a monitor mix man called Martin O'Grady, and he knows *exactly* what I want: old school, belt the volume up. But if it's too loud, I can't be giving gestures to him, so [manager] "Rambo" Stevens has a set of monitors on the side as well. He knows if it's too loud, so he does all that hand signaling, because if ever I have to do that myself, it really distracts from the song and you've lost your place and you've lost the emotion. You really need back up and support like that going on. That's a neat little team and helps the voice to no end. I absolutely think that frustration onstage can really wreck a voice. You shouldn't have to be competing with equipment.

Do you keep anything onstage to help you through the gig?

BRAAAANDY! [*Laughter*] It's to gargle in between numbers because I put a lot of effort into what I do and that can shred the back of the throat. So, to get through that huskiness without pain, I found that brandy takes the pain away from reaching the higher notes. It also gives you a raspiness on the bottom end. Not cheap brandy either. I made that mistake. Nice expensive VSOP, thank you. And electrolytes, of course! I love electrolytes. They come in little green sashays. I mix it up with water. It's everything you need, but mostly Vitamin D, Magnesium, and Zinc. The one I love is called Electro Mix. And that I *will* drink, but very little because if you start swallowing anything onstage, you ain't gonna have the energy to get into it.

You mean you'll start feeling lethargic?

It's like a boxer, I suppose. You have to spit it out. It'll wind you something terrible. You bloat yourself, and then the body's trying to digest, and while it's doing that, it's certainly not helping you with the singing side of business. Each to his own, you know. I found my methodology. Had to learn it bloody quickly too. I'm afraid that first band of mine were an impatient bunch of fellas! [*Laughter*]

Is there anything after the show that helps keep your voice in shape?

I go straight to sleep because I'm so totally drained. Vaguely shaky. Just nothing left in me. It's an effort just to sit up because you get incredibly run down. Tour buses are good because you get straight off the stage, onto your bus, and into your bunk. But then, you're wallowing in air conditioner. The air conditioning on the buses and hotels really takes its toll on you. And it's a major problem to find hotels with windows that open. These hermetically sealed tanks are no good for us. They dry out the throat; they dehydrate you. They're very anti-social, I find. I don't care if there's traffic whizzing by with all the car fumes in the world; that seems to be healthier than air conditioner.

In general, how do you take care of your voice on the road?

You have to limit the amount of gigs you do in a week. Three would be ideal, but let's face it, nobody could afford to tour that way. And I can't eat before a gig. I'll eat like a horse after, but it's always gonna be temporary food. This is the trouble about putting weight on. It's none of the fine dining the band get beforehand because I couldn't handle that. It's always a rushed thing like a pizza, and all that fat induced food that ultimately catches up with you and slows you down. It's a Catch-22, and I don't know any way around it. But no catering company in the world is gonna wait around 'til 2 a.m. for me! [*Laughter*] The emphasis on *me*. "Fuck you, we've gone home!"

When you start getting sick, what do you do?

There's nothing you can do except hit the vitamin trail. Very rarely, you have to get a doctor in to have a look at you because you can feel you're damaging yourself at this point. And whatever they'll give you, they're all just a problem in themselves. I found that the steroids stop the pain just like the brandy, but I prefer the brandy. If you haven't got the voice, it just isn't gonna come. That's when all them rehearsals that I hate so much come in to play. [*Cracks up*]

What's rehearsal have to do with not having a voice?

You learn little running patterns on where to breathe into songs. Sometimes onstage you can forget that because you get carried away with the excitement of it all. But those things are really damn important, and I hate them. I'm so self-conscious and see myself as a failure in a rehearsal. [*Groans*]

Why is that?

I don't know why. I'm shy. I'm in the wrong career, really, for someone who's shy and retiring. [*Laughter*] I should take my clothes a little less seriously. Look at the trouble it's got me into!

Are there songs where you wonder if your voice will be there that night?

Ohhh, yeah, many! "Rise" because it's so many words that come in so quickly, and hardly a huff or a puff between that and the chorus. *The chorus is way higher!* That's a difficult one. Or a song like "Religion" you'd think would be easy because it's mumbling away and moaning about the state of the world, and then, in comes this supersonically high chorus of [*sings*] "This is religion!" It's way up there, and I'm always fearful of clawing up to that note.

Are there songs where you've had to adjust the key live?

I've suggested it to various members over the years, but it never works. It doesn't sound the same. And then it's tough tits on me. I think it's easier to adapt the voice sometimes than it is the instrument, and again, that's practice. I would never recommend anyone live next to a singer.

Are you singing in your house a cappella?

[*Sings operatically*] YEEEESSSS! [*Laughter*] I find shouting does me a world of good. But that's not what the neighbors are viewing it as.

What was your most embarrassing vocal mishap ever?

This was at a festival in Estonia. It was really quiet before the gig. We all walked to the stage and—*ROAR*—there's 175,000 people, and my bum just hit the floor. For the first two or three songs, I was squeaking. Not singing. Squeaking. With the sheer nerves of it. But, *grrrr*, you have to pull through, you have to find it in yourself, and eventually you do. There's an even worse one once in Belgium. It was Paul Cook's birthday, and I bought all this champagne for him, and he, of course, didn't wanna drink it. Someone had to. And I volunteered. [*Laughter*] Wow. It was so awful what was coming out of me. I nicknamed myself Honkey Donkey from that point onwards. Most hilariously of all was Neneh Cherry. She come up and said, "John! That gig was the best I've ever seen!" [*Laughs harder*] I suppose the spectacle we made of it became more important than the indulgence of, "Oh, listen to that set of beautiful notes delivered by a virtuoso." Show business is really bloody important up there. *It really is*. Not only just to cover up, but actually to *add*. It's another form of expression. It's another tool in the box.

Do you remember a performance where you surprised yourself?

Recording is difficult for me because I'm so damn shy, but making the last two albums, Walter [Jaquiss, engineer] suggested that I sit in the room next door with just a mic and my headphones and practice it. I was *hoping* he was secretly recording it, and he did! And it was great! [*Laughter*] The pressure was off me, so I was just lulling away, and finding myself inside the melodies. It was a really clever way around it. Trickery, I highly recommend. At the same time, no matter what the lead singer says about, "Turn that camera off," or "Turn that microphone off," DON'T LISTEN TO HIM!

Do you have a favorite vocal performance you're really proud of?

Nooo. It's not like that. Because it's always for me, once I've done the thing, to get onto the next project, not hang on the laurels of it. And, indeed, not to hang around too long on any one song in the studio. If you haven't got it by five or six takes, you're never going to. Give it up. Move on. Get on to something else until you find another way around that. What happens with endless takes, the repetition begins to be permanent, and you just keep on making the same mistakes. At least with me. I get trapped and too much contained inside a thing, and I need to break free of it.

It's interesting that you mentioned finding another way to do something because as you were talking, it was making me think of your song "Another Way."

That's exactly what was on my mind when I wrote it! [*Laughs*]

You're singing, "I've got to find another way," and you're singing it in a voice that we haven't really heard from you yet.

Don't know where it came from, really just wanting to find other ways out of things. I'll tell you, it carried on for a long time, the entrapment of punk. It became a huge trap of people wanting to see or view or hear things in that clichéd manner. When we started, we were no cliché. There was nothing like us. To expect us to carry on in that way for the rest of our lives is ridiculous. If you don't progress, well, you might as well not bother.

That's what's so interesting about *Never Mind the Bollocks*, because in a weird way, there shouldn't have been a second record.
I agree. Looking back on it, it's like, "Well done, move on."

"Here's one album. We just changed the fucking world. See ya later!" [*Laughter*]
You know? We didn't like each other, bye-bye! [*More laughter*] We really do get on alright outside of work. It's just one of those situations. I'd much rather we be friends.

I feel like when people think about you, this outspoken, larger-than-life character comes to mind. But the downside of that is sometimes the actual talent gets lost in the conversation. To me, the reason you're so important is because you're applying the *real* definition of punk rock to your voice as an instrument. Because after the Pistols broke up, you could've played it safe and done that thing forever.
Yeah, yeah, and sound like every other Two-Bob.

Exactly. But what you've been able to do so profoundly with PiL is, you've given yourself the ability to use your voice in every way imaginable without trying to be anything other than what comes into your head. *That's* actually the most punk rock thing you should be known for! You're completely free when you step up to the mic. Not a lot of singers can say that.
Yeah. I thought about this years ago. In the beginning was the human voice, and the human voice was imitating nature. Then we invented instruments, and we asked the human voice to imitate the instruments and ignore its nature. [*Chuckles*] So, that's how I view it.

You know, the word "affectation" can be seen as a negative, but I'm using it in the positive when I say, you have a couple affectations that have become part of your vocal style, and you've been doing it from day one. "Holidays in the Sun" officially kicks off your recording career. First song, first album.
Well, one of my biggest affectations would be the way I roll my Rs. [*Rolls his tongue so it vibrates, then breaks into a laugh*]

That's right! The opening line is, "I wanna see some history," and you go, "I wanna see some histo-*llllllll*-y!" How did rolling your tongue become a part of your arsenal?
I love trebling up my Rs [*does it again, even higher, laughing harder*] Please, do laugh, I got that off a cartoon called Speedy Gonzalez. [*Mimics Speedy Gonzalez*] "Arriba! Andale, andale, andale!" [*Rolls his tongue again, cracking up*] That's the sound he used to make, and it just stuck in my range. When I was very young, I'd watch that on TV and be mesmerized. I must've

been four or five, and I wanted to imitate that sound. And I was ever so pleased that so few people in the world can. Unless you're born into it. [*Laughter*]

You also have a really wicked vibrato. On "Worry" off the 9 album, it just blends so perfectly with the music.

Ahh, yes, it almost syncopates. Good fun, that! I love that song, and I love experimenting with it live. PiL is the kind of band that will do that. We won't set deliberate traps for each other, but if somebody makes a mistake, we'll integrate it. And yes, I can warble in any direction possible at that point because I'm in the groove with the fellas.

I could never do that. You can just turn that on and off?

It's just there in the brain. You don't have to go looking for it. It just automatically fits the purpose. Again, it's back to the toolbox, isn't it?

What's changed the most about your voice since you started?

Depth. The gravity that I can put into things. When you're first out, you're a little squeaky, and you develop all these other skill sets and tones that you can add in there, textures and layers and singing outside of your usual way. Always challenging myself, I am.

If you could duet with any singer—living or dead—who would it be?

Oh, Kate Bush! She asked me once to write a song that we could do together, and I did. I called it "Bird in Hand," and it was about saving parrots from the Venezuelan parrot trade. [*Laughs*] She went, "No, thanks!" [*Laughs harder*] What I was doing was a bit mad for her, and I was astounded, because I always thought her singing was way excellent nuts.

Who are your top five favorite singers of all time?

Doris Day.

For real?

Yeah, for real. I love them old films where she just hums and belts out a tune. *God. The perfection of it.*

Who are your other four?

Roy Orbison, Chris Isaak, Horace Andy, Bryan Ferry. My record collection is vast. I'll have it all, please! I'll quite happily sit at home and try and emulate those kinds of voices, knowing that I can never, ever, in a billion years sing like them. That's why I find them so encouraging because there's nothing that reminds me of me in it. But a bigger influence, oddly enough, would be Benny Hill and Jack Benny, two comedians. I would be glued to Jack Benny when I was young. His sense of timing, the way he spoke, was like a song. It had a distinct melody and a pattern that I really, really liked and understood. And there's where the humor lay, in the delivery of that.

I think I know what Benny Hill did for you.

Benny Hill, of course, because of the implications he'd put in innuendos. He'd sing songs with that wry smile, and the whole thing being completely silly, but wonderfully, bloody, importantly, funny. And a lot of human quality in it too. Vulnerability. I also love Gaelic singers, Irish singers, the balladeers, particularly the blokes because of the [*affects a deep voice*] "tooooones" they put in things. I just love a nice, melancholy ballad about everybody dying a slow, miserable death because of the lack of love in the world. [*Chuckles*] Oddly enough, that stuff cheers you up because it forms compassion in your heart and sense of empathy, and that's what I find folk music does for me. That's why I love just about all women in country music.

I heard you were a big Dolly Parton fan.

Yes, huge. Love her voice. Don't care what she's singing. Those tones, it's like being wrapped up in something lovely and fluffy, like an ostrich blanket.

If you could ask any singer about their voice, who would it be and what would you ask?

Ugghh, there's nothing they could actually teach me here at this point. I do it for a living, and I do it my way, and I found out what works for me. I'm fully not prepared to run up and down the music scales before I go on, or do any of that bollocks.

Well, I'm gonna send you this book when it's done, and I hope you'll flip through it.

I'll definitely give it a read! But as for asking them questions about themselves, no, because I think singers are too tormented as it is. [*Laughs*] We might be seen with a jealous eye from the band members, but worse than that, we're the first on the chopping block in the press. It's a no-win situation, really, and you don't wanna torment your fellow compatriots. [*Laughter*] "Hello, here's a mundane question for ya!"

Well, thanks for letting me torment you!

It's funny, Chrissie Hynde's got a wonderful voice. Love her voice. It's really good. I seen her the other night on a YouTube thing with Neil Young, oddly enough—there's one of my favorites! Definitely him—but the two together was really lovely. And all those naughty, gnarly, Neil Young guitar bits. Fuckin' most excellent! You know, for a laid-back hippie, the boy can let it rip! But Chrissie taught me how to play guitar, and I never, not once, asked her how to sing. And she never, not once, suggested it! [*Laughter*] And I never learned to play the guitar!

AIMEE MANN

"WE HAVE TO SIT THERE and think about mucus."

Aimee Mann just summed up the glamorous life of a singer. For the moment, however, let's turn our attention elsewhere because this woman deserves it. We fell in love with her as the singer of 'Til Tuesday, one of the great '80s bands. But Aimee Mann kept moving forward, and as a solo artist, has released one great record after another, becoming one of the most well-respected, critically acclaimed, singer-songwriters of our generation.

Her cinematic music helped inspire Paul Thomas Anderson's *Magnolia*, which is jam-packed with Mann's music, for which she received an Academy Award nomination. But even though she has two Grammys and the Academy can suck it, that's not what's important.

As Aimee says, there are certain artists, certain songs, that have a pull to them. That's all you want—a voice that pulls you in and draws you close. For Aimee, it didn't come easy. She fought for it with hard work, repetition, and the passion to find her own space. And in case you forgot, she was also the nihilist's girlfriend who cut off her toe in *The Big Lebowski*. So, let's remember who we're speaking with, dude...'cause she really ties the room together.

Who first exposed you to singing?

I don't think anyone did. I sang in the choir at school, but it certainly wasn't some overt display of talent. I was really shy, a kid who just kept stuff to myself. When I got mono, I was out of school for three weeks and had to stay in bed. One of my brothers had gotten a guitar for Christmas that he never played, so I got it out of the closet and started teaching myself some Neil Young songs with a songbook and kind of sang along to that.

Were you emulating anyone when you started out?

When I started playing guitar, it was Bob Dylan and Neil Young songs. I was just trying to sing them in tune; I wasn't trying to emulate anybody. But when I started this punk band, it was very shouty, new wavey, and experimental, so I was just trying to be weird. I thought Nina Hagen was fascinating because she had this crazy, operatic style of punk music.

How did you find your own voice?

I was trying to sing over electric guitars and drums, and terrible monitors, and you can't hear yourself, so I just kind of shouted. That was really my style. If you listen to the first 'Til Tuesday record, that's basically what I'm doing. I'm trying to hear myself. [*Chuckles*] There's no other tone goal. But in order to find your own voice, you have to do a thing over and over and over. Mastering the craftsmanship of something will enable you to find out who you are within the craft of it. But it's worthwhile to find your own sound because why sound like everybody else? That space is already taken. Find your own space.

Did you ever have any vocal training?

Occasionally I've taken singing lessons. They have you do stuff and you're like, *I don't know if this is helping or not.* [*Laughter*] I also went to Berklee College of Music to be a voice major, not because I had a lot of musical talent, but I had this idea that if I learned about music, then maybe I would know if I had any talent. They had a summer session that anybody could go to, and I really, really worked hard. But it just felt like, *I don't think this is working.* So, I switched to being a bass major and learned how to play bass.

What wasn't working for you?

Whatever they were telling me, the exercises, the warm-ups, the scales, and breathing from your diaphragm. I was like, *What?* [*Laughs, confused*] How do you know when you're breathing from your diaphragm? *Like how do you know that?* [*Laughter*] The conclusion I drew was people can either sing or they can't. It just didn't seem teachable to me, and I still kind of feel that way.

Are you nervous before you perform?

In my first band, I would just drink through the whole thing., so I must have been. They sold Grapefruit juice in glass bottles, and I would pour out a third of it and fill that stuff with vodka and drink that onstage. I don't think of myself as much of a drinker. Then, I think about that, and I'm like, that's *kind of* a lot of alcohol. [*Laughs*]

How are your nerves beforehand these days?
It's usually fine. But it's almost always connected with whether anything is different. Like if there's a different musician or somebody in the crew is different, or if it's a venue I'm unfamiliar with, or if there's a problem at soundcheck. Some shows can be weird. Outdoor shows can be weird. There's things that throw you off.

How do you calm yourself in those times?
I just allow the music itself to calm me down. And playing with my friends. I'll look at the bass player and say something dumb to him, or I'll make eye contact with my fellow musicians. It's a team effort.

Do you do vocal warm-ups before shows?
No, I find that doing scales and stuff does not help me. It just doesn't engage my voice in the same way. What helps is if we have a long soundcheck, or if I'm playing songs backstage. Just having played a bunch of songs will help. If we had a show where we didn't get to soundcheck, it would be hard to walk right onstage and sound good for the first couple songs.

Is there anything after the show that helps keep your voice in shape?
Alcohol is hard on your voice, so I don't drink a lot. I found out the hard way that screaming can screw your voice up. [*Laughs*] I went to Disneyland with a couple of kids, and for fun, you scream on all the rides. But it fucked my voice up for a couple weeks.

So, how do you take care of your voice on the road?
If I have a cold or I'm congested, I'll drink ginger tea. But I'll tell you what really worked: I had a bad cold, and I could barely croak out a few words, and I found this advice to "Warm-up by very lightly humming one note." Just to yourself. [*Calmly hums*] When you feel a little more confident, maybe hum two notes. Just go up and down. Long, slow, and quiet. But do that all day. It fucking worked. By the time the show came around, I could sing. I was shocked.

Are there songs where you wonder if your voice will be there that night?
If it's that hard, I just lower the key. There are no heroic parts. My vocal style is very conversational. There's no showboating. I don't like showboating. I couldn't do it even if I liked it. I just don't have that kind of voice.

What was your most embarrassing vocal mishap ever?
It's happened a few times where I'll inhale saliva, or my vocal cords get irritated, and I'm coughing because something's happened, and I just can't croak out anything. Sometimes you can stop singing, and people don't notice if the song continues. But, if you *can* talk to the audience, you can just, "Give me a minute," and kind of joke around about it. This is not super

pleasant, but when I start the falsetto stuff, sometimes it'll make my throat a little more mucusy, and the danger of that is, you have to be careful of your breathing, because if you breathe in a little piece of mucus, it goes right on your vocal cords.

[*Laughter*] Isn't it crazy, all the shit that goes along with this?
I know! We have to sit there and think about mucus. Do you wanna know what I've been doing? This is very recently. I've been breathing through my nose, and it's easier to sing longer and steadier notes. You should try it. It's really helpful for a passage where you're running out of air. There's a song I have called "Goose Snow Cone," and there's this line, "Lookin' into the face of the goose snow cooo-ooo-ooo-oone," which is a long fucking time to extend one note. And for like two bars, I'll breathe in through my nose, and then, I'll have enough. But if I take a big gulp through my mouth, it's not enough. It's a different quality of air.

Do you remember a performance where you surprised yourself?
Not really. When I write a song, I know exactly how it's supposed to sound. There's kind of an exact blueprint in my mind. Singing for me is telling a story, and it's about the song, so I'm trying to stay out of the way. I don't like the singers that tell you how you're supposed to be feeling. I like the singer to just present the story and *you* have the feeling about it.

How are you with hearing your own voice?
I'm not one of those people who's like, "Ewww, yuck!" Having said that, I don't think I'm a very good singer. There's definitely circumstances where I'm like [*makes a fart sound*]. I've never sung in tune on television because I'm always nervous, and I can't control my breath.

Do you have a favorite vocal performance you're really proud of?
I think the vocals on *Mental Illness* are really good. I'm really happy with the performances on that record. If it goes on the record, I'm usually pretty happy with it.

"Voices Carry" is one of the most iconic, new wave anthems of the '80s. It's also a vocal placement master class, if you're trying to understand how to seamlessly transition to different parts of your voice throughout a song. For example: you start off singing low in the verse. Then, you switch to your mid-range during the pre-chorus. Then, you slide into your falsetto for the chorus, "Hush hush." But the next line, "Keep it down now," you go low again, Then, you climb back up to the high note on "Voices carry." Then, at the end, you're screaming out and sustaining some high notes like you're in a real fight, and now you don't care that voices carry.
Yeah, yeah. It's a hard song to sing, so that's probably true. I agree with you.

What's changed the most about your voice since you started?
I think the biggest change was probably the second 'Til Tuesday record. Just being in the studio and actually being able to hear myself, I started to sing differently. The songs were no

longer written in a rehearsal space where I couldn't hear anything. Who knew that hearing yourself would be a prerequisite to sing well? [*Laughter*] It seems shocking!

If you could duet with one singer—living or dead—who would it be?
Colin Blunstone.

Aww, that would be great! You guys would sound good together.
I think so too. Best rock vocalist ever. Beautiful, velvety voice.

Who are your top five favorite singers of all time?
Sinatra, Colin Blunstone. I think Elton John's voice is fantastic. Great falsetto.

Oh! Another great song to practice vocal placement is "Razor Face" by Elton John.
That's so funny because I was recently listening to that song! Fantastic, right?

The way he transitions between his falsetto to his head voice? [*Sings*] "Needs a man who's young to walk him 'round…"
I know! It's amazing. And it has so much feeling in it. I love Donald Fagen's voice because it's so him. Nobody else sounded like him. He just sounded like this weirdo from New York. It was just so idiosyncratic. I love singers where you can really tell it's them. I do think there's a thing with singers today where they just all sound the same. They all have great pipes, but they all have the same style. You know that little baby hipster voice that the girls have?

Yeah, there's a weird thing a lot of female pop artists are doing where they'll pronounce words with a certain affectation?
Absolutely. And they all sound the same. It drives me crazy because nobody sounds like themself, and it's just not that interesting. I like Elliott Smith's vocals for the same reason. He sounds like himself. Obviously, Paul McCartney has got a great voice, but I was trying to learn "Martha My Dear," and talk about fuckin' transitions! It's super low, then it goes super high. It's all over the place, and he's fucking perfect in every section of his vocal. *Perfect.* I think that adds up to at least five. And I have to stick my husband, Michael Penn, in because I always describe his voice and music as if The Beatles were Jewish. [*JTG agrees, laughing*] There's a little Dylan and a little Lennon, and it's a really interesting mixture.

If you could ask any singer about their voice, who would it be, and what would you ask?
I'm so curious about real singers like Adele, or people who can really bring it. I just don't know how they do it. [*Laughs*] I feel like my vocal cords don't work the same. Or I have a very quiet voice. I probably have the same equipment, the same diaphragm, but how do they get this big, giant sound, and I can't? But I don't think that's answerable.

CHAN MARSHALL

"AMATEUR."

That's the first word Chan Marshall says to me as I fumble to get my tape recorder to work. I already love her. Chan is known to most of the world by her stage name: Cat Power. It doesn't matter if she's playing garage rock, R&B, folk, gospel, Americana, or hip-hop, her deliberate execution and unconventional production make her the type of singer who can draw from any genre to build something completely new.

Her voice can be painfully vulnerable, bloody and brutal, sweat-soaked and seductive, or beautifully playful, sometimes all within a single lyric. And even though she's been releasing records since the '90s, it feels like she's just getting warmed-up.

I knew Chan would be awesome to speak with, but I never expected she'd be mixing up magical potions to help us out when times get tough. I should have, especially after all my thoughts above, because this woman is at her best when she's mixing it up. No matter what life throws her way, she always comes out on top, better than before. A true artist. A true survivor. A freedom fighter. And a vampire killer.

Chan Marshall, you're the greatest.

Who first exposed you to singing?

I always thought it was my dad or my stepdad because they were in bands. But I was at home with my son, cooking some stuff for him and singing, and I realized it was my grandmother. She raised me since I was about one to four and a half, and she was always singing country. We'd go to church and clap and sing the hymns, so my influence was definitely southern country. She died right before the pandemic, and I realized, *Oh, my God, I can't call her*. But I found myself doing what she did. I'd be alone, cooking and singing.

Were you emulating anyone when you started out?

My grandmother used to tape record me when I was little, and she'd tell me what songs to sing. One of them was "The Gambler." She's like, "Oh, play 'The Gambler!'" But her favorite one for me to sing was "Salty Dog." She liked me to sing it real slow, so I had to emulate country for her to enjoy. She'd always make me sing. Even near the end.

How did you find your own voice?

I sang all the time. Growing up, I was always going to different schools, and was always the new kid. I struggled to find friendships, and it was hard because, generally, the people who were into music were dudes. And boys didn't want to talk to me about music. If I was somehow chirping up and saying something about the Circle Jerks or [Hendrix drummer] Mitch Mitchell...

Mitch Mitchell, God bless you!

You know what I'm saying? But I was never invited into the conversation of music. They just assumed that they knew more than me 'cause "She's just a girl," and that fuckin' vibe as usual. I just got used to it. But in PE class, you always had to shower, and I would wait in the toilet and not shower. Then, when everybody was gone, I would sing alone in the locker rooms because every locker room always has a lot of tile and tall ceilings, and there would be no one around in between classes. I would just sing, sing, singety sing. Sometimes the Black girls would catch me, and say, "Ohhh, she's singin' again!" And they'd egg me on, you know, "Play that one from *The Color Purple*," and I'd do "Miss Celie's Blues (Sister)." They'd be laughin' and singin' with me, and that was like the only time anybody ever heard me sing back then.

Did you ever have any vocal training?

At church with my grandmother. [*Sings*] "I'll fly away, Oh Lordy, I'll fly away." You just learn the notes, and you sing 'em with happiness. When I started singing, I felt like I did it for my stepdad, for my father, for my friends who passed away who were in bands. I thought, *I have to do this if I'm getting asked*. I felt like I had to do it for everybody who deserves this. The opportunity. I'll do it because a lot of people don't get the chance to do that. That became like a private, secret commitment. I've never told anyone that.

Well, I love that you did. Are you nervous or confident before you perform?

I always feel nervous when we're literally writing the set list. I said *literally* in the correct form! [*JTG laughs*] Usually, when we're doing that, I can't think straight, and I can't focus. Last night was my first show since the pandemic, in my hometown of Atlanta. My fingers went numb, I couldn't feel my leg, and I got nervous in a very different way. Normally, my heart rate will just increase all of a sudden like [*rolls her tongue super fast*] and sometimes I'll get in a state where I was last night where everything starts vibrating. It usually starts with my hands, and then my knees and my face. My whole body, the whole show, will just be vibrating, and that's usually when I have the best show. Strange.

Do you do vocal warm-ups before shows?

Absolutely not. I usually have a couple cigarettes, some tequila. I have a Throat Coat Tea with two tablespoons of honey, and that's what I have onstage. I'll put a little in the back of my throat, and then I'll spit it out, or sip it. I have that every single night.

Do you have any rituals before you hit the stage?

Privately, I like to light a candle if I have one. A lot of people I love have passed. I'll have the picture of the person on my smart phone, light the candle, and have incense. I didn't have it last night, which is why I might have been trembling in a way I'm not familiar with. Usually, I'll bring the incense with me onstage, and that really calms me down. That's the ritual. A gentle prayer to the universe.

So, it's almost like the show is being dedicated in their honor?

Yeah. If they're with us. 'Cause they are. It's like an invitation.

Is there anything after the show that helps keep your voice in shape?

A bottle of wine with a friend I haven't seen in a long time. Maybe two cigarettes. I just relax.

How do you take care of your voice on the road?

I don't do soundchecks and I always sleep. When I have my son on tour, I'm so busy in the day with him. We always go to a museum, or a science center, or the park, or a swimming pool. But when I'm alone, I always sleep. My dad was a singer, so I learned that through him. I noticed how he slept, and I noticed that helps my nerves, my focus, and my voice.

When you start getting sick, what do you do?

Oh man! I have this whole situation. When I feel it coming on, I take Effervescent. It's like Alka-Seltzer, but it's vitamin C. I'll do that every time after I pee, 'cause you lose your vitamin content out of your body. Then I'll do like twenty drops of Echinacea with an aspirin twice a day. If that doesn't knock it out, I have these Chinese herbs that I take three times a day to knock out the mucus that's forming. I'll drink Chamomile 'cause it's anti-viral, and just a lot of warm liquids to burn it to death and get it flushing all the bad cells out of the body. And inhaling a lot of essential oils. Eucalyptus can open the chambers up, but Rosemary oil can actually kill mucus in the lungs.

And how are you inhaling the oils, a humidifier?

That, or I'll just hold it under my nose and take deep breaths. Hold one nostril closed and do like five on each side. Just walk around with it in your pocket and do it whenever.

And you find that works?

It does. Also, what works is this soup that I make. I've always been sick. When I was born, I was in an incubator, so I have auto-immune problems. But I found that if I smash a few cloves of garlic, it takes about fifteen minutes for the natural chemical called allicin to form. Garlic is like a natural antibiotic. You know, it's a killer of vampires. [*Laughter*] Leave it on the side for fifteen minutes, and while you're doing that, get some vegetable stock, and put some onion, carrot and fresh thyme in there. Thyme is also antiviral. Then add the garlic to the vegetable stock on low heat. Then add the juice of two lemons, and four heaping tablespoons of Manuka honey. Then roll two Zinc tablets up in a paper towel, smash 'em with a hammer, and dust it inside. Don't let it boil, 'cause you'll kill it. Just let it simmer. Then you mince the stems of some cilantro and put the leaves in there. Then you add eight more ounces of water, and turn it off, put the lid on and let it steep. You can leave it on a low heat. The longer you do, the more delicious it is. Then you get a strainer and just pour this liquid gold over your glass. But the trick is not to drink it like you're thirsty or in a rush. Just little sips during the day, and it'll basically kill whatever virus is in your sinuses.

Thanks for the recipe!

Everybody I know's like, "Oh, I'll get some medicine." I'm like, "Really? What kind of medicine?" [*Meekly responds*] "Nyquil." I can't take that shit, it's disgusting. It's like you got deadly boogers in your chest and pouring liquid glue over it.

Are there songs where you wonder if your voice will be there that night?

Always. All the loud, high ones. But you just have to do it. Even if you're afraid it's not gonna work, you just have to say, "Why worry?" Just fucking try it out.

Are there songs you've recorded where you've had to adjust the key live?

No, never. But I just did this memorial for a friend of mine who passed, and the song was Marianne Faithfull's cover of a Kurt Vile song, "The Ballad of the Soldier's Wife." The musical director said, "What key is good for you?" I said, "I don't know." So, I went up to the rehearsal, and everyone kind of lost their shit, and stopped playing during the song. I look at them like, what's going on? As a young adult, I learned about free jazz and improvisation, and that's kind of my ball game when I'm singing. I like to enjoy singing and fit myself where I feel warm and safe and cozy, and then, do what I want. But I realized, working with these actual sheet music people, that I was fucking them up because they were expecting me to play my voice like an instrument is on paper. So then, I had to very quickly, sing every single fuckin' note, and I delivered, of course, but everyone's freaking out. Like, "Can you not sing in that key, low?" And I realized, "Oh, you want me to sing like Marianne Faithfull." It's the same notes, but they wanted me to sing in the same register.

What was your most embarrassing vocal mishap ever?
Once I was at the Knitting Factory, it was my birthday, I think I turned twenty-one, and I accidentally smoked pot like a fool...

Wait, how do you accidentally smoke pot?
Well, when I was younger, I smoked pot all the time. It was second nature. I hadn't done it for a few years, and then I thought, *Oh, this is why I don't do that anymore.* [*Laughter*] I used to turn my back to the audience. I may have been playing "Rockets," and I almost fell offstage 'cause I was so stoned. But accidents happen in every song, in my opinion.

You used to turn your back on the audience? I'm interested in that.
When I did the first show for this record called *The Greatest*, it was the first time in my life that I wasn't playing guitar or piano. And when I stood on the stage, I saw the audience. *I never saw the audience.* I always had my hair in my eyes or was always on my guitar or the piano. I'd always close my eyes, I never looked at people, and now I didn't have anything in my fucking hands! So, I was just standing there, and I couldn't distract myself, and I was forced to see their faces. Every one of those motherfuckers was smiling, and they were all younger than me. It hit me like an arrow. *Damn, you see how asleep you've been?* I realized they were all there for me. They weren't there to be cool or posture or get laid; they were there for me. That tour was the first time I sang in my heart since I was probably six years old for my grandmother.

Do you remember a performance where you surprised yourself?
Whenever I go to a studio, I like to sit at every instrument and get comfortable, and make sure the mics are in the right place, get the levels so they're not hot when they're recording and stuff. So, I started on the piano, just warming up, and I played this song by Rihanna I had never played before called "Stay." It was the first time I had worked with [engineer] Rob Schnapf, and the surprise was, a couple days later, he said, "Can I play you something?" I said, "Sure." He had recorded it. That was on my last record, *Wanderer*.

How are you with hearing your own voice?
I have to listen to it over and over to find what my brain hears in my head. When I listen back, there's all this stuff in my head, and I have to decide if I'm gonna do it or not. Once I'm done and it's sealed, I usually don't listen to it ever again. Then live, I like to fly freely, if I

feel like changing it, or doing something new, because I always like to continue the journey of the song.

Do you have a favorite vocal performance you're really proud of?

Patti Smith's daughter, Jesse, has this company called Pathway to Paris, and they were doing concerts around America to help people understand the necessity for action on climate change. I played three songs on a grand piano at Carnegie Hall. Remember I told you about the vibrating? That was one of the nights I was vibrating from beginning to end. That was a really good performance. Another one would be at The Apollo. Two nights in a row. I got the mic and went down in the audience. That was probably the most fun I ever had singing.

How about on record?

I like this Kitty Wells cover, "It Wasn't God Who Made Honky Tonk Angels," on the new record [*Covers*]. It just felt so natural to sing in that style. I really like my delivery on that. It sounds fun even though it's really sad.

A lot's been made about you being the queen of lo-fi in the early years where everything was just recorded pretty raw. But the production of your voice made a big leap on *You Are Free*, and then again on *Sun*. All of a sudden, you're doing all these rad, melodic background vocals, and layering yourself in interesting ways. Can you talk about the evolution of your voice in the studio? Those records really see you embrace the studio as an instrument.

Yeah, I was using my voice like a poet, a live poet that had an opportunity to record. But every record's a learning curve. I had to fight with engineers in the past who were working on the albums to please just do what I ask. "Can you please just rewind that portion, and put it on a different track, and then slow it down and replay it?" And it was just like, [*mocks an engineer/producer getting frustrated*] "Awww!" They just couldn't cope. I don't know if it's 'cause I'm a woman or something, but I don't want anyone telling me what to do. If it's coming from me, it's my lesson. I know that sounds egotistical, but it's not that. I've always worked with producers and engineers, and then got credit stolen from me. So, that's why I'm always like, "I produce everything," and now I'm really vocal about it. But I was just wanting to try something new, do something different. I never really know what I'm doing. To me, that's the fun part. Not making a cage or a box for myself, just flying with it, making sure that it comes to me, giving it space to come to me. Before, I never did that. I never gave it space. I just documented the song and got the fuck outta there.

There a tune on *Sun* called "Peace and Love" where you basically rap some of the lyrics. "Black" off *Wanderer* has the same kinda vibe. But rap done wrong is horrifically embarrassing, especially if you're a white girl, yet it sounds like you instinctively have the knowledge in you. It's not like you're trying to be someone else. You're doing it organically, with your phrasing, and you really know where the moves are. How did that come about for you?

I love hip-hop and rap. It's one of the greatest expressions of the word. *Thank you!* I feel it's a rap too. There's so many rappers that I love. And yes, half of it is the delivery: Tupac, Biggie, Jay-Z, Trick Daddy, Juvenile. The other halves are the tone, the cadence, and the story. So, just with that, you've got a great singer there. Talib Kweli says that the great rappers to the core are just really big music nerds. I think that's what I am and where it comes from. I always knew a lot of different music, so the knowledge is there. And it's stored in a place that will live forever. It's not that I set out to, "Oh, I wanna do a rap song," I'm just making music, and it's all coming from one big source.

Yes, that's exactly right, 'cause it doesn't feel like someone that's trying to do something that's out of your realm for you to do. It feels like it's—
My life.

What's changed the most about your voice since you started?
It's come back around to being the voice my grandmother made me happy to sing with.

If you could duet with one singer—living or dead—who would it be?
That's not fair. It has to be one male and one female.

Do it.
Billie Holiday and Otis Redding.

You and Eddie Vedder have sung on each other's records as well. Have you learned anything from singing with him?
To be gentle with myself. He's very gentle with me. The father figures I have, I consider myself their son. You know the whole "They" and "Them" thing that's been happening? I've been questioning, am I "They?" I wear eyeliner like my mom, but I don't wanna show my tits and my ass, ya know? That's something private to me as a female, and he taught me through the dignity and honor that he showed me that I have to honor myself too, and that's really beautiful to come from a man who's a friend. With boys there's like a pecking order. [*Speaks like a young boy*] "How do you know about Black Sabbath? How do you know about Corrosion of Conformity? Or John Lee Hooker, or Elizabeth Cotten, or John Fahey?" Eddie taught me that I don't have to explain shit to anybody.

Who are your top five favorite singers of all time?
Oh man. There's so many. But Bob Seger is probably the most underrated singer. Obviously, Dr. Nina Simone and Bob Dylan, because of what they taught humanity. Billie Holiday because of her soul. She knows that she doesn't have a chance in hell, and that's why hearing her voice is like the sweetest sound to me. Because, yes, you can hear all that pain, but when she's singing it's like she's allowed to be a butterfly. She's allowed to belong to the universe,

and to be soft and gentle and free and light and happy. And Hank Williams. He wrote like 800 songs!

If you could ask any singer about their voice, who would it be and what would you ask?
I'd ask Bob Dylan, [*mimics his Muppet style vocal tone*] *Why did he change his voice?*

On *Nashville Skyline*?
Yeah, why? Why? Why? Why?

And with that, we begin to sing a duet of "I Threw It All Away," like Bob Dylan on Nashville Skyline.

MICHAEL MCDONALD

ALL YOU GOTTA DO IS LISTEN to the opening line of "Takin' It to the Streets" by The Doobie Brothers and you'll hear a voice that single-handedly sums up an entire era of music that so many of us hold dear. That moment in the mid-'70s when Michael McDonald's velvety smooth vocal tone and layered harmonies set the standard for the perfect drive down the California coast at sunset. You do that today and the world still feels wide open with possibility.

The Doobie Brothers were already established when Michael joined up with them, but it was his unmistakable voice and songwriting talent that would carry them to three Grammy Awards and an induction into The Vocal Group and Rock & Roll Halls of Fame. His solo career would lead to another Grammy, a string of top-ten hits, and the award I'm bestowing him as the most enjoyable singer to imitate. And what about those iconic background vocals he became known for with Steely Dan? Or writing for Van Halen? Or singing with Ray Charles? I got it all covered.

"You don't know me but I'm your brother..."

Who first exposed you to singing?

My dad was a singer. He mostly did it for his own enjoyment, but he did perform quite a bit around the St. Louis area in different pubs and saloons. He was a guy that everybody kind of loved to hear sing the old songs, stuff from the '30s, '20s, ragtime stuff. He classically had an Irish tenor voice. By the time I was ten, I followed him around in all his haunts where he sang. For a guy who never drank, he was in more bars than probably anyone who's ever set a record for it. But he just loved singing with different piano players around town. So, I kind of grew up in that environment, performing live, more or less spontaneously. Seems like I've been doing it my whole life. Since I was about four, they put me on a bar and I sang some way too serious song for a four-year-old, and everybody thought it was funny and clapped for me. That was the big mistake. I couldn't get enough of it.

Were you emulating your dad when you started, or trying to sing like someone else?

No, at that age, I was just singin' my heart out. Probably out of tune too. But over the years, being in Top 40 bands, you had to play as much of what was on the radio as possible. So, I found myself studying a lot of singers of the time. For instance, when we would do a Ray Charles or Marvin Gaye song, I would go to school on their phrasing and inflections and emulate those as much as I could to make our performance sound just like the record. If you could achieve that you had a good shot of becoming popular on the local music scene.

That's so interesting 'cause on your *Motown* [covers] records, I notice you lean heavily toward the Marvin Gaye stuff, like it really influenced you growing up.

Yeah, most definitely. Taking on that project had a lot to do with that. I really couldn't figure out why they would ask me of all people to do that project. But I thought, I should just say yes because one thing's for sure, I've gone to school on this stuff my whole life, so maybe I can bring something to it from that angle. Maybe I've been training for this without realizing it.

How did you find your own voice?

In the end, it was probably an amalgam of many other singers who I emulated coming up, going back to Nat Cole, Ray Charles, Frank Sinatra, Tony Bennett. Those were the artists that my dad and I listened to together when I was a kid, in his car, driving around. When Ray Charles or Frank Sinatra would come on, it was like the whole world filled up with the voice of these guys, and bein' a little kid, barely able to see over the dashboard, it really made an impression. And, of course, enjoying that music with my dad was a real bonding experience, so those are precious memories for me.

Did you ever have any vocal training?

Not really, no. When I felt like I needed to take some protective measures, I worked with a vocal trainer in LA for a couple sessions, and he gave me some valuable lessons about warming-up. I think that's important, loosening your vocal cords. But one of the most important things a singer can do is train yourself to relax, especially being in front of a loud band where hearing yourself is limited. A large part of my training was learning not to sing too hard, and find my voice in a more relaxed state so that I could endure throughout the evening. And then, find a way to bring passion to that, so it sounds like you're screamin' your head off, but you're not.

Are you nervous or confident before you perform?

Typically, if I start yawning before a show, I realize I'm kind of hyperventilating. A natural reaction is you feel sleepy, and you start yawning a lot. You're actually not breathing right, you're kind of hyperventilating, and that's your body's way of getting oxygen. So, when I start doin' that, I realize I must be a little nervous about tonight for some reason. We change things up a lot, so we'll rehearse things at soundcheck that are a little different from how we normally do it and that always causes me a little bit of anxiety. *Do I remember exactly how that works?* But I don't really get nervous 'cause mostly I enjoy playin' with the guys so much that I look forward to it, and the audiences are usually great.

So, tell me about your vocal warm-ups before shows?

One of the most important ones I've ever learned is to stay low. I'll hear a lot of singers pushing at the top of their range before a show, and I used to do that too. Just seein' how high I could get, or where my voice is at that night because, in the course of touring, there's a little wear and tear with that.

But now when you warm-up, you stay low?

As low as I can. I find those low notes rattle my vocal cords in a way that tends to relax them. It's like massage therapy. If I can stay low with my exercises, the lowest notes I can sing, I find that I do my voice a lot more good than if I were trying to open it by gettin' in my upper ranges. It's kind of a mental exercise too because you wanna sing a little higher, see what you've got, but I avoid that temptation. I convince myself that if I just stay low and relax my cords as much as possible, I'll have the most I'm gonna get by the time it comes to sing in the upper ranges. That usually works. Sometimes, I'll go to the lowest two notes I can sing, and just pivot back and forth from the second lowest note I can sing to the lowest note I can sing, doin' whatever I can to stretch those muscles in my neck so those muscles aren't any more tense than they have to be. I find that nothing seems to help my voice on a bad day more than exercises.

How do you take care of your voice on the road?

Sleep is important. Inherently, with the road, you start to live like a vampire. In the old days, we were young and partyin', and I don't think I really thought that much about what shape my voice was gonna be in the next night. I was used to having a certain amount of natural talent and I took it for granted. In The Doobie Brothers, a lot of our background stuff was high. I had a lot of falsetto in the songs we wrote and prided myself on being able to get up in the upper ranges in my head voice. But as I got older, I realized that that's not my strength anymore, and if I really wanna have that range at all, I gotta sleep cause that falsetto is the first thing to go.

When you start getting sick, what do you do?

That's always a nightmare. I have probably done more Z packs than most people 'cause I try to get on it right away. The sooner you knock it down, the more chance you have of finishing the tour and not canceling shows. Knock on wood, I haven't had to do that much. But as recently as this last tour, there were a couple shows I had to cancel because my voice gave out. I got the flu and couldn't sing through it. The audience are amazingly understanding when you're sick, and they appreciate you makin' the effort, but there comes a time where you're goin', *I'm not giving these people anything that's worth payin' money for tonight*. [*Chuckles*] So, the better part of valor is to cancel and make up the show another time when you can actually sing for them.

Do you have any rituals before you hit the stage?

I mostly try to relax and play the piano as much as I can an hour or two before I go up. But I'll sit and hang with the band and the crew at catering even if I'm not gonna eat. I like to spend that time with the guys that I work with 'cause we enjoy each other's company. Then we do some VIP meet and greet stuff a lot, so I try to get as relaxed as I can before that. I don't like a lot of activity, and to feel harried any more than I have to, and then go right onstage.

Do you get concerned about your voice during the meet and greet?

Sometimes I do. I try not to overdo it and talk too much. But I like to visit with folks and give 'em time, and make 'em feel like I'm present and accounted for.

Is there anything after the show that helps keep your voice in shape?

What I try to *not* do is talk too much. Singing, by comparison, is the easiest thing to do with your voice. But when you just sang a whole show, and then you go backstage and you start talking to people, especially in a crowded room, that's probably the most damage you do in the whole night to your voice.

Are there songs where you wonder if your voice will be there that night?

Probably from the first one. I always see where I'm at on "Yah Mo B There," our opening song. A lot of times I'll pick an opening song that helps me open up. No matter how much I sing backstage, it's never the same as when I get onstage and I really start to put out. I don't seem to be able to do that in my dressing room. For some reason, psychologically I can't really bring myself to sing the way I sing onstage at home, or in a closed room, when it's just me. So, when I get onstage, I know that I'm gonna be pushing harder than I have, so it's always a good idea to start with a song not too hard in the upper ranges. "Yah Mo" is one of those where I'm just kinda pokin' at it up there in the high parts and ad libs because I'm not sure I've got it, and I don't wanna go off a cliff. But you can find other ways to make the song work.

Like an alternate melody or somethin'?

Yeah, an alternate melody, and what you might do improvisationally. That's one of the most important things about being a singer who performs a lot: you gotta know your "go to" stuff, your alternative licks that you have in your pocket where you can still put the song over with a certain amount of emotion and passion. You don't wanna have one way of singing a song, and then if you can't sing it that way, you're screwed. You wanna have a "go to" range, so if your upper range isn't there, you still have some idea of how you'll put the song over.

Are there songs where you've had to adjust the key live?

I've lowered some keys over the years. I find that as I get older, there's no sense in fighting. For the longest time, it was kind of an ego thing for me to keep the songs in the original keys. I did that as long as I could, then I suddenly realized, I'm not doin' anybody any favors here. [*JTG cracks up*] So, I went ahead and lowered 'em, and after all that, it was really a good thing, instead of dreading, *Oh God, here comes that one.*

What are the craziest ones for you?

"I Keep Forgettin'" and "What a Fool Believes" are probably the highest keys, and the most strenuous to sing. Just bring 'em down a key. Nobody knows the difference and *you don't even know the difference* after you've sung it enough. We even tried to do "Real Love" in a lower key, but it just felt so weird that I said, "Let's just keep it in F." That's the song every night where I think, *Oh God, here we go*, but we usually get through it okay. I just have to be careful that I don't hurt myself and the rest of the show suffers.

Is it the line, "Well, we've both lived long enough to know"?

Absolutely. That little lift is the hardest part to sing. It's important for me to really concentrate on relaxing so I can get up to the notes pitch-wise and not be pushing too hard. That's only gonna do more damage than good.

What was your most embarrassing vocal mishap ever?

There was one night at the Thousand Oaks Performing Arts Center where I literally had no voice, but, for whatever reason, I decided that I just needed to get out there and do the show. On the third song in, I realized, *This is not good.* I was worse than I thought. I was just limping through the show. At one point, I even apologized to the audience, which is something you're *never* supposed to do. [*Chuckles*] Promoters hate when you do that. They think people are gonna start asking for their money back, but I said, "I'm sorry, I'm a little sick tonight, but I'm gonna do my best for you, and I hope you'll understand." The audience were almost more supportive than usual, but it was like I was living my worst nightmare. That's probably the hardest show I ever had to do.

Do you remember a performance where you surprised yourself?

I was one of those people that would get onto a record and listen to it incessantly. All my favorite songs were on *Stevie Wonder's Greatest Hits*, like "You Met Your Match." I just studied those so much, and I think, mentally, was kind of tracing his voice. There are a couple licks he did where a couple nights later, I was in a nightclub singing, and just accidentally fell into one of those riffs. All of a sudden, I opened up this whole style of singing that I'd never tried before. I didn't consciously mean to try it, but listening to all those songs that week, my brain had kind of charted it, and, in an unguarded moment, my brain decided to sing that lick, and I remember thinking, *Wow, that was interesting!* And I started to pursue that kind of vocal approach, a little more classical R&B style of singing.

How are you with hearing your own voice?

I think every singer has some reason to hate their own voice. The first time you hear yourself back on tape, that's a shocking moment. You think you know how you sound, and then you hear yourself back, and go, *That's what I sound like?* Then, from that moment on, you're kind of reconciling with that reality and see your glaring bad habits—of course, pronunciation has always been a problem for me. But you see all the things you find unpleasant about your voice, and I think you spend the rest of your life trying to clarify those things, or work on those things, and get a better understanding of what you really sound like.

Have you been able to do that?

I love singing live 'cause I don't really worry about it so much. I hate singing in the studio 'cause all of a sudden, I get all tight. Some artists do it with more ease than I do emotionally and mentally, but it's not my favorite thing. What I've learned over these last few projects, the *Motown* projects especially, was to go ahead and just keep singing twenty, thirty takes of the song, because that's when I actually relax and sing the song, connecting with my inner self better. I get a better performance.

Do you have a favorite vocal performance you're really proud of?

The *Motown* records are some of the ones I've enjoyed listening to the most. And then, I enjoyed the *Blue Obsession* record. I think I've come to a better understanding with myself in the latter years of singing.

You don't dig your earlier work?!

With the Doobies, I remember listening to old roughs where I was just mumbling half the melody and singing what words I had. Typically, those were the best vocals. I'd listen back to 'em and go, *Shit, I wish I could've sang it that way when I actually had all the lyrics in place*. It didn't seem nearly as heartfelt or spontaneous 'cause I wasn't thinkin' about it. And when I'm comping, a lot of people will say, "They all sound exactly alike, they all sound good," but I like to find the lines that are the most heartfelt. Then, of course, my neurosis about pitch—I wanna make sure it's in pitch. I don't wanna hear this later and think, *Oh, yeah, it might be okay to everybody else in the world, but I feel I was flat on that*. A lot of vocalists go, "I hate to tune my voice," and I'm not against any of that if it makes a better listening experience in the end. I like to drive around later and listen to a vocal that's been comped and tuned, and take credit for it. [*Laughter*]

I want you to think about the entire arc of recorded music. All the singers we've heard over the span of our lives. All the incredible voices, all different, all unique in their own ways. And out of *all* those voices, and *all* those amazing singers, *WHY ARE YOU THE MOST FUN TO IMPERSONATE?* [*Laughter*] Do you have any perspective on this?

I think a lot of people try to imitate me as a joke. It's like me and Ed Sullivan.

No, it's no joke! It's done out of love, man!

Well, you're nice to say that. I don't know. I think with the Doobies there was a certain era where people sounded so different from one another, like back when we were all comin' up in the '70s. Although, we all borrowed from each other, and we all listened to each other intently to pick up little things. But if you imitated someone too much, it was like the kiss of death. It was like, "Well, we already have a Ray Charles or a Stevie Wonder, we don't need some guy imitating them." But these days, it does seem like vocalists kind of fall into a thing where they all try to sound like each other in a way.

Yes.

But back then there was Donald Fagen, and Boz Scaggs, Randy Newman, James Taylor, any number of artists. They were very distinctive sounding singers. People tend to imitate your timbre because they're reminiscing about an era of music.

What's wild is how much your voice really defined the sound of that era. Call it "Soft rock," "Yacht rock," "Blue-eyed soul," any of those ridiculous labels that people try to put on it. But it was *your* voice that really stood out during that time. And it seems like everyone wanted you to be a part of their music for that reason. Forget lead vocals for a second; even your backing vocals have become iconic. You showed up on so many hits from that period. Two of my favorites being "Peg" by Steely Dan, and "Ride Like the Wind" by Christopher Cross. Those really showcase how incredible your backgrounds are. Is there a specific approach you have when you're recording those?

Many times, the approach was something I had done early on when I made my own demos, which were pretty bare bones instrumentally. Just me playin' the guitar or piano and singing. And then, I would sing those backgrounds myself 'cause I really couldn't afford to hire singers. So, I would sing all the harmonies and then double 'em. There was a certain sound to that, but it honestly didn't ring a bell with me or anything.

So, how did those vocals catch fire the way they did?

When I went in to work with Donald Fagen, the first song I ever sang for those guys in the studio was backgrounds for "Bad Sneakers" off the *Katy Lied* album, and I remember Donald specifically wanted me to sing all the background parts myself for some reason. Something about the way [engineer] Roger Nichols recorded them and the key the song was in; everything kind of conspired to make the backgrounds have this certain kind of phasing and ethereal quality, like a shimmer. That was strictly due to the fact that it was just me singing with myself. Had I sung with other people, it would've been fine and nice, but it wouldn't have had that sound that you get when you sing with yourself and then double it.

Yeah, there is something to that.

Something about your own timbre next to itself on tape creates a weird, pronounced, cho-rusing effect that you only get that way. I kind of rediscovered doing that through Donald, and he encouraged me to do that on the other stuff I sang with them. Frankly, it had never sounded that good to me before, but then, people started to hire me and go, "How do you get that sound?"

That was like a whole other career as a singer for you.

I was in that group of LA background singers who were solo artists, but made extra money singing backgrounds in the studio. Myself, John Townsend, Bill Champlin, James Ingram, Phillip Ingram, David Paich, and females too: Kim Carnes, Gloria Jones, Siedah Garrett, all these wonderful singers I did so many sessions with. I always enjoyed those sessions because of the camaraderie and excitement of hearing what somebody was doin' before it was released. And it was so representative of what I got from being in LA and being close to the pulse of the music business.

What a great time for music.

I loved every minute of it, but, after a while, I was encouraged to stop doin' it by manage-ment. Even radio would say, "You know, we've heard enough Michael McDonald on the backgrounds of records." [*JTG laughs*] But I couldn't bring myself to stop because it was so much a part of my life that I enjoyed. I didn't really care if it damaged my career; it just wasn't somethin' that I would've given up.

I'm glad you didn't, man. Something else I've always wanted to know is your side of the story regarding "I'll Wait," the song you co-wrote for the Van Halen album *1984*. How did that come about?

[Producer] Ted Templeman put us together. They had recorded that album, and they had the track, but they didn't have a song, really. Ted sent me a cassette and said, "Can you apply some lyrics and a melody to this?" I said, "I'll give it a shot." So, he set an appointment for me to write with David Lee Roth to make sure it was something that David could sing and *would* sing. David and I got together at Ted's office, and I had gotten some ideas and lyrics together as a starting place, and we hashed out the lyric so that it was something he liked, and then they went in and recorded David's vocal on it.

Is there a recording, or a demo version of you singing it?

No. That's a good idea though! [*Laughs*]

You should record that song!

I should do that. I'll come up with a samba version of it or somethin'.

What's changed the most about your voice since you started?

One thing with the instrument of the voice, you'll become aware that it changes with your age. The voice is a changing instrument, and you just have to follow it. It isn't gonna be the same when you're thirty as it was when you were nineteen, and it's not gonna be the same when you're sixty as it was when you were thirty, so you have to go with your strengths. Certain parts of your range are gonna get stronger and certain parts are gonna go away. I don't have that high falsetto range anymore. I find that there's a good and a bad with it. I just had to learn to sing differently as I got older.

How do you wrap your head around that, especially with your range?

I remember Ray Charles tellin' me once, he was about seventy then, "You know, man, I'm still singin' all my songs in the original keys." That became like a goal of mine. I was never gonna bring any of my songs down a key. Finally, I was talking to Little Anthony, and he goes, "Man, have you not dropped your keys yet?" I go, "No, I didn't wanna do that," and he goes, "What, are you crazy?! I dropped every one of my keys. Why put yourself through that? You'll be so glad you did it, and you'll feel you can put your best foot forward instead of goin', 'Uh oh, here comes that line! Am I gonna fuckin' choke?'"

Right, right...

It was the best advice I got. Lower the damn key and sing it comfortably. Sing it well. I started to sound like a screeching owl tryin' to get up there. Don't be wonderin' how this is gonna go right before you play the song; that's not a good headspace to be in. I've done that. The timbre of my voice has changed, so I just look for what's good. The hardest thing for me at this age is to sing in tune. I was never one of those guys who sang in comfortable keys, the crooner. Even though I'm credited with that, I was always singing at the top of my range, and especially live, just belting it out, so I'm paying for that now. I'm having to negotiate a way to still sing these songs how they're meant to be sung, but without shortening my career any more than I have to.

If you could duet with one singer—living or dead—who would it be?

I would like to do a duet with Buika. She's a Spanish singer who's sang all different styles of music, but she's sung flamenco and tango, kind of more traditional Spanish. To me, she's got one of the most passionate, alluring voices I've ever heard.

And who are your top five favorite singers of all time?

Ray Charles, for sure. Marvin Gaye. Loved O.C. Smith, his voice. Aretha, of course. Buika.

If you could ask any singer about their voice, who would it be and what would you ask?

I always marveled at Ray Charles, how he sang in such wonderful pitch, and yet I know he had that very hoarse timbre to negotiate. Buika has that smokey timbre to her voice for a female, but it's so beautiful and sensual. When you're one of the more hoarse singers by nature, you have to work a little harder physically to make sure you're in pitch. You can fall short of notes because you're not pushing enough air. Tony Bennett was a great example of that. He and Ray Charles are two of the singers I marvel at the most, their mastery of their phrasing and their pitch, when I know that their voices both had that challenge of having to push a little harder to make a voice like that respond.

So, what would you wanna know?

I would ask them about their head voice, which is what singers like that, myself included, have developed. There's a certain thing that a singer learns to do to keep from straining their voice too much. You learn to get up there and sound like you're beltin' it out without the phys-ical strain you might have put on yourself when you started out. You stop singin' like Alfalfa and start singin' a little more like somebody with a beautiful ability to get in the upper ranges smoothly, like Julie Andrews. You learn techniques to achieving the same thing without the punishment. If I could find a way to have that conversation, I think that's what I would ask.

Did you learn anything from singing with Ray?

We really never had that kind of time. I sang with him live a couple times, which was a great experience, but we only sang in the studio on that one track together ["Hey Girl"]. Frankly, I was so emotionally overwhelmed by the experience of standing in the middle of a sound stage with Ray Charles, who I had idolized from the time I was eleven years old, surrounded by a forty-piece orchestra. I'm sittin' there thinkin', *Am I gonna wake up from this? Is this a frickin' dream? What is goin' on here?* My life was passing in front of me. Everyone I ever knew who I grew up playin' music with, we all loved Ray Charles. He was like God when we were kids. I could see every one of their faces goin', *Geez, imagine this*. I felt like I was livin' that experience for everyone I ever knew. It was almost difficult for me to pay attention to what I was doing. But it was wonderful. And it was the last time I saw Ray. He passed away a couple weeks later.

SAM MOORE

"COMIN TO YA ON A DUSTY ROAD. GOOD LOVIN', I GOT A TRUCKLOAD."

When you hear it, you turn it all the way up. That's how it goes. Sam Moore and the late Dave Prater came together in 1961 and formed one of the greatest vocal duos of all time: Sam & Dave. Combing their love of gospel with R&B, Sam's high tenor and Dave's baritone created such enduring classics as "Soul Man" and "Hold On, I'm Comin'."

Hailed by Bruce Springsteen as one of his favorite vocalists of all time, all you gotta do is hear the man wail to know exactly why Sam & Dave were inducted into the Rock & Roll Hall of Fame, the Grammy Hall of Fame, and the Vocal Group Hall of Fame: they could sing their asses off. But that's not the only thing I love about Sam Moore. He laughs his ass off too. All the time! And whether it's on a record or during an interview, Sam's lively, humble, and joyful spirit is the reason you just have to listen.

Who first exposed you to singing?

No one. To tell you the truth, I didn't want to be a singer. I wanted to be a minister. Then, when I got into junior high school, I joined this octet. Then, they put me in the big choir, but I didn't sing *lead* on anything. I think the first time I did a professional lead was when I got with Dave—begrudgingly because I never liked to stand out front. I was always the kind of a performer that liked to make others sound good. If I could do something in the background to make them sound good, I felt as though I was doing my job.

So, what inspired you to actually become a singer?

It was a fluke. I had been doing amateur hours in predominately Black clubs, and I was getting my little twenty-five dollars for first prize, but I only knew one song. I sang that wherever I would do the contest. I was with my friends one night, walking past this club called The King of Hearts here in Miami. My buddy said, "Hey Sam, I bet you won't go up and ask for that job." I looked and it said: "Wanted: Singer, Emcee, and Host." You know when you want to impress your buddies and all that stuff? I walked up and told a lie that I could do that job. The owner's father said, "Where did you work before?" I said, "Oh. Fountain Blue!" He said, "Who did you host behind?" I said, "Sinatra, Sammy Davis Jr, Danny Thomas, Billy Eckstine." A BIG LIE. He said, "Sam, most of those guys, they didn't have to have emcees," I said, "Yeah, there were times." I just *liiiied!* [*Laughter*] He said, "When can you start workin'?" I said, "Whenever." He said, "What about tomorrow night?"

How old were you?

I was in my twenties. I went in and I sang "Danny Boy" the way I'd been doing on the contest. But the thing about it: *I did it every night, that one song!* [*Chuckles hard*] Eventually, he said, "That the only song you know? You gotta learn some more songs." Now, this is how Dave and I got together and started singing. Dave came to the club and signed up on the amateur hour. At the time, I had heard about Dave doing all the songs by Sam Cooke, but, for some reason, he said he wanted to do a song by Jackie Wilson. So, I got onstage and said, "This is a young man who's going to sing 'Doggin' Me Around' by Jackie Wilson." Little did I know that Dave didn't know all the words, and I'm standing up there…

If this is how you guys became Sam & Dave, I'm gonna freak out.

Dave forgot the words. *I knew the words.* Dave had a process and he starts sweating and that process went to recess! [*Laughter erupts*] *Stop laughing, Jason!* From there, Dave and I were together from 1961. The next thing I knew, Dave and I got signed to Atlantic, and I was put in a position to have the lead voice. I thought we could do like The Everly Brothers, but, anyway, the rest is history.

Nooo way. Wow.

Did I give you something?

Is that a famous story because I've never heard that?

Naaaw, I never heard anything about it. But that's how Dave and I got together.

When you started singing, were you emulating anybody?

No, no, no. I was singing gospel songs by The Soul Stirrers and whatnot. I liked Sam Cooke, Jackie Wilson, Willie John, and Clyde McPhatter, and, believe it or not, I heard your grandfather do a song one time, and they told me not to emulate that because, "First of all, you're not Lebanese. You're not Jewish. You're not Italian. Be who you are and find your own voice."

So, how did you find your own voice?

I haven't found my own voice. I still struggle with what others are thinking about me. But I can share this: I'm a singer that likes to preach. I like songs I can get my teeth into. If I don't think I can make the song my own, I won't tackle it. I don't care how much I may admire it, I won't sing it.

Was vocal training ever a part of your process?

No. Never. Always been this raggedy, raggedy behind voice. [*Laughs*]

Are you nervous or confident before you perform?

Listen, out of sixty-five years being in the business, if I can get past the first two or three songs, I'm fine. Other than that, yes, I'm very nervous. I wanna throw up, and I'm hoping I don't forget the words. [*Cracks up*] If you playin' drums behind me and you see me turn around and look at you, it's because I have forgot the words! But I'll make up somethin'.

Do you do any vocal warm-ups before shows?

Noooo. Do you think I should've done that in those days 'cause I don't know?

Hey man, if I could sing like you, I would never do vocal warm-ups.

I've never done 'em. As I've gotten older, there are certain registers that it's a little [*makes a shaky noise*]. I'll stretch for that high note, I'll go for it. But I don't do it as regularly as I did when I was with Dave.

How do you take care of your voice on the road?

I go to the hotel, I undress, take a shower, brush my teeth, gargle so my breath won't smell in the middle of the night, and I go to bed. Get up the next morning and have breakfast, and that's it. I don't do no vocalizing or nothin' like that. I talk loud, and usually when I wanna put some flavor, and when I say flavor, when I wanna put some saliva into my throat, I'll put a penny in my mouth because it gives more saliva. It lubricates.

Are you kidding?

No! I'll put a penny in there. I don't keep it in there long.

How about some gum, Sam? Why do you have to put a penny in your mouth?
WELL, TO GIVE…

YOU BETTER WASH THAT PENNY!
I WASH THE PENNY, JASON! YOU'RE SUCH AN ASSHOLE! I WASH THE DAMN PENNY!
[*Hysterical laughter*] I have a thing called Entertainer's Secret. It's a device I got from Conway Twitty's wife to lubricate my throat. If I get too hoarse, Joyce [Sam's wife and manager] will make a concoction of tea: calamine and hot water, no lemon, because that raws-up the throat. And I'll spray my throat just ten minutes before I go on, and I'm fine, and scared.

Do you have any other rituals before you perform?
I don't have no rituals. I'm already scared as hell. Sometimes I ask, "Can I go on first?" Get it over with, man. [*Laughs at himself*] This sounds real stupid, but it's really true!

Is there anything after the show that helps keep your voice in shape?
[*Enthusiastically high pitched*] *Nooo. I don't do all that.* Listen, you got the kind of person that you're talkin' to—it's not I'm old school, it's something I just DO. I go into a zone. I don't even stand there lookin' for all that clapping and that stuff.

What was your most embarrassing vocal mishap ever?
I was singing one night at the Apollo Theater, and *ohhh boy*, at that time, I was on drugs, right? I was singin', and I thought I was really killin' 'em. *Oh, I thought I was really getting over.* There wasn't that many people there, and I was just goin' through those songs like laxative goes through the body. And when I got through, I walked off. There was a comedian named Moms Mabley. She said, "Where you goin'?" I said, "We through." She said, "Well, let me tell you somethin'. First of all, you didn't sound good. Second of all, falling on your knees, that was dumb. Number three, you didn't finish the songs out." I said, "Well, it ain't that many people." She said, "You know what? If that's the attitude that you take, then maybe you can find somethin' else to do because that's not fair. If they payin' you $5,000 or $500,000, you perform for that little crowd as well as you would do for a big crowd. You don't ever cheat anybody." And you know what? After that, I never cheated like that again. If you're gonna leave it, leave it with them. You leave your gift and your presence with them. Because you know what? They deserve it. And they paid to hear you do this, so *sing*.

Were there songs where you wondered if your voice would be there that night?
If you threw a song at me and I hadn't rehearsed it, that most likely would throw me off a little bit.

Are there songs where you've had to adjust the key live?
I probably would've kept the songs in the same key they were recorded in, but my wife went behind my back. When I say, "Behind my back," I wasn't nowhere around. She got with one of my band members, and she lifted the keys, Jason!

She lifted them?
Yeah!

Higher?!
Yeeeaaah, Jason, she did that to me!

What was she thinking?
I was singin' one night, and I went to a song that I'd been singin' for years. But when it got to the next level, where I was supposed to go...I farted. [*JTG cracks up*] You laughin', but I farted! It was too high! I said, "What the?" And I looked over towards the curtain, and she looked away like, "Why you lookin' at me?" I called my music director in. I said, "What the fuck was that?" He said, "Oh, no, it wasn't me, boss. Joyce said you sound dull, and to give those songs a lift and make it brighter." Wait a minute...[*Sam's wife takes the phone out of his hands*]

JOYCE: Yes, I raised the keys. I did that. But then, here's the punchline: one day, to [producer] Isaac Hayes, I said, "The keys that you cut the songs in, were those the right keys for Sam?" He goes, "Oh no, we had to lower those keys and adjust to accommodate for Dave." Dave was kind of baritone and gravelly. So, I said, "Well, I raised all the keys 'cause everything sounded dull when Sam was singin' 'em solo." He said, "You were right." So, *ha ha ha*. The original songs gave Sam the platform to do all of the gymnastics, even though the keys were lower, because there was a bed from which to springboard. But when he was singing the songs himself, they were just limpy wrist and had no energy or excitement, so I said, "Raise 'em up," and it worked! So, no, I'm not takin' the push, but I'm givin' the answers. Hold on a second, here's Sam.

[*Sam gets back on the phone*] So, you got the picture, my dear brother. [*More laughter*]

So, now do you keep the keys higher, or do you lower them to be more comfortable?
Between you and me, Jason, some of 'em are still a little high. But that's okay. I work it out some kind of way. I can do it.

Do you remember a performance where you surprised yourself?
Yeah, I did something in London one time. We were playing this club, and, for some reason, I went into a zone. What that means is, the crowd was so wonderful I did two hours onstage. I almost passed out when I came off, but I had a good time, man. I sang some of *everything*. Sly & The Family Stone, "Take Me to the River," and, *oh man*, I'm not a James Brown voice, but we did "Papa's Got a Brand New Bag." We just hit 'em for two hours. Ohhh man, did I like that. I'll never try that again though. Not now!

Do you have a favorite vocal performance you're really proud of?
You know, I'm-a-share this with you: I have never come offstage pleased that I've done a good job. But this one time, I think I was in Japan, and I think within myself, *I think I did a great job*.

How about on record?

I liked the album that I did with Randy Jackson, *Overnight Sensational*. I like the way Randy produced me. But that was a test 'cause I hadn't sung in so long. I didn't have a record company, I wasn't gonna get signed by anybody, but I was pleased with that because I'm here by myself doing this. But I'm still looking for the great performance that I'll be proud of. I really feel as though, eventually, *somewhere*, I'm gonna find that note. Yeah, I think I'm gonna find it, Jason. *I'm gonna not look for it*, but if it comes, I'm not gonna back away from it, I'm just gonna go with it.

How are you with hearing your own voice?

I'm the kind of singer who hates their own voice. *Oh, you know about that, do you?*

How can Sam Moore hate his own voice, tell me that?

I do, I do, I do. When I walk around, I don't sing, I whistle. It gets on Joyce's nerves because sometimes I whistle and it's waaaaay shrilly! And I know it is! She'll look at me, roll her eyes, "Will you stop?" [*Howls out, laughing*]

Well, I see why there's so much laughter on your songs over the years. [*Sam howls harder*] You don't really hear that kind of spontaneous joy on record that often. You and Sam Cooke really made laughter a beautiful thing to hear in music.

I guess we did, I guess we did.

Where did that come from?

Church. When the minister would preach from the pulpit, and the sermon got so emotional and got so good, he would go, "Ha-Ha-Ha!" Then he would set his tempo from right there, and that's where I got it. All gospel singers usually do that. If you listen back to Mahalia, somewhere in the song, you'll hear a laugh. But it's an emotional laughter. When Dave and I first started recording, there were times when the song would be so good to me that you'd hear me say, "Boy, this is gooood. I wish my grandma was here right now," stuff like that. I did it in every song, and that got kind of like [*groans*]. I figured that out myself, *Hey, enough of that now*, you know, you gotta find something else. But the laughter is gonna always be there. *If it's good, Jason. Yeah. If it's poppin'*.

Bruce Springsteen was lucky enough to have you sing on his *Human Touch* album, and if you listen real close, we can hear you laughing at the end of "Soul Driver."

There's some laughter there. It was good! It was really good!

You guys have sung with each other a bunch over the years. What is it about Springsteen's voice that moves you?

When you do a thing with Bruce, he's not trying to sing like Dave. He's Bruce. I'll give you a for instance: I did his Christmas show, and it was cold that year, and I got a cold. I was *sick*. Joyce called Bruce and let him know, "Sam has bronchitis, and his throat is *gone*." His wife was nice enough to give Joyce the number to a doctor. The doctor said, "I'm gonna give you a steroid. But I want you to know, you're gonna be singing, and out of the clear blue, your voice is gonna shoot to the top. It's gonna get outta control."

So, you still ended up doing the show that night?
Bruce and I are singing. But Bruce was singing my part. And I was, "Good, I'm so glad he can do that." [*Cracks up*] In the middle, my voice came back and went *BANG!* And he said it right onstage, Jason, "About goddamn time 'cause singin' your part is 'bout to kill me!" I started laughing. Everybody started laughing. [*Cackles in hysterics, almost in tears*] We had a good time. We can just bang it out on each other. I like singin' like that.

You're obviously one half of the greatest soul duos of all time. Does having someone else beside you pull something more out of you?
No. It pulls away from me. Can I tell you something? Especially men, when they wanna sing with me, they wanna sing better than Dave. Most men, they wanna make a contest or make a game out of it. "I can get that note over, Sam," and "I can make that turn better than Sam." I say, "Why you wanna do that? I just wanna have a good time and bang each other's brains out singin'. I don't want a contest. *I don't want to prove anything*, that you better than me, or I'm better than you, I don't like that." So, I really don't do it that much with male singers.

If you could duet with one singer—living or dead—who would it be?
Pavarotti. He and I were born the same day, month, and year. Ain't that somethin'?

Who are your top five favorite singers of all time?
Eddie Levert from The O'Jay's. Dennis Edwards who just passed from The Tempts. Bobby Womack. Uhhh, a little softer, I like the way BeBe Winans sings. And the fifth would have to have been, in her time, Aretha. But the kids today, I don't think so. [*Laughs*] It's not that they don't have the talent! But [*sighs*] I won't fit there. My voice wouldn't fit what they're doing, let's just put it like that.

If you could ask any singer about their voice, who would it be and what would you ask?
I learned a lot from this man when he was alive. If I could have done a duet with him, I would've been happy to do it; that would have been Sinatra. The control, the diction. I would ask him, what did he do? And how did he know? How did he know he could do that?

Do what?
Could he *perform* like that? Could he *record* like that? I mean, he would take a song and [*mimics a note as if it were a car racing past*]. And I'll tell you somebody else. I have to add a sixth person. I have to add Ray. *Ray Charles? UH! UH! UH! UH!* The genius? *Oh God*, those people is some of my favorite people.

Well, man, you're one of my favorite people.
Thank you, my friend.

Robby Krieger on
JIM
MORRISON

LOS ANGELES, 1967. The Doors release their self-titled debut album and a new chapter in the history of music arrives with some "MO-JO-RIII-SIN!"

Jim Morrison and The Doors took this country—took the world—and turned it upside down. They put the same danger and sexuality into their music as Chuck Berry, Little Richard, and Elvis Presley had done just a decade earlier. But it was Jim's distinctive voice, electrifying stage performances, and unpredictable behavior that would make The Doors one of the most influential, controversial, and iconic bands of all time.

By 1971, Jim's wild lifestyle had caught up with him at the age of twenty-seven. His legacy, however, is another story. Having sold over 100 million records, The Doors have been inducted into the Grammy and Rock & Roll Halls of Fame, and their music continues to appeal to the rebellious and poetic nature of younger fans today.

Door's guitarist Robby Krieger stood to Jim's left, playing his instrument in a way that would perfectly encapsulate the era. But he came into my life, personally, over a decade ago, when he and the late artist Scott Medlock founded the Medlock/Krieger Golf Tournament to benefit St. Jude Children's Research Hospital. Throughout the years, Robby and his friends have raised so much money and awareness for the kids and their families that I'll never be able to thank him enough. So, thanks again, Robby. That said, we're gonna need a Parental Advisory Warning for this one. (Especially for Jim's parents!)

When was the first time you heard Jim sing?

It would have been the first time we played together with The Doors. I really couldn't tell much about what kind of singer he was at that time because he was more of a writer. He'd never sung before, but he had written all of these songs.

What was your impression of his voice?

I didn't really say, "Oh wow, this is a great singer!" At first, he wasn't really much of a singer. He was kind of shy, and he didn't have much of a voice. Never had a singing lesson in his life. Couldn't read music. Didn't really play anything except a little piano. But he just had a natural voice that turned out to be amazing. It was kind of a learning process for him with our first bunch of gigs. It took him maybe three-four months of doing parties and little gigs here and there to really get a grasp on it.

Was he self-conscious about it?

I think so. In fact, he would never face the audience when we first started. He would always face us because that's how we rehearsed. We'd all face each other. [*Laughs*] It wasn't really until we got to this place called The London Fog, which was right down the street from The Whisky, that he started coming out of his shell and really singing.

He had such a distinct vocal sound, the way he would sort of croon his lyrics in his lower register, and then explode into this guttural scream at certain points.

He had quite a range. If you listen to the last chorus of "Light My Fire," not many guys can sing that part without going into a falsetto.

Do you know where his style came from, or who he was influenced by?

He liked a lot of people. He liked Sinatra, Elvis, of course, the blues guys like B.B. King and Albert King, Robert Johnson. But he never really tried to copy anybody. Always had his own voice, really. In fact, I think that was true for all of us in The Doors.

More than most musicians, there's so much mythology around Jim. That must get frustrating because you knew him as a normal guy and your friend. You must have to shake your head sometimes and go, "Listen. He was just a guy too."

Yeah, *The Doors* movie made him out to be so crazy, *and he could get that way*, but he wasn't like that all the time. People don't realize what a genius he was as far as writing lyrics, and, like you say, sometimes the image overrides what a great singer he was. I know because I've had many people try to sing Doors stuff with me.

That must be fascinating.

The guys that try to look like him and act like him, to me it just makes it silly. My son, Waylon, he sings the stuff pretty much correctly, but he doesn't try to sound like Jim Morrison and do all the little things, which I think is a good way to go about it because nobody could be as good as him.

How did Jim approach recording? Did he spend time punching in and trying to get takes just right?

On the first album, we didn't have a lot of time to mess around recording, so we pretty much did it together. But he was in a vocal booth, so he could re-do his part if we needed it. At first, he didn't like punching in. He wanted to do it all as a band. We all did. But that's hard to do—for everybody to play good all at the same time. So, we did end up re-doing a lot of the vocals, and we kept him on a separate track. We only had four tracks, so that first album is pretty live. But then, the second album, we did have a lot of time because we made a bunch of money off the first album. [*Laughs*] Our budget was a lot higher so we spent a lot of time doing vocal overdubs. At first, he didn't like doing it, but he got really good at it. If you look at some of those pictures of him, he had a really big throat. His neck was like eight inches across or something, and you can see where that sound came from. It's like Pavarotti. If you ever notice his throat, it's kind of like Jim's.

I've seen footage of you guys in the studio, and Jim has two mics in the vocal booth that [producer] Paul Rothchild put up, one on top of the other. Sonically, what was the reason for that? What were they trying to achieve?

It might've been to get a stereo vocal sound. You put them out of phase with each other so one is recording kind of sideways, and the other's up and down, and that way you get the fullest sound. Not that many people know about that.

Was Jim nervous or confident before shows?

At first he was nervous, but by the time we got to The Whisky, there were no nerves left. [*Laughs*] He was totally into it.

Did he do something to prepare himself before he got out onstage?

No, he didn't really have a warm-up routine or anything like that. His warm-up was drinking. [*Laughter*]

How much did he drink before he went out?

Well, you never knew, and that was the problem. If he had just the right amount, then it would be a great show. If he had a little too much then it wouldn't be so good. [*Chuckles*] It was very unscientific.

Did he take care of his voice on the road?

No. Never worried about it. He never lost his voice. It's amazing, the way he screamed and stuff, staying up all night. He was lucky, he had that big, full voice that never, ever seemed to wear him down.

I wanna take you back to the recording of "The End." There's that final section of the song where Jim is going nuts. [*Robby laughs*] What's he doing in the room physically? Is he throwing himself around?

He couldn't really throw himself around much because then you'd be off mic, but that was definitely a live take. We did the whole song twice, and I think we made an edit halfway through, so, it's really two takes cut into one. That was the acid phase. He was on a lot of LSD that night.

So, he was on LSD when you guys recorded "The End"?

Very much so. And you know what "The End" is about? It's about the Oedipus complex. "Mother, I want to fuck you. Father, I want to kill you." Before we recorded it, he was taking all this acid, and he sat down at the table, and I'll always remember, he says, "Fuck the mother, kill the father." He kept saying that over and over. I don't know whether it was to get himself in the right mood or [*laughs*]...I mean, it sounded like he really believed it.

This is before you guys went into record, he's just sitting there saying that?

Yeah, it was crazy. [*Mimics Jim*] "Fuck the mother, kill the father, that's where it's at." When he took acid, he would see his mother's face in the moon. His dad was an admiral in the Navy, so he was kind of a hard ass. His mother was kind of nuts as well. I think that it was just that he was such a sensitive person, and a genius, so that type of shit bothered a guy like that more than your normal. His brother and sister were totally normal people. Didn't bother them.

When you hear his voice now, what do you remember most?

Just playing with him live. And in the studio. I never realized what a great voice he had back then until I started doing these songs with other singers and had them try to recreate it. His vocalizations were so unique. It's like he had his own style that nobody had come close to yet. A lot of guys copied him afterwards.

But there can be only one. [*Robby laughs*] It's so interesting because there had to be a Jim Morrison. There had to be The Doors. Somebody had to be it, and you guys *were* it, you know?

Well, I guess. Yeah. For sure, we were there at the right place at the right time. And the four of us were just the right combination of people that could've pulled it off.

MESHELL NDEGEOCELLO

HOW CAN A VOICE TOUCH YOU SO DEEPLY with almost a whisper? Grammy Award–Winner Meshell Ndegeocello has been doing that her entire career. It's a sound that's conversational and confessional, sweet, warm, and subtle, or blood-thirsty, sharp, and cold. Whether it's funk, soul, jazz, reggae, hip-hop, or rock, Meshell's also one of the baddest bass players out there. But it's the poetic lyricism, unconventional phrasing, and engaging melody of her voice that always leads you to a place you've yet to discover inside yourself.

I first heard Meshell when her debut album, *Plantation Lullabies*, came out in 1993. It felt like an instant classic, almost picking up where Curtis Mayfield left off: a vibe from the past, reimagined for the modern age. Since then, she's taken her voice even further, always expanding her style, finding new places to go. And while I am aware of how on-the-nose this may be, I caught up with Meshell while she was out exploring in her car, seeing where it would take her, before driving back home. And that's exactly what she does best: explores the unknown, gets what she needs, then drives it on home.

Who first exposed you to singing?

I only sing because I wanted to be a songwriter. Singing was not my goal. But when I was making demos in high school, singers would want me to pay them, or they just wouldn't show up, so I just started singing myself. I had a hard time. People didn't like my voice, producers I was working with, it was a really hard road. But I got better after the third record [*Bitter*] where I just started to explore different aspects of my voice.

Were you emulating anyone when you started out?

I'm not good at emulating. I come from Jazzheads, and when you come from Jazzheads, it's about discovering something. I hate that word jazz, sorry. When you come from an improvisational music background, it's very important to have your own voice. The things that always moved me the most about any musician is their tone and pocket. So, as a singer, I was like, if I can have good pitch and make it feel good in the melodic aspect, it'd be great. And being a huge fan of Sting, it was important to hear the words. I really liked that he was one of the few groups where I could actually hear the poetry in the words. It was amazing.

So, how did you find your own voice?

You have to ask yourself: should I find my own voice? Or should I be the type of singer that can sing any type of song so that I can participate in theater? Or I can do sessions. Or I can be a vocal acrobatic kind of person. I think Prince bridged that gap. If you gave him any type of song to sing, he could've sung it. He could've sung a theater piece; he could sing a funk piece. All that was in him because he studied all the things that made a singer great, which is pitch, technique, and virtuosity. But then you have Tom Waits where it's like his state of mind, his connection to words, and the everyday struggle. I think that is just as much about his singing technique as anything else.

It's funny you mention him because I always say that Tom Waits is the greatest soul singer of all time. You hear his soul so beautifully in every song. There's no trickery there. It's real soul, blood, and guts.

Yes. Also, singing is physical, and it's generated from the actual flesh and bone and vibration from the body. There are people that can transform your being with the sound of their voice.

Did you ever have any vocal training?

No, I've only started to. For the last five years I have been struggling to play the bass and sing because the bass strap lays directly on a muscle that has weakened, which affects my breath. And it's affecting my posture, which is not allowing me to project, so I'm learning how to sing in a whole 'nother way without having the bass, which is interesting.

How are you learning to sing now?

I have been doing Alexander class.[5] Dancers do it, theater people, singers love it, because it's a way of creating mindfulness towards what your body is experiencing, which can really help you with anxiety and projection. It's really been a life changer for me. It's helped me make my body more attuned so that I can use the instrument better.

And how does it affect your voice?

I can sing much louder, and I'm able to have less neck pain when I sing. I was having neck pain even when I didn't have the bass on, and that's why I'm rethinking the singer. I find myself trying to find video clips of certain kinds of singers and how they hold the mic, different ways of moving in their body. Singers like Lou Rawls I find interesting now. And I'm listening to a lot of country singers. I saw that documentary [*Country Music*] by Ken Burns, and now Hank Williams haunts my dreams. Just trying to find other ways to express myself with my voice and see where I can feel differently just being a singer, disconnected from this other instrument that people associate me with.

Did you ever study Marvin Gaye, the way he held the mic?

Oh yeah, he definitely has one of the coolest techniques. It's funny you say that. If I am trying to mirror anybody lately, it's a little bit of Marvin Gaye, a little bit of Shirley Horn, and the aspects of Billie Holliday that people haven't commercialized. The thing about her is the phrasing. Her and Frank Sinatra. To me, Billie Holliday, Frank Sinatra, and James Brown are all about pocket, the placement of the phrases.

Are you nervous or confident before you perform?

Oh God, I had to do stuff in a go-go band when I was about seventeen, eighteen, and there's no room for being nervous. These people have paid to have a good time, so you go do your job, and you do it well. That's always the mindset I have when I go onstage—to somehow be like an athlete, don't hear the crowd, and just focus on the thing I'm supposed to do well. I don't feel anything. If I go out onstage, and I actually were to have that discussion within my mind, I would never go out because I have been extremely nervous, and it's paralyzing. I become angry, and it's not pleasant. [*Laughs*]

How did you get rid of that nervousness?

I started surrounding myself with musicians that are more rooted in understanding that we are a team, and we must function well emotionally together. I get less nervous when I'm playing with people I trust because I know they're not going to try to trick me harmonically or play loud. As a musician who sings, I realized all the times I disrespected a singer by being too loud, or just fuckin' playin' over shit. Recording a record is different than playing live. A

---

5   The Alexander Technique is a method which helps a person discover a new balance in the body by releasing unnecessary tension. It can be applied to sitting, lying down, standing, walking, lifting, and other daily activities.

lot of people act like they're playing in the studio when they play live. But live, there's a lot more air. There's a lot more things that are happening that are not gracious. [*Chuckles*] You should be kind to the singer so that they can do the best job they can. If I trust in them, that will buoy me to just focus on pitch, delivering the story well, relaxing, and interacting with the audience, which is the other thing about being the lead singer.

What's that?

You gotta be a special person to want to be the lead singer. You want people to look at you, and look towards you to fulfill something in them. There's a little megalomania in there. That can come from not having enough attention, or it could come from really liking the attention. My nervousness didn't come until that was over. Once I realized I no longer needed this to generate the love I needed for myself, that's when I got nervous. Then I had to ask myself, because I needed it for my livelihood, *What is the best way to get through this?* And that was to trust in everybody, to have a common bond, and just try to create beautiful sonic experiences.

Do you do vocal warm-ups before your shows?

Yes, I do with the drummer. We do that lip thing [*does a lips trill*], and then, he's teaching me Solfège.[6] But the biggest practice for me is just singing the song. Before I go onstage, I just sit with the guitar player and go through a song, which is just the best warm-up ever, to just sing a few songs to get open with singing.

Are you doing songs from your set or just anything?

Songs from the set. I'm a big believer in repetition. Repetition makes you better at something.

Do you have any other rituals before you hit the stage?

I drink a lot of tea with licorice, or Throat Coat and honey. I just try to make my physical self a vessel and get the body aligned. And I sleep a lot, literally, until a few hours before I have to play. I have an understanding that it's physical and emotional, and I must clear my mind.

Is there anything after the show that helps keep your voice in shape?

Oh, yeah, I do have something. I just thought he was being an asshole, but Prince would like... there's no yelling, there's no talking. I try to limit the talking. It is an instrument, so, I just kind of limit the bullshit after shows. I don't really wanna talk to anybody, you know, keep it mellow.

---

6   Solfège (also called solfa, or solfeggio) provides a framework for melodies by establishing recognizable relationships between pitches and training your ear to hear patterns. It is an excellent system for learning the architecture behind music and is a fundamental concept of ear training. You can practice with a piano by playing the major scale in the key of C as you sing, "Do-Re-Mi-Fa-Sol-La-Ti-Do." Sing up and down the scale. Once you can sing the scale in tune by yourself, without the help of the piano, try moving around the scale in stepwise motion.

When you say you thought Prince was being an asshole, that's funny 'cause when I interviewed Mavis Staples, she was telling me that Prince used to tell her to shut up after shows and not talk! Did Prince say that to you?

Oh no, he'd just talk so soft sometimes. You'd be like, *C'mon, man. I can barely hear you* [*laughs*], but it's like, "Relax your instrument so you can be prepared."

When you start getting sick, what do you do?

Ohhh, I panic. I do not handle throat colds well. What do you do?

I interview people like you and try to learn some tricks! But, yeah, I'll do the no talking, and the teas, and if there's a juice bar that has those immunity shots that's like garlic and oregano, I'll take two of those and try to knock it out. Or I end up going to a doctor to try to get it knocked outta me. Whatever it takes!

I do the ginger shots or the oregano oil. I'll do a hot bowl of steam. If I did get super wealthy, I would definitely build a sweat lodge on my property because I definitely sweat it and steam it out of my nasal passages. I've never been a neti potter. I know a few singers that neti pot, but I couldn't do that. I just put the oregano oil in the hot water and sit under a towel until I can get it out.

There are so many acts of voodoo and ritual you go through trying to make sure this thing doesn't go over the top.

Yeah, it's very scary. I stress out.

Are there songs where you wonder if your voice will be there that night?

Oh God, yeah. I had to sing "Purple Rain." I do this Swedish version, and there's a weird melody in it, so I get a little nervous there. I'm doing some shows where I honor Prince, and there's a couple little songs where I'm like, *Woo!* Like little melody phrases that I'll hit that are just outside of my melodic sense. I get nervous on stuff like that. But I will stop myself if I'm too unsure and try to re-envision it. I've been known to sing a line over and over 'til I get it. It just depends on how I feel, but if I make a mistake lately, I will definitely try to re-address it.

Live, you mean?

Yeah, live, I'll re-address it. If I miss something, I'll literally be like, "Uhhh, let me try that again," and the band'll know, and I'll just loop it until I find it and get it.

Amazing! And are there songs where you've had to adjust the key live?

I don't like to adjust the keys. I'd rather just re-envision it melodically. That just weirds me out for some reason. It changes the spirit of the harmony to me. The only person I like when they change the key, or when they throw the whole arrangement away in general, is Bob Dylan.

How do you feel when Sting does it?

See? That's funny. He's a supreme musician. I trust most everything he does. [*Laughs*] I feel he's so musical, even if he had a bad night, he's still pretty incredible. Those songs are life-forms themselves, and they speak through him and without him.

What was your most embarrassing vocal mishap ever?

You know what? Let's be honest. I'm embarrassed every night I sing. Every night, it's hard, and I'm embarrassed for different reasons.

What's the embarrassment about?

That I should be better.

Do you remember a performance where you surprised yourself?

When I listen to *Ventriloquism*, I can't believe that's me on a couple songs. I just go, *Wow, I would listen to that*. "Tender Love," I think I sang that really well. The melody's good, plus it's just a good song.

How are you with hearing your own voice?

I hate the sound of my speaking voice. *Hate it!* I'm one of those people like, "Mute me in the session when I come in to listen. I do not want to hear myself."

That's so fascinating because I think you have the most soothing speaking voice. I'm very soothed by speaking to you. It's so funny the way we perceive ourselves.

I know.

The thing I love most about your voice is how conversational and confessional your tone is. I hear you and I feel like you're being honest with me. You're not tryin' to be anybody else but you. The whole *Bitter* album is a great example of that. And it wouldn't be nearly as soulful if you had some singer being all pyrotechnic. None of the songs would resonate! I mean, the actual song, "Bitter," has physically hurt me. You could actually bleed out listening to it. [*Laughs*]

Awww, man. Yeah, that one's sad.

Do you have a favorite vocal performance you're really proud of?

"Fool of Me." I just like it sonically. In terms of performance, I think my best performance is *Comfort Woman*. I think the vocals are really interesting on there. Otherwise, I don't know yet. I gotta make some new music. *That* could be the best!

You've always been awesome at layering your vocals, using your low voice, and then a couple high ones behind it, but I really dig the falsetto and the layering on "Dead End" off the *Weather* album.

Oh yeah, I forgot about that one! That's a cool singing record. There's a singer named Benji Hughes, I did that one with. He wrote "Oysters." He's the one that was like, "Just create these different characters to sing in," and that's how I approached a lot of *Weather*, especially songs like "Dead End," just being all the different people in my mind.

Shout out to Benji Hughes. That tune made me get into his stuff! Really cool singer.

He's a genius.

What's changed the most about your voice since you started?

At first, I sang with a husky rough edge, contralto, with bits of speaking intertwined. Then, I found that I enjoyed melodies and tried to grow in that way. As I age, I have lost range, and I smoke, so the instrument has suffered. But I try to approach with heart, and hopefully create a good song that wants to be heard.

If you could duet with one singer—living or dead—who would it be?

Eugene McDaniels.

That would sound great! And who are your top five favorite singers of all time?

Stevie Wonder, Chaka Khan, Sade, Cat Stevens, and David Byrne.

If you could ask any singer about their voice, who would it be and what would you ask?

Sly Stone. I'd ask him if he sang softly or loudly on the *Fresh* album.

LUKAS NELSON

Y OU WOULDN'T BE DOING LUKAS NELSON a great disservice to simply write
him off as Willie Nelson's son. You'd be doing a disservice to yourself. I found that
out the hard way. But let's face the facts: most die-hard music fans are also music snobs,
and we kind of suck for that. We often judge things we don't even know about, or blow
them off because it's easier than stopping to take a listen. But when you get humbled,
you get humbled hard.

From playing with his own band, Promise of the Real, to singing with his father,
to joining forces with Neil Young, Lukas Nelson doesn't need to earn our respect. His
incredible voice, his remarkable range, and his unique gift are all it takes to shut down
anyone who ain't givin' it.

I was stoked to come clean about misjudging Lukas during our conversation. But
what I didn't see coming was the deep wisdom and beautiful philosophy about the
voice that a young man half my age would soon be sharing.

Who first exposed you to singing?

Dad first exposed me to singing. He's the first musical memory I have.

Is that who made you feel you could do this?

I had a dream when I was a kid that I was on a stage and there were like millions of people out there, and I was terrified. Then, this voice told me to shrink into my chest and look out at the audience through my chest and sing from that part of my body. I started to sing from there and the whole crowd went wild. All my fear disappeared about bein' up onstage. I was about six years old, and I knew that's something I was meant to do. I was meant to play music, and I went on that path after that.

Do you still sing from your chest when you're singing?

Well, it was a metaphor now that I look back. Comin' from the heart was the metaphor. The Great Spirit was telling me to go do life, sing from the heart, and make sure that everything came from there, and then I would be okay. So that's where I try and live.

Were you emulating anyone when you started out?

I probably learned how to sing like Dad cause that was the first thing I ever heard singing-wise. I just felt his voice was what the normal voice sounded like.

How did you find your own voice?

I'm still workin' on my voice. I'm still tryin' to get it to the place where I really am happy with it. I'm honing it in. [*Chuckles*] I'm feeling comfortable singing live more than I used to, but it's an ongoing process. You just get better and better at it as time goes by. You start developing, understanding how your throat works as an instrument. It's such an individual thing. Singing is like putting in golf. It's a feel. Everybody's got their own way of doing it. And I think that's why it's so hard to teach, and maybe there's not that much written about it, is because it is such an individual thing.

Tell me more about how singing is like golf?

There's obviously the normal sort of fundamental stroke. You push the putter back and you move it forward and it pushes the ball along. So, you have to know that part of it, you have to know how to sing. You have to know how the air passes through and uses the walls of your throat, and the angle, and then the pressure you have to apply to make certain notes appear. It's a wind instrument. It's how much air is going through. You regulate that as you sing. It just takes time to get really in tune with that. How hard do you have to blow with the shape of your own throat, and the expanse of your lungs, in order to get the same tones that you hear?

Did you ever have any vocal training?

I had a few people give me breathing exercises, but I just listened to all my favorite music and tried to emulate it as much as possible. I listened to people's voices that I loved: Neil [Young] and Dad. The thing about Dad and Neil, and all of our voices, it's very vulnerable. We're not singing, we're just being. It's almost conversational. Because the song is really the ultimate vehicle. The song is really what connects. You're inserting yourself into the story, so you have to be sort of a character in the song. And you have to figure out how to be the best character who can hit the notes with the same passion.

Are you nervous or confident before you perform?

The only time I get nervous, really, is when it's a talk show like *Conan* where you feel like, *Oh fuck*. It's like you got one shot, and it's live. But ever since that dream, I've felt more comfortable onstage than I do anywhere else, to be honest.

Do you do any vocal warm-ups before shows?

No. Ultimately, I just sing all the time, every day to keep my vocals warm. I don't have too many routines to protect my voice. I just intuitively know what to do and what not to do in terms of where I won't hurt it too much. But, when we're with Neil, everybody in the band gets together beforehand, and we do vocal warm-ups. We go [*sings a run of scales*].

With Neil?

Yeah. We all get together before the shows and sing those. But when I'm just doing Lukas Nelson & Promise of the Real, I just go up and wing it. I don't wanna rely on routine because that can fuck me up mentally. I get onstage, and then if I haven't done the vocal warm-ups, then I'm thinkin' about that. I wanna be able to just drop and perform anytime, anywhere. So, I keep myself constantly ready to be able to play.

How do you take care of your voice on the road?

I try to eat healthy. I try not to smoke out of pipes. Or when I'm smokin', I try and keep it to a few hits off a joint. I don't smoke cigarettes. But, I can't say that any one thing really works because Sinatra smoked cigarettes his whole life and his voice was fuckin' great. The Beatles, John Lennon, they all smoked cigarettes, and they sang awesome, and could hit those high notes like nobody's business.

Do you have any rituals before you hit the stage?

We do a circle, like a huddle, before we go up and play. The band gets together and talks about what we're wanting to manifest from the show.

Is there anything after the show that helps keep your voice in shape?

It's just such a spiritual thing for me. Being able to sing has so much to do with being in the right energy and the right state of mind and having the right perspective on life. I just try and keep a good relationship with music completely, and then I don't worry too much about routine.

When you start getting sick, what do you do?

That's a terrifying time for a vocalist. The only time I need vocal rest is when I get sick. You can't really stop the common cold; it just comes when it comes. You just do what you can to live a healthy lifestyle, keep my immune system rockin', and try to keep a positive attitude 'cause I think that also affects whether you get sick or not.

Are there songs where you've had to adjust the key live?

Yeah, sometimes you change the key to fit your voice in a better way. But it's more about tonality rather than if I can hit the note. Can I get more roundedness out of my voice? Can I get a deeper sound if I go in a lower key? That sort of rounded, deep fullness is a good thing to have in the voice.

Do you remember a performance where you surprised yourself?

Oh, that happens every time we're in the studio. Magic, you know?

Let's talk about your song "Surprise" where you sing, "Surprise, you didn't expect me, did you? I'm comin' through your window, and I've only got time." That feels like it could be about you as a singer. Being the son of Willie Nelson, that must be part of the fun and fire for you, winning people over based on the magnitude of your own talent. Does that play into it when you're performing? Like, "You think you know me because you know my dad, but you have no idea what I can do."

I think there's a certain element of that, for sure. I like the feeling I get when people love us for who we are, and I can tell that it's a genuine sort of love and inspiration. That makes me feel good.

You have this soft sweetness like your dad has, and that beautiful kind of phrasing, but then you have this other element where you can really rock your ass off and can scream and do things in a way that your dad doesn't do. There's even an operatic element that really surprised the hell out of me the first time I heard it. "If I Started Over" is a great example. Where does that come from?

I feel like I can do anything if I put my mind to it. I try not to limit myself. If I wanna hit that note, I just go for it. I try to fill my lungs with as much air as possible and hit that note. I think about it like I'm an athlete. Athletes don't let any doubt affect what they do. There's no doubt in their mind they're going to win; the best ones, that's how they feel. They put so much emphasis on being the best at what they do. They practice so much. I practice all the time.

There's another lyric in "Surprise" where you say, "I've been a witness to greatness. I can't settle for anything less." That sounds like what you're sayin' here too.

It is. That's exactly it. I forgot about "Surprise." [*Laughs*] Yeah, that's a good one.

Being a witness to greatness in your life, I'm wondering what that's taught you about being a singer, first starting with your dad.

He just taught me that it was important *to be* a singer. That having a unique voice is really important if you wanna have a career. It really is about havin' a character in your voice, not just about being able to hit the notes.

Speaking of characters, I heard a rumor that Bradley Cooper asked you to teach him how to be a singer for his remake of *A Star Is Born*. Is that true?

No. He was already a singer. I was just helping him bring it out. It's just training your voice to hit those notes all the time, and that's just muscle memory. It's just repetition. If you know what the good note is, that's 90 percent. The rest of it is just being able to hit that note on command, and that's just practice.

How'd you help him get there?

Just sat with him. We sang and we recorded. We would listen to the songs back. He was a musician already. It was just a small piece of development, of exposing that talent even more within himself.

Is the theory here that you believe all people are really musicians?

If you have the ability to discern pitch, then you have the ability to be a musician. If you can tell the right note from the wrong note. For example, if you're singing along to a song and you can recognize that your voice isn't doing what the other voice is doing, then you're able to discern. You know when it's right; it sounds good. It's just a matter of putting the time and the effort into it like anything else. Most people don't have time; that's really the bottom line.

How are you with hearing your own voice?

I criticize it often, but I don't hate it. The older stuff I have a hard time listening to.

Do you have a favorite vocal performance you're really proud of?

I did a version of "Southern Accents" by Tom Petty that I really like, but it's not out yet. Just sittin' there.

That's what made me fall in love with you, by the way. Tom Petty.

What? Really?

Because of the stuff I was saying before about the baggage your name can bring and judging somebody when you don't even know them yet. Not that I was judging you, but the first time I saw you live was a couple days after Tom Petty passed away. I was devastated. His music meant so much to me, and I was in no mood to go watch *anybody* play. But my buddy, Joel, got the gig doing your sound and kept raving about you. So, I begrudgingly went to see you at The Fonda. Had the arms folded,

the whole trip. [*Lukas chuckles*] **The lights go out and you come onstage wearing a Tom Petty top hat and launch into "American Girl." Man, you delivered everybody in the room from their pain. It was exactly what we needed in that moment. From that point on, you put on this amazing rock show. You weren't just Willie's kid. You were purely your own, and so confident, and in your own skin, and it was a beautiful thing to see. I was like, "Alright. I'm down with this guy."**

Well, that makes me feel great, man. I'm so happy that that's how people saw that show 'cause I felt the same way.

What's changed the most about your voice since you started?

It's gotten stronger, fuller, rounder, sort of deeper, and I've gotten better at hitting the notes.

If you could duet with one singer—living or dead—who would it be?

Probably Paul McCartney.

Who are your top five favorite singers of all time?

Ohhh God. Skip that one. I can't do that one. No, no. I can't go there. I don't like to rate and rank. No. No.

If you could ask any singer about their voice, who would it be and what would you ask?

Probably Sinatra, just in terms of his control, his attention to detail, where he places syllables, and where he comes in on the rhythm. Dad learned a lot from Sinatra, so he would probably be the one, although he probably wouldn't say shit to me, probably just, "Hey, take it easy, have a cigar."

That's alright, you'd be able to have a cigar with Sinatra.

Yeah...

WILLIE NELSON

ISHOULDN'T HAVE TO write anything else. "Willie Nelson" pretty much sums it up. At ninety years old, Willie has been writing, recording, and performing on the world's biggest stage almost his entire life. His ingenious songwriting, brilliant guitar playing, and iconic voice helped usher in the outlaw country era of the early '6os, a new sound that flew in the face of the conservative style of the day. But Willie doesn't play by "Their rules." And he never will.

Whether it be his advocacy for Native Americans, farmers, biofuel, or the legalization of marijuana, Willie has always done what's felt right in his heart. Even when that meant pushing past the clowns who told him his voice was never gonna cut it.

Well, that voice became a member of the Country Music Hall of Fame, has received the Kennedy Center Honors, has won 10 Grammys out of 52 nominations, and the list keeps going. Willie's face will forever be chiseled on the Mount Rushmore of American vocalists. And while he may be a man of few words, the Tao of Willie always speaks volumes.

Who first exposed you to singing?

My grandfather was a voice teacher. And my grandmother, who raised me, played piano and organ. They were both great musicians. All I remember was singin'.

Were you emulating anyone when you started out?

The Stamps Quartet were a great gospel group. I grew up listenin' to their music. But as far as any one particular singer, I don't think so.

How did you find your own voice?

I played with my sister [Bobbie Nelson] a lot on piano, me sittin' next to her with a guitar, and we'd do "Stardust" and "Moonlight in Vermont," and all those songs.

Did you ever have any vocal training?

My grandfather coached me, but he died when I was pretty young. But what I learned from him I think was real good. I learned to sing what I felt.

Are you nervous or confident before you perform?

I've been doin' it all my life, and I enjoy crowds, so I don't get worried or scared, or any of those things.

Do you do any vocal warm-ups before shows?

I may do a little warm-up before. I like to turn on country radio and sing along. I'll sing harmony with 'em or whatever. I don't really make it a point, but sometimes it just happens where we'll do a little pickin' and singin' before the show.

Do you have any rituals before you hit the stage?

No.

You don't smoke one before you get out there?

Oh, I used to a long time ago, but I quit smoking, because it was kind of hurtin' my lungs a little bit. I don't do anything! I don't drink anymore; I don't smoke cigarettes. Just kinda goin' natural.

Is there anything after the show that helps keep your voice in shape?

There's not anything I do intentionally.

How do you take care of your voice on the road?

Singing is the best exercise for anybody, really. Because you're using your lungs different. I just go out there and I sing!

When you start getting sick, what do you do?

I go home. [*Laughter*]

Are there songs where you wonder if your voice will be there that night?

If it was okay last night, I'm sure it's gonna be alright tonight. I don't worry about it. If I have a bad night or somethin', that pisses me off, but normally, I'm confident that I'm gonna be okay.

Are there songs where you've had to adjust the key live?

I think I'm still in the keys that I did a long time ago. I still do "Whiskey River" in G.

What was your most embarrassing vocal mishap ever?

I got too high one night and that taught me a lesson. I just left the stage. *This ain't the night!* [*Laughter*]

How are you with hearing your own voice?

I don't mind that at all.

Do you have a favorite vocal performance you're really proud of?

Not really. But I've been singin' pretty good the last few years. The more I sing, the better I sing. When we had to take off all that time, that really affected my singin', and I had to do things to keep it. Sing along with the radio! I'd do anything I could to keep my voice up because if you don't use it, you lose it.

You have such a unique way of phrasing. Where did that come from for you?

My favorite singer of all time is Frank Sinatra, and one of his things I enjoyed most was his phrasing. He never sang the same line twice. He did it as he felt it each time, and that's the way I sing.

When you first started, you were told that your voice didn't fit the traditional sound at the time, so you wrote for other people. What gave you the strength to keep believing in your own voice?

I didn't believe anybody that said anything. [*Chuckles hard*] I didn't pay any attention to those folks.

You've now made over seventy albums and you're a national treasure. How's that make you feel, thinking back on those folks who said you couldn't do it. Anything you want to say to them now?

Awww, I think they know what I would say. [*Wicked laughter*]

You were a member of one of the greatest supergroups ever, The Highwaymen. Waylon Jennings, Johnny Cash, Kris Kristofferson, and you. How do four guys get in a room, each a superstar in their own right, and make their voices blend so beautifully?
It was a natural thing. We all loved each other and were big fans of each other, so whatever they did was fine with me, and whatever I did was fine with them. We didn't have any problems about anything.

Years ago, I was at one of your shows, standing directly in front of your mic, singing along with you, and you're having a blast as you always do. And, at one point, I'm thinkin', *Man, I want that bandana on his head!* Right as I'm thinking that, you pull the bandana off your head, lean down and hand it to me. After playing this many shows, do you feel a psychic connection between you and the crowd, as if you can read their minds? Because it was so magical. I still don't quite know how that happened.
Well. I do connect with the audience. I sing to different people in the front row. I wrote this song called "I Fall in Love with the Front Row Every Night," and it's true. So, thank you, and you're welcome. [*Laughter*]

What's changed the most about your voice since you started?
Other people could probably answer that better than me, but I kind of feel like my voice has been pretty steady for a long time.

"Dusty bottles pour a finer glass of wine." When you sing that line, it reminds me of your voice.
Yeah, alright! Thanks!

You've sung duets with just about everyone, but if you could duet with one singer — living or dead—who would it be?
Well, it's Frank Sinatra.

Who would be your top five favorite singers of all time?
Frank Sinatra, Hank Williams, Eddy Arnold, Tony Bennett, Connie Smith.

When I interviewed your son for this book, he refused to answer that question!
Oh, he did? [*Cracks up*] That's funny, that's funny.

If you could ask any singer about their voice, who would it be and what would you ask?
Well, my favorite singer was Frank Sinatra, and I read somewhere that I was *his* favorite singer, so that's as good as it gets right there.

AARON NEVILLE

SOMETIMES YOU CAN FEEL THE EXISTENCE OF HEAVEN just by listening to someone's voice. There's something that can't be described in words. You just feel it, you just KNOW IT. Go listen to Aaron Neville sing, then tell me I'm wrong.

Born in New Orleans, Louisiana, of African-American, Caucasian, and Choctaw descent, Aaron's vocal sound reflects his heritage. He carries the weight of the world but does so with one of the most distinctive voices R&B has ever produced. His angelic tone has earned him multiple number one records, Grammys, crossover hits, and also led to the formation of The Neville Brothers, the iconic group he formed with...(I'm hoping you guessed it).

It could not have been more of an honor to speak with Aaron before he announced he was officially retiring from the road. So, while we may not see him as much as we did before, he's here now to share decades of wisdom from being out there, telling it like it is.

Who first exposed you to singing?

My brother, Art Neville. After that, it was the Nat King Coles and the Clyde McPhatters, all the doo-wop groups, and the gospel quartets, and the cowboys—you name it. I was a big Hank Williams fan.

Were you emulating anyone when you started out?

In a sense, yeah. Just taking little things here or there, but not really tryin' to mimic 'em. I used somethin' from them and used my own thing. I used to like Nat King Cole, how he pronounced his words, his diction and all. Clyde McPhatter, he's just a great singer. And Pookie Hudson and The Spaniels, and Billy Ward & The Dominoes, and Sonny Til and The Orioles, all them guys.

How did you find your own voice?

I never really was tryin' to sound like nobody else. When I was a kid, my grandmother used to rock me on her lap, and we'd listen to the gospel station. Most of the gospel singers back then, they was doing a lot of screaming. When I was thirteen years old, I heard Sam Cooke sing a song so smooth with the gospel, and I said, "Wow, that's what I wanna do." That helped guide my direction.

You have such a specific style.

It's comin' through me. I wish I could make a note to cure cancer. A lady told me about a little boy who was autistic, and they said they couldn't do nothin' with him. The only thing that would calm him down is if they put a headset on him with my voice goin' through it. That shocked me. Gave me a, "Wow." I said, "Well, it ain't me. Must be the God in me touchin' the God in him."

Wow.

Yeah, that was heavy.

Did you ever have any vocal training?

None. My brother, we used to harmonize together. He had a doo-wop group when I was about eight or nine years old, and they figured if I could hold a note, they'd let me sing with 'em. They showed me how to do all the harmonies, so, I can do each part of the harmony, just not at once. [*Chuckles*]

Are you nervous or confident before you perform?

I'm confident, anxious.

Like, excited?

Yeah. Rarin' to go.

Do you do any vocal warm-ups before the shows?

I don't really know what I'm doin'. [*Laughs*] I just use my voice to hit notes. Just mess around, hit notes, make sure when I go out onstage, I have 'em.

Do you have any rituals before you hit the stage?

I do apple cider vinegar and honey with a little cayenne pepper, a little lemon. I guess I be psychin' myself out 'cause I don't know if that stuff works or not. [*Laughter*]

Is there anything after the show that helps keep your voice in shape?

Sleep is the main thing. I try to go to sleep early. But you gotta unwind when you come off the stage, back to the hotel. You gotta watch some TV or somethin', a game show or whatever, then go to sleep.

Are there songs where you wonder if your voice will be there that night?

Sometimes. Probably "Everybody Plays the Fool." That's a kind of a challenging one. I mean, I've done all them songs twenty some years, and I played with The Neville Brothers for almost close to forty years. We did all the same songs in the same keys all them years. That kind of hurt my throat a little bit. I used to wind up with bruised vocal cords or nodules.

What were the symptoms of the nodules?

Just being hoarse.

What did they say you were doing wrong to get the nodules?

What I was doin' wrong was singin' over loud bands and not changin' keys. Like if the key is in B flat, I shoulda brang it down to A flat or somethin'. It's a precious gift, so you gotta nurture it and take care of it.

How long did it take you to heal?

That took a long time 'cause I didn't know what it was, and before I really realized it, I had damaged it.

So, how long were you on vocal rest?

A few months. Now I sing every day, me and my keyboard player, Michael Goods. We get on speakerphone, and he plays the piano while I sing. We rehearse songs.

And you find that keeps your vocals in shape?

Yeah, you gotta use 'em or lose 'em, you know?

Are there songs where you've had to adjust the key live?

Oh yeah, definitely. That's the thing, if you can't do that, you gonna be in trouble.

What was your most embarrassing vocal mishap ever?

I was never embarrassed about nothin'. I mean, things happen, but the audience doesn't know. If I'm getting ready to hit one note, and I feel it's gonna be weak, I jump to another octave.

Do you remember a performance where you surprised yourself?

I've done that a bunch of times. I've hit notes, and I surprised myself, like a song called "Feels Like Rain."

The John Hiatt song?

Yeah, yeah, doin' it live. I went higher than I usually go on the notes.

How are you with hearing your own voice?

I hate my speakin' voice, I love my singin' voice. I remember the first time I heard myself talk in the studio, *Uggggh! Dang!* [*Laughs*] It's like, *Hey man, that ain't me!* But the singin' was alright. It was cool.

Do you have a favorite vocal performance you're really proud of?

Yeah, a bunch of stuff I did with my brothers like the "Yellow Moon," "Brother's Keeper," the stuff with Linda Ronstadt. I got a Grammy with Trisha Yearwood. We sang "I Fall to Pieces." I did a thing with Rob Wasserman. He was doin' the album of duets, and me and him picked "Stardust," which was recorded at Willie Nelson's studio in Austin, Texas. I did all the vocals, and all the background vocals. Then, I did the "Mickey Mouse March" with Dr. John. He's playing keyboard, and I'm doing all the vocals, all the harmonies, and singin' the lead. Did you ever listen at the album from the '70s with "Hercules" on it?

There's a couple different records with "Hercules" on it.

I recorded "Feelings," "One Fine Day," and a song called "Performance."

What is it about those records for you?

They were like the first time in my life where I was, I don't know, just the innocence of the songs. It was a great time for me singin'.

I think a perfect example of how beautiful and complex your vocals are would be on a song like "Have Faith" off your first solo album. You listen to it, then put your head in your hands and go, *How is he doing this?* [*Aaron laughs*] How are you able to sing a melody—*sustain the note*—while having the octaves fluctuate inside of it, *and* keep it in the same key, all at the same time? Are we just supposed to assume that's your vibrato 'cause it feels like there's something else going on there?

It's a spiritual thing. That's why a lot of times I have to sing with my eyes closed. The music is the most important thing. I guess it's my life comin' outta my voice. Things I done done, and things I done watched or witnessed in this world. Just wantin' to try and mend a lot of the wrongs that's goin' on in the world through the vocals. Does that make sense?

It does on a spiritual and emotional level. But vocally, it's as if you're walking up and down the stairs like, "Oh no, I forgot that note, I'll go back down there and pick that up, then I'll go back up there." [*Aaron chuckles*] But it's all in the same melody, you know?
Mmm hmm, yeah. It's how you're feelin' on a certain night.

"True Love" off The Neville Brothers *Family Groove* record gives me that same feeling.
Me too. My brother Art wrote that. I love that song.

I hear you singing that, and I go, *Where does he get the nerve to sing like this?* [*Aaron laughs*] Is there something about singing with your family that brings out another side to you, something that singing on your own doesn't?
Oh yeah, we had been together two or three of us at a time, never all four of us, until 1976 when my uncle, who was the big chief of The Wild Tchoupitoulas Mardi Gras Indians, called us to do his album with him. We didn't have to say, "You take this note," or "You take that note," everybody just fell in right where they were supposed to. It was a natural thing. So, 1977, the brothers got together, and we ran up and down the highway almost forty years. But, yeah, it's the blend. It's the respect thing. Each vocal respects the next vocal. Nobody's tryin' to overdo the note or nothin', you just want it to blend.

I gotta ask you about the song "Heaven" off your *Apache* album, 'cause it may be my favorite song of yours.
That's a great song. It touches me every time I hear it. It never gets old.

It was released in 2016, which means you're how old at that point?
I must've been 76 or 75.

Yet your falsetto feels stronger than ever, and there's a raw quality to your voice that makes it even more soulful than recordings you did as a young man. How is that possible?
I've seen a lot more. [*Laughter*] Gotta lotta wrongs I'm tryin' to right.

What's changed the most about your voice since you started?
The most that's changed is me havin' asthma. I was born with asthma and I outgrew it, but it came back with a vengeance around 2003. After that, I was windin' up in ERs everywhere. It hasn't happened in a long time, knock on wood. You just gotta work around it.

How do you work around it?

My band can take up the slack if I don't hold the note as long. They can hold it longer. I gotta take a deeper breath. But I'm livin' with it, and I ain't lettin' it get me down.

If you could duet with one singer—living or dead—who would it be?

Well, too bad she can't sing again, but it would definitely be Linda Ronstadt, one of the greatest voices ever.

Yeah, you guys had a real good thing, huh?

Yeah. She said that our voices were married, like we musta sang together in another life. [*Laughs*]

What was it about her voice that moved you so much?

It's a respect thing. She respects me and I respect her. And when we harmonize together, it's the ultimate blend.

You guys made a real beautiful sound. Who would you say are your top five favorite singers of all time?

My brother, Art. Linda Ronstadt. Nat King Cole. Sam Cooke. Pookie Hudson and The Spaniels. Johnny Adams and Marvin Gaye. I used to call him The Man with the Tear in his Voice. You could hear his hurt. He was hurt.

If you could ask any singer about their voice, who would it be and what would you ask?

It's gotta be somebody like Nat King Cole. What would I ask him? I don't know. He died too young, man. All them guys back in the day were smokers. I smoked for a long time, but I quit in 1980, so I guess that kind of helped me out. But Nat King Cole, Frank Sinatra, Dean Martin, all them guys. It was a fashion statement to see 'em with a cigarette in their hand while they're singin'. And all of 'em died with lung cancer, throat cancer, whatever.

So, what would you ask Nat King Cole?

I would ask him what you askin' me, "How do *you* keep your voice in shape?" [*Laughter*]

STEVIE
NICKS

YOU JUST READ THE NAME ABOVE and can't help but think of this beautiful, mysterious, and mystical songstress, twirling around in her flowing dress, a tambourine in her hand, singing with a voice so uniquely her own that it moves your soul to no end. The world would learn of her distinctive vocal sound when she and Lindsey Buckingham joined Fleetwood Mac in 1975. Her contribution to *Rumours* would catapult the band to superstardom, making it one of the bestselling albums of all time.

Her tumultuous, on and off career with Fleetwood Mac has become almost mythic at this point, generating sales of well over 100 million records. But she didn't stop there. Stevie has become one of the most iconic singers of our time by being an incredible solo artist in her own right as well, and is the only woman to be inducted into the Rock & Roll Hall of Fame twice.

It meant so much to speak with this legend about her definitive approach to singing. Our conversation would also lead to some beautiful and personal memories of Tom Petty and drum up a bit more Fleetwood Mac drama than I anticipated. But something else happened when the interview was over: I told Stevie that my sister's birthday was coming up in a few days and that Stevie was her all-time hero. I asked if she'd say, "Happy Birthday" on my recording, so I could give it to her as a birthday gift. Stevie said no, she'd sing it to her instead. Like I said...a legend.

Who first exposed you to singing?

My grandfather. He was a country singer who never really made it but tried his whole life. When I was in the fourth grade, he brought a truckload, literally, a *truckload* of 45-inch singles over to my parent's house in El Paso, Texas. Brought 'em all into my room downstairs in the basement, and we listened to 'em all. Some of them were very country, some were a little more bluesy country. But a lot of them were like Ricky Nelson, and there was The Everly Brothers [*sings "All I Have to Do Is Dream"*] "Dreeeeam. Dream, dream, dream." I loved that song! And I loved Buddy Holly's "Everyday."

Was it your grandfather who made you feel you could do this?

He really did. I learned *all those songs*. I would sing along, and I remember him saying, "You're a harmony singer." I'm like, "What's that?" He's like, "You don't sing in unison with these people. You instantly go to the harmony above or below, and I don't have to teach that to you, you just know it." But then, I turned completely rogue, because Top 40 radio turned into R&B radio, which I loved. That was The Supremes, and The Temptations, and all the girl groups, The Shirelles, the people that Carole King and Gerry Goffin were writing for, and I just went totally towards that. My grandfather was like, "What happened?" [*Laughter*]

You knew you were gonna be a singer from an early age, didn't you?

Oh, I even choreographed a tap dance for the talent show where I was wearing a black skirt, black dress, black tap shoes, black socks, black stockings, and a black top hat. It was like I was already making up my outfit for Fleetwood Mac, *in the sixth grade*.

That's amazing!

I'd be singing in the back seat of the car in Texas and my parents would turn around and go, "Seriously, who are you?" And I'm like, "Well, I'm going to be a singer." My father was like, "Ohh, this is not good." They believed me. Because my grandfather was married, had three kids, and every two years, he just left and went on the road, rode the rails and played in all the bars across the country. He's not a good husband, and not really that great of a father, because he was determined. He didn't make it. When the *Buckingham Nicks* record was released, and I handed it to him, I could see just a flash of bitterness go across his face. He was in his early eighties when he died, and it was like, *She's gonna do it. These two are gonna make it, and I didn't.*

How did you find your own voice?

I think I was just born with my own voice. I wrote my first song when I was fifteen and a half, and from that moment, I just started writing full on. My mom said, "You can be a singer-songwriter, but you're going to college." And I did. I went to five years of college, and the last three years of that, I was in a band with Lindsey. We played with every famous band that was playing up and down the Peninsula in San Francisco. We opened for Janis Joplin a couple times, Jimi Hendrix, Chicago at the Fillmore, Buffalo Springfield at Winterland in San

Francisco. That's where we started. But the perk of being an opening band, even if you were eighth on the bill, was that you got to stand on the stage and watch the headlining band. So, I got to take what I learned from Janis, and Grace Slick, and Jimi Hendrix, who actually saw me standing on the side of the stage and dedicated a song to me.

Wild! Can you give me some examples of things you were able to learn?

From Jimi Hendrix I learned humility and to be really kind and sweet and fun, 'cause he was all those things. And then, of course, he'd start playing the guitar and singing, and he was just a monster. From Janis, I learned how to just stomp out there on the stage and take hold of the audience. I just watched her do it a couple times and figured it out. That was where Lindsey and I got our experience. That's why it wasn't hard for us to walk into Fleetwood Mac. We'd already been there in front of thousands and thousands of people.

Are you nervous or confident before you perform?

I do get nervous. In that last hour, I'm not very friendly to everybody. [*JTG laughs*] But it's just because I'm goin' into myself. I get butterflies, and sometimes the butterflies are a bit more like bees. It's just excitement, but sometimes it hits you, and you think you're having stage fright. Bad stage fright is throwing up in the bathroom and I never had that. I just get very quiet because once make-up is done and you start to change, that's it.

Did you ever have any vocal training?

I didn't until I did. I was getting ready to go on a Stevie Nicks tour, and I had invited five hundred people to a dress rehearsal. I got really sick and was gonna cancel it. But one of my best friends, who was a singer as well, said, "I know a vocal coach. We can get him to your house, you can do thirty minutes with him, and I guarantee you'll not have to cancel this." Not for a minute did I believe her. "This is bullshit; this is never gonna work." But Steve Real came over and sat on my bed with his electric piano. It's like [*runs scales*] "Na-na-na-na-na-na-na." *Oh, I'm sure that's gonna help me.* I was really hoarse. I worked with Steve for thirty minutes, and then he said, "Now go back to sleep for two or three hours. Always put three hours between when we finish and when you start." So, I went back to sleep, woke up around five, and started "La-la-la-ing" around the house, put on some music, started singing a little bit, and was like, *I think I can do this.*

How was the show?

I walked onstage and did a two hour set. From that moment onward, I never went onstage without Steve being with us. He was able to make me a cassette tape, so, whether I had him or the tape, I never went onstage, *ever once*, without doing the tape.

What's your vocal routine?

If we're going on at 8:00, I do twenty-seven minutes at 3:00. Then, at 4:30, eleven more minutes. So, it's thirty-eight minutes. Three hours between the last "La-la-la-la-la" you sing, and going onstage.

And what exercises are you doing?

It starts out with [*runs some scales while doing tongue trills*]. And then, [*does some scales using*] "Do-do-do-do-do-do-do." So, there's the long versions and the short bursts. [*Does lip trills, then hums some scales using "Mmmm."*] And then, you do "Nays," [*runs scales, singing*] "Nay-nay-nay-nay-nay." And then, you do "Duh." [*Sings*] "Duh-duh-duh-duh-duh." And then, the long one is, [*sings a longer version of the same*]. And then, you go back, and you throw a "Brrrr" in 'cause a [*lip trill using the Brrrr sound*] vibrates the gunk off your vocal cords. I never have a bad night now, not even if I'm sick. And, boy, if I could go back to 1975 and have this vocal tape, I would do it. Because at seventy-one years old, I am singing as good, if not better, than I ever sang in my whole life, because I'm a full on trained singer, and I love that. I know exactly what to do when I'm having problems.

Can you give me an example of a problem you've been able to overcome?

If you're having trouble hitting a note, if you're gonna go, [*sings*] "Thunder only happens when it's rainin', players only..." For some reason, that second line gets me every time, "Players only *LOOOVE you*..." When you go up to that note in "Dreams" you'll raise your neck up. That's the natural thing to do when you think you're not gonna hit a note. As soon as you look towards the sky, your cords come together and they shut down, and then you start singing right out of your throat. When you're a trained singer, you sing out of your diaphragm. Steve always says, "Just keep lookin' at that microphone, don't look up."

That's true?

Yeah. And since I've been working with him, I'm singing three or four steps higher than I was when I started. It's wonderful and gratifying to say I am a *trained singer*. I study voice.

How do you take care of your voice on the road?

You just have to try to get as much sleep as you can. Smoking's terrible for you, smoking pot's terrible for you, drinking's terrible for you. When you're high, you'll do things that you wouldn't do. You'll strain your voice.

When you first start getting sick, what do you do?

You try to put on the brakes somehow and not let it go to a place where you're gonna have to cancel a show. If you're really sick, there's not a lot you can do. But if you just have a bad cold, then you just stay in bed. I hate to burst everybody's balloon, but there's a certain rap song that says [*sings*] "I'm livin' like a rockstar," I'm like, "You have no idea!" [*Laughter*] You have no idea what it is like to do that many three hour shows and then get on an airplane and fly two hours after the show to get to your next destination and unpack. You're *lucky* to get to bed by 4:00 or 5:00 a.m. Then, you get up at 5:00 p.m., eat dinner, watch *Law & Order*, and then you go back to bed because you have a show the next day. You are simply recovering from last night and preparing for tomorrow night.

Yeah, there's a lonely side to all this.

It's brutal. It's all about the show. Everything you do out there, it's about that three hours. *Are the shows fun?* Yes, absolutely. It's a lot of self-gratification, and the audiences are great, but *is it really fun?* No. It isn't. It's fun onstage. The rest of it is brutal. But being a trained singer, it's 50 percent less brutal. You never have to worry about anybody saying, "Stevie Nicks wasn't on last night." There ain't nobody ever writes that. And that's all you play for; to be able to walk on and do a good show for the people who paid a lot of money to come see you. You have to be the master of your own fate, and studying voice is a good place to start. That's why I tell all my young friends, "You better get a vocal coach 'cause it will save you so much grief."

Do you have any rituals before you hit the stage?

When you're me, you become Stevie Nicks slowly. You get there, and then you have rollers in your hair, and you get your makeup done, and then you start to become her, and all of a sudden, "It's time to change!" You change into your chiffon, take the rollers out, put a few curls in with the iron, scrunch up your hair, and the final thing is, *Okay, time to go in the boots*. When my little feet go in those black velvet boots, that's when I become me. Everybody starts to smile, you walk out into the hall, the rest of the band's there, and it begins.

Your mic stand is always bedazzled with scarves and silver chains and everything. Are they just decorative or do some have a special meaning for you?

The ones on there now have been on there a long time. I've only changed it a couple times in my whole life, I think. Same with my tambourine and all my ribbons; they've been on there forever. If the tambourine was lost, that'd be terrible. It can all be redone, but there's something to having those things that are really old and beloved.

Yeah, they've been through the wars with you.

Getting used to a new tambourine would be hard for me. *It is ritualistic.* It's kind of tribal.

Is there anything after the show that helps keep your voice in shape?

We change, go to the airport, get on a plane, and the best thing you can do on that plane is not talk. I sit in the very first seat because I figure I'll be quieter if I sit by myself. I try and wind down on the plane whereas other people have fun, have a glass of wine and dinner. But I eat when I get to the hotel. [Stevie's assistant] carries a cooler thing, and she'll heat food for me. Part of it is like being a nun. You have to cloister yourself a little bit. You can't be getting on the plane and rabble-rouse and yell and laugh and talk because that's the beginning of preparation for the next show.

I know you spoke about that note in "Dreams." Are there other songs where you wonder if your voice will be there that night?

If you just concentrate on your training, you're gonna be fine. Even though your brain says you're not, you are. And if you know you're not gonna hit it, you just go down to the next note.

That seems to be the move. Or get the audience to sing.

We have two background singers that have been singing with us forever, and I'll always give 'em a heads up if something's going on with me. There's a *really* high part in "Second Hand News." If I feel like I might not be able to sing that, I'll just look over at Sharon [Celani] like, "You sing it," and I'll just pretend to be singing. [*JTG laughs*] That doesn't happen often, but it does every once in a while. I'm not gonna strain my voice when I don't have to 'cause then you're screwing up your voice, and you'll pay a price. So, background singers do beautiful harmonies and stuff, but every once in a while, they actually save your life.

Are there songs where you've had to adjust the key live?

There used to be before Steve. It's like Robert Plant saying to me, "Well, I lowered all those damn keys," and I'm like, "We did too," but now we don't have a reason to lower them.

What was your most embarrassing vocal mishap ever?

This is the worst one that I can remember. Fleetwood Mac was doing "Stand Back." At the end of the verse, it's like, [*sings*] "No one looked as I walked by. Just an invitation would have been just fine. He said no to him again and again." [*Scats the final line*] and then it goes into the chorus, "Stand back, stand back!" Well, either I went into another verse and the band went into the chorus, or I went into the chorus and the band went into another verse, but it was a train wreck of epic proportions.

[*Laughs*] Ahhh, those are the worst! I love it.

Just terrible. Nothing to love about it. Because in the Stevie Nicks band, they know to follow the singer. Waddy Wachtel, my musical director and lead guitar player, he says, "Always follow the singer." Fleetwood Mac did not follow the singer, and they couldn't figure out what the hell happened. It was like they all dropped to their knees and put their coats over their heads. By the time we found our way back, we were into the solo. But the brain is such a weird thing. About ten days later, the same thing happened again. That was *really* a bummer because that is when I said, "I want a teleprompter." I'm not gonna suffer. I don't need to suffer. I'm too old to suffer. I want a little teleprompter right at my feet, and I won't look at it unless I need it, and the first two words go outta my head.

They're kinda controversial among singers. Some hate 'em, some love 'em.

I hardly ever look at it, but every once in a while, it'll just shut down, and I see it go black, and I get afraid. It's like, *Oh my God, where's the teleprompter just in case I need it?* All you need to do is forget two words and you're screwed. It takes you like three songs to recover. You're never supposed to apologize to your audience, but I have before! [*Cracks up*] I've said, "Well, that went well, huh?" Then, the whole audience is laughing with you. Better they're laughing with you than at you.

It's so awesome that twirling around onstage has become your signature move in a way, like James Brown doing the splits or Pete Townshend doing the windmill. Since we're talking about embarrassing moments, have you ever fallen over while spinning around?

I've never fallen over by spinning around, but I did fall once in "Edge of Seventeen." There was a case pushed up against the edge of the stage, and I thought it *was* the stage. I stepped on it, and it went out. My right leg went down and the rest of me stayed up.

Oh shit.

Thank God I *can* do the splits. It was the scariest thing that ever happened to me onstage. I didn't fall off, but *I almost did*. Luckily, I was able to throw my body back towards the stage, and I got up and finished the song. I'm very careful up there. When I'm twirling, I'm very careful.

Do you remember a performance where you surprised yourself?

When you're recording, sometimes you can do stuff that you absolutely think you could never do. In "Wild Heart," there's a part that goes, [*sings*] "Even in the darkest places of your mind!"

Yeah, towards the end!

It's *really* high. When we recorded it, I couldn't sing near as high as I can now, and I was like, "I can't do it!" But my sister-in-law, Lori, said, "You *can* do it. March out there and hold your head up high!" [*Laughs*] I did it. Now, because of my vocal training, I probably could do that part.

How are you with hearing your own voice?

I actually quite love my voice 'cause my singing voice is a lot like my speaking voice. In the old days, if I was calling information, there were times when an operator would say, "Are you Stevie Nicks?" I'd go, "Funny enough, I am." They hear my singing voice in my speaking voice.

Do you have a favorite vocal performance you're really proud of?

I make sure that I'm always proud of every vocal because you only have that one chance. I work really hard on all of them, and I don't let them go out until I think that they're spectacular. Once that song leaves you, it's gone to the world. It doesn't belong to you anymore, and you can't call it back. It's like a spirit. It's gone.

I want to talk about a specific vocal. But I also know that the song is pretty contentious, so I wanna preface this by saying that Fleetwood Mac's history has been documented enough so please don't feel like I'm digging for more drama because I only wanna discuss what happens to be one of your greatest vocal performances ever. The problem here is that the song happens to be "Silver Springs." Your vocal is just so fucking glorious. The anger in your voice on that final chorus. You don't usually scream like that on record. We're really listening in on a real argument.

Yes, you are.

I'd love to know how you recorded that in the studio, because you really captured the emotion in such a real and raw way.

It was quite a long time into Lindsey's and my relationship. And it was for all the things that don't work between you and me. "I will follow you down 'til the sound of my voice will haunt you. You'll never get away from the sound of the woman that loved you." That's how I felt. Every time I sang it, that's how I sang it. And he sang it with me, so I didn't do that vocal alone. We sang those choruses together.

How do you do that?

You are in the studio together, singing on the same mic, and you're glaring at each other. [*JTG laughs*] And then they say, "Do it again," so you do it again, and you're still glaring. I would say we probably didn't have to do that vocal very often. We probably did it once or twice. It was an angry song onstage. And it was still an angry song onstage up until the last time we did it.

I'm so sorry for the pain it caused you. But it is an unbelievable song. [*Laughter*]

I know. I have a good friend that always goes to me, "Oh, tragedy, tragedy, tragedy, *cha-ching, cha-ching, cha-ching!*" But Lindsey and Mick [Fleetwood] told me in a parking lot that "Silver Springs" wasn't going to be on *Rumours*. It was gonna be the B-side of "Go Your Own Way," and there was nothing I could do. I was furious. I had no power...*then*. I had also given that song to my mom for Christmas because there was nothing I could really give her except a piece of jewelry or something, and I wanted to give her something really special. She really loved that song so I gave her publishing, writer's royalties, everything. Then they took it off the record. It messed up my gift and hurt my feelings.

After Fleetwood Mac was broken up for a few years, you guys reunited and made that live album, *The Dance*, and finally got to release "Silver Springs" properly!

It became the first single, and it did amazing. Suddenly, my mom was calling me, going, "Oh my God, it's raining money!"

I feel like backing vocals are an art form that don't get the credit they deserve, and I really love the way you build yours so beautifully. What's your approach to that process?

When I'm working in *my* band, the lead vocals are recorded, and I just sing counterpoint. Then, I send the girls out to sing along with that, and those become a three part. I hired Lori and Sharon in 1979. I said, "I don't wanna sound anything like Fleetwood Mac. I wanna be Crosby, Stills, and Nash. I'm gonna be the Stephen Stills, and Lori, you're gonna be the Graham Nash, and Sharon, you're gonna be the David Crosby."

What's the difference doing backgrounds with them compared to Fleetwood Mac?
It's kind of the same way Christine and Lindsey and I approached our vocals: letting either of the three of us go out and just sort of vamp, and then taking those vamps and making them into your backgrounds, instead of just doing classic "Ohhhhs."

Oh, that's brilliant. Vamping and finding something inside of it to turn into a part.
We can use "Dreams." It's like, [*sings the lead*] "Like a heartbeat drives you mad, in the still-ness of remembering what you had." The backgrounds go, "Heart-beat...still-ness...lon-ley...uuuu-uuu, uuu-uu-uuu—uuuu." Then there's a high one that Christine does on the record. That's *behind* the other part that I sang first. It becomes a real counterpoint melody that you've got going on. It's really one of the funnest parts because the leads are always done very fast, so the background vocals we take a lot more time with.

"Gypsy" has this beautiful vibrato throughout that song where it seems that you just turned on a switch and it was there.
I always thought that [*makes an exaggerated goat sound*] "N-a-a-a-a-a" thing was irritating. So, I worked on making that vibrato less. It's still there. It's just now I've learned to sing and to control my voice. When I need to use it, I use it, and when I don't wanna use it, I don't.

It's just in you? It just comes out?
Yeah. You can't ever change your vibrato. You can get rid of it sometimes, but you can't change the one you were born with. [*Laughs*] There's a *South Park* episode; Fleetwood Mac's in it, and I'm a little goat in a little chiffon outfit with boots, and I'm like, [*makes the vibratory goat sound again*]. I get kidnapped by the Taliban or something, and the United States sends the Army in to get me—you know *South Park*, it's so insane—and it was all about that vibrato. I'm like, "Oh, great. Now the whole world knows that I sound like a little goat!" [*Laughter*]

Were you laughing when you watched it?
I had to okay it. And listen, you want to go along with the *South Park* people because they can turn on you. [*Laughs*] So, you're like, "Yeah, whatever, it's fine."

So, what's changed the most about your voice since you started?
It's just stronger. That's the beauty of being a trained singer. You can do four shows a week instead of two or three. Without the training, you're out there spending a whole lot of money with too many days off. But you need it 'cause you're not trained, so you're gonna scream your voice out every time you go onstage. Your voice doesn't just get stronger cause you sing a lot. Your voice gets stronger because you know how to sing.

If you could duet with one singer—living or dead—who would it be?

I did a duet with LeAnn Rimes called "Borrowed (Re-Imagined)," and I think it's my favorite duet I've ever done. The song itself is gorgeous, and super sad, so it was really fantastic. I think she's the best singer I've ever sung with. You have to really be on your toes to sing with her. Singing with her was hard because she's so good. I had to really learn to sing with her, and I had to listen to it a lot.

Is there someone you'd still love to duet with?

I'd like to sing with Ed Sheeran. I love his voice.

I'll bet you could arrange that.

I'm working on it.

Since we're on the subject of duets, I would be remiss if I didn't ask you about Tom Petty's voice. He really meant everything to me, for so many reasons, and the duets you guys did together over the course of your careers are just perfect. Your voices blended so beautifully. What was it like to sing with him?

I started singing with Tom in 1980 when we were doing *Bella Donna*, and he gave me "Stop Draggin' My Heart Around." Had he not given me that song, which was the single, I don't know if *Bella Donna* would've taken off like it did. It kicked *Bella Donna* straight into the universe and he and I became like brother and sister friends. I wanted to be him in a lot of ways. We were kind of the boy and girl version. When I was signing my record deal with Atlantic, that's what I said to them, "I want to make a girl Tom Petty record, a really good, hard rockin', swampy record." The fact that Tom was able to come in and be a part of it—our friendship never ended until the last day of his life. I just loved his voice and felt super close to him, always. His first wife said to me, "I think that besides me, you were the best friend he ever had." So, it was as much about our friendship as it was our singing. The Heartbreakers, they were their own tribe, and they always said, "No girls allowed," but coming up to the end, he gave me a platinum silver Sheriff's badge saying, "To the only girl in The Heartbreakers." On the inside, it said, "Love, Tom Petty." It had little teeny diamonds scattered all over it, and little bits of 24 karat gold. Whenever I would want to come in, they'd say, "Can she borrow him for a minute?" He would say, "Well, she has a badge." I'll always have that.

[*Laughs*] That's awesome.

It was awesome. And the loss has been awesomely bad. He can never come again, and never be replaced, so it's just really, really sad.

I can't imagine what you're going through. But what a beautiful thing you guys have given the world. Can you tell me about how you recorded those songs?

Some of them we did right next to each other on two different mics. We usually sang like that. If we wanted to tweak something, we'd each go out by ourselves. But it was very easy to sing with Tom because we sort of took on the same personality when we sang together.

"Insider" gets some love here and there. But "I Will Run to You" is such a great one too, and I don't think it gets enough play out there in the world.

That is a really good song. But you know what? All those songs, and the things that we did, they just go out there and simmer in the world. He's not dead. He's here.

Well, that's the beautiful thing about music, it keeps you alive in so many ways.

Yeah.

Who are your top five favorite singers of all time?

LeAnn Rimes, especially after singing with her. Natalie Maines from The Chicks. Sheryl Crow. I'd have to say Bonnie Raitt. And, well, I've only sung with Carrie Underwood once, but it was pretty spectacular so we could say her. And then, Christine McVie. That's probably six, right?

You're Stevie Nicks, you get six. But if you could ask any singer about their voice, who would it be and what would you ask?

A voice that I really love is Robert Plant. Even though he prefers to not be in Led Zeppelin anymore, he said to me, "I would just prefer to follow the music around the world." I get that, because he has such a fascinating voice. I turned on the TV over in Europe and it was a Robert Plant concert. It had only been on for about fifteen to twenty minutes, but it was like four in the morning, and I watched the whole thing. I just really enjoyed listening to him, watching him sing. He doesn't sing quite as high as he used to, but he sang so high that nobody could be expected to do that. But he still sings great, and his songs are still great, and he's still a great performer.

So, what would you ask Robert Plant?

"How long are you gonna do this? I hope forever. Don't stop. Keep following the music around the world."

KAREN O

I BELIEVE EVERY YOUNG SINGER OUT THERE should hear what Karen O has to say right now. Because while a lot of people play rockstar, she truly is one. And even though she's one of the most captivating performers you'll ever lay eyes on, it's her voice that can either sweet talk or claw its way into your soul. There's just something about pure honesty, raw vulnerability, and intense passion that never fails.

That's why when you listen to Karen O, she never fails.

As the lead singer of the Yeah Yeah Yeahs, Karen and her band were nominated for a Grammy after the release of their debut album, *Fever to Tell*, in 2003. Since then, they've taken their exhilarating style of indie rock and turned it into an exciting career.

Karen's solo projects and collaborations have shown us a restless spirit, continually seeking out new ways to inspire her vocal approach, each one just as good as the last. And that happens to be just what she wants for you. As a matter of fact, this magnetic force of nature is actually challenging you.

Toward the end of each interview, I always ask, "If you could duet with any singer, who would it be?" It's a tough question I've tried to ask myself over the years. And Karen O might just be my final answer.

Who first exposed you to singing?

It probably started with the fact that my dad was a music lover. His favorites were The Everly Brothers, The Beatles, doo-wop or country or rock 'n' roll. It's kind of where I got the building blocks of what later would become my sense of melody.

Were you emulating anyone when you started out?

When I was nineteen, I went to Oberlin College in Ohio, and they send you home for winter term. It's just this really brutal time in the winter where they didn't want the kids going to school 'cause they got kinda depressed. So, they sent you home, and you had to choose what you wanted to do for that term. I chose to take acoustic guitar lessons with this guy Rick who had a mullet haircut from Jersey. [*Laughter*] Once I learned four or five chords—I still basically know the same amount—I started writing songs. It was the mid to late '90s, and I think I was emulating a bit of Cat Power, and maybe a little PJ Harvey, because she had this *4-Track Demos* record that blew my mind—just how free and unbridled she was. They were the only two women in indie rock that were making a splash at that time that I connected to. Maybe a little bit of Björk too. But then my voice is really different from all those ladies. [*Laughs*]

How did you find your own voice?

The way that I created the style that I used for the early Yeah Yeah Yeahs *Fever to Tell* songs, and the first EP, was really because in the beginning when Nick [Zinner, guitarist] and I were writing, I did a lot of the demos using this little toy megaphone. It had "Deep Voice," "Alien Voice," "Megaphone Voice," and "Super High Voice." I would do most of the demos through the "Megaphone Voice," which is quite distorted. I was using my voice as an instrument through this toy megaphone.

Was there a benefit to that for you?

I had total freedom to play with my voice and do a bunch of vocal styles and acrobatics because I wasn't associating my voice with just a voice. I was associating it with the sound that was coming out of this toy. It was an interesting way to start figuring out what my style was gonna be with the band. And it took me a while after that because I loved playing with the effects. It would just bring out so many different ideas and exploration experimentations. I didn't associate my voice with myself for a really long time in that band.

But even without all that, you have such a specific style that's your own, and it always feels so vulnerable and uncensored to me. There're songs where you're willing to bleed, like "Mysteries," where it's almost like you're purging some sort of demon from your soul.

Yeah.

And then, there's that other side of you like "Beast" [off Karen's solo album *Live from Crush Palace*] where your voice is really delicate and haunting. You do both so well.

Thank you. There are certain qualities of a singer that immediately resonate with me. For instance, Sam Cooke is probably my favorite singer of all time.

Mine too!

He's the king. [*Laughs*] He must be a lot of singer's favorite singer, right? Because he's so special. He had this...oh my God, I don't even know what it is! It's a disservice to put adjectives to what he does, but there's a purity there, a warmth, a spirituality. And those inflections he did. I guess he kind of stumbled onto it with gospel. I'm definitely attracted to a lot of singers that started off in gospel. But it's singing your heart out, as you're saying, that's what attracts me most about wanting to sing. Being able to sing your heart out, and kind of touch the divine with it. You're reaching for the heavens with your voice, and sometimes you can just about get there and move people in that way.

Yeah, I think when singing kind of moves you the best is when there's a combination of the spiritual, the sexual, and the vulnerable. You have all that.

Thank you! Those are all very important to me with singing. Those three aspects are all equally important.

Did you ever have any vocal training?

I was never interested in being technically trained because I saw what that style was, and it didn't really trip my trigger. I was almost suspicious of it. I felt like it would be a construct or a trap that I didn't really wanna be in. Once I got into high school, I started going to the city to see indie rock bands, and that was quite inspiring and influential for me to start singing.

Are you nervous or confident before you perform?

I'd say like 90 percent of the time, really nervous before I go on, and then as soon as I step onstage it switches over. But there've been times where I've lost my nerve onstage. Thankfully, they're kind of few and far between, but no one's immune to all of a sudden becoming really self-conscious up there for some random reason or another.

I'm always fascinated when certain people say that because they sure don't show it.

The first time I ever performed as the lead singer for the Yeah Yeah Yeahs, it was just as much about the exposition, and the sort of pageantry, and creating a persona as it was about the singing. The singing was probably the last on the list of important things. [*Cracks up*] I *performed*. And I think many margaritas were involved. We were opening up for The White Stripes at the Mercury Lounge, which is why all the margaritas were happening. Once I was on, it was completely cathartic. I turn into someone else, and I don't feel nervous.

Your first show with the band was opening for The White Stripes?

We were first out of four. This was during their second record, *De Stijl*, before they really blew up. They were just starting to get a bunch of buzz around them. I cut hearts out of black duct tape and had those as pasties underneath a tank top, and doused myself in olive oil 'cause I wanted to look like I was all sweaty when I got on there, but the olive oil was running into my eyes, and stinging my eyes. It was a mess. But it was quite unusual.

Do you do vocal warm-ups before shows?

I never did until the last five or six years. I feel like my voice has dropped a little, so it takes a bit more work to hit all the notes that I used to. I do a basic five-minute warm-up. Then, I'll put some music on and sing along to it right before I go on, just to warm-up my voice.

What's that warm-up consist of?

If you put "Five-minute vocal warm-up" in Google, it's the one that pops up. It's on YouTube. It's the one that you go [*vibrates her lips in a trill*]. Then you just do a couple different sounds up the scales and down the scales, and that's about it.

How do you take care of your voice on the road?

It's so much pressure on you to deliver. All I do on the road is try not to get sick. [*Laughs*] It's like being struck down to hell; it's so horrible. It's also not just your voice; it throws off your hearing by being congested, and it throws off your ability to hit the right notes. Just *UGH!* Such a nightmare. So, I drink tons of tea, which is generally Throat Coat. A hint of Manuka Honey in there can help bring your voice back. I have Manuka Honey drops I suck on too, and these little dried pods you throw in hot water. They expand into this gelatinous mushroom looking thing, but it lubricates and moistens your throat and vocal cords.[7]

I gotta try those at some point.

I'd say just as bad as getting sick is having to withdraw from all the fun and activities on the road. Everybody's having a party, and I'll just be hanging out in the hotel room feeling sorry for myself, watching TV or something, because I can't afford to get sick. Your instrument's your voice. If anything happens to your well-being, that can shut down an entire show, or a tour. *You* have to be almost like the monk on tour.

Do you have any rituals before you go on?

Getting dressed, and putting make-up on, getting my stage clothes. The costume is part of the ritual. Listening to some jams that get me and the boys excited while maybe drinking a little bit of tequila, pouring some on the floor for homies that aren't with us anymore. And dancing a bit to warm-up the joints, the old aching bones.

---

7   Boat Sterculia Seed

Are there songs where you wonder if your voice will be there that night?

There are definitely songs like that. Sometimes I struggle when I'm up there 'cause I structure the set list more on an emotional arc rather than a vocal and physical arc. I might have a song where I've just totally blasted out my vocal cords screaming, and then it might go right to a song where I'm supposed to sing really soft and be in key.

How do you manage that transition for yourself?

One of the tricks for that is I'll have the mic down by my waist, and I'll start singing the song off mic to find the right key, with everybody watching me. Then, when I feel ready, I'll bring the mic up and start singing. So, I have a moment to find it for myself and hopefully be where I need to be.

That's a smooth little move. Do you ever adjust the keys live?

We almost did that with "Skeletons," which is a bit of a reach, but when we tried adjusting the key, the emotion changed. I'm sure someone has broken it down, maybe it was even David Byrne, to the science of how music works with our brains and emotional centers. But, it just didn't have the same emotional resonance so, I was just like, "Screw it, let's just keep it at the same key and I won't buckle. I'll make it happen." [*Laughs*]

How do you trick your mind into reaching that note?

For one thing, you're not doing yourself any favors with self-doubt. Ask for what you need, because there are certain songs where I'm supposed to come in on the right note, but sometimes I'm just overwhelmed up there and, as you know, now being a singer yourself, you don't really know what it's going to sound like on that stage. It could be a muddy mess. I ask one of the players to give me the note before I come in. I put myself in the best position possible to succeed. Sometimes, I'll still come in on the wrong thing. If I do, I'll just laugh it off, and I'll start again until I get it right. [*Cracks up*]

That's one of the things I love about watching you onstage. You're not self-conscious, and you're able to say, fuck it, and kinda laugh at whatever is going on. If it's not perfect, you're still smiling and having a good time. The audience is so much more into the experience than going, "She didn't hit the note." I think *there's* a lesson to the way you approach performing live. There's a zen approach to it that's really cool.

I think that singing is so much more than hitting the right note. It's about connecting with the audience, connecting with something divine to a certain degree. It's connecting to your most primitive and deepest intuition, and to your nature as a human on this planet. It always strikes me how a lot of the best songs in the world are bad poetry. [*Laughter*] When you sing something, you can give it this whole other meaning than if you were reading it on a page. It's like seduction to a certain degree. But it's also transcendence.

Do you remember a performance where you surprised yourself?

On this record I did with Danger Mouse, there's a song, "Ministry," where there's like this style of singing that's very '60s, a little bit psychedelic. For instance, the lead singer of The Zombies, Colin Blunstone, has this really sort of sleepy, effortlessly beautiful, dopey, pure voice, but it kind of sounds like he just rolled out of bed and got on the mic.

That's true. And that's exactly how I would describe what you're doing on "Ministry."

Especially in the bridge, some of the vocal inflections in there I had never done before. My voice is really soft, but it's on top of the mix so you really hear it. It was a different place I had never been before. I was stoked because I really love that style.

How are you with hearing your own voice?

I'm okay. I don't sit around and listen to my records all day long. [*Laughs*] If I hated my voice, it'd be a problem because I'm very particular about capturing emotion in a performance, and nailing that vibe that you need, that tone for it. I have to listen to my performances with a very discerning ear. Like, *What little inflection will make it feel this way or that way?* Stuff like that. If I hated my voice, it would be torture having to do that. Luckily, I don't. I'm kind of like a detective/investigator after I sing, but more on an emotional level, trying to find the take that has the best feeling. Again, that doesn't mean the most perfect.

Do you have a favorite vocal performance you're really proud of?

There's a song on the *Where the Wild Things Are Soundtrack,* "Hideaway." It's not like I'm doing anything that special, it's just a really special song to me. I feel like there's something timeless and emotionally resonant about the performance that really stands out to me. I'm not sure why, but that comes to mind.

You also covered "Worried Shoes" by Daniel Johnston on that album, and that's one of my favorite songs of his. Are you a fan of his voice, because it can be pretty divisive?

I'm a huge fan of his voice. There's a purity and a naiveté to it that's just gut wrenching. His songwriting too. A lot of the content of the songs are just like, *Oh my God*. They're just tragic.

But they're so true, and moving, and vulnerable, and melodic!

Yeah, yeah, the vulnerability, and the melody, and the purity and innocence of his voice is something else. The unselfconsciousness of it too. That's the thing. I think it's harder and harder, growing up in a world where you could be four years old and become an instant sensation on the internet, to be kind of naive.

Let's walk down that road a second. I think it's important.

When I was coming up, starting to write music with the band, there's so many gatekeepers to decide whether or not you were worthy for the world to hear. Then, the internet kind of took that away. "No more gatekeepers! It's a free for all for everybody!" Which is awesome 'cause it's like a party. You get to hear all these voices that maybe never would've broken through. But it also steals something innocent from the intention of singing. It goes from singing because you need to, to singing because you might be famous. The shame in that is that it's harder for people to find their own voice. People associate getting famous with being liked. If you do stuff to be liked, then you're going to start following what other people like. It can be as big a difference between you informing what other people like, to being informed to sing what other people like. [*Laughs*]

You laugh, but that's some profound wisdom.
That's a really big challenge for up-and-coming singers.

What's changed the most about your voice since you started?
I have more confidence. I feel less cynical about what I should and shouldn't do. I feel more open, trying styles that maybe I wouldn't have tried before. But, yeah, it all comes down to if it feels right or not. I really don't know what's changed about my voice. It might be the same except just like half a step lower. That's a more accurate response.

If you could duet with one singer—living or dead—who would it be?
I'd like to pair up with Willie Nelson. I think my voice would complement his nicely maybe.[8]

Who are your top five favorite singers of all time?
Sam Cooke, Nina Simone, Patsy Cline, Neil Young, and Billie Holiday.

If you could ask any singer about their voice, who would it be and what would you ask?
I'd ask Axl Rose how he has the stamina to belt in a soprano key for hours in concert, which is like an octave higher than his speaking voice.

---

8   Before this book was released, Karen did end up doing a duet with Willie Nelson on "Under Pressure" by Queen & David Bowie.

T Bone Burnett on
ROY ORBISON

BOB DYLAN BRILLIANTLY DESCRIBES the iconic voice of Roy Orbison in his memoir, *Chronicles*, by saying: "He sounded like he was singing from an Olympian mountaintop and he meant business. He was now singing his compositions in three or four octaves that made you want to drive your car over a cliff....There wasn't anything else on the radio like him."

And there hasn't been since. Orbison will always be one of a kind. His solo career in the '60s would see him land twenty-two singles in the Billboard Top 40 between 1960 and 1966. He won five Grammys and a Lifetime Achievement Award, and he's in practically every music hall of fame there is. But, like most artists of his era, he would be cast aside for years in the wilderness.

Roy, however, found his way back to the radio in the late '80s as a member of the Traveling Wilburys [with Bob Dylan, George Harrison, Tom Petty, and Jeff Lynne] and by collaborating with another music legend: producer, guitarist, and songwriter, T Bone Burnett. Winner of 13 Grammy Awards, an Academy Award, and a man who will, no doubt, one day be in the Rock & Roll Hall of Fame himself, alongside his friend who will be there waiting.

When was the first time you heard Roy sing?

The first thing I ever heard was that Cindy Walker tune "Sweet Dreams Baby." I'm from Fort Worth, Texas, and Orbison lived in Fort Worth when he was a teenager. He absorbed all that music goin' on downtown. There was all kinds of crazy, beautiful cowboy music and blues music happening there. It was a culturally and musically rich area.

When did you guys meet?

I guess it was in the 1980s.

Was re-recording "In Dreams" for the *Blue Velvet* soundtrack the first thing you did together?

I think we did some recording before that too. The thing that was amazing to me was that he never wanted his vocals in the headphones when he was recording because he said he had gotten used to the feelings in his bones. He had worked for twenty to thirty years without monitors, so he had just gotten used to the way the vibrations felt in his jaw, and that's the way he could hit the notes.

Wow.

The other thing that was fascinating was he sang so quietly. If you stood ten feet away, you couldn't hear him. It was just pure, pure tone. Pure, amazing, round, solid, soft, incredibly soft tone. When you got close to it with a microphone and turned it up, it would seem incredibly loud because it was so powerful.

You're blowin' my mind right now, man, because it always amazed me how he hardly opened his mouth yet could blast out so much sound and range and volume. He was almost operatic at times, and his mouth was sewn shut! How was he doing that?

All support and tone. I went to school with Betty Buckley. She was a great jazz singer and did a lot of Broadway work. She was also in *Tender Mercies*, but she's been doing heavy duty vocal lessons for decades now, and she showed me how her teacher was teaching her to hold a note as if were coming out of her mouth in a tube. So, she could just keep pushing the note out, and it would travel slowly, but completely keep its shape. It was all through breath control. She made this sound that was other worldly, like it was coming from another dimension. That's exactly what Orbison was doing.

How did Roy approach recording vocals in the studio? Was he going for whole takes or just trying to get a comp?

He sang live with the band. We would do a few takes, but he wouldn't labor over it. If we were overdubbing, he might take one just to tune up, and then, the second take would be brilliant. He had a genius voice that nobody had really heard before. Because it was a voice that was playing the microphone as a horn.

That's a great way of putting it.

There are people who can use the technology in an interesting way, and that's one of the things about Roy as well, how he sounded when a microphone got close to him. I'll tell you one interesting thing he told me about "In Dreams." He said, "You know, the way I write songs is, I just start with my lowest note, and then I start a melody and I don't repeat any parts, I just keep writing new melodies 'til I get to my highest note." That's how he wrote "In Dreams"; by going through that process of just writing one melody, and then following it with another inversion of the melody, and following that with another inversion until it leads to a new section. By the time you get to the fifth section, he's out in the open, you know?

Yeah, he's in Tuscany, on a balcony. [*Laughter*] In 1989, you work together on *Mystery Girl*, Roy's comeback record, and then, you produce his *A Black & White Night* album, which is one of my favorite live records. That concert film is amazing too—Roy performing with you, Tom Waits, Springsteen, k.d. lang, Jackson Browne, Elvis Costello. And as part of his backing band, you have Elvis Presley's rhythm section. That must have been unreal.

That was an incredibly great, unforgettable night. *Leonard Cohen was in the audience*. All sorts of artists and face cards. There was this air of expectancy. Then, sure enough, the show lifted off and the people in the hall were just in ecstasy. At the end of the night, we had to get out of there because the fire marshal was throwing us out. And just as we got home, there was an earthquake. There was a big round chandelier that must have weighed 800 pounds right over where Orbison was, and it fell.

Oh my God.

If that earthquake had happened two hours earlier, or if we stayed later to do more takes—

That would've hit him cause Roy's not movin'.

[*Laughs*] Yeah, yeah, yeah!

His vocals during that show are even stronger on some of those hits than they are on the original recordings. That falsetto on "Crying" is so beautiful!

He said, back in those days, sometimes you would have to take the best band track, even if it wasn't the best vocal track, because the whole thing felt better. He told me a lot of those vocals were not his best vocals, but the whole record was so good, they used it.

On that album and on *Mystery Girl*, Roy does a cover of "The Comedians" by Elvis Costello. How did that song come to him? It's perfectly suited to his voice.

Elvis had put that song out on [*Goodbye Cruel World* in 1984]. I called Elvis and asked if he had anything, and he said he had written this song for Orbison. I listened and said, "This is a really good song. You should check out Orbison's range and write it between his low note and his high note [*laughs*], which he did! Orbison said, "God, he is so smart. He found my low note and my high note."

Do you have a favorite vocal track of his?

I love "Running Scared." It's hard not to love that song. I love "Sweet Dreams Baby"—God, I could just start and go for a long time. I've spent a lot of my whole life being influenced by Roy Orbison.

When you hear his voice now, what do you remember most?

We used to hang out up in Malibu. One day we were driving down PCH, and he had a beautiful, dark brown, Mercedes convertible—it was a classic. There was a guy sitting at the light, and we pulled up, and the guy looked over at him and said, "Hello, Elvis!" Orbison turned and looked at him, and the guy said, "Oh my God, it's Roy Orbison!" He floored it and blew the light! [*Laughter*] *He was gone!* Probably afraid Orbison was gonna drink his blood or something. [*More laughter*] I loved him. I really loved him.

OZZY OSBOURNE

WE ALL CARRY IMAGES IN OUR HEADS of Ozzy Osbourne as this maniacal, bat-biting, hell-raiser. But the reality is much more compelling.

As pioneers of the heavy metal sound, Ozzy and his mates in Black Sabbath took music somewhere it had never been when they released their debut album in 1970.

Combined with his own solo records, Ozzy's music has sold over 100 million records, and, in 2006, he and Sabbath were inducted into the Rock & Roll Hall of Fame. And it's that insanely underrated voice that led the way. But don't be fooled by the image and the album art; Ozzy is much more spiritual than you would believe, way more disciplined than you could know, and one of the biggest Beatle fanatics you'll ever have the pleasure to meet.

With his melodic, sing-song, British delivery that never fails to make you laugh, Ozzy is impossible not to love. But it takes a ton of hard work to do what he's done his entire career. With a live show that never disappoints, I always love when he screams for the crowd to, "GO CRRRAAAZZZYYY!"

And we always do. 'Cause when the Ozzman Cometh, you've got no choice.

Who first exposed you to singing?

My mother used to sing, and we'd get together with my siblings and have little pretend shows. We were a bit of a singing family. We'd have sessions where we'd mimic Mick Jagger, The Beatles, Chuck Berry. My sisters were great at harmonizing like The Everly Brothers. So, it wasn't exactly new to me when I took it over as a profession.

What made you want to take it over?

I was living in virtual poverty, and I knew I wanted to get out of there. So, when I first heard "She Loves You" by The Beatles, it completely blew my head off, and that was it. My father got me a little 100-watt PA System with a microphone, and because of the fact that I had my own equipment, people wanted me in their bands.

I love how much you dig The Beatles.

I was a Beatle freak. I still am. I don't think there will ever be a band, EVER, to have an impact on the world like they did. Every one was a winner. The only one I'm not crazy about is *Please Please Me*, but after that, everything. *With the Beatles, Rubber Soul, Sgt. Pepper*. I mean, Jack [Osbourne] says to me, "What is it with you and The Beatles?" I said, "Let me explain something to you. Can you imagine going to bed in one world, and you wake up, and it's a bubbly exciting world you're waking in?" That's what it was like for me. I was unhappy, I heard "She Loves You," and it made me feel fucking great! What they fucking did for this planet was unbelievable.

Were you trying to emulate one of the Beatles when you started singing?

I saw Paul McCartney and said, "You know what I love about you guys?" and he said, "What?" I said, "You always had the best fucking melodies," and he smiled. What I got from The Beatles was melody.

Yeah, sometimes it feels like they stole every great melody from the sky and now we're all just left trying to scavenge the rest of 'em.

I've been co-writing songs the best part of my adult life. Sometimes I'll go, "That'll do" but "That'll do" ain't as good as "That's great!" I like it when your hair stands on your arm, that emotion. Then you know it's a winner.

How did you find your own voice?

I don't know, it just kind of happened, really.

Did you ever have any vocal training?

No, but later in my career, I had to learn to warm my voice. I was always getting in trouble 'cause I'd go cold from screaming like a fucking stuck pig onstage. Can you imagine going to an athlete, "You got a game tomorrow," and they go, "Yeah, I'll be fine," and you haven't done a fucking ounce of training?

It really is a recipe for disaster.

There were times in my crazy past where I'd be up there, hungover from the night before, and it was disrespectful to the audience that had worked jobs, pumping gas, delivering shit to people. I got to the point where, how would I feel if I saw The Beatles and they were all fucked up? I would be very pissed off.

So, you do vocal warm-ups before shows?

I work out for forty-five minutes every night before I go on tour. And every night before I go onstage. I have to do that now or my voice will go. I find that if I don't warm-up, if I don't do my ritual, pray for the audience, I'm not doing my job. All I gotta do is an hour and forty-five-minute show. If I can't get around that, there's something very wrong with me doing it.

What's your warm-up look like?

My vocal guy does it. I got his recording, which is like gold dust to me. I listen to the tape in my dressing room with one headphone in my one ear, and the other one free so I can hear myself. [*Does some lips trills*] I do scales, then I repeat *them* [*runs scales, "Mum, mum, mum, mum, mum"*]. I do three cycles before I go on, and the whole cycle's like fifteen minutes. I've been doing the same tape for a lot of years and it works.

Do you have any other rituals before you hit the stage?

It sounds crazy, but get a piece of a crispy apple and chew on it.

Hold on, what is this about?

It's something in the apple. I'll tell you how I know that: my tour manager used to work for Pavarotti, and Pavarotti used to do that before any show. He'd chew a piece of apple. And it works, man.

Pavarotti would eat a little piece of an apple before he went onstage?

It starts your lubrication. You've got to be lubricated. If you got a dry mouth, you're gonna sing like a fuckin' asshole. When you're frightened, you get cotton mouth so, you gotta find a way of getting over it.

You mentioned that you pray before you perform.

I hand it over to God, so you're not walking around with this whole gig in your head. It's too much for ya. I ask God, "Help me to have a good show. If you'd like to, show up and show the audience a good show." Then, you just rock 'n' roll. We're only human. The thing about being a singer is, I'm stuck with what I've got.

How do take care of your voice on the road?

I try not to talk a lot. The day after, you don't wanna talk. At very extreme times, I'll take a steroid, but I don't recommend doing that too much. But there's Entertainer's Secret [the spray], Chinese tea's good as well. I got these German throat sweets. I got all kinds of things in my arsenal. [*Joking*] Also cyanide, which is really good. A lot of it stems from emotion as well. If you've had a fucking row with someone, if something's fucked your day up, it'll come out in your voice. If you've been on the phone to your old lady, fighting on the phone, it fucks your gig up.

Are you nervous or confident before you perform?

The first gig I ever played was a gig at a Birmingham, England fire station. I've never been so frightened in all my life. There was about three people, and you would've thought I was gonna be shot. I was nervous as anything. To be honest, I still sometimes get a bit of stage fright, and the reason why I don't mind it so much is because it shows that I care.

Are there songs where you wonder if your voice will be there that night?

A set is like a journey. There's always a point where I go, I just gotta get over these hurdles and I'm sunny. There's one or two songs like that. I get over the jump, and go, *I'm saved!* But I also work the audience.

In what way?

You might need some time to recuperate. If I've done too much in a previous song, I'll just interact with the audience—"Let me hear you shout!" and that sort of stuff. It's tricks that you learn. Talk to the audience a bit, and say "Hi." When you're rocking and you're going fucking nuts, you don't wanna go [*talks rapidly*] "Right now we're gonna do a song called 'I Don't Want to Change the World'" and go straight in, 'cause that's panic. You're running on panic. I try not to panic onstage.

Are there songs where you've had to adjust the key live?

What you do is tune down a notch. You'll hear the band go, [*grumbles disapprovingly*] "YOU AIN'T GOTTA SING FOR TWO HOURS!" It's a completely different thing to guitar players or drummers. Believe me, if somebody had offered to give me anything when my voice was gone, they wouldn't have had to ask twice, because it can either be heaven or fucking hell.

What was your most embarrassing vocal mishap ever?

I did a gig at the Hammersmith Odeon in England. The FIRST NOTE, my voice goes OUT, and I'm thinking, *Oh, God. Scotty, beam me up, I wanna fucking die!* I just danced around more.

Do you remember a performance where you did something that surprised you?

When I did Monsters of Rock in England years ago, I was on before AC/DC, and, the night before, I got fucking hammered in the hotel. The next morning, I come 'round, and I go, "I'm gonna be singing like a fuckin' asshole today." It was one of the best shows of my career. It was just fucking awesome.

How are you with hearing your own voice?

There's only one person who sounds like Ozzy Osbourne, and it ain't you!

If you could duet with one singer—living or dead—who would it be?

Lennon.

Who are your top five favorite singers of all time.

Robert Plant, Paul McCartney, John Lennon, the guy from Journey. You ever heard him sing? Steve Perry. He's got one of the most amazing fucking voices, man. He does everything fucking brilliant. And who's the last one? ADELE!

If you could ask any singer about their voice, who would it be and what would you ask?

It'd be two: John Lennon and Paul McCartney. And the question would be, "When did you know you had the perfect voice combination?"

I feel like you've got the most iconic laugh in rock 'n' roll history. What made you start laughing on your records?

The last record, the producer said, "I'm not gonna put your laugh on this record." I said, "You're putting it down the toilet." You know what? I didn't put a laugh on there, it didn't do too well. [*JTG cracks up*] So, fuck producers. When you record an album—this is very important—if there's a song on an album that you do not like and you don't fix it, that will haunt you 'til the day you fucking die. I've got tracks on various albums, I get so pissed off, I jump the track.

But how did this laugh become so iconic? How did it come about?

I just laughed. [*Laughs maniacally*]

STEVE PERRY

S OMEWHERE IN THE WORLD RIGHT NOW, someone has stumbled onto the stage of a karaoke bar with a bit too much confidence and is belting out the lyrics to "Don't Stop Believin'" by Journey. And it is not going well. "STREETLIGHT PEOPLE—WHOA-UUU-AHGGRRGHG!" I've sent flowers to the hospital.

From the day Steve Perry joined this bay area band, they were on their way to the Rock & Roll Hall of Fame. Steve came in and took this jazzy, progressive rock outfit with three albums under their belt and turned them into a classic rock hit machine, destined to become the soundtrack of our lives. Having sold over 100 million records, they are one of the bestselling bands of all time. You just can't deny those songs. Or that voice.

Since leaving the band, Steve has become one of the most enigmatic figures in music, resurfacing every so often with a new solo album, and vocals as enviable as ever. I had my first conversation with Steve over two decades ago when we sat next to each other in traffic school. He was humble, self-effacing, and had a great sense of humor. He has something else as well: the right "requirements."

Who first exposed you to singing?

I would have to say my father. He always wanted to be a singer. His family was musical, and he would sing me to sleep as a child. Then, I watched him perform when I was four years old at the Hanford Civic Auditorium in Hanford, California. He and my mother were in a local production of a musical, and I was sittin' in the front row in these fold-up chairs, and I remember my little shoes, which were sandals with white socks on, and they're just swinging, not touching the ground. I'm lookin' up and he's singin', and my mind said, "I can do that!" I knew what he was doing was something I had in me too. From a very early age, I was not very good at expressing my feelings verbally as I was expressing them vocally. So, around the house, I would just sing. My mother said I used to hit a high C that would go through her head! You know how kids can scream "*Ahhh!*" [*Hits a high note*]. That pristine little, squeaky, piccolo voice...man, that thing must've been painful. [*Laughter*] I had a real high falsetto.

Was your mom supportive?

My mother put me in boy's choirs and barber shop quartets. Then, I was introduced to a pair of green, metal flake bongos that I insisted my mother buy me, and that's what started my drum career! [*Laughs*] By the time I was twelve, I was playing a trap set to music I was listening to, whether it was the rock of that era, which was surf music, "I Get Around" by the Beach Boys or whatever. I was in my first band around the age of thirteen, and I was the drummer/singer. I remained a drummer/singer until I got the phone call to go join Journey.

Were you emulating anyone when you started out?

When I first started out, it was R&B almost exclusively. "Ninety-Nine and One-Half (Won't Do)" by Wilson Pickett. Otis Redding and Carla Thomas, "Otis, you're a tramp!" Singing "Knock on Wood" in high school bands. And Sam Cooke, of course, I did a little bit. But it was more important to emulate the emotional approach I liked about these singers. You know, [*sings "Knock on Wood"*] "I don't wanna looo-oooose this good thiiiing, *that I got!*" [*Phrasing the vocal to the beat*] Just that pocket, two-three. "*That I gaaaa—ot.*" Waiting. For the *moment* to come back in with the next phrase. [*Sings*] "If I do" [*hums, waits a beat*] "I would surely" [*beat*] "surely lose a lot." See, the phrasing and the spacing actually sets up what you're about to do by what you don't do. It sets a certain feel in motion that is so important for the voice to have a *swing* to it. A *pocket* to it. The way you're phrasing and swingin' the syllables sets up almost everything you need.

You know who's great at that? Stevie Wonder. He'll even break up a word by syllables!

Ohhh, one of the best!

How did you find your own voice?

It started to evolve when I was drumming and singing in Hanford, in a club called the El Rancho. It was a pretty rowdy, ratty bar, but we worked there a long time, and I learned so much. Like singing when there's only ten people at the bar, the rest of it is empty, and still trying to dig in and hope somebody will listen. Doing covers of "Bridge Over Troubled Water," loving Art Garfunkel, but wanting to take it to a place that's more *mine* helped me reach for a more legato and more soaring kind of voice. He was a great teacher for me to reach for things. As was Streisand, Aretha, Gladys Knight. Those are some amazing voices that became my teachers. Growing up, I had parental guidance to a degree, but my parents split up when I was seven, and there went my voice—my father. After that, when it came to what I was *really needing* to live life, I was taught by my big parent, which was music.

I understand.

Singing songs like "Bridge Over Troubled Water" at the El Rancho gave me a real insight as to some of the things that were possible to do with my voice. *And another thing*, it had red carpet in it. And it was filthy. Everybody spilled their drinks on the carpet. And in would come these women in their mini-skirts, wearing this horrible perfume. "A smell of wine and cheap perfume" came from that club.

Oh, nice!

Swear to God. "For a smile they can share the night." [*Laughter*]

Did you ever have any vocal training?

The only vocal training I had was Mr. Nichols, who was the barber shop quartet leader/music director, when I was about eight, nine years old. When I got to college, Mr. Fritz was the choir teacher there. And there was some guidance. [*Laughs*] He used to look at me and tell me I'm singing kinda loud. [*Laughs harder*] "Tone it down." He wanted me to blend with the group. But I'll tell ya, it's something I miss terribly and would love to do: form a section of four to five voices and sing live with that. There's something really amazing that happens when singers sing together.

Going from playing the drums to becoming the singer is the trippiest feeling. Do you remember the first time you came out from behind the kit and stood up front?

It was at the El Rancho. You had to play "What is Hip?" and "Down to the Nightclub" by Tower of Power. It was getting harder and harder for me to play the Dave Garibaldi drum parts and sing good enough to pull it off. So, I hired a drummer, and that's when I stepped out front. For the first time, I didn't have cymbals in front of me, and I felt naked as can be. I'm out there singin' to sing to someone else's drum pocket, not the one I remember my whole life.

[*Laughs*] IT'S HARD, RIGHT?

A challenge, I would say it's been ever since. I think I sing better to my own pocket than I do to anybody else, with the exception of five drummers: Vinnie Colaiuta, Larrie Londin, Steve Ferrone, Josh Freese, and Steve Smith. Those are pockets I can relax into and not think about drums and be a singer.

Are you nervous or confident before you perform?

I'm never nervous. I hadn't been onstage in twenty-five years, and then, I went to walk onstage with the Eels in Minneapolis, and that was pretty freaky. Emotionally, I had a great time. Vocally, I don't know how good I did, but I had to not worry about that for once. I just said, "You know what? I don't have room for that. I'm gonna go out there and do the best I can with what I've got to give after all these years." It was an indie crowd, and I thought, *It's a totally different generation, and most of 'em may not even know who the hell I am, so I'm just gonna have a good time.* Because I love the band, and that's all that mattered to me. So, when I walked out there, I was pleasantly surprised that they were excited I was there.

Do you do any vocal warm-ups before shows?

I used to do different ones than I would do now. Back in the day, my voice was like steel; it was pretty hard to break, so I didn't have to do a lot of warm-ups. I would use the first two-three songs and pedal through those, and not put my foot down until that warmed me up. But as any singer gets older, that changes. The voice never stays the same.

What would you do to warm-up?

The venues would usually have some sort of shower area, or locker room, because they're usually sport-oriented venues. I would go in there 'cause it made me feel comfortable hearing a little echo, and I would do half-steps. For some reason, I thought it was important not just to do the whole steps starting low, but to do half steps starting low—half steps going all the way up, and half steps going all the way down. Then, I would do all the A vowels—*A-E-I-O-U*—all the way up, all the way down. Then, I would try to do some diphthong vowel versions of the whole thing.

What's diphthong mean?

Like the vowel A is comprised of A and E together. You can't say the vowel A without having an E at the end of it. It won't make the word A. It's Aeeeee. You hear it? E is at the end of A.

Ohhh, interesting! You're right, what a trip!

[*Laughs*] I used to try and have a good E vowel 'cause it's kind of everywhere.

Did you have any other rituals before you'd hit the stage?

I used to do a little bit of a running in place thing to keep some edge off. Just to keep my nervous energy placed somewhere.

Is there anything after the show that helps keep your voice in shape?

I tried to get a good night's sleep. It's probably one of the biggest things you need. If you wake up kinda hoarse and grumbly sounding, take a shower with lots of steam. I got a cold steam humidifier, and I'd walk into my room after the show, and it would look like a fog bank. When you sleep with that much moisture in the room, no matter what city you're in, no matter what temperature change, the room would be consistent. And I'll tell ya, most people think you're a moody, pain in the ass singer, but don't talk. Talking is more destructive to your voice than singing!

So, you wouldn't talk at all on show days?

I wouldn't ever talk on show days. I wouldn't do interviews. I wouldn't talk to anybody. I had to do what I had to do. Rock 'n' roll back then was like an Olympic sport. You *really* had no wiggle room. There were plenty of groups that went out there and [*screams like a banshee*], but if you were doing songs that had requirements, melodies…

[*Bursts into laughter*] "Requirements…"

[*Cracks up*] If you were doing songs that had requirements vocally, range-wise, and with consistency all night, those requirements are demanding. There's not much room for a lot of F-in' around.

When you start getting sick, what do you do?

I would have to look down at Bennie, our production manager, and act like I'm cold, and give him the "cut across the neck" because some of the venues had air conditioners blowing down on the stage. The air conditioners, with the cigarette smoke in the venues in those days, would make my nose start to run down the back of my throat, and I'd wake up with a sore throat. You can't take any drying agents to stop the dripping 'cause it dries your voice.

So, what's the move?

I'd put warm water with salt, pour it in my hand, and snort it up my nose and let it run out, to try my best to disinfect without drying it out. That was the biggest nightmare of all, and it can make any singer absolutely, fearfully neurotic, 'cause you don't know what you're gonna have 'til you open your voice in soundcheck. Then, it's too late to cancel the show because soundcheck ends at 5:00-5:15 and doors are at 6:00! Guess what? You're scared. I don't think nobody understands how fearful and neurotic singing can be.

Were there songs where you wondered if your voice would be there that night?

How 'bout all of 'em? [*Laughs*] Name one right now. Gimme one of your favorites!

"Who's Crying Now."

YES. [*Laughter*] The part that I was concerned about was the bridge, [*sings*] "Only so many tears you can cry…O-O-UUU-OOO-OOO." All that was somethin' I did on the record that I loved, and I had to have it live. I gotta get there!

So, you suffer from the thing of, "Oh shit, I just wrote this, now I gotta deliver it."

[*Sighs*] Yeah. I would say that's correct.

Are there songs where you had to adjust the key live?

The entire For the Love of Strange Medicine Tour, we tuned the band down to E flat.

What was your most embarrassing vocal mishap ever?

The first one that comes to mind was on a Journey tour. I went back to the band after I had my first solo album, *Street Talk*, and I had a hit called "Oh Sherrie." For some reason, I had a mental block on the second verse. I would sing the first verse in the second verse position. I'd look at the audience with my palms up, "What can I tell ya?" [*Laughter*] So, then I started putting paper in front of my monitor with the second verse there so I could glance down and go, "Ohhh, right."

Do you remember a performance where you surprised yourself?

That came after I made the first record with Journey, *Infinity*. It was challenging to come up with the definitive versions of what those songs should be. Then came the second record, and I thought, *Boy, it's gonna be a lot easier*. The surprise was that every time you write something, it's absolutely like doing it from the ground up again, and no growth curve can be applied from the previous one to this one. You can't because it has a total different set of requirements based on what it needs to be, and it has nothing to do with the earlier record!

Is that a songwriting surprise or a vocal surprise?

That's a vocal *and* songwriting surprise!

How are you with hearing your own voice?

Oh, there's self-loathing all over it. [*Laughter*] Just the other day I was listening to a Journey track on the radio, and I said, "Damn, I didn't know that I was doin' that stuff. Wow, that's pretty good." I can appreciate it now. You do have to get away from it, you know?

Do you have a favorite vocal performance you're really proud of?

I'm proud of all of 'em for different reasons. Of course, I love "Don't Stop Believin'," I love "Who's Crying Now," and then you step into a different character of "Faithfully," and then you step into another character of "Separate Ways." I like doing these slight vocal characters that I think fit the intensity, or the lack of intensity of a song. "Walks Like a Lady" is a totally different vocal character. They're all me, but they've got a little different insistence on them.

There's a ton of songs that get overlooked in your catalog because you've had so many hits, but I wanna talk about "Somethin' to Hide" off *Infinity*. Toward the end of the song, you start singing along to the guitar melody, and you end up going so high, it's not humanly possible. Those must be the highest notes of your career. Do you remember anything about recording the vocals for that?

Those are the same high notes that are in the end of "Mother, Father" too; that's the same falsetto kind of thing. I do remember that, and that is one of those things that, musically, the song was asking to be. I reached for it and went and got it.

What's so commendable about you being able to hit those notes is the restraint. Because you could've littered all those songs with those kinda notes, showing off. But what's great is that you had it, but you only pulled it out when it felt right. You gotta respect that.

I would've fucked myself over! That was the only one that really called for that, in my opinion. I find it amazingly fascinating that you asked about that song. I always loved that song. I thought that song was a hit. I particularly love the bridge, all the voices I layered in there. [*Hums the background melodies, then sings the lead*] "There's somethin' inside you that I know that you're not tellin' me..." That bridge was my favorite. "You've got somethin' to hide" was a great melody, but I also knew it was gonna be comprised of 50 percent falsetto and 50 percent regular voice.

Were you hitting that scream in falsetto at the end?

That's a hard falsetto. I did some on my solo record, *Traces*, at the end of "Sun Shines Gray" and "We're Still Here."

"Wheel in the Sky" has some buried in the solo that almost feel like another instrument.

It was a high falsetto in the background. Like some girl singing high, angelic notes by herself, in echo, while [*guitarist*] Neal Schon is playing this beautiful solo. I just thought it was complimentary and sorta needed to be there. I didn't wanna step on his solo, but I didn't think that it did 'cause it was in the back, just floating like another instrument.

Over the years, you've been so vocal about your love of Sam Cooke's voice, and obviously, his melodic influence can be heard on everything from "Lovin', Touchin', Squeezin'" to "Missing You." What do you think made Sam Cooke's voice resonate so strongly for you?

When I heard Sam Cooke, there was something emotional that came into me and spoke to me in a way that I wanted to know why that makes me feel so good. I wanted to know, *Could I feel that by trying to sing like that?* That began my absolute infatuation with the velvet smoothness and throat positions of Sam Cooke.

Explain throat positions.

Singing is about finding throat positions for these vowels. Like there's an "Ahhh" vowel that goes, [*sings "Ahhh" at the front of his mouth*]. Okay, that's just an open "Ahhh." Then, there's [*sings "Ahhh" from the back of his throat*] more in the back and honking [*alternating between the two tonalities of the sound*]. You hear the difference? One's in the back with a bit of a "Honk" sound in it. The other one's just comin' out your mouth like you're talkin'. If you listen to Sam Cooke, he would go back in his throat with a certain vowel, and once he was back there, he'd stay there. He would put his vowels in the pocket of the back of his throat. I was fascinated by that.

That is wild.

Let me just tell you one more thing that nobody knows: At the age of seven-eight years old, I was fascinated with ventriloquism. I loved all these ventriloquists on television. So, I got a Jerry Mahoney doll for Christmas and started practicing talking in the back of my throat and not moving my lips or my teeth. Having to do those vowel sounds in the back of my throat, practicing ventriloquism, began something when I started hearing singers like Sam Cooke. If you watch him, and most great singers, they very seldom open their mouths very big when they're singing big.

You know who's the king of that? Roy Orbison.

Yeah, listen to his tone. His tone has an Italian term I think it's called Squillo. A steely ring to the voice. He has such a *riiiiiing* when he sings. He's doing everything in the back of his throat. When I was in Journey, I started really working that spot, for the high notes to go back. When they'd go back, they'd drop down my throat, and, all of a sudden, there was *another voice* that came out that didn't seem to have any range limits on it. Then, when I started to overwork my voice, I fell out of the pocket and started to get more laryngeal with it, more insistent. And you don't wanna do that.

At the end of "Young Hearts Forever," you sing a piece of "Old Flame" by Thin Lizzy, and Lincoln Brewster plays a piece of "The Boys are Back in Town" on guitar. Phil Lynott is one of the most underrated singers in rock 'n' roll. He was one of those guys that made me feel like I could do this. I knew I could never sing like Steve Perry, but Phil's voice had something that felt like, he's just kicking back, talking to some friends. It really wasn't about his range. It was about his delivery and his confidence, and he had some of the coolest phrasing ever.

Talk about a unique singer that had a unique sound, with unique phrasings, and unique choices of vowels and words. I loved him. He's such a character! I would say that he was one of the first talk-singers. I think that some singers tell stories; like Bruce, they're vocal poets. [*Does a solid Springsteen impression*] "I was walkin' down the street with my hands in my pockets, and the streetlights were burnin.'" You know, they're talkin' and singin', and I think the first time I heard anybody do that was Phil, and that was a long time ago!

There's a song called "Here I Go Again" by him that was an outtake on a box set...

Was it [*sings the chorus melody*] "Here I go again...?"

Yeah! The first verse, he goes, [*sings with Phil Lynott's phrasing*] "So we packed our bags and headed for the north sea. There was Eric, Brian, Freaky Pete, Charlie, Frankie Lee, and me..." It's like, are you fuckin' kidding?

See what I mean? He *sings* amazing poetry. It's just a new place he came up with. What a shame when he passed so young. We played a lot of shows together.

Did you learn anything about singing from him?

A lot of phrasing from him, you betcha.

So, you take twenty-four years before releasing any new music and come back with this brilliant solo album, *Traces*, and your voice is still as melodic and as strong as ever. I'm in love with "You Belong to Me." That's a soul singer doin' it for real. There's a raspiness to your voice that's so perfect. Is there a secret to getting a good rasp before you record?

The secret to that song is that's the demo vocal. Barry Eastmond and I wrote that, and I was sittin' there with my legs underneath the coffee table, with my M49 hangin' down in front of my face, with a little preamp and compressor API box into my laptop. We're sketchin' the song, comin' up with ideas, and I'm singin' the lines as I'm droppin' 'em in, and that became what that is. I didn't wanna go back and re-create that moment because it was showing up with an honesty and a "rasp," as you call it. I could've sung a little cleaner, but there was an honestly that I thought was important, vocally.

After being away so long, how much time did it take to feel good again as a singer?

It's always a problem. You stop singing for two weeks, and it goes down. You stop singing for years, it goes down too. [*Laughs*] It takes a while. I think the older you get, the more preparation the voice requires. If you're tired, sad, happy, angry, lonely, depressed, heartbroken, if you didn't sleep well, some of these emotions can help the singer sing, but some will completely get in the way because the instrument is you!

What's changed the most about your voice since you started?

I've taken some of the condemnation off my shoulders. There's hardly any singers who like their own voice. If you watch the Linda Ronstadt documentary, she still says, "There's much better singers than I am," and I'm goin', "Girl, you gotta be crazy, okay? You gotta be outta your goddamn mind!" Talk about versatile. I'm listenin' to her sing every kind of music that NO singer can do! And she's pulling it off—not only beautifully, but with *absolute* perfection of intention and heart and soul. She probably has some loathing that it's not good enough, and I think that is just part of the vocalist's curse, the self-condemnation thing. If anything's changed, I'm *really* workin' on gettin' that off of my back.

If you could duet with one singer—living or dead—who would it be?

Sam Cooke. And he would make me sound so bad. [*Laughter*] He would kick my ass! *Sooo bad*!

I don't know, man. Don't sell yourself short!

That would be a scary night, I'll tell you that. I had an opportunity in Journey. My attorney calls me and says, "You know, I represent Barbra Streisand, and she's gonna be doin' a Broadway record, and she wants you to sing one with her." I said, "Excuse me?" You don't know how much I listened to Barbra Streisand while I was touring. I said, "I can't do it, I'm too much of a fan. I can't do it." Years go by and I'm in the studio at the Record Plant in Los Angeles, and [producer] David Foster sees me in the hallway and says, "I'm here with Babs. You ever met her?" I said, "No. I have a little bit of a story, so I don't know." He goes, "Oh, she's wonderful, she'd love to meet you." So, I walk down there, and said, "It's such a pleasure to meet you. You have no idea how much you've inspired me." She said, "Wait a minute. Weren't we supposed to sing together?" I said, "*Ummm... well...?*" She said, "Why didn't you do it?" I said, "I was scared to death; I'm too much of a fan." "Oh, don't be ridiculous!" she said, "It would've been great!" "I'm just too much of a fan, I'm sorry." [*Laughs*] That's what I told her!

Who are your top five favorite singers of all time?

It's impossible to name five! It's an unrealistic request from you. [*Laughs*] Of course, Sam Cooke, Marvin Gaye, Natalie Cole, Nat Cole, Joni Mitchell, Smokey Robinson, Barbra Streisand, Aretha Franklin, *Jackie Wilson...oh my God!* Jackie Wilson was a beast! Major Lance. Oh, I loved Major Lance in high school. He did "Monkey Time." [*Sings the vocal and the horn part*] "Do the monkey time! Ba-bada-booom-bop-bada..."

Oh yeah, that's a good tune!

Then, he did the "Um Um" song. He was so great; I just loved his pocket. Joe Tex. One of the best underrated singers. Otis Redding, of course. Brian Wilson influenced me in so many ways. In fact, the bridge on "No Erasin'" is me tipping my hat to Brian Wilson. Growing up, I loved Andy Williams. Talk about a tone *in the back of his throat*. Listen to those live performances. When he goes back, his voice will ring like a bell up there! Tony Bennett, of course. I love Jimmy Durante for his phrasing. If you listen to Jimmy Durante, he's kinda got a little Phil Lynott in him. [*Sings like Jimmy Durante*] "Smile though your heart is aching. Smile. What's the use in..." He's just poetic with his phrasing. He's not an amazing singer, but emotionally, he kills me with his songs. Sarah Vaughan, Bonnie Raitt, and did I mention Trevor Hall? Don't forget new voices like Ray LaMontagne, Remy Shand, James Morrison, and of course, Ariana Grande, and Olivia Rodrigo. There's too many.

If you could ask any singer about their voice, who would it be and what would you ask?

I always wanted to work with [Motown songwriting team] Holland-Dozier-Holland. I never had the pleasure, but I got to work with Lamont Dozier. We wrote this song that's on one of my solo records called "Love's Like a River." I was agonizing, and I thought he could help me with a phrase and a lyric that we had written. I thought, *This one phrase doesn't seem to transition from the one before it, and it doesn't set up the one that's coming. Should we re-write? Is it the melody? What is it?* And Lamont, sitting behind me on the couch, said, "Oh, don't worry about it." I said, "What do you mean?" He said, "All we're trying to do is sell a feeling." I went, *Man*. The challenge from then on was, I only need to sell a feeling. I really loved him. All the singers, what would I ask them? I'd rather tell them I love them than ask them anything.

Well, guess what, man? I love you!

Awww, thanks, bro. You know, if you were to ask me, "What would you say to any up-and-coming singers?" I'd say start listening to more than you're listening to because I can tell by the way you're singin' that you're not listening to a broad range of voices. Listen to some Dinah Washington, Patti Page, Pat Benatar, Steve Marriott, and never leave out Tony Bennett. I prefer the Joni Mitchell of recent years to the earlier one because her voice is *unbelievable* now. I think her recent records kill her earlier stuff. There's a tone and a grain in her voice that wasn't there years ago....You know what brings on that maturity? Living a long time, and life having its way with you. It can bring out a different interpretation of your own voice. Because there's more behind it than there used to be. We've all lost more, we've all experienced more, we've all been through more. And the voice is you. The instrument is you. So, if that's where you're at, and that's what you've been through, then that's gonna show in there.

Jimmy Iovine on
TOM PETTY

MUSIC REALLY IS MYSTERIOUS. I mean, I've never met Tom Petty. But I've probably spent more time with him than most of the friends I have. These voices we love, these songs that move us, why do we choose them? Or do they choose us?

I only know that from the moment I stole the debut album by Tom Petty and the Heartbreakers from my sister's bedroom, I was a changed man. At five years old. Since then, that dirty blonde dude in his black jacket and a billow of smoke behind him, taught me the lessons throughout my life that still hold true.

"Even the losers get lucky sometimes," "Even walls fall down," and "Most things I worry about never happen anyway."

Tom and the Heartbreakers were inducted into the Rock & Roll Hall of Fame in 2002. He won Grammys with the band, as a solo artist, and as part of the Traveling Wilburys, a little supergroup featuring Roy Orbison, George Harrison, Bob Dylan, and Jeff Lynne. That's a team you ain't playin' for unless you're hittin' at the highest level. And that's exactly what Tom did 'til the day he passed away.

Jimmy Iovine is one of the great record executives of our time, co-founder of Interscope Records, and along with Dr. Dre, founder of Beats Electronics. He has been honored by the Grammys, inducted into the Rock & Roll Hall of Fame, and has produced everyone from John Lennon to Bruce Springsteen, Stevie Nicks, U2, Pretenders, and Patti Smith. He also made three records with Tom Petty and the Heartbreakers. And today, he made me cry.

When was the first time you heard Tom sing?

It was like everybody else in the early '70s. I may have heard "Breakdown," and a little bit of the follow-up album [*You're Gonna Get It!*], and then I really started paying attention. I just thought he sounded great with those songs. That's how I listen to music. I listen to how it all fits together; and if it's workin', it works.

You started out with Tom by producing *Damn the Torpedoes*, which was the critical third record for the band.

At that time, I did three third albums. I did *Born to Run*, I did *Easter* by Patti Smith, and that led into *Damn the Torpedoes*. That was in four years.

How did you approach recording his vocals?

I always did live vocals. I don't like recording takes without the guy singing, whether we kept the vocal or not. I did three albums with John [Lennon], two albums with Bruce [Springsteen], and one with Patti, and they all sang live. Everybody records live with the band. That's the only way I knew how to record.

Did you ever have to comp with Tom, or was it all live?

Yeah, we did all that, but I wasn't one of those producers that was like, "Let's record the drums, and then, the bass." I was like, "Let's record like we're a band!" Lennon taught me that because we had eight guys in the studio when we were recording John. I said, "Okay, this is how you do it."

Was Tom tough on himself recording vocals?

He was tough on himself about everything: lyrics, vocals, guitar parts, *their* guitar parts, *your* guitar parts, the drum sound. We bonded on that album. We were like one person, two sides of the same coin. We just weren't gonna let go.

On the *Classic Albums* documentary about the making of *Damn the Torpedoes*, you talk about how Tom is taken for granted as a songwriter, and you're so right. But he's also totally taken for granted, overlooked, and underrated as a vocalist.

I always felt Tom was never fully appreciated.

He was almost like a one-man Beatles. His catalog is that consistent and that great.

It's as good as any of the greats. He's tremendous.

"Here Comes My Girl" is one of the most original vocal tracks ever. First off, he's talking through the verses, real honest and confessional, then he ratchets up the strain in his voice when he gets to the pre-chorus, almost as if he's annoyed that you would question his decisions. And then, the chorus hits and that release is just filled with so much melody and romance. I mean, when people talk about having character in your voice, look no further.

To make that interesting on his part, he had to do a lot of work in creating the character. I think he was trying to come up with a singing verse, and he didn't, and he just decided to do that.

Hard Promises **has "Insider" on it, which is another beautiful duet between Tom and Stevie Nicks. You also recorded "Stop Draggin' My Heart Around" with them during this time as well. From your perspective, what made those two voices sound so perfect together?**

Stevie's the most natural singer I've ever worked with, and the greatest harmony singer in the world, even though she's a great lead singer. She loved Tom's voice, so she knew how to wrap her voice around Tom. Part of him was a country singer, so you put those two voices together, there was no way that wasn't gonna work. Not a chance.

Was it just instant out in the room, or did they have to work at it?

They don't even think about it, they just do it like they're wakin' up. It just happens in one take, two takes. [*Chuckles*] In those days, left to her own, she would always sing the harmony, even when it was her record!

Tom was great at harmonizing with himself too. You listen to "Straight Into Darkness" on ***Long After Dark*, and he's singing so much higher than people give him credit for. He's deceptively high!**

He was deceptively talented! I love that song. The Tom Petty songs that I play the most are "Rebels," "Even the Losers," and "Straight Into Darkness." By the way, if Stevie Nicks had sung "Straight Into Darkness" with him, that would have been a hit record.

No Shit! **I've thought about that so many times! It's the missed duet between them, isn't it?**

Yeah! Whatever they sing together, if it's close to a record like that, it's gonna go. I swear, I played "A Thing About You" today, and if Stevie sang that song with him, that's as big as song as "Stop Draggin'." In those days, you put a woman singing those aggressive, male lyrics, it just worked.

Do you know if Tom was nervous or confident before he would perform live?

He was focused.. I'd call Tom strong. Not confident, just strong. He was strong of character and strong of will.

You obviously had the honor of working with John Lennon, and I always felt that Tom and John shared a common bond with their voices, but could never place what it is. I'm sure you would know more than most, but am I nuts?

Without insulting either one of them, they're on the thinner side. Like John, we always doubled his voice. He didn't like the way it sounded singled. Those vocals are all doubled.

And Tom really chose the moments to double, huh?

Yeah, he didn't need to. *John didn't need to!* He just chose to. [*Laughs*]

When you hear Tom's voice now, what do you remember most?

I hear my friend. When I hear "Refugee," I still just get upset. I think I play it on purpose. There's nothing I hear about Tom that doesn't make me miss him, so there's no other emotion in it. I'm proud of the records we made together. I used to say to him, "Hey Tom, I just heard 'Refugee' on the radio. It sounds better on the radio." And he would say, "Why's it sound better on the radio?" I'd say, "'Cause it's on the radio!" [*JTG laughs*] That was our standard joke. And when he passed, that's what I said to him.

Ohhh man. You went to see him?

Yeah. But he was already gone. But I said, "Tom, I just heard 'Refugee.' It sounded great on the radio. You know why? 'Cause it's on the radio."

And with that, we hang up the phone, and tears fall down my cheeks.
God bless you, Jimmy.
And God bless Tom Petty.

DOUG PINNICK

I WANNA DEDICATE THIS INTERVIEW TO ALL THOSE IN THE STRUGGLE. Be it with your voice, your confidence, your faith, fears, family, band, church, or friends. There's a lot of heavy, confessional truth you're about to read from the singer of one of the greatest rock bands ever!

For over forty years, King's X have consistently put out new music without ever breaking up or changing a member, placing them in a rare musical category that basically includes only three other bands: U2, Rush, and ZZ Top. When their debut album, *Out of the Silent Planet*, was released in 1988, nobody had ever heard a sound quite like King's X. Their mixture of hard rock and Beatles-esque harmonies made them instant heroes to anyone who was paying attention. Pearl Jam, Alice in Chains, and Soundgarden were some of the groups who were. And while Doug Pinnick was absolutely killing it on bass, it was his powerful and passionate voice that gave the band an anchor rooted in soul.

Now, at seventy-one years old, he's still bringing that same soul to the stage every time they perform. His bandmates, Ty Tabor and Jerry Gaskill, sing lead sometimes as well, but it's always been the combination of their voices that's lifted King's X high above their contemporaries. A place they remain to this day.

Who first exposed you to signing?

My mother said I was singing before I could talk. She told me she played records around the house, and I would dance and get so excited that when she would stop the record player, I would start crying and yelling, "Gimme yay! Gimme yay!" She didn't know what I was sayin', and I'm thinkin', she was playin' blues, so I probably heard a song that was, "Yeah, yeah, yeah," and that's what I kept trying to tell her.

Was your mom a big influence on you?

She was actually kicked out when I was three, and they took me from her. My great grand-mother didn't allow any other music in the house but Christian music, which sounded like a funeral. So, after my mom's gone, there's no music around. But every now and then, a couple relatives would pop in with a Mahalia Jackson record or a Staples Singers record, and I would just sit mesmerized at Mahalia Jackson singin', "I'm gonna move on up a little higher." That's probably the first song I remember tryin' to learn.

What was it about that song?

I was enthralled by the melody and how she sang it. Mavis Staples was the same. When they played a Staples Singers song, and Mavis would go into her scatting and do all those riffs around the family, I was just mesmerized. But those were the only two people I heard, so that is my heart when it comes to what I've always tried to accomplish singin'.

That's fascinating 'cause there's a lotta church in your voice for a rock singer.

The church that I went to as a child, I had to sit with my grandmother up front. I hated that because the preacher would just yell fire and brimstone. If you're dancin', if you smoke, if you drink, if you listen to rock music, if you do anything, you're goin' to hell. Period. I mean, *every-thing*, it didn't matter. But when I would go to a relative's house, somebody would always have come down from Chicago with the latest Muddy Waters song, or the latest song from the Chicago blues thing that was happenin' at the time, and I would just listen and listen. Then, when I got home, I tried to remember the songs. Many times, I would take a piece of cardboard, and use a plate, and cut a circle around it. Then, I would take a glass and draw another circle and draw the label I remembered, and the name of the song on it. Then, I would sit it on a little square thing, and I would find these different sticks that looked like nee-dle arms, and I would just rig up my own record player. I would sit there and move the needle across, and try to sing the song. [*Gets choked up*] I'm havin' a hard time with this right now 'cause I really forgot. I just saw that as I told you, and that's pretty sad.

It's kinda beautiful though, too.

All I had was music. I was obsessed with it, and there was nothing else in my life *but* music because my mom was gone. My great grandmother, she just didn't understand how to nur-ture. I think she loved me, but you would never know it.

You did a great job discussing that experience within the live version of "Over My Head" off *Best of King's X*. I love it so much I can't even listen to the studio version now.

Wow. Thank you. I can't listen to it because it's so personal. People tell me how powerful it was, but I felt like I slit my wrist in front of everybody and said, "Oh, look at poor me." That's not what I wanted.

No, you took what was already a rock/gospel number and made it real. It needed the audience, that call and response.

I'm gonna have to watch it after we get done talkin' 'cause I haven't since '94. I remember my grandmother sayin', "Pride comes before a fall." It's a self-realization, that to this day, I don't accept or understand anyone's admiration, or any reason why they would like my voice or care about it.

Well, we got a long way to go in this interview, homie. You're not gonna make it. [*Laughter*]

I've just been taught through self-shame and ignorance that I'm a piece of shit, and I'm not any good and nobody cares anyway. Then, to go ahead and prove it, King's X never had a hit.

Alright, hold on. The narrative on King's X has always been, you guys are one of the greatest bands ever who never got their fair shake commercially. But the real story and the real victory is that regardless of all that, you never broke up, you never gave up, and you're still killing it. How many bands can say they've been together for over forty years, with the same guys the whole time? You're talkin' about King's X, U2, and Rush. Who else?

And ZZ Top. That's it.

***AND* you never achieved their level financially, and you *still* stayed together, meaning it's much tougher on you. So, I don't even wanna hear that shit.**

[*Laughs*] One good thing I notice is that we've been around so long with the internet, there's new generations of kids. It's kind of nice when I run into some twenty-somethings and they can pull out Led Zeppelin, Hendrix, and King's X, and sit there and listen to all three equally. It's refreshing to see that is the reality of it when I start to beat myself up.

Did you ever have any vocal training?

I was in the school choir for all eight years of grade school and high school. And when I went to college, I was in the Madrigal. That's supposedly the best vocal singers of the college. It was like twelve of us, and you got chosen. It was pretty cool. The teachers taught me so much about music. They'd play the piano, and make me sing things, and put me in contests, and I always won—never lost one. Got an A+ every time, singin' "Blue Moon," showtunes, and Frank Sinatra. I was always in front of somebody singin'.

Were you emulating anyone when you started out?

When I got to high school, I moved in with my mother in another town, and she let me play the radio all day long. And what's on is WVON in Chicago! That was one of the biggest soul stations in the United States. All I heard was Motown and Stax music all day until they turned off at night. At 6:00 in the morning, I woke up, turned the radio on, and sang along with everybody. I learned how to sing singin' those songs. Smokey Robinson, Temptations, Aretha Franklin. "Respect" and "Dr. Feelgood." I would try to copy her, try to sing every inflection. And I sang in the house as loud as I could 'cause nobody said I couldn't. People used to tell me to shut up sometimes 'cause I got on their nerves after a while. [*Laughter*]

How did you find your own voice?

I don't know if I ever did; that's the problem. There's a lot of things I've done vocally that I wouldn't have done if I knew how to use my voice correctly. I punish my voice. I notice when they get older, who keeps his voice and who doesn't. Then I look back at what they did when they sang. Mick Jagger always sounds like Mick Jagger. *Why does his voice sound just as young as it did when he started?* Because he sings in his speaking voice. I didn't learn that you should sing in your speaking voice 'til I was in my sixties. Jimi Hendrix is my vocal range. His voice is where I should've been singin' everything. Listen to Aretha Franklin and how many key changes she changed to fit her voice because she can't do it either. Or Mariah Carey.

Are you nervous or confident before you perform?

I seldom remember getting nervous until King's X got a record deal. All of sudden, there's pictures, and there's magazines, and there's articles, and all this attention you're getting that you don't know what to do with. And you're aware of how people perceive you now. They're describing you and saying how amazing it is. Then other people come along and go "Uhhh, I like so and so better." You're readin' all this stuff and the fun ends, basically. After that, you second guess everything you do. But I had an epiphany a year and a half ago about my voice, so...we'll get to that.

Okay, when you're ready.

I remember one night in the early '90s, I was at the hotel, just nervous, talkin' to my friend, really havin' a hard time, and I go, "What do you do?" He goes, "Dude, that's just the adrenaline." He said his mama used to say that the reason you feel antsy and nervous is because all that adrenaline is buildin' up inside you because you're gettin' ready to go out there and bare your soul to the world. She said, "You're not nervous, you're just windin' up. You're like a racehorse at the front line ready to go. So, don't fight it, embrace it." That's what I did. I still had it, but I embraced it and just dealt with it.

Do you do vocal warm-ups before shows?

I can't do that stuff. I got ADD. As soon as I take one riff, my brain is gone and I'm thinkin' about somethin' else or lookin' at a text message. I'll just pull out my guitar, put my headphones on, and go through about five King's X songs in a room by myself. When we go onstage, my voice is warmed-up. That's the only way I can do it now. I'm not gonna go into a room and do exercises. I just hate it.

Do you have any rituals before you hit the stage?
Nowadays, I do about two or three shots of tequila or Jack and honey. I hardly ever drink at home, but when we play, I always take a shot because it'll put me in a better mood. One time, I decided to play without havin' a drink, and I was just too aware of everything. Everything mattered. Every tone, every sound, every note, every clap. After like four songs, I said, "I ain't had a drink since I got onstage and I need one." Somebody brought me a drink, and within about two minutes, I was okay. I loosened up, I could be me, and the things that bothered me didn't anymore. I'm such a sensitive person that it drives me fuckin' crazy sometimes.

If you really think about it, whenever somebody has an issue in life, good or bad, they just do what they do and handle their business. *Singers* are so sensitive that they have to fuckin' break out into song! I mean, you're *singing* how you feel, that's how sensitive singers are! Only a lunatic breaks out into song! [*Laughter*]
That's true! All of a sudden you're singin' [*like a Broadway singer*] "AAAALLL OF THE WOOORLD!"

[*Sings dramatically*] "*This happened to meeeeee!*"
[*Cracks up*] I never looked at it that way. That's awesome. That's exactly how we are. Oh my God.

Is there anything after the show that helps keep your voice in shape?
I've been told I need to shut the fuck up, and, instead, we have meet and greets for an hour. After that, I hang out with my friends and we yack, and I'm yellin' and screamin' and drinkin' at the after party. I go to bed hoarse and wake up the next day and don't say anything all day until it's time to go on.

How do you take care of your voice on the road then?
That's it. Literally. It's pretty bad.

When you start getting sick, what do you do?
Oh, I don't get sick. I ain't been sick in twenty years. I've had a couple colds, but I just keep goin'. I blow my nose and go! [*Laughter*]

Are there songs where you wonder if your voice will be there that night?
I wonder if my voice will be there for any of them every night, and I always have to prepare myself to do alternate things in case it ain't workin'.

Do you adjust the keys live?

Never have. That's probably what the problem is. There's a point in your voice where you belt it, and there's a point in your voice where you can croon. I never explored those two positions to correctly utilize them. I just did everything in E and A, and nobody came around and said, "Man, it'd be easier for you if you sang that note a half step lower," or "You need to do this in E instead of F."

What was your most embarrassing vocal mishap ever?

[*Chuckles*] The thing is, all of 'em are bad to me. But when I go down the list of all the things that I think were bad, *noo!* Because the magic always happened regardless of whether I knew it or not. Most of the time, I didn't. I could walk off and go, "That was horrible!" and people are crying. I've seen people crying when I sing as long as I have lived. I really don't understand it, and I probably never will, but that's the truth. I'm kind of oblivious to a lot of things. I don't know why.

You've definitely given some clues. [*Laughter*] Do you remember a performance where you surprised yourself?

One time. Jason Touchette, the lead singer of Podunk, who can sing his ass off, and long ago on a tour, he would always come onstage and do "Over My Head" with us. At the end, where I do my vocal scats, we would go back and forth like two guitar players, vocally. But one night, he went out there and started whippin' me, and I'm keepin' up with him, but I'm goin', *woooo!* On the final note, he did one that brought the fuckin' house down. Honest to God. I stood there thinkin', [*whispers*] *Fuck. Fuck.* And as soon as he was done, I opened my mouth up, and *Walked. All. Over. It.* And the whole place went up! And he looked at me, and put his head down, and I don't know what happened, but it was like the adrenaline came and it opened up.

How are you with hearing your own voice?

I hate my voice. Sometimes I like it, but I hate it more than I like it. There's a song called "This Time Around" on the Carmine Appice *Guitar Zeus* album, and that is what I was trying to accomplish when I would listen to "Maybe Your Baby" by Stevie Wonder or Aretha's "Dr. Feelgood." Every lick in those songs is exactly the right fuckin' thing, with emphasis on the right words, like 101 on how to sing a verse and a chorus.

Do you have a favorite vocal performance you're really proud of?

That's the one. And "Yeah X 3" off the 24-7 Spyz album. I sang the second verse and chorus, and went, "Now that's what I've been waitin' to hear." [*Cracks up*]

So, two songs that aren't your own originals?

Oh yeah!

There's something going on here that we're gonna get to the bottom of.
I remember when we were gettin' ready to do the fourth album, I wrote "The Big Picture," but I hadn't put vocals on it yet. It was 7:00 at night, and I rolled a joint and went for a walk because I always hear music in a different, spiritual way as I'm walkin' in the woods. When I came back, I went, *I'm gonna try a vocal on here.* And my voice wouldn't open up at all. It was just like, *Douglas, what are you doin'? You just smoked weed, it's late at night, and you're tired.* Then, I thought, *Well, why don't I distort it?* So, I took a SM57 and plugged into a Pignose, sang into it, and went, *That's cool.*

That is cool. I didn't know you were singing that through a Pignose.
I sang that whole thing in one take and left it. When I went into the studio, I couldn't re-do it. So, we took it off of my 6-track and flew it onto the record.

You're pretty much the lead singer of the band, but we'd be doing King's X a huge disservice if we didn't talk about the other two voices that make up the sound. Ty and Jerry sing lead on different tracks as well. Especially Ty. But it's that vocal blend, creating all those incredible melodies and harmonies, that really takes your music to another level. Can you talk about what each guy brings to the party?
Ty is usually 99 percent dead on pitch all the time, so he's the relevant pitch when everybody sings. And he's tuned into his guitar. I'm kind of a loose singer, so I'm kind of *around it.* Jerry is kind of like a cross between me and Ty. If me and Jerry are singin', our voices automatically lock together. But when Ty comes in, he doesn't lock. He's dead on himself. And so, this friction-like harmony happens. The sound that we have is very happy, almost pretty. It was always somethin' that I didn't like, though it's one of our strengths, so I never say no. But whenever I'd make up these dark melodies, as soon as the guys would sing, it was butterflies. [*Laughter*] So, you just have to leave it at that. It's a part of who we are, and I embrace that.

How do you and Ty decide who takes the lead?
Ty doesn't like to sing. But one day he did tell me it's real hard singin' next to me. This is the only time he's ever said it, but he said, "I gotta sing next to the greatest singer in the world." But when "It's Love" came out, he was the singer of that song. I was supposed to sing the chorus, and I wasn't singin' it the way that he wanted. I was tryin' to sing it like Doug would sing it, and it wasn't workin' for him. So, I just said, "Fuck it, you sing it!" and I walked out the door, mad. And he sang it, and it was our biggest selling hit. And that broke me down real hard. I thought, *That's why we never had a hit. I'm the one that's holdin' the band back.* That kinda never left me. Even though I won't entertain it, it still nags me.

All the vocals from this band are an artistic achievement. On your first album, *Out of the Silent Planet*, you guys pretty much made it clear that you were gonna have some of the most incredible backing vocals ever. [*Doug laughs*] And that's carried on through your entire career. Tell me how that choice came about.

Back in the day, there was always harmonies and stuff goin' on. But when [ex-manager and producer] Sam Taylor came into the camp, he pretty much forced us all to sing. Ty and Jerry love The Beatles, and as soon as we opened up our mouths, it was The Beatles. We didn't even try, it was like, *Oh fuck*.

What do you think some of the best King's X backing vocals are?
"It's Love." "Lost in Germany." "Black Flag." "Chariot Song."

"Chariot Song" has gotta be number one, right?
I guess so. Ty wrote all the songs I mentioned. I think the way he makes up melodies and vocals are like a music teacher goin' to class. They're just incredible pieces of music: the way they're executed, how they're mathematically constructed. My harmonies are more gospel.

Let's talk about the background vocals on "We Were Born to Be Loved."
I came up with all those. For me, that was The Andrew Sisters. [*Sings*] "He was the boogie woogie bugle boy of Company B," you know that song? They were three sisters who used to do three-part harmonies that were identical to each other. It wasn't even real. They could tongue twist songs [*sings a quick, summersaulting vocal melody*], all exactly alike but in harmonies. I thought about that when I was doin' "Born to Be Loved," [*sings*] "I can shout from a rooftop how I really feel!" That's totally Andrew Sisters.

That has to be one of the funkiest, most insane endings for a song that I've ever heard in my life. I've seen you do it live and it's like, *How are you pulling this off?*
[*Laughs*] It's all counting, and if you're not lookin' at somebody, you gotta be *real steady*. We are trusting each other, because all we know is everybody's groove has to be the same. And Ty and Jerry have impeccable timing. Jerry's insane with timing, but Ty is even beyond that, and can tell when Jerry's speedin' up or slowin' down. And Jerry says Ty is speedin' up or slowin' down too, so there's always an argument there.

***Welcome to bands!* [*Laughter*]**
Yeah! I love playin' with those guys. It's like the three of us playin' basketball and showin' off.

It must be so rewarding that now when you guys perform "Goldilox," none of you sing at all. The entire audience sings the whole thing in harmony with each other.
I've been doin' it for thirty years now, and it's still hard every night. I don't know how to react. I don't know what to say. I don't know what to think. Every night we just turn the mics out and they sing it. One night, I thought, *I wanna sing it! It's been so long since I sang it*. I opened my mouth up and started singin', and as soon as I got to "*I can't believe*" the crowd sang so loud that I couldn't find my pitch. I just backed up and let them sing it.

They stole it from you!

They stole it. It's theirs. I'll probably never sing it live again.

Well, it's gotta be a great feeling.

It is. My life has been so exciting. We're human, and we get used to things, and we don't appreciate things, and we take things for granted, and I'm just like that. But I want to get out and feel that drive. If you think you're the shit, you're never gonna get better, and I avoid that like a plague. I always say, whenever I write that song that impresses me, and that I get goosebumps from, and I turn into a fan of myself, that's the last song I'll ever write. I've written almost 500 songs, and one day, maybe, I'll have that hit. But if I have that hit then I ain't got nowhere to go. So, I think it's more fun to keep tryin' to write that song. Yeah, I gotta get over that. I want to write a song that the whole world would deem is the greatest song ever written. At least for a few months! [*Laughs*] I used to say, "For all time!" [*Laughs harder*]

Well, every time you've released a record, there've been songs where I've gone, "These are the greatest songs...for these few months!" [*More laughter*] There's stuff across all the things you've released. Whether you know it, or wanna accept it, that's on you, but I feel it.

Thank you.

What's changed the most about your voice since you started?

It's just gotten lower and lower. Took me 'til fifty to hit puberty and now you gotta re-learn to sing. The high stuff was a little unnatural anyway. I had to pretty much yell everything to hit those notes, and as a result, I pushed so hard that I just wore my voice out. It's a different voice now. I got a song I just wrote, and it's the range where I'm talkin' right now. I can't do the old Doug. That's what frustrates me when I'm doin' a record. Everybody wants to hear Doug yellin' and screamin', and I can't. Even though *they feel* the passion, *I feel* the roughness, and hear myself strugglin' to hit the note. There's a fine line between yelling and having passion.

I agree. Some of your best work, and some of your most emotional work, are songs like "Picture" off *Ear Candy*. You're kinda speak/singing that one, but it's so moving, and you're so connected, and passionate. You don't need to scream. It's intimate.

Sly [Stone] could do that. That's where I got that. He's probably my favorite singer.

That's a given. [*Laughter*] But if you could duet with one singer—living or dead—who would it be?

Chris Cornell. We dabbled with it. It came across our conversations every now and then. It just never happened. I would've loved to. Love that guy. What a voice.

Who are your top five favorite singers of all time?

My top five are people that have changed my life. So, that's Sly Stone, Mavis Staples, Mahalia Jackson, Stevie Wonder, Aretha Franklin. And Paul Rodgers was like a mixture of all of them; that's why I loved him so much. Paul opens his mouth up and I hear every one of 'em.

If you could ask any singer about their voice, who would it be and what would you ask?

Celine Dion. I would ask, "Can you teach me how to sing that good?" [*Laughs*] You weren't expecting that!

I was not. When we first started talking, you said you had an epiphany about your voice that you were gonna share.

I used to have a hard time before I'd go on. But doin' the Experience Hendrix Tour [2019], I really put a lot of pressure on myself because this was a big deal for me. Humongous stage. I'm playin' with [guitarist] Joe Satriani and [drummer] Kenny Aronoff. Kenny's played on every hit that's ever been, and Joe is a platinum-selling player and asked me to do this. What I was told, under the radar, was that he took his paycheck and paid for a tour bus, and me and Kenny's salary, and he made no money. He did it for fun. Okay?

That's amazing.

We went out there and did five Hendrix songs. And dude, I ruled that motherfucker. I can do Hendrix. It was standing ovation every night. It wasn't just me, the band was somethin' to be reckoned with. But every time we got ready to play, I was beatin' myself up. I was nervous, I was scared. It's Satriani and Kenny Aronoff, and I'm "That guy." That's my legacy. "Who's that guy singin'? He sounded pretty good," and they go home. So, I'm thinkin', *I'm not holdin' my own, Joe's gonna fire me*. So, every night, before I went on, I grabbed my bass, and sang the whole set in the bathroom, at the same volume I would onstage. That was the first time I really started warming-up, and found a way to do it. And it worked because when I walked onstage, I was ready to go. But I still was nervous. So, I walked around in circles, and prayed to my muse that I'd have a good night tonight. I've always felt like there was somebody there, and I just believe this is my muse. And I heard this voice in my head say, "You don't need me anymore." I stopped and went, *What?* All of a sudden, my brain went, "What have you been doin' all your life?" *Singin'*. "What have people been doing when you sing?" *Cry*. "What happens when you go onstage, no matter what mood you're in, no matter how bad you feel, or how bad the monitors were?" *People were moved*. And the voice said to me, "Go do what you're supposed to do." I walked onstage, and there was no fear anymore. I haven't had it since.

Well, after everything you've been through, it sounds like you stopped listening to the voice of religion, and started hearing the voice of God.

YEAH! Dude, don't sue me. [*Speaks as he writes*] "Stopped listening to the voice of religion and started hearing the voice of GOD!" What a defining line. Sounds good to me!

Wendy Melvoin on
PRINCE

"WENDY...IS THE WATER WARM ENOUGH?"

That's who I'm talking to right now. Wendy from The Revolution. Guitarist, producer, singer-songwriter, and professional badass.

If you're a fan of Prince Rogers Nelson, you know Wendy Melvoin like she's family, and you're completely starry-eyed just talking to her. You grew up with her. You rocked out to her. You grieved with her when The Revolution broke up. And you did again when Prince passed away.

Prince recorded his first album in 1978, playing all the instruments himself. But before he left this earth, he sold more than 150 million records, was inducted into the Rock & Roll Hall of Fame, won seven Grammys, an Academy Award, and too many others to mention. More importantly, Prince changed our lives for the better.

Untouchable, enigmatic, mischievous, and prolific beyond compare, he was one of the most incredible live performers ever seen. One of the greatest guitar players ever heard. One of the most legendary songwriters of all time. And then, there's that voice. That range. That scream. That playful charm, that hunger for sex, and thirst for God, all rolled into one.

MAN, I MISS PRINCE!

"Shall we begin?"

When was the first time you heard Prince sing?

When I was around thirteen years old, my twin sister [Susannah] and I snuck out of my dad's house during the summer months and would go to this nightclub in Hollywood called The Starwood. The Starwood had two rooms. One was for live rock acts and the other was this really cool underground disco. My sister and I were little disco babies, and we loved to dance. We went dancing one night, and the DJ was playing this song. I ran up to the booth and was like, "Oh my God, what is that song you're playing? Who's that woman that I'm hearing?" He goes, "It's not a woman. His name is Prince. He's nineteen years old, and the song is called 'Soft and Wet.'" It was from his first record [*For You*]. From thirteen until I joined the band at nineteen, I did all my research, and I became obsessed with Prince. I was completely in awe of his abilities.

He not only plays every instrument on *For You*, he starts out with the title track, singing this intricate a cappella melody where he proceeds to tell us his mission statement as an artist within the first two lines! "With love, sincerity, and deepest care, my life with you I share." I mean, he knew right from the start what he was up to, didn't he?

[*Chuckles*] Oh, he knew. He was born one of those guys that knew where his creativity was gonna go. It's very difficult for us mere mortals to comprehend the kind of laser focus he had, even as a small kid.

Nothing was frivolous, was it?

No, no, no. He was his best audience, so nothing was frivolous. [*Laughs*] Everything had intention. He was doing most of this pleasing himself, first and foremost, with the result of connecting millions and millions of people around the world to his creative output. But he was something else. He took great care with his spark.

Was he just that confident right out of the gate?

It's an interesting thing about Prince. He was the most self-conscious human being I've ever met in my life—and I've known *really* self-conscious people—that when they walk into a room, they're so paranoid that there's eyes looking at them, that everybody starts looking at them. Self-consciousness kind of breeds attention. It's a weird kind of cognitive dissonance. The thing about Prince, with how self-conscious he was, he was that gifted. But the gift was so much stronger than his self-consciousness that it just eclipsed, and that's what helped turn him into a rock star. "Don't look at me offstage, but keep your eye on me when I'm onstage."

Was he nervous or confident before shows?

Never nervous, no. After he did *Dirty Mind*, he was not nervous about anything. Prior to that, there were performances where he was nervous, but he was young, he was nineteen and twenty. But once the *Dirty Mind* record was done, all bets were off.

Did you ever get to see his approach to recording vocals in the studio?

I saw it, but he would have everybody leave the room when he would press record. When he was recording vocals with [engineer] Susan Rogers and she *couldn't* leave the room, like if she was screwing around with some outboard gear that would help facilitate whatever his vocal was, he would literally put the microphone in a corner of a room and face the corner so she wouldn't see his eyes while he was singing.

Does that play into what you're talking about, the self-consciousness?

He would be self-conscious about trying to create a narrative about a character he was gonna sing about, or try and tap into something super vulnerable about himself. He was encompassing a character, trying to dig into the psychology of what it was that he was trying to say, and he didn't want to be watched while he was trying to dig.

It doesn't sound to me that he was loose with a vocal. He would probably grind that thing in the ground to get it *just* the way he wanted.

He would get it exactly the way he wanted but it didn't take him long to do it. He was known to cut two to three original songs in a day. He's not spending a lot of time fuckin' around with overdubs and redoing shit. It's like, hit it or quit it. That's how gifted he was. This is a guy that would have a full arrangement of an entire song in his head. He'd start playing the entire song on drums, without a click, then go back into the control room and add bass, guitar, keyboards, and then, his vocals.

The spoken word intro to "Computer Blue" between you and [keyboardist] Lisa Coleman has got to be one of the coolest, most iconic openings to a song ever. I remember hearing that as a kid, and it was just so sexy and mysterious. How did that come about?

It was the three of us in the studio trying to come up with something evocative, and Prince loved to play off the fact that me and Lisa were a couple. It was part of the allure of, "Are Wendy and Lisa gay or not?" Well, let's be suggestive. And is Prince like watching them? Or *What is this?* It came out just by pure drama and intrigue. But we did it in the room together as an overdub at the very end.

Was that something that he had written out for you?

Oh yes! Absolutely.

He had so many alter egos living inside of his voice, even going so far as to name some of them. Can you talk to me about Camille and some of his other personas?

It helped him pretend to be different people. It was like being an actor for him. They're parts of him. His Camille voice ["Shockadelica"], his Jamie Starr voice ["I Wish U Heaven part 3"], his Bob George voice ["Bob George"]. The integrated personality would be Prince, and all the other ones are like fractured people, but they're part of him. He just *was* it. He'd walk in one room and he'd be singing like Camille. And then, you knew he was in a certain type of mood if he was singin' like Jamie Starr. You knew he was in a definite kind of mood if he slowed his voice down and did Bob George. You could tell what mood he was in by the vocal technique. And when he went to falsetto, that was a completely different person as well.

Can you walk me through what those moods were with each character?
Camille is definitely playful. He used that voice to be more in touch with the frisky, playful, rebellious person, 'cause he always had like a slightly sped-up tone, and it almost sounded like he was being a Gremlin. When that voice came round, his personality was very mischievous. Bob George was pissed off; that low, slowed down voice was either the sound of God talking to him, or it was like dark and mean and violent. Listen to the song "Bob George." It's dark, and that was a dark period for him. I think he was working out his anger on something. Jamie Starr was more of an alter ego; the synonym he used for producing Vanity 6 and The Time, but it was very closely related to Camille.

He almost sounds like Morris Day a bit when he's Jamie Starr! Who does shit like this? No one comes close. And then he's got that amazing falsetto.
His falsetto was sexy. Eddie Kendricks, I loved his falsetto. I loved Sylvester Stewart's falsetto. Philip Bailey was a great falsetto singer, but I think Prince had the best falsetto of them all. It was natural, the vibrato was beautiful, he knew how to control his voice really well, *and it was really sexy*. He knew how to use his maleness to counter the femaleness of how sexy that falsetto was so well. If you were listening to "Do Me, Baby," it didn't matter if he sounded like a woman on those high notes, you still were like, "Oh my God, that's the sexiest man I've ever heard." He knew how to play those parts.

Originals had a bunch of demos on it, and "Baby, You're a Trip" has some of the most wicked Prince screams ever. Have you ever heard anyone top Prince when it comes to screaming a melody?
No. No. No. I've talked about that a million times to people. There's some blues singers that have a crunch to their voice in the upper register that's beautiful, but as far as being the most famous person alive? No. Not even Robert Plant during his heyday of Zeppelin, nothing could compare. Although, I'll tell you who could scream/sing really well: Paul McCartney.

Yeah, McCartney's amazing. But there's something to scream/singing a melody, and then, to sustain it and keep it locked in there the way Prince does.
Like on "The Beautiful Ones"?

That's a perfect example.
When he breaks into the latter half of that song, there's no denying how honest he's being with that scream, and how controlled it is. I don't know of another artist that could translate that kind of pain as well as he did.

The ending of that song gives you chills. He's also just coming from the falsetto in the verses, which is so smooth and sexy, and then when he hits you with that scream, you're like, "Oh, man, he means it!"

He sure does. There's a little bit of that in "Darling Nikki" towards the end, but that one has a little bit more of a desperation, pissed off kind of quality to it. "Beautiful Ones" is coming from his broken heart, and it's incredible.

Did you ever ask him how he hit those high notes without tearing his voice apart?

I never did because he never seemed like he was struggling. Sometimes his eyes would get really red, and you could see he was pushing so hard in his vocals. And when you'd watch him onstage, and he was hitting notes like that, there'd be like fog, almost like you were in cold air and you see your breath outside. You could kind of see that with Prince when he sang. It was very odd. It was like the heat from his vocal. Depending on the room, you could see condensation. That's how hard he would be singing.

That's intense. Wow. Did he do any vocal warm-ups before going onstage?

Yes. He was always singing huge falsettos in his room. Always.

Was he doing an actual warm-up routine, or was he singing along to anything?

No, just singing falsetto. If he was listening to anything it would be listening to himself and his own music. He wasn't one to put on other people's music before a show. [*Laughs*] As a matter of fact, he didn't like that very much. So, sometimes it would be to a rehearsal, sometimes it would be to an unreleased thing he did, but most of the time, it was just him practicing licks, singing falsetto, and warming his voice up. We would get to soundcheck around 2:00 in the afternoon and would not leave until the show was done because our soundchecks would run about three hours long. So, right after soundcheck, there'd be like an hour and a half to get ready. He'd already been singing onstage, but he wouldn't be blowing it out completely. He never really lost his voice!

How did he take care of his voice on the road?

There was always a humidifier going in his hotel room. Always humidifiers everywhere he went. There was always hot tea and lemon everywhere he went, and he sucked on Halls Vapors constantly. That was his regimen. He took care of it. Obviously, he didn't do much talking, so that saved his voice, and when he did speak it was very airy. He had a very airy quality to it, and he didn't push too hard. But when he sang, he pushed it.

There was a period after The Revolution broke up where it felt like there was no more interaction between Prince and his old bandmates. And from a fan perspective, it was a huge deal in terms of how unresolved it all seemed, especially between you, Lisa, and Prince. And it really stung because you had such an amazing run of records, and the chemistry was so undeniable. But, years later, *Emancipation* came out, and

there was a track on that album called "In This Bed Eye Scream," and I remember reading the liner notes, and he had dedicated it to you and Lisa. The lyrics seemed to be Prince reaching out, in the only way he knew how, by singing.

That's right.

I was so excited that maybe you guys would hear it and get back together, and I always wondered what you guys thought of that song when you heard it.

Like you just explained it, we felt that was his way of trying to talk to us, and we reached out. I'm telling you, there were so many times we were almost back together again, and he just changed his mind. [*Sweetly*] He just changed his mind. He just didn't wanna do it. We tried. We were gonna do a tour as The Revolution with Prince, maybe six months we were talking about it before he passed away. Just awful. We were never enemies. We were kind of a divorced couple who had children together and loved each other still, but just couldn't be married. That's kind of what it felt like. But there was no animosity. There was just disappointment.

That line "How did we ever lose each other's sound?" That just...*ugh*...

It's really sad. We did some *amazing* stuff together. It's heartbreaking. But I'm also so grateful to know my life has him in it, and not a lot of people can say that.

The music that you guys made together, it will always be. It's part of the Mount Rushmore of music. And you and Lisa, and the rest of the band, obviously, had so much to do with that. There's a reason why that run of records is so monumental. That chemistry changed my life. It really did, starting very early.

Wow. That's so sweet.

The things that are happening, even sonically, on those records, just aren't happening today in the same way. You just can't top 'em.

I know, I know, *I know, I know, I KNNNNOOOOW!* [*Laughter*] Oh God, I know.

When you hear his voice now, what do you remember most?

I just miss him when I hear it. I don't tear it apart, or think about it in other terms, it's more visceral still. I'm still grieving him. It's awful to not have him here. It's awful.

Marky Ramone on
JOEY RAMONE

JOEY. JOHNNY. DEE DEE. TOMMY...AND MARKY!
Once upon a time, these eccentric characters from New York City were in a group that many consider the first punk band ever. And although they had wildly different personalities, they all changed their last names to one word: Ramone.

What set the Ramones apart was their adherence to a militant set of rules. Their songs would be short and loud. Their bangs would hang down onto their faces. Their uniform would be jeans, t-shirts, and black leather jackets. And their gangly lead singer, wearing black sunglasses, standing 6'6" at the mic, would be Joey Ramone.

While the band rocked hard, Joey delivered his vocals as if he were a crooner from the '50s. It was the exact ingredient needed to make them one of the most influential groups of all time. Joey would be gone from cancer by the age of forty-nine, but what he left behind are some of the best rock 'n' roll songs ever recorded.

The Ramones have received a Lifetime Achievement Award from the Grammys, and have been inducted into the Rock & Roll of Fame, but the tragic irony is that this legendary band always stood outside of the mainstream success they truly deserved. With their iconic logo shirt selling more than their records ever have, the band always held true to the musical mission, and begrudgingly, to each other.

Stepping away to produce, Tommy Ramone left his drum seat after the first four years on the road. He was replaced by Marky Ramone from Richard Hell and the Voidoids, who played the role beautifully with the band for years, until each of them sadly passed on. But Marky still carries the flag as Marky Ramone's Blitzkrieg.

So "Hey! Ho! Let's Go!"

When was the first time you heard Joey sing?
We were all at CBGB. My band started out way before the Ramones, and they used to come into the club and watch us. So, we were all friends. When I first heard Joey, I said, "Yeah, this guy is very unique. He has a look, he's six foot six, and he's influenced by really great vocalists." He loved the British Invasion, the girl group stuff that Phil Spector produced, Alice Cooper, and David Bowie, and he loved The Kinks. So, you throw that up in the air, the omelette comes down and it's Joey.

It was revolutionary because, for so many bands, it was about the pyrotechnics or the gymnastics, or sounding sweet and soulful. Joey came along and said, "I'm gonna just be myself. I know my range and I'm not straying from it." He was so real and so human, and just gave the song exactly what it needed.
He had his own style.

Did he ever discuss his voice with you? Either his frustrations, or if he loved it?
He wasn't one to toot his own horn. But before we'd go on the stage, he would warm-up, and go through the exercises of certain notes.

So, he did vocal warm-ups before going on?
Definitely. He would do the [*sings scales*] "La-la-la-la-la-la-la," all that stuff. It helped. He was very into presenting the audience the best quality of his vocals that he could.

Did he have like a tape or something?
He went to a teacher. The teacher would make him a cassette to listen to, and he would bring that backstage, and the teacher would go, "Okay, Joey, go, 'La-la-la-la-la-la-la,' and he would do it, wait a little bit, and then the teacher would go, "Okay, Joey, do this." He would follow that.

Did he do anything else to take care of his voice on the road?
He would drink tea and honey. A few cough drops here and there. There really wasn't that much to do; he had it in him. It's evident on the live shows, the albums, everything.

In your book, *Punk Rock Blitzkrieg: My Life as a Ramone,* you speak about Joey's obsessive compulsive disorder and how hard it could be for the band at times. But it

was a serious thing, it was just that no one really knew much about it back then. I'm curious if his OCD had any effect on how he recorded his vocals.

He would piece together the vocals. We would definitely try to aim for a whole track, but sometimes certain things had to be corrected. In '82, we did the US Festival, which was run by Steve Wozniak. He was one of the inventors of computers and all that stuff. This show was in front of 100,000 people in San Bernardino. It was about 104 degrees in the desert, and we're all wearing our leather jackets. [*Laughter*] At one point, we're doing a song, and Joey's mic went out. So, the tech came out, changed the mic, but he wanted the old mic back! That's when the OCD kicked in. But you can't do that in front of 100,000 people. So, he had to continue with the mic he had. But he didn't sing. If you look back, you'll see what I'm talking about. He was just standing there a little frustrated and upset that he didn't have the original mic, but the show went great.

Was he nervous or confident before he would perform?

Confident. We did so many shows that the confidence better be there! You know what I mean? Through experience, through the constant touring, through the recordings…

Do you have a favorite vocal performance of his?

"I Just Want to Have Something to Do." "Sheena is a Punk Rocker." "I Wanna Be Your Boyfriend." "The KKK Took My Baby Away." I liked "Havana Affair." There's so many that it's hard to list just one, but I really liked the slower songs too because he was able to use his vibrato in that. "Needles and Pins," which was originally done by a band called The Searchers. His vocals are great on that.

Do you have any memories of him recording that stick out to you?

The Phil Spector sessions [*End of the Century*]. When I got the recording of Joey's vocals on "I'm Affected." Really good.

A lot's been made of those sessions over the years, and it's become this kind of rock 'n' roll myth that Spector held you guys at gunpoint.

I know. He never pulled guns out on us. He would put them on the side of the console, or he would hang them up on a clothes rack that was in the corner, but he never pointed a gun at us. Me and Joey loved him. He didn't get along too well with Dee Dee and John. Look, everyone can't get along, but you have to understand each other and work with each other.

What was his approach to recording vocals?

With the vocal department, Phil was very simple. He just wanted a natural vocal. He will do forty takes of something. When he started out in the early '60s, he would do so many takes, it would take hours and hours and hours. He's considered one of the greatest producers of all time, so we all put our trust in him.

How did Joey hold up, having to do that many takes for him?

He loved Phil and he went along with it. He had to. The more work you put into it when you listen to a great producer like that, the better it's gonna be.

When you hear Joey's voice now, what do you remember most?
The depth of his singing, the phrasing's great, his vibrato, and he was versatile, very versatile. I don't listen to the albums, but every time I hear a song on the radio, or doing my thing on SiriusXM [*Marky Ramone's Punk Rock Blitzkrieg*], I'll go, "Hey, that's great." He had his own style, and I like stylists. It takes time to create a style. We all subconsciously put our influences with our own way of doing what we do, and we hopefully, eventually, have our own style. That's what he was about.

Steve Cropper on
OTIS REDDING

IF THERE'S A SOUL SONG you love with all your heart, there's a good chance that Steve Cropper either wrote it, produced it, or played guitar on it. Widely considered one of the greatest guitarists of all time, Steve came onto the scene as part of the Stax Records house band, Booker T. & the MG's in Memphis, Tennessee. There, he backed everyone from Sam & Dave to Wilson Pickett to Carla Thomas and Johnnie Taylor.

Later in life, Steve was even a member of The Blues Brothers with John Belushi and Dan Aykroyd. But it was his work co-writing, producing, and playing with Otis Redding that took him to a whole other level of "Respect." Just think of those songs: "Try a Little Tenderness." "Hard to Handle." "These Arms of Mine." "Pain in My Heart." "(Sittin' on) The Dock of the Bay." Those are just a few of the many hits that Otis and Steve Cropper brought to the world, all within the span of three short years.

Redding's life was cut short in an airplane crash at the age of twenty-six, but he will always remain one of the most iconic singers in the history of popular music. He and Steve were both inducted into the Rock & Roll Hall of Fame for their contribution. So, when it came time to speak with someone about the Big O. Mr. Pitiful. The King of Soul. Well, it's just gotta-gotta-gotta be no-no-no-no one other than The Colonel himself.

When was the first time you heard Otis sing?

We were cutting a band he was singin' in called Johnny Jenkins and the Pinetoppers, and they had an instrumental hit called "Love Twist." What I didn't know is that they had a singer. I thought he was their driver. They drove up to the studio from Macon, Georgia in a Cadillac, and this big, tall guy gets out, goes to the trunk, and starts gettin' stuff to carry in. I saw some mics, and I go runnin' down there, and said, "Hey man, we've got our own mics in the studio!" [*Laughs*] During the session, our drummer, Al Jackson, came to me and said, "You know that guy that drove Johnny up here? He wants you to hear him sing." I said, "I don't have time now, we're in the middle of a session." At the end of the session, Al came back, and said, "He's buggin' me to death. Will you just take five seconds to get him off my back?" I said, "Well, I guess so. Have him come down to the piano and sing for me."

I can already see this scene in the movie!

This is a true story! Otis comes down there, and I said, "Okay, play me something." He goes, "Well, man, I don't play any piano. I only play a little guuu-tar." [*Laughs*] He says, "Can you play me some of them church cuuu-wads?" Not "chords," but "cuuu-wads." I said, "Like this?" I played in B flat or whatever. He said, "Yeah," and started singin' "These Arms of Mine." I went, "Holy Mackerel! Stop it!" He said, "You don't like it?" I said, "Hold it right here, don't move!" I go up and grab Jim Stewart, who was the owner and engineer at the time, and I said, "Jim, just drop what you're doin', you gotta hear this guy sing." So, he comes down there, and the next thing you know, he said, "Get the band back together!" because he'd already sent everybody home. And [Donald "Duck" Dunn] reminded me, I come runnin' out on the sidewalk. He said, "I was puttin' my bass in the trunk of the car, and you said, "Get your bass back out, we gotta cut this song on a guy!" And that was Otis. [*Sings*] "These arms of miiiine." I swear, he said those four words and the hair on my arms stood up.

The way he sings the first two lines of "Pain in My Heart" is all anyone ever needs to know about soul. The lyric, the vocal, it's all right there. It's just amazing to me that at that young of an age you can go, this is what soul is. How old was he when you guys recorded the first record?

[*Sings*] "Pain in My heart." Golly, I have no idea. Twenty-four, twenty-five maybe? Well, from '63-'66. Three years we did all that.

That's insane, Steve. *That's insane.*

Yep.

"Hey Hey Baby" is another one from that album that just blows me away.

Yeah, I love that one!

Otis and Little Richard were the only guys who could sing rock 'n' roll like that, where there's a natural distortion built into their voices that's almost impossible to replicate. Am I romanticizing that in my head, or have you ever seen anything like that?

No, I've been sayin' for a long time: if you took a jar of Sam Cooke and a jar of Little Richard, and poured 'em together and mixed 'em, you'd get Otis Redding. He could rock 'n' roll and sing hard just like Little Richard, and sing soft and beautiful just like Sam Cooke as a crooner. He had that ability. Not too many artists can go both ways.

How did Otis approach recording his vocals in the studio? Was he going for one take?

Absolutely. There's so much feeling in it, and that's why it created all those great tracks. Very seldom at Stax did we overdub vocals because we went for the right take in the studio with everybody live. Sam & Dave was cut on 4-track, but they sang all that live in the studio with the band. There was not any overdubs that I know of.

It must bring so much joy to your heart when you listen to the radio and hear Sam Moore say, "Play it, Steve!" on "Soul Man." That's gotta make you smile when you're riding around.

[*Laughs*] It was one take, and that happened to be the take everybody liked so we used it.

It's one of the greatest shout-outs in music history.

Yeah, I didn't think that much about it until Belushi did it when we were with The Blues Brothers, and he'd always sing, "Play it, Steve!"

Did you play guitar on "Remember Me?"

Absolutely.

It's hard to find anything about that song. It feels like that one just slipped through the cracks somehow. But it's got to be one of the most understated, great soul performances. That little lick you do? [*Hums the guitar melody*]

[*Laughs*] The one I like is "Pain in My Heart" where I go [*sings his guitar melody*]. I don't know what made me think of that. [*Laughter*] And I'll tell you another one, and it may not be a favorite of yours 'cause nobody knows much about it, it's called "Nobody's Fault but Mine."

Are you kidding? [*Sings*] "Nobody's fault but mine."

I love that song! I love what I played on it! But I always said on most of the older stuff, it you take his vocal stuff off, most of the stuff that I'm doin' sounds pretty country. But when he *sings* it, it sounds really funky and R&B.

You gotta go listen to "Remember Me" because your guitar playing on there…

Okay, I will. I don't listen to his stuff too much. It's real hard to do. After he passed away, I don't think I listened to anything he did for about seven years.

This is probably a myth, but I heard that the whistling at the end of "Dock of the Bay" was just a placeholder because Otis was gonna come back and sing some more, but he never got the chance to. Is that true?

That might be true. When you wrote with Otis, you didn't write fade outs because he always came up with something, so we didn't that time as well. He didn't know what to do, so he started whistlin'. There's some outtakes where [engineer, Ronnie Capone] says somethin' like, "Otis, you'll never be a whistler." And Otis showed him. That's the one and only take he whistled it right.

Awww, man, that's beautiful.

Earlier, he was tryin' to do seagull sounds and he sounded like a dyin' crow to me. [*Mimics Otis*] "Caw-caw-caw," [*laughter*] kinda silly. The history books will tell you "Dock of the Bay" was the last thing he recorded. *It was not*. We cut a lot of things in that couple of weeks. "Ton of Joy," "Champagne and Wine," "Direct Me," "Pounds and Hundreds."

Was Otis nervous or confident before he would perform?

Otis had a lot of confidence. He wasn't nervous at all. Eddie Floyd's one of those guys who can't say his name right before he goes on. [*Laughs*] Then, he just goes up there and does it.

Did Otis do any vocal warm-ups before going onstage?

No. Otis was not a classically trained singer.

Do you know if he took care of his voice on the road?

Obviously, he didn't or he wouldn't have had to have an operation.

I didn't know about this. What was the operation about?

After the Stax/Volt tour, we did the Monterey Pop Festival, and several weeks went by before Otis came in to record. This time we were gonna get him longer than a day or two because normally he was on the road all the time. Ronnie said, "Do you realize how well Otis is singing?" I said, "Yeah, I've never heard him sing better." We started pulling old outtakes and tracks off the shelves and havin' him re-do them at night 'cause we couldn't do them in the session. I guess he had some polyps taken off his throat 'cause it was getting a little raspy. I just thought he was getting a little tired from all the touring we were doing, 'cause the man, every night, was singin' and screamin' at the top of his lungs. But he never lost his voice that I know of. Never missed a gig.

When you hear his voice now, what do you remember most?

"These Arms of Mine." [*Chuckles*] He was somethin'. Well, his voice was about as good as it gets, but I remember him as a guy. What I do remember, which is real stupid on my part, is I never had a picture taken as a buddy with Otis Redding. People didn't have phones and weren't runnin' around with a camera all the time. And one of the greatest times for me was when we were in New York to do a show, and somehow, it got canceled. We were runnin' around Manhattan for three or four days, and he was so streetwise, I couldn't believe it. He was just wiser than me. He knew everything. I always looked at Otis as an older brother. Did not know we were the same age until they said in the paper what his age was. I went. "We were the same age? *He was older than me!*" [Promoter] Alan Walden put it together one time in an interview, he said, "Otis had a million-dollar smile," and I never thought about that. You were his new best friend when he walked up to you. He treated everybody that way. That's the way he was. And you can say this about him. I know he had a great voice, but he was probably one of the most non-prejudiced human beings I have ever met. There was no such thing as color in the Stax days. It didn't exist. If they looked at me as a white guy, they never told me that. I never looked at them as Black guys, they were just my best friends. And we were all makin' music together for the same reason: tryin' to get a hit record. That's all we were tryin' to do, get a hit record. [*Laughs*]

I think you did alright in that regard, my friend.

Well, we did okay, yeah. [*Laughter*]

LIONEL RICHIE

AS ONE OF THE BESTSELLING ARTISTS OF ALL TIME, Lionel Richie has been giving us vocal lessons in soul, funk, and pop music his entire career, selling more than 100 million records. From his early days in the Commodores to his solo recordings, the man has proven himself to be a hit machine of the highest caliber.

After we did this interview, he would go on to become one of the judges on ABC's American Idol, and an inductee into the Rock & Roll Hall of Fame. But right now, he's gonna talk to us about making friends with your voice, having your own style, and those notes that will haunt you forever.

Sometimes you can tell an interview is going to be great just by the way the conversation starts. Well, I knew we were in good hands when Lionel rang me after a couple weeks of failed scheduling attempts, and immediately pronounced, "Young man! It's only been forty years! I thought before I turned ninety-seven, we might do the interview. Good God!"

So, let's not keep the man waiting any longer.

Who first exposed you to singing?

It was probably my grandmother. My grandmother was a classical pianist, and an instructor at Tuskegee University. There was also a guy by the name of William L. Dawson. He was a fabulous composer, and he was in charge of the Tuskegee choir. Now, to give you the history of the Tuskegee choir, when they inaugurated the Empire State Building, the Tuskegee choir was brought to New York to sing for it. And William L. Dawson was a very dear friend of my grandmother. I was probably nineteen years old, a freshman. I was probably the shyest kid in the world and didn't know I could sing. Not knowing that I was a singer or writer, I joined a band and we started singing cover songs. My first band, ever in my life, was called the Commodores.

You've got to be kidding me.

No, no, no. And I had no idea of my singing ability. At. All. It wasn't until we auditioned for Motown Records, and for the Jackson 5 tour. I had to be prodded into being the lead vocalist because I didn't have any confidence in my singing because I didn't really know what the hell I was doing. If I had to draw a cartoon of Lionel Richie's climb to fame, it would be Lionel Richie with nineteen people behind me, with their foot pushing me out onto the stage.

But how did you join the Commodores if you weren't a singer?

I joined the Commodores as a saxophone player.

That's right, I forgot about that!

The bass player and the drummer were the lead singers. In the beginning of the Commodores, I only had two songs to sing in the whole set. And if I told you "Little Green Apples" was one of the songs, you'd understand how heavy I had to sing. Not at all. But as time went on, Michael [Gilbert] had to go to Vietnam, and now the responsibility of who was gonna sing some of those songs fell on my shoulders and whoever else came in. It was clearly not in my life plan, or set of ego, anywhere along the line, that I was going to be the lead singer for the group. [Laughs]

Were you emulating anyone when you started out?

When you're starting out, you just mimic everybody. You cover songs, so if it's Archie Bell & The Drells, you mimic Archie Bell & The Drells. If it's Jerry Butler, Jerry Butler. If it's The Temptations, it's The Temptations. Whoever you were copying, you wanted to sound just like the record. And, of course, we did.

How did you find your own voice?

I know very, very famous actors that don't like to see themselves in the movie because they don't like to see themselves up close. It took me five or six years just to get used to hearing my voice on a record. The first time you hear yourself sing, you don't know anything about unique. You don't even know you have a sound, or what being a stylist is all about. But as time goes on, you learn, that's my little niche right here. Okay, I know how to do that. You learn by doing. The hardest thing I had to do was go solo, because when you're in a band, you've got five other guys who can be wrong all the time. You can blame somebody. When you're solo, it's all your fault. [*Laughs*]

So, you slowly started feeling comfortable in your role?
Yeah, you start finding out what your thing is. If it's a ballad, which I wrote and felt comfortable with, okay, that's my voice. And then, okay, I'll do "Sail On," which is a country sounding voice. On "Three Times a Lady," I was classical. Then on "Brick House," I was this other voice. And you develop your own style. The first time I started singing, I didn't sound like Lionel Richie. It took years of developing over time.

Did you ever have any vocal training?
The greatest thing that ever happened was I had no training whatsoever. I remember, after years of singing, going to a vocal coach, and he said, "Now let's take Mr. Brown for example. Now Mr. Brown sings incorrectly." I said, "*James Brown?*" He said, "Yes." I said, "Okay, I don't need to do vocal lessons anymore. Because if Mr. Brown is singing incorrectly, then I don't want you to change my style at all." You follow me?

You can't mess with James Brown. That's no way to win hearts and minds.
That's what I tell people all the time. You can go see opera singers, or people on Broadway, and they may have the most incredible voice ever. Now. Will they ever sell a pop record? No. Because Broadway voices, classical voices, and classical training, does not work for pop music. Because that's actually all about your style. It's the way you are. Some people sing through their nose. Well, that's their style! Everybody has their thing. What you don't want is for somebody to break the habit and try to sing "correctly" and blow your style. Being a kid, I loved watching tennis, and they were saying about Rod Laver, "Rod Laver is playing unorthodox. All of his shots are just improper execution of how you're supposed to hit the ball." And then, the other commentator said, "Yes, but he won all the tournaments." [*Laughs*] So, do we care about proper or improper? No! *Did he win?* Yes! Okay, then that's how he won. *Who cares how he hit the ball?*

Are you nervous or confident before you perform?
The first time you sing onstage, you can hear your heartbeat through the microphone. Remember now, I didn't want to be the singer. I liked the horn parts. I was the guy that was foolin' around in the corner. Once you grab the lead mic, everybody's lookin' at you, and I was scared to death. And it took many years—even to this day—if you're not a little stage frightened before you go out there—I call it "Healthy Respect"—if you're not a little pumped, a little fear factor in there, then you're not really present.

Do you do anything to keep centered before you go out?

I just tell a couple jokes backstage with the band, make sure we're laughing hysterically, then walk out onstage. There has to be a certain amount of lightness. I have to look like I'm relaxed when I walk out onstage. I don't wanna get out there and then relax. I just wanna go out there lookin' like I've been onstage for forty minutes. Part of the whole thing, the attitude, is making the crowd feel comfortable, like it's no big deal to you, but you're excited to see them. That's how you get the crowd to be comfortable. But I really don't relax until the end of the first song. By then, you know how your ears sound, how the band sounds, you know the stage is cool, you know where you are, you know the crowd is gonna be in that mode, and then, you go kill it.

Do you do any vocal warm-ups before you perform?

Oh, absolutely. I do ten to fifteen minutes of full on getting the vocal cords engaged. Plus, in the shower before I go over to the show, I use the steam to do my first vocal warm-up, because I have plenty of moisture in the air.

What do those warm-ups look like?

You do your scales, your octaves, your [*does tongue trills*]. Then, you go into your mid-notes. And if your mid-voice—not an octave lower, not your high range—but if the mid-voice sounds clear as a bell, everything else is possible. Then, I'll probably sing the highest part of "Easy" or "Truly" just to make sure that the highs are there. My highest note of the night.

"Truly." That's a real note right there.

That's a real note. [*Cracks up*]

And it's long. You gotta hold that out.

And it's loooong. And they wanna hear the whoooole thing; that's exactly right.

When you wrote it, were you like, "Oh shit, I'm writing myself into a corner?"

Yeah. Every once in a while, you go, *What did I just do to myself for the rest of my life?* When you're recording, you have to remember, this is the note that is going to be haunting you for the rest of your life. I've seen some artists hit some incredible notes, and I say, "I wanna see him do that ten years from now. I don't believe it." But to let me know where I am every day, in my career, in my life, "Truly" is that note. And the last note on "Endless Love." [*Sings*] "I'll *giiivvve* it all to *yooouuu...*" That note right there. That is the note you don't play with.

How do you take care of your voice on the road?

Sleep, sleep, and sleep. Water, water, and water. Humidify, humidify, humidifier.

Do you sleep with a humidifier on?

Yes, 'cause most the time it's dry, dry, dry. For example, when you tour in the summertime on the east coast, it's fabulous because there's nothing but humidity, and you can just take deep breaths all day. When you get to the west coast, it's drier. Now you need moisture in your room because the more you take a deep breath in, the drier the air is. You have to kind of know where you are, and what time of the year it is. And when I'm touring, I don't drink. I do water, water, water, and I sleep, sleep, sleep. The only problem you have when you're touring is flying is not your friend because it's dry up there. So, I do a lot of moisturizing before I fly to the show. And lots of water. And tomatoes, you stay away from completely. And nuts, you stay away from.

Really, why nuts?

If you wanna cough faster than anything else in the world, eat some nuts. It gets into your vocal passages when you take a deep breath in.

And tomatoes are acidic, so that could bring on some reflux.

We're in the business of eating late at night, and that acid will come back up and burn your vocal cords. So, you have to prop yourself up at a certain angle so that the food or the acid stays down. Or you may need an Antacid. Either Maalox or Gaviscon. You only learn this when you turn ninety years old. When you're nineteen, you don't care about anything. You can drink all night, do everything wrong. But when you start learning what destroys your range or your vocal cords, you realize they are a delicate muscle just like your hamstring or something else. It'll start scaring you to death.

Anything after the show that keeps your voice in shape?

I just dump two bottles of water right away; just dump it. You gotta hydrate immediately.

Are you doing any warming-down exercises?

Yeah. Again, you go back to the shower. There's all the steam you need in the world, and you just have a little [*does some light trills again*] just to get it to calm back down.

Are there songs where you wonder if your voice will be there that night?

Those early Commodores songs, and the range that was, versus where your voice is now? *Can you hit the top, top note?* No. But we just take it down a half step and play in another key. The worst thing in the world is to try to keep your ego where I can hit the note that I used to hit when I was twenty-one years old. Forget about that.

What was your most embarrassing vocal mishap ever?

[*Laughs*] I think every artist will probably tell you the mishap of life is where you walk out onstage and sing the wrong verse, or can't remember the lyric. But you learn a little trick with that. At the end of the song, you go, "Okay, for all of you that were technical geniuses, so I fucked up," and they go, "Ahhh-hahahaha!" But they love that 'cause now they were there the night you screwed up "Penny Lover" or whatever. But, oh my God, have I done it? Yes. You can't avoid your career without that. You will walk out onstage one day and go, "What's the second verse to that song?" [*Laughs*] But now, we have little gimmicks onstage where somebody can actually whisper in your ear opposed to where you're standin' out there being stupid for four to six bars.

Do you remember a performance where you surprised yourself?

Oh yeah! Let's just talk about any song I've written. There's a moment in time where you're possessed, you're pregnant with that idea, and it goes from just being an idea to where it's actually playing back to you. And there are moments where every song, *every song*, feels like it's been here for the last hundred years, and you go, *Oh my God, that's—that's amazing!* [*Laughs*] It's almost magical. To where I can have something humming in my head, and a couple hours later, it's singing back to me, and actually better in certain cases, than it was humming in my head. That's when you just have to be in awe of the mystical, magical powers of God and the universe.

Speaking of God, I wanna take you back to 1980. The *Heroes* album. And those howls you do at the end of "Jesus Is Love."

Listen. I'm an Episcopalian, okay? If you know anything about the Episcopal faith, and the Catholic faith, we don't deal too much with feelings. We just deal with [*hums in monotone*] "Da-da-da-da-da-duh-da," right? So, I needed a howl. I needed a yell. I needed a scream. It required that. I opened my mouth, and I'll tell you, it was one of those magical moments where even I had to turn around and go, "What was that?" [*Laughs*]

I knew it. There's something in those howls. 'Cause it's not what you normally do.

Truthfully, I never knew I could hit those notes until I hit those notes. The voice doesn't sing, the mind sings. If you just let go and not think about it. If you get out of the way of somebody telling you that's an incorrect way of hitting that note. If you get away from all that, and just deliver what your mind is thinking, your voice will do anything you wanna do. You just have to get away from the handicap, which is your mind. I know there's no logic to me being able to write the songs I'm writing based on training. *There is no training*. Now, if you say, "This is what I heard," and you're not afraid of expressing it that way, then you can write anything you wanna write. But you can't let someone tell you, "You're singing improperly."

Do you have a favorite vocal performance you're really proud of?

"Jesus Is Love" and "Wandering Stranger." Those are the two that I was possessed with. I am squealing notes, not screaming. Go back and listen to "Wandering Stranger," you'll hear what I'm talkin' about. I'm just squealing it out.

It doesn't sound like you're the kind of singer who hates their own voice.

No, I had to make friends with my voice. My job is: you take all your clothes off, and you stand in the mirror. Do you like that person? 'Cause that's what you gotta work with. That's the same with voice. There's a moment in time where you're like, I wanna sing like Sam Cooke, I wanna sing like Prince. And then, one day you go, no, I like singing like Lionel Richie. No matter who else stands in the room with you, you gotta say, no, that's Prince, and I'm Lionel Richie. And you gotta like that person! Because Mick Jagger can't sing like James Brown. It comes out sounding like Mick Jagger. You know? I mean, "You Are," I was trying to sound like Stevie Wonder. Well, I sounded like Lionel Richie. [*Laughter*]

What's changed the most about your voice since you started?

It's all intact, thank God. I guess all entertainers think about the high notes, but the highs aren't that high. If you got enough rest, they'll be there.

If you could duet with one singer—living or dead—who would it be?

Oh my God. McCartney would be the one. I would love to do something with him.

Who are your top five favorite singers of all time?

That's the hardest question you'll ever ask 'cause I'm a fan of all of 'em. [*Sighs hard*] Sam Cooke would be one. Definitely. He was just ridiculous. McCartney would be one. There's so many. Top five is tough. [*Groans*] Man, let me think about that and give you the right ones. I'll send that back to you.

Alright. Last one. If you could ask any singer about their voice, who would it be and what would you ask?

Of course, it would be James Brown. And the question would be, "How the hell did you keep your voice intact for your entire career?" Screaming at the level he was screaming? Unbelievable.

Is he in your top five?

James Brown would be in my top five, always, yeah, put him in. I like that, I like that.

Alright, I'm gonna hold you to two more.

You can hold me to two more.

(Note to Lionel: I'm still waiting, man!)

LEANN RIMES

SOME PEOPLE ARE JUST BORN WITH IT. While so many of us come to our voice through a twisted funhouse of fear, struggle, and hard-fought determination, there are those who are simply touched by God. That's not to say they take their gifts for granted and don't have to work as hard to build a successful career. It simply means that most people aren't considered the second coming of country legend Patsy Cline right out of the gate. Most people don't have their debut album go multi-platinum overnight and win three Grammy Awards. And most people don't have this happen at the age of fourteen.

But most people aren't LeAnn Rimes.

LeAnn has been making jaws drop with her incredible voice since she was a little girl, and this woman is still making us shake our heads in wonder, still nurturing her talents, and still ready to take on whatever challenge comes next.

Just tell her she can't do it. Just root for her to fail. Then, watch what happens.

Who first exposed you to singing?

My mom says that I came out singing. But both my parents were really into music, so there was always music around the house. My dad has tapes of me singing when I was eighteen months old, and you couldn't understand a word I was saying when I was talking, but when I started singing, you could understand clearly. So, it was truly something I came into this world with.

Were you emulating anyone when you started out?

The songs that I was singing along with when I was little were like The Judds, Whitney Houston, Reba [McEntire], and Judy Garland. I listened to her a lot from watching *The Wizard of Oz* a zillion times. My Godmother was into Broadway and showtunes and classical. My dad was into classic rock and country. My mom was into Motown. I kind of got a little bit of everything fed to me from a very early age, but I pulled from different women.

What did you pull from who?

Patsy Cline was such an emoter. I remember listening to her and *feeling* something, like, *Oh, I wanna do that*. Then, as I got older, I would listen to Janis Joplin, and I was like, *Oh, I want that type of freedom*. And Barbra Streisand and Judy Garland, there's such a control to what they did, which is so interesting: to want the freedom of Janis, and the control of Barbra and Judy, and the emotion of Patsy. But I don't think I was ever trying to truly emulate anyone. We all pull from other people, then make it our own.

So, how did you find your own voice?

Oh God, I'm still lookin' for it. I am still developing it in some ways. The authenticity of it. How deeply authentic can I be with my own voice? Finding more truth to it. But I had like crazy pitch my whole life, which I know has been a piece of my gift, and something in me just knew how to express emotion through my voice. And part of my voice is actually understanding what the song is about in order to express it. I remember my dad trying to explain "Fancy" by Reba to me when I was about seven, and I still wanted to sing that song, and no one would let me. [*Laughs*] I'm like, "Why? It's so good."

Did you ever have any vocal training?

Not until my mid-twenties, 'cause I was working a lot. My doctor sent me to this guy in LA a couple of times just to teach me how to warm-up.

Tell me about your first time onstage as a singer. You were a child, right?

I was five. My dance teacher convinced my mother to put me in this song and dance competition, and there was no one in the "six and under" category, so they just lumped me in with the "twelve and under," and thought for sure I wouldn't win. I won the whole event. [*Laughs*] There were so many pissed off mothers. It was not good. That was my first taste of like, *Oh, people may not like the fact that you're good.* It was a really interesting thing to experience as a five-year-old.

Whoa. That's kind of gross.

Yeah, I really saw the worst in people. [*Laughs*] But my dad was there, and he sat me down and said, "Is this something you love? Is this something you wanna do?" It was fun. And it was also the way I probably expressed myself, the way that I couldn't, maybe *as a child*. It all came out through my voice.

Were you nervous or confident up there?

I don't think I've ever been nervous until my early thirties. [*Laughs*] It doesn't happen every time, but what I call nerves is anticipation, really. It's not, *Can I pull this off?* It's more like, *Let's get going. I'm sick of sitting around.* But I'm really glad I started as a child 'cause I went for years and years without questioning anything. Then life happens, and the only thing that started to get to me was the fear of judgement. I've been the best at what I do, and at some point, I was waiting for the other shoe to drop that one time when I'm not. That came from being in the public eye and knowing that our society kinda builds people up to tear them down. Then, social media became a piece of my life, and it was just so easy to instantly attack, or *be* attacked, and that played into things. Now that's outta my system. But yeah, there's some anticipation, for sure.

Do you do vocal warm-ups before shows?

I probably do half an hour of vocal warms-ups. Like fifteen to twenty minutes of scales, and then, I'll put on songs that I like and sing along to them. I definitely don't walk out cold.

Do you have any other rituals before you hit the stage?

I usually meditate and get myself centered and focused. Where this all comes from is my heart, and when my heart is connected, it's a whole different show. So, I really try to focus on connecting with that space in me, and being a conduit for whatever needs to flow through me to flow through. My intention now is so much different than when I was younger. I connect with people so deeply when I walk onstage, it's like, what message needs to be sent? Who needs to hear what I have to say? What song is gonna touch a place in them that they walk out of here feeling a little lighter, or a little more open? I'm walking out to connect in a different way these days.

Is there anything after the show that helps keep your voice in shape?

Sometimes I'll warm-down. It's kind of like scales going from top to bottom.

What situation would require you to warm-down?

There's a point in my voice where if I've sung a lot of high stuff, it almost feels *so* open that it's really hard for me to get back down and control the lower register of my voice. If it feels like I'm having trouble controlling that lower register, I'll start to warm-down a bit.

How are you taking care of your voice on the road?

To me, it's more mental than it is anything. I don't like to overthink it. But if it's really dry, like when we're touring in the winter, I'll have a humidifier around. Mucinex is always a great thing if I am feeling a little under the weather, just to get mucus off the vocal cords. I'll do a Neti Pot if I'm really stuffy. Hydration is key. I drink a lot of water. At least a gallon a day.

When you start getting sick, what do you do?

The doctor. [*Laughs*] I up my Vitamin C when I'm on the road, which is key. I take a lot of supplements too, just on a daily basis to keep myself as well as I can. You know, there's always steroids when we don't have a voice, which I've had to do before. It's not my favorite thing, and sometimes I will make the call not to. I'd rather cancel a show and come back full voice than not. It's really important for me, especially when you're a singer and people are there *to hear your voice*. There's no tracks backing me. There's no 20 percent mic, 80 percent track going on. I do everything I can to be able to walk out sick, but if there's half my voice there...my songs aren't easy to sing, so I need that energy, and I need that voice to be able to carry me.

Are there songs where you wonder if your voice will be there that night?

If I'm well, no, not at all.

Are there songs where you've had to adjust the key live?

Oh yeah, especially when I'm sick. I mean, there's some songs I did when I was really young that maybe we've dropped the key a half step now: I joke that my balls dropped when I was in my teens. [*Laughter*] At some point, my lower register came, *which I love*.

Yeah, that must be wild, when you have to sing songs you recorded as a kid.

I had this thought drilled into me that I had to make it sound exactly like the record when people come to see it. But my dear friend, Darrell Brown, who's my manager and creative partner, was like, "Don't hit that note if you don't want to! Just don't do it if it's stressing you out tonight." It was good for me because I finally let go of that, and it freed me up to sing some other cool stuff. Starting so young, there's this box you think you have to fit in. As you get older, you realize there's a lot more freedom than what I thought.

Your voice was so round and warm and mature for your age that people were comparing you to Patsy Cline. You became the youngest person to ever win a Grammy for your performance of "Blue," which you recorded when you were thirteen, and you take home Best New Artist! Did that freak you out like, "What if I morph into having a grizzled, old smoker's voice when I'm twenty?"

It's funny because I hit puberty really young. *Really young*. Like if my voice was gonna change, it would've changed by fourteen. But as I got older, there was a different tone that started to come out. I also think that has to do with a different emotional approach too. There was this richness and wisdom that came out that I didn't have at fourteen. Yes, it was round, and yes, it was warm, but to me, it sounds thin compared to how I sing these days. It's actually gotten better. Thank God, it hasn't gone the other direction! [*Laughs*]

What was your most embarrassing vocal mishap ever?

I was eight, and it was *Star Search*. It was my second time on the show, and I did "You Lie" by Reba. They pre-record all the music for the show so, when they did, it was like two or three beats off the original way it was done, and it totally threw me for a loop. I was just so scared 'cause I didn't have it in my head, and you could just see it written all across my face. Where I would normally do this break thing in the song, my voice cracked. That led to me losing, and then, *that* led to a place called Johnnie High's Country Music Revue in Fort Worth, Texas. I performed there every Saturday night from the time I was seven 'til the time I signed a record deal at eleven. My dad wanted me to sing that same song *there* the following week to get my confidence back. And I forgot the words.

***Oh no!* [Laughs]**

Yeah, that was like a one-two punch of, *UGH. Okay. That sucks.* So, now when I forget the words, I just come out and say it. "I don't know what I'm singing right now, hold on a minute." I have no shame in my game when it comes to forgetfulness. Usually, they're yelling out lyrics and I'm like, "Thank you." It doesn't happen often, but when it does it's like, *What's happening right now?!*

Do you remember a performance where you surprised yourself?

My dad got the "Blue" demo when I was ten or eleven, but threw it in the trash because the demo was horrible. It did not sound like the same song. He left, and I dug it out of the trash, and listened to it, and that's when I added that whole yodel thing at the beginning. He came back and was like, "Oh, the song's not so bad!" That was just a kid's creativity and intuition, and that song would have never been if I wouldn't have done that.

That's amazing.

Yeah, sometimes things come out, and you're like, "Whoa, that was awesome!" There's a song on the last record called "Long Live Love," and we were in the studio, and Darrell's like, "Improv here!" We were trying to fit a yodel in and whatever came out of my mouth was so cool, we were all like, "Whoa! What was that?" It sounded like this Indian chant, really hypnotizing thing. I'm glad that was on tape. [*Laughs*]

How are you with hearing your own voice?

I've gotten a lot better about it. I had to come to terms with, and understand, that these are moments captured in time, and that's who I was, and where I was at that moment. You can always listen back and say, "Oh, I'd sing that differently now," or "I could've done *that* better," but I listen from a different perspective these days.

Do you have a favorite vocal performance you're really proud of?

This is not coming from an egotistical place at all, but most of them. If I'm fully connected—body, mind, heart, soul, spirit, it's all there—and I'm on pitch, then I'm proud of what I'm doing. When I get lost in those moments, that's when life is good.

I recently spoke with Clive Davis about Whitney Houston's rendition of "The Star-Spangled Banner." I feel like that song was written to test your mettle as a singer, and you've been doing it since you were nine! I'm curious about that experience because my assumption would be that you're walking into a pretty unforgiving sports arena, full of people who are amped up, and maybe even secretly rooting for you to fail. And when you pull it off, they go nuts. Is that accurate?

[*Laughs*] That fuels me. That fuels me like no other. And, yes, people kind of *are* waiting on that, and I know that's not gonna happen. But yeah, I learned it from Whitney. That was the ultimate National Anthem, and I'm like, *I can do that*. And I put my own spin on it after listening to her sing it. So many, many deep bows to her.

Deep bows to you, after hearing her sing that to casually go, "I can do that."

I know, that was my kid brain! That's still very much in me, like, *Oh, I can do that!*

That's why you can.

You know? It's taken me a long way in life. [*Laughter*]

What's changed the most about your voice since you started?

The depth of it. The way I can convey an emotion in a song. It's like, what's the emotion of the song? What does it make me feel? How can I feel that as deep as I can possibly feel it? And how can I take others on that journey? That's kind of how I approach music. Whether that be the joyest of joys, or the lowest of sadness, I want to reach into people in the places they don't normally touch. That's what I have fun with now. And I think that life experience has definitely given me the ability to be able to do that.

If you could duet with one singer—living or dead—who would it be?

Only one? [*Laughs*] Oh shit! I can't do this!

No, you're the girl who can do anything, remember?

I think everyone, including myself, would love to sing with Patsy Cline if she were still around.

When I interviewed Stevie Nicks, she said her duet with you is her favorite she's ever done. And she also said you're the best singer she's ever sung with.

Whaaaat? She's so cool. What a cool woman who's been through everything in life and still brings it to the table. When you're looking at her singing, she's so interesting. She was really watching me sing. Being in a band that sings harmonies, she loves getting intimate with your tone and exactly where you're placing things. She would just face me in the studio and really intensely watch me. That was one of my favorite experiences ever with another artist 'cause she really wanted to be there, so I love her to death.

Who are your top five favorite singers of all time?

Whitney Houston, Patsy Cline, Aretha Franklin, Steven Tyler. There's so many. Let's go with Janis. She was so unafraid to make whatever sound she wanted to make. It didn't have to sound pretty. She just reached in and let whatever come out that needed to be expressed.

If you could ask any singer about their voice, who would it be and what would you ask?

Oh my God. Well, let's go with Steven Tyler. "How the hell do you do that screech thing all the time and not lose it?" [*Mimics Tyler's famous, staccato vocal riff*] "Yak-ak-ak-ak-ak-ak-ak-ak-kow!" We honored him the other night at a Grammy event, and I'm watching him onstage, at his age, doing this crazy ass thing with his voice, like, "How are you not hoarse when you walk off every night?" So, yeah. I'm amazed at that man. He's still got it.

CHRIS ROBINSON

OH MY LORDY, I VIVIDLY REMEMBER The Black Crowes releasing their debut album, *Shake Your Money Maker*, in 1990. I can still hear "Twice as Hard" right now and have the same thought I did back then: "That's it right there." You just know the real thing when you hear it. Chris, his brother Rich, and the rest of the band had released one of the greatest debut albums of all time. I mean, "Twice as Hard" was one thing. But then you got "Jealous Again," "She Talks to Angels," "Sister Luck," "Hard to Handle," and "Seeing Things."

And that was just the first record.

Since then, The Crowes have gone on to release one classic album after the next while Chris has released some amazing solo records as well. And all of it has one thing in common: it's some of the best damn soul singing you'll ever hear.

This conversation took place right before The Black Crowes announced they were finally reuniting after years of discontent between the brothers. I'm not saying that what you are about to read had anything to do with it, but you be the judge.

Who first exposed you to singing?

My father was like a be-bop, rock 'n' roll singer in the late '50s. Had a couple Top 40 records under his name, Stan Robinson. Then, in the early '60s, he immersed himself in folk music, was signed to ABC/Paramount Records, and made a few singles as a folk duo called The Appalachians. By the time I'd come along in '66, my dad had left his dreams and ambitions behind and was living another life. You know what a Schmatta is? He's in the garment business.

Yeah, you ever see *Save the Tiger* with Jack Lemmon?

Yeah, it's like Willy Loman, *Death of a Salesman*. He really hated when I brought that up. But he would pull out the old Martin E28 and play on the weekends, and that's the first real like, *Oh, this music's alive!* Music in the house. Someone singing. It's real intimate. I realized a lot of kids at my school didn't have dads sitting around on a Saturday morning, singing train wreck songs and murder ballads. [*Laughs*] My dad was a good singer. He had a very good, quality voice. But I'm Southern too, so people are always singin'.

Was your father the one who made you feel you could do this?

My father told me I was completely talentless. Couldn't sing, ever, when I wanted to sing with the family. I couldn't sing the right harmony, he'd tell me to shut up. Yeah, it's sad. I was fairly estranged from my father as an adolescent and as an adult. Those are his hang ups and his resentments, I guess. When we made it big, I'm sure it was a real trip for him, but, I'm sure he was proud. But initially, I don't know if it was jealousy that he didn't make it, or didn't want it. Either way, I was never encouraged to be a vocalist.

Who inspired you to be one?

Music's always been such a huge gravitational force. To this weird, scrawny, dyslexic kid from the deep south, music was a place with no dogma, no judgment. It was free. By the time I'm a teenager, punk rock was something that was an open doorway too. Like the energy. You don't have to be good. I would say R.E.M. was where I could put all the ideas together. *Oh, you can be in a band that's like art-driven that has '60s elements, but in a modern band?* I sing nothing like Michael Stipe, but at that time, that sort of delivery, and those murky, muddled, strange images and lyrics.

Were you emulating anyone when you started?

Otis Redding looms large in there. Sam & Dave. And my voice being a little higher, I was really into the female singers: Tina Turner, Ann Peebles. Between The Rolling Stones and the Faces and all the funk, soul, and R&B, those are the people I was emulating. I started The Black Crowes because no one wanted to do it, and no one could do it. The sort of "Blackness" in my voice or that "soul" sound is all the records I listened to: Sly & The Family Stone, Parliament-Funkadelic, even Prince. But, growing up, I felt if I start sounding like that then I'm perpetra-tin'. [*Laughs*] Fuck it, there's no rules.

How did you find your own voice?

Just throw yourself into the void. There was no brass ring of fame and money. It was just to be doing it. I come from a time and place where status wasn't really a part of it, you know. It was about pure expression and pure energy, about wanting to be a part of something that's counter to what everyone else was doing in *my* world. But the harder the music got, and the funkier it got, the more I had to find that kind of dynamic in my voice. The guitars are loud so you have to start singing louder. It's truly rock 'n' roll stuff, man. I'm probably the worst person to talk to 'cause for years I said, "One thing I never think about is the singing, I just do it." It's all instinctive.

So, no vocal training ever?

Never. I have people come up to me at my daughter's school or my son's soccer game and they go, "My daughter wants to sing," and I go, "Don't send 'em to a vocal coach." [*Laughs*] "Don't do it." Lots of people can sing, but to me, it's never been about hitting the right notes. It's a visceral connection. That's why I never really sing it the same. It's always been representative of freedom.

Are you nervous or confident before you perform?

I felt oddly comfortable onstage pretty early on.

Do you do vocal warm-ups before shows?

When *Shake Your Money Maker* started, I had some little scales that I ran. We were doing six nights out of seven. First tour, I had fifteen nights in a row.

No, sir.

I had some bad nights. And a hard time with my stamina. Your vocal cords are just muscles like anything else. If you were in a race car for the first time, you would throw up after a couple laps, you know? [*Laughs*] You don't have your endurance built up.

Well, how do you take care of your voice?

I don't. At all. [*Laughter*] I don't even think about it. I just do what I do. You just sing.

So, you don't stop talking on your day off or anything like that?

No. You've heard me sing. *What am I, American Idol bullshit?* I don't give a fuck. I wanna sing good, and it's important, but I'm not like a pop singer. I'm a folk singer. [*Laughs*] I'm a blues singer. A little more rough 'n' ready. I don't think Otis Redding did vocal warm-ups! And you don't have to dig too deep to realize I know Otis Redding. He's the greatest soul singer of all. *Still*, the guy that I put on, and I just...I'm in a puddle. There's a lot of great singers, man, but the Big O, he was givin' it to ya.

Without question. You have any rituals before you hit the stage?

No, just super laid back.

Is there anything after the show that helps keep your voice healthy?

I drink tons of water. All day. That's one of the only real health things that I've done without even thinking about it. Forever. I've just always drank a lot of water. When I was young, we would drink beers or whatever, but alcohol doesn't really help with the singing.

With The Crowes, were there songs where you wondered if your voice would be there that night?

Oh, of course, of course. The chorus in "Cursed Diamond" is super high up there. Songs like "Virtue and Vice" or "Twice as Hard." But we could drop it down a half a key or a full step. Just a half step would help me after twenty-five years of doing it. [*Laughs*]

What was your most embarrassing vocal mishap ever?

Completely shit faced in Pensacola, Florida in the mid-'90s. Oh, worst, worst. I'm so happy they didn't have social media, because at the time, I'm sure there would've been videos and stuff. But people didn't want their money back, they were just worried about me. [*Cracks up*] Just got up there too drunk. Our opening band was the Dirty Dozen Brass Band from New Orleans. They drove up with like thirty pounds of crawfish and beer. We just partied before the show and it was like, *Whoop*, didn't put the brakes on.

Do you have a favorite vocal performance you're really proud of?

Maybe something like "Oh Josephine" on *Warpaint*. I don't really think about it like that too much, 'cause once you sing it, that's just that one time. Being a live musician, any song I've written is gonna always change. Adam [MacDougall] plays a little something on the piano and could make me change where I'm putting the melody. I want those things to show themselves as they're happening. One spark is another spark is another spark. It's just about being available to the people, and the material, and the vibes around you. You're always looking for the moments that make it magic.

How are you with hearing your own voice?

I'm super cool with that. It's just that it's the past. It's like, "What's next?"

Do you remember a performance where you did something that surprised you?

The last verse of "Sometimes Salvation." That just came out of me. I didn't write it. That would've been one of those things, like, *Wow, where did that come from?*

In my opinion, you have one of the greatest screams in rock 'n' roll history.

I used to! I can't even do it anymore. [*Laughs*] My God, it hurts.

But you're in the pantheon of the greats.
Tina Turner had the best one of all time.

She's insane. But "Bad Luck Blue Eyes Goodbye" and "Sometimes Salvation" have some screams at the end that must have drawn blood.
Well, that's the Joe Cocker, you know? You gotta do "A Little Help from My Friends." I think that's probably where that comes from, besides all the soul music where those kinds of inflections are. That kind of music would bring out that thing of, what color do we need here? And that color is what I would *feel*. Once I got the freedom to not have a producer sit there and tell me what to do, I had the freedom to let it all go. I needed that.

"Blackberry" has some screams that would make James Brown proud.
I'm from Georgia, man, so we got James, Ray Charles, Little Richard, Otis, Percy Sledge. There's a lot of people from Georgia that can sing.

"Cursed Diamond" has one coming out of the solo that's completely insane. Do you remember that one?
Steve Marriott could do that. Robert Plant had a good scream too.

STOP MENTIONING OTHER PEOPLE! YOU'RE DOING THIS!
Yeah, yeah!

Those screams sound like they're tearing straight through your throat. How do you pull those off without blowing your voice out?
I did it every day. That's when I was young, man. You're young, you know? [*Cracks up*] I was twenty-three years old and I had to open for Robert Plant and Steven Tyler, back-to-back, as a young man. Robert was forty-two years old. Shit, I'm eight years older than he was when I met him. And he couldn't really do some of that stuff anymore, and I would be like, *wow*, not really realizing like...*fuck*...*time*...It's funny now, Robert is a person I really look up to as an artist, as a singer, and as a person in this industry light years ahead of what some of the other people from his generation are doing.

When you guys went on tour with Jimmy Page doing Zeppelin songs, did you have to adjust the key there?
Yeah, it's Led Zeppelin. I can't sing like Robert. I'm not that kind of singer. I had to find my own voice in those songs that still had respect for the blueprint, and the piece that everyone knows, yet get my own vibes in there.

What was the hardest one for you to sing?
I *hated* singing "Celebration Day." [*Laughs*] Every time. [*Sings in a high register*] "My my my, I'm so happy. I'm gonna join the band!" I was like, *ugh*, I couldn't even wrap my head around it.

What's changed the most about your voice since you started?

I probably lost some range. But the quality of my voice is better, the control I have, how I want the sound to translate to what I'm singing, the imagery, the melody. I think it's better. When I listen back to stuff from the mid to early '90s, my voice is only doing one thing in a way, and now my voice can do so many different things.

Well, you've done the higher, crazy stuff. But your solo performances are coming off just as soulful, they're just not as loud.

Exactly. If we can make a soulful connection, that's all there is. That's it in a nutshell.

If you could duet with one singer—living or dead—who would it be?

Bonnie Raitt would be amazing. Ann Peebles would be another one. Emmylou Harris would be fuckin' ridiculous. Yeah, those big three pop into my mind.

Who are your top five favorite singers of all time?

Oh my God. Well, Otis is at the top. And then, I have to put Garry Shider from Parliament-Funkadelic, and Glenn Goins. I would put Freddie Stone in there, Sly Stone's guitar player. And probably Jerry Garcia. And Bob Dylan's one of my favorite singers of all time.

If you could ask any singer about their voice, who would it be and what would you ask?

I would ask that guy from the Crash Test Dummies, remember that song? [*Sings low and mumbles*] "MMM MMM MMM..." "What the fuck are you doing? It's freaking me out. Baritone voices freak me out. Why're you doing that? Stop it." That should be only for The Temptations, you know what I mean?

SMOKEY ROBINSON

"BABY, BABY, DON'T CRY. BABY, BABY, HERE'S WHY."
A man with too many hit singles and Grammy Awards to count. A Rock & Roll Hall of Fame inductee who was also awarded the Library of Congress Gershwin Prize for his lifetime contribution to popular music. But forget all that a second and think about this: If it wasn't for Smokey Robinson, there may never have been any Motown music in this world. Smokey and Motown founder, Berry Gordy, meeting exactly when they did gave us Stevie Wonder, Marvin Gaye, The Supremes, the Four Tops, The Temptations, and so many other legends.

But it was Smokey & The Miracles, fueled by Smokey's incredible songwriting and iconic voice, that helped start it all. And thank God he did, because a world without Motown ain't a world worth living in.

A short while after this interview, I had the good fortune of directing Smokey in a commercial for Music Gives to St. Jude Kids. We ended up traveling together, and I got the chance to watch him out in the world. And here's what I saw: Everyone he came in contact with, whoever wanted a picture, a hug, or a word, Smokey gave it to them with an open heart. It's not a burden to him, it just comes naturally, like shutting down a bunch of my questions. And the process of singing itself.

Who first exposed you to singing?

I grew up in a home where there was nothing but music all day long. Every single solitary day. Music of every type. Gospel to jazz to classical to blues, it was being played there.

Who inspired you to become a singer?

I wanted to be a singer by the time I was four years old.

Really?

Yeah, I always wanted to be a singer.

Were you emulating anybody when you started out?

I don't know that I was necessarily trying to sound like anybody, but I had several guys who were my singing idols. My number one singing idol was Jackie Wilson. After him was Sam Cooke. And then, there was Ray Charles, Clyde McPhatter, Frankie Lymon, and a guy named Nolan Strong who had a group called The Diablos out of Detroit.

How did you find your own voice?

I just had my voice. I was always a high singer even in high school. When I was in the choir, I sang second soprano and first alto.

Did you ever do any vocal training?

No, I've never done that.

Are you nervous or confident before you perform?

I'm nervous every time, man. That never stops. When I'm standing in the wings, waiting to go on, there's *always* that anticipation, butterflies in the stomach, until I get out there and sing four or five notes, and then I'm cool. Because you never know what's gonna happen. You can't take it for granted that you're gonna go out there and be great. You just go out there, do your job, and hope the people enjoy it.

Do you do vocal warm-ups before shows?

Not really, man. I sing a little bit at soundcheck.

How do you take care of your voice on the road?

They got all these myths about singers: "Drink some hot tea with lemon," "Take some cough drops." The best thing in the world for your voice is rest and taking care of yourself normally. I know that this is the only body I'm gonna get. This is the only voice I'm gonna get. So, I work out, and I stretch *every* morning. I've been doing yoga for thirty-five years, man. And I used to run marathons, but my knees gave out. Just take care of yourself. That's the best thing for your voice.

Do you have any rituals before you go onstage though?

I pray before every show that God will bless us, and let us be able to entertain the people, and do a good show in his name.

Is there anything after the show that helps keep your voice in shape?

You mean directly after the show?

Yeah, some people hum, some people…

I have no idea who does that, man. [*JTG cracks up*] I don't do nothin'. I go back to my dressing room, I change my clothes, I go to my hotel, I look at some TV 'til I go to sleep. That's what I do.

Do you have songs where you wonder if your voice will be there that night?

You know what? There's a lotta songs. Like sometimes on nights when my voice is tired or something like that. But over the years, you learn how to play your instrument so, I know what I can do on a certain night and what I can't do, vocally. I just go by that because I've been doing this for…way, way, way before your parents were born. [*Laughter*] If there's a certain song where I need a little more to reach that note, I'll just sing another note.

What's your most embarrassing vocal mishap ever?

Shit, man. No, no, no, you can't ask me that. I've been doin' this too long for you to ask me that. [*Chuckles*] You wanna hear the top *thousand*?

Yeah, gimme a good one!

I discard that, man. Those are not memories I wanna keep. [*More laughter*]

Do you remember a performance where you surprised yourself?

It's a night-by-night adventure, you know what I mean?

Do you have a favorite vocal performance you're really proud of?

No, babe. No, I don't.

Well, it's safe to say that you have the most iconic falsetto of all time. But I'm curious how you hit upon using your falsetto as your main singing voice?

Well, I appreciate you, man. But that's a myth. I don't use it as my main singing voice. I just have a real high voice.

Is that right?

Yes. Most of the songs that I sing, I'm singing in my natural—unless I go, *[in high falsetto]* "Ohhhhh!" or something like that. I'm not singing in falsetto. I don't know how I got that reputation.

Wow. Smokey, that is a startling revelation. But there is something about your voice that I feel gets overlooked, and that's your vibrato. For me, that's one of the most mystifying things about the vocal cords as an instrument.
Yeah.

How do you have such control of your vibrato? I'm thinking of songs from your *Timeless Love* record especially.
Thank you very much, my brother. I don't try to control it necessarily. When I'm singing, I'm just tryin' to feel what I'm singing. See, I never considered myself to be a *great* singer. You know, *I feel. I'm a feeler*. So, I feel what I'm singing.

But when I listen to you sing with that vibrato, and it's so in tune, and it's so in control, that's just naturally comin' outta you?
That's just my natural voice, man.

You are blessed by the Lord above, my friend.
I agree with that. I'm so blessed because I get a chance to live my life, earning my living, doing what I absolutely love. And I love singing. And people pay me. [*Laughs*] I can't beat that. Anybody who gets a chance to live their life doing their love—it doesn't have to be entertainment—it's a blessing.

How are you with hearing your own voice?
Are you kidding, man? [*Laughs*] No, I don't hate listening to my own voice.

You shouldn't!
But I could have a record that's been out for years and I'll listen to it, and I'm critiquing what I coulda done right there. *I coulda done this or I coulda done that*, you know? Especially after you've sang them live for so many years. The performance is never the same as the record.

What's changed the most about your voice since you started?
My register. But I did that on purpose. When I left The Miracles, I used to sing really, really high on all the records. I left with the intention of never coming back to show business again in that light. I was just gonna write songs for other people, produce some records of other people. I was vice president of Motown and that was gonna be the rest of my life. I did that for about three and a half years, and went crazy, okay? So, when I decided that I was gonna come back, I said, "First of all, I wanna play some places I have not been playing: Las Vegas, Atlantic City, Tahoe. I wanna play nightclubs, places like that." The Miracles and I played stadiums, so I wanted to change my format. I wanted to be able to sing in Vegas. So, I dropped my keys down. I could still reach those notes if I wanted, but I don't want to. I want to have another sound.

So, you're cool with adjusting the keys live?

Yeah, yeah, yeah. It's to be psychologically comfortable 'cause I just don't want to be singing way up in the stratosphere the way I used to when I was a kid. I don't want to sing like that anymore.

Your voice seems to have grown stronger and more soulful with age.

I was gonna say that too. It's much stronger than it used to be, man.

Because a lot of singers, as they grow older, can lose things. It seems like you're *gaining* things. Do you feel that?

Well, I appreciate that too, my brother, 'cause I'm trying to. But, like I said, it all starts with taking care of yourself. Remember that, man. *Remember that*. It all starts with taking care of yourself. Because your voice, your vocal cords, your larynx, and all that stuff, is a part of your body. They're a part of you. So, when you take care of you, you're encompassing all of that.

I can already feel you trying to buck me on this, but I'm asking anyway. If you could duet with one singer—living or dead—who would it be?

Ohhh, boy, now once again, you've posed one of those questions that I have no answer for, man.

Who are your top five favorite singers of all time? Can you gimme that?

Come on, man.

[*Cracks up*] I ask everybody!

Well, my answer to that is you can't ask me that. [*Laughter*]

Alright, last one, Smoke. Make it count! If you could ask any singer about their voice, who would it be and what would you ask?

It would probably be an opera singer. Andrea Bocelli, somebody like that. Especially the tenors who are singing out loud, and their natural voice is in the stratosphere. I'd ask them how they maintain it.

JOHNNY RZEZNIK

"AND I DON'T WANT THE WORLD TO SEE ME, 'CAUSE I DON'T THINK THAT THEY'D UNDERSTAND."

I mean, can Johnny Rzeznik write a chorus? It's always the combination of that perfect hook combined with Johnny's heartfelt vocal tone that has given the Goo Goo Dolls such an enduring catalog. Some voices just feel good to sing along with.

Rzeznik and [bassist/vocalist] Robby Takac formed Goo Goo Dolls in Buffalo, New York in 1986. Since then, the band has had nineteen top 10 singles, and written some of the biggest hits of the '90s: "Name," "Broadway," "Slide," "Black Balloon," and "Iris," which held the number one spot for eighteen weeks on the Billboard Hot 100. Eighteen weeks!

The band have also been amazing supporters of St. Jude, always seeking out new and exciting ways to donate their time and money to the kids and families at the hospital. And all that makes singing along with John feel even that much better.

Who first exposed you to singing?

Well, my mother was a musician. Not professionally—she was a schoolteacher—but she played the flute, she played the piano. She was like a crazy Renaissance kind of woman, so music was always in the house. Then, I went to a Catholic school, and we had to take music class where you'd sing along with the teacher. I hope they still do that in school. That was the first place I sang, and then, of course, you'd have to sing in church. Otherwise, they'd poke you in the back with a stick. I also remember listening to my sister's records all the time, and singing along with them. They had this Rolling Stones compilation called *Hot Rocks*, which everybody in the world had, and I remember singing along to "Satisfaction" at seven years old, and just thinkin' it was the coolest thing I'd ever heard.

It seems like it took you a second to really wanna do it professionally though.

I didn't bother singing for a long time. Then, we were recording our second album, and I'd gotten drunk enough to say to Robby, "Let me try to sing this one song." It was called "Up Yours." I went up to the microphone and sang it. And he was like, "Wow, man, you should sing!" I don't know if he regrets that now, or if he's okay with it. [*Laughs*]

So, that's the track on the album?

Yeah, we put the song on the album. And I started to gradually gain more confidence.

Were you emulating anyone when you started out?

The guy I was probably trying to emulate the most would've been Rod Stewart or somebody like that. But the voice that came out of my mouth was kind of the voice I had. You're always imitating two or three people, and then your own voice grows out of that.

When I hear "You Know What I Mean," I'm like, "That's Johnny." You know how everyone has their distinct sound? That's the classic you.

I forgot about that song. I really like that song.

Did you ever have any vocal training?

Around our third record, we were working with a producer named Armand John Petri, and he told me that I was gonna have to learn some technique if I was gonna survive and actually sing better than I was. I needed help with my pitch, which I still, you know, we all need help with our pitch. So, he started teaching me.

What did he teach you?

How to breathe from my diaphragm. He showed me how to practice scales to get better pitch. And he had a friend who gave singing lessons, so I went to her. But singing lessons are so expensive, it's crazy. I took a few lessons, and brought my little recorder, and recorded them so I could do them over and over again. I didn't take any other lessons until we did *A*

Boy Named Goo. I started to study singing because I was always losing my voice and blowing it out.

What did you learn from your studies?

More emphasis on the mechanics. I never wanted to learn any stylistic things. I wanted to maintain the character and the attitude of what I was doing, but I didn't want to lose my voice. And I wanted to extend my range. When I moved out to Los Angeles, I worked with Eric Vetro, mostly learning survival techniques. It's about practicing what you learn. Now, with YouTube and the internet, there's a lot of really good stuff out there, but it's about keeping your voice active and practicing. A teacher named Dave Stroud has an app called SingPro, and it's exercises I do driving in my car, or every night before we go on.

So, tell me the vocal routines you're doing before shows.

It's a combination of David Stroud's techniques and Eric Vetro's techniques. I highly recommend both. You do ascending and descending scales, and lip trills, and then different humming of the vowel sounds. Then, look this guy up if you've never heard of him. His name's Ingo Titze, and he's like a vocal scientist. He does these exercises where you take a small drinking straw, and you vocalize through the straw. [*Hums scales*] It really clears up your voice if it's tired. You can find him on YouTube, and it's really interesting.

Are you nervous or confident before you perform?

There's still times right before I go onstage that I'm a little nervous and I have to run out there. If I don't, I'm afraid I'm gonna turn around and run in the other direction. I get up in front of people and I sing my songs, and I really want them to love them, and I really want to connect with these people. When there's songs that people don't like, it hurts a little, but you know, you keep going. It's really strange doing what we do because in one sense you have to be incredibly vulnerable and honest and in touch with yourself at all levels. And then, when you go out into the world to do it, you have to be incredibly tough because you are gonna be met with resistance, discouragement, bad nights. I've had hundreds of beer bottles thrown at me. [*Laughs*] But, every time someone told me I couldn't do it, or "Fuck you," or "You suck," it just made me wanna do it more, and made me wanna do it better.

How do you take care of your voice on the road?

I get a little raw after six weeks, but I do my best to stay away from any steroids because they're terrible for you, and eventually you're gonna hurt yourself with that. If your vocal cords are inflamed, it's because of something you're doing, so, stop doing that. If it means you can't sing for a couple of days, well, on your days off, you gotta shut up. I sit in my room, I shut up. I text people. I don't drink or smoke. You gotta drink a lot of water, and make sure you exercise. It's a lot of survival skills because I'm not Tony Bennett. I wish I could be that guy. So, any kind of sprints, high intensity interval training—I don't wanna get too wonky about it.

No, dude, get as wonky as you want!

Well, it's all about being physical. The more lung capacity I have, and the more control I have over my diaphragm, is important. Doing your diaphragmatic breathing and strengthening your core. The stronger you are at the core of your being, the better you're gonna sing, and the longer you're gonna be able to sing. The most important thing, before any formal training, was I heard myself sing and went, *Okay, this is who I am*. Each person's voice is like their fingerprint. It's important to understand what makes you unique. Then, if you need help to develop the physical skills to make that soulful part of yourself come out, that's where the technical stuff comes in.

Do you have any other rituals before you hit the stage?

I stand on the side of the stage before I go on and the intro to the show will be playing. I just tell myself how lucky I am to still be here. I know that sounds corny, but it's the honest to God truth. Dude, if I lose my gratitude, I'm done. I had a lot of years of my life where I was so ungrateful. I wasn't an asshole about it, but I was just sorta, "Yeah, yeah, whatever, whatever..."

What changed for you?

A few years ago, something metaphysical slapped me in the head and said, "Don't you know how lucky you are? You get to do this." Just stayin' in that frame of mind keeps me sober, keeps me happy, helps me keep my friends. [*Laughs*] I mean, I've never been in the biggest band in the world, but...

[*Bursts out laughing*] What're you talking about?

We had a lot of big songs, but we were never playing stadiums like U2.

I guess it's all relative, but there was a point in time where you couldn't go anywhere in America—probably the world—without hearing your songs.

Yeah, that was awesome. I'm really grateful for that, man, but we never got to that iconic status. Very few people do. I know a lot of guys who never got to that place and they're pissed about it. But I'm just happy to be where I'm at.

You guys have written some iconic songs. Just to have written such iconic music, and then, to still be able to perform at the level you're performing and making a living, is huge. Especially when you think of the bands that dropped off.

Are you kidding me? Oh my God! 'Cause it could have went south. I always credit Robby with this: Robby was the guy who kept the band together, no matter how shitty things got. Before we got a break, we were traveling around in a van, sleeping on people's floors for ten years. I was married, and was like, "Listen, there's a certain cut off. If we're not making a living, I gotta stop this, I gotta go to school. I wanna have a family, ya know?" He was always the guy, whenever I'd go, "I'm done, I quit." Now, I still have the band. I lost the wife, but I still have the band. [*Laughs*] I think I did okay with the band. But the thing is, we all get our turn, right? And we've had a long turn, and we've done really well, man. It's been great. But we got off the subject.

This *is* the subject. Everything it takes to do this.
What do you do? What do you do for your voice?

I'm learning a lot from these interviews, but right now, I'm a monk on show days. Even the night before, I watch what I'm eating, try not to drink whiskey...
Don't ever drink whiskey. [*Laughs*] That's my other advice: Don't. Drink. Whiskey. Because if you start refluxin' on whiskey, you can knock your voice out for a month. Oh my God, I have a very bad habit. People have commented on it, but it helps me a lot. I chew gum when I sing 'cause it keeps my mouth wet. It's gotta be a certain kind of gum though. It can't have milk sugar in it 'cause that gives you phlegm.

So, what are you doing, just storing it in your cheek as your singing?
Yeah. I also keep some Fisherman's Friend [cough drops and lozenges] on the side of the stage too. Whatever you can do to thin out the phlegm and keep your mucus as thin as possible. "Don't forget to keep your mucus thin." I can't believe I'm talking about this shit! I don't think I've ever talked about this stuff with anybody except a vocal coach.

[*Laughs*] You do anything after the show to keep your voice in shape?
I try to keep quiet. And the key is sleep, man. Sleep, sleep, sleep. We generally travel by bus after the gig, so I get my bunk all cozy. I bring my pillow from home. [*Laughs*] And we got a really good driver that kind of rocks me to sleep.

Are there songs where you wonder if your voice will be there that night?
Oh, every time I gotta hit that high note in "Iris," I'm like, *Aww shit!*

Lionel Richie and I were just talking about "Truly." He said when he wrote it, he was like, "Oh no, what did I just do to myself for the rest of my life?" And I was thinkin', I bet John's got the same thing in "Iris."
It's amazing! Oh yeah, it's always that note. If I can knock it out two, three times in the bathroom right before I go out onstage, you know? [*Laughs*]

That's exactly what he said!
Right! You hit it two or three times and you're like, "Alright, I'm good." I had to really unscrew my head because there was a time I sang "Iris," and I didn't hit that note with a huuuge audience, and something happened. I got caught up in my own head. Every time I went to sing that note, I started getting scared—*You're not gonna hit it, you're not gonna hit it*. So, I started cheating it down. Some nights I'll still cheat it down if I don't think I can hit it.

You mean, the melody?

The melody, yeah. I'll just sing it down instead of up. [*Sings the chorus to "Iris" with a lower melody*] Like that. Or I'd stick the microphone out into the audience. [*Laughter*]

Are there songs where you have to adjust the key live?

I have in the past. There's nothing wrong with lowering the key to a song if it helps you perform it better, if it can give you a more confident, consistent performance every single night. You can't forget when you're a singer: you're there to bring it to the people. They don't give a shit about your problems. You're there to take their problems away from them and let them have a good time. Is the majority of the audience gonna know you slipped it a half step down? Nobody is ever gonna know. All they know is that you're there bringin' it as hard as you can to them. That's what you gotta do. That's what it takes. Every night. You adjust the key as long as you can keep the emotion in the song. That's the most important thing: getting the emotion across to the audience so that they connect. The only reason to sing is to connect.

What was your most embarrassing vocal mishap ever?

[*Laughs*] We wanted to do a cover of a Depeche Mode song, "Somebody." It's a beautiful love song. But if you're not an English new wave guy, you've got no business singin' that song. I got done doing my vocal takes, went into the control room, and said, "Play it back for me." The guy played about fifteen seconds, and I was like, "Get rid of it. Nope. Not happenin'." My voice was so inappropriate for that song. I swear to God, it was a sign from the universe, you're not supposed to be singing this song.

Do you remember a performance where you surprised yourself?

I'm horrible at harmony. So terrible at it. I always need a producer to work with me because I can't naturally do them. But on a song called "Cuz You're Gone," I actually went out in front of that microphone, and sang this melody, and I was so shocked that I actually did it. I was like, *Where the hell did that come from?* I don't know, but it was supposed to be there. It's like discovering something. I love that.

Do you have a favorite vocal performance you're really proud of?

Nah, not really. There's songs of mine I like more than others. There's also a lot of songs I listen to where I go, "Man, if I had only done this," or "Shit, I wish I had done that."

How are you with hearing your own voice?

I've learned to be okay listening to my singing voice. Except when I'm pitchy, that drives me nuts. But when I hear my speaking voice, it bums me out. I'm like, "Ugh, turn it off, I don't wanna hear myself talking." It's a weird thing with me, but I can't do it.

What's changed the most about your voice since you started?

My voice has matured. I'm still physically capable of hitting the highest note I sing, but there's a different quality to it. Just feels thicker, more leathery, like I'm a little more in control of it, whereas like fifteen years ago, I wasn't in control. Sometimes my voice would crack a little more.

If you could duet with one singer—living or dead—who would it be?

[*Laughs*] I think I'd like to sing Stevie Nicks's part with Tom Petty in "Stop Draggin' My Heart Around." That would be funny.

Who are your top five favorite singers of all time?

This has nothing to do with their music. I just like the way they sing. I love Rod Stewart. Great singer. Paul Westerberg. I like Mick Jones from The Clash. Janis Joplin. I could listen to her sing anything. Aretha Franklin. She could sing the phone book, I would die. Mahalia Jackson. *Man*. Tony Bennett, so rich. His voice is just made of wood and silk. Beautiful, beautiful, beautiful.

And what's your favorite vocal performance by Robby?

I like Robby's vocal on "Another Second Time Around" because I can really feel the emotion of what he's singing about.

If you could ask any singer about their voice, who would it be and what would you ask?

I might ask Mariah Carey how she did that crazy bird sound. I don't know how many octaves up it went. You know that song? [*Sings*] "You got me feelin' emotions." She's like [*sings up some octaves*] "Uhh-Ahh-Ahhh." It's crazy. Or like Mimi Ripperton when she sang [*sings*] "Lovin' you is easy cause you're beautiful." You might be too young. Look up that song. She does this thing where she just goes up, I don't know how many octaves, but you're like, "Whoa! What the hell?" Beyond falsetto. It's like a freakish trick. Not that I would do it, but I'm just interested in how someone can manipulate themselves that way. Or a guy like Tom Waits. Same thing. "What do you do? How did you learn to sing that way?"

Al Schackman on
NINA SIMONE

I ENCOURAGE EVERY SINGER to watch the documentary *What Happened, Miss Simone?* The opening scene shows Nina Simone appearing onstage before a live audience. What happens next is mesmerizing to behold. The way she takes her time, standing before them, not saying a word, the applause dying down. But she just stands there, leaving the crowd in a state of uneasy confusion. "Does she want more applause?" It's not that. It's something internal that only she knows. A sense of menace, of real violence flickers past. She could kill them all right now if she wanted to. Then, out of nowhere, someone in the crowd makes her laugh, and within an instant, her whole demeanor changes. A giant smile sweetly bursts forth, the danger subsides, and, as she slowly begins to sing, everything appears to be okay for the moment.

That is the mercurial, enigmatic, and extraordinary nature of the High Priestess of Soul. Already a gifted pianist by the age of three, she was denied admission to the Curtis Institute of Music in Philadelphia because of the color of her skin, but that only served to embolden her fight against oppression.

Today, her influence on popular music can be felt across all genres. (Just read the revelation in Michael Stipe's interview.) Twisting and turning blues, jazz, folk, pop, and classical melodies into an art form that was completely her own, Nina sang herself straight into the Grammy Hall of Fame, the Rock & Roll Hall of Fame, and through a career as tumultuous as the relationships, and times, that inspired the songs.

But there was always one place where she could find solid footing on shaky ground: with her guitarist, musical director, and close friend, Al Schackman. Nina's longest running musical colleague. Al was gracious enough to speak with me like you would about a beloved family member. And although I knew it was gonna be a wild conversation...wow.

When was the first time you heard Nina sing?

1957. I was in New Hope, Pennsylvania, playing at a club/restaurant with my trio, and she had a gig at the Bucks County Playhouse Inn. Friends of hers had dinner at the place I was playing and thought it would be a good idea to put the two of us together. I went and sat in with her and heard her sing for the first time. The two of us played Bach fugues that night. She just got up on the stand and never looked at me or told me the key or anything. But we both had perfect pitch, so I knew what key she was in. She started on a counter point in fugue—a variation on the Bach piece—and I started in on the third part, and man, we just took off, and right in the height of this, she started singing the first verse of "Little Girl Blue."

What did you think?

I've never heard such isolation. It was amazing.

And you guys played together for over forty years, from basically '57 to 2000?

Right. I was actually the first musician that she ever played with 'cause she played solo. But we just bonded. To me, her natural voice was kind of like alto going on contralto, like Marian Anderson. It was such a beautiful, rich voice. There was something in her voice that had this uncontrollable vibrato, which, through the years, got less. Eartha Kitt had that same vibrato. It was just an unusual element in her singing.

What was her approach to recording vocals in the studio?

She was like Frankie. You know his system when he recorded?

Sinatra?

Yeah. He would do one take for the orchestra rehearsal. He would do a take for the control room, to get their settings right and the microphones adjusted. And "the take" for himself. He would not record one track more than three times. Nina was more strict than that. She would just sit down and do it, and you'd be lucky if you got two or three. She wouldn't do more than three. She'd say, "That's it, I'm outta here."

Did she take care of her voice on the road?

Oh, she took care of her voice meticulously.

What would she do?

She yelled. [JTG laughs] She was angry so much of the time. Something would anger her, and if it was the day of the performance, she really yelled a lot. She never took care of her voice. She never felt she needed to because she never felt she was really a singer. She was a concert pianist, but that got screwed because she was Black, and that was always a thing. She was refused a scholarship. It was always a point of tension there.

Was she nervous or confident before shows?

We had our little ritual. Nina and I would stand just offstage, behind the curtain, and usually, she liked to hold hands. [Laughs] We would have a little glass of champagne, and then, she'd say, "Okay, go on out," and we'd come out and usually play her on. There were occasions when she would be nervous. Fragile. I think it was over the fact that she was going to expend so much energy, and she knew it would be like going to war. Sometimes she was going out angry about something, so she would throw that anger out to the audience, and it wouldn't work well.

She could be incredibly confrontational with her audience sometimes.
Always.

What was it like to be onstage with her during those moments?
It was tough. She'd be going on and on about something that happened, or she was dissatisfied, or some injustice, or the money, how she was being paid, or working like a dog, stuff like that. I would start to noodle the introduction of the next song, and sometimes she would pick that up, and say, "Aww hell," and start. But there were other times, she'd turn around and say, "Shut up, Al!" [*Laughter*] Jason, what I'm telling you is nothing compared to some of it. It'll be in *my* book. [*Chuckles*]

She's just endlessly fascinating on so many levels.
Sometimes she would be so embroiled in the emotion of the piece that she was doing, like "Pirate Jenny," the Kurt Weill/Brecht piece from *Threepenny Opera*. It's an amazing piece of music. *It was an amazing show*. She would sing the part of Pirate Jenny, and part of the verse is, "Kill them now or kill them later?" She would just pause and say, [*in a deep, murderous voice*] "Kill them now." But one time we did it, she suddenly stopped, and said, "KILL THEM NOW!" As she's saying this, there's a child in the audience who started screaming, and the parents had to get the kid outta there. [*Laughter*] That's how intense Nina could be. I don't know another vocalist, another artist, that changed their energy so dramatically as Nina could. Every song, every piece of music that Nina did had such a dramatic element to it. If you listen, the song has the theater of the character in it, and that was so unique about Nina.

In 1964, after the bombing of a church in Alabama that killed four little girls, and the racially motivated murders of Emmett Till and Medgar Evers in Mississippi, Nina wrote and recorded "Mississippi Goddam." There were a lot of people who were more horrified by her language than they were by the murders themselves, even banning the record in some places. To see someone who's not only your bandmate, but your friend, going through something like that, especially as a white man, must have been heartbreaking. But it also must have been something you were really proud to have been a part of.
Oh, I was on the front lines. Both Nina and I. We met Dr. King for the first time, and before they even said anything, before saying "Hello," she said, "I just want you to know I'm not non-violent!" But "Mississippi Goddam," the first performance of that was just she and I in Selma.

I know you guys took part in the march from Selma to Montgomery with Dr. King, and performed that song after crossing police lines earlier that day. That's really using your voice. That could've ended with one of you dying. Was that ever discussed?

One sentence: Nina was fearless. I would pity anybody that got in her way when she was trying to get through. She breezed right past the police line in Montgomery, "GET OUT OF MY WAY!"

Oh my God. What did they do?

They got out of her way.

Holy shit.

It was quite an experience. And she could get into trouble. I mean, no joke trouble. She was bi-polar. Sometimes we protected people from *her*. I think the only time she ever attacked me was in Finland. There was a period of time where she didn't want any musicians around her, just the two of us, and frankly, there were parts of that that I loved. She had demanded a new fee of $30,000 a concert, and she wasn't gonna work for less. Unheard of. In Finland, somehow, she got it. I wasn't making that much because we only managed two or three concerts a week, because she demanded a travel day, and a rest day, and a concert day. That's five days already. It was tough to make what we really could've made out on the road. So, she got this $30,000, and I said, "Nina, can I make a little more now?" She was funny with the money, like the song says, [*Laughs*] and she came at me and attacked me in her suite, "You son of a...! You're fired!" And she swung at me!

How'd you get out of that one?

I just packed up and went to the airport. At the airport, she liked to be rolled around in a wheelchair. She was heading home to Holland, and I was heading back to the States. I cleared customs, and I'm walking, and suddenly they're heading toward me, and she's in her wheelchair eating a hot dog. [*JTG laughs*] So, I walk by her—she was going one way and I was going the other—and we pass, and she raised her hand and gave a little wave. I raised my hand and gave a little wave to her. That was the last time I saw her until our next concert a few weeks later. [*Cracks up*] In other words, it was never spoken about, and I got the raise.

Incredible.

But then, on the lighter side, there's a Kurt Weill/Bertolt Brecht piece of music that we did called "Moon Over Alabama." There's a video you can find on YouTube—you'll know it's the right video because there's a fake tree behind her. I'm right offstage, and you'll see she's having a wonderful time. You get another glimpse of her that people don't see very often. You can really see her having fun, and hear the fun in her voice, and that, to me, was tremendous to be able to hear that once in a while. You can hear my guitar and the interplay with her.

When you hear her voice now, what do you remember most?

My sister. The loss. And good stuff.

MATT SKIBA

IT ALWAYS STARTS WITH A SONG, RIGHT? The first thing that grabs us and says, "Pay attention!" Matt Skiba's rock band, Alakaline Trio, began releasing records in 1997, but it was the actual song "'97" that made me pay attention. The track had a reckless energy, a forthright melody, and a voice unafraid of its own vulnerability.

After extensive touring and a string of impressive albums, Matt was asked to become the co-lead singer for the legendary punk-pop band blink-182. This wasn't just any old outfit. Just like Sammy Hagar, Brian Johnson, and even Chuck D, Matt would be stepping into the shoes of a singer that their fans already knew and loved.

It would take strength, humility, and discipline to pull this off, but Skiba doesn't back away from a challenge. He pushes himself even harder, as you'll see in this brutally honest and surprisingly spiritual conversation that's about to take place....

Right after he's through brushing his teeth.

Who first exposed you to singing?

It's so weird that you asked that question. The first person that exposed me to singing is my grandmother who I'm still very close with. She's not with us anymore here. You know, I never really had any huge questions or concerns either way about the afterlife, but after my grandmother died, I've had some things happen where I'm like, "There is no way that is not her." I was riding home to do this interview, and there was a lilac tree I used to sit underneath with my grandmother. I stopped and took a picture of the lilac tree and sent it to my folks ten minutes ago. Then you asked about my grandma, and that's probably her too.

Was your grandmother a musician?

She had a beautiful voice and would sing all these Polish and Czech folk songs to me. She was a killer harmonica player too.

Is she the one who made you feel you could do this?

She always told me, "You're going to do something incredible with your life. I know it as clearly as I see right in front of me, and whatever it is, you know you can do whatever you want." She would always tell me that I'm one of God's children all the time. I'm trying not to start crying right now...that's the most beautiful thing anyone's ever said to me. She was ingraining into me that, *You got this. You can do whatever you want.* She instilled this, I wouldn't say confidence, but everything she said I took as absolute truth. I absolutely have her to thank for everything.

That's awesome, man. Were there any other singers who influenced you at that age?

As a young kid, and to this day, I am a huuuge Neil Diamond fan. That warm, smoky voice. *The Jazz Singer* soundtrack, I have the original pressing of that, and it's worn the fuck out 'cause I would listen to that record over and over again as a kid. And *Hot August Night*, that double live record. Neil Diamond was the first guy where I started learning someone else's music. Then in '89, I saw my first real punk show. I was like twelve. [*Laughs*] I took the train with my friends to see Social Distortion. Mike Ness's handsome ass walks out with his eye-liner, and all the girls wanted to fuck him, and every guy wanted to be him, and twelve-year-old me was like, *I wanna do that!* For all the wrong reasons, but that sexy motherfucker was it.

Who were you emulating when you started out?

I remember singing along to that Green Day record, *39/Smooth*, and I caught myself singing correctly, where it felt effortless. He's belting. Billie [Joe Armstrong] can sing. He helped me get interested in voice lessons, and learning you can still be punk rock and be good at shit. You don't have to be a waste case.

How did you find your own voice?

I haven't found anything. It's like enlightenment. You never really achieve it while you're alive, but you're always working towards it. That's kind of the same thing with singing. Every time

I go in the studio, I learn something new about my voice, literally and physically—my voice, my throat, the sounds that it makes. I'm still always wanting to be better. Even when I write, I'll fuck with a word, enunciating it different ways, the cadence or whatever. There's always a different way to do it. It's still a journey.

You mentioned getting vocal lessons.

I couldn't go a few days without blowing my voice out. I'm like, "What am I doing? I don't have complete control over this." I had an ENT look down my throat and say, "You need to quit drinkin', dude. Your shit is all enflamed, and you have acid reflux. That's why you wake up and you can't talk 'cause you're gurgling up." He saved my ass. He helped me seek recovery and get to a place where I'm healthi-*er*. I'm not the healthi-*est*, but if I can't sing then what the fuck am I doing here? [*Laughs*] There's also a point where that just becomes sad. Kids are paying money, and the older you get the more it hurts, and the more obvious it is that you're fucked up. It ain't cute when you're in your forties and you're a mess. *I can't even imagine picking up a beer now. I'm sweating my balls off.* I'd equate it to dying of thirst in the desert and just like drinking a hot cup of piss. It's just like, *What is the last thing I wanna do?* So, the show is the party for me, and now that I've figured that out, I couldn't be more grateful.

And it's such a better high than anything else.

Man, that's the moment. When you're up there playing for those people, maybe someone just found out their dad died, or God knows what shit people go through. Music is the salva- tion, as it was for me, as I'm sure it was for you. We all go through hard times and music is the savior so, to be a part of that energy is such an honor. And in honoring that, I personally don't think it's a great idea to get fucked up and do it.

Are you nervous or confident before you perform?

When I joined blink, there were nights I really didn't know where the fuck I was. I felt like I was on Pluto or something up there. It took me a second, and I think it would be weird or unnatural if it didn't. If I just got up there and was all comfy immediately, like, [*chipper*] "I'm in the band now and here it is!" It's like, naw, there's some growing pains that have to happen.

You were also introducing yourself to a whole new audience.

Yeah, exactly.

I'm sure a bunch of the audience loved you from before anyway, but there's still gonna be some hardcore fans going, "Who the hell's this guy?"

Oh yeah, you still gotta take your lumps and earn that shit.

How do you keep calm?

I would get nervous to a point where it wasn't good. I was like quivering and couldn't play. That happened to me during a couple shows. But I did see a doctor, and I was like, "I don't wanna take Xanax or anything that's gonna make me out of it for the show." This doctor recommended a beta blocker. It's like a non-narcotic alternative to Xanax. People that do a lot of public speaking oftentimes will take beta blockers. It just helps you feel like, "I got this." Luckily, now I don't take it anymore because it helped me overcome stage fright. I've played with blink-182 enough to where it feels very fun and at home and natural. I'm not so worried. I've solidified my position there.

Do you do vocal warm-ups before shows?
Every night.

What's your routine?
I went to a coach named Eric Vetro who I only saw one time. It was an hour lesson, and he recorded it to put on my iPod. I do the whole hour lesson before a show. The whole thing about singing is muscle memory; that's how you sing correctly. That's how you hit those notes the same way every night. If we're on the road and somebody's struggling, there's warm-ups that'll take down swelling in your throat. You should never have the veins in your neck popping out when you're singing. Whether you're singing soft, or screaming in a death metal band, it's all the same shit.

So, walk us through your practice.
For the nervousness, I do transcendental meditation. For the vocal thing, when I hear the first band start, that's when I [*begins scales combined with vocal trills*]. There's a falsetto warm-up that I do, and I'll just be making tea, walk around, and sometimes it'll sound super awkward, but it's not something where I go, "Alright, everyone get out, I have to warm-up." At first, I felt kind of naked and weird, but that's the thing that makes me able to sing the same way every night. Fuck what anybody thinks. Just walk around warming-up different parts of your range, different parts of your throat, really light. I've played with people who are trying to sing as loud as they can before they go onstage. It's like, "Bro, you need to wake some shit up before you try and do that." There's a lot of parallels between training and working out. It's a very physical thing.

A lot of singers have spoken to me about how they feel like athletes. Even being the drummer my whole life, I never considered that I was an athlete. But now that I'm a singer, I do see the parallels. Drumming is a different type of athletics. With singing, if I'm throwing my body around, when that note comes in the next verse, I'm not gonna be prepared for it. You have to know when you can rock out, and when you can't. There's a physicality that engages every part of your body and every ounce of your breath.
I equate singing to lifting weights. If you're lifting weights, you're focusing on a certain part of your body. Doing vocal warm-ups is exercising your throat and getting it warmed-up. It's a muscle just like anything else. Another thing I've learned is that the first sweat of the day

should not be onstage. Before I work with my trainer, I get to the gym a half hour early and walk on the treadmill, start jogging, start breaking a sweat. Same thing with singing. You need to do some cardio, get a jump rope, get on a bicycle, get off your ass. It's gonna make your show ten times better, for sure.

How does working out come into play?
Your whole body comes into play when you're singing. If you feel stronger, you stand up straighter, and if you stand up straighter guess what you do better? *Sing!* You're a column of air so you want to be standing up as straight as you can. Even the way that my microphone is positioned is so that I'm not crouching, 'cause if I have to lean forward, then I'm gonna start straining because my body's jammed up. That should be a wide open column of air. A powerful, strong, relaxed column of air.

How else do you take care of your voice on the road?
I just know that when we start getting into warmer temperatures, more humid temperatures, that you don't wanna blast the AC. You want that shit off.

How do you deal with people on the bus that are like, "It's too hot!"
Playing in blink-182, I have my own bus. [*Laughter*] With Alkaline Trio, luckily all three of us are singers and we all feel the same way. When you turn the AC on, watch people start getting sick, that's the way it is. Blowing that bullshit into the air. It's just another variable. Not *no* AC, but *low* AC. I just close the vents in my bunk.

Do you have any rituals before you hit the stage?
Everything that I have backstage travels with me so, I have all my Perfect Push Ups, my jump rope, and all the shit I use to open my body and work out.

I feel like you have a whole system laid out.
Right when I get there in the morning, I'll drink a couple glasses of Throat Coat or whatever decaf tea, and then do my early meditation. Then I'll do that again maybe three hours before a gig. That way, if I pass out, I'm not trying to wake up like forty-five minutes before we play, and I'm frazzled and rushing. I have a thermos that's filled to the brim with like three bags of Throat Coat tea floating in it. Then I put honey, and two Ricola [cough drops] in there, and let the shit seep for a couple minutes. It all melts, and once the tea bags have been in there for five to ten minutes, I'll pull them out, cap that thermos, and take it to the stage with me. Then, water, water, water, water, all fuckin' day and night. Just pounding water. And not speaking. Any sort of press, I'd prefer not to do on a show day. Something I learned from Mark [Hoppus, blink-182 bassist] is, he always brushes his teeth before he goes onstage. Now, I can't not do it.

What's that about?

You just feel so much better after that, like after you take a shower. You do that before you get up onstage, it's like everything's handled. I think it's a psychosomatic thing.

Is there anything after the show that helps keep your voice in shape?

I try not to talk for about an hour after we get offstage, and I'll do things like [*does vocal trill type scales by vibrating his lips*]. A warm-up and a warm-down should be very gentle. And getting eight hours of healthy sleep.

Are there songs where you wonder if your voice will be there that night?

Not anymore. That would suck if I was going through all this trouble and that was still happening. People are like, "Why do you meditate?" and I'm like, "'Cause it works." I wouldn't be wasting my time with something if it didn't have a profound effect.

What was your most embarrassing vocal mishap ever.

I continue to forget words, but we call those punk rock mistakes. Good enough for punk rock. But the things I can control, I do. It's been a bit of a journey to figure them out, but there's always something to learn. You can always get better.

From Alkaline Trio to Matt Skiba and the Sekrets to blink-182, there's a style you have that I've noticed progress. You do a great job of layering melodies on top of each other. It's not like when you first started out, maybe you double tracked here or there; now it feels like you've got this other thing that's become yours.

Yeah, I sing the octave that is the lead vocal, and underneath it, I sing an octave lower, sometimes two octaves lower, and sing it exactly the same way, and it tucks in there.

Do you remember a performance where you surprised yourself?

When we were making an Alkaline Trio record, there was a backup I had to do that actually became the lead vocal. I was like, "There is no fucking way I'm gonna be able to hit that." I warmed-up and just thought about it like, *The minute you stop reaching for it, you'll land it*. First take, BOOM! Everyone was like, "HOLY SHIT! HOW THE FUCK DID YOU DO THAT?" I was like, "I don't know, man. I don't know." That was one of the first times where I was like, "Damn, I guess I'm officially a singer now."

What song was that?

"I Found Away" on *Agony & Irony*. The end I sing, "I found away, I found away, I found away." I'm way up in the stratosphere of my range; like it's black outside the windows of my spacecraft, you know? Like, holy shit, we did it. The wings are still on the ship, we're here!

I love how weathered and beat up your voice is on "Blue in the Face." A lot of people would record that and try to make it a pretty ballad, but it sounds like you sung it after a two-hour show.

Ugh, I fuckin' hate it! When we were making that record, that was my breaking point. I was living in Los Angeles, kind of against my will. My bandmates had all gone home because I was going through some fucked up shit. I was drinking heavily and just not happy being myself, and that was the last song we recorded. My voice was cooked. I was so depleted, and defeated, and bummed, and [producer] Jerry Finn was like, "Let's set up one mic and just sing it as best you can." So, I can't really listen to that record. That voice and that person, I'm just like *Ugh*. But, hey man, if you like it, then it was all worth it. Even if it was just you. But there's a lot of other people who say, "Fuck you, that's my favorite record," so if all that self-destruction made a record that people loved, then it was worth it. I lived through it.

Tom Waits and Keith Richards work together a lot, and I've heard them talk about how if a song's too pretty, it doesn't work for them. There has to be a hair in the frame, like an old movie. It has to be a little ugly to have the soul. "Blue in the Face" has that.

Well, there isn't a higher compliment, so I appreciate you saying that. It's like Patricia Arquette's crooked teeth. Part of the reason she's so beautiful—it's like, if you ever fix those teeth, we're gettin' divorced! It has so much character, it's so sexy. I love the hair in the frame analogy. I'm gonna use that. I just didn't have the option of anything else.

The option you had was, "I'll just sing it two days from now and give myself some rest." You could've sung it again and made it really pretty. But the fact that it sounds so weathered and beat up, especially in the context of the lyrics. The song is called "Blue in the Face," and the last line is "Your coffin or mine?" This is a dying man, and if it had been pretty, it wouldn't have worked.

You got me. You're right, I'm wrong. It's like being married. You're right, I'm wrong. [*JTG laughs*] I'm too close to it to see that, but I love that, and I'm honored that that's how you hear it. I'm glad that the dying man didn't die.

How are you with hearing your own voice?

I'm good with it now. What choice do I have? It's kind of like looking at yourself in the mirror. Do you wanna look at yourself in the mirror? I personally don't. But I need to shave, and I need to keep this shit together as much as I can, and it's the same thing with the voice. You might as well enjoy it, and get good at it, and have fun with it.

What's changed the most about your voice since you started?

I've learned how to use it correctly. It took me a long time to be able to say that, and that's why it's so rewarding. I don't wanna sound cocky, I just know a lot about singing because I've put the time in, put the work in, and I still do every time I sing.

If you could duet with one singer—living or dead—who would it be?
Who's the Kate Pierson to my Iggy Pop is how I'm thinking about this. And right now, I'd like to duet with Alison Mosshart from Dead Weather, The Kills, and Discount. I love her voice.

Who are your top five favorite singers of all time?
Jehnny Beth, Ian Curtis, David Bowie, Bob Mould, *aaaand*...I mean, we can't really talk about singing and not talk about Freddie Mercury.

If you could ask any singer about their voice, who would it be and what would you ask?
I would ask David Bowie how he sang so well on all that cocaine and cigarettes. 'Cause his cocaine career was brief, but man, was it nasty. The Thin White Duke, that was all his cocaine shit. I'm like, "How are you singing and still look cool on all that blow?" If I do blow, it looks like I did a bunch of blow. [*Laughter*]

ROBERT SMITH

THERE'S A HIGH DEGREE OF PROBABILITY that this book never gets written, and I never become a musician without the influence of Robert Smith in my life. I was barely a teenager, just about to start playing drums, when The Cure reached out, took hold, and never let go.

Robert's mysterious voice contained the sorrow of the world, but just like that, he could switch, becoming wildly eccentric, foolishly playful, or even explosive with anger. But it's the authenticity and emotion he constantly reveals that's earned The Cure a place in the Rock & Roll Hall of Fame and Robert a Godlike Genius Award from the NME.

Since 1979, The Cure have helped define and shape the sound of every genre from post-punk to new wave to goth, pop, and rock. Then, just when you think it's all over, they come back stronger than ever.

I caught up with Robert as he was close to finishing The Cure's new album and I couldn't wait to have this conversation. But then, I thought of his stage persona, his trademark, quirky, black bird's nest of hair, his red lipstick, black eyeliner, and make-up. What character was I about to meet? Would he be shy, aloof, bizarre, a drag? "Never meet your heroes." You hear that all the time. Well...Robert Smith proved 'em wrong again.

Who first exposed you to singing?

I played guitar from about the age of seven, learnt piano around the age of ten, but I never really sang, and I never wanted to perform in front of an audience. Whenever school productions came around, I always put my hand up to do the backstage stuff: putting things together and taking things down and packing things up. I never wanted to be onstage, but I ended up there in 1976, as rhythm guitarist in Malice, our school punk band, and I sang a cover of "Suffragette City," mainly because I wanted to see what it felt like to sing in front of people. And I kind of hated it. [*Laughter*]

So, how did we get here?

The band changed its name to Easy Cure and went through a succession of auditions for singers, and nobody really sounded right. I had started writing words, sketches of songs that I wanted us to play, and, in a kind of desperation, I just started singing them myself. After a few rehearsals, I started to think, *Maybe I can do this for real*. We played our first paid show in the summer of 1977, and that's really the day I became *a singer*. We changed our name one last time, signed a deal, and recorded an album the following year, but I was still pretty unsure of my voice.

How did you get your confidence?

The first three albums that we made: *Three Imaginary Boys*, *Seventeen Seconds*, and *Faith*, and maybe even the fourth, *Pornography*—I wanted the vocals mixed low. Even playing the live shows, I didn't want to be a voice sitting above the instruments. I'd say to the front of house engineer, "Every single noise this band makes is as important as my voice." And although this was done primarily because I was lacking a bit in confidence, I did grow to really like the sound of the low vocal. It was pretty unusual and became a part of The Cure sound! I liked the feeling of the listener having to really *listen* to make out what I was singing.

When did you start feeling more at ease being the singer?

We made three singles in 1983, "Let's Go to Bed," "The Walk" and "The Lovecats." Around that time, I had a change of perspective, and started to experiment more with my voice. I started to feel more comfortable about being the focal point. The vocal point? From then on, I really started to *think* about singing, and realized I had never *really* stretched myself. The *Pornography* album was about the closest I had come, but that was more about the screaming than the singing. I was getting angsty, but I really didn't know how to *control* my voice. It took a while to figure out; as with any instrument, you practice, you develop, and you reach a point when suddenly one day, you think, *Hey! I can do what I want with this instrument!* That kind of happened to me in 1983.

Were you emulating anyone when you started out?

As a youngster getting into music in the late '60s and early '70s, I was inspired by The Beatles, The Stones, Jimi Hendrix, Pink Floyd, Nick Drake, David Bowie, Alex Harvey. But I wouldn't say I ever really *sounded* like any of them! There are lines on the first album where I'm definitely trying to *sound* a bit like Bowie with some of the inflections and stuff. Obviously, I don't get that close, but I'm in the same kind of world, I think.

I've heard you say that Hendrix had a profound effect on you.
Hendrix was my musical hero. I never wanted to play lead guitar like Hendrix, but I loved his rhythm style, and I wanted to sing like him, write songs like him, and live the life that I imagined he was living! I read that he didn't really like his own voice that much, and maybe I picked up on that a bit. But when he really got into a song, there was always that moment when I would think, *Fuck me*, and hear *it* in his voice. I think I sensed subconsciously how powerful it must be to be able to do that. There was no way my life as a ten-year-old, at school in the south of England, was like the life that Jimi Hendrix was living. [*Laughter*] But inside my head, I was actually in the Experience.

How did you find your own voice?
I remember in my early teens reading an interview with a singer, and they said one of the secrets of being a great singer is to sing how you talk, to make sure that the inflections you sing are the same as those you use naturally. If you need to exaggerate, do, but don't try to sing in a way that makes you feel uncomfortable. It will likely make any listener uncomfortable too. Speak the song lyrics, notice how you pause and where you breathe, and what stresses you put on certain words and certain lines, and only then, try singing it. That's something that I've always done. My favorite singers are the ones that sing like they talk. I usually *hate* singers that open their mouths and suddenly become a different person—born in London by way of Los Angeles! But I love great opera singers, for example, and they generally don't sound like opera when they talk. [*Laughs*] I hope you know what I mean: a singer who sings as they speak has a certain...authenticity? It always seems to feel more *real*, and authenticity and emotion in a voice are much more important to me than technical excellence.

Did you ever have any vocal training?
No, but my dad sang all the time at home. He sang amateur dramatics. I think he wanted to be a singer, secretly, because he was always rehearsing Gilbert & Sullivan, all that sort of stuff. My mum played piano, so there was always live music in the house, and you couldn't help getting caught up in it. But, like I said at the start, I listened, but I never really thought about singing along. The only time I ever sang along was at Christmas and birthdays! [*Laughs*]

Are you nervous or confident before you perform?
I've never really experienced nerves before a performance, maybe because I've always been onstage in a band. I love being the singer in The Cure, it's fantastic. But I always think, *This is the noise that the band makes*. And maybe I'm never nervous because, although I *want* people to like us, if they don't, I don't care! Yeah, *that's* my secret to not being nervous! [*Laughter*] I

was taught at a very young age not to pay too much attention to critics. "Those that can, do. Those that can't, *criticize*" is an old adage I remember from childhood!

Do you do vocal warm-ups before shows?

I've always gone through the same kind of routine, but I'm not sure that it qualifies as a proper warm-up! I do my make-up, and when I'm finished, I shout at myself in the mirror for a couple of minutes. It starts low and then it gets louder. I do it until I'm at the point where my throat and my whole head's vibrating, and then, I think, *Right, I'm ready to go*. It's psychological as well as physical. It just frees me up. It's a good way of releasing any underlying tension, and just kind of making sure that my voice is there.

What are you shouting at yourself?

No words, just sort of primal screaming, that kind of thing. Nothing too angsty though. You know when you sometimes go, *aaaaaAAAGH!* Without hurting my own voice, I just kind of do that. Wave my hands about, jump up and down, and bellow at myself. It's a crucial part of my pre-show preparation! And I drink a hot honey and lemon, or a Throat Coat tea, and suck a handful of Ricola and Vocalzone Pastilles just prior to a performance. I suck a lot of those sweets when I'm recording as well. This year I've been doing vocals for the next Cure albums, and I've got through about a hundred packets so far! I also find sucking licorice can help my voice.

Black licorice, right? I've heard that.

Yeah. It also reminds me of childhood, which is an added benefit!

Do you have any other rituals before you hit the stage?

After the soundcheck, I do the set list. Then, I sit in the dressing room and play the basic chord parts on my guitar and sing maybe one or two lines from each song in the order that we're going to play them, just to convince myself that it's the right set list, the right flow, and that I know what key each song is in. [*Laughs*] And the band always gets together for a while before we go onstage, to make sure that everyone's tuned in, and that no one's suffering unduly. I usually have a couple of pints of the local beer, just to get me to the point where I'm feeling kind of...vibey? But there's no group hugs or prayers or anything like that. We know what we all expect from the performance, and it's up to each individual in the band to do as well as they can.

Is there anything after the show that helps keep your voice in shape?

Generally, the first hour after we come offstage, I lay on the ground on a towel, crying. [*Cracks up*] Once the buzzing inside my head stops, then I'm fine. So, without having to think about it, I don't talk much because I am usually shattered when I come offstage. A lot of it's just common sense, acknowledging ageing, and acknowledging what physically happens to your body and your throat. If you want to be a singer, you can't just keep hammering it.

How do you take care of your voice on the road?

We always stay in hotels that have opening windows. I try to avoid all air conditioning. We always travel on a bus with fresh air vents. The main thing I hate about flying is the horrible air. Bad air always hurts my throat. I just look after myself a lot more than I used to. I never drink alcohol the night before a show. I hardly ever have a night out on tour anymore. I completely gave up smoking about ten years ago. And I need sleep. That's crucial! If I've not had enough sleep, however much I want to sing well, I can't. It just doesn't happen.

When you start getting sick, what do you do?

A couple of the band are very conscientious about "5 A Day,"[9] so we always have a juicer backstage. There's always beetroot and carrots and celery and stuff they stick in the blender and insist that I take a glass. The band do try to look after me when we're touring. I got really sick on the 2008 tour, probably the worst I've ever been. When we arrived in America, we had two days before the first show, and I made a mistake and went out with everyone for a meal. As we were waiting to be seated, someone in the crew sneezed on me. I didn't make a fuss; I went to the bathroom, blew my nose, washed my face, laughed it off. Three days later, I could barely talk. I felt dreadful the first ten shows, like I was letting myself and everyone else down, and I couldn't seem to recover. It just kept coming back worse and worse.

Did you get it checked out?

I saw three doctors inside a week, and each one gave me a different diagnosis, and each one gave me different pills and sprays. I really thought I was developing a serious throat problem, and once you start worrying about that, you're fucked! You start thinking, *This is it. I am definitely losing my voice forever!* I still did the shows, and pushed through, hoping things would improve, but in Kansas City, I did pretty much lose my voice.

What do you do onstage when that happens?

I sang the whole show a couple of octaves down, which was bizarre. I sounded like Lee Marvin doing Cure covers! I told the crowd at the end of the show, "We'll come back, and I'll sing to you properly." Now I tell everyone on tour, "If you come near me with a bug, and you give me that bug, there *will* be consequences!" And I'm serious about it because if the singer can't sing, everyone may as well pack up and go home.

Are there songs where you wonder if your voice will be there that night?

"Prayers for Rain" from *Disintegration*. Occasionally, I'll stick that in the set, and I'll see how long I can hold the word "Raaaaaaaiiiiiiiiin." [*Laughs*] It's like a battle I have with myself; can I get through sixteen bars while holding this note? I say to myself, "Look, if you don't behave,

---

9   The 5 A Day campaign is based on advice from the World Health Organization [WHO], which recommends eating a minimum of 400g of fruit and vegetables a day to lower the risk of serious health problems, such as heart disease, stroke, and some types of cancer.

we'll do this song every night." [*JTG laughs*] And there were some songs on *The Cure* album which I never felt comfortable singing live. Ross Robinson, who produced it, pushed me to a point where I was often at the limits of my voice, and I knew that I couldn't sing those songs four, five nights a week. It was physically impossible for me to do it.

Yeah, the studio versus live gets you every time.
That's a totally different thing. Singing those songs in the studio a couple of times, trying to get *the performance*, psyching myself up and then really going for it, knowing I wouldn't have to sing the following day. That's one of the reasons a lot of those songs never stayed in the set because they're so hard to sing! Usually, when I'm singing, there might be a point in a song where I really push my voice, but it's just *that* point, and it's to *make* a point. I don't really want to sing a song where I'm having to strain my voice for four or five minutes, because I know that's going to kill me! I do try to think about playing live when we're recording and imagine how the song will work onstage.

Are there songs where you've had to adjust the key live?
No, I haven't reached that point yet. I know people do it all the time. It's no big deal. But if I had to ask the band to play songs in a different key, they'd simply ask me, "Why don't you just sing them lower?" [*Laughter*]

What was your most embarrassing vocal mishap ever?
Does silence count? There have been quite a number of times when I've completely blanked! If we're playing forty songs in a show, there are moments when I think, *Here comes the opening line, and I have no idea what it* is! [*Laughter*] But I'm also in the enviable position where I can extemporize. So, I think, *Right, tonight I want to sing something different, so I will. I wrote this song. I can do what I want.* And I generally get away with it! I don't really think too much about embarrassing...Well, okay, I went onstage once when I had eaten quite a lot of magic mushrooms. That was probably my only really embarrassing show because I lost it about halfway through. I was just standing there, looking at my guitar like I'd never seen a guitar before! Strangely enough, the vocals were the last thing to go. The mic would appear in front of my face, and I would just start singing; whatever words happened to pop into my head. I suppose I wanted to see what it was like; I never did it again because it really wasn't that much fun.

Do you remember a performance where you surprised yourself?
There are moments all the time when you do something and think, *Cool, I didn't think I could do that!* Sometimes you even reach a point where things are so effortless that you almost don't feel like you're actually *doing* it at all. That's the feeling that I strive for. It's almost like an out of body experience. In the studio, I was proud of how far I could push my voice on *The Cure* album. But at the same time, I went a bit too far on some of the songs, and didn't quite sound like me. But I was surprised at how far I could push my voice if I wanted to.

Yeah, you're really belting. "(I Don't Know What's Going) On." That's a great one!

There's a song on there called "(I Don't Know What's Going) On"?

That's what I just said!

Yeah, that one! I remember being surprised that I could do that vocal. As I was doing it! [*Laughs*] I didn't think I could sing like that. I am proud of a lot of the vocal stuff on *Bloodflowers* and *4:13 Dream* too.

How are you with hearing your own voice?

I like my own voice when I sing well. It is a bit difficult to understand why you'd be a singer if you didn't like your own voice. Despite what Jimi said, I think it's the one thing you sort of *have* to like! [*Laughs*] But I don't really like my interview voice. When I'm singing, I feel like it's a performance, and I'm trying to communicate with people in a totally different way. Although it's still words, most of the time, it's also non-verbal.

In what way?

Singing isn't *just* about words. It's about *sound* and *emotion* too. Mothers singing to babies and stuff, cooing. It's a definite bonus if you've got great words, but say like scat singing [*does a jazzy scat*] "Do-do-ba-dee-bop." Sometimes that's all you need. Sometimes you don't need words. Over the years, I have wished that my range were a bit *lower*. Maybe that'll come as I age. I can sing a note or two lower now than I could a couple of years ago. Maybe I'm heading down into Lee Marvin world whether I like it or not.

Do you have a vocal performance you're really proud of?

We did a show in Hyde Park in 2018 to celebrate the fortieth anniversary of the band, and when I said earlier, I was *never* nervous, I must admit I was a *bit* nervous that night because we were filming it, it was a big crowd, it was the anniversary, and it was a one-off. I thought, *If I mess this up…*[*laughs*] There's really nowhere to hide. But, about five songs in, I knew this is going to be a good show. I was so relieved. Then I really started enjoying it. I *tried* things, vocally. I got more and more confident. The band caught fire, and I just spread my wings! By the end, I felt *really* great. So, that was my favorite vocal performance. Of the last ten years, anyway! [*Laughs*]

I'd love to know how you came up with the "Flicka-flicka" opening lines for "The Caterpillar," because it's so genius that the melody and those lyrics feel as if we're listening to a butterfly flapping its wings.

Andy Anderson, who played drums on *The Top* album, usually wore leather trousers, and he started playing that rhythm on his thighs as I was playing him the tune on guitar. The sound that his hands made sounded like butterfly wings. I just followed the rhythm that he was playing, and started singing, "Flicka-flicka-flicka-flicka." It really was that simple! But I must admit, that's a pig of a song to sing live sometimes, trying to get that "Flicka-flicka" thing right when it's like two and half hours into a show and my lips are getting tired!

[Laughs] "Push" off *The Head on the Door* is one of my favorite Cure songs, but I'm always so impressed by the restraint you show with the vocal. The song begins, but you don't even start singing until 2:30 into the track. You've shown that same type of restraint throughout your career where you're not afraid to let the music speak for a while, and I'd love to know how the inspiration for that came about, because most singers would never dream of doing something like that.

On the new album, there's a song that plays for more than seven minutes before I start singing, how about that? [*Laughter*] With "Push," it's always a really nice moment in the set when we play it live, because it gives me two or three minutes where I can just kind of rock out with the others. It's one of the few times I can walk away from the mic and not have to worry about getting back there in time; I go for a wander and have a look around and see what's happening. The song is kind of about a train journey, and musically it is in two distinct halves. I always thought the first half was about looking out the window, and then the train stops, and passengers get on. And the second half of the train journey is way more agitated. Something like that anyway! [*Laughs*]

Well, this brings us to one of your greatest songs, in my opinion, which is "The Hungry Ghost" off your last album, *4:13 Dream*. It's so amazing that you're still able to hit those high notes so beautifully, and the ones in that song in particular seem really tough.

It's funny you were asking earlier about dropping the key. When we play it live, I do actually drop most of the vocal part down a fifth, and a couple parts down an octave. I love playing that song live. It is one of my favorites, but when I listen to the album version, I just think, *Ouch, how did I sing that up there?* [*Laughs*] I couldn't sing it in that register night after night. It is in the upper reaches of where I can go. But I wanted the song to have a tension in it, because the whole song's about the horror of just wanting more and more and it never being enough. I felt that singing the lyric just on the edge of my voice breaking was a way of communicating that emotion. The song just sounded a lot stronger when I sang it higher.

As a philosophical thing, are you like, "I'm gonna sing higher on the record because more people are gonna hear the record than see me live?"

I remember in the '80s, we became the most bootlegged band in the world. We overtook The Rolling Stones and The Grateful Dead at one point based on the number of cassette bootlegs that were available! We've always had a lot of fans that are wonderfully obsessed by every aspect of the band, particularly live shows. Live performances are unique and special, and live recordings can be as good or even better than *the studio version*, but I will listen to *Are You Experienced*—going back to Hendrix again—and for me, the album performances just *are* the performances. I've got endless versions of songs by Hendrix that I've accumulated over the years, but the *definitive* version is pretty much always the album version. I don't think that invalidates any of the other performances in any way, but if there has to be a definitive performance, I think the studio version is almost always it.

What's changed the most about your voice since you started?

I think my voice is definitely getting better as I age! In 2019, we headlined thirty-five major festivals around the world, and I think the level I sang at through the year, the *way* I sang, was actually better than at any other time I've ever sung. Something's probably got to give at some point soon though. [*Laughs*] I am expecting the sky to fall in, because my voice can't possibly just *keep* getting better. As I've grown older, I realize there's less time for me to play these shows, sing these songs, and so, maybe I'm just putting more into it. Maybe.

Well, your voice at the last show in LA was unbelievable. You sang better than ever on your last album. You haven't lost shit. It's really impressive, and really interesting.

Yeah, it's funny. It's become one of the first things people mention when they review the band. "Robert Smith's voice sounds the same." I should really have lost some range or something by now. But I don't seem to have. Yet.

If you could duet with one singer—living or dead—who would it be?

That dream already came true because I sang with David Bowie, and the experience was unreal. He had the most *phenomenal* voice. I was seriously, *seriously* overwhelmed. There was so much *power* in his voice. When I arrived at Madison Square Garden, I went to the mixing desk to introduce myself to the front of house engineer, and the PA was off. Bowie was onstage, just singing words and phrases, kind of warming-up. And I could hear him like he was next to me! The throw of his voice was absolutely incredible.

What was it like to sing with Bowie?

I was crying with happiness when I walked off. It was definitely a dream come true.

Who are your top five favorite singers of all time?

Five? Fucking hell! Well, Alex Harvey would have to be in the top five because he was the first person who I thought could get away with being almost like a cartoon version of himself, but at the same time, could also be incredibly powerful. Hendrix, of course, just because he was always there for me. And Bowie. Hmmm…Can I have McCartney and Lennon as one voice?

I'll let it slide this once.

Thank you. Because when they sing together, for me, that's like a perfect voice. I'll probably need Nick Drake in there too because he touches me so much. Elvis! Billie Holiday! Mick Jagger! Neil Young, John Martyn, Tom Waits, Ian Curtis, Kurt Cobain, Frank Black, Billy Corgan, Trent Reznor, David Gray, Chino Moreno, Aretha Franklin, Carole King, Janis Ian, Evelyn "Champagne" King, Chrissie Hynde, Liz Fraser, Amy Winehouse, Kristin Hersh, Kim Deal. And, of course, James Graham from The Twilight Sad. He has got a beautiful voice that engages me instantly. There are at least as many again as I have listed. Most times, it's just that indefinable *something* that makes me want to listen to that person sing. When someone's got that, they've got it. And when they haven't, it doesn't matter how hard they *try* to be a singer, they'll never really be a *singer*. When someone opens their mouth, and they have that *it*, I just can't stop listening to them. [*Pauses*] And Frank Sinatra. Is *that* five? [*Laughter*]

If you could ask any singer about their voice, who would it be and what would you ask?
Over the years, I have been lucky enough to meet and talk to a lot of singers I really admire, and at some point in the conversation, I usually ask them about the feeling they have when they sing in front of an audience. I think you expose yourself in a very particular way when you do that. You definitely cross a line. So, I ask about their experience, their emotion when they do it, nothing technical about how they sing. I just ask about the actual experience of singing live in front of people. And if I am honest, I don't think I have discovered a magical common thread. But the conversations are usually good! [*Laughter*]

Well, when you're singing live, what is that experience for you?
Singing live in front of an audience makes me feel like I am experiencing *myself*. I think because I'm kind of a quiet person in real life—I'm really not that effusive, not that ebullient—onstage I can tap into a part of me that...Well, I kind of let go. And I feel like, "Whoa, this is me experiencing *myself*. So, *this* is what I'm like!" I also really enjoy being part of a communal event, something that's happening in real time, and no one is really sure what's going to happen. I open my mouth and I think, *Here we go*. And something always happens. I tap into something, which is like, *There is nothing else other than this singing moment*. That's what I enjoy most about it. That and the love I get from the crowd! [*Laughs*]

BRUCE SPRINGSTEEN

SPRINGSTEEN SAID YES?!
I knew I wasn't going to be able to keep my cool. My only hope was that he wouldn't be too uncomfortable from all the love he was about to receive from a psycho-fan. But all his fans are lunatics when it comes to this guy. Now, ask yourself why.

Is it the 150 million records sold? No. Is it the twenty Grammy Awards? No. The Academy Award? Nope. The Golden Globe? The Tony? The Rock & Roll Hall of Fame induction? No, no, and no.

We are obsessed with Springsteen for one reason: He does what most people in our lives never seem to do. He gives us everything he's got. And he not only gives it, he demands it. From his early days singing in New Jersey clubs to selling out stadiums around the world, Bruce Springsteen is the epitome of what a rock 'n' roll singer and performer should be.

Part poet, part preacher, part teacher, and the ever-lovin' leader of, "The heart-stopping, pants-dropping, hard-rocking, booty-shaking, love-making, earth-quaking, justifying, death-defying, legendary E. STREET. BAND!"

Ladies and gentlemen, I give you…. BRUUUUUUUCE!

Who first exposed you to singing?

It's all around you. My mother sang. My grandparents. They all sang me lullabies, so that would be the first thing I remember is just little children's lullabies. "Pony Boy," those are really your first experiences with singing, I think. And my grandfather owned an electronic store and was a radio repairman, so the radio was a prominent fixture in our home. It was constantly on, and I was exposed to opera, and all different types of singing since I was a toddler.

Was there someone who specifically inspired you to do this?

I suppose the rock 'n' roll singers. Elvis. Even though Elvis had a spectacular voice, you weren't really gonna emulate him. But a lot of the rock 'n' roll singing you heard on Top 40 at the time made you think, *Yeah, some of that. I might be able to catch some of that.* But, initially, I was a guitarist, and singing came later. I sang in my room.

So, how'd you come up front?

My first time onstage as a lead singer was singing "Twist and Shout" at the Elk's Club with my first band. It was adrenaline through the roof, and thrilling. I don't know if it was any good, but I belted it out, and I felt proud of myself afterwards. [*Laughs*] Later on, in The Castiles, I started to share lead vocals with our lead vocalist, George Theiss. Eventually, we sang half the songs each, and my voice got better. I was interested in singing and fronting, slowly, and that's how it came around. But, it's a very different thing than just playing alongside in a band. You're effectively leading a group, and you have that direct vocal communication with the audience, which is very powerful.

Were you emulating anyone when you started?

We were initially a Top 40 band. We played the hits, but we also played a lot of rhythm and blues and soul. And so, you were naturally attempting to emulate some of the greatest singing alive. If you were attempting to emulate the Motown records or soul music, or, for that matter, great rock music, you are attempting to emulate the greatest pop voices of your time, and so, you're immediately measuring yourself by that bar.

How did you find your own voice?

That took me quite a while. I was very influenced by Bob Dylan, of course, and some others. But I just sort of stumbled into my own voice because once I heard it coming back at me from a speaker, I realized, *Whoa, that's the way I sound. I don't like that.* [*Laughter*] That's your first thought. *Who's that? That doesn't sound like me.* Because you don't sound like that in your head. Inside your head, you sound much better. But outside of your head, the tape tells you what you sound like. And at the end of the day, it has the last word.

From The Castiles you start singing for Steel Mill, right?

By the time I got to Steel Mill, we had a little southern blues feeling going along with our metal and prog thing. There was a little Gregg Allman at that time, and I loved the guy from

Moby Grape. Moby Grape was one of my great heroes. My mind is blanking on his name now. Let me get my computer, see if we can find him. It's important, hold on. [*Leaves to get his computer*] *Allll right*. Also at the time, there was a guy named John Finley in a group called Rhinoceros who I loved. [E Street guitarist] Steve Van Zandt and I were huge Rhinoceros fans.

Was he a local guy?

No, Rhinoceros was sort of a recording supergroup. They made two or three records at one time in the '60s or early '70s, and John Finley was the main lead singer. He really, really affected me a lot. I tried to sound like him. If you listen to me in Steel Mill, I'm probably trying to sound like John Finley. John Finley or...Bob Mosley from the Grape! These were guys that had this full-throated voice that I loved. I just loved it. So, there's all these obscure people that really influenced you at a moment, but you don't get past much more than an emulation at best. You're not at the essence of your own voice yet. That takes a while.

Did you ever have any vocal training?

No.

Are you nervous or confident before you perform?

I get nervous to this day, and you always question your voice! I mean, I never thought I had a great voice. I thought I had a voice that was pretty versatile and I could work it in a lot of different ways. So, I use it well, but it's not a natural gift or anything.

Do you do vocal warm-ups before shows?

No.

I knew you were gonna piss me off. Any routine or anything?

We will come to the show early and do a soundcheck. Sometimes it lasts ten minutes, and sometimes it lasts an hour, depending on what we're learning and what we're doing. I will simply sing at the soundcheck. But I've also walked onstage cold and started singing. If I feel a song's coming up where I need to use my voice intensely, I may take a sip of tea with pepper.

With pepper? I've never heard of this. What does that do?

I don't know. They say it loosens your voice up a little bit, and I find that it does.

So, how do you take care of your voice on the road? *You especially*.

I don't have to do anything. I've been gifted with a work horse of a voice, and I've never missed a show because of a vocal problem, and I've never done any warm-ups. I've never done anything particular to take care of my voice except to use it wisely. I don't over-sing. No matter how hard it sounds like I'm singing out there, I'm not over-singing. I'm singing within the parameters of where my voice sings well and safely.

But I've seen what you do up there!

If you start pushing it, you end up hurting your voice. I never do that, even though I can sound like I'm throwing my guts up. [*Laughs*] You learn how to manage your voice. If you manage your voice well, and if you are gifted with a bit of a work horse, then you shouldn't have any problems. The only time I have a problem with my voice is if I get ill, if I get a sinus infection, and it affects my vocal cords.

When you start getting sick, what do you do?

You usually end up going to the Medrol pack and taking a few steroids for a few days, and hopefully that takes the swelling down.

Do you have any rituals before you hit the stage?

I generally like it quiet. Sometimes, I'll catch a nap, sit and play the guitar. I just don't like a lot of commotion, mainly 'cause it's like you're a bomb that's gonna go off. [*Laughs*] I like reserving the energy on that day until that moment. Then, when the moment hits, that's when I like to feel that release. So, on a show day, I'm relatively collected and calm, and I don't expend a lot of energy doing a lot of other things, even though I do more now than I used to do 'cause I'm not as superstitious as I used to be.

Is there anything after the show that keeps your voice in shape?

If you sing hard and long, your voice wants rest after that. I know so many singers who talk their voice out when they're not onstage. After the show, before the show, they're talking their voice out. I've seen it happen. So, I always make it explicit to people who sing with me, if I see they're havin' a problem, you gotta stop talkin'. [*Laughs*] You can't go out and party, party, and talk, talk after the show. But at this stage, all professional singers are aware of how to take care of their voice and do so responsibly.

You're revered for playing some of the longest rock 'n' roll shows ever. Officially, what's the longest one you've ever done?

Four and a half hours maybe? Our fans would know, but I'm not sure. Over four hours.

Oh my God. And how was your voice the next night? Do you remember?

It was fine.

I've probably seen you live more than any other artist, in all types of venues, from stadiums to intimate acoustic shows to your show on Broadway. And I can honestly say I've never seen anyone give as much to a performance as you. You'll literally break yourself in half to make sure the audience leaves transformed. As a vocalist, how do you carry on when you start to get tired up there? Is it pure will, or is there something you tell yourself to keep up that endurance and physicality?

I have a lot of adrenaline and that takes up a lot of the slack. Plus, your pride is on the line. And to me, that still matters. Your self-respect is on the line. You come out and you blow it off, I'd be less than who I thought I was; to come out and rush through it or treat it like it's just another night. I still go on the assumption that you can have great impact on someone's night, in one evening, in a relatively brief period of time. And that person, you don't know where they're going to go, you don't know what they're gonna do, you don't know how you've helped them, or how you've shaped a small, tiny piece of their life for a moment. But I do know those things are possible because I've had them happen to me. Through music. My main responsibility each evening is to go out there and provide an experience where that possibility is present. I take that seriously.

That was beautifully put. I once heard you say, "Nothing exists until you go, 'One-two-three-four.' Then, you and the audience, together, manifest an entire world, an entire set of values, an entire way about thinking about your life and the world around you, and an entire set of possibilities that can never be taken away." Only you could take the four count and turn it into a life-or-death situation. But you're so right.
[*Laughs*] That's what happens.

I love that you've pretty much trademarked the four count. Any singer who yells, "One-two-three-four!" to kick in a song, I feel like we owe you a couple of bucks.
That's funny.

Are there songs where you've had to adjust the key live?
I usually move the key up when we play live. I've never moved a key down. I'll move it up a whole tone, just to get more excitement out of it, and get my voice in a slightly higher range. I haven't had any of those kinds of problems.

Is there a song where you wonder if your voice will be there that night?
There's always that spot at the end of "Jungleland" where you really have to open it up, in a very specific sort of way, and that still has a little challenge to it. It's usually there, but it's a big vocal exercise.

Yeah, that's a big one. What was your most embarrassing vocal mishap ever?
Forgetting words, or starting the show when the entire band wasn't onstage. [*Laughter*] Those are the kinds of embarrassing moments I've had, but nothing vocally. Occasionally, there'll be a din that gets so loud that towards the end of the night that your ears will play a trick on you, and you'll find yourself, *I'm a half tone up*. [*Laughs*] *I better straighten this out.*

Do you remember a performance where you surprised yourself?
The vocal on "Born in the U.S.A." had a lot of power to it. And that end of "Jungleland" was something that just spontaneously came out of me at a particular moment, and that was it. It wasn't planned or written. I was just singing to the chords playing at the time.

Do you have a favorite vocal performance you're really proud of?

Naw, I can't say I do.

How are you with hearing your own voice?

I've learned how to live with it. [*JTG laughs*] I love many other voices, you know? Rod Stewart or Bob Seger or Sam Moore, pick any of the great soul singers. There's many, many voices that have a gift that's greater than mine. But I've done okay with what the good Lord gave me.

There's so many vocal performances I'd love to talk to you about, but I'm gonna limit myself to five and ask for some quick thoughts on each one. First off, the entire *Live in New York City* record is the greatest live album ever. You cannot touch the E Street Band on that record. It's the only live album I've ever heard that really makes you feel the energy of actually being at the show. I mean, that thing is a fight for your very soul, and I can sum it all up in one specific moment. At the end of "Land of Hope and Dreams," you guys are ringing out the chords, building tension, vamping, and you're going, "Come on this train...Come on this train..."

Right...

And then, you do this gospel scream where the chords change beneath you, and you go, "Say...YEAAAAAHHH!" You know what I'm talkin about?

Yeah, I do.

Ohhh man, the devil don't stand a chance right there! Can you tell me about that moment?

[*Laughs*] We're deep into the gospel thing, as deep as we can get. And that's the "*Take me to Jesus*" moment of the night, you know, "*People Get Ready!*"

Alright, this one can tear a man to pieces if it comes on at the right time, driving late at night, and you're all alone. The piano version of "The Promise" off *18 Tracks*.

Oh, that was one take. A lot of it just depends on how deep in you get at a particular moment, how involved you get with the lyrics and the story. And then something wonderful can happen.

The next one may be your most soulful performance in a way. "Back in Your Arms."

Well, that's where I'm gettin' as close to my soul roots as I can. I'm doin' it like, not exactly the original thing, but not bad, you know? [*Laughs*] It's a good song. I'd like to see it covered by somebody who could really sing it.

The next one I'm curious about is "Lift Me Up," because you're singing in this real fragile falsetto we don't normally hear from you.

As I got older, I gained a falsetto, which I didn't have when I was young, so I started to put it to use. I said, "Well, let me try singing an entire song in this falsetto," and that song came along.

It was part of a John Sayles picture, and it just worked out very nicely. I actually like that cut quite a bit.

Alright, number five: I'd love to hear about the vocals on "Good Eye" off *Working on a Dream* 'cause it's such a badass performance. What was your inspiration for that?

Oh, "Good Eye!" I liked, "I had my good eye to the dark and my blind eye to the sun." I had that line, so I said, "Well, I gotta make somethin' outta that." It just turned into this little blues, and I think we distorted my voice over some funky microphone, and that's how it ended up sounding that way.

You do this amazing howl toward the end that I love, where you kind of like walk your voice up a few octaves. You know that howl? [*Mimics Bruce*] "Hey-hey-*HEY-HEY-HEY?!*" That's a badass scream, man! [*Laughter*]

Yeah. Yeah.

What's changed the most about your voice since you started?

I have a higher range than I used to have when I started. I have a falsetto that I never had. Why those things developed, I'm not sure, but they did rather naturally, and outside of that, I wouldn't say there's been any super big changes in my voice over the years.

If you could duet with any singer—living or dead—who would it be?

Oh, that's a tough question. God, it could be anybody. It depends. Who would I wanna be shown up by, is that the question? [*Laughter*] Sam Cooke, Elvis Presley, you know, it all goes down the line. Any of the great singers.

Well, speaking of that, you got a chance to be a part of Roy Orbison's backing band for that *Black and White* concert, and you got to share the mic with him a couple times! What was it like to sing with Roy Orbison?

Very enjoyable. That was a lot of fun. Just a great night. Great to sit behind him while he sang those songs so beautifully. That was singing.

Who are your top five favorite singers of all time?

That's very difficult. I have to have Sam Cooke up there. I'd have to have Elvis. Little Richard. I'm gonna be leaving a lot of people out. The early guys were great. You know, Jerry Lee Lewis was actually a hell of a singer. Talk about a guy that was so expressive as a country singer and a rock singer, just totally believable. Sometimes, it's not the greatest voice, it's this sort of authenticity and credibility that whenever they utter a note...there are a lot of guys that cover that ground. Fats Domino and Mick Jagger. I think Mick is the greatest white rock singer of all time for my money. Just the combination of sound and attitude. But then, there's Rod Stewart. Rod Stewart had one of the great white rock voices, still does. I could go on endlessly. Sam Moore, Smokey, of course. You have to put Smokey up there. There's a guy that in just a few syllables can melt everybody in the audience. I've seen him with just an opening line have the crowd go insane. This is a guy singin' as soft as can be, drivin' the audience wild. [*Laughs*] So, I don't know, too many to go on about.

If you could ask any singer about their voice, who would it be and what would you ask?
I don't know if I have any questions 'cause people get gifted. You gotta have the gift, and then learn how to sing well. There's people with good voices who don't quite know how to sing. You see them on the talent shows all the time. There's a lot of good voices that come up there, not that many people who know how to sing and have something particular to say. Those are the combinations that make a good voice. You gotta have a good voice. You gotta know how to sing. And you gotta have something to say with that voice.

BILLY SQUIER

IF YOU GREW UP IN THE 1980s, you are no stranger to the arena-sized anthems of Billy Squier. His 1981 *Don't Say No* album is widely considered one of the greatest rock records ever, and what followed were even more platinum records and hit singles. The dude was an absolute hit machine. But what propelled him forward wasn't just the strength of his songwriting; it was that voice. Just ask Freddie Mercury his feelings on the matter.

Those of you who weren't even alive during this golden age of music are still reaping the rewards of what Billy Squier brought to the party because he also happens to be one of the most sampled artists in hip-hop history. His signature sound has been used by everyone from Jay-Z to Run-D.M.C. to Alicia Keys, and on and on until the break of dawn.

This interview was a humbling one. If you're feeling a bit down, or discouraged, I think you may really appreciate what Billy Squier has to say, and what he was brave enough to reveal. Now start humming the riff to "Everybody Wants You." 'CAUSE THEY'RE GONNA!

Who first exposed you to singing?

The first memories I have of singing was going to church. The melodies and the organ would kick in, and it was moving to me. I enjoyed singing the hymns. I did start singing in glee club, which would've been high school, but none of it was serious at that point. It was fun.

When did you become serious about it?

It took a long time for me to even think about being a singer because guitar was my first love. But the key thing was that the singer in our group was more concerned with being a pop star. For him, it was like the teeny bopper magazines. My heroes were Clapton and Keith Richards and Jimmy Page, and guys who were serious, serious musicians. One night, we were onstage doing a show, and I looked at him and said to myself, *If I keep playing in this band, this guy's gonna kill my career.* And I left. I was twenty-four, and having quit, I decided I would become a singer, 'cause I was already a better singer than him. The difference was I never tried to be a great singer.

How do you become a great singer?

I had a guy who lived across the hall from me who was an opera singer. I would hear him warming-up and doing scales and breathing exercises. I thought, *I'm gonna see what I can learn from this!* And he gave me a couple pointers.

Do you remember the pointers?

You gotta breathe from down low. You gotta support your diaphragm, filling your lungs up from the bottom. Your whole singing apparatus is gonna be supported by the whole system." And it was very easy to do, breathing in. So, that was cool. And then, doing vocal exercises was understandable enough because I'd like my range to expand, because now I was thinking about who I wanted to sing like.

Who was that?

Rod Stewart and Paul Rodgers were very prominent. Both of whom could sing considerably higher than me at that point. I couldn't do what they could do. Hearing them sing was like, *Whoa! Look out!* [*Laughs*] If you try to sing like those guys, and you're not careful, you could hurt yourself. Because they're not really singing that way! *Nobody tells you that!* [*Laughter*] Nobody tells you how to go about that properly. But, I formed this band called Piper. It was the first time I had to come to grips with being a lead singer. *Really.* Because we got a record deal, and that's where I started struggling with singing; partially because of what we were talking about with Rod and Paul. I wasn't totally hurting myself, but I was trying too hard. I was trying to man up to them, kind of. And I would get this one particular pain under my rib-cage. It didn't mean I couldn't sing, but the psychological effect it left on me would be really debilitating because I've always had difficulty believing that I was any good.

It's been so wild hearing this from so many of my heroes.

A lot of artists have that issue. But growing up, I had certain role models that led me to believe that I really wasn't first rate, and it gave me a bunch of problems. So, when something like that would happen, I would blow it out of proportion, and it would really affect me. In my private world, I was worried, I was unhappy, I was struggling, and I didn't think I could do what I set out to do.

How do you find your way past those demons?

It's difficult. That's a tough answer because the other side of my persona is that despite of the way I grew up, not believing in myself, I always believed I could do this.

[*Laughs*] Isn't that the most fucked up thing about what we do? It's just this overconfidence and self-loathing all at once.

Yeah. When I was seventeen years old, my father said, "What are you gonna do? Are you gonna go to college? What are you gonna be?" I remember saying to him, clear as day, "Dad, if I do what I plan on doing, I'm gonna be fine. I'm gonna make plenty of money." And I wasn't doing it to make money, but he realized fifteen years later when I bought them a house and sent them around the world. [*Laughs*] I was determined, and I was dead serious about doing this, and I wasn't going to lose. But I would create a situation, which plays to my character, where I'm really not good enough, and people are gonna find out that I'm really a loser and all that.

So, when you were going through that, how did you get your voice to perform?

I'd be a little more careful in rehearsals. I'd pay a little more attention to getting the sound in my head, projecting it, keeping it away from the areas where I would feel pain, and then, it would just come. By the time it had to be right, it was right. There's a song on the second Piper album called "Little Miss Intent." I'm listening to it back going, *I got it! I got it! I'm singing like Paul Rodgers. I'm done. I can do it.* A lot of it was psychological.

I think that area often gets overlooked.

Mentally, we have so much effect on what we do, and what our bodies do. If you're not right in your head, you can work your tail off, and be a singer or a guitar player or whatever you want, and you won't get it right because you're standing in your own way. I'm a big believer in self-awareness, and it's really hard. You can improve your self-awareness your whole life. The more you know about yourself, the more you can get the most out of who you are.

Are you nervous or confident before you perform?

Only the requisite amount, which is you should always feel nervous before you play a little bit. [*Laughs*] It was scary because I never wanted to be a front man. I didn't wanna talk to an audience or come up with cool stories. I'd seen lots of great front men, but wanting to be true to myself, I had to take a little time to figure out what I was comfortable with that might fulfill the requirements of that job. It didn't happen overnight, but you go tour, and you learn, and find out the things you can do.

What did you find out?

I gave it a lot, and obviously, a lot of people reacted to it in a positive way. So, I'm better than I give myself credit for, but I wouldn't call it my greatest accomplishment. And I'm not trying to be self-effacing. I think I was good. Maybe I was *really good*. I know that I've written some great songs, and I can go out now and I can play these great songs, and I can sing the shit out of them. And I can do them better than I used to because I'm more comfortable now. I'm a better singer now. I'm a better guitar player now. And I'm not *trying* to be a great front man. I can just go out and be me. I have nothing to prove.

Are you doing vocal warm-ups before shows?

I never needed to. I learned how to sing right. I'm not trying to trivialize it, but once I get it, I got it. I've never warmed-up before shows, I've never lost my voice, so I guess, I learned my lessons well.

How do you take care of your voice on the road?

The place I do the most damage to my voice is after shows in situations where it's very loud and I have to shout to talk to people. So, no clubbing, no loud parties, stuff like that 'cause I'll lose my voice in a second. That would be the main thing, curb the excesses. It's not the show that's gonna hurt you, it's what's around it.

When you start getting sick, what do you do?

Call a doctor. Depending how sick you are, they might give you something for it. Sometimes they just say, "Stay in bed," and then it's up to you. But you can sing when you're sick, unless you have laryngitis or something. You can have a fever, or physical problems and feel like hell, but still sing if you just get yourself up for it.

Do you have any rituals before you go onstage?

I like to take a nap. At least half an hour. When you're on the road a lot, you gotta learn to catch some sleep when you can. That's really the ritual. I always want that time. I like to compose myself or quiet myself, because usually before the show I have stuff I have to do. I've got meet and greets or interviews, or shit's going on. I never wanna go from a flurry of things to just walking onstage. I want to go off by myself and get in "show mode."

Is there anything after the show that helps keep your voice in shape?

I realized that one of the dangerous things about being on the road is being in places where there's nothing to do after the shows. You're kind of high as a kite to begin with, and I think that's why we end up taking drugs and drinking, because you're already *going*. And you don't really wanna come down.

Or it's impossible to come down, so you start taking stuff *to* come down, and that can be dangerous too.

Yeah, that can happen too. I used to like to go out and hang with the road crew. They'd be breaking down, and I'd go out on the stage, and be talking with them, and maybe moving something—*not really doing the work*—but hanging out and enjoying the family. I preferred that to the potential wildness that existed outside the hall. That's kind of ritualistic. I did that a lot.

Are there songs where you wonder if your voice will be there that night?

Occasionally, yeah. It could be little bits and pieces. But as long as I know I can do it, then I don't worry about it too much. If it was something that I couldn't do consistently, then that would be a different story. Again, that would come down more to my mental frame of mind. If I wanted to make things hard for myself, then I could start worrying about stuff like that. *I could make the chest pains come back, you know what I mean?* It's like, I see the enemy and he looks like me.

Are there songs where you've had to adjust the key live?

Never. The only song I dropped a key in recently was "In the Dark," and it wasn't because I couldn't sing it. I did a different arrangement that sounded really good with the guitar capo'd up, and the key dropped from E to D. I know people drop it all the time. I don't believe in that. I feel like that's taking the easy way out. If I do "Lonely Is the Night" in C, you're not even gonna like it. It's not gonna work! It gets heavier, it gets weightier, so I don't believe that should ever happen. Unless you never cared to begin with.

Well, some people need to do it, or it might sound like shit, or they'll hurt themselves.

It should never happen! [*Laughter*]

Do you remember a performance where you surprised yourself?

When I did the first record, I was working with [producer] Eddie Offord up in Woodstock and needed to do background vocals. He knew this guy named Alex Ligertwood who had just become the singer of Santana. He said, "We should get Alex to come out, he's a great singer, and you guys can do it together." The day before, I got *brutally sick*. Eddie's girlfriend, in the tradition of Woodstock, was a real hippie and took me down to the organic store and got me like a thirty-two-ounce slurpee of beet juice and said, "You gotta drink this." I hate beets. If you ever try to drink beet juice, you'll just die. I mean, *that* almost killed me. But the next day, we did everything. It flushed everything outta my system. And one song from that record got tons of airplay, "You Should Be High Love."

Great song.

If you listen to the end, that's Alex and I scatting back and forth, completely live, not rehearsed at all. I remember listening back and going, *Man, I was doin' stuff. I wasn't prepared to do that!* I was really proud of that. I still am. I hear that and I'm like, *That's it, that's where it's at.* When the music takes control of you, that's what you want. A lot of times, if you know what you're doing and you're pre-programmed to do it, trying to do it a certain way, you don't let the ecstasy creep into it. That was the moment where we were just completely free flying. I really enjoyed that.

That's cool. Plus, you introduced beet juice as a sickness remedy!
That's true, miracle cure. Oh yeah, I highly recommend it.

How are you with hearing your own voice?
I think I have a great voice. [*Laughs*] No, I'm having too much fun with this interview now!

No, man, you should feel that way!
I think I have a great *sounding* voice, which is more to your question, not like I'm the greatest singer who ever lived. The sound of my records, the sound of my voice, I have no issues with at all. I think I'm a very consistent singer, and I believe in trying to get the most out of my voice in every song. I remember being surprised to hear myself on the radio, not knowing who it was, and going like, "This is fucking great! *Oh, that's me!*" [*JTG laughs*]

Do you have a favorite vocal performance you're really proud of?
I love "Little Miss Intent," which is the first time I really felt like a singer. There are some like "G.O.D." from *Hear & Now*; very hard song to sing because it's long, it doesn't stop, and it's high. That was an accomplishment as a writer too. It wasn't a three-minute single. It was doing something else. That's a tough vocal performance.

I love your falsetto on "Nobody Knows." How come you never broke that out more?
When I wrote it, I wasn't thinking about falsetto. When I came in to do it, it just worked perfect for that song. I also believe that's one take. But you're right, it's a very unique performance. Everything on *Don't Say No* worked perfectly, but it's a special song. I just didn't write anything that made me wanna approach it like that again.[10]

At the end of "Everybody Wants You," you give this little laugh as the song fades. Was that intentional or was something going on and you kept it there?
That was intentional, having grown up with lots of records where you'll hear stuff like that, and go, *Oh, that's cool*. ZZ Top or something. I laugh at the beginning of "Keep Me Satisfied" too.

I wanna acknowledge the musical chemistry between you and Bobby Chouinard (Billy's late drummer). He was one of my favorite drummers, and the way your vocal phrasing played off his drums was so perfect that I actually thought that *you* may

---

10   Turns out we were both wrong. Billy hit me with an email later saying, "BTW, there is indeed another falsetto performance (again, one take), and it IS on Happy Blue. "Two" is the last track on the CD and was written for my godson's second birthday (that's him on the front cover).

have started out as a drummer as well. But I read an interview with him where he said that you're the best drummer he knows that can't actually play the drums. Can you speak to that as a singer?

What Bobby says is true. I couldn't play it, but I knew he could. I could look at the drum set in my mind and go [*mimics an opening drum fill*]. That was "Catch 22." I did the whole pattern for him, he would get it, and just kill it. And that's not to take it away from Bobby, that's how much I was involved. It was really important to me. We were a great team and that's why it worked so well, because it went perfectly with what I was gonna do singing and playing on guitar.

Like on "Rock Out/Punch Somebody," or even "The Stroke," your vocals lay back within the drums, you know?

I do, but you're the first person that's ever made me aware of it. As you say it, it's completely obvious. When I hired Bobby, he played ahead of the beat. I loved him for his energy and his attitude and his personality, and he had *talent*. But he wasn't my kinda drummer. I taught him to back up. I basically took John Bonham and just laid it on Bobby and said, "This is how it is."

That's interesting 'cause I heard him say Bonham wasn't an influence on him.

He wasn't, I was. [*Laughter*] But what you said makes perfect sense, because when I get him to feel it the way I feel it, then I'm not fitting my voice to him. It's already fit.

It's like your phrasing *is* part of the groove, if that makes sense.

It does. This is kind of an "Ah-ha" moment. When we talk about this, it excites me because we're touching on something that I've done for a long time and never recognized necessarily how special it was.

There is a reason why the hip-hop community has embraced you the way they have. It's because of *the beat*. You and Bobby just had a very special combo that a lot of singers and drummers don't have.

It makes really good sense, so thank you for bringing that up front in my consciousness; something I was aware of but never really thought about in that way.

Something I don't think a lot of people are aware of is that Freddie Mercury sang background vocals on some of your records. Not only was he the greatest front man in rock 'n' roll history, but arguably the greatest singer too. What a testament to how much he thought of *you* as a singer and songwriter. And your voices sound so great together, like on "Love Is the Hero!" How did that come about?

First of all, my heart just pounds when I hear that. Some of the greatest experiences and friendships of my life was with Freddie. And he gave me a tremendous amount. I knew them since 1973, but fast forward to 1982 when they asked me to go on tour with them. I said, "Yes, of course." That was a great tour. Freddie and I sang together onstage and that was absolutely...wait a second...I get a little emotional when I talk about him 'cause I'm looking at a picture of him and me at the Forum in Los Angeles, singing to each other. I'm talking to you, and I looked over and went, *"Awww."* It's kind of overwhelming, but...it was fantastic.

Awww, man.

It's stuff that has meant more to me as the years have gone by. It meant a lot then, but it's meant more. And that led to other things. He sang on "Emotions in Motion." He does the heavy breathing.

Is that him whistling too?

Yeah! And then Roger [Taylor] sings at the end of it. Roger's doing the higher harmony. I had definite experiences with them, but the one that's really important is in 1986. I was making *Enough Is Enough* with an English producer named Peter Collins. Freddie had just moved into a big new house in Earls Court and found out that I was in town and wanted me to come over. So, we went over, and he asked, "What're you doing?" "I'm making a record." He says, "Can I hear it?" So, I got some tapes together and started playing them for him, and he loved them. We ended up staying up all night and working and listening to what I had, and he's going, "No, we're gonna do *this*." He re-wrote "Lady with a Tenor Sax." I would never come up with a title called "Lady with a Tenor Sax." [*JTG laughs*] That's Freddie. He said, "Darling, no, no, no, it's gonna be 'Lady with a Tenor Sax.'" I mean, I'm not saying no to Freddie. But "Love Is the Hero" wasn't intended to be a duet. That song was kind of done, but all of a sudden, he was there doing it. And at the end, it's fantastic when we're just singing back and forth. Talk about ecstatic moments, I mean, you could just kill me right then.

Did he just sing to your track or did you guys sing together?

Oh, we sang it together, yeah.

That's so awesome.

It was much more than that. We became friends, and I realized that he really respected me. I get emotional when I talk about him because he gave me so much. He made me believe in myself.

In what way?

I was trying to get him to sing some part on one of those songs, and he said, "No. You do it much better than I could." Like, *"What? No! No!"* He would say things like that, and he meant it. I've never forgotten it. To have someone of that magnitude—I mean, you hit the nail on the head, arguably the best front man of all time, a great writer, hugely creative, completely his own man. If you ask me for a highlight of my musical life, that's it.

Watching him sing, was there anything you picked up that helped you?

You could never quite do it as well as him, but he believed so much in his power when he was onstage. When he walked on, he'd go, *That audience is mine*, and you didn't have a choice if you were in the audience. He was able to overcome anything. Think about what he looked like. When he came out of the closet, he was the worst dresser in the world. I mean, he had no taste in clothes whatsoever, right? So, *he doesn't look good*, his mustache, his hair short, he didn't care! He didn't think for a second! If I did that, I'd be panicking! [*JTG cracks up*] He'd walk there, [*mimics Freddie*] "*Day-O!*" and just wait. "Oh, you didn't hear me?" "*DAYYY-O!*" And they'd do it! He could get away with stuff like that, which I couldn't do. But I learned from him, that.

Did you ever put it to use?

In fact, I got asked to do a show in Chicago by a radio station called The Loop. Def Leppard was headlining, and I had not been performing for a while, and had basically walked away. But I had made this acoustic record called *Happy Blue*, and I was intrigued by this idea: *I'll just go out and do it myself. I know people aren't gonna like it, but I don't care. This is where I'm at.* So, I worked up a little version of "Everybody Wants You" that I could do, an acoustic version of "The Stroke" called "Stroke Me Blues" and stuff from *Happy Blue*. Then, I got out there, and was in the dressing room, like, *You're a fucking idiot. What are you doing? You're gonna get crucified. This is a big mistake. They are not gonna like you. They don't want that. They want Billy Squier as they know him!* I started thinkin' about Freddie. I specifically started channeling Freddie. I said, "I've got to go out and I have to own them. I can't give them the option of not liking me." So, time came—totally by myself, no drum loops or anything, just me and a guitar—and it's probably like 15,000 people outdoors in an amphitheater. As soon as I came out, I just put my hands out in front of me, my palms up, and waited. And the place went nuts. I had 'em. That was Fred. He saved me that night! [*Laughter*] Ten minutes before showtime, I was in a lot of trouble.

That's great. So, what's changed the most about your voice since you started?

Remember how I talked about the way you think or feel about yourself can influence your physical performances? *Now* I feel good about myself, so I'm very relaxed.

What helped you get to that place?

I started doing more shows by myself, and what that's done has taken away a lot of the bombast of a big show. I still commit as much. I want every show to be the best show I've ever done. But I don't have to live up to anyone's expectations about the band. I can be a better singer than I was then, I can be a better guitar player, but I can't go back in time and play the music in the times it was played in. All that was a part of what made "Billy Squier" such a phenomenon. I can't bring all those intangible forces to bear that made those shows so great. But if I go out *now* and I do this, it's *new*. This isn't Billy Squier trying to go back and be "Billy Squier" like everybody else does. I have no desire to be in the round robin summer fests of bands that go out every year and play the same stuff over and over again. I can't imagine anything more boring. If you see me now, I'm sitting on a stool. But wait 'til you hear me play guitar, and wait 'til you hear me sing.

If you could duet with any singer—living or dead—who would it be?

I'd love to sing with Aretha, but I don't know how I would do it! [*Laughs*] I'd just be listening to her! I'd be on my knees, just worshiping at the altar. But it'd be worth a try!

Who are your top five favorite singers of all time?

Oh boy. I'm gonna go with Paul [Rodgers], I'm gonna go with Rod Stewart. After that, there were people who influenced me in different ways. For instance, Jagger influenced me. Do I think Mick Jagger's a great singer? Not necessarily. But is he a great vocalist? Yeah! I mean, his expressions, his attitude, the slang, the way he delivers stuff. Even someone like Jim Morrison, the power of the delivery, it's like, wow! Then, we're gonna throw in Freddie, of course.

If you could ask any singer about their voice, who would it be and what would you ask?

Whoa. That's a really hard question. Okay. Paul McCartney. And I want an in-depth answer: "What was it like to sing with John Lennon?"

That's a great question.

And it's gotta be more than a phrase. He can't just say, "Great."

He would probably look at you and say, "Only if you tell me what it was like to sing with Freddie Mercury."

And we can do it! [*Laughter*]

PAUL
STANLEY

I T'S BEEN FIFTY YEARS SINCE KISS FIRST HIT THE STAGE as larger-than-life characters wearing face paint, eight-inch platform boots, breathing fire, spitting blood, and belting out crowd-pleasing rock songs at maximum volume. And Paul Stanley, The Starchild, is always right there in the center, his shirt off, wielding his electric guitar and sharing most of the vocal duties with his partner in crime, bassist, Gene Simmons, The Demon.

KISS have sold over 100 million records, making them one of the bestselling bands ever. They've been inducted into the Rock & Roll Hall of Fame and their iconic logo is recognized as one of the most famous in rock history. And whether Paul is shouting out loud to a crowd of 137,000 in Rio, starring as The Phantom in the stage production of *The Phantom of the Opera*, or singing classic R&B with his side project, Soul Station, he is always studying different aspects of the voice, paying attention to the changes that come with age, and staying "Too cool to sweat."

Who first exposed you to singing?

In my family, music was central to everything. My parents, my sister, and I had very good voices, and we used to spend a lot of time, particularly in the car, if not in our apartment, singing together. And everybody had a fairly innate sense of harmony. We never sang unison. We would break out into harmonies on various songs, and it was very natural to me. Singing was really a bonding process.

What made you go, "I'm gonna do this for a living"?

Music, or anything where you're gonna go against the grain, has to be something you're compelled to do. So, when someone comes to me and says, "I'm thinking of being a musician," I go, "Don't." If it's something you have to think about, you're in the wrong game.

Were you emulating anyone when you started out?

I was mimicking anything I heard and listening to the nuances. I'm talking about being a six-year-old, seven-year-old. [*Laughs*] I was taken with the nuances of what I was hearing, whether it was Dion and the Belmonts or hearing Jussi Björling, a Swedish tenor, I wanted to be able to do those things with my voice. The voice is such an interesting instrument because it's really the only instrument that is manipulated by your brain. You don't touch it, you don't blow on it, you don't use your feet or your hands on it. It's totally an ethereal connection, so it presents its own problems and challenges. But it's kind of like learning to navigate a jet with your mind. It's like the earliest form of *Star Wars*.

How did you find your own voice?

For a long time, my voice was a product of honing my limitations, and then, at some point in the '80s, I found my head voice, and it was like opening the door to the attic. All of a sudden you have all this head room. At that point, I could make dogs run into the street. [*JTG laughs*] That was eye opening to me, and there was quite a while where I was more focused on how high I could sing rather than why I was doing it. But it was very freeing, and gave me more command and understanding of the instrument.

Did you ever have any vocal training?

I was never keen on vocal training, except at one point where I had some questions, and I was fortunate to find somebody who wanted to preserve the characteristics of *my* voice and *my* technique while addressing the problems I was having.

That's a big fear with coaches, that they'll take away what you naturally have.

I've found that most teachers tend to turn out cookie-cutter singers. I'm familiar with enough of them where I think they replace a lot of your innate personality and imperfection in your voice, and replace it with gloss and technique, which, certainly in terms of rock music, tends to turn singers into some sort of bastardized Broadway singer.

Do you feel nervous or confident before you perform?

When I was in grade school, they would put on children's adaptations of musicals. Every year, I would go and try out and freeze. Although I had a really good voice and good projection, as soon as I would get in front of people, this little mouse squeak would come out. So, every year, I would swear that *that* year I was going to conquer it, and didn't. But the practical reality is that if you truly want to front a band, or perform onstage, and you have the ability, then you better find a way to break down that barrier—the shyness and the insecurity—otherwise you're dead before you start.

What helped you break through that wall?

Necessity. You climb up the ladder to the top of the diving board, and you're either gonna climb back down or you're gonna jump. I've always been one for jumping.

All these years later, are you nervous or confident before you perform?

I understand nervousness before you perform, but nervousness to me comes from not being sure of yourself. And I understand that when you first start out. But as you build your confidence—and confidence should be based on experience and positive feedback—why would you be nervous? If anything, I have anticipation to get out there because I know that I can do what's expected. Once I established what I was doing, and knew I was in control of it, that was really the key. Are you in control of it? If you're in control of it, it's like driving. Why would you be nervous? You know how to drive.

Do you do vocal warm-ups before shows?

When you're young, you're invincible, or so you think, so vocal warm-ups were never something that I did. The more demanding things became, I found myself warming-up, particularly to break into the upper register 'cause that was a door that needed to be oiled and opened. It needed some nurturing or prodding, so warm-ups became important.

What's your routine?

It can be doing some phonetics and different scales and intervals. Sometimes it's just about warming-up my cords, not necessarily singing loud or even singing, as much as just letting them vibrate. Humming along with music that I'm playing in the dressing room.

Do you have any other rituals before you hit the stage?

Because of the physicality of what I do in KISS, I do crunches and curls and stretching, so that I can do what's expected and keep it fairly effortless. It's another aspect of the machine.

Including make-up and everything, what's the order of how you prepare?

We get to the show by about 4:00. As a rule, I may not have eaten but a small snack. At 4:00, I'll eat somewhat of a small meal. And we're not on 'til 9. Then, there's all kinds of things that need to get done, and somewhere during that, I'll get on a big, inflatable exercise ball and do crunches and stretching, and then I'll do push-ups, and then I'll do bicep curls and triceps, and do whatever I need to do to get—I don't wanna say pumped up cause I'm not in it to look like The Rock.

[*Laughs*] No, but there's a certain physique you need to have in order to be The Starchild. I mean, you're a fuckin' action figure!
Yeah, you know, unfortunately I compete with my past! [*Laughs*] So I'm mindful of that, and then I listen to some music while I'm getting ready and sing or hum along with it. Then, make-up usually starts. If I'm in a rush, I can do it fairly quickly.

Wait, you're doing your make-up yourself?
Oh, totally.

I never knew that.
Yeah, yeah, since the beginning.

How long does it take to apply your own make-up?
It can take an hour and a half, or it can take thirty-five minutes.

I've always wondered this: Black star first, white make-up around the star? Or do you do the white make-up, then put the black star over the white?
White face with an outline of where the star will be, then black.

It must get pretty hot onstage with all that gear and pyrotechnics. Do you keep anything up there to help you through the gig?
No, I'm too cool to sweat. I leave that to the other guys. [*JTG laughs*]

Is there anything after the show that helps keep your voice in shape?
Not really. My voice has always been pretty durable. That all goes back to technique. If you were really screaming your head off onstage, you'd have no voice left. It's really knowing how to do what you do.

How do you take care of your voice on the road?
I don't drink alcohol the day before a show. I only drink when there's a day off. Alcohol tends to dry out your vocal cords and certainly my sinuses. It just takes away a lot of the lubricant that's really important. I learned that to preserve my voice, you don't wanna go onstage with dry cords.

When you start getting sick, what do you do?
If you understand singing enough, then you should be able to shift your voice to another part of your cords. It doesn't always work, but I think singers can modify where they're singing from in terms of your vocal cords. But your best defense is always water and staying hydrated.

You had some vocal surgeries, didn't you?

Mine were more exploratory, just to check out my vocal cords in a way that couldn't be done with a scope. I was interested in finding out if there was a way to extend your vocal longevity lifespan, because, in the end, singing is biomechanics, and like any other sport or athletic endeavor, muscles change over time. In this case, it's your vocal cords.

What did you learn from doing that?

As time goes by, your cords begin to stiffen. They don't have the same flexibility or ability to vibrate like they once did. So, you're trying to compensate by forcing more air to get them to do what they did. That's why people drop keys, because you can't muster the air it takes to get your cords to hit the highest notes. I was curious if there's a way to extend that, and there really isn't. So, if you listen to a lot of singers and go, "Gee, they don't sound quite like they used to," well, you know, Dr. J can't shoot baskets like he used to. I mean, it's just the deterioration or the lifespan of something.

Are there songs where you've had to adjust the key live?

Well, you don't always do that because of whether or not you can hit the note. It also has to do with, sometimes, tonally, your voice may hit a sweet spot that delivers the song better in one key than the other.

Do you have songs where you wonder if your voice will be there that night?

I'm pretty good at making it happen. I have to be honest enough to go, if you were looking at it under a microscope, it wouldn't necessarily have the same richness or the same effortlessness that it once had, but in the context of a live performance, that's okay because you're not listening under a microscope. Recording is a different animal because you're gonna hear it over and over, and you don't have the luxury of the ambience of a hall and the excitement of a crowd. So, you don't need the same subtly that you would want to have in the studio. But a performance of a catalog of songs is not made or broken by one crack, or the human failure in a song or two. You have to look at the whole picture.

What was your most embarrassing vocal mishap ever?

There's been times where my voice might crack, and that didn't happen thirty years ago. But I also remember, decades ago, going to see Robert Plant and Jimmy Page, and going, "Oh gee, his voice is cracking." Well, welcome to the real world. Once again, I think you have to look at the entire evening, and if you're watching a basketball game and somebody shoots and misses, well, that doesn't mean that the team's not gonna win, that doesn't mean that the next is not gonna be a three-pointer.

Do you remember a performance where you surprised yourself?

In the '80s and '90s, I surprised myself a lot, because anything I wanted to do, if I could hear it in my head, I could do it. Hitting high Cs was nothing, let's go for Es and Fs. But those are times that don't necessarily last forever. It goes back to human frailty, and that's something that every athlete—and I consider singing an athletic sport—modifies, and has to, based upon the evolution or de-evolution of age.

How are you with hearing your own voice?

When I first started singing on recordings, I didn't like my voice, and over time I thought it was pretty friggin' good.

Do you have a favorite vocal performance you're really proud of?

I can't say a particular one. I pulled a lot of stuff off, live, that was pretty amazing to my ear, a lot of singing and vocal gymnastics that were effortless. That's the interesting point, to do it without any effort. Even on KISS *Unplugged*, I think "I Still Love You" is an example of being able to do virtually whatever I wanted.

That might be my favorite vocal of yours.

Thanks. The thing I appreciate about a lot of those performances was that they were effortless, and I could do it twenty-five times. It wasn't like climbing a mountain, it was like soaring over one.

Do you have a favorite Gene Simmons vocal performance?

A lot of his earlier stuff tended to be a bit campy, but it was so much his personality. Sometimes I tried to steer him away from it, and I was kind of missing the point. That's so much a part of what he does. Some of the later things were really definitive. Some of the stuff on *Revenge* is great, and some of the stuff on *Sonic Boom* is great. "I Love It Loud" is terrific. He's got a very definite delivery, and the interesting things is, when I first met him, he had a very melodic, lyrical voice, and he kind of transformed it into a character voice.

"Hard Luck Woman" is one of my favorite KISS tracks, and the story I've heard is that you actually wrote that song for Rod Stewart, but you guys ended up keeping it for Peter Criss to sing. Is that true?

Yeah.

Man, it's the greatest Rod Stewart song. He should have covered it!

I sometimes approach songwriting as a puzzle or as a challenge. Can you write a song like this? "I Was Made for Lovin' You." Can you write a dance-disco song? I've always been a big fan of Rod because his roots have always been Sam Cooke and David Ruffin. But when I heard "Maggie May" and "You Wear It Well" and "Mandolin Wind," I thought, *Gee, I can write a song like that*. I sat down and pulled out my twelve string guitar and started playing what was "Hard Luck Woman." Then "Beth" became a hit, and we needed a follow up. So, we decided to do "Hard Luck Woman," and instead of me singing it, we'll have Peter sing it 'cause he has that raspy voice.

Did Rod ever comment on that song, or was it ever discussed?

No, I don't even know if Rod's heard it. I could ask him.

You've also had the unique experience of starring onstage in *The Phantom of the Opera*. As a vocalist, I'm curious about the difference between being in a rock band and being in a Broadway musical.

Well, it's extremely demanding because it calls for precision. You're not playing it by ear, you're singing classic material that people know and expect to hear delivered with an authenticity, staying true to the framework and the format. And you also answer nightly to a director who will tell you if you're on target or if you need to work on something.

You have all this freedom to do whatever you want in KISS. What was it like to suddenly be in a position where you're receiving notes and input from other people about your voice?

I had to do a full on audition, 'cause, frankly, they don't need Bozo the Clown to come in and ruin a billion dollar franchise. It was a big challenge because it took a different technique of singing, staying away from certain parts of my voice, and living in a different part of my voice. And you can hear a pin drop when you sing something like "Music of the Night." There's also a need to stay very, very true to it and respectful. And there's one "be" in there that if you don't hit, you fall on your face in front of everybody. I was pleased to find out that I wasn't the only person who, once in a while, wouldn't make it.

[*Laughs*] That's gotta be such a crazy feeling!

Doing something like that eight times a week takes a huge amount of focus and discipline. I had two weeks rehearsal before they threw me into the show, and the show had been running for ten years, so you don't rehearse with the cast, you rehearse with some of the understudies. Preparing was exhausting, but it was also exhilarating. It's one of the most satisfying creative outlets I ever had. I was supposed to be the second to last Phantom, but they wound up buying out the contract of the person who was supposed to replace me, and I stayed and did the final shows.

That's amazing. And were you warming-up beforehand?

I warmed-up for a good half hour before each show.

"Odyssey" off *Music From "The Elder"* has a Broadway feel, and that's one of my favorite vocals of yours.

I really don't like it. It's very hokey and Broadway-esque without being the real deal.

But there's a character thing about your voice that I really love in it.

I think so much goes into delivering a song well, and part of delivering a song well is knowing what you're singing about. It's clear to me that some of the singers I see on talent shows don't know what they're singing about. I can always tell that they don't understand the lyric. For somebody to sing something well, they need to sit down and read lyrics, not memorize them. In the same way that an actor reads a script, the best singers are the ones who deliver a song from their heart, and deliver a song understanding what they're singing, not just as gibberish to go along a melody.

And you felt you were doing that on "Odyssey?"
Yeah, because I learned so much during *Phantom*. There was a day where I was rehearsing with one of the understudies, and one of [producer] Hal Prince's people from New York came up and said, "Let's all sit down and read the lyrics to the song." We sat down and read them, and talked about the lyrics, what they meant and why the person was singing that. That completely changed the song. Because I had a tape of me singing one of these particular songs before I joined the show, and it was clueless. I hit all the notes, but it had no depth to it. That's my point. The need for you to understand what you're singing, and in a case like "Odyssey," I felt more like a kid trying to sing opera-ish; it wasn't genuine. To project a song, you have to either have lived it, or understand where the lyric comes from.

I couldn't agree more. But can we agree I like "Odyssey," and it's still pretty good?
We can agree that *you* like it. [*JTG laughs*]

What's changed the most about your voice since you started?
Hmm. Tough question. Can't answer it.

If you could duet with one singer—living or dead—who would it be?
Oh boy. Sam Cooke.

Who are your top five favorite singers of all time?
Pavarotti, Tony Bennett, Robert Plant, Rod Stewart, and Steve Marriott.

If you could ask any singer about their voice, who would it be and what would you ask?
Robert Plant. "When did you realize your high notes were going?" I remember going to see Plant live in '69 and just being gobsmacked, just completely baffled by how he was hitting those notes, particularly because he wasn't singing falsetto. He was singing full voice. I would find out decades later nobody can do that forever.

MAVIS STAPLES

"THANK THE LORD, I GOT A NEW BORN SOUL."
That's what it feels like when you hear Miss Mavis sing. Together with her father, her sisters, and her brother, Mavis Staples, as a member of The Staples Singers, changed the sound of gospel music for good. From the time she was a little girl, Mavis and her family became known as "God's Greatest Hitmakers." But The Staples sound really began to evolve when they joined up with the Rev. Dr. Martin Luther King to become the musical voice of the civil rights movement, turning their faith-filled, powerful songs into a glorious call to action.

Inducted into the Rock & Roll Hall of Fame and the Blues Hall of Fame, Mavis has continued touring and recording on her own, well into her eighties. To say that she is an icon is a massive understatement. So many of the singers interviewed in this book consider Mavis both an inspiration and touchstone for their own voices. And what a voice. What a soul. What a spirit. Alright, Mavis, let 'em hear it!

Who first exposed you to singing?

My father [Roebuck "Pops" Staples]. I was always singin' around the house, but Pops really started me to singin'. He was with an all-male group, and these guys wouldn't come to rehearsal. He just got disgusted, and one night, came home, pulled out this little guitar, set us down in a circle on the floor, and began givin' us voices to sing. Now my voice comes from my mother's side. My mother and grandmother had really strong voices. 'Cause, you know, Pops has a little fine voice [*impersonates Pops singing*] "Will the circle be unbroken?" [*Chuckles*]

Were you emulating anyone when you started out?

I loved Sister Mahalia Jackson, and Pops would tell me, "Mavis, don't try to sing like Sister Mahalia Jackson. Get your own voice style. Sing like Mavis." Pops was always playin' these gospel records, but they would always be men, you know, The Soul Stirrers, The Dixie Hummingbirds. One day, I was back in my little play area, and I heard this lady's voice, and it moved me on into the livin' room where Pops was. I asked him, "Who is that daddy?" He said, "That's Sister Mahalia Jackson." I said, "*I like her*." Pops had to play Sister Mahalia Jackson for me every day when he'd come home from work. Then, one day, he came and said, "Guess what? They want us to open up for Sister Mahalia Jackson on Monday night." Well, I had to wait the whole weekend 'cause that was a Friday.

That must have felt like forever!

I was so excited, and after the show, she told me, "You're a good little old singer." Then, I grabbed my jump rope and was on my way out the door, and she said, "Where you goin'?" I said, "I'm goin' outside to jump rope." I was eleven years old. Us children, we always brought our ropes to church. She said, "Outside?" She felt my chest, she felt my neck, she say, "Don't you know that you're damp?" I said, "No, ma'am." She say, "Yes, you're damp, and you don't go out in the air after you sing like that and you're damp. You wanna sing a long time like me, don't you?" I said, "Yes, ma'am." She said, "Well, when you get through singin', you take all this off, and you tell mama to give you one of your brother's t-shirts. You get dry before you go outside." She taught me how to take care of my voice and became my friend, my teacher, and my idol. And to this day, Jason, I get dry. I take a t-shirt with me to the concert. *Not my brother's t-shirt*, [*laughter*] but I still do that.

How did you find your own voice?

I would just sing, and I guess my style came to me. Nobody really taught me. It's just my gift. God blessed me. He gave me my voice. I don't even know what key I sing in. My father, when he passed, I said, *Ohh Lord, Pops passed and left me, and I don't know what key*... When I got with Jeff [Tweedy] or any other producer, they would always ask, "What key?" I say, "I don't know. You have to work with me and let me find what's comfortable for me."

I don't know what keys I sing in either.

I sang the National Anthem one time for the Lakers, and the organist asked me, "What key would you like, Miss Staples?" I said, "Ohhh God, that's a good question." [Laughter] I had to run, find a phone, call Pops, and I said, "Daddy, what key would I sing this National Anthem in?" He said, "Wait a minute, let me get my guitar." He got the guitar, and he said, "Okay, show me where the highest point is" [hums "And the rocket's red glare, the bombs bursting in air."] I showed him that. He say, "Okay, you tell 'em you want the key of A." That's always been a problem with me after Pops passed. Because anywhere my father would hit his guitar, I knew where to sing. I knew the sound.

Did you ever have any vocal lessons?

I've never had any voice coachin'. I just drink lots of ginger tea with honey. Prince told me one time, he said, "Mavis, you're talkin' too loud. You have to save your voice." I said, "Well, Prince, in my family, if you wanted somethin', you had to talk loud. There were five of us children." Prince and Roberta Flack were two of my friends that told me, "Mavis, you're talkin' too loud. You'll mess up your voice." But to this day, Jason, I still talk loud. I can't help it!" [Laughter]

Are you nervous or confident before you perform?

I was always scared to death. But after I get one or two songs out, then I'm comfortable.

Are you doing vocal warm-ups before your shows?

I do. I had polyps one time and had surgery on my vocal cords. After the surgery, the doctor gave me this lady to go to to strengthen my vocal cords again.

How did you get polyps? From singing?

I think I got them 'cause I was smokin' back then, I'm sorry to say. But I sure did stop. You know, in high school, you get caught up, and you wanna do what everybody else is doin', not knowing it was bad for my voice. I said, "Daddy, I can't make my highs." 'Cause I have a good range, that was why Pops started me to singin', because when we first started, my brother Pervis was the lead singer.

Right, you took over for your brother at some point.

Pops told me, "Pervis can't make the highs anymore. You can sing high and low, so you have to do it." I was singin' baritone. Baritone is the prettiest voice in the group to me. But Pervis, he reached puberty and his voice got too heavy. When I had to do it, I said, "Ohhh God." I did not want to do it. "Uncloudy Day" was the first song that I had to sing lead on, and I was singin' bass. I was about twelve or thirteen years old!

Didn't some people think you were a man too?

I had to be a man or a big fat lady. People would have bets that I was not a little girl. And my brother and I, we would fool the people. When it came time for me to say, [sings in a deep *baritone*] "Well, well, well. Oh Lord, they tell me now," Pervis would pretend he was goin' to the mic, and you'd hear all over the audience, "I told you that wasn't no little girl!" But while they were goin' through that, I'd ease up to the microphone, [*sings*] "Well, well, well..." Lord, the place would go crazy! One man got mad at me. "Little old girl, I bet my whole paycheck on you!" [*Laughter*]

So, tell me about your warm-up routine?

I do the lowest register and come from my gut. [*Speaks low, vibrating her cords by saying*] "Yeaaaah—Noooooo." Feel my vocal cords rattling, you know, like vibratin'. That's the only thing I do. Everybody else be [*mimics people doing scales*]. I don't do that! [*Laughter*]

Do you have any other rituals before you hit the stage?

I go in that dressin' room, I pray a little prayer, and I go to my heart. Like my father taught me, I go to my heart. I do my little exercises if I need to. And then I go onstage. I'm eighty years old, but I don't pitty-pat onstage. I sing hard, I work hard. [*Laughs*] I can't believe I'm still doin' it at this age and don't let up. I still sing just as hard as I did when I was twenty years old. It's just my style.

It's really amazing, Mavis. How else do you to take care of your voice on the road?

That's one thing that the throat doctor told me, "You shouldn't talk before you sing or after you sing. That'll keep your voice." And I do that. We call it "From stage to car."

Do you do anything after the show to keep your voice in shape?

My little tour manager, he gets me straight to the car and back to the hotel. Because if I stay there any longer, I got to be shakin' hands and talkin' to people, so that's not good. But I can't sleep right away because I'm still wired up. I'm thinkin' about how good the show was, or somethin' may have happened that wasn't such a good thing, and that's mostly on the band. They have to keep the tempo. You want a nice groove, and sometimes the drummer gets too fast, so I have to jot that down, or send the band leader a text: "Things were rushing. We have to keep a groove." Pops always taught the musicians, "You can't play too loud. You have to compliment her."

When you start getting sick, what do you do?

I very seldom get sick. Now, I might catch a cold, but I will toil on through it. If I'm sick, the show must go on. I don't come up with any excuses. "I can't do it tonight, y'all, I got this cold." *I sing through that cold!* And God is with me. Certain notes I can't reach, I'll go somewhere else, but I'll make it work.

Are there songs where you wonder if your voice will be there that night?

Well, if there's a song like that, we just won't do that song. We'll pull it out of the show. There's so many songs that I can sing that if something like that happens, we don't have to do that song. You gotta be flexible, Jason! [*Laughter*]

Now you tell me!

[*Screams out, cracking up*] *Yeah!*

Are there songs where you have to adjust the key live?

Oh, I don't have to adjust the key. Sometimes I have to remember certain songs. I had my tour manager get me a little teleprompter. As long as I was in my seventies, I was fine. Since I hit eighty, I think I be tellin' myself I'm old. But I gotta stop that, I'm really not; I feel good. I'm doin' everything I was doin' when I was younger. I'm grateful. I'm blessed to be the age I am, and God has blessed me to continue, and people still wanna hear me. That's what amazes me after all these years. I sit and I think about my father sometimes. *Pops, if you only knew, I am still singin', you wouldn't believe it.* You know? 'Cause I don't believe it.

Well, we're all real lucky that we get to hear it, Mavis. We're real lucky.

Ohhh, thank you.

What was your most embarrassing vocal mishap ever?

Listen, man. [*JTG cracks up*] This one takes the cake—and I have fallen on the stage too—but for some way, I'll hold the mic, and I'll continue to sing while I'm on the floor. But my most embarrassing was in the Apollo Theater. This lady had made Cleedy [Mavis's sister] and I these gowns. And the gowns were sheer. So, she made us these cotton slips to go on to the floor. But instead of puttin' elastic in the waist, she put a hook in the [eye of the dress, locking it together]. And we do this clap, and as we're clappin', I raised my arms, and I could feel that slip comin' off me, goin' down. So, I told my brother, I said, "Pervis, when we get ready to go off, I'm gonna step out of this slip. You pick it up and ball it up." I step out of it, Jason. That boy, he picked that slip up, and he flung it like when somebody's fightin' and they wave the white flag. And people laughed! I mean, they must've laughed for five or ten minutes. I was so embarrassed.

Do you remember a performance where you surprised yourself?

I've done that a lot of times. Sometimes I'll come off the stage and I can't believe I did that. Things come to you that you haven't done before, and I might not ever do it again, but I was shocked at myself. *Where did that come from?*

And how about in the studio?

Pops would always let us know, "When you go in the studio, be ready. Have your song ready. Because that's not the place to be rehearsing. That's money. You have to pay money to be in the studio." So, I always rehearse before goin' in the studio. But certain things that you might hear in the music, that you didn't hear before, it'll make you do something different, it'll make you go further. And it always turn out to be better when you do somethin' that you haven't done. You surprise yourself. And when you play it back, "Ohh my, I have to keep that. I have to do that again! That sounds good." Yeah, it happens.

How are you with hearing your own voice?

Oh yeah, I'm okay.

Do you have a favorite vocal performance you're really proud of?

I love to sing "Freedom Highway" because that's a song that my father wrote for the Movement, and when we sing it, I get a chance to preach. So, that's my favorite, but I don't do it every night because it's a long, long song. I stretch it out. I tell the audience all about why we're singin' that song. My father wrote it for the big march from Selma to Montgomery.

Your *Livin' on a High Note* Album has a such a beautiful track called "MLK Song" where you sing in tribute to Martin Luther King. You and your family played such an important role in the Civil Rights Movement, working so close with him. And this was a moment in time where using your voice to fight for equality and injustice could actually get you killed. And yet, you, your father, and your sisters were right there on the front lines, using your voices in the most powerful way there is. I'm curious what it felt like for you to sing during that pivotal moment in history?

It felt good because we were doing good. We met Dr. King in the '60s. The Movement hadn't begun yet. He had a radio show that my father would listen to all the time, and we happened to be in Montgomery, Alabama on a Sunday mornin'. So, Pops called my sisters and I to his room, and told us that this man, Martin, has a church here. "I wanna go to the 11:00 service. Would you all like to go?" And we told him, yeah. So, we went to Dexter Avenue Baptist Church, and someone let Dr. King know that we were in his service, and he acknowledged us. He said, "I'm glad to have Pops Staples and his daughters here this mornin', and we hope you enjoy the service." Well, we enjoyed the service. And when the service was over, Dr. King would stand at the door to shake the worshippers' hands as they filed out. My sisters and I shook his hand, and when Pops got to him, he stood there and talked to him for a bit. When we got back to the hotel, he said, "Y'all know, I really like this man. I like his message. And I think that if he can preach it, we can sing it." That's when we started writin' freedom songs. We joined the Movement, and Pops and Dr. King became friends.

Did Dr. King ever tell you what song of yours was his favorite?

"Why (Am I Treated So Bad?)." That was his favorite song. Anytime we'd be goin' to the meetin', he would tell Pops, "You gonna sing my song tonight, right?" And Pops would say, "Oh yeah, Doctor. We're gonna sing the song." We would sing about twenty minutes before he would speak. And I tell you, I'm just so grateful that Pops was hearin' him on the radio and wanted us to sing these songs that he could preach.

If there's ever been a more powerful example of how important singing is, and how important music is, it has to be things like the Civil Rights Movement. That's where singing matters most.

That's right. That's right. And music is healing. You know, people will hear some messages through a song that they don't hear in a speech. So, yeah, it's the *best*.

Well, I wish Dr. King could've heard "MLK Song."

I wish he could have too.

What about Dr. King's singing voice, could he hold a tune?

No, I don't think so! [*Laughter*] I never heard Dr. King sing! No, Dr. King would be singin' in his preachin', if you wanna call that singin'.

He had a melody! So, what's changed the most about your voice since you started?

Well, my voice is heavier. I don't sing as high as I used to. But I like it because it's different. All of the other girls sing in these *tiny little voices*. I'm still singin' baritone and bass.

If you could duet with one singer, living or dead, who would it be?

Ohhh, Sister Mahalia Jackson. That's easy.

And who are your top five favorite singers of all time?

Sister Mahalia Jackson, Aretha Franklin, Sam Cooke, Odetta, and Nina Simone.

If you could ask any singer about their voice, who would it be and what would you ask?

It'd be Jimmy [Carter] from The Blind Boys of Alabama. I call him Jumpin' Jimmy. He's my little boyfriend. I would like for him to show me how he hold that note. He holds a note so long, Jason, I would have fainted by now! Man, little Jimmy Carter, he can hold a note for a good ten minutes, and it just goes on and on, [*sings*] "Ahhhhhhhhhhhhh..." I can't do it. I asked Dizzy Gillespie one time in New York, I said, "Dizzy, can you give me someone here that teaches voice coachin'. I wanna know how to hold a note." Because they do it. Trombone Shorty does it too on his horn, they hold the note. And Dizzy Gillespie, I hate to say it, he cursed me. He said, "Goddamnit, you got it already! You don't need no voice coachin'! You gonna mess up!" I said, "Okay, Dizzy, I won't." He got mad at me! So, that's who I would ask: Jimmy Carter, "What do you do to hold that note like that?"

All I can say is God bless Dizzy Gillespie.

[*Bursts into laughter*] Oh boy, you are somethin'. And you right! You are exactly right! God bless you, Dizzy.

ROD STEWART

IN 1964, AFTER SEEING LONG JOHN BALDRY PERFORM, Rod Stewart was singing the blues and playing harmonica in Twickenham railway station. A man passing by heard the sound of Rod's voice, ran over to him from across the tracks, and asked him to join his band. It was Long John Baldry.

There ain't a singer alive who wouldn't want to sing like Rod Stewart. He opens his mouth, we shake our heads. It's really that simple. His perfect blend of melodic R&B, raspy rock 'n' roll, and long-suffering soul has made him one of the bestselling artists of all time, selling over 250 million records! He's also been inducted into the Rock & Roll Hall of Fame—TWICE! Once as a solo artist, and again as the main vocalist of Faces.

In 1969, this guy started singing for one of the greatest rock 'n' roll bands ever, then had the balls to release his first solo album the very same year. His output has remained that consistent, and his distinct and iconic voice has carried him through the shifting genres of popular music, even thriving through the disco era, discovering new heights into the 21st Century, and singing jazz and pop standards with the incredible success of the Great American Songbook. That was a long-winded way of saying, few have what Rod's got—a voice for all time.

Who first exposed you to singing?

I suppose in terms of singing in front of the public, that would've been Long John Baldry. But I was singing well before I met John in the early '60s.

Were you emulating anyone when you started out?

Yeah, I used to like Lonnie Donegan and a lot of the skiffle artists of the day, and moved on to Ramblin' Jack Elliott, Woody Guthrie, and Bob Dylan. I loved all that folk stuff, especially Bob Dylan's first album.

How did you find your own voice?

Copying others, really. 'Til I found me own voice, I used to sound like Sam Cooke or Muddy Waters. And then, the Rod voice came out around the late '60s, early '70s. I never worked on making it raspy. People put it down to smoking and whiskey. But I've never drunk whiskey and I've never smoked. It's just come out like that. It's very hard to describe what's going on in one's vocal cords. My vocal cords are fairly large, but it's a mysterious thing.

Did you ever have any vocal training?

The only training I got started about fifteen years ago. And that wasn't training, it was how to warm-up properly, which is very, very, very important. I wish I'd have known about it twenty years hence.

So, you're doing warm-ups before shows?

It's really just going through the scales. The scales were given to me by a wonderful Jewish cantor in Los Angeles. He gave me a warm-up tape around '85-'86, and that changed me a lot. So, I owe him a lot. And I still do it.

Are you only doing scales, or anything else?

I start off with the easiest song I could possibly sing. That would be "Handbags and Gladrags" followed by "Have I Told You Lately that I Love You?" "First Cut Is the Deepest," and then onto other songs like "Some Guys Have All the Luck." By the time you're finished, you're singing the song that's the highest in your range, and then you're ready to go on. Takes me about an hour and ten minutes to get in the groove.

You sing those songs all the way through before you go on?

Yeah, more or less, oh yeah.

Are you nervous or confident before you perform?

It's more hesitation where I can't wait to get out. It's not those nerves where you get dry in the mouth. You gotta remember when I go out to sing, everybody wants me to be good, and so they're all on your side as opposed to a football match or anything like that—half the crowd want you to lose, and the other half want you to win. With me, as long as I'm in good voice, I can win.

Do you have any other rituals before you hit the stage?
I have to have my period of quiet where I get in the zone and get changed, so I kick everybody out. I finally get changed, and then, I'll have a little Bacardi and Coke, and that's it, I'm gone. That's all I need.

Is there anything after the show to keep your voice in shape?
I only just four years ago learned how to warm-*down*, which I never used to do, and that is *so* important. It's completely turned my life around because I can now comfortably do four shows a week, two hours a night.

What's the warm-down look like for you?
As opposed to the warm-up, which is loud sounds, you do little tiny sounds like [*makes the small sound of a bird chirping*] "Ee-ee-ee-ee-ee-ee." And one of the things I do is "Jingle Bells." [*Makes the small sound to the melody of "Jingle Bells"*] Very, very quietly. I'll do that just ten to fifteen minutes, and I'm warmed-down, ready to go again.

How do you take care of your voice on the road?
Two liters of water a day, not too much shouting, try and keep your voice at a minimal. The ideal thing is to go home and go to bed, but it's really hard after you've done a show.

When you start getting sick, what do you do?
Panic. You get that itchy throat and runny nose, and post-nasal drip, and you're, *Oh, please, not now, we're right in the middle of a tour*. But as I explain to the fans that have bought tickets, there's nothing you can do. I would give my right arm to be able to perform for them but it happens to all of us. Most people can go to work when they got a cold; I can't.

Is there any special thing you do to knock it out?
Rest and water are the best things. There's a wee steroid you can take, which'll get you through one show beautifully. Takes the swelling in your voice down, but you can't keep taking them. They're disastrous. If they're swollen, they gotta stay swollen and go down naturally.

Are there songs where you wonder if your voice will be there that night?
Not really. I've got an embarrassing amount of confidence when it comes to my voice. [*Laughter*]

Do you have any songs where you have to adjust the key live?
If the first song is too high, then I'll just drop it half a step, but most of them I'm comfortable with. I don't do "Tonight's the Night" in the same key I did in '76, and a few of them, 'cause, obviously, *anybody's voice* drops with age. Then, I had throat cancer, which helped me in a way, because I went into the American Songbook. 'Cause my voice was lower, and it gave me

a certain maturity, I suppose. Other than that, I can still reach the notes I want to, and I've got better control now than when I first started, that's for sure.

Do you remember a performance where you surprised yourself?

When I started doing the American Songbook and heard the first couple of tracks back, I got such a great deal of confidence 'cause I was brought up with those songs, and they're beautiful to sing, and not *everybody* can sing them, especially rock singers. So, I was very pleased with those five albums and enjoyed every one of them.

How are you with hearing your own voice?

I love me voice. I don't like some of the tracks I did over the years 'cause I look back and go, "Uhhh, I coulda done that better," but I think all musicians are like that. Your classic songs—you know, "Maggie May" and "Sailing" and "Hot Legs"—they couldn't be bettered, but some of the things I could've bettered. I actually like the sound of me own voice. But I do prefer Sam Cooke's. [*Laughter*]

Do you have a favorite vocal performance you're really proud of?

At the anniversary of the Apollo, while I was wearing a yellow suit, I sang "Dock of the Bay," and the vocal performance was great considering it was done by Otis Redding! I was proud of that.

Whenever I hear "Man of Constant Sorrow," that's the voice I wish I had.

Yeah, that was a lovely song to do. 1969 I did that.

We gotta cut right to the chase. What is the deal with your voice? How is it perfect? You have the perfect rock 'n' roll voice that all singers want.

It's God's gift, mate. It's really funny because Bruce Springsteen said in his book [*Born to Run*], "I always wanted to sound like Rod Stewart and Muddy Waters," or somebody. That was a great compliment. But listen, pal, it's God given. I was given a gift and I honed in on it, and worked on it, and I'm a very fortunate man.

There're certain singers like you—Little Richard, Sam Cooke, and Otis Redding—that seem to have this mechanism that gives your voice the perfect amount of strain and distortion.

God's gift. Put it down to God's gift.

I will. That makes me feel better, actually.

And don't forget, James Brown once said I was the greatest white soul singer who ever lived, so put that in your pipe, Elton John! [*Laughter*]

You've also covered a bunch of Tom Waits songs throughout your career, and he may be my favorite soul singer of all time. Does that make sense when I say that?

Yeah, are you kidding? Tom? He's wonderful! I love Tom, yeah, we're in the same school!

What is it about his voice that moves you so much?

Some people are not technically great singers, and I'll name Bob Dylan and Tom Waits, but they have style. Jagger has style in his voice, although it's off-key and it's flat, but it's stylistic. So is Bob Seger. Bob Seger's a great singer, and so is your man—"Downtown Train." But they're not technically great singers, and neither am I, really, but I have a great range. But he is one lyricist. *Oh my God*, I love his songs. Yeah. I love Tom Waits. Brilliant.

What's changed the most about your voice since you started?

Probably control. I haven't got the best pitch in the world; I'm very critical of that, and I work on it. Other than that, it's gotten better. I don't know how much better it's gonna be, but it's as good as it's gonna get at the ripe old age of seventy-five.

When you're recording and there's a pitch issue, do you work on it 'til you get it? Or do you just have them flip a switch?

I'd rather go in and do it again, but sometimes the producer might say, "You know, the pitch is wrong, but the *feeling* is there." And that is more important than anything else. Don't worry about the pitch if the feeling is there. So many people can sing perfectly in tune without any soul whatsoever.

If you could duet with one singer—living or dead—who would it be?

Oh, Sam Cooke, without a doubt.

And who are your top five favorite singers of all time?

They're all Black, that's for sure. I would say Billie Holiday, Ella Fitzgerald, Muddy Waters, David Ruffin, Sam Cooke, and Otis. That's six. Bobby Womack's one of my favorites as well.

Aww, Bobby Womack's so good.

Ohhh man, he was tremendous.

If you could ask any singer about their voice, who would it be and what would you ask?

Usually, I ask singers the same questions you asked me: "How do you look after your voice?" "What do you do after a show?" "What do you do before a show?" I used to meet up with David Ruffin every time the Faces played in Detroit, and there's a great picture of me looking down his throat. And then him looking down my throat. [*Laughter*]

MICHAEL STIPE

THE MARK OF A GREAT SINGER isn't just someone who can sing a tune, it's about the personality the singer gives the vocal—that distinctive tone that lets you know who's calling on the line. When Michael Stipe from R.E.M. calls, you know damn well who it is: the voice that helped inspire everyone from Paul Westerberg to Thom Yorke, Eddie Vedder, Kurt Cobain, and Courtney Love. A Rock & Roll Hall of Fame inductee whose band has sold more than 85 million records.

When the band decided to break up amicably in 2011, it hurt. I felt like after thirty years, they were just getting warmed-up, making some of the best music of their career. So, I have two regrets about this interview. Number one: I didn't ask about the incredible background vocals by bassist Mike Mills, the secret weapon of R.E.M. And number two: I believe with a bit more time, I could have got the band back together.

Michael Stipe has long been one of the most captivating and enigmatic front men in music, and I knew he was gonna be fascinating to speak with. But there was a lot more I didn't know, and I couldn't be more grateful that he shared all of this with us.

Who first exposed you to singing?

My father was a whistler, so he would whistle through the house. You just can't be in a bad mood when someone's whistling around you, and I kind of feel the same way about singing. It's like stretching.

In what way?

If you own a cat or a dog and you observe them...I made a rule for myself once: every time my dog stretched, I had to stretch. I realized my dog stretches like a hundred times a day. That's a lot. Singing is like stretching for me inside. It's a way of allowing your body to move and breathe. I sound like a total hippy here, but I am a hippy so, it's just a way of stretching and moving your body from the inside out. But it's also something that's a complete joy.

You know what's fascinating? A lot of people forget about the joy of singing.

There's nothing more joyous than singing along to a song that you love or going to a concert and jumping up and down with a crowd of people. Singing is this incredible, very human, very beautiful, almost holy, thing. It's a way of bringing light and happiness to yourself or to the people around you. But singing professionally is a different thing altogether 'cause there are constraints that our bodies have, and there are issues we have to deal with.

As a drummer, I have a required set of physical demands. Every limb is working and spoken for. But when you step up to that mic with nothing else to do but sing, it's a really naked feeling at first—what you do, and how you move your body.

It is really awkward to not know what to do with your body. I love watching other singers 'cause I can always tell if they go into a trance state, or you can see when someone is moving for the crowd, or when they're moving for their voice. There's a big difference there. I think the very best performers are those who acknowledge the almost trance like state you go into when you're performing, and the way that your body, your hands and your arms particularly, move in order to support the note, in order to help create the melody or the rhythm, the meter of the song, you know?

I'd love to hear more about this.

What you do with your body is a really complex and difficult question because a lot of people do super dumb things with their body when they're singing. But if you allow the natural thing to happen, that thing kind of becomes an extension of the voice, and it's really beautiful to watch someone who isn't focusing so much on what their body is doing as just allowing themselves to be completely present in the moment.

Do you have an example of someone who's great at that?

Opera singers. The way that they move their arms and their hands, it's really supporting the lungs and the note and the melody. The melody rises and rises, and drops again, and you can see in the hands and the movement when someone is in that kind of beautiful trance state.

You're in that a lot. I see you do this thing with your fists where you kind of raise up your elbows. You know what I'm talking about?

Yep. I did a thing that Courtney Love used to call "The Michael Surfer Move." I was like, "What are you talking about?" She was like, "You know, your move." And she got up on the table and showed me, and I was like, "Oh my God, that *is* me. That *is* what I do."

Were you emulating anyone when you started out?

I was fifteen when I heard Patti Smith's first album, and I instantly was like, "Okay, these are my people." I was a teenager going through all kinds of changes, but one of the most profound was recognizing my own otherness. In particular, I'm talking about my sexuality. Most people around me did not represent the way I was feeling and the questions I was asking myself. But I found this world that felt like it represented an otherness, and something that was outside of society and what we consider normal, which is a wonderful thing to discover at such a young age.

That's an important piece of the process, finding who you are. But you weren't singing like Patti necessarily.

No. There are early tapes of R.E.M. floating around and I'm actually singing like Elvis Presley more than anyone. I'm doing this rockabilly hiccup thing, and was just kind of exploring, not really knowing what my voice was capable of.

How did you find your own voice?

By making records. Live, the adrenaline takes over and you just sing, and that's that. You don't really think too much about it; you try to hit the note. But once you're recording, it's really a different story. You realize when you go flat—*I go flat a lot*. You realize when you go sharp, when you're off meter with the band. So, listening to my voice on tape is really how I honed what became my style of singing. I was like, *Oh man, I gotta work on this*. It took like three albums to get there. That doesn't diminish *Murmur* or *Reckoning*, they're both beautiful records, but it really is this unbelievable naivete.

How so?

There's no calculation. It was just what we did live put down on tape. By *Fables of the Reconstruction*, the band's third album, I was like, I really need to put some energy and focus into this. I can't just sing nonsense.

I know you were finding a style, lyrically, but your vocal sound was distinct and unique from the start.

I didn't realize until really late that my voice was as distinctive as it is. I knew that we were successful, and that people responded to my voice, but didn't realize until probably the mid-2000s that my voice was absolutely recognizable to a lot of people.

I'm shocked it took you that long.

I just didn't hear it. I still don't, to tell you the truth. I know when I'm moved by the choices that I make as a singer, but I really didn't know it was that distinct. But I love that I have such a distinctive voice and that it serves as a catalyst for emotional, cathartic feelings or experiences for people.

It's pretty amazing how people can connect so deeply to a vocal.

I love the power of music. Singing along to a favorite song, finding harmonies and melodies within it that you love, that's such a powerful thing. That's such a powerful community thing. It really helps bring us together in a beautiful way. Singing is one of the most natural and beautiful things we all share. What we don't share is the ability to hold a note [*Laughter*]

Was vocal training ever part of your process?

This is not a story I've told before, but, as a teenager in high school, I slept with men and women. I had a girlfriend at the time who was a singer, and she was having lessons by this vocal coach, so I went to see this guy. He was a very, very old man, and he was a classically trained singer, and I didn't like the way he touched me. I felt really violated by the way he touched my body when he was trying to show me how to sing and where to sing from, so I never went back.

Oh my God.

Yeah, it's not...you know, I'm not gonna write a book about it.

I also don't have to put that in here if you don't want.

No, I chose to tell you. So consequently, I had one third of one singing lesson before realizing I didn't like the way things were going with him, and I never looked back. By the time R.E.M. formed, I had the audacity to get onstage. I don't know where it came from because I was, and remain at my very core, an extremely shy person. But I had that need and desire to get up and perform, and to make music and to entertain.

Are you nervous or confident before you perform?

I get excited and I kind of black out, so I don't really have that much recollection of what happens onstage. Like when you're standing there and people are applauding, you don't really hear it. That's a weird thing to say, but it's really true.

Do you do vocal warm-ups beforehand?

I've never done any kind of vocal warm-up. What I do is ground myself physically by stomping the ground, just reminding myself, *This is where I am. I'm right here, this is the ground, these are my feet, this is my body*. We always have our head somewhere. And a great singer will make it look easy, but singing is not easy. It's an extremely physical thing to do. Your whole body is going through contractions to push the note, to hold the note, to move the note around, to figure out when to breathe and how to breathe, to make it a great performance and experience for everyone.

One of the biggest shockers when I started was just how physical it really is.

In 1995, I had to have hernia surgery in the middle of the tour, and I had about three weeks for the stitches to heal. I was like, "How am I gonna do this?" My body had been cut open at the bottom of my belly where you push all your notes from, right at the top of your pubic bone. We were on the road with Radiohead, and I went to Thom Yorke and said, "Where do you sing from? I can't sing from here right now." He said, "I sing from my head." And he showed me how he would place the note at the back of his skull, and that's where he would sing from. So, I used that to hit some notes that I wasn't able to hit singing from my belly.

That's great. Placement is a whole other trip. Where you place your voice.

We did a festival show with PJ Harvey, and it's when she was wearing this hot pink, skin tight, cat suit. She's a thin woman, and she's an astonishing performer, and, as we all know, an incredible singer and songwriter. But I couldn't see her belly moving in and out. So, at the end of her show, I was like, "Where are you singing from?" And she said, "I sing from my back."

What? [Laughter]

I was like, "*What?*" She showed me the back of her ribs, and that's where she's pushing the note from, that's where she's storing the air. So, I tried it and it worked! At this point, my band had been together for fifteen years and seven, eight records under our belts. I knew how to sing Michael style, but now in my tool chest, I had Thom's style and Polly's style, so my body could heal from the hernia operation, and I could kind of shift around the note in my body to prevent myself from hurting myself again. I have those two to thank for that.

That is really interesting about the back. I'm not sure if I even understand it.

It's a part of our lungs we completely forget about. But if you practice sitting in a chair, and you breathe into the part of your belly that's underneath your bellybutton, which, I guess, is right under your ribs where your stomach is, then you breathe into your lungs. So, physically, think about the back of your lungs and the back of your ribs, and breathe very slowly, and open up the back of your ribs, and then exhale. Practice that, and you'll find a new way to place your voice, and that's all thanks to PJ Harvey.

She's so rad. Are there songs where you wonder if your voice will be there that night?

The harder ones were not about being able to hit the note, but about pitch. "Everybody Hurts" was really hard. I don't have a great range and a perfect pitch. When I've been around singers that have perfect pitch, I always find myself a little—it's my insecurities coming forward, in a quite beautiful way—but I find myself a little jealous 'cause I've never had perfect pitch.

So, what would you do to prepare for "Everybody Hurts" onstage?
Just get scared shitless and then, when the time comes, you just do your best.

Are there songs where you had to adjust the key live?
If I covered other people's music, I would have to change the key to fit my range, but with R.E.M in particular, I never had to go up or down.

Did you ever have a really embarrassing vocal mishap?
Anything live for TV was always really stressful because there's no saving that. You can't stop the song and start it again. You're just out there, and if you fuck up, you really fuck up. There was a television show host who made a really off-color joke right as we were about to start our first song, and I was so thrown off by his lack of humor. It was so awful that I started singing the wrong words to the wrong song.

Do you remember a performance where you surprised yourself?
Um...no. [*Chuckles*]

How about a favorite vocal performance of yours that you're really proud of?
Yeah, there a song called "Electron Blue." I'm really proud of that.

I love that song. What about it?
It's just so emotive. It feels like *Blade Runner*. It feels like the future to me. And we really nailed it on that song.

I feel like you have some of the most mysterious and versatile vocal cords in music. You have the classic Michael Stipe, higher range, head voice like the chorus of "Everybody Hurts." But in a song like "Low," you go so low that it's almost impossible to retain the melody, but you do somehow. And then, there's songs like "Disappear" where you speak the verses, but your voice still has this vibrato running through it. And that vibrato is like an electric current that powers all of your songs.
Yeah. I know. I don't know how to do that. All I do is sing.

It's not something you fashioned, it's just your cords doing this?
I think it's just the way the cavities in my head resonate sound. I always heard that Freddie Mercury had such a beautiful voice because he had buck teeth, and the sound kind of rolled off the top of his palette. Now I don't know if there's any truth to that, I kind of doubt it. But it might have helped that he had buck teeth a little bit.

So, it's just a natural thing that's in you?
Yeah, the body resonates sound, and it does in a different way for each of us.

How are you with hearing your own tracks?

I like my singing voice. I don't like hearing my speaking voice. It kind of grates on me. I think I sound really pretentious and full of myself.

What's changed the most about your singing voice since you started?

My range got bigger. It's kinda weird. I lost my falsetto as I grew older, but my range got deeper, and my natural vocal range got bigger.

That's so interesting because when I hear "I Don't Sleep, I Dream," I get mad at you a little bit. You had such a beautiful falsetto on that song, and that's the one area of your voice I always felt you never gave more to.

I actually love that song. "Tongue" is the other one I sang completely in falsetto.

"Tongue" as well! Those are great performances.

I've tried to sing those since then, and I think I kind of lost that part of my voice. But I quit smoking ten years ago and that really helped.

If you could duet with any singer—living or dead—who would it be?

There's a beautiful countertenor named Anthony Roth Costanzo who I just love hearing his voice. My voice is so low, and his voice is so high, that it would be a really interesting combination. I love singers who sing at the top of their range. I'm not one of them, but I love singers who really push their voices 'cause you can push it and really make the hair on people's necks stand up on end. Paul Westerberg from The Replacements would be a good example of that. He would go up into the top of his range and what we feel emotionally when someone is doing that is quite intense. It creates that beautiful tension.

Yeah, I love the way Westerberg does it.

Who else does that? Dylan does that. Oh, the singer for The Knife is always kind of pushing the top of the range and it works. They're incredible. My voice sounds very strained if I sing in that certain area of my range, so it's not pleasant. It's not moving.

Who are your top five favorite singers of all time?

I sat around a table this summer with several amazing singers and one of them said, "Who's the top singer of all time?" I said, "Well, present company exempted, because we can't talk about ourselves, that's embarrassing, we're at lunch." [*JTG cracks up*] It was myself, Elton John, Bono, and Patti Smith, and our friends and family sitting around the table. We all arrived at a list of our top five favorite singers, and at the very top, our number one, unanimously, was Nina Simone.

Can't go wrong there! Alright, you got four more to go.

Present company exempted? [*Laughter*]

Yes! You can't say your name!

Two people who radically changed my life through their own music were at that table—Elton John, and Patti Smith. And then, Bono who I grew up with. We've been exchanging stories and secrets forever, so those three are right up there for me. I mentioned Thom Yorke, Polly Harvey, Courtney Love. These are all people who I hold in the utmost respect as performers, as songwriters. *Dolly Parton*. I'd love to sing with Dolly Parton. That would be extraordinary. She's such an astonishing songwriter. Talk about a unique voice. That voice is like no one.

If you could ask any singer about their voice, who would it be and what would you ask?

I'm more fascinated by the choices people make with meter, with rhythm, and with exploring the different aspects of their voice, how conscious or unconscious that is. Maybe someone like the nephew of Nusrat Fateh Ali Khan. I'd be very interested in hearing his take on the emotive power of his voice and his singing style. That's what I'm talking about though. I never realized until I was in my mid-forties that my voice was that unique, so it's nice to know. I'm not quite sure what to do with it or where to go from here. [*Laughs*]

You better do something with it, Michael. I wanna hear some new music.

Thank you, Jason, that's very sweet. I do like my voice a lot, so I'd like to use it again.

JEFF TWEEDY

THE FIRST TIME WE HEARD JEFF TWEEDY'S VOICE was when his previous band, Uncle Tupelo, were helping to bring country music back to its original roots, a place it hadn't been for a long time. It was a movement that started the "No Depression" sound that emerged from the alt country world in the early '90s.

Jeff's role in the band was more of a supporting one, but after their demise, he started something new, taking charge of the lead vocals and songwriting himself. And Wilco was born. Playing with his own band, solo, or with his other side projects, Jeff always creates a sonic landscape that covers more ground than most would ever dare. This Grammy Award–Winning singer has built a career by experimenting with the boundaries of genre and taking a sledgehammer to all preconceived notions of what can and can't be.

His live shows are always a high-wire act where it seems like anything can happen. And when it does, Jeff's artistic integrity and honest vocal performance is always the one constant, holding it all together, keeping the music believable, vulnerable, and true. Now tell that drunk dude in the back to cool out. Jeff's about to speak.

Who first exposed you to singing?

Records meant so much to me so early. I kind of feel like I introduced myself to singing by singing along with records really loud and feeling the power and catharsis of raising your voice to sing. When I got an electric guitar, I would play by myself in my bedroom, trying to sing over my guitar amp. I'd really have to project just to be able to sing correctly that loud.

So, you were already in training from a young age. Is that what gave you the confidence?

Singing along with The Byrds records is what gave me the confidence to sing harmonies, and that's primarily what I did early on in Uncle Tupelo. I always credit Jay Farrar for making me sing because he didn't want to sing the songs I was writing. I always wanted him to sing them, but he didn't want to.

Were you emulating anyone when you started out?

Probably Roger McGuinn. But I had a bit more of an affected twang to my voice early on. I think there's an instinct to disguise yourself a bit that I recognized later. It's a little easier to take on a persona or something. For whatever reason, I had a bit more of a pronounced southern accent when I sang than I did when I talked, and that kinda went away over time as I got more confident and more comfortable in my own skin and was able to sing as who I am.

How did you find your own voice?

By looking at it as purely a way to communicate things that you can't just say. And singing to people. One on one, just singing to my mom [laughs], singing to a few people at a party, just feeling that intimacy and that crazy, scary vulnerability, and getting comfortable with it. Then, developing some sort of antenna to figure out if what you're singing is being heard. It's hard to know what's getting through. Everyone listens in a different way. Sometimes when you wanna say something, I think the only way to figure out if it's coming across is to sit and play it for somebody. I love it when people stop by the studio because you can always hear it a little more with someone else's ears when they're sitting there. It's just a different energy in the room.

Did you ever have any vocal training?

No. Sheer repetition and bad PAs forced me to sing louder. Not having good monitors for years taught me how to project a little bit. Nothing official.

Are you nervous or confident before you perform?

I'm pretty comfortable onstage in general. I do still get nervous, but not in any kind of debilitating way. I don't really have a lot of stage fright. The only time I really get nervous is when I'm physically not in the condition I want to be in. I can tell my throat is tight or raspy or something. If I got a cold, or if I feel like there are things that are outta my control.

Do you do any vocal warm-ups before shows?

No. I feel that people that get mired in routine kind of psyche themselves out more often than not. [*Laughs*] It's superstitious to me, like hot tea or anything. I don't think any of that shit makes a difference. I think water is all you really need to drink.

So, you just go out cold?

I try to sing a little bit, but that's more just to feel the guitar in my hand. But I don't always do that. I feel like if I got into a routine, it would be more detrimental to me if I couldn't do the routine for some reason. Does that make any sense?

Totally. But how do you take care of your voice on the road? 'Cause there is that.

I don't think that my voice is a particularly pristine instrument. It changes, and gets raspy, and a little frayed around the edges. As the tour wears on, I'm pretty comfortable if my voice starts to show some of that wear. But I'm comfortable because I still know how to sing with that voice. I can shift and go, *Okay, today I have a fuzz box in the chain.* [*Laughs*] Just purely looking at it as an instrument, I feel inspired by it when it changes a bit and there's a little more emotion coming from just the pure sound of it. For some reason, I've never had to struggle with keeping my voice, even when I'm screaming my head off a lot more. It's just always seemed to be there when the show would start.

Is there anything after the show that helps keep your voice in shape?

I stopped going to the after show meet and greets and pretty much go straight to the bus. I'm quiet for a long time right after, and that helps a lot. Talking is way harder on your voice than singing, especially over a loud room of people. Over the years, that really damaged my voice on a tour, spending time trying to communicate after the show.

Do you have any rituals before you hit the stage?

I hate having to pee when I'm onstage, so the one thing I do is I stop drinking liquids about an hour before stage because I don't wanna have to pee. And I never drink anything onstage because the second I take a sip of water I have to pee.

Are there songs where you wonder if your voice will be there that night?

Not really. I don't think anybody comes to hear my songs because my voice is perfection. I think they identify with some of the fallibility in my voice. I'm pretty comfortable with that. It would be terrible if everybody was relying on my voice to be something infallibly beautiful.

Some things are beautiful because they're imperfect.

Right. The whole point of singing is to communicate, and some people have voices that have to fight through their limitations to communicate. A lot of my songs make no sense if they're sung by somebody with a pristine, well-trained, perfect voice. I think a lot of my songs would have very little to say in that context. I write songs for my voice.

I think the honesty in your voice is your secret weapon.

Well, it's a necessity. I had to prioritize getting the lyrics across over dazzling people with my vocal gymnastics. [*Laughs*] That's not in the cards.

But you also don't have to pull out any pyrotechnics because we come to you for your honesty and for the soul in your voice. A lot of people can sing perfectly, but not everyone connects to that.

Well, thank you. I don't dismiss those things. I can't do very much of what people would consider pyrotechnics. [*Laughs*] I can sing pretty loud, maybe that's impressive sometimes. But I love technically incredible vocalists like Colin Blunstone. I can marvel at how beautiful that is, and I aspire to get better as a singer and be able to sing more complex melodies and not just simple melodies over cowboy chords. I've tried to expand my understanding of how melodies work over chords, and I recognize things that can be improved. And I do work on it, but it's not the main thrust of what is happening when I'm onstage.

You have some songs that are deceptively high though. Like "I Can't Keep from Talking" off the *Golden Smog* album. That seems like a tough song to sing well, but the strain is part of what makes it work.

Yeah, that's a tough one. [*Laughs*] A lot of times, you need to hold off singing those until a couple days into a tour. Only time I ever sing those songs anymore is when I'm by myself on a solo tour. My voice loosens up after a couple of shows and I can really get there. But I'm holding off on tuning my guitar a half step down.

Are there any songs where you have to adjust the key live?

It will probably happen at some point. I'm just trying to keep that card under my sleeve.

What was your most embarrassing vocal mishap ever?

God, there is one that was just so egregious. I think it might have been "You Are My Face." I just very clearly replaced one of the lyrics in the first verse with "Fart" for some reason. Pretty major brain freeze, and that happens when things get rote.

Do you remember a performance where you surprised yourself?

In the earlier days of touring, like on *Being There*, when Wilco was playing tons and tons of shows every year, my voice would get to some point where I could sing a few notes at one time. I had a scream, and I could almost make a train whistle sound with my voice. Like a Mongolian throat singer, there were these overtones. It's as close as I ever got to being David Lee Roth.

You do an amazing squeal toward the end of "I'm a Wheel."

Yeah, yeah, that was one of the last places it appeared. But that was always a surprise, when I would open up my mouth, and that's what would come out. At some point, I got to where I could control it a little bit, but it's not something that's normally a part of the arsenal.

I wanna stay on "I'm a Wheel" 'cause I always wanted to know, right after the guitar solo, you go, "Ummm," as if you're thinking. Were you starting another verse and realized there wasn't one there? Or was that something you did because it's awesome?

I just thought that I hadn't heard "Um" in a song before, and I wanted to put "Um" in a song. [*Laughter*] It's really what I wanted to say. I could put "Um" in all of my songs and it would feel right to me.

How are you with hearing your own voice?

I'm totally okay listening to my own voice and feel like I've had to. I want to produce myself, and I want to be a good advocate for my songs, so I've had to kind of learn how to listen to my voice the way I think other people would. It's crazy, but I have to be able to make myself cry. I have to be able to make myself feel it. So, I have to be able to listen to it with that kind of intensity, and I do. I love it.

That's a great way of looking at it.

I can dismiss my voice for all the reasons that it would make me self-conscious talking to someone like you in a book about my voice, because I know how it compares to truly great vocalists. But having said all that, I love my voice. That's who I am, and I am able to listen to it and understand what's working and what's not, and what needs to be improved. I can't stand my speaking voice. I would never want to listen to the audiotape of this conversation, for example.

[*Laughs*] So many people hate their speaking voice. But do you have a favorite vocal performance you're really proud of?

Probably something I'm working on. Generally, that's the thing I'm most connected to.

Your vocal on "The Lonely 1" kills me every time. There's an intimacy and a vulnerability to your voice that places us directly inside what it feels like to be alone in the world. Very few songs can do it on that level. Do you remember anything about recording that song?

On the expanded version of *Being There*, there's a version where we recorded a bunch of walking to the convenience store and back. Then, we cut the tape, and made a collage out of it, and played it over that track as a way to create some distance from myself. We didn't end up using that version but I remember there was some effort on my part to make it not be the way *you* perceived it. [*Laughter*] The song always sounded a little too earnest to me. And that's always something you should look for in a performance. So, maybe the singer, being the worst judge, should defer to the people in the room, especially when you're feeling a little uncomfortable. It usually means that there's something emotionally vulnerable about it.

I recently saw you play at Largo on the final night of a four-night solo run. I've seen Wilco so many times over the years, but this was my first time seeing you alone. And it's worth noting that it was also one of the funniest stand-up comedy shows I've seen.

Wow.

You had the entire crowd laughing their asses off. But the show got me thinking about *Sunken Treasure,* **that documentary about your solo tour from years ago. There's this one moment where you're onstage, and some dick heckles you by screaming, "'Black Eye' sucks!" It kind of throws you a beat, but you come back strong. I'm curious if over time you've found a way to use your voice, by singing quieter, or any tricks like that, to cool off an audience when they're getting obnoxious.**

I just got off a fair amount of acoustic solo touring, and there were some shows where I thought to myself onstage, *If I had started even ten minutes later, I probably wouldn't have survived these shows.* [*Laughs*] In other words, it took every single second I had ever spent making music or playing in front of people, to kind of soothe myself in the moment.

Walk me through how you survive that without throwing punches?

The worst thing that can happen to you onstage is that you can be confronted with an emotion that you didn't prepare for. Like you get mad at somebody in the audience, or you get frustrated; anything that leaves you feeling out of control onstage is really, really disorienting. Over the years, I've gotten better at a lot of things, and I've also realized, you can't always be perfect, and that you're gonna lose control, occasionally, of an audience. You don't have any control over what somebody does when they get drunk and decide to make the show about themselves. But you can learn how to stand your ground.

What have you found that works for you?

I don't have it at my fingertips, maybe now it's an instinct, if that's possible. We've also learned to control some of the outside aspects of the atmosphere too, like trying to make sure that if there's a bar in the room, that it's shut down during the show, instead of people throwing beer bottles across the room into a trash can. [*Laughs*]

Certainly, playing venues like Largo helps, 'cause it seems like they've cultivated an audience that's really there for the music.

That's why I like playing there so much. It's just an ideal space, the perfect size audience. It's a clientele that has been kind of conditioned to behave in a respectful way. I kind of think most people that go to Largo are onstage themselves a lot, or have been, you know? [*Laughter*]

You've produced a bunch of records for Mavis Staples. Is there anything you've picked up from her in regards to singing?

We're such completely different instruments. It's more her overall attitude towards music making, and the joy she gets out of being a singer, and being able to share her gifts. I always felt like this is something I wanna do, and I don't wanna stop doing it. So, when I work with someone older than myself who is still excited and up for it, I find that extremely inspiring and encouraging. And I've never met anyone more up for it. Up for being challenged, up for a new idea, just up for the whole thing, she's ready to go. Nobody more than Mavis. That's the thing I got the most out of being around her.

What's changed the most about your voice since you started?

The thing that always strikes me when I hear earlier recordings is how I was hiding behind a bit of an affected accent. It's common that when someone starts singing in front of people that they have a bit of a persona or something. So, aside from getting stronger as a singer, and my voice deepening a little over time, I feel much more confident hitting notes, and I'm not trying to sound like anything other than what I hear in my head. Early on, I wanted to sound like something that I thought should be on a record. [*Laughter*]

If you could duet with one singer—living or dead—who would it be?

Karen Dalton?

Interesting, you know who else said that? Nick Cave.

Oh wow, that's amazing.

Who are your top five favorite singers of all time?

Oh man, I needed a heads up for this! Howlin' Wolf. Karen Carpenter. Bob Dylan. Karen Dalton didn't really put out enough stuff to put her in the top five even though I just mentioned her. John Lydon. Aretha Franklin.

If you could ask any singer about their voice, who would it be and what would you ask?

"Any singer a question about…" Just buying time by repeating the question. [*JTG laughs*] My brother always told me something that sounded like urban mythology about Rod Stewart's voice, that he had gotten his voice to sound like that by standing in front of a mirror and screaming until he damaged his vocal cords. My brother told me that when I was a little kid. So I'd ask Rod Stewart if that's true.

PS. It was omitted from his interview, but I did ask Rod Stewart about this when we spoke. And I'm sorry to break the news, but your brother's a liar, Jeff!

DIONNE WARWICK

THIS SIX-TIME GRAMMY AWARD–WINNING LEGEND is one of the reasons we're all here right now because Dionne was the very first person I asked to participate in this project. Our families have been friends for years, so I decided to go for broke and make the call. The truth is that I had no idea if any of this would work. But Dionne immediately said yes, and that was enough to get me going.

But man, I wasn't ready at all! This was Dionne Warwick I was about to talk to here. If she were a sports figure, you'd have to have her card because her stats are crazy. Dionne's immense soul and extraordinary command of her instrument can make an audience spring up on their feet, or bring 'em down to their knees. She's sold over 100 million records, is one of the most charted vocalists of all time, and is still out there showing us how it's done at over eighty years of age. Now, let's add in all she's done for the world, serving as the U.S. Ambassador of Health, and her groundbreaking HIV/AIDS activism. But it's her full-bodied, beautifully round and warm voice, and her powerful charisma that has given Dionne such monumental longevity, paving the way for too many young women to possibly name.

And while we're on the subject of names...

Dionne, it's so fitting that you're the first singer I'm interviewing for this book because my sister was named after you. You were the first singer's name that I ever knew!
[*Laughs*] F'n A right.

Who first exposed you to singing?
It was my grandfather. My grandfather used to be a minister, and I was six years old the first time I sang in front of people. He called me to his pulpit and asked me to sing the song that I sang in our Sunday school class, and that song was "Jesus Loves Me."

Were you emulating anyone when you started out?
I come from a singing family, so I'm kind of a loose mixture of every voice that was a part of my family. My mother and aunts and uncles were gospel singers, and in fact, they were the first gospel group [The Drinkard Singers] to record on RCA/Victor records. So, what I sound like is all part of what my family sounds like.

So, you didn't have any vocal training?
No, it's just if you got it, you got it.

Your first time singing was in church. By the time you got onstage to perform as a solo artist, was it any different for you?
Oh yeah, quite different. It was not the sanctity of people that knew me, you know, they were people that knew my recordings. But I've always treated it as if I have invited a bunch of people to sit around and hang out with me, and they want me to sing a few songs, and that's what I do.

You always look so confident onstage. You don't get nervous, do you?
No. Sometimes I suppose that I must be missing something. [*Laughter*] Every performer that I know, especially the icons of the industry—I remember Ella Fitzgerald—she was a nervous wreck every time before she went onstage. I would never had known it, but I did have the good fortune of meeting her. She was appearing at the Coconut Grove. I went backstage to say hello to her, and she was a jumble of nerves. So, I just kind of crept on out, let her be to herself for a minute, 'cause I had never seen anything like that before.

Do you do any vocal warm-ups before you go on?
No, the only thing I do is put God on my shoulder and out there we go.

How do you take care of your voice on the road?
What keeps me lubricated is a cough drop. I keep a cough drop in my mouth.

Onstage?
Nobody ever knows or sees me put it in there. That's the only thing I do.

Do you have any rituals before you perform?
Yeah, like I said, I carry Him out there with me, so I'm constantly in prayer.

Is there anything after the show that helps keep your voice in shape?
No, I go and eat something as fast as I can! Usually, after the show, you want to get back to the hotel 'cause there's a 7:00 flight the next morning. What we really need to be able to do, and none of us can, is to get as much rest as possible. No doubt. And limit talking. Talking is quite a different use of vocal cords than singing.

Are there songs where you wonder if your voice will be there that night?
No, 'cause you find out when I do! [*Laughs*] Nah, if I have a bit of a problem with my throat at the time, I use my musical education to work around those kinds of things. It's like, *Okay, you're not gonna make that D so why don't you do an A instead.*

Have you ever had an embarrassing vocal mishap onstage?
When you open your mouth and nothing comes out! [*Cracks up*] But I have no problem laughing at myself. I laugh with people at me! So, if I happen to not be, vocally, as good as I want to be in the moment, I let people know that if a squeak comes out, just ignore it 'cause I am. "And we're just gonna ball our way through this."

I love the conversational tone you take with your audience.
Well, you know, they've come for one purpose, and I certainly appreciate that, and think they should be as much a part of the show as I am.

Do you remember a performance where you surprised yourself?
I have done a couple of shows that I've been super proud of, where I did things vocally that were, in my estimation, kind of over the top. *Hey girlfriend, that was pretty good.*

What made it "pretty good" for you?
Other notes as opposed to what I normally would sing, where I got applause from my band, and it was like, *Whoa, okay!*

How are you with hearing your own voice?
I'm okay listening to them. Once I've recorded and carried the project to finish, that's usually the last time I listen to it. I don't listen to me. I listen to everybody else but me.

What's changed the most about your voice since you started?
Well, as I've matured, so has it. It's that simple, really. Certain notes just aren't there anymore, and it's okay. That's why there's a little thing called, "Change the key." [*Laughs*]

When your voice started to change, was it traumatic or was it like, "Okay, I'm just gonna roll with it?"

No, it was one of those things that was obviously expected and all I did was alter the key.

Who are your top five favorite singers of all time?

Sarah Vaughan, Ella Fitzgerald, Sammy Davis, Jr., Barbra Streisand, Nat King Cole.

If you could duet with anybody—living or dead—who would it be?

Oh, it still might happen too: Earth, Wind, and Fire. We've been procrastinating about getting in the studio together. It's my favorite group of all time!

Dionne, I'm so glad I got a chance to ask you all this. Thanks for being the first one.

Thank you, sweetheart, for thinking of me!

How could I not? You're an icon for crying out loud!

Oh, well, sometimes that's questionable.

ROGER WATERS

"WHEN I SAW THE REQUEST TO DO THIS BOOK, I, of course, had the immediate response, 'What the fuck is he talking about? I'm not a singer!'"

This is what Roger Waters, the visionary behind Pink Floyd, just said to me. And he's way off base. But our talk was profound in ways I didn't expect. Or maybe I did. We've both suffered from self-doubt as vocalists, we both share the same feelings on human rights, and we've both sold over 250 million records. (Google it).

When Pink Floyd's original singer-songwriter, Syd Barrett, departed the group in 1968, bassist Roger Waters stepped in as their main songwriter, co-lead singer, and conceptual leader, and they became one of the most critically acclaimed and commercially successful bands of all time. *The Dark Side of the Moon*, *Wish You Were Here*, *Animals*, *The Wall*. These records earned them a place in the Grammy and Rock & Roll Halls of Fame. But beyond that, they are the stuff of legend.

When Roger left Pink Floyd, he went on to a solo career, and from 2010-2013, his extraordinary live show of *The Wall* became the highest-grossing tour by a solo artist ever. Not bad for someone who thinks they're not a singer.

His passion is lyrical, empathetic, and intense. His generosity is heartwarming and sincere. And, yeah, he still got a couple licks in at his old mates in the Floyd, but that's why we love him. He's knows exactly what the function of a singer can truly be.

So...here we are.

Who first exposed you to singing?

God, I've no idea. Frankie Vaughan? I never aspired to, or was inspired, really, to become a singer. It may be that somewhere between the Atomic Energy Research labs in Aldermaston and Trafalgar Square, I looked at some tall, handsome bloke, a bit older than me, playing the guitar, and how adoring the young women were. Funnily enough, I'm thinking of one specific person, now that you come to mention it. He was this sort of skinny type, black curly hair, and he played the fucking guitar, which he carried on his back and would suddenly burst into a Woody Guthrie song. Maybe that had something to do with it. I thought, *Fuck me, if I'm ever gonna get laid, this is obviously the route.* [*Laughter*]

Were you emulating anyone when you started out?

I don't think so. I do remember going and singing folk songs on tube trains in London with Juliet Wright, the woman who actually married Rick Wright. I suppose it was at that point I realized that I could sing a bit. So, I guess, I spent the next twenty-five years of my life banging my head against the "mad bugger's wall." The mad buggers being [guitarist] David Gilmour and [keyboard player] Rick Wright, but mainly Gilmour, who in order to maintain some kind of equilibrium in the band, spent their lives explaining to me that I was completely unmusical, that my voice was awful, that I couldn't hold a tune, and was tone-deaf, and that I was absolutely useless at everything. So, they'd obviously spotted, even then, that I was a fucking genius and that they were in my shadow! [*JTG cracks up and Roger follows*]

You know what it reminds me of? Those old Buffalo Springfield stories about how they all talked shit to Neil Young about his voice. And yet, Neil's the guy that we all fuckin' love!

Yeah, of course.

Did you ever have any vocal training?

I didn't up until a very few years ago. When I started going back on the road after I left Pink Floyd, and after I went through the great years of developing character and soul.

I wanna know what that means.

You know what's good for the soul? Fucking misery and pain and defeat. When those assholes went out on the road in 19—whatever it was—87, I was going out with my second album, *Radio K.A.O.S.*, and as soon as we hit the road, life became unbearable for me. I remember one evening, I was playing to about 1,500 people in a 4,000-seat arena in Cincinnati. I had a cold sore on my lip and I banged the mic. And there I was, covered in blood, singing my songs in front of a few people, looking very, very empty. And, by coincidence, the very next night, Pink were playing in a Stadium to 70,000 people, singing all my fucking songs. I thought to myself at the time, *You know what this is? This is character forming.* And it was. And it is.

God, that must have been crushing.

The propaganda machine has churned out this weird story that a lot of the trolls believe, that I was horrible and autocratic, and what a lovely chap David Gilmour is. It's something that I live with, but I don't really like it. I think it's part of leaving, which Neil did, of course, funny enough. Whether it's Buffalo Springfield or whatever, Neil has been leaving bands all his life because he felt the need to be himself and to express himself, and he felt he was being held back in that endeavor at certain times.

Because once Syd was no longer the singer, everything sort of fell on you.

I was doing all the work—*all of it*—and I came to realize there was no way I could continue to work in Pink Floyd. They'd never had an idea or a feeling about anything that interested me at all. And yet, they didn't really like my ideas and feelings. But there *weren't* any other ideas and feelings in the band. [Drummer] Nick Mason, who I adore, we've mended our schisms years and years ago. He still makes me laugh, and he's one of my favorite people. But the other two, I wouldn't give you thruppence for either of them. They were just fucking miserable. Gilmour, bless him, I hope somebody blesses him at some point apart from blessing him with a great voice, talking of voices, and a great ability to play the guitar. But if somebody were to bless him with a bit of imagination or a bit of heart that would be great for him.

You know what's fascinating? Even though you were in that small club, feeling horrible, you're now the biggest-selling concert tour in history.

Yeah. Well, all the way through those difficult times when we were really over, but clung together because we were scared shitless of what might happen outside the umbrella of what became a very powerful brand name, and still is, Pink Floyd. Through all of those years, fighting my way through this turgid fucking swimming pool full of the treacle of envy and misery, which I did for year after year, he wrote one song. "Fat Old Sun." There's nothing wrong with it, but *fuck me*, we were in it together for twenty years!

You said you never had any vocal training until "After I went through the great years of developing character and soul." These were obviously those years. Are you saying that this is the training you had? Building something up to release through the voice?

No, I'm not. This is me, meandering about a subject that I rarely ever talk to anybody about, so I'm just unburdening myself. Yes, I did.

[*Laughs*] Well, I'm here for you, brother! Anytime. So, what was the training?

In the early 2000s, I went, *Maybe I'll go and see somebody to actually learn a bit of something because here I'm fifty-three years old, going back on the road, got a lot of singing to do if I'm gonna do this seriously*. I thought maybe I should learn, technically, and I went to see Katie Agresta on the Upper West Side in New York, and I really liked her. I would stand by her piano and sing scales on different vowel sounds. I've only recently started to implement it, on the US + Them Tour, twenty years later, because I had some lung problems, and it became difficult.

So, singing the scales is helping your lungs do what?

It's singing fifths and things, up and down, up and down, but what she was trying to teach me was the relaxation of all the muscles in your face, neck, and head. You're trying to create sound by using your diaphragm to push air through your larynx over your vocal cords. So, very recently, I've found myself singing notes by using my diaphragm and allowing air to make a note as it passes my vocal cord and comes out. I thought, *Fuck! That's what she was talking about.* Very late in my career. So, when I saw the request to do this book, I, of course, had the immediate response, *What the fuck's he talking about? I'm not a singer!*

You're so wrong. Look, I was a drummer my whole life. And when I became the singer for my band, I was like, *I can't do this!* But the truth is, *I am a singer. I can do this, in my own way, with my own truth.* You're one of my heroes, *as a vocalist,* because I believe in singers that tell the truth and are honest and soulful.

Well, thank you. Thank you for that. And I agree with you. Notwithstanding the fact, if I'd gone my whole life without hearing "E Lucevan Le Stelle" by Franco Corelli, I would feel that there was a fruit that was magnificent that I'd never tasted. So, I do recognize the beauty of voices that can do things, technically, that feel impossible and are extraordinarily moving, and blah blah blah. However, I equally, like you, find Neil, obviously, Dylan, obviously, and other people who express their truth. I love the fact that you believe that. I don't think it's the *only thing* that matters vis-à-vis Franco Corelli, though he had his own truth.

What I'm saying is, if I compared myself to Sam Cooke and Donny Hathaway, there would be a real problem, and I would never open my voice to sing. But if I just be myself, without hopefully being too offensive when it comes out, and there's something there to cling to, which is, God willing, my soul, then, we've got something.

Yeah, I agree.

What did it feel like the first time you stood onstage as the lead singer of the band?

I can remember being onstage at the Albert Hall in London, and opening our concert, playing acoustic guitar on my own and singing "Grantchester Meadows," and that being terrifying beyond all imagination. 'Cause A: I didn't think I could play the guitar, which I couldn't, really, [*Laughs*] and B: I didn't think I could sing. It was frightening because there were 5,000 people or whatever, but it was, theatrically, the correct thing to do at the time. However, I haven't really got comfortable with what *you're* talking about until recently.

What's that, just being yourself?

I've made a demo of a new song over the last few weeks. It's called "The Bar," and it's probably the best thing I've ever written. It's just me playing the piano, which I was never able to do, and now I can play the piano and sing at the same time as well. What's important about this new song is that it's me writing and me singing what I've written. [*Recites the lyrics to a painful and personal, political song*] So, I am poking my finger in the eye of American exceptionalism, and at this murderous country that I live in, and I'm singing about it. And because it's real and my feelings are real, and it's something I've written, nobody else can sing it. Or they can but it's different.

That's exactly right. Nobody else could sing a song from *The Wall* and have it work on an emotional level the way it can with *you* singing because *you* lost your father. It's *your father*. Nobody else, no matter how great a singer they are, can move you in the same fashion because that's buried inside the DNA of your voice.

I know what you're saying, but you're obviously wrong. [*JTG laughs*] Well, no, you are to some extent! It's a bit like David claims to have written "Comfortably Numb," which he does all the time. God knows where he gets the brass neck to do it. I wrote "Comfortably Numb" for my solo album, and so, when we needed it for *The Wall*, there it was; I already had it. That song is *not* about my father. That is part of a theatrical narrative that I wrote about a character called Pink and a conversation that he has with a doctor as part of a dramatic narrative that *is* part of that musical piece. [*Sings the opening verse of the song*] But when it comes to the choruses and David sings, "There is no pain you are receding," which he does beautifully, he can sing that, and it can be moving, even though he had nothing to do with writing it. Well, he did, actually. He wrote the chords to that middle eight. That was his contribution to "Comfortably Numb."

And that's why his voice sounds so good when he sings it there!

Maybe you're right. Maybe because he wrote the chord sequence, that's why it sounds good.

Obviously, there's a tiny bit of hyperbole in what I'm saying—*a tiny bit*—but as you said before, "Why would he want me for this book?" Well, this is fuckin' why! Because I do believe in that. I believe it with all my heart.

Yeah.

So, back to the stage a minute. Are you still nervous before you perform?

No. Not at all.

Do you do any vocal warm-ups before shows?

Yeah, I do twenty-five minutes about an hour before I go on. And I'll tell you what Katie's other thing is: you hold your tongue in a face cloth, and pull it out of your mouth [*starts making noises*] holding your tongue, removing that huge muscle from any involvement in the movement of your vocal cords.

When you're holding your tongue, what are you doing vocally?

I sing [*in a "Jingle Bells" type melody*] "Gee-gee-gee, gee-gee-gee" and I go down the scale doing that. They're extremely useful to me.

Do you have any other rituals before you hit the stage?

We gather, we huddle, and we say this in unison, "Tonight we will perform with..." and then we all smile, and then we say the word "Genuuuuiiiiine," and then we sing the word "Love" for as long as we can. It's cool 'cause it's an exhalation of breath down to the last possible amount that you have, which is extremely good for your lungs, and for your vocal cords, and for your health, in general.

Yeah, we forget to breathe.

There's a great book out by a guy called James Nestor called *Breath*, and if you're interested in this shit, it's extraordinary. It's about how the human race has forgotten how to breathe. We over-oxygenate all the time by breathing too fast, and, in consequence, we are denying our lungs and our blood and our body the CO_2 that it craves and desperately needs in order to function properly. It's worth reading.[11]

Do you chew gum onstage? I think I see you chew gum.

No. Well, hang on. What do I chew? *AHHH!* I know what you might have seen me with! Hall's sugar free cough things. Yeah, that's what it is. They're sugar free cough drops. It's a saliva inducer so, it stops you getting dry-mouthed, which is a nightmare, because you're sweating so much and you're putting out so much energy that it's very easy to dehydrate.

Is there anything after the show that helps keep your voice in shape?

Only dry martini cocktails. Gin straight up with a twist. But I do limit myself to two.

How do you take care of your voice on the road?

Just by doing Katie Agresta's vocal exercises. I do that in the morning, and I do it before the show. That's just about an hour of exercises every day.

Are there songs where you wonder if your voice will be there that night?

Sometimes there are songs where you just sing different notes 'cause you know you can't hit the highest note, so you sing another inversion.

Are there songs where you have to adjust the key live?

Lots of them. The whole *Wall* show, most of them are down a tone. Anything that's problematic, I drop by about a tone. Almost everything that was in E minor has been dropped to D minor. "Run Like Hell" has gone down a tone from D to C, which means detuning the guitars from E to D. I don't play, I was just looning around in a Nazi costume.

Because you mentioned that costume, it's so brilliant at the end of that show when you guys are playing "Outside the Wall," that everyone's in their real clothes. They

---

11   I bought the book as Roger advised, and he was right. Worth reading!

finally become themselves, just real people at the end. That's such a brilliant little touch. All the walls are torn down, and now you're just a human being wearing a regular t-shirt.

Yeah, it's nice, innit? But the truth of that song never escapes me. I use it in conversations all the time with people. I go, "After all, it's not easy, banging your heart against some mad bugger's wall," because so much of life is like that. And certainly, we're seeing today, everything that happens in American politics now is banging your heart against some mad bugger's wall, 'cause they're all fucking mad.

I couldn't agree more. [A political coversation takes place before getting back to the matter at hand.] Do you remember a performance where you surprised yourself?

I find it hard to believe just how high I could sing thirty years ago. That range. I used to scream by taking air in, not by breathing anything out. It was dragged past my vocal cords, inwards. Using the technique, that was probably 120 decibels. It's that scream I used to do in the middle of "Careful with That Axe, Eugene." If I was to do it now—I won't try and make a loud noise—but it's [*shrieks wildly*].

Damn! [*Laughter*] So, how are you hearing your own voice?

Often, I listen to it and think, *Fuck, that's good*. And very often, I try to explain to other people how to sing it, and realize how difficult it is to copy my phrasing. It's just as difficult to copy my phrasing as it is...well, you talked about Sam Cooke. "A Change Is Gonna Come." To try and copy that is almost impossible because the phrasing is so delicate and important, but I bet every time Sam Cooke sang "A Change Is Gonna Come," he phrased it the same.

Going back to our conversation about, can somebody cover a song, and do it with the same amount of innate soul? I think Otis Redding was the only person that got anywhere near Sam Cooke's performance of that song.

Yeah. I agree. Otis Redding had such an extraordinary instrument that he could do almost anything with it, and it is amazing.

Do you have a favorite vocal performance you're really proud of?

Nothing that pops out. If I went through and listened to stuff, I would probably go, "Maybe that," but it's not something I carry with me, or can get out at a dinner party and go, that one. It's not a stock question that I get asked.

Well, this isn't some bullshit interview, Roger. [*Laughter*] I really love how your voice sounds on "Broken Bones." It almost feels like a cousin to "Paranoid Eyes." There's a real intimacy to those vocals that cut right to the heart of the lyric. Do you have a certain way you record songs like that?

Very close to the fucking mic, so I have to use a pop shield. I have an old favorite Neumann U48 microphone that I sing on. I monitor it very loud in cans, so I can hear it like nobody else will ever hear it, almost as if I'm in my own head, because my voice is very quiet. It develops an intimate quality where you can hear every little bit of saliva on the lip, or movement, and that's what I like. I only have two volumes in my singing: one and eleven, to go a bit Spinal Tap! [*Laughter*]

Right, you have that very intimate sound, like we're talking about on these songs. And then you have the, "I'm giving you marching orders" voice. [*Mimics Roger screaming as he does toward the end of "The Happiest Days of Our Lives."*]
Yeah, exactly! [*Laughs*]

Do you have a favorite vocal performance by Syd?
Well, I have a favorite song, but it wasn't in Pink Floyd, which was "Dark Globe." I really love "Dark Globe." The kick in the way he used words was always fascinating. For instance, if you think of the first verse of "Bike" [*Sings Syd's phrasing*] "I've got a bike, you can ride it if you like..." Up until there you think, *Well, that's nice*. It's alliteration and it's rhythmic, but then it's got the kick, "I'd give it to you if I could, but I borrowed it," which doesn't rhyme, and it's weird, and it's also perfect.

That's a great example of how unique he was.
It's really fucking cool. So, my admiration for Syd's writing was in his ability to kick off into uncharted territory if you like.

Do you have a favorite vocal performance of David's?
Of David's? It's very difficult for me. I mean, I mentioned the choruses of "Comfortably Numb," but it's hard, you know? He sings a lot of the songs beautifully.

That's interesting because once Syd was gone around '78, you stepped up the song-writing and kept the band going. But it feels like you leaned on David to sing more in the beginning, then at a certain point said, "Alright, I got this," and started singing more stuff yourself. How would you decide who would sing what between you two?
We would decide together. But Dave has a much greater facility with producing notes in an order than I do. What he doesn't have, because they're not his fucking songs, is the capacity for it to be real. The only bone I have to pick with the corporate body that was Pink Floyd at the time was how I got railroaded out of "Have a Cigar," which Roy Harper sang on. I always really regret that I didn't just go, "No, fuck you, I'm singing this," because at the time I got so much, "Oh, for fuck sake, you can't sing, you're always out of tune, and you're useless" from Rick and David.

Such a bummer. So, what's changed the most about your voice since you started?
I can't hit the high notes like I used to, but what I've realized is, if I just relax and sing where it's comfortable in my range, I express the emotion, and that's when it is great.

If you could duet with one singer—living or dead—who would it be?

Oh, my Goodness. Duet. Well, I've had very little of that experience in my life, but I've already done it, and he's just died, and it's John Prine. We did a duet on "Hello in There" in 2015 at the Newport Folk Festival, and I'm getting a bit teary. I wouldn't give up that memory for all the fucking Cincinnati stadiums in the world. I loved the man, and I loved his music so much. So, when he asked if I'd sing with him, I went, "Fuck yeah." And it was stunningly beautiful. Funnily enough, I asked him to sing a duet with me on *Amused to Death* in 1992. I could hear him singing on the choruses of "Watching TV." He tried to do it, but could not figure out how to sing along with what I was doing. I thought, *That's really interesting*. We just laughed and had another drink, and put it away with no embarrassment or anything. Don Henley did it instead. *Not instead!* But Don Henley, who I knew as well, sings high vocal harmonies over the choruses in "Watching TV."

John Prine's another guy just singing from his heart. No special effects needed.

When you hear "Donald and Lydia" or "Sam Stone" for the first time, if you don't fall in love, there's something fucking wrong with you. When he started his career, Kris Kristofferson took him to a club in Chicago, and he got up onstage and sang three songs. He was a postman at the time, and the guy who owned the club offered him a job. He says, "Doing what? I'm not much good at washin' dishes." And the guy said, "No, idiot! Singing your songs!" Prine went, "You're kidding," and he went, "I'm not kidding. I want you here next Thursday. Do an hour set." You know what? The three songs he'd just sung were the only three songs he'd ever written. And they were "Sam Stone," "Hello in There," and "Paradise." He then went off, desperately writing new songs so that he could go to work. Isn't that fuckin' amazing?

Wow.

Yeah, wow.

I'd love to know your top five favorite singers of all time?

Billie Holiday. Sam Cooke. You've already said Otis Redding. Let me think...Franco Corelli. Alright, you've mentioned him today, Neil. I'm a huuuuge fan of Neil's. Huuuge.

If you could ask any singer about their voice, who would it be and what would you ask?

Oh fuck. [*JTG laughs*] Well, it's Franco Corelli. When he started, they told him he was a baritone. It took him years and years to persuade people that he was actually a tenor. So, he had a big range, but where did it come from? "When did you realize...? Or were you just some kid who went to a conservatory somewhere and learned to sing cause you...? How did that happen...?" Listen to the 1967 recording of Franco Corelli singing "E Lucevan Le Stelle" which is in the third act of *Tosca*, just before he's going to be executed. Listen to the beauty of his delivery of the long held, very high note, but then glissading down to the end of the phrases, which he holds at the middle and end of that aria, and I think you will understand why I've probably listened to it a thousand times.

What would you ask Corelli about that?

"How does it feel to be able to do that?" Because for those of us who've ever sung a note in our lives, to *hear him* do that feels superhuman. To be able to technically, and physically, control those little muscles and your breath, to the point where you can *make that* communication with other people is stunning to me. But that's a technical side of singing that produces an extraordinary result, which in terms of the kind of singing I do, or Neil does, or even, dare I say, Sam Cooke or Billie Holiday, it's a completely different thing. *It's not that*, however exquisite what they do might be. I don't feel connected to Corelli's pain when I listen to "E Lucevan Le Stelle." When you listen to Billie Holiday, every note of Billie Holiday, you feel the pain. Every. Single. Note. Same with Bessie Smith. Most of my favorite singers go back to the blues.

Well, after everything you've been through in your life, to build yourself back up, and to stand in front of the biggest selling audiences in concert history and have all those people chanting back to you, "Tear down the wall! Tear down the wall!" how the does that feel?

You've brought back a memory. What's the line in "Hey You" that the audiences all shout out? "Together we stand, divided we fall," which is the last line. I swear to God, a football stadium in Istanbul was the loudest audience I've ever heard. They actually shook that cardboard wall that lay between the band and them. They were amazing. That felt extraordinary. We all looked at each other and went, "Fuuuuuck me, can you hear that?" [*Roars*] "*TOGETHER WE STAND, DIVIDED WE FALL!*" And they're right. That is exactly the message. The ruling class is desperately trying to persuade everybody that to be divided is the *only* way to survive, that we *have* to fight everybody else. Their philosophy, both politically and in terms of their humanity, is the exact opposite of "Together we stand, divided we fall." They think, "Divided we stand. Together we *would fall*. We cannot be together with you. Because that would be the end of our supremacy. We need to be divided in order to feel supremely superior. That is what we stand for." It's only recently, I had to ask myself, "Should you go on shouting into the darkness? Or should you keep your powder dry and save yourself for a different battle?" When I asked myself that question, I remembered that when I was about thirteen, my mother said, "You know, you're going to have to make difficult decisions in your life. So, when you come to make a decision, you need to look at all the information you have. Look at all sides of the question. And when you've done all that, done all your research, then will come the easy bit." "Oh, yeah, Mom, what's the easy bit?" "*You do the right thing*." And the right thing is to go on tellin' 'em to fuck off as loud as I can, in whatever way I can, and at whatever risk to my reputation, or my welfare or my security. I said, "You are in a very lucky position in that you have a voice. You have to go on making as much noise as you can, and fuck 'em!" So, I'm glad to know now that singers have a function 'cause that would be it. There we are.

ANN WILSON

H EART'S DEBUT ALBUM WAS RELEASED in 1975. It's now 2022, and not a decade has passed where this band has not had a top ten record in the charts. Led by the songwriting duo of Ann Wilson and her sister, guitarist/vocalist Nancy, their sound has crossed multiple genres throughout the years, from hard rock to pop, folk, and whatever else they've felt like doing.

When the grunge era arrived, driving a nail into the coffin for so many artists of the time, Heart not only survived, they were idolized by the Seattle music community they helped create. Bands like Soundgarden and Alice in Chains were not only singing their praises, but it wouldn't be long before they were singing with Ann as well.

Just listen to her voice on any classic from "Barracuda" to "Crazy on You," then fast-forward to songs like "No Other Love" or "I Jump" from just a few years back. This is how you get inducted into the Rock & Roll Hall of Fame: you sing like Ann.

I was thrilled to speak with her about the power of the big hand, how she brought Robert Plant to tears, and how she helped break down barriers for women just by singing from the...(DON'T YOU DO IT!)...heart.

Who first exposed you to singing?

I come from a family of people who love to get together and play ukuleles and sing old English pub songs and stuff like that. My parent's generation and their parent's generation were just a bunch of singers, so, as kids, we were never shy about sitting around in a big bunch and letting our voices ring. But it's a big jump from that to actually going out and doing it professionally.

What made you wanna do that?

I don't know. Just a big hand pushing me.

Were you emulating anyone when you started?

Oh, everyone. Peter, Paul, and Mary, The Limeliters, Ann Peebles, Aretha Franklin, Janis Joplin. And then, I started in on males. Mick Jagger, Robert Plant, Rod Stewart, Elton John. I took instruction from all of them.

How did you find your own voice?

Just by singing constantly. After a while, any affectations of someone else's style started to fall away. For instance, if you say, "We're gonna write an Elton John song," once you're actually singing your own melodies and making it your own, it doesn't sound anything like Elton. So, I imagine, that's kind of the process.

Did you ever have any vocal training?

No, I never did. But in both junior high and high school, I was in the choir, so I was working with a music teacher who was pretty brilliant. He was in the chorus in the Seattle Opera, and he taught me a lot about how to breathe, and diction, how you say your words. Because how you pronounce words when you're singing is such a big deal.

Do you remember your first time onstage as a lead singer?

I was in a band at my high school, and we were playing in the school theater for some rally or something. I got so nervous that my voice shut down on me, and I couldn't sing. Now I understand it's 'cause I was so anxious.

What gave you the courage to continue doing it after a moment like that?

Well, like I say, the big hand. The thing that makes you go audition for the school talent show, that makes you just gotta get up there. There's some kind of a high involved when the lights go down and you're in the spotlight onstage in front of people, and you have complete license to express yourself and then get a response. That's magic.

Do you still get nervous before you perform?

These days I don't. Back in the '80s I did. I just got comfortable with the idea of not being scared; just like, *What's the worst thing that could happen?* [*Laughs*]

Do you do any vocal warm-ups before shows?
Usually, for at least forty minutes before I walk out there, I'll just sing along with somebody else's album or sing a cappella. I don't run scales or anything like that. It's too boring. Anything that can open up your throat, but more importantly than your throat, your soul, 'cause that's what opens everything up.

Is there something that does that for you?
I like anything by Daniel Lanois. The songs are in the right key for me to sing along with.

Aww, he's so great. Do you have any other rituals before you hit the stage?
I just try to remain super calm and peaceful. I wanna go out there and sing from the place of complete relaxation.

Is there anything after the show that helps keep your voice in shape?
I found that Arnica pellets really help my voice. They give Arnica to people to help with bruising or swelling. But if I take mega doses of these pellets during the day, my voice will heal way faster and better than without. Because your throat is bruised and enflamed from hitting it so hard. You can get them any place where they sell homeopathic stuff.

How do you take care of your voice on the road?
I don't smoke, I don't drink, I don't inhale anything granulated. [*Laughs*] Those things will dry out your throat and irritate it. I have this stuff that Neil Young turned me onto called Satori. It's a little vocal restorative spray that's got a bunch of different herbs in it.

When you start getting sick, what do you do?
The Arnica thing is preventative, and it really works. B12 shots help with energy. I take a whole lot of that gentle vitamin C. If it's a really bad situation, I'll see a rock doc and get a steroid shot, but I don't recommend stuff like that.

Do you have songs where you wonder if your voice will be there that night?
As long as I'm not sick, I don't have any problem with my voice.

Are there songs where you've had to adjust the key live?
I've never done that because when you record these songs, and you arrive at the key it's gonna be in, you do that for a reason. It's important, 'cause the melodies, the sound of the voice and everything is right for that key. If you start changing keys, you take the shimmer off the top of the song. Some of the electricity goes out of it if you start making things lower, so I've always fought against doing that.

What was your most embarrassing vocal mishap ever?

Strangely enough, it was with "Stairway to Heaven" when I was still in a bar band, probably right around the time *Zeppelin IV* came out. We were playing in this tavern, and we went out on a break, smoked a bunch of pot, got really high, and then came back in to do our next set. Well, "Stairway to Heaven" was in the set, and I'm sure you know how many verses there are. [*Laughter*] So, I start singing, and I forget where we are. I don't know what verse it is, I don't know what comes next. Oh my God, it was so awful.

I don't think anyone comes close to playing Zeppelin songs better than Heart. Then in 2012, they receive the Kennedy Center Honors, and you're suddenly performing for the band and President Obama. You come out with Jason Bonham on drums. You got horns, strings, a gospel choir—all wearing John Bonham's trademark bowler hat—and you unleash the most incredible cover of "Stairway to Heaven" you'll ever hear. And it's so moving because every time they cut to the band, Jimmy Page is beaming from ear to ear, John Paul Jones is smiling away, and then you have Robert Plant fighting back tears, almost haunted by the emotions that are coming up for him. And knowing all that he lost during Zeppelin—from his son to Bonham to part of his relationship with the band—I may be projecting, but I felt like it was all on his face as you were singing.

I don't think that you are projecting at all. I think that's what was really happening with Plant. People like to say, "You brought Plant to tears." Well, that's way too easy. I think he was looking down on that spectacle, and the incredible power of the lyrics that he wrote, and he saw Jason Bonham on drums. Jason had been a little kid, running around at their band practices, and I just think he was overcome, like you say, by the memories of that time, and all the horrible things that happened back then.

Did he say anything afterwards about your performance?

Yeah, he did, but he's pretty famously a cool cat, so he wasn't that effusive. But he did say, "You know, usually I hate it when people do 'Stairway to Heaven' because they always butcher it. But I like your version."

Awww, man. I totally get why he wouldn't want to go out and do Zeppelin stuff anymore, but did Jimmy Page ever approach you about you fronting the band? I think people would love to see a run of you guys doing that.

No, he didn't. And, believe me, I dropped handkerchiefs everywhere. [*Laughter*]

Do you remember a performance where you surprised yourself?

Heart started out with me as the chick in the band who sang the ballads, right? And then, the men in the band would sing the rock stuff, and it was kinda this traditional way the gender roles were split up. But "Crazy on You" was the one where I went into the studio with [producer] Mike Flicker, and it was like the top lifted off my voice. I could get up to those high notes, and it wasn't anything I was consciously trying to do, that's just what the song called for. I remember sitting in there, listening to myself and going, *Wow!* I was inspired by Gino Vannelli, of all people. He had that same Italian ability to go way up high, full voice. So, I may have been channeling him, but once I got there, I knew how to do it.

On that live, acoustic version of "Crazy on You" off *The Road Home*, you're doing things with your voice that truly makes your hair stand on end. It's just beautiful.
Thank you.

When Chris Cornell inducted you guys into the Rock & Roll Hall of Fame, he said, "Ann Wilson is a uniquely great vocal force of nature." The place went nuts, but you were shaking your head. Were you just being humble, or do you have a hard time with compliments?
Both probably. I think because it was coming from Chris Cornell, who I consider to be a vocal force of nature, and one of those people who, when he sang, told the truth, and there was no separation between fantasy and reality for him. He was all the way real, right down to the bone. So, to hear him say that, I probably was going, "Ohhh Jesus..." [*Laughs*]

But for a lot of people, your voice broke down so many doors. I hate even segregating it; being women in rock or men in rock, because great singers are great singers, but what you did with your voice really paved the way for so many women in rock.
It's funny because when we were starting out, the first reviews Heart was getting in the late '70s didn't know how to classify me and my vocal style. A lot of the time, I'd get negative reviews because I wasn't singing in this delicate, kind of pretty, feminine way, and they didn't know what to do with that! A couple of times it was like, "Ann Wilson, putting the foghorn business out of business," and these really weird things. They didn't get it. But that dissipated.

Every time I hear "Barracuda," I'm always dumbfounded by how you came up with that melody and phrasing for the verses. I'll never understand how you got there. It doesn't make sense. Do you know what I mean? It's just the craziest thing how you do that.
Yeah, where does that come from? [*Laughs*] That's one of the great mysteries of songwriting. It just arrives. *I love that when that happens!*

How are you with hearing your own voice?
It depends on the era. [*Laughter*] We have so many different eras now. I think there are times when I sound better than others. The times I'm not that fond of are the times when I was partying the most, like in the '80s. I can hear the strain, and it's not a good type of strain. It's like an anxiousness that's in the way of the true expression. But, most of the time, I don't mind it. If I can relax and go, "You can't change it, so accept it. You can't go back and overdub and fix that." [*Laughter*]

Do you have a favorite vocal performance you're really proud of?

Yeah, there are a few of them where I don't know who that is. I like them so much it seems like somebody else to me. Things in the '90s in the Lovemongers, and on *Desire Walks On*. Like on "Mistral Wind." Just a song here and there when I went out of body with it, and I wasn't thinking.

Let's talk about singing with your sister a second. Your voices blend so beautifully. Is there a song she sings where her vocals really impress you?

"These Dreams" is my favorite. That's a really good marriage of voice and song.

What's changed the most about your voice since you started?

It's gotten lower, but I'm fine with it as long as I can still get up to the top. Everything changes, I just have to take more care with my health now when we're on the road. I didn't used to have to care so much! But the body does not recover the way it did when you're nineteen or twenty-five, so those are the biggest changes. You have to be a lot more careful.

If you could duet with one singer—living or dead—who would it be?

Lucinda Williams. I think she's the best Americana-country singer goin' right now. She's so down and so simple and straight ahead, and no pretense. That appeals to me.

Over the years, you collaborated with Alice in Chains a bunch, singing on each other's stuff, but a real highlight is the duet you did with Layne Staley on your *Desire Walks On* album. You guys cover "Ring Them Bells" by Dylan, and we get to hear this other side of Layne that we never experienced before. It's like he had this soul singer living inside of him that stuck his head out on that track.

Totally. Layne was a really soulful person. Especially for being as young and as troubled as he was. He had the ability to transport his soul all over the place. I thought he was a really good singer. I was really pleased when he agreed to do that with us. We also have a version of Chris Cornell singing that with us, but at the time, the management of Soundgarden didn't want him to be associated with Heart because of image reasons. Heart was considered to be a middle of the road band from the '80s, and that didn't jive with the Soundgarden image that they were trying to make. So, they pulled back the version we did with Chris, but Layne said, "Hell, I don't care! Alice in Chains is one of the darkest bands in Seattle, and we'll do it with ya!" So that's how that happened.

Who are your top five favorite singers of all time?

Joni Mitchell...oh wow, so hard...Robert Plant, of course...Alison Krauss...Lucinda...and Elton John, in the day.

If you could ask any singer about their voice, who would it be and what would you ask?

I would ask Plant about his voice. Because he has so many voices. He's got at least four or five different voices. I'd say, "What is your soul in each one of these?" It sounds like a weird question, but the voice emanates from the soul, so I'd like to hear him talk about that.

THOM YORKE

THE GREAT TOM WAITS ONCE SAID, "Singing is just doing interesting things to the air, elongating it and twisting it into shapes." That quote always reminds me of Thom Yorke, because, on a primal level, I can't think of anyone who does that better.

As the lead singer of Radiohead, and a slew of other side projects and solo records, Thom uses his voice not just to sing the melody of the lyric, but as another musical instrument to explore the sonic possibilities of a song. And that creative spirit has earned him a place as one of the most influential singers of all time.

Yorke and his band have sold millions of records, won multiple Grammys, and have been inducted into the Rock & Roll Hall of Fame. But more importantly, they've taken rock music as an art form and expanded it beyond where it stood before they came along. Their live shows are an experience that always feels sacred, ecstatic, and euphoric. Thom's voice can truly lift you off the ground and transport you to another planet.

But back down on earth, he taught me how to disappear completely.

Who first exposed you to singing?

How do you mean?

Who or what gave you the realization of, *This is something I want to do.*

I didn't want to do it.

Welcome to the club! [*Laughter*]

I always expected someone else would be doing it, because I didn't see myself as the sort of character that could put myself in front of a microphone. When I was like eight years old, I decided to learn to play guitar, and I told my first guitar teacher that I was gonna be a rock star. I was really into Queen, but I never saw myself as Freddie Mercury. I was always Brian May in my head, surprisingly. And it sort of changed because I couldn't really find anyone else to do it. [*Laughs*] Couldn't get anyone to fit the job description. Because I started writing my own songs, it sort of happened like that. I didn't actually think that I could do it.

So, when did that appear on the horizon?

Probably around the age of thirteen or fourteen. I'm now at school, and I'm starting to write songs and record them using my own voice, and even passing tapes out. But even then, I was thinking, *I'll find someone else to sing them*. And then, I started singing more because the band started forming. But my first proper, real experience of saying to myself, "Okay, I'm a singer," wasn't really in that situation.

What was the situation?

I was well supported by the head of music at my school. I couldn't read music so, normally, I would've been dismissed, but he kind of saw something in me. He said, "You should take singing lessons just to protect your voice because you're straining your voice," which is what people do when they've never sung before.

So, you had vocal lessons in school?

My singing teacher was like the cultural, polar opposite. He made me sing Schubert, and I didn't know what the fuck was going on. I mean, I could just about tell the notes were going up and down, but it's in bloody German. But weirdly, I quite enjoyed the challenge of having to do something so structured and classical and the specific technique of how to use my body. And I did a recital of a Schubert thing in front of about twenty people, and that's the first time where I said, "Okay, I guess I'm a singer," because people really liked it, or rather I was surprised by the sound that was coming out. I didn't really expect it.

When you started to sing your own stuff, were you emulating anyone else?

Oh yeah! [*Chuckles*] For quite a few years, I would say. [*Laughs more*] It was always mostly Michael Stipe, sometimes a little bit of Morrissey. I would emulate most of the singers who were quite low down. I was really into David Sylvian's voice, but my register wasn't there. It was much higher. It was sort of a comedy when I tried to sing like that.

How did you find your own voice?

It took me years. The hardest lesson to learn is to be yourself. It's like you try all these different outfits on. There was no way I was gonna be Michael Stipe because my register wasn't the same, I wasn't from Georgia, but I really admired how he wrote lyrics. So, I took a lot of that kind of thing from him. But I always felt that my register was uncomfortably high or awkward, or that my voice was too soft. When I was eighteen, I took a year and recorded music for most of it. Then I sent the tape off, and it won like "Demo of the Month" in this free music magazine, and this review said, "Who is this guy? He sounds just like Neil Young!" I went, "Who's *Neil Young?*" [*Laughter*] I'd never even heard Neil Young, so I went out and bought *After the Gold Rush* and was like, *Wow! It's okay to sound like that?* Because he's slightly higher than me, but there was like a softness, and a naiveté in the voice which I was always trying to hide. Then, it was like, Oh, maybe I don't need to hide it.

Did that affect the way you started to approach your vocals?

It took me a few years after that because starting off as a rock band, everything was all about force and energy. It took me a long time to go, "I don't need to do that." When we were doing the second record [*The Bends*], I went to see Jeff Buckley before he died. Again, that was one of those, *It's okay to do that?* And it reminded me of this vulnerable part of me that I was choosing to hide. I remember I recorded "Fake Plastic Trees" on my own to begin with. Then, when we came together to listen to it, the others said, "We'll use that!" and I was, "No, no, we can't use that, it's too vulnerable. That's too much me." [*Laughs*]

Years ago, I read an article that said when you were listening to the playback of that song that you just melted and started crying 'cause it was so vulnerable. Is that true?

Yeah, absolutely. Because when you record, you're going through one set of feelings, but the one thing you're not really aware of is *you*. You're not aware of your own identity, so it's like meditating. Even when you play, if you perform something well, you have a sort of feeling that goes beyond that. You're not even aware of your own vulnerability, you're just off somewhere, and then you come back. It's like seeing yourself in the mirror for the first time, catching yourself unaware. It's an odd feeling, but at the same time, that's what recording vocals has become for me. When we were doing *OK Computer*, [*laughs*] I had this whole thing about how I must be off my face in order to record the vocals so that I'm not self-conscious. But, you know, it just sounds like a drunk bloke. Endless weeks of disastrous vocals until I sobered up. [*Laughter*]

I'm down to hear that alternate record, of you drunk-singing *OK Computer*.

Not really! I remember being totally half-cocked, trying to sing "Let Down." God. Awful.

That's the one to sing drunk!

[*Laughs*] It really isn't! You gotta be so accurate! But you spend a lot of the time, probably like actors do, trying to achieve ways to not feel self-conscious so it just becomes about singing itself. Much like being an actor, in order for it to be believable, you have to remove yourself. The lack of consciousness about what you're doing is really an important bit.

How do you remove that consciousness?

It's this weird feeling. You have this whole preparation, like a physical thing that you must prepare and analyze, and then, by the time that you record it, you have to totally forget about it. That's what athletes do. In order to get into the zone, you have to prepare for it, and then not think about it. I always get the feeling that the good takes from singers are the ones where they remove themselves identity-wise from what it is, Neil Young being a classic example. You have the sensation that on those records in the '70s, that it was a moment [*snaps his fingers*] and then it's passed. Maybe they did five, and then they chose one. That's how we used to work all the time—five, maybe six, seven, top whack. I wouldn't be aware of what's in there, but Nigel [Godrich, producer] would be. Usually, an emotion will come through despite itself, despite all the practicalities. "Is this in tune?" "Is that the right intonation?" Something else will come through.

If it's a little out of tune, but the emotion is there, how specific do you get?

I try not to bother about that. When we first started recording with Nigel, we made an agreement where you try to keep as much of the mistakes as you can bear, if it's got that other thing. Occasionally, you might tune a note, one note, but that's about it. Try and keep it as human and as real as you can get away with.

My guitar player and I call it "The thing." I do a pass and go, "What do you think?" He'll go, "Well, it was technically good, but it didn't have the thing."

That's kind of what I mean, yeah. It's not often in the first round of recording a vocal that I'll get anything technically good. It's like getting out the charcoal stick and going, "Well, it's gonna look like this." It's like you have to walk the path of the vocal, and go away for a few weeks, then come back familiar with the path, and do it properly, because there is a technical level you've got to get to, but then, "If that's what you call a mistake, then, *Yeah right!*"

Did you ever have any vocal training outside of school?

No, that was it. Basically, the guy taught me how to pitch and open up my throat, and to sing to the crown of your head. That was kind of enough. One time, I went and stayed in Spain where Björk was recording and woke up the day we were supposed to do the session, and she was doing scales *really, really loud*, first thing in the morning. I came downstairs going, *What the fuck…is that?* I'd never done scales in my life. She'd lost her voice or something six months previous, so that made me think, *Oh. Alright. Well, I know how to do scales.*

Do you do vocal warm-ups?

Not every day, but on tour, doing proper warm-ups and warm-downs, that's super important. If you warm-up, you know where your weaknesses are before you start. *Okay, there's
something wrong here. I can't push it today because of this.* You get a bit nervous, but at least
you're not surprised by it when you start singing onstage. A lot of the time, tension in the
body will affect the voice so, I'm very fortunate that we have a chiropractor who comes on
tour with me and goes [*mimics the sound of bones cracking as they adjust*] with my neck sometimes, and then [*makes a wondrous sound of relief*]. It's quite an amazing feeling when your
voice just opens up like that. It's mental. But this is what happens when you're touring a lot,
you have to have someone fix you up if you throw yourself around like I do.

That's a great thing to be able to have.

The funny thing is now that I've stopped heavily drinking or abusing myself, the healthiest I
feel is on tour! [*Laughter*] Because there's someone looking after you! Hold on, I gotta let the
cat in. [*Opens a sliding glass door, says to the cat*] "Don't just stand there."

Are you nervous or confident before you perform?

I started getting nervous later, when it started being something real, when we signed a
record deal, and when we played Astoria, for example, in 1994—just terrified. [*Laughs*] Or
when we did Arsenio Hall. That was a car crash. TV's a nightmare. That makes you really
super nervous. It's live, you can't do it again, something always goes wrong, it's always over
the top because you're all really hyped up, and you make a mistake, and you walk off and go,
"*FUUUUCK! I WAS SHIIIIIT! FUUUUUUCK!*" [*Laughter*] And there's nothing you can do about
it. Yeah, that makes me nervous. I'd be worried if I wasn't getting nervous, actually. I mean,
sometimes you can walk on and be quite casual about it, but not often.

Tell me more about the vocal warm-ups before you perform?

I'm big on preparation before the show. I literally have my own space on tour, which I'm a bit
embarrassed about sometimes, but I have to have my own room. I do yoga as well because,
like I said, the body and the voice are all tied up so, if the body's relaxed, the voice is relaxed.
Also, the yoga helps with preparing you for when things go wrong onstage.

What kinds of things?

Working in high pressurized situations like a festival when your entire headset goes dead or
starts giving you white noise, you gotta be able to react in a way that's not, "*Holy shit!*" You've
gotta be calm mentally, not just vocally. They go together because if you're tense, then your
voice tenses up. And if your voice tenses up, then you push it too hard, and that has consequences. So, whatever it takes to stay open.

So, what's your vocal warm-up before you go on?

About ten to fifteen minutes of scales. More than doing major and minor scales, I force myself to try and learn weird scales instead. Jonny Greenwood [*guitarist*] is the one who's really into weird scales so, I kinda got that off him.

Do you have any other rituals before you hit the stage?

I meditate for about twenty minutes if I can. What else? Stand on me head.

Is that true?

Yeah. That's for about three or four minutes. Then, there's a mad dash at the end of all this. [*Laughs*] I never allow myself quite enough time between doin' all that nonsense, and then I've got, like, "Oh fuck, get changed! Shit! *GO!*" [*Laughter*]

You mentioned you warm-down after the show. What's that look like for you?

Pretty anti-social. You just sing softly to yourself. Scales, or if there's a song in my head, doesn't really matter. It's just the act of singing softly and dropping it down, that's what's important. Then, resist the temptation to reach for the first drink that someone gives you. For at least the first ten minutes.

What other ways do you take care of your voice on the road?

Try not to get fucked up. AC is another lethal one. Really lethal. AC on buses is a bad one. There's no real way round that because there's certain times where you really don't have any choice but to be in an AC environment. The only way to counteract that is to try and find a few hours in the day to make sure to spend a few hours out of AC. Even if it means walking around the block a few times. Otherwise, it's weird how much you can end up being in AC and not even realize it.

When you start getting sick, what do you do?

Panic. I try and sleep as much as I can. I have these great pills called Vocalzone. I don't know what's in them, but they're great. But only sort of as a low maintenance, [*feels his throat*] "Oh, it's a bit rough." [*Waits a beat, then pantomimes chugging the entire box, breaking into laughter*] In terms of routine, you're supposed to drink lots of hot fluids, don't touch any dairy. Dairy's lethal. *FUCK ME*, this is the most geeked out I've ever talked about my voice. [*Cracks up*] All the things I don't even bother taking to anybody else about, other than my tour manager. [*Pretends to cry*] "*I need some more Vocalzone!*" By the way, I've always resisted taking steroids. Some singers I know seem to be on tour on steroids all the time. I really hate that shit.

Yeah, it's really dangerous too.

It's really dangerous. Luckily, things have kind of changed, but in America you'd have this situation where the promoter knows the doctor, and the doctor turns up and goes, "Oh yeah, you're fine. Take these." And it'd be like some fuck off, crazy steroid, and you'd take it and be jumping around the room and want to kill everybody. It makes you *super* aggressive. I stopped doing that because I don't trust any of these fucking people.

"The promotor knows a doctor." I'm sure it's fine. [*Laughs*]
If I can't sing, I can't sing, it's bloody obvious. And say you do that show and you're sick, you're wiping out the next five shows. In fact, that is the worst thing about being a singer, full stop. Everything else about it I love, it does amazing things to you. But the one thing I fucking hate is having to cancel shows, or, even worse, think you can do a show, persuade yourself you can, and then, lose your voice halfway through and have to walk off. It's only happened to me like three times in my life. There is nothing worse.

Gimme a good one.
There was one in Australia in front of like 12,000 people. I had to walk off, and it was just the most horrendous thing. Eventually, you forgive yourself. You say, "You know what? You're only human." But at the time, some people don't get it. Even when Ed O'Brien [guitarist] went back onstage and said, "We're really sorry, but he can't carry on," people started fucking booing, and you're like, "What? *Seriously?*"

Because they think it's like some star trip or something.
Yeah, do we look like Guns N' Roses to you? [*Laughter*] Come on.

Are there songs where you wonder if your voice will be there that night?
There's ones from the early years. What happens with voices is voices drop. One time I met Neil Young. He was talking about how the early songs for him are harder because they're higher, and it's the same for me now. "Creep" is an absolute bastard, the bit in the middle, although you can go falsetto, but I try not to. Anything that's got like a high G, or higher than that, these days, starts to be a bit tough.

Are there songs where you have to adjust the key live?
No. I haven't got to that stage yet. I hope not to because that would just be, in terms of the guitar playing, a total nightmare so, I hope that doesn't happen.

What was your most embarrassing vocal mishap ever?
[*Laughs*] There was one time we played in San Francisco in this really nice outdoor place, Shoreline. It was a great show, really, really fun. The audience were brilliant. Then, before the final encore, I smoked a blunt with Jonny. I went back on and started playing "Everything in Its Right Place" and got completely lost. I think I sang the second verse first, and then I was looking at the keyboard going, *What's this?* [*Laughter*] Then, I went to sing the next verse, and I realized, *I've just sung that*, and I looked at the others, and they were all going [*makes a face*] "Get us out of this one." I'm just going around the riff, looking at the audience, and they're all

singing the words, and I'm going, "What?" [*Tries reading their lips*] I was so high, I just got up from the piano and [*puts his hands up in surrender*] walked off. [*Laughs hysterically*]

That's incredible because the song only has like three lines in it!
Exactly! [*More laughter*] It's not fucking rocket science!

Do you remember a performance where you surprised yourself?
When we were doing "Paranoid Android," I was having what could be loosely described as a bad day. I went AWOL, left the others and went off with [artist] Stanley Donwood, and we ended up in the pub for most the day. Then, we wobbled back on bicycles, up the hill to the studio, and they'd done a whole lot of the track, and it was really great. They were working on the end bit, and I was sitting, going, "It needs someone shouting," and Nigel's like, "Okay." I went in and shouted into this little Dictaphone. [*Mimics himself screaming in gibberish*] I had no idea what I was saying. Then, I finished and went, "Well, that's not gonna work." And he's like, "Wow, that's great!" A lot of the time there's that feeling where you say, "This isn't gonna work. This is obviously shit." And then, you go in and go, "That's really cool!"

How are you with hearing your own voice?
I probably should like the sound of my voice a bit more than I do. What tends to happen is the more emotionally attached I get to a song, the harder it is. Or the more I struggle to finish a song, the harder it is to listen to my voice because I spent months imagining how it should be. The longer I'm doing that, the tougher it is to listen back and accept that I'm actually only human, and it's only going to be like that, because the longer you think about it, the more you think about the possibilities, especially with lyrics.

Do you have a favorite vocal performance you're really proud of?
I really like "Bloom." On the surface, that's quite simple, but actually is a real bastard, which is what's nice about it. You kind of have to sing it in this way that's *reeeeeally* open. But when you do it live, it's much harder because there's a lot of technical shit going on, and you have to totally forget about the chaos and come in with this really open voice. It's a bit like playing trumpet because you're not thinking about the words, you're making just this sound—*Raaaaaaaa*.

When I interviewed Tony Bennett, he said that his vocal coach told him to imitate other musicians, "piano players and trumpet players and saxophone players. But don't imitate singers." When he said that to me, I thought of you immediately.
Really?

Yeah, because to me, your voice sounds like a violin. Does that make sense?
As long as it's not an oboe, mate, I don't mind. [*Laughter*]

But does that make sense to you, or is that a bizarre statement?

No, that makes sense. Most of the vocals I write are wordless for quite a long time except for maybe one key phrase. I work on it like that, and I think of it like that, but I totally agree. I think of my voice as an instrument, but it's not like any normal instrument because, no matter what you do, you're naked. I guess, maybe that's why I'm sort of fascinated with effects on the voice. One of the things I enjoyed recently was watching Jonny experimenting with microtonal stuff where you're moving between the notes. So, you have the almost semitone scale, and then you have all the notes in between. And I did this thing where I set up a modular synthesizer to go between all the notes, and then I copied it with my voice, and it's like a twenty-minute piece.

This is getting very Radiohead right now. What's that sound like?

You have these slowly dropping and ascending lines, and I had to treat it like my voice is an instrument, as a violin or something, because I had to follow the shifts in the pitch, micro-shifts, bit by bit, so literally, breath by breath. I didn't want to hear any of my breath. So, I sang each note, cut out the breaths, sang the next bit of the note, cut out breaths, sang the next bit of the note, cut out the breaths. Took me weeks. *Weeks*. It's on the *Suspiria* soundtrack.

What's the track called?

"A Choir of One." I wanted it to feel like a choir, but it's a choir of one voice, basically. Then, I did various different pitches. But all the notes are clashing and it makes you feel really, really uneasy. It was a horror film.

That's fascinating because there's a very orchestral component to a lot of your vocals where you don't just settle for the lead. You make the voice part of the atmosphere behind a track. "Present Tense" or "Judge, Jury, and Executioner" are two awesome examples of that.

It's something I get quite anxious about because, a lot of the time, I will be really into a piece of music as it is, and the vocal is simply a punctuation for that. The core of the thing we're working on is not necessarily the voice. Especially with Jonny, it may be something to do with the rhythm, or with the way the chords fall, or an arpeggiation he's written. My job is to simply find my way to sit inside it, which I really, really enjoy!

But not a lot of singers do that. Marvin Gaye was the first time I noticed a lead singer on one track, and then behind that, there's four or five other Marvin Gaye's doing stuff.

Marvin Gaye's an interesting example because if you've seen that documentary about the *What's Going On?* record, he basically scatted all the lines and everybody scored it out. And that's like my dream world. [*Laughter*] I guess I don't think in terms of "lead vocals" that often because I feel like it's a trap. If you think, "Now I must do the lead vocal," it's like saying, "Now I must do something more important than what's already there," which, to me, is like, *No, that doesn't compute at all*. In fact, I used to really fight that during the *Kid A* period where on "Pyramid Song," all the music is in the music. I'm singing one fucking note all the way through, and there's all this melody going around me. So, I'm choosing to sort of frame the rest of the melodic action by being the human being. Does that make sense?

Yeah, because you really don't approach singing as a lead singer. It's almost like you approach it as a painter or something.

That's literally how I do it sometimes because the method of painting, the stuff I did learn at college, was sometimes the only way to get where you need to go is to lay stuff down on top of itself until you have what you need. You don't really know what's gonna stick. Sometimes the most exciting thing to do with a piece of music is: it starts here, and then something happens here, and then something else happens, and we're over there now! *That's the story*. And that to me is painting. That's not songwriting. *Blood on the Tracks* is one of my favorite records because Dylan takes the idea of storytelling and songwriting to the ultimate place. It doesn't get any better than that, really. I've never been able to do that because I'm as excited about sounds, whether the sound of my voice or the sound of an instrument, as I am about the lyrics or the drum rhythm. They're equally exciting to me.

I see what you're saying, but you're underselling yourself a bit as well. One of my favorite songs is the live version of "True Love Waits" off *I Might Be Wrong*, and that's just you and an acoustic guitar, and that's all you need.

That was one of those songs where it happened as an acoustic guitar song, and it was like, *Well, that's too easy, we can't do that*. Because it's just on acoustic guitar and a voice. I've done that. Poor thing, it became a victim of its own simplicity.

But that song is perfect as is. Then, you went and re-recorded it with all this other stuff, and I always wondered why you felt you had to do that?

I don't know. Unfortunately, there's lots of songs like that. One of my mistakes is dismissing things because they're simple. Nigel, more so than the others, would say to me, "You're making a mistake because you want to see something in it that's not there so, stop fucking trying to change it." Things have fallen by the wayside that shouldn't have for that reason, because I'd had some sort of belligerent agenda, which can smother a song and refuse to let it grow. "True Love Waits" was a bit like that. It was one of those things where it was almost made to be at the end of a show. It wasn't even necessarily made to be recorded. It was made to say, "Okay, guys, goodnight. Thanks."

YES! That's hilarious, because at the end of the live version, you go, "Thank you, everybody," and I swear to God, I say it along with you whenever I listen to it. It's part of the song. [*mimics Thom*] "Thank you, everybody." [*Laughter*] So, this happens to me a lot with your music: I'll be listening to a new record for the first time, I'll hear the music, and think, *How the hell is he gonna do this?* Then, you'll come in with the vocal, and I'll go, *This motherfucker! I can't believe it!* You find a way to take music

that almost doesn't feel tethered to the ground, and you'll reign it in with this incredible melody, and somehow it locks the song into place.

You and my band both, mate. [*Laughter*]

"Backdrifts" is a perfect example. How you got there is crazy!

I had that piece of music for ages, and I was always playing it going, "Check this out, this is great," and everybody's like, "What the fuck is that, man?" I was like, "Fine, I'll put the vocal down." Then, everyone goes, "Ohhh, I get it!" See, I have this terrible habit where I can hear something in a piece of music, and I just assume everybody else can, because I can hear the melody that's gonna go with it. It's really obvious.

What's changed the most about your voice since you started?

Just age. Your voice just changes naturally. It's softened up a bit and got a bit more woody sounding. Whatever it is, I definitely prefer the sound of my voice now than I did before because it's open in a different way, and the register has slightly moved, tonally, down a bit, which I kind of like.

If you could duet with one singer—living or dead—who would it be?

John Lennon. It would sound awful though, *awful*, *UGH*. It wouldn't mix well at all.

Who are your top five favorite singers of all time?

I'm obsessed with Ella Fitzgerald at the moment. There's a performance you can find of Ella Fitzgerald playing with Duke Ellington. They're on this famous TV show in the '60s, a black and white show. She does two jazz standards, and her technical singing is *fucking insane. In. Sane.* She's like belting the crap out of it. She's so loud, and she doesn't miss one note. She does one *super, super fast*, jazz scat thing, which is just...I mean, it's physically impossible. I've not seen anyone do anything like that. And then, obviously, there's Nina Simone. And then, there's Scott Walker, and then, there's Michael Stipe. That's four, right?

Yeah, you got one more.

Goddamn, that's really hard. I wanna say Billie Holiday. Oh! Tom Waits! "Tom Traubert's Blues." That and "Simple Twist of Fate" by Bob Dylan are the two songs that are guaranteed to reduce me to tears every time I hear them. *Guaranteed*. I can't get through either song without falling to pieces.

If you could ask any singer about their voice, who would it be and what would you ask?

It would be John Lennon. Lennon's whole attitude to singing, I'm a little bit obsessed with, because, on the surface, he has this whole, raw, doesn't give a fuck...just the way he sings is weirdly brutal. I'd want to talk to him about how he was always so incredibly accurate, but always sounding on the edge of like, *He's gonna miss it, he's gonna miss it*. And, specifically, all these ideas he had in his head about how his voice should be treated. I was like, *How do you see it?* Because what they did with his voice, they had pretty simple tools, but they did really interesting things. So having a conversation with him about that...or yoga.

PHOTO CREDITS

Bryan Adams @ Scott Legato, ScottLegato.com / **Seth Avett** by Lindsey Akiyama / **Tony Bennett** at the State Theater by Andy Witchger (courtesy of Flickr) / **David Bowie** by Richard E. Aaron, courtesy of Kenny Nemes / **Ben Bridwell** @ Scott Legato, ScottLegato.com / **Jeff Buckley** by Martyn Goodacre / **Belinda Carlisle** by Kevin Mazur/Getty Images, courtesy of Lauryn Levin / **Neko Case** by Denise Truscello / **Nick Cave** by Josh Fogel, joshfogel.com / **Alex Chilton & Big Star** by Michael O'Brien, © 1972–2022 / **Chuck D** by Philippe Bareille / **Kurt Cobain** by Jeff Kravitz / **Citizen Cope** by Joel Didriksen / **Chris Cornell** by Debi Del Grande / **Roger Daltrey** by Kevin Mazur/Getty Images, courtesy of Lauryn Levin / **Britt Daniel** by Andrew Mather | KCConcerts.net / **Joe Elliott** by Kevin Mazur/Getty Images, courtesy of Lauryn Levin / **Perry Farrell** @ Scott Legato, ScottLegato.com / **Patty Griffin** at Lincoln Center Americanafest by Steven Pisano (courtesy of Flickr) / **Sammy Hagar** by Matt Becker, melodicrockconcerts.com (courtesy of Wikimedia Commons) / **Emmylou Harris** by Dave Golden / **Davey Havok** by Alex Okami / **Jimi Hendrix** by Henry Diltz / **Whitney Houston** by David Corio / **Brittany Howard** @ Scott Legato, ScottLegato.com./ **Chrissie Hynde** by Urko Dorronsoro Sagasti / **Jim James** by Justin Wise / **Joan Jett** by Philippe Bareille / **Brian Johnson** by Martin Philbey / **Norah Jones** "50/365" by Jeff Drongowski (courtesy of Flickr) / **Janis Joplin** by Henry Diltz / **Simon Le Bon** by Eva Rinaldi (courtesy of Flickr) / **Geddy Lee** by Randall Tomada / **Little Richard** by Henry Diltz / **John Lydon** by Richard E. Aaron, courtesy of Kenny Nemes / **Aimee Mann** by Andy Dudley / **Chan Marshall** and Cat Power en el Primavera Sound 2008 by alterna2 (courtesy of Flickr) / **Michael McDonald** at the Yamaha All-Star Concert by Justin Higuchi (courtesy of Flickr) / **Sam Moore** courtesy of Sam Moore and Joyce Moore (courtesy of Wikimedia Commons) / **Jim Morrison** by Henry Diltz / **Meshell Ndegeocello** by Hans Bürkle / **Lukas Nelson** @ Scott Legato, ScottLegato.com / **Willie Nelson** by Roberta/RobbieO (courtesy of Flickr) / **Aaron Neville** by Henry Diltz / **Stevie Nicks** by David Rose, davidrose.com / **Karen O** by Shirlaine Forrest / **Roy Orbison** by Paul Natkin / **Ozzy Osbourne** @ Scott Legato, ScottLegato.com / **Steve Perry** by Emma Holley / **Tom Petty** by Amber (courtesy of Flickr) / **Doug Pinnick** by L Scott / **Prince** by Richard E. Aaron, courtesy of Kenny Nemes / **Joey**

Ramone by David Corio / **Otis Redding** at Monterey Pop Festival 1967 (c) Ray Avery, CTSIMAGES, Cynthia Sesso. Used with permission / **Lionel Richie** by Raphael Pour-Hashemi / **LeAnn Rimes** photo by Yaelyphotographer.com (courtesy of Flickr) / **Chris Robinson** by Paul Hudson (courtesy of Flickr) / **Smokey Robinson** @ Jc Olivera/VipEventPhotography.com / **Johnny Rzeznik** by Andrew Mather | KCConcerts.net / **Nina Simone** by Joe La Russo / **Matt Skiba** by Ant Palmer / **Robert Smith** @ Scott Legato, ScottLegato.com / **Bruce Springsteen** by David Rose, davidrose.com / **Billy Squier** by Sarah McLean / **Paul Stanley** @ Scott Legato, ScottLegato.com / **Mavis Staples** courtesy of the LBJ Presidential Library (cropped and edited) / **Rod Stewart** @ Scott Legato, ScottLegato.com / **Michael Stipe** by Joel Didriksen / **Jeff Tweedy** by Joshua Mellin / **Dionne Warwick** by Ray Attard, Malta Today (courtesy of Flickr) / **Roger Waters** by Mary/swimfinfan (courtesy of Flickr) / **Ann Wilson** by Criss Cain / **Thom Yorke** by Martin Philbey / **Jason Thomas Gordon** by Josh Fogel, joshfogel.com

ACKNOWLEDGMENTS

Mom. None of this happens without your faith, love, and undying passion for music. Thank you for that, Ma. I love you so much.

I am forever in debt to all the vocalists who gave so much of their time, talent, and heart to this project. The same can be said for Bruce Kluger. The greatest "Champion" a writer could ever hope to have. Thank you for all of your passion, humor, and guidance throughout this process. I could not have made it across the finish line without you, man. Shane Visbal, Abe Velez, and Sarah Branham, your invaluable support led me to David Dunton at Harvey Klinger Agency, and I'm so thankful that it did. David, thank you for taking a chance on me. Jacob Hoye, what a rock star you are as an editor. Your enthusiasm for this book has been a true blessing. Thank you and your incredible team at Permuted Press. Thanks to Rick Shadyac, Emily Callahan, Tom Carolan, Chris Boysen, Glenn Keesee, Jennifer Poyner, and the entire Music Gives team at ALSAC/St. Jude. All my love to Cary Beare who forced the mic into my hand. And to the rest of our Kingsize family: Matt Delvecchio, Andrew Crosby, and Svend Lerche.

And a huge debt of thanks to everyone else who made this book possible:

Alex Lifeson
Alexander Ford
Alison Oscar
Amy Hairston
Andy Buckley
Andy Kipnes
Andy Mendelsohn
Arturo Cisneros
Barbara Carr
Bennett Cale
Bob Crawford
Brian Message
Bruce Allen
Carole Kinzel

Carolyn Rosenfeld
Cary Jones
Clive Davis
Christine Stauder
Dan Rothchild
Daniel Romanoff
Danny Bennett
Darrell Brown
David Elliot
David Rose
Dennis Arfa
Dionne Kirschner
Dolph Ramseur
Elaine Schock

Emily Bragg
Emily Carlstrom
Emily McMannis
Emmajane Salsedo
Eric Mayers
Erin Hanson
Esther Collins
Fran Defeo
Gunter Ford
Harvey Leeds
Jack DeBoe
Jack Osbourne
Jason Ashcraft
Jeremy Westby

Jessica Linker
Joe Sugerman
Joel Eckels
Joel Hoffner
John Wolk
Jolyn Matsumuro
Jonathan Levine
Jordyn Bruyns
Joyce Moore
Judy Miller Bailey
Julie Calland
Juliette Carter
Kate Watkins
Kathi Whitley

ACKNOWLEDGMENTS

Katy Krassner
Keith Foti
Ken Weinstein
Kenny Laguna
Kerry Gordy
Kevin Arbantes
Kevin Calabro
Kevin O'Neil
Larry Gordon
Laura Bergstein
Lotus Donavon
Marc Allan
Marlo Thomas
Mark Fenwick
Mark Rothbaum
Matt Cornell

Meg Symsyk
Michael Eisele
Michele Fisher
Michele Stephens
Mike Kobayashi
Morgan Feldman
Ngoc Hoang
Nicki Loranger
Olivia Harrington
Paul de Barros
Paul Kremen
Pauline Egan
Penny Guyon
Peter Katsis
Peter Paterno
Rachel Flotard

Rachel Willis
"Rambo" Stevens
Raymond Gonzales
Renata Ravina
Robby Krieger
Ron Kaplan
Rosa Canepa
Sally Jaye
Sam McAllister
Samantha Steuer
Sharon Cho
Sheryl Louis
Sky Nicholas
Stacie Surabian
Steve Barnett
Steve Masi

Sylvia Weiner
Talia Beltran
Tarquin Gotch
Taylor Thompson
Taylor Weekly
Thomas Cussins
Tom Consolo
Tony Magherita
Trevor Kirschner

Thanks to the photographers and their teams
who graciously provided the pictures in this book!

Alex Okami
Amanda Hatfield
Ameoba Hannigan
Andy Dudley
Andy Witchger
Ant Palmer
Bruce Kluger
Criss Cain
Cynthia Sesso /
Ray Avery Estate
Dave Golden
David Corio
David Rose
Debi Del Grande

Denise Truscello
Emma Holley
Eva Rinaldi
Hans Bürkle
Henry Diltz
Jc Olivera
Jeff Drongowski
Jeff Kravitz
Joe La Russo
Joel Didriksen
Josh Fogel
Joshua Brasted
Joshua Mellin
Justin Higuchi

Justin Wise
Kenny Nemes
/ Richard E.
Aaron Estate
Kevin Mazur
L Scott
Lindsey Akiyama
Martin Philbey
Martyn Goodacre
Mary Bieze
Matt Becker
Michael O'Brien
Paul Hudson
Paul Natkin

Philippe Bareille
Raphael
Pour-Hashemi
Ray Attard /
Malta Today
Ray Avery
Robbi O
Sam Milgrom
Sarah McLean
Scott Legato
Shirlaine Forrest
Steven Pisano
Urko
Dorronsoro Sagasti

ABOUT THE AUTHOR

Jason Thomas Gordon is the lead singer/drummer of the Los Angeles rock band Kingsize, a screenwriter, and creator of *Music Gives to St. Jude Kids*, a campaign that raises funds and awareness for St. Jude Children's Research Hospital through music-based initiatives. St. Jude was founded by Jason's grandfather, entertainer Danny Thomas, in Memphis, Tennessee, in 1962. Jason also serves as a National Committee member of the hospital's board.

@Kingsizetheband / Kingsizetheband.com